MORNING
AND
EVENING

An Updated Edition
of the Classic Devotional
in Today's Language

CHARLES H.
SPURGEON

Foreword by Haddon W. Robinson

EDITED BY ROY H. CLARKE

THOMAS NELSON PUBLISHERS
Nashville • Atlanta • London • Vancouver

Dedication

This book is lovingly dedicated to my mother,

URSULA NICHOLL CLARKE,

a saint whose prayers have reached
the very throne of God.

© 1994 by Roy H. Clarke

Published in Nashville, Tennessee, by Thomas Nelson, Inc.

Unless otherwise indicated, Scripture quotations are from the *New King
James Version of the Bible,* © 1979, 1980, 1982, Thomas Nelson, Inc.,
Publishers.

Library of Congress Cataloging-in-Publication Data

Spurgeon, C. H. (Charles Haddon), 1834–1892.
    [Morning and evening daily devotions]
    Morning and evening : an updated edition of the classic in
today's language / Charles H. Spurgeon ; edited by Roy H.
Clarke.
        p.   cm.
    Previously published as Morning and evening daily devotions.
    Includes index.
    ISBN 0-7852-8239-4
    1. Devotional calendars—Baptists.   I. Clarke, Roy. H.,
1930–   . II. Title.
BV4811.S6669   1994
242'.2—dc20   94–8843
                                                                CIP

Printed in the United States of America

1 2 3 4 5 6 7 8 — 00 99 98 97 96 95 94

FOREWORD

Once or twice in a century God hauls off and creates a servant so mighty in gift that the only proper response is "Wow!" Charles Haddon Spurgeon was one of God's special projects in the nineteenth century.

Spurgeon was not an original thinker, and he made no claims as a theologian. He was a communicator, the outstanding preacher of his day. Before the rise of the megachurch or the invention of microphones, six thousand people crowded into his congregation to hear him preach twice every Sunday. He preached to other gatherings as many as ten times a week. His Sunday sermons were taken down by stenographers and printed throughout England. They were cabled to New York on Monday and reprinted in leading newspapers throughout the United States. In 1865, Spurgeon's sermons sold 25,000 copies a week. They were translated into more than twenty languages. Spurgeon occupied the same pulpit for forty years and did not preach himself dry. God created a bush that blazed with fire and yet was not consumed.

God made this "Prince of Preachers" feel the humbling of rejection and sickness. From the time he came to his London pulpit at nineteen, he was the butt of cruel jokes in the press and the object of scorn from other clergy. Depression was a frequent and perverse companion. He suffered from gout, a disease that produces tortuous misery, and pain hounded him during the last twenty years of his life. His wife, Susannah, became an invalid at thiry-three and could seldom attend church to hear her husband preach. Yet, among the concluding words of what, unknown to him, was his final sermon, Spurgeon testified of Christ: "He is the most magnanimous of captains. . . . He is always to be found in the thickest part of the battle. When the wind blows cold, he always takes the bleak side of the hill. The heaviest end of the cross lies ever on his shoulders. If he bids us carry a burden, he carries it also. If there is anything that is gracious, generous, kind, and tender, yea lavish and supernatural in love, you always find it in him. These forty years and more have I served him, and

I have nothing but love from him. I would be glad to continue yet another forty years in the same dear service here below if it so pleased him. His service is life, peace, joy."

Charles Haddon Spurgeon's writings are read more widely than those of any other preacher in history (besides the Bible). Today there is available more material written by Spurgeon than by any other Christian author, living or dead. Over a hundred years after his death, his sermons and writings still refresh the reader. They are a bubbling spring whose waters require little filter or treatment. This updated edition of Spurgeon's *Morning and Evening* demonstrates how the Great Communicator can reach across years to speak God's word to hurting, struggling, bewildered men and women today.

The late German theologian and preacher, Helmut Thielicke, urged ministers: "Sell all that you have and buy Spurgeon." That is sound advice. Thanks to Roy Clarke, however, we don't have to pay that price. By simply keeping this book by our bedside or on our kitchen table, we can read Spurgeon to open and close our day.

Haddon W. Robinson

PREFACE TO THE
UPDATED EDITION

During a very difficult period in my life, I turned to the writings of Charles Haddon Spurgeon. Every page comforted me, and I soon discovered the reason: In his devotional writings, as in his sermons, Spurgeon was predictable (although never boring). Begin in Scripture wherever he might, this Prince of Preachers led listeners and readers directly to the fountain of comfort, Jesus Christ.

In this edition of *Morning and Evening,* offering perhaps the finest of Spurgeon's devotional writing, I have aimed only to update his language, replacing a word here or recasting or condensing an expression there in contemporary American English. My purpose has been to help Spurgeon lead today's readers (believers and unbelievers alike) to Christ as effectively as he did over a century ago.

Morning and Evening consists of daily devotions first published separately as *Morning by Morning* and *Evening by Evening.* Written with the assistance of the Reverend Joseph William Harrald and Mr. John Lewis Keys, these splendid worship readings are characterized by Spurgeon's rare ability to put rich, warm, deep spiritual truths in simple language. Yet Spurgeon avoids the common and the dull, attributes he considered the vices of most preaching and religious writing.

Spurgeon was a man of the whole Bible. His devotional writings draw, as do his sermons, from every book of the Bible. This edition is the only one that identifies Spurgeon's many brief Scripture quotations and allusions. A Scripture Index at the back of the book shows Spurgeon's wide-ranging use of the Bible and affords the reader access to each use. Besides the Bible, Spurgeon also drew deeply from the well of Puritan writings. John Bunyan's *The Pilgrim's Progress* was his favorite, and readers of *Morning and Evening* will find frequent references to its allegorical characters.

I undertook this project only after immersing myself in as much of Spurgeon's writing as I could. This feast for the soul included *The Treasury of David,* a seven-volume commentary on the Psalms; over sixteen hundred of his sermons; his three books, *Lectures to My Students, Addresses to Ministers and Students,* and *All of Grace;* articles by Spurgeon for his monthly magazine, *The Sword and The Trowel;* and *The Autobiography of Charles Haddon Spurgeon* (compiled after his death from his diary, letters, and records).

Several biographies were especially helpful: *Spurgeon, Prince of Preachers,* by Lewis Drummond; *The Life of Charles Haddon Spurgeon,* by Russell H. Conwell; *Charles H. Spurgeon,* by W. Y. Fullerton; *Spurgeon,* by Arnold Dallimore; and *Lamplighter and Son,* by Craig Skinner.

To further assist me in reading Spurgeon's nineteenth-century English accurately, I used *The Oxford English Dictionary,* 1929 edition. Fowler's *The King's English* helped me to properly translate the idioms of the nineteenth century, and the work of replacing Scripture from *The Authorized Version* with Scripture from *The New King James Version* further acquainted me with Spurgeon's inheritance of the Puritan influence on English.

The result of these efforts is, I hope, a faithful, careful revision that, like the loving restoration of a beautiful piece of antique furniture, provides an honored classic for enduring contemporary use.

Spurgeon's friend, John B. Grough, said, "I have seen Mr. Spurgeon hold thousands in breathless interest. I knew him as a great man, universally esteemed and beloved. But as he sat by the bed of a dying orphan boy he was grander and greater than when he swayed multitudes."[1]

This is *Morning and Evening,* Spurgeon—one on one, encouraging, teaching, inspiring, and worshiping.

Engraved on Spurgeon's tomb are two verses from his favorite hymn, "There is a Fountain," by William Cowper. The second verse is prophetic:

> Then in a nobler, sweeter song,
>   I'll sing Thy power to save,
> When this poor lisping, stammering tongue
>   Lies silent in the grave.

Dear Charles Haddon Spurgeon, this you have done. You are both teacher and friend as together we have joyfully

---

[1]*Spurgeon, Prince of Preachers* by Lewis Drummond; Kregel Publications, 1992.

praised and worshiped God the Father, God the Son, and God the Holy Spirit.

My dear reader, through the power of the Holy Spirit, may this same blessed experience be yours.

Roy H. Clarke
January 1994

AUTHOR'S PREFACE

Morning by Morning

In writing these brief reflections on biblical passages, our goal was to assist believers in their private meditation and devotion to Jesus Christ.

On several occasions a child suggested a thought that encouraged my despondent heart, or a flower, smiling upward from the grass, turned my thoughts toward heaven. As you read these simple pages it is my hope that, by the Holy Spirit's grace, you will hear "a still, small voice" speaking the message of God to your soul.

Because the mind wearies of the same thing, readers will find a variety of approaches and methods, such as exhortation, soliloquy, verse, and first, second, and third persons.

In the wide range of topics, readers of our sermons may recognize many thoughts and expressions, but most of the material is fresh and new. And, as much as possible, the presentation of common salvation is original.

We have written out of our hearts, and most portions are memories that refreshed our own experiences. I hope the Spirit of God will rest on you as you read these pages and that the time spent with these devotions will be a blessing.

Our ambition has led especially to the hope that this little volume will assist morning family worship, where God's altar is honored. If it has been your custom to read other inspirational authors, we do not wish to usurp their place. *Morning by Morning* aspires to earn a position among them. Our happiness will overflow if this book blesses you. In importance, family worship is beyond measure, both for the present and succeeding generations.

To be a chaplain in your home is a very great honor.

Charles Haddon Spurgeon

Author's Preface

Evening by Evening

Our Master set His seal of approval on our earlier volume, *Morning by Morning*. This has encouraged us to give our best efforts to the *Evening by Evening* series of devotions. It goes forth with prayer to be a blessing. Already, more than twenty thousand readers are among our fellow morning worshipers. May each of you receive grace from the Lord Jesus through these readings.

We have striven to keep out of the common track and thus have selected unusual texts and neglected subjects. The vice of many Christian books is their dullness, and from this we have tried to be free. Only you can tell if we have succeeded.

If the material leads just one heart upward that otherwise might have drooped, or if it sows in a single mind a holy purpose that before had not been conceived, we will be grateful. The Lord has sent such results in thousands of instances, and to Him be all the praise.

The longer we live, the more deeply we are conscious that only the Holy Spirit can make truth profitable to the heart. Therefore, in earnest prayer, we commit this volume and its companion to His care.

Charles Haddon Spurgeon

HEAVENLY FRUIT ON EARTHLY GROUND

"They ate the food of the land of Canaan that year."
—Joshua 5:12

Israel's wanderings had ended. The promised rest was attained. No more moving tents, fiery serpents, fierce Amalekites, and howling wildernesses. They entered the land that flowed with milk and honey, and ate the food that others had planted.

Perhaps this year, beloved Christian, we may enter that land. Joyful are the prospects, and if our faith is active, it will produce absolute delight. To be with Jesus, "there remains therefore a rest for the people of God" (Hebrews 4:9). This is indeed a joyful hope, and to expect this glory soon is a double delight.

Unbelief shudders at the Jordan that still rolls between us and the good land. But rest assured, we have already experienced more ill treatment than death at its worst can cause us. So banish every fear. Rejoice with exceeding great joy in the prospect that "we shall always be with the Lord" (1 Thessalonians 4:17).

Yet this year many of us will live to serve the Lord. If so, the New Year's text is still true. "A promise remains of entering His rest" (Hebrews 4:1). The Holy Spirit is the assurance of our inheritance. Preserved in Christ Jesus we are as secure as the saints in heaven.

There they triumph over their enemies, and we also have victories. Heavenly saints enjoy fellowship with their Lord, and this fellowship is not denied us. They rest in His love, and we have perfect peace in Him. They sing His praise, and it is also our privilege to praise Him.

This year we will gather celestial fruit on earthly ground (Exodus 16:21) because faith and hope have made the desert bloom like the garden of the Lord. Man ate angel's food once, why not again (Psalm 78:25)?

Oh for grace to feed on Jesus, and to eat the fruit of the land of Canaan this year!

A GOOD BEGINNING

"We will be glad and rejoice in You."

—Song of Solomon 1:4

We will not start this year with the sorrowful wail of a primitive trombone, but with the sweet strains of the harp of joy and the high sounding cymbals of gladness: "O come, let us sing to the Lord! Let us shout joyfully to the Rock of our salvation" (Psalm 95:1). Let others mourn over their troubles. We have the sweetening tree of Moses to cast in Marah's bitter pool. We will magnify the Lord with joy (Exodus 15:25).

Eternal Spirit, our powerful Comforter, we who are the temples in which You dwell will never cease from adoring and blessing the name of Jesus. We *will*—we are resolved: Jesus must have the crown of our heart's delight.

We are ordained to be the musicians of the skies. Let us rehearse our everlasting anthem before we sing in the halls of the New Jerusalem. We will *be glad and rejoice.* Two words with one meaning, double joy, blessedness on blessedness. Is there a limit to rejoicing in the Lord today? Do not people of grace find their Lord to be a precious fragrance, a rare ointment, a sturdy palm, and an aromatic spice? What better fragrance do they have in heaven itself? We will be glad and rejoice *in You.* That last word is the meat of the dish, the kernel of the nut, the soul of the text. What heavens are laid up in Jesus! What rivers of infinite blessings have their source and every drop of their fullness in Him!

Oh sweet Lord Jesus, You are the present portion of Your people. Give us such a sense of Your preciousness that from the first day of this year to the last day, "we will be glad and rejoice in You."

Let January open with joy in the Lord and December close with gladness in Jesus.

A PRAYER FOR THIS YEAR

"Continue earnestly in prayer."

—Colossians 4:2

It is interesting to note how large a portion of Scripture is devoted to prayer. We are furnished many examples, precepts, and promises. We scarcely open the Bible before we read, "Then men began to call on the name of the Lord" (Genesis 4:26). And just as we are about to close the volume we hear the "Amen" of an earnest prayer (Revelation 22:20).

Instances of prayer are plentiful: a wrestling Jacob; a Daniel praying three times a day; a David with all his heart calling on his God. On the mountain we see Elijah, and in the dungeon Paul and Silas.

We have multitudes of commands and myriads of promises that teach the sacred importance and necessity of prayer. We may be certain that what God emphasized in His Word, He intended to be conspicuous in our lives. He has said much about prayer because He knows we have a great need for it. So deep are our needs, that until we are in heaven we must never stop praying. A prayerless soul is a Christless soul.

Prayer is the lisping of the believing infant, the shout of the fighting believer, the requiem of the dying saint falling asleep in Jesus. It is the breath, the watchword, the comfort, the strength, and the honor of a Christian.

If you are a child of God, then you will seek your Father's face and live in your Father's love. Pray that this year you will be holy, humble, zealous, and patient. Pray that you will have closer fellowship with Christ and pray that you will frequently visit the banqueting house of His love (Song of Solomon 2:4). Pray that you will be an example and a blessing to others. Pray that you will live for the glory of your Master.

The motto for this year must be, "Continue earnestly in prayer."

RENEWING YOUR STRENGTH

"Let the people renew their strength."

—Isaiah 41:1

Everything on earth needs to be renewed. No created thing can continue by itself. "You renew the face of the earth," said the Psalmist (Psalm 104:30). Even the trees that have no cares and do not shorten their lives with hard work, need to drink the rain of heaven and feed from the hidden treasures of the soil. The cedars of Lebanon that God planted (Psalm 104:16) live only because they are full of sap drawn daily from the earth.

Your life cannot be sustained without renewal from God. Just as it is essential to replace the body's energy by eating, the soul must be revitalized by feeding on the Book of God, by listening to the preaching of His Word, and by the soul-filling table of communion.

How depressed we become when renewal is neglected! How poor and malnourished are the saints who live without the diligent use of the Word of God and secret prayer. If our faith can live without God, that faith is not from God; it is only a dream. But if our faith is from God, we will wait for Him as flowers wait for the dew.

Without restoration we are not ready for the perpetual assaults of hell, or the stern afflictions of Heaven, or even our inner strife. When the storm strikes, it is a disaster for the tree that has not taken fresh sap and grasped the rock with many intertwined roots. When hurricanes strike, it is a catastrophe for the sailors who failed to strengthen their mast, or drop anchor, or seek shelter. If we permit the good to grow weaker, evil will surely gather strength and struggle desperately to be our master. Then painful affliction and sad shame will follow.

In humble prayer, draw near to the footstool of divine mercy, and realize the fulfillment of the promise, "Those who wait on the Lord shall renew their strength" (Isaiah 40:31).

JANUARY 2, EVENING

ATTRIBUTED TO YOU

"I will . . . give you as a covenant to the people."

—Isaiah 49:8

Jesus Christ is the sum and substance of the covenant. He is the property of every believer. Can you comprehend what you have in Christ? "In Him dwells all the fullness of the Godhead in bodily form" (Colossians 2:9). Consider that word *God* and its infinity. Meditate on *perfect man* and all His beauty. As God and Man, all that Christ has is yours. Given as a pure free favor, handed over to be your unalterable property forever. Our blessed Jesus as God is omniscient, omnipresent, omnipotent. Does it comfort you to know that all these great and glorious attributes are yours?

Does He have power? His power is yours to support and strengthen you in overcoming your enemies and to keep you even to the end. Does He have love? Every drop of love in His heart is yours. You may dive in the immense ocean of His love and say, "It is all mine." Does He have justice? It may seem a stern attribute, but even justice is yours. He will by His justice see that everything promised in the covenant of grace will be secured for you.

All that Jesus has as the "perfect man" (Ephesians 4:13) is yours. As the perfect man, Jesus delighted in His Father. He stood accepted by the Most High. Oh believer, God's acceptance of Christ is your acceptance. The love the Father set on a perfect Christ, He now sets on you. All that Christ did is yours. Jesus' perfect righteousness, His life that was free from sin and stain, His keeping of the law and making it honorable, all this is yours. Christ is in the covenant:

> My God, I am thine—what a comfort divine!
> What a blessing to know that the Savior is
> Mine!
> In the heavenly Lamb thrice happy I am,
> And my heart it doth dance at the sound of His
> name.

A GRAND HIGHWAY

"Every valley shall be filled and every mountain and hill brought low. The crooked places shall be made straight and the rough ways smooth."
—Luke 3:5

I will pay attention to the Master's proclamation and give Him a road in my heart, a road built by His gracious operations through the desert of my nature. The four directions in the text must have my undivided attention.

"Every valley shall be filled." Low and sordid thoughts of God must be given up. Doubt and despair must be removed. Self-seeking and sensual delights must be forsaken. Across these deep valleys a glorious causeway of grace must be constructed.

"Every mountain and hill brought low." Proud self-assurance and boastful self-righteousness must be leveled to make a highway for the King of kings. Divine fellowship is never guaranteed to proud, arrogant sinners. The Lord respects the unpretentious and visits the broken-hearted, but the proud are an abomination to Him (Proverbs 16:5). My soul, seek the Holy Spirit to guide you here.

"The crooked places shall be made straight." The undecided heart must mark a straight path of decision for God and holiness. Double-minded people are strangers to the God of truth. My soul, make sure that in everything you are honest and true, because the heart-searching God is watching.

"The rough ways smooth." Stumbling blocks of sin must be removed. Thorns and briers of rebellion must be dug up. Our great Visitor must not find muddy ways and stony paths when He comes to honor His favored ones with His company.

This evening Lord, find in my heart a highway made ready by Your grace. May You triumphantly progress through the utmost borders of my soul, from the beginning of this year until the end. Amen.

GROWING IN GRACE

"Grow in the grace and knowledge of our Lord and Savior Jesus Christ."

—2 Peter 3:18

"Grow in the grace." Grow not just in one grace, but in all grace. Grow in that root grace: faith. Believe the promises. Let faith increase in fullness, consistency, and simplicity.

Grow also in love. Ask that your love be more extended, more intense, more practical, influencing your every thought, word, and deed.

Grow likewise in humility. Listen to know more of your own nothingness. Grow downward in humility and grow upward with a closer approach to God in prayer and a more intimate fellowship with Jesus.

May God the Holy Spirit enable you to "grow in the grace and knowledge of our Lord and Savior." If you do not grow in the grace and knowledge of Jesus you are refusing to be blessed. To know Him is "life eternal," and "to grow in the grace and knowledge" of Him is to increase your happiness. If you have no desire to learn more about Christ, you know nothing of Him.

Whoever has sipped this wine will never be thirsty. Christ satisfies, yet it is a satisfaction that never fills, but stimulates the appetite. If you know the love of Jesus, "as the deer pants for the water brooks" (Psalm 42:1), you will long for deep drinks of His love. If you don't want to know Him better, then you don't love Him. Absence from Christ is hell. But the presence of Jesus is heaven.

Do not rest until you have increased your acquaintance with Jesus. Learn more of Him in His divine nature, in His human relationship, in His finished work, in His death, in His resurrection, in His present glorious intercession, and in His second coming.

An increase of our love for Jesus and a more perfect concept of His love for us is one of the best ways to grow in grace.

JANUARY 4, MORNING

JESUS KNOWS US

"So Joseph recognized his brothers, but they did not recognize him."

—Genesis 42:8

This morning we meditated on growing in the grace and knowledge of our Lord Jesus. His knowledge of us was divinely perfect long before we had even the faintest knowledge of Him. "Your eyes saw my substance, being yet unformed. And in Your book they all were written. The days fashioned for me, when as yet, there were none of them" (Psalm 139:16). Before we had a body we were in His heart. When we were His enemies, He knew us. He knew our misery, our madness, and our wickedness.

When we wept bitterly in despairing repentance and saw Him only as a judge and ruler, He viewed us as His beloved. In His heart He loved us. He never abandoned His chosen. He always holds us as the object of His infinite affection. That "the Lord knows those who are His" (2 Timothy 2:19), is as true of the prodigals who are feeding pigs as it is of the children who sit at His table.

But to our sorrow we did not know our royal Brother, and from this ignorance grew a multitude of sins. We would not give Him our heart. We failed to trust Him. We refused to believe His words. We rebelled against Him. We would not reverence Him. The Sun of Righteousness shone and we failed to see Him. Heaven came down to earth, and earth ignored Him. Praise God, those days are over!

Even now we know so little about Jesus compared to what He knows about us. We have just started to understand Him, but He knows everything about us. How thankful the lack of knowledge is not on His side, for then our situation would be hopeless.

He will not say, "I never knew you; depart from Me" (Matthew 7:23). But He will confess our names before His Father (Revelation 3:5). Until then, He will make Himself known to us, but not to the world (John 14:17).

JANUARY 4, EVENING

LIGHT

"And God saw the light, that it was good; and God divided the light from the darkness."

—Genesis 1:4

Light is good since it came from God. "Let there be light" (Genesis 1:3). We who enjoy the gospel light should be far more thankful. We need to see more of God in it and through it. Solomon said, "Truly the light is sweet" (Ecclesiastes 11:7), but the gospel light is infinitely more precious because it reveals eternal things and ministers to our immortality.

When the Holy Spirit gives us spiritual light, we see ourselves as we really are. We see our sins in their true colors, and our eyes are opened to see the glory of God in the face of Jesus Christ. When the Most Holy God reveals Himself we see the plan of mercy He offers. We see the world's future as the Word describes it.

Spiritual light has many beams and colors. There is knowledge, joy, holiness, and life. All these are divinely good. Now if the light we see is this good, what will the essential light be? How glorious will be the place where He reveals Himself. Oh Lord, since Your Light is so good give us more and more of You, the true light.

Light and darkness have nothing in common (2 Corinthians 6:14). Children of light must not have fellowship with the deeds, doctrines, or deceits of darkness. The children of the day must be sober, honest and bold in their Lord's work (1 Thessalonians 5:5). We must leave the works of the darkness to those who live in the dark.

Our churches should by discipline divide the light from the darkness, and we by distinct separation from the world must do the same. In judgment, in action, in hearing, in teaching, in association we must discern between the precious and the vile (Jeremiah 15:19). We must keep the same distinction the Lord made on the world's first day.

Oh Lord Jesus, be our light all day long, for Your light is the light we need. Amen.

THE LIGHT IN YOU

"And God saw the light, that it was good."

—Genesis 1:4

This evening we see the love our Lord has for the light. The Lord looked at the light with satisfaction and saw "that it was good." If the Lord has given you light, He looks on that light with a special interest. It is precious to Him as His handiwork, and it is like Him, because "He is light" (John 8:12).

What a wonderful thought to know that God's eye is tenderly watching the work of grace that He started. He never loses sight of "this treasure in earthen vessels" (2 Corinthians 4:7).

At times we cannot see the light, but God always sees it and that is far better. Better for the judge to see my innocence than for me to think I see it. It is comforting to know that I am one of God's people. But whether I know it or not, as long as the Lord knows, I am safe.

This is our foundation: "The Lord knows those who are His" (2 Timothy 2:19). You may hurt and groan over inbred sin. You may weep over your darkness, but the Lord sees the "light" in your heart because He put it there. And all the clouds and gloom of your soul cannot hide your light from His gracious eye.

You may be in deep depression. You may have sunk into despondency and despair. But if you have any desire for Christ and if you are seeking to rest in His finished work, God sees the "light." He not only sees it, He preserves it. "I the Lord, keep it" (Isaiah 27:3). This thought is precious when you watch, worry, fret, and feel totally helpless. The light, preserved by His grace, will someday develop into the splendor of noon and the fullness of glory. The light in you is the dawn of eternity.

A CURE FOR WORRY

"Casting all your care upon Him, for He cares for you."

—1 Peter 5:7

A wonderful way to overcome sorrow is to realize, "He cares for me."

Christian, do not discredit your Lord by worrying. Come, throw your burden on Him. You are staggering under a load your Father would not feel. What to you is a crushing burden, is to Him a speck of dust on a scale. Nothing is so sweet as to:

> Lie passive in God's hands,
> And to know no will but His.

Suffering child, be patient. God has not forgotten you. He who feeds the sparrows will furnish your needs (Matthew 6:26). Do not despair. Hope on. Hope forever. Take the weapons of faith against a sea of trouble, and your opposition and distress will end.

There is One who cares for you. His eye is on you. His heart beats with pity for the difficulties you face, and His omnipotent hand will bring you help. The darkest cloud will scatter in showers of mercy. The blackest night will give way to morning. If you are His, He will bind your wounds and heal your broken heart. Don't doubt His grace because of your trials. He loves you as much in times of trouble as in days of happiness.

What a pleasant and quiet life you might have, if you left the providing to the God of Providence! With a little oil in the jug and a handful of flour in the bin, Elijah overcame the famine (1 Kings 17:16). God can do the same for you!

If God cares for you, why do you worry? Can you trust Him for your soul and not for your body? He has never refused to carry your burdens. He has never collapsed under their weight. Stop worrying. Leave all your concerns in the hand of a gracious God.

JANUARY 6, MORNING

THE TOUCH OF HIS HAND

"Now the hand of the Lord had been upon me in the evening."

—Ezekiel 33:22

The Lord's hand may be on me for judgment. If so, I need to understand why. I need to hear not only the rod, but Him who planned it. I am not the only one chastened during the night. So may I cheerfully submit to the affliction and carefully learn from it.

The hand of the Lord strengthens my soul and lifts my spirit to eternal things. Oh that I may feel the Lord dealing with me. A sense of the divine presence dwelling in me carries my soul toward heaven as if on the wings of eagles.

At times like this I am full to overflowing with spiritual joy. I forget the cares and sorrows of earth. The invisible is near, and the visible loses its power over me.

Oh that this sacred experience of divine fellowship would be assured this evening. The Lord knows that I need it greatly. My grace languishes. My perversion rages. My faith is weak. My devotion is cold.

His hand can cool the heat of my brow. His hand can stop the turmoil of my palpitating heart. That glorious right hand that molded the world can create my mind anew. The hand that never grows weary, the hand that bears the earth's huge pillars, can sustain my spirit. The loving hand that holds all the saints can cherish me. The mighty hand that breaks my enemies in pieces can subdue my sins. These are the reasons I need His healing hand.

Why should I not feel that hand touching me this evening? Oh my soul, speak to your God with this powerful plea; Jesus' hands were pierced for your redemption. Tonight you will surely feel the same hand that once touched Daniel and put him on his knees that he might see visions of God (Daniel 10:10).

JANUARY 6, EVENING

TRUE LIVING

"For to me, to live is Christ."

—Philippians 1:21

Believers did not always live for Christ. Not until God the Holy Spirit convicted them of sin, not until grace brought them to see the dying Savior making a propitiation for their guilt, not until the moment of the new and heavenly birth did they begin to live for Christ.

Jesus is the one pearl of great price, and for believers to obtain that pearl they must sell everything (Matthew 13:46). He has completely won our love. For His glory we live. In defense of His gospel we would die. He is the pattern of our life. He is the model after whom we would sculpture our character.

Paul's words mean more than you think. They imply that the aim and the end of Paul's life was Christ. His very life was Jesus. In the words of an ancient saint, "He did eat, and drink, and sleep eternal life. Jesus was his very breath, the soul of his soul, the heart of his heart, the life of his life."

As a Christian, do you live to this standard? Can you honestly say that to live is Christ? Your business—are you doing it for Christ, or doing it to become richer? Or are you doing it for your family? Are these valid reasons? The Christian who professes to live for Christ cannot live for another goal without committing spiritual adultery.

Who would dare say that they live wholly for Christ? Yet this alone is the true life of a Christian. Its source, its sustenance, its fashion, and its end are all gathered up in one word: Jesus Christ.

Lord accept me. I give myself, praying to live only in You and for You. Let me be like the bullock that stands between the plow and the altar, ready to work or ready to be sacrificed. Let my motto be, "Ready for either."

SACRED LOVE

"My sister, my spouse."

—Song of Solomon 4:12

With intense affection the heavenly Solomon addresses His bride, the church. "My sister": one close to me by relationship, partaker of a mutual affinity. "My spouse": one nearest and dearest, united with Me by the tender band of love. My sweet companion, part of Myself.

My sister, by My Incarnation I am bone of your bone and flesh of your flesh. My spouse, by heavenly marriage I have taken you to Myself in righteousness. My sister, whom I knew so well and over whom I watched from infancy. My spouse, taken from among the daughters, embraced in the arms of love, and promised to Me forever.

It is true, our royal Kinsman Jesus is not ashamed of us. He takes boundless delight in this two-fold relationship.

We have the word *my* twice in our text. It is as if Christ dwells with rapture on His possession of His church. "My delight was with the sons of men" (Proverbs 8:31), because they were His own chosen ones. He, the Shepherd, sought the sheep because they were His sheep. He seeks and saves the lost because the lost, long before they were lost, were His. The church is the exclusive possession of her Lord. No one else can claim a partnership, or even pretend to share her love. Jesus, your church delights to have it this way. Let every believer drink comfort from this well.

Christ is near to you in ties of relationship. Christ is dear to you in bonds of marriage, and you are precious to Him. He grasps both of your hands with both of His, saying, "My sister, my spouse." Remember these two firm grips that enable your Lord to get a double hold on you that He cannot and will not ever let you go.

Beloved, do not be slow to return His sacred love.

THROUGH THE EYE OF FAITH

"The iniquity of the holy things."

—Exodus 28:38

What a veil is lifted and what a disclosure is made by these words. It will be both humbling and profitable to study this sad situation. The iniquities of our public worship: its hypocrisy, formality, lukewarmness, irreverence, wandering of heart, and forgetfulness of God. What a list!

Our work for the Lord—its rivalry, selfishness, carelessness, slackness, unbelief. What a mass of defilement!

Our private devotions—their laxity, coldness, neglect, sleepiness, and vanity. What a mountain of dead earth!

Look carefully and you will find this iniquity is far greater than it first appears. Dr. Payson, writing his brother, says, "My church, as well as my heart, resembles the garden of the sluggard. And what is worse, I find that many of my desires to improve both proceed from pride or vanity or laziness. I look at the weeds which overrun my garden, and I breathe out an earnest wish that they were eradicated. But why? What prompts the wish? It may be that I want to walk out and say, 'In what fine order is my garden kept!' This is pride. Or it may be that I want my neighbors to look over the wall and say, 'How splendid your garden flourishes!' This is vanity. Or I may wish for the end of the weeds because I am weary of pulling them up. This is indolence."

You see, even our desires for holiness may be polluted by wrong motives. Under the greenest lawns worms hide, and you don't have to look long to find them.

Here is a thought to cheer you. When the High Priest bore the iniquity of the holy things, he wore on his brow the words, "HOLINESS TO THE LORD" (Exodus 28:36). And while Jesus bears our sin, He presents before His Father's face, not our unholiness, but His holiness.

Oh for grace to see our great High Priest through the eye of faith!

JANUARY 8, MORNING

BETTER THAN WINE

"For your love is better than wine."

—Song of Solomon 1:2

Nothing gives the believer more joy than fellowship with Jesus Christ. Like others, we enjoy the good things of life plus the added benefits of the gifts and the works of God. Yet in each of these, and in everything added together, there is nothing equal to the substantial delight that is found in the matchless person of our Lord Jesus.

Jesus has wine that no vineyard on earth could ever yield. He has bread that all the corn fields of Egypt could never produce. In my opinion, the joys of earth are no better than garbage when compared to Jesus, the heavenly manna. I would prefer one mouthful of Christ's love and one sip of His fellowship than a whole world of carnal delights.

What is the chaff to the wheat? What is an imitation gem to the true diamond? What is a dream to the glorious reality? What are yesterday's joys, at their best, when compared to our Lord Jesus?

If you know anything about the inner life, you will confess that your highest, purest, and most enduring joys are the twelve fruits from the tree of life (Revelation 22:2). There is not a spring which yields such sweet water as the well of God which was pierced with the soldier's spear.

All earthly pleasures are earthy, but the comforts of Christ's presence are like Him, heavenly. When we review our fellowship with Jesus we find no emptiness. There are no dregs in His wine, no dead flies in His ointment. The joy of the Lord is solid and enduring; it is not empty. An examination with discretion and prudence will testify that it stands the test of time. The joy of the Lord in time and in eternity will be worthy to be called "the only true delight."

For nourishment, comfort, exhilaration, and refreshment, no wine can rival the love of Jesus. Drink deeply this evening.

REJOICE, WITH UNSPEAKABLE JOY

"I will be their God."

—Jeremiah 32:38

Christian, this truth is all you need. If you want happiness you need something that will satisfy, and this verse is enough. If you can pour this promise into your cup, then you can say with David, "My cup runs over;" "more than my heart could wish" (Psalm 23:5, Psalm 73:7). When "I am your God" becomes reality, then you possess everything.

Desire is as insatiable as death. Yet He who fills all in all can fill our desire. The capacity of our wishes can not be measured, but the immeasurable wealth of God can more than overflow it.

Let me ask, are you complete when God is yours? Do you want anything else but God? If everything else failed, isn't His all-sufficiency enough to satisfy?

God is the Maker of heaven, and this is music fit for heaven. All the music blown from sweet instruments or drawn from living strings cannot produce a melody as sweet as this promise: "I will be their God." This declaration is a deep sea of bliss, a shoreless ocean of delight. Come bathe your spirit in it. Swim as long as you like and you will not find a shore. Dive throughout eternity and you will not find a bottom.

"I will be their God." If that doesn't make your eyes sparkle and your heart beat with happiness then most assuredly your soul is not healthy.

But you want more than present delight. You need hope. And what more can you hope for than this great promise: "I will be their God." This is the masterpiece of all the promises. Its joy can make heaven on earth, and it will make a heaven above.

Dwell in the light of your Lord. Let your soul delight in His love. Get the resources and energy this promise yields. Live up to your position. Rejoice with unspeakable joy.

A DELIGHT AND A JOY

"Serve the Lord with gladness."

—Psalm 100:2

Delight in God's service is a sign of His acceptance. Those who serve God with a sad face because what they are doing is unpleasant are not serving Him. They are bringing a form of homage, but life is absent.

God does not require slaves to grace His throne. He is Lord of the empire of love and His servants dress in robes of joy. The angels of God serve with songs, not with groans. Just a murmur or a sigh would be mutiny because obedience that is not voluntary is disobedience. The Lord looks at the heart, and if we were forced to serve, He would reject our offering.

Service coupled with joy is heart service, and heart service is true service. Take away joyful willingness from the Christian and you have removed the test of sincerity. If you are forced into battle, you are not a patriot. But if you march into the conflict with flashing eye and beaming face, singing, "It is sweet for one's country to die," then you have proved your patriotism.

"The joy of the Lord is your strength" (Nehemiah 8:10). Joy removes difficulties. Joy is to our service as oil is to the wheels of a railroad car. Without oil the axle grows hot and accidents occur. If there is no holy joy to oil our wheels, our spirit will soon be clogged with weariness. The person who is joyful in God's service can sing;

> Make me to walk in Your commands,
> 'Tis a delightful road.

Let me ask you a question. Do you serve the Lord with joy? Then show the people of the world, who think our religion is slavery, that serving God is a delight and a joy. Let gladness proclaim that we serve a good Master.

JANUARY 9, EVENING

MY INHERITANCE

"There is laid up for me the crown of righteousness."

—2 Timothy 4:8

Are you concerned that you will not make heaven? Worry no longer! All the people of God will be there.

I love the old story of a dying man who exclaimed, "I have sent all before me. God's finger is on the latch of my door, and I am ready for Him to enter." But someone said, "Are you afraid that you will miss your inheritance?" "No," said he, "No! There is one crown in heaven that the angel Gabriel could not wear. It will fit no head but mine. There is one throne in heaven that Paul the apostle could not fill. It was made for me."

What a joyous thought! Your reward is secure. "There remains therefore a rest" (Hebrews 4:9). Can you forfeit it? No, it is unalterable. If I am a child of God I cannot lose it. It is mine as surely as if I were there.

Let's sit on the top of Mount Nebo where Moses sat, and view the pleasant land of Canaan (Deuteronomy 34:1). Do you see that little river of death glistening in the sunlight? Across the river, do you see the pinnacles of the eternal city? Look at that pleasant country and all its joyous inhabitants! If you could fly across that valley you would see written on one of the many mansions: "Reserved." Reserved for you. You will dwell forever with the Lord.

Poor doubting one, that magnificent inheritance is yours if you believe on the Lord Jesus and have repented of your sins. If you have been renewed in your heart, if you are one of the Lord's people, then there is a place reserved for you. A crown is waiting for you (Revelation 2:10). No one else will have your reward. It is reserved in heaven just for you. There will be no vacant thrones in glory when all the chosen are gathered in.

NO GREATER JOY

"In my flesh I shall see God."

—Job 19:26

This was Job's devout anticipation: "I shall see God." Job does not say, "I shall see the saints," though doubtless this will be wonderful. He says, "I shall see God." He does not say, "I shall see the pearly gates, I shall behold the walls of jasper, I shall gaze on the crowns of gold," but "I shall see God." This is the sum and substance of heaven. This is the joyful hope of all believers.

We delight to see Him now by faith. We love to behold Him as we pray. But in heaven we will have an open and an unclouded vision. "We shall see Him as He is" (1 John 3:2). We shall be made completely like Him. Like God! What more could we ask? To see God! What more could we desire?

Some would read this passage, "Yet I shall see God in my flesh." They find here an allusion to Christ. "The Word became flesh and dwelt among us" (John 1:14). An allusion to the splendor of the last days when we will see Him in all His glory. Whether correct or not, this is certain: Christ is the object of our eternal vision. There will be no greater joy than seeing Him.

And though it is but one source of delight, that source is infinite. All His attributes will be subjects for contemplation, and because He is infinite under each aspect, there is no fear of exhaustion. His works, His gifts, His love to us, and His glory in all His purposes and actions are ever new themes.

The patriarch Job looked forward to the personal enjoyment of seeing God: "Whom my eyes shall see for myself, and my eyes shall behold, and not another" (Job 19:27).

Visualize heaven's jubilation. Think what it will be. All the brightness of earth fades and darkens as we look at heaven. This is a brightness which can never dim, a glory which can never fade: "I shall see God."

JANUARY 10, EVENING

GROWTH

"These have no root."

—Luke 8:13

My soul, examine yourself this morning in the light of this text. You have received the word with joy. Your feelings have been stirred and enlivened. But remember, to receive the word in your ear is one thing, but to receive Jesus into your soul is quite another. Superficial feelings are often joined with an inward hardness of the heart, and good feelings do not always last.

In the parable, this particular seed fell on a thin layer of soil having a rocky bottom. When the seed began to take root, its downward growth was hindered and so its strength was spent pushing its green shoots upward. Without moisture from a deep root the plant withered.

Am I like this? Have I put on a good show in the flesh without having a corresponding inner life? Good growth takes place upwards and downwards simultaneously. Am I rooted in sincere loyalty and love to Jesus? If my heart remains hard, not fertilized by grace, the good seed may germinate but it will ultimately die. It cannot flourish on a rocky, unbroken heart. I fear a godliness that grows as rapidly and with as little endurance as Jonah's plant (Jonah 4:6,7).

Let me count the cost of being a follower of Jesus. Above all let me feel the energy of His Holy Spirit, and then I shall possess an abiding and enduring seed in my soul. If my mind remains as unyielding as it was by nature, the sun of trial will burn, and my hard heart will increase the heat more dreadfully on the ill-covered seed. My religion will soon die, and my despair will be terrible.

Heavenly Sower, plow me first, and then sow the truth in me. Let me produce a bountiful harvest for You. Amen.

A PLEA

"I have prayed for you."

—Luke 22:32

What an encouraging thought that our Redeemer never ceases interceding for us. When we pray He pleads our case to God. He advocates our cause. His supplications shield us from unseen danger.

Look at the comfort in His words to Peter. "Simon, Simon! Indeed, Satan has asked for you, that he may sift you as wheat" (Luke 22:31). But . . . But what, "Go and pray for yourself"? That is good advice, but it is not what He said. Nor did He say, "But I will keep you watchful, and so you will be preserved," even though that would be a great blessing. No, Jesus said, "But I have prayed for you, that your faith should not fail" (Luke 22:32).

We do not know how much we owe to our Savior's prayers. When we reach the hilltops of heaven and look back on how the Lord our God led us then we will praise Him. We will praise Jesus who, before the eternal throne, undid the mischief Satan was doing on earth.

How can we thank Him enough? Jesus never stopped pleading for us. He never held His peace, but day and night He pointed to the wounds on His hands and carried our names on His breastplate. Even before Satan had started to tempt Jesus He hindered him and entered a plea in heaven for us. Mercy outruns malice.

Mark it! He does not say, "Satan has sifted you and I will pray," but, "Satan has asked for you." He checks Satan's desires and nips them in the bud. Jesus does not say, "But I have desired to pray for you." No! He says, "I have prayed for you. I have already done it. I have gone to court and entered a counterplea even before an accusation is made."

Oh Jesus, what a comfort to know you have pleaded our cause against an unseen enemy. You have eliminated his charges. You have identified his ambush. This gives me great joy, gratitude, hope, and confidence.

I AM CHRIST'S

"You are Christ's."

—1 Corinthians 3:23

"You are Christ's." You are His by donation because the Father gave you to the Son. You are His by His blood purchase even though the price of your redemption was great. You are His by dedication since you consecrated yourself to Him. You are His by relation because you are named by His name. He made you His child and His joint heir (Romans 8:17).

Work hard to show the world that you are the servant, the friend, the bride of Jesus. When tempted to sin, say, "I cannot do this wickedness because I am Christ's." Eternal principles forbid the friend of Christ to sin. When wealth can be gained by sin remember that you are Christ's and so have nothing to do with sin. Stand firm in the evil day. Remember you are His.

Are you employed where others sit idle and do nothing? Then work with all your power. When the sweat stands on your face, when you are tempted to quit, shout, "I cannot stop because I am Christ's. If I were not purchased by His blood I might be like Jacob's son, Issachar, 'lying down between two burdens' (Genesis 49:14). But I am Christ's. I must work."

When pleasure's sweet song calls you from His path, say, "Your music cannot tempt me, I am Christ's."

When the cause of God calls you, give yourself to it. When the poor need your help, give not only your goods but yourself also.

"You are Christ's." Never disguise your profession of faith. Let your manners be Christian. Let your speech be like the Nazarene's and your conduct and conversation so full of heaven that everyone will recognize His love and holiness and know that you are the Savior's.

"I am a Roman!" was once reason enough to practice integrity. How much more should your motive for holiness be, "I am Christ's."

IF YOU CANNOT PREACH LIKE PAUL

"There are yet words to speak on God's behalf."

—Job 36:2

There is no need to seek publicity for our virtue or to demand notoriety for our zeal, but it is a sin to hide what God has given us. A Christian is not a hidden village in a valley. A Christian is "a city set on a hill" (Matthew 5:14). We are not to be a lamp under a basket but a lighted lamp shining to all (Matthew 5:15).

Seclusion may at times be fine, and to hide one's self is considered modest. But to hide Christ in us is never justified. Failure to speak the truth about what is precious is a sin against others and an offense against God. We may be shy and withdrawn, but let us not indulge this trembling tendency or we will be useless to the church. In the name of Him who was not ashamed of us, let us forget our feelings and tell others what Christ has done.

If you cannot speak like a trumpet, use the still small voice. If the pulpit is not yours, if the press does not carry your words on its wings, say with Peter and John, "Silver and gold I do not have, but what I do have I give you" (Acts 3:6). If you cannot preach a sermon on the mountain then talk to the Samaritan woman by Sychar's well (John 4:5).

Praise Jesus in your home if not in the temple. Praise Him in the field if not in the market place. Praise Him with your family if not in the world. From hidden springs within you let satisfying, flowing rivers of testimony run out. Give a drink to every passer-by. Don't hide your talents: use them, and bring good interest to your Lord and Master. If you speak for God you will be refreshed, the saints will be encouraged, it will be useful to sinners, and the Savior will be honored.

SHIPWRECKED

"Jehoshaphat made merchant ships to go to Ophir for gold; but they never sailed, for the ships were wrecked at Ezion Geber."

—1 Kings 22:48

Solomon's ships had returned safely, but Jehoshaphat's vessels never reached the land of gold. In the same business, in the same location, Providence prospers one and frustrates the plans of another. Yet the Great Ruler is good and wise in both situations. As we think on this verse may we have grace to praise the Lord for ships sunk at Ezion Geber as well as for vessels that arrive loaded with material blessings.

Let us not envy the successful or complain about our losses as though we were singularly and specially tried. Like Jehoshaphat, we may be precious in the Lord's sight even though our plans end in failure and disappointment. Jehoshaphat lost his ships because of an alliance with a sinful family and fellowship with sinners. This is the cause of much suffering among the Lord's people today. In 2 Chronicles 20:37, the Lord sent a prophet to Jehoshaphat to declare, "Because you have allied yourself with Ahaziah, the Lord has destroyed your works." This was a fatherly chastisement that appears to have been a blessing, for in the following verse Jehoshaphat does not allow his servants to sail in the same vessel with the servants of the wicked king.

Would to God that Jehoshaphat's experience might be a warning to the Lord's people today. "Do not be unequally yoked together with unbelievers" (2 Corinthians 6:14). A life of misery is generally the lot of those who are married to, or in any other way of their own choosing yoked with, the people of the world.

Oh for such love to Jesus that, like Him, we may be holy, harmless, undefiled, and separated from sinners. If not, then expect to hear the words, "The Lord has destroyed your works."

THE IRON FLOATED

"He made the iron float."

—2 Kings 6:6

The borrowed axe head was hopelessly lost underwater. The honor of the prophetic band was threatened because the name of their God would be compromised. Against all expectations the iron rose from the stream's bed and floated. "The things which are impossible with men are possible with God" (Luke 18:27).

A few years ago a Christian I knew was called to a project that far exceeded his ability. It was so difficult that the very idea of attempting it bordered on the absurd. Yet he was called and his faith rose to the occasion. God honored that faith and unexpected aid was sent. The iron floated.

Another member of the Lord's family was in a disastrous financial situation. He would be able to meet all of his obligations and much more if he could sell part of his estate. When it did not sell he was placed under great pressure. In vain he sought the help of friends, but then faith led him to the unfailing Helper and the trouble was averted. "God enlarged his path under him, so his feet did not slip" (2 Samuel 22:37). The iron floated.

A third individual had to deal with a friend who was terribly depraved. He taught, reproved, warned, invited, and interceded, but the stubborn spirit would not relent. Then came an agony of prayer and soon a blessed answer from heaven. The hard heart was broken. The iron floated.

Beloved, what is your desperate problem? What heavy trial hangs over you this evening? Bring it to the mercy seat. The God of the prophets lives. He lives to help His saints, "that you may lack nothing" (1 Thessalonians 4:12). Believe in the Lord of hosts! Approach Him. Plead the name of Jesus. The iron will float.

You will see the finger of God working miracles for His people. "According to your faith let it be to you" (Matthew 9:29). And, once again, the iron will float.

JANUARY 13, EVENING

A MIGHTY SAVIOR

"Mighty to save."

—Isaiah 63:1

With the words, "mighty to save," we can fully understand the great work of salvation. This indeed is total mercy.

Christ is "mighty to save" those who call on Him. He is mighty to make sinners repent. He is mighty to give us new hearts and to work faith in us. He is mighty to make those who hate holiness love it and to make those who despise His name bow before Him. He is mighty to carry to heaven those who believe.

This is not all, for divine power is equally evident after conversion. The life of a believer is a series of miracles from "the Mighty God." The bush burns but is not consumed (Exodus 3:2). He is mighty to keep His people holy and preserve them in His love until that day when He fulfills their spiritual existence in heaven.

Christ's might does not make people believers and then leave them to struggle alone. "Being confident of this very thing, that He who has begun a good work in you will complete it" (Philippians 1:6). Jesus not only imparts the first germ of life in a dead soul, He also continues the divine existence and strengthens it until every bond of sin is broken. Then the soul leaps from earth perfected in glory.

Here is some encouragement. Are you praying for someone you love? Oh don't stop praying. Remember Christ is "mighty to save." You are powerless to reclaim the rebel but your Lord is Mighty. Grab hold of that omnipotent arm and ask Him to put forth His strength.

Are you personally troubled? Fear not, "My grace is sufficient for you, for My strength is made perfect in weakness" (2 Corinthians 12:9). Jesus is "mighty to save." The best proof is that He has saved you. What a thousand mercies that you did not find Him mighty to destroy!

A BRIEF PRAYER

"Beginning to sink he cried out, saying, 'Lord, save me.'"

—Matthew 14:30

Sinking times are praying times for the Lord's servants. Peter neglected prayer when he started his venturous journey on to the water. But as he began to sink the danger of drowning made him pray, and although his cry was late it was not too late.

In hours of bodily pain and mental anguish we are driven as naturally to prayer as a shipwreck is driven to shore by the waves. The fox runs to its hole for protection, the bird flies to the woods for shelter, and the believer in difficulty hastens to the mercy seat for safety. Heaven's great harbor of refuge is All-prayer. Thousands of weather-beaten vessels have found a haven there. The moment a storm begins, rush to the mercy seat.

Short prayers are long enough. Not length but strength is desirable. There were only three words in Peter's gasping petition, but they were sufficient. Urgency is a great teacher of brevity. If our prayers had less prideful tail feathers and more wing they would be better prayers. Wordiness is to devotion what chaff is to wheat. Precious things come in small packages. Everything that is real prayer in many a long address could have been uttered in a much shorter petition.

Our desperate distress is the Lord's opportunity. An immediate sense of danger forces our anxious cry to Jesus, and with our cry His help does not linger. We may appeal at the last moment, but His swift and effectual hand makes up for our delay.

Are you nearly engulfed by the boisterous waters of affliction? Then lift up your soul to our Savior and rest assured; He will not let you perish. When you can do nothing Jesus can do all things. Enlist His powerful aid and all will be well.

CLAIM A PROMISE

"Do as You have said."

—2 Samuel 7:25

God's promises are not to be thrown away like pieces of scrap paper. He intended that we should use them. God's gold is not miser's money. God's gold is to be minted and traded. Nothing pleases our Lord more than to see His promises put in circulation. He loves to hear His children say, "Lord, do as You have said." We glorify God when we claim His promises.

Do you think God will be poorer for giving you His promised riches? Do you believe God will be any less holy for giving you His holiness? Do you imagine God will be any less pure for washing you from your sins? "Come now, and let us reason together," says the Lord, "though your sins are like scarlet, they shall be as white as snow; though they are red like crimson, they shall be as wool" (Isaiah 1:18).

Faith does not delay the promise by saying, "This is a precious promise, I wonder if it is true?" Faith goes directly to the throne and pleads, "Lord, here is the promise, 'Do as you have said'." Our Lord replies, "Let it be as you desire" (Matthew 15:28).

When you have a promise and don't take it to God you dishonor Him. But when you hasten to the throne of grace and cry, "Lord, I have nothing to recommend me but this: 'You have said it'," then your prayer will be granted. Our heavenly Banker delights to cash His own checks.

Do not let the promise rust. Do not think that God will be troubled by your importunities. He loves to hear the loud cries of needy souls. It is His delight to bestow favors. He is more ready to answer than you are to ask.

The sun is not weary of shining or the fountain of flowing. It is God's nature to keep His promise. Therefore go at once to the throne and tell Him, "Do as You have said."

JANUARY 15, MORNING

A DAILY BUSINESS

"But I give myself to prayer."

—Psalm 109:4

Lying tongues were busy against David's reputation, but David did not defend himself. He moved the case to a higher court and pleaded before the great King. Prayer is the safest method of replying to words of hatred.

The Psalmist gave himself to prayer warmly. He threw his whole heart and soul in it. He strained every sinew and muscle, as Jacob did when wrestling with the angel (Genesis 32:24). This is the only way to speed to the throne of grace.

A shadow has no power because it has no substance. A prayer that is not presented in agonizing earnestness and passionate desire is utterly ineffective. It lacks driving force. An old Puritan divine said, "Fervent prayer, like a cannon aimed at the gates of heaven, makes them fly open."

Our problem is that we are easily distracted. Our thoughts wander here and there. Like quicksilver our minds run this way and that way and we make little progress toward our goal. What a great evil! It harms us, and even worse it insults God. What would you think of a citizen who played with a ball or attempted to catch a fly while having an interview with the president?

The intent of this text is for us to continue and persevere in prayer. David did not cry once and stop. His holy clamor continued until it brought down the blessing. Prayer must not be infrequent. Prayer must be our daily business, our habit, our vocation. As artists give themselves to their models and poets to their classical pursuits we must be addicted to prayer. We must be so immersed in prayer that we "pray without ceasing" (1 Thessalonians 5:17).

Lord teach us to pray that we may be more and more influential with You. Amen.

JANUARY 15, EVENING

FEAR NOT

"I will help you, says the Lord."

—Isaiah 41:14

This morning listen to the Lord Jesus speak. "I will help you. It is a small thing for Me, your God, to help you. Consider what I have already done. What! Not help you! I bought you with My blood. What! Not help you! I died for you. Since I have done the greater, will I not do less?"

"Before the world began I chose you. I made a covenant for you. I laid aside my glory and became a man for you. I gave my life for you. Since I did all this, then I will surely help you now. In helping you I am giving you what has already been purchased. If you needed a thousand times as much help, I would give it! Your requests are nothing compared with what I am willing to give. You need much, but it is nothing for me to grant your needs. Help you? Fear not! I will help you."

Is this not enough? Do you need more strength than the omnipotence of the United Trinity? Do you need more wisdom than exists in the Father? Do you need more love than is displayed in the Son? Do you need more power than is manifest in the Spirit? Bring your empty pitcher! This well will fill it easily. Hurry! Gather your wants, your emptiness, your woes, your needs, and bring them here. See! This river of God is full to meet your needs. What else do you need? Oh my soul, go forward in His strength. The eternal God is your Helper:

> Fear not I am with thee,
>   Oh be not dismayed;
> I, I am thy God,
>   And will still give thee aid.

CONSECRATION

"Messiah shall be cut off, but not for Himself."

—Daniel 9:26

Blessed be His name. There was no cause of death in Him. No original or actual sin defiled Him. Death had no claim on Him. No one could justly take His life. He had done no wrong. No one could have slain Him by force unless He was willing to die.

Look: one sins and another suffers. We offended justice, but He paid the penalty. Rivers of tears, mountains of offerings, seas of the blood of bullocks, and hills of frankincense could not remove our sin. But when Jesus was cut off for us the cause of wrath was immediately cut off and sin was put away forever.

Here is wisdom, in which substitution, the sure and speedy way of atonement, was devised. Here is condescension, which brought the Messiah, the Prince, to wear a crown of thorns and die on a cross. Here is love, which led the Redeemer to lay down His life for His enemies!

It is not enough to admire the spectacle of the innocent Christ bleeding for the guilty. We must have an interest in it. The Messiah's death was the salvation of His church. "Just as the Son of Man did not come to be served, but to serve and to give His life a ransom for many" (Matthew 20:28).

Was the Lord Jesus our representative? Are we healed by His stripes? It would be a terrible thing if we fell short of a share in His sacrifice; better to have never been born. As solemn as this question is, it is a joyful circumstance and can be answered clearly and without mistake. To all who believe on Him the Lord Jesus is a present Savior and the blood of reconciliation has been sprinkled on us.

Let all who trust in the merit of the Messiah's death be joyful every time He is remembered. Let our holy gratitude lead us to the fullest consecration to His cause.

HEAVEN AND CHRIST

"Then I looked, and behold, a Lamb standing on Mount Zion."

—Revelation 14:1

The apostle John had the privilege of looking inside the gates of heaven and describing what he saw. He begins, "I looked, and behold, a Lamb!" This verse teaches that the primary object of heaven is "the Lamb of God who takes away the sin of the world" (John 1:29). Nothing else attracted the apostle's attention like Jesus Christ. He is the theme of the songs sung by glorified spirits and holy angels.

Christian, this is joy! You have looked and you have seen the lamb. Through tears you have seen the Lamb of God taking away your sins. Rejoice! In a little while "God will wipe away every tear from their eyes" (Revelation 21:4), and you will see the same Lamb exalted on His throne.

What a joy to have daily fellowship with Jesus and to anticipate a greater joy in heaven where we shall live with Him forever. "I looked, and behold, a Lamb." That Lamb is heaven itself. As good Rutherford said, "Heaven and Christ are the same. To be with Christ is to be in heaven, and to be in heaven is to be with Christ. Oh my Lord Christ, if I were in heaven without you, it would be a hell. And if I were in hell with you it would be a heaven, for you are all the heaven I want."

> Not all the harps above
>   Can make a heavenly place,
> If God His residence remove,
>   Or but conceal His face.

All you need to be blessed, supremely blessed, is "to be with Christ."

WEAPONS OF THE DEVIL

"Then it happened one evening that David arose from his bed and walked on the roof of the king's house."

—2 Samuel 11:2

In an evening David saw Bathsheba. We are never out of the reach of temptation. At home or away we are likely to be allured by evil. The morning begins with peril and the shadows of evening still find us in jeopardy. We are safe under God's protection, but woe to those who go forth unarmed. Those who think they are secure are in great danger. The armor-bearer of sin is self-confidence.

David should have been off fighting, but he remained in Jerusalem enjoying life. He got out of his bed in the evening. Idleness and luxury are the devil's weapons. Noxious creatures swim in stagnant water. A neglected garden soon produces a dense tangle of weeds and briars. We need the constraining love of Jesus to keep us active and useful for Him.

When I see the king of Israel lazily leaving his bed in the evening and falling into temptation it is a warning to me. I need to set a holy watchfulness to guard the door of my heart.

Could it be possible that the king went to the roof for meditation and devotion? If this is true, remember that no place, however secret, is a sanctuary from sin. Our hearts are combustible and sparks are plentiful. Use everything you have to prevent a blaze. Satan can climb housetops and enter closets. Even if we could keep that foul fiend out, our own corruptions would ruin us unless grace prevented it.

Watch out for evening temptations. Do not think you are secure. The sun may have set but sin is up. We need a watchman at night as well as a guardian during the day.

Oh blessed Spirit, keep us from evil tonight. Amen.

JANUARY 17, EVENING

Rest

"There remains therefore a rest for the people of God."

—Hebrews 4:9

Heaven will be much different than earth. Here we are weary of toil and suffering. There, in the land of the immortal, fatigue is unknown. Trying to serve our Master on earth we find our strength falls short and our constant cry is, "Help me to serve You, O my God." Here there is too much work. I am willing, but I don't have the strength. I am not weary of the work; I am wearied in it.

Ah, believer, this weariness will not last forever. The sun is nearing the horizon, but it will rise again with a brighter day than you have ever seen, upon a land where they serve God day and night but still have rest. Here rest is partial. There rest is perfect. Here we are always wandering and never arriving. There they are at rest and have reached the mountain top. They have ascended to the heart of their God and they can go no higher.

Ah, toilworn laborer, just think: you will rest forever. Can you imagine it? It is rest that remains an eternal rest. Here my greatest joys carry the label "mortal." My beautiful flowers fade. My delicious drinks are drained to the dregs. My sweetest birds fall to death's arrows. My pleasant days are shadowed into nights. The flood-tides of my pleasure ebb in sorrow.

But there everything is immortal. The harp doesn't rust. The branch doesn't wither. The eye doesn't dim. The voice doesn't falter. The heart doesn't waver. There we will be totally absorbed in everlasting delight.

Happy day! Happy day! When we shall put on immortality and our Eternal Sabbath shall begin.

TEACHER AND LESSON

"He expounded to them in all the Scriptures the things concerning Himself."

—Luke 24:27

The two disciples on the road to Emmaus had a profitable journey. Their companion and teacher was the finest of instructors, the one in whom are hid all the treasures of wisdom and knowledge (Colossians 1:9).

The Lord Jesus stooped to become a preacher of the gospel. He was willing to hold a class for two, and He is willing to teach even one person. Seek the company of this excellent instructor, for until He makes you wise, you shall never be wise unto salvation.

This unrivalled tutor used as His textbook the best of books. Though capable of revealing fresh truths, He preferred to expound the old here. He knew how He wanted to teach and spoke immediately from Moses and the prophets. He showed that the only certain road to wisdom was not found in speculation, reasoning, or human books but in meditating on the Word of God. The fastest way to be spiritually rich in heavenly knowledge is to dig in this field of diamonds, to gather pearls from this heavenly sea. When Jesus sought to enrich others, He worked in the quarry of Holy Scripture.

These greatly blessed disciples were led to consider the best subject: Jesus speaking about Jesus and expounding the truths about Himself. Here the diamond cuts the diamond, and what could be better? The Master of the house unlocks His own doors, leads the guests to His table, and places His food on it. He who hid the treasure in the field guides the searchers to it. Our Lord often talked about pleasant subjects, and He could find nothing sweeter than His own person and work. Always search the Word with this in mind.

Oh for grace to study the Bible with Jesus as both our teacher and our lesson!

SEARCHING

"I sought him, but I did not find him."

—Songs of Solomon 3:1

Tell me where you lost your fellowship with Christ and I will tell you where you can find Him.

Did you lose Christ by forgetting the prayer closet? Then that is where you must seek and find Him.

Did you lose Christ through sinning? Then the only way to find Him is to give up your sin and ask the Holy Spirit to discipline you.

Did you lose Christ by neglecting to read and study the Scriptures? Then you will again find Him in the Scriptures. The old proverb is true, "Look for a thing where you dropped it." Look for Christ where you lost Him, for He has not gone away.

It is difficult to go back and look for Christ. Bunyan tells us that Pilgrim found the road back to be the hardest to travel. Twenty miles forward is easier than one mile back. When you find the Master, stay close.

How did you lose Him? One would think you would never leave a friend so precious. His presence is sweet. His words are comforting. His company is desirable. Why did you not watch Him every moment? Were you not afraid of losing Him?

Even though you let Him go, what a miracle that you are now seeking Him. Even though you groaned, "Oh that I knew where I might find Him, that I might come to His seat" (Job 23:3), keep on looking. It is dangerous to be without your Lord. Without Christ you are a sheep without a shepherd, a tree without water, a leaf in a wind storm blown from the tree of life.

With your whole heart seek Him. "You will seek Me and find Me, when you search for Me with all your heart" (Jeremiah 29:13). Give yourself fully to the search and you will discover Him to be your joy and your gladness.

JESUS' COLLEGE

"He opened their understanding, that they might comprehend the Scriptures."

—Luke 24:45

Jesus not only opens the Scriptures, He also opens our understanding. In opening the Scriptures He has many workers, but in opening our understanding He is alone. Many can bring the Scriptures to mind, but only the Lord can prepare the mind to receive the Scriptures. Other teachers reach the ears, but our Lord Jesus is different because He instructs our hearts. Others deal with externals; He imparts an inward taste for truth.

The most uneducated become skilled scholars in the school of grace when the Lord Jesus, through His Holy Spirit, unfolds the mysteries of the kingdom (Mark 4:11). He grants them a divine anointing to see the invisible (Hebrews 11:27). They are happy when their Master gives clear understanding and strength.

How many people of profound learning are ignorant of eternal things! They know the killing letter of revelation, but not its living spirit. They cannot comprehend. They have a veil over their heart through which the eyes of carnal reason cannot see.

We were that way. We who now see, we were once totally blind. Truth was to us as beauty is to the dark, unnoticed and neglected. If it had not been for the love of Jesus we would have remained in complete ignorance. An infant could climb the pyramids and an ostrich could fly to the stars easier than we could attain spiritual knowledge apart from His gracious opening of our understanding.

Jesus' College is the only place where God's truth can be learned. Other schools may teach what to believe, but only Christ can show us how to believe it.

Sit at Jesus' feet and earnestly pray for His blessed aid to make our dull minds grow brighter, and our feeble understanding able to receive heavenly knowledge.

JANUARY 19, EVENING

THE GREAT KEEPER OF SHEEP

"Abel was a keeper of sheep."

—Genesis 4:2

As a shepherd, "Abel brought the firstborn of his flock and of their fat. And the Lord respected Abel and his offering" (Genesis 4:4).

This early type of our Lord is clear and distinct. In a similar way, Abel reveals the coming of our Lord. Abel was a shepherd, but also a priest who offered a sweet-smelling sacrifice unto God. In this act he points toward our Lord, who brings before His Father a sacrifice that pleases Jehovah forever.

As Abel was hated by his brother, Cain, Jesus was hated without cause, as our Savior. As Abel was murdered, and so sprinkled his altar and sacrifice with his own blood, he is a symbol of the Lord Jesus, who was slain by hate-filled men while serving as a priest before the Lord. "I am the good shepherd; and I know My sheep, and am known by My own. As the Father knows Me, even so I know the Father, and I lay down my life for the sheep" (John 10:14–15).

Abel's blood spoke. The Lord said to Cain, "The voice of your brother's blood cries out to Me from the ground" (Genesis 4:10). The blood of Jesus has a mighty voice too, and its theme is not vengeance but mercy. It is precious beyond all preciousness to stand at the altar of our good Shepherd, to watch Him bleed as the slaughtered priest and then hear His blood speak peace to all His flock. Peace in our conscience. Peace between Jew and Gentile. Peace between man and man's offended Maker. Peace down through the ages of eternity for blood-washed saints. Abel is the first shepherd, but our hearts will always place Jesus first in order of excellence.

Great Keeper of the sheep, we the people of Your pasture bless You with whole hearts when we see You slain for us.

WORTHLESS THINGS

"Turn away my eyes from looking at worthless things, and revive me in Your way."

—Psalm 119:37

There are many worthless things: the cap and bells of a clown, the laughter and music of the world, the dance, the cup of drunkenness, titles and educational degrees. The world knows that all of this is worthless.

Far more treacherous, however, are those equally worthless things: the cares of this world and the deceit of riches. If you spend your life amassing wealth your days will pass as a worthless show. Unless we follow Christ each day and make God the great object of our lives we differ only in appearance from the most foolish. We need to take to heart the first part of our text, "Turn away my eyes from looking at worthless things."

"Revive me in your way." The Psalmist confesses that he is dull, heavy, moody, and all but dead. I may feel like this. I may feel so sluggish or moody that the best motives cannot revive me. Will hell revive me? Can I think about sinners perishing and not wake myself up? Will heaven revive me? Can I think about the reward that awaits the righteous and still remain cold? Will death revive me? Can I think about dying and standing before God and still be sloppy in my Master's service? Will Christ's love motivate me? Can I think of His wounds on the cross and still not be stirred with fervency and enthusiasm? It seems so!

Only God Himself can revive me. Thus the cry, "Revive me." The Psalmist pours out his soul in passionate pleadings. His body and soul unite in fervent prayer. "Turn away my eyes from looking at worthless things, and revive me in your way." This is a good prayer everyday.

Dear Lord, in my case, hear it tonight. Amen.

JANUARY 20, EVENING

IF ONE WAS MISSING

"And so all Israel will be saved."

—Romans 11:26

The joy of knowing that all Israel was safe caused Moses to sing at the Red Sea. Not a drop of spray fell from that solid wall of water until every citizen of God's Israel was safe on the other side. Once that was accomplished the sea returned. Part of Moses' song was, "You in mercy have led forth the people You have redeemed" (Exodus 15:13). When all the elect shall sing the song of Moses, it shall be the claim of Jesus, "Of those whom You gave Me I have lost none" (John 18:9). There will not be a vacant throne in heaven:

> For all the chosen race
>   Shall meet around the throne,
> Shall bless the conduct of His grace,
>   And make His glories known.

As many as God has chosen, as many as Christ has redeemed, as many as the Spirit has called, as many as believe in Jesus—all shall safely cross the dividing sea. Of course, we are not all safely landed yet:

> Part of the host have crossed the flood,
>   And part are crossing now.

The advanced guard of the army has already reached the shore, but we are still marching through the depths. We are this very day following our Leader into the heart of the sea. Be of good cheer. The rear guard will soon be on the shore, and the last of the chosen will soon be across. Then when all are secure we will hear the song of triumph.

But oh! If one was missing. Oh! If one of the chosen did not make it. There would be an everlasting discord in the song of the redeemed. The strings of the harps of paradise would be cut, never to make music again.

JANUARY 21, MORNING

THE AFTERMATH

"Then he became very thirsty; so he cried out to the Lord and said, 'You have given this great deliverance by the hand of Your servant, and now shall I die of thirst?'"
—Judges 15:18

Samson was thirsty and ready to die. This difficulty was totally different from anything the hero had previously experienced. To have his thirst quenched was nothing compared to being delivered from a thousand Philistines, but a very thirsty Samson felt this small problem was worse than any of the great difficulties from which God had so specially delivered him.

After a great deliverance it is common for God's people to find that a minor problem overwhelms them. Samson kills a thousand Philistines, stacks their bodies, and then faints for a little water! Jacob wrestles with God at Peniel and overcomes, but he becomes lame (Genesis 32:25).

Is it not strange that our muscles shrink after we win a victory? It is as if the Lord must teach us how little and how nothing we are without Him. God has many ways to humble His people. Dear child of God, if after a great mercy you are laid very low, your case is not unusual. When David assumed the throne of Israel he said, "And I am weak today, though anointed king" (2 Samuel 3:39). Expect to feel the weakest after you have enjoyed the greatest triumph.

If in the past God has given you a great victory, your present difficulty is only like Samson's thirst. The Lord will not let you faint or permit the world to triumph over you. The road of sorrow is the road to heaven, but there are refreshing wells of water all along the route.

So tired Christian, let Samson's words cheer your heart, and then rest assured God will soon deliver you.

PRIDE

"Son of man, how is the wood of the vine better than any other wood, the vine branch which is among the trees of the forest?"

—Ezekiel 15:2

These are words to humble God's people. We are called God's vine but by nature we are no better than anyone else. It is only by God's goodness that we are fruitful. Planted in good soil, we are trained by the Lord to grow up the sanctuary walls and produce fruit for His glory.

What are we without God? What are we without the constant influence of the Spirit who makes us fruitful? Oh believer, learn to reject pride. In you there is no room for it. Whoever you are, whatever you have accomplished, you have nothing to make you proud. The more you have the more you are in debt to God, and there is no reason to be proud that you are in debt.

Think about where you came from. Look back at what you were. Where would you be today but for His divine grace? Look at yourself. Does your conscience bother you? Do your thousands of failures tell you that you are not worthy to be called His son?

If He has done anything for you, you know it is only grace that made the difference. Great believer, you would be a great sinner if God had not made you different. You who are courageous for the truth would have been courageous for error if grace had not seized you.

Do not be proud. Even if you own a large estate it is a wide domain of grace and all you once owned was sin and misery. How strange an idea to think that we who have borrowed everything would exalt ourselves.

We are merely poor dependents who rely on the bounty of our Savior. We are vines that will die unless we receive fresh water from the streams of life in Jesus (John 7:37–38). And yet we are proud. Oh foolish hearts!

THE REWARD

"Does Job fear God for nothing?"

—Job 1:9

This was Satan's wicked question concerning that upright man, Job. Today that same question could be asked of many.

There are people who love God only because He prospers them. If things went bad they would give up their boasted faith. If after their supposed conversion they clearly see that the world has prospered them, they will love God in their poor carnal way. But if adversity strikes they will rebel against God. They love the table but not the host. They love the cupboard but not the master of the house.

True Christians expect their reward in the next life and anticipate enduring adversity in this life. The promise of the old covenant was prosperity, but the promise of the new covenant is adversity. Remember Christ's words, "Every branch in Me that does not bear fruit He takes away; and every branch that bears fruit [What?] He prunes, that it may bear more fruit" (John 15:2).

"What!" you say. "That is a terrible promise." Yet this affliction yields such precious results that the Christian who goes through it learns to rejoice in trials. This evening rejoice in the blessed assurance that as trials increase so does His grace.

Let me promise you this, child of God, you will be no stranger to the rod. Sooner or later every bar of gold must pass through the fire. Do not worry. Rejoice. Such fruitful days are ahead that you will forget this world and be ready for heaven. You will be delivered from clinging to the present to looking forward to eternal things soon to be revealed. When you feel that you are serving God for nothing, rejoice in the infinite reward of the future.

JANUARY 22, EVENING

FOOTPRINTS

"I have exalted one, chosen from the people."

—Psalm 89:19

Why was Christ chosen from the people? Answer my heart, because heart thoughts are best. Was it because He would be our brother in the blessed tie of blood relationship? Oh what a relationship there is between Christ and the believer. The believer can say, "I have a brother in heaven. I may be poor, but I have a brother who is rich. I have a brother who is a king, and He will meet my needs while He is on the throne! He loves me. He is my brother."

Believer, wear this blessed thought like a strand of diamonds on the neck of your memory. Wear it like a gold ring on the finger of your recollection. Use it as the King's own seal. Stamp your petitions of faith with the confidence of fulfillment. He is a brother born for adversity; treat Him as such.

Christ was also chosen from the people that He might know our needs and sympathize with us. "He was in all points tempted as we are, yet was without sin" (Hebrews 4:15). In all our sorrows we have His sympathy. Temptation, pain, disappointment, weakness, weariness, poverty—He knows them all for He has felt them all.

Remember this, Christian, and let it comfort you. No matter how difficult and painful your road, it is marked by the footprints of your Savior. Even when you reach the dark valley of the shadow of death and the deep waters of the swelling Jordan you will find His footprints there. Every place you go, He has already been. He is our forerunner. Each burden we have to carry was once placed on Immanuel's shoulders:

His way was much rougher and darker than mine;
Did Christ, my Lord, suffer and shall I repine?

Take courage! Royal feet have left a blood-red track on the road, and they have consecrated the thorny path forever.

JANUARY 23, MORNING

WE REMEMBER

"We will remember Your love more than wine."

—Songs of Solomon 1:4

Jesus will never let His people forget His love. If all the love He has given should be forgotten, He will visit them with fresh love.

"Do you forget My cross?" He asks. "I will make you remember it. At My table I will again reveal Myself to you. Do you forget what I did in the council chamber of eternity? I will remind you, for you will need a counsellor and I will be ready when you call."

Mothers do not let their children forget them. If a son moves far away from home and does not write, his mother writes, "Has John forgotten his mother?" Then a sweet epistle comes back, proving the gentle reminder was not wasted.

It is the same way with Jesus. He says, "Remember Me." And we respond, "We will remember Your love. We will remember Your love and its matchless history. Your love is as ancient as the glory You had with the Father before the world was formed. Dear Jesus, we remember Your eternal love when You became our guarantee and gave us Your engagement ring."

We remember the love of Your sacrifice. It was the love that, until the fullness of time, thought about its sacrifice and eagerly awaited the hour which was written, of You, in the volume of the book, "Behold I come" (Psalm 40:7).

Oh Jesus, we remember Your love as it was shown to us in Your holy life. From the manger in Bethlehem to the garden in Gethsemane we follow You from the cradle to the grave. Your every word and deed was love. We rejoice in Your love, a love that death could not stop. Your love shines in the splendor of Your resurrection.

We remember that burning fire of love which will never let You rest until Your chosen arrive safely home, until Zion is glorified, and until Jerusalem is settled on her everlasting foundations of light and love in heaven.

JANUARY 23, EVENING

THE TRAP

"Surely He shall deliver you from the snare of the fowler."

—Psalm 91:3

There are two ways God delivers us from the snare of the fowler. First, He delivers us from the snare by not letting us enter it. Second, if we should become trapped, He delivers us out of it. The first promise is the most precious to some, while to others the second promise is the best.

"He shall deliver you from the snare." But how? Trouble is often God's method of deliverance. God knows that backsliding will end in our destruction. Thus in mercy He sends the rod. We question, "Lord, why?" Little do we know that trouble is often His method of delivering us from a far greater evil. Sorrow and crosses have saved many from ruin by frightening the birds away from the fowler's net.

At other times God keeps us from the snare by giving spiritual strength so great that when tempted we may say, "How can I do this great wickedness and sin against my God?"

What a blessed thing to know that if, in an evil hour, the believer goes into the net, God will bring him out. Oh backslider, be cast down but do not despair. If you have drifted away, listen again to your Redeemer. "Return backsliding child . . . for I am merciful" (Jeremiah 3:12).

You say you cannot return because you are captive. Listen to the promise: "Surely He shall deliver you from the snare of the fowler." You will be delivered from the evil you have fallen into. Even though you may need to continue to repent of your ways, He that loves you will not cast you away. He will receive you. He will give such joy and gladness "that the bones He broke may rejoice" (Psalm 51:8).

No bird of paradise will ever die in the fowler's net.

THE FIRST THING

"But Martha was distracted with much serving."

—Luke 10:40

Martha's fault was not that she served. After all, a Christian is a servant. "I serve" should be the motto of all the members of heaven's royal family.

It wasn't Martha's fault that she had "much serving" to do. We cannot do too much. We need to do everything we possibly can. Our head, heart, and hands must be engaged in the Master's service.

It wasn't Martha's fault that she was busy preparing a feast for the Master. Happy Martha, to have an opportunity to entertain so blessed a guest and to have the willingness to throw her whole soul heartily into preparing dinner.

Martha's fault was that she was "distracted with much serving." She forgot Him and only remembered serving. She allowed service to override fellowship. We need to be both a Martha and a Mary. We need to serve and to have much fellowship with Jesus at the same time. To accomplish this we need great grace.

It is easier to serve than to have fellowship. Joshua never grew weary of fighting the Amalekites. But Moses on the mountaintop in prayer needed two helpers to hold up his hands (Exodus 17:12). The more spiritual the exercise the quicker we tire. The choicest fruit is the hardest to grow. The most heavenly graces are the most difficult to cultivate.

Beloved, while we do not neglect external things that are good in themselves, we must make certain that we enjoy a living, personal fellowship with Jesus. Do not neglect sitting at the Savior's feet.

The first thing for the health of our soul, the first thing for His glory, and the first thing for our own usefulness is to keep in continual fellowship with the Lord Jesus. See to it that a vital spirituality of our relationship with Jesus is maintained over and above everything else in this world.

JANUARY 24, EVENING

MEMORIES

"I will mention the lovingkindnesses of the Lord and the praises of the Lord, according to all that the Lord has bestowed on us."

—Isaiah 63:7

Can you do this? Have you ever experienced mercy? Even if you are depressed, never forget that blessed hour when Jesus met you and said, "Come to Me" (Matthew 11:28). Remember that wonderful moment when He snapped your shackles and dashed your chains and said, "Therefore if the Son makes you free, you shall be free indeed" (John 8:36).

Even if you have forgotten your love of Christ, you must have a precious memory that is not quite overgrown with moss where you can read a happy tribute of His mercy. Were you seriously ill and He restored you? Were you poor and He supplied your needs? Were you in great affliction and He delivered you?

Go to the river of your own experience, dig up a few bulrushes, and make an ark for your infant faith to float safely on the stream. Do not forget what God has done.

Open the book of your memory and think of days passed. Can you remember the hill Mizar? Did not the Lord meet you at Mount Hermon? Have you never climbed the Delectable Mountains (Psalm 42:6)? Have you never been helped by God in time of need? I know you have.

Go back just a little way to yesterday's choice mercies. It may be dark now, but if you light the lamps of the past they will glitter throughout the darkness and you will trust the Lord "until the day breaks and the shadows flee away" (Song of Solomon 4:6).

"This I recall to mind, therefore I have hope. Through the Lord's mercies we are not consumed, because His compassions fail not. They are new every morning. Great is Your faithfulness" (Lamentations 3:21,23). "Remember, O Lord, your tender mercies and your lovingkindnesses, for they are from of old" (Psalm 25:6).

REJOICE IN OBEDIENCE

"Do we then make void the law through faith? Certainly not! On the contrary, we establish the law."

—Romans 3:31

When a believer is adopted into the Lord's family the relationship to the old Adam and to the law immediately ceases. The believer is under a new rule and a new covenant.

Believer, you are God's child. Your first duty is to obey your heavenly Father, not like a slave but like a beloved child. Obey your Father's slightest suggestion. Does He ask you to fulfill a sacred duty? Do not neglect it or you will be disobeying your Father. Does He command you to be like Jesus? Then it is your joy to do it. "Therefore you shall be perfect, just as your Father in heaven is perfect" (Matthew 5:48). Work to be perfect in His holiness, not because the law commands but because your Savior pleads.

Does He ask you to love one another? Do it, not because the law says "you shall love your neighbor as yourself" (Leviticus 19:18), but because Jesus says, "If you love Me, keep my commandments" (John 14:15). And this is the commandment He gives: "love one another" (John 13:34).

Are you told to give to the poor? Don't do it because charity is a burden you must perform. Do it because Jesus teaches, "Give to him who asks you" (Matthew 5:42).

Does the Word say, "You shall love the Lord your God with all your heart" (Matthew 22:37)? Look at the commandment and reply, "Oh commandment, Christ has already fulfilled you. I do not need to obey for salvation, but I rejoice to be obedient because God is my Father and He owns me."

May the Holy Spirit make you obedient to the constraining power of Christ's love so that your prayer will be: "Make me walk in the path of Your commandments. For I delight in it" (Psalm 119:35).

Grace is the mother and the nurse of holiness, not the apologist of sin.

MY HEAVENLY FATHER

"Your heavenly Father."

—Matthew 6:26

We are God's children twice over. First by creation and second by adoption. We are privileged to call Him, "Our Father in Heaven" (Matthew 6:9). Father. What a precious word.

The Father has authority and the children are obedient. Here is affection mixed with an authority that does not provoke. The obedience of God's children is a loving obedience that is willingly and happily followed. We do not serve God as slaves of a taskmaster, but we rush to do His commands because He is our Father and this is His way. "Present yourselves to God as being alive from the dead, and your members as instruments of righteousness to God" (Romans 6:13). Righteousness is your Father's will, and His will must be the will of His children.

Heavenly Father. The very words are a kingly attribute covered so sweetly in love that the King's crown is forgotten in the King's face and the King's scepter is no longer an iron rod but a silver scepter of mercy. Indeed, the very scepter seems forgotten in the tender hand of Him who holds it.

Heavenly Father. The very words are honor and love. How great is the Father's love for His children. What friendship cannot do, what kindness will not attempt, a Father's heart and hand must do for His children. They are His and He will bless them. They are His and He will be their strong defense. If an earthly father watches over his children with unceasing love and care, how much more will our heavenly Father watch and care for us?

Abba, Father. If you can say that, it is sweeter than the music of angels and cherubim. There is heaven in the depth of that word *Father.* There is all I can ask, all my needs could demand, all my wishes might desire. I have all in all to all eternity when I can say Heavenly *Father.*

WONDERFUL THINGS

"And all those who heard it marveled at those things which were told them by the shepherds."

—Luke 2:18

We must never cease to marvel at the great wonders of our God. It would be exceedingly difficult to draw a line between holy wonder and real worship. When our soul is overwhelmed with the majesty of God's glory, though we may not express it in song or speak with bowed head in humble prayer, we silently adore. Our incarnate God is to be worshipped as "Wonderful" (Isaiah 9:6).

That God would even consider His fallen creatures is marvelous. That God would not sweep us away like trash in the gutter but send His Son to be our Redeemer is indeed wonderful. As we examine ourselves in the light of this great truth, redemption is astonishingly marvelous. What a miracle of grace that Jesus would give up the thrones and royalties of heaven to suffer shame and disgrace on earth for us.

Lose yourself in wonder, for in this case wonder is a practical emotion. Holy wonder will lead you to grateful worship and heartfelt thanksgiving. It will give you godly watchfulness. You will be afraid to sin against this great love. Feeling the presence of the mighty God in the gift of His dear Son, you will take off your shoes because you are standing on holy ground (Exodus 3:5).

You will be moved to glorious hope. If Jesus has done such a marvelous thing for you, then heaven is not too great an expectation. Who can be astonished at anything after being astonished at the manger and the cross? Is anything wonderful remaining after you have seen the Savior?

It may be from the quietness and loneliness of your life that you are hardly able to imitate the Bethlehem shepherds, who told what they had seen and heard (Luke 2:17). But at least you can fill up the circle of worshippers before the throne by marveling at those wonderful things God has done.

FULLNESS

"And of His fullness we have all received."

—John 1:16

These words assure us there is fullness in Christ. There is fullness of essential Deity. "In Him dwells all the fullness of the Godhead" (Colossians 2:9). There is fullness of perfect manhood. In Him, bodily, "the glory of the Lord shall be revealed" (Isaiah 40:5). There is fullness of atoning in His blood. "The blood of Jesus Christ His Son cleanses us from all sin" (1 John 1:7). There is fullness of justified righteousness in His life. "There is now no condemnation to those who are in Christ Jesus" (Romans 8:1). There is fullness of divine sufficiency in His plea. "He is also able to save to the uttermost those who come to God through Him since He always lives to make intercession for them" (Hebrews 7:25).

There is fullness of victory in His death. "Through death He might destroy him who had the power of death, that is, the devil" (Hebrews 2:14). There is fullness of power in His resurrection from the dead. "His abundant mercy has begotten us again to a living hope through the resurrection of Jesus Christ from the dead" (1 Peter 1:3). There is fullness of triumph in His ascension. "When He ascended on high, He led captivity captive, and gave gifts to men" (Ephesians 4:8).

There is fullness of blessing of every kind and shape and fullness of grace to pardon, regenerate, sanctify, preserve, and perfect. There is fullness of comfort in affliction and of guidance in prosperity. There is fullness of every divine attribute, of wisdom, power, and love, a fullness that is impossible to survey, much less to explore. "It pleased the Father that in Him all the fullness should dwell" (Colossians 1:19).

Come, believer, ask great things and you will receive great things. This *fullness* is inexhaustible. This *fullness* is treasured where all the needy can reach it. It is treasured in Jesus, Immanuel: God with us.

JANUARY 27, MORNING

PONDER THIS

"But Mary kept all these things, and pondered them in her heart."

—Luke 2:19

This blessed woman exercised three parts of her being: her memory, she kept all these things; her affection, she kept them in her heart; her intellect, she pondered them. Her memory, her affection, and her understanding were all involved as she considered the things she had heard.

Beloved, remember what you have heard about your Lord Jesus and what He has done for you. Make your heart the golden pot of manna to preserve the memory of the heavenly bread (Hebrews 9:4). Let your memory treasure everything about Christ that you have felt, known, or believed. Then let your affections hold Him forever. Open the broken alabaster box of you heart and let the precious ointment of your affections stream over His pierced feet (Luke 7:37–38).

Meditate on what you read. Do not stop at the surface but dive into the depths. Be not like a bird that does not touch the water with its wings, but be like a fish that penetrates an ocean's depth.

Abide with your Lord. Do not treat Him like a stranger. "Constrain Him, saying, 'Abide with us for it is toward evening and the day is far spent'" (Luke 24:29). Hold Him. Do not let Him go.

Ponder means to weigh. Get out the scales of judgment. But who has scales that can weigh the Lord Jesus? "Behold, the nations are as a drop in the bucket, and are counted as the small dust on the scales; look, He lifts up the isles as a very little thing" (Isaiah 40:15). "Who has measured the waters in the hollow of His hand, measured heaven with a span and calculated the dust of the earth in a measure? Weighed the mountains in scales and the hills in a balance" (Isaiah 40:12). On what scales can we weigh Him?

If your mind cannot grasp the Lord Jesus in your understanding, embrace Him in the arms of affection.

PERFECTION

"Perfect in Christ Jesus."

—Colossians 1:28

Are you imperfect? Does everyday prove it? Does every tear that trickles from your eye weep *imperfection?* Does every sigh of your heart cry *imperfection?* Does every harsh word from you lips mutter *imperfection?*

You know your heart too well to imagine even for a moment that there is any perfection in you. Yet in the middle of this sad awareness there is comfort, for you are "perfect in Christ Jesus." In God's sight you are "complete in Him" (Colossians 2:10). Even now, at this very moment, "He has made us accepted in the beloved" (Ephesians 1:6).

But there is a second perfection yet to be realized. It is delightful to look forward to the time when every stain of sin will be removed from the believer and we shall be presented faultless before the throne (Jude 24). On that day the Church of Christ will be so pure that not even the eye of Omniscience will see a stain, or a wrinkle, or any such thing. We will be so holy and so glorious that Hart did not stretch the truth when he wrote:

> With my Savior's garments on,
> Holy as the Holy One.

Then we will know and taste and feel the happiness of this enormous but short sentence: "Complete in Christ" (Colossians 2:10). Not until then will we "know the width and length and depth and height—to know the love of Christ which passes all knowledge" (Ephesians 3:18–19).

Does this not make your heart leap for joy? Dirty as you are, one day you will be pure. Filthy as you are, one day you will be clean. What marvelous salvation! Christ takes a worm and transforms it into an angel. Christ takes a filthy, deformed thing and makes it clean and matchless in His glory, peerless in His beauty, and fit to be the companion of seraphs.

Oh my soul, stand and admire this blessed truth of perfection in Christ.

SEEN AND HEARD

"Then the shepherds returned glorifying and praising God for all the things that they had heard and seen, as it was told them."

—Luke 2:20

What was the subject of the shepherds' praise? They praised God for all the things they had heard. Let us copy them and sing about what we have heard, a song of thanksgiving for Jesus and His salvation.

They praised God for what they had seen. What we have experienced, what we have felt, what we have made our own, that is the sweetest music. "My heart is overflowing with a good theme; I recite my composition concerning the King; My tongue is the pen of a ready writer" (Psalm 45:1).

It is not sufficient to hear about Jesus. Hearing may tune the harp, but the fingers of living faith create the music. If you see Jesus with the God-given sight of faith, don't let cobwebs accumulate on the harp, but with loud praise to His sovereign grace sing your psalm and play your harp.

One reason they praised God was because of the agreement between what they had heard and what they had seen. Look at the last part of our text: "as it was told them." Have you discovered that the gospel is exactly what the Bible told you it would be? Jesus promised rest. Have you enjoyed sweet peace in Him? He said you would have joy, comfort, and life by believing in Him. Have you not received all these? "His ways are ways of pleasantness, and His paths are paths of peace" (Proverbs 3:17).

Surely you can say with the queen of Sheba, "Indeed the half was not told me" (1 Kings 10:7). I have found Christ to be sweeter than His servants said He was. I looked on the likeness they painted, but it was a crude image compared to Him. Our King in His beauty outshines all imaginable loveliness. What we have "seen" far exceeds what we have "heard."

Let us glorify and praise God for a Savior so precious and so satisfying.

JANUARY 28, EVENING

SOON

"The things which are not seen."

—2 Corinthians 4:18

In our Christian pilgrimage we need to look ahead. Before us lies the crown. Onward is the goal. Whether it is for hope, joy, consolation, or the inspiring of our love, the future has to be the grand object of the eye of faith.

Looking into the future we see sin cast out and the body of sin and death destroyed. We see the soul made perfect and ready to take a portion of the inheritance of the saints in light.

Looking further, the believer's enlightened eye can see death's river crossed, that gloomy stream forded, and the hills of light in the celestial city attained. We enter the pearly gates hailed as more than conquerors and are crowned by the hand of Christ. We are embraced in the arms of Jesus, glorified with Him, and seated with Him on His throne, just as He has overcome and has sat down with the Father. These thoughts can relieve the darkness of the past and the gloom of the present. The joys of heaven will surely compensate for the sorrows of earth.

"Quiet!" my fears. This world is just a narrow span, and it will soon pass. "Quiet, quiet!" my doubts. Death is only a narrow stream, and it will soon be forded. Time, how short; eternity, how long! Death, how brief; immortality, how endless! Even now I think I am eating Eschol's grapes and sipping from the well inside the gate (Deuteronomy 1:24–25). The road is short. I will soon be there:

> When the world my heart is rending
> With its heaviest storm of care,
> My glad thoughts to heaven ascending,
> Find a refuge from despair.
> Faith's bright vision shall sustain me
> Till life's pilgrimage is past;
> Fears may vex and trouble pain me,
> I shall reach my home at last.

WITH ME

"The dove came to him in the evening."

—Genesis 8:11

Thank you Lord for another day of mercy. Even though I am weary from toil I sing my song of gratitude to You my preserver.

The dove returned to the ark because she found no rest outside. Today I have learned that there is no satisfaction in earthly things. Only God alone can give my spirit rest. My business, my possessions, my family, and my accomplishments are alright in their own way, but they cannot fill the desires of my spiritual life. "Return to your rest, O my soul, for the Lord has dealt bountifully with you" (Psalm 116:7).

It was evening and the gates of day were closing when the weary dove came back to its master. Oh Lord, enable me this evening to return to You. The dove could not endure a night hovering over the restless waste, and I cannot bear to be away from You even for another moment. Jesus, You are the rest for my heart, the home for my spirit.

The dove did not land on the roof of the ark, "the dove came to him." Oh my longing spirit, look into the secret of the Lord. Pierce the interior of truth and enter that which is inside the veil. Reach my Beloved in actual deed. I must come to Jesus. Nothing less than love and the closest fellowship with Him will do.

Dear Lord Jesus, reveal Yourself, and spend the whole night with me. And when I wake, be with me still. Amen.

I notice that the dove brought in her mouth an olive branch, a memorial of the past day and a prophecy of the future, and I wonder if I have anything to bring home to please You? Do I have a pledge or deposit of lovingkindness? Yes, my Lord, I acknowledge my grateful thanks for Your tender mercies that are new every morning and fresh every evening (Lamentations 3:21–23).

Now I pray, "Put out Your hand and take Your dove into Your heart." Amen.

JANUARY 29, EVENING

THE SOUND OF MARCHING

"When you hear the sound of marching in the tops of the mulberry trees, then you shall advance quickly."

—2 Samuel 5:24

We need to be prayerful. We need to seek the anointing of the Holy One to rest in our hearts. We need the kingdom of Christ to come. "Your will be done on earth as it is in heaven" (Matthew 6:10).

There are times when God seems especially to favor Zion, such as "when you hear the sound of marching in the tops of the mulberry trees." This is when we need to be doubly prayerful, doubly earnest, and wrestling more than usual at the throne. Actions need to be prompt and vigorous. The tide is flowing. Row, row for the shore. We need a Pentecostal outpouring and a Pentecostal work.

"When you hear the sounds of marching in the tops of the mulberry trees," you have great power in prayer. The Spirit of God gives you joy and gladness. The Scripture is open to you and the promises are applied. You walk in the light of God's countenance. You have a special freedom and liberty in devotion. There is closer fellowship with Christ than you thought possible.

On joyous occasions, "when you hear the sound of marching in the tops of the mulberry trees," that is the time to touch God. When God the Spirit is helping your weakness, that is the time to get rid of any evil habit. Spread your sail, but remember what you must sing:

I can only spread the sail;
Thou! Thou! must breathe the auspicious gale.

Make sure you have the sail up. Do not miss the wind for lack of preparation. Seek God's help to be more earnest in duty, more strong in faith, more constant in prayer, and to have more liberty at the throne, that your lifestyle may be more holy as you live closer to Christ.

JANUARY 30, MORNING

THE INHERITANCE

"In Him also we have obtained an inheritance."

—Ephesians 1:11

When Jesus gave Himself for us, He also gave us His privileges and rights. As eternal God He has exclusive rights, yet as the Mediator, the federal Head of the covenant of grace, Jesus' heritage is ours.

All the glorious results of His obedience to death are our joint riches. It was for us He accomplished the divine will. See, He enters glory, but not only for Himself. "The forerunner has entered for us" (Hebrews 6:20). Does He stand in the presence of God? Oh yes, "Now to appear in the presence of God for us" (Hebrews 9:24).

Consider this, believer, that you have no right to heaven. Your only right is in Christ. If you are pardoned, it is through His blood. If you are justified, it is through His righteousness. If you are sanctified, it is because He is made your sanctification. If you are kept from falling, it is because you are complete in Him.

Jesus is magnified, for all is in Him and by Him. Thus your inheritance is certain because it is obtained in Him. Each blessing is sweeter and heaven itself brighter because Jesus your Beloved has obtained all.

There is no one who can estimate your portion of the divine inheritance. Weigh the riches of Christ on scales, weigh His treasures on balances, and then try to count your riches and treasures. Reach the bottom of Christ's sea of joy and you will still be unable to comprehend the blessing God has prepared for those that love Him (1 Corinthians 2:9). Leap over the boundaries of Christ's possessions and all you will be able to do is dream of a limit to the inheritance of the elect.

"For all things are yours, . . . and you are Christ's, and Christ is God's" (1 Corinthians 3:21,23).

JANUARY 30, EVENING

IMPUTED AND IMPARTED

"The Lord our Righteousness."

—Jeremiah 23:6

It always gives me great calm, untroubled comfort, and peace to think about the perfect righteousness of Jesus Christ. Frequently the saints of God are downcast and sad. I do not think they would be if they could always see their perfection in Christ.

There are some who are always talking about corruption, the depravity of the heart, and the innate evil of the soul. But why not also go a little further and remember that we are "perfect in Christ Jesus" (Colossians 1:28). No wonder those who dwell on corruption are downcast. Surely if we recall that Christ is made righteousness we will be of good cheer.

Though distress afflicts me, though Satan assaults me, though there are many things to be experienced before I reach heaven, these are all done for me in the covenant of divine grace. There is nothing lacking in my Lord; Christ has done it all.

On the cross He said, "It is finished" (John 19:30). And if it is finished then I am complete in Him. I can "rejoice with joy inexpressible and full of glory" (1 Peter 1:8), "not having my own righteousness, which is from the law, but that which is through faith in Christ, the righteousness which is from God by faith" (Philippians 3:9).

This side of heaven you will not find a holier people than those who have received the doctrine of Christ's righteousness. When the believer says; "I live on Christ alone; I rest only on Him for salvation; I believe, even though unworthy, that I am still saved in Jesus;" then there rises a motive of gratitude: shall I not love Him and serve Him, since I am saved only by His merits?

"For the love of Christ compels us, because we judge thus; that if One died for all, then all died; and He died for all, that those who live should live no longer for themselves, but for Him who died for them and rose again" (2 Corinthians 5:14). Saved by imputed righteousness, we greatly value imparted righteousness.

JANUARY 31, MORNING

RUNNING

"Then Ahimaaz ran by way of the plain, and outran the Cushite."

—2 Samuel 18:23

Speed in running isn't everything. The course selected is also important. A swift runner racing up and down hills can not keep pace with a slower traveler on level ground.

What about running my spiritual journey? Am I pressing up the hill of my own works and running down the ravines of my own humiliations and resolutions? I must run the level way. I must "believe that [I] shall also live with Him" (Romans 6:8).

How blessed it is to wait on the Lord by faith. "Those who wait on the Lord shall renew their strength; they shall mount up with wings like eagles. They shall run and not be weary. They shall walk and not faint" (Isaiah 40:31). Christ Jesus is the way of life. He is the level way, the pleasant way. He is the way suitable for the tottering feet and feeble knees of trembling sinners.

Am I traveling in His way? "Whoever walks the road, although a fool, shall not go astray" (Isaiah 35:8). Have I been delivered from proud reason and been brought as a little child to rest in Jesus' love and blood? If so, by God's grace I will outrun the strongest runner who chooses any other path.

In my daily cares and needs I must remember this great truth. My wisest course is to go at once to my God and not wander to this friend or that associate. God knows my wants and can relieve them. I will go to Him through prayer and the plain argument of the promise. I will not talk to the servants but hasten to their Master.

In reading this passage, it strikes me that since we compete with each other in common matters then we must also run with total dedication to obtain the grand prize. Lord help me as, "I press toward the goal for the prize of the upward calling of God in Christ Jesus" (Philippians 3:14).

JANUARY 31, EVENING

REASONS TO SING

"Yes, they shall sing of the ways of the Lord."

—Psalm 138:5

Christians begin to sing when they lose their burden at the foot of the cross. The songs of angels are not as sweet as the first song of rapture that gushes from the innermost soul of the forgiven.

Do you remember how John Bunyan described it? When poor Pilgrim lost his burden at the cross, he gave three great leaps and went on his way singing:

> Blest Cross! blest Sepulchre! blest rather be,
> The man that there was put to shame for me!

Believer, do you remember the day your burdens were lifted? Do you remember the place where Jesus met you and said, "I have loved you with an everlasting love" (Jeremiah 31:3)? "I have blotted out, like a thick cloud, your transgressions, and like a cloud your sins" (Isaiah 44:22). Oh, how sweet it is when Jesus takes away the pain and load of sin.

When the Lord first pardoned me, I was so happy I could hardly keep from dancing. As I left the house where I had been set free, I thought that I must tell the stones in the street of my deliverance. I was so full of joy that I wanted to tell every falling snow flake of the wondrous love of Jesus, who had blotted out the sins of one of the chief rebels.

It is not only when we are saved that we have a reason to sing, but as long as we live we will discover new motives for song. As we experience His ongoing lovingkindness we will say, "I will bless the Lord at all times; His praise shall continually be in my mouth" (Psalm 34:1). Make sure you praise the Lord today:

> Long as we tread this desert land,
> New mercies shall new songs demand.

WONDERFUL LOVE

"Your love to me was wonderful."

—2 Samuel 1:26

We need to speak about wonderful love, not David's love for Jonathan, but the wonderful love of Jesus. And we will not talk about what we have heard, but about the things of the love of Christ that we have tasted and handled.

Jesus, Your love to me was wonderful when I was a stranger wandering far from You, fulfilling the desires of my flesh and my mind. Your love kept me from self-destruction. Your love held back the axe when Justice demanded, "Cut it down; why does it use up the ground" (Luke 13:7). Your love drew me to the wilderness and stripped me; it made me feel the guilt of my sin and the burden of my iniquity.

Your love spoke comforting words when I was utterly dismayed: "Come to me all who labor and are heavy laden, and I will give you rest" (Matthew 11:28). Your love is matchless. In a moment You washed away my sin. You made my polluted soul, crimson from the blood of my birth, filthy from the grime of my transgressions, as white as the driven snow and as pure as the finest wool (Isaiah 1:18).

With great love You whispered, "All mine are yours and yours are mine" (John 17:10). How kind were your words that "the Father Himself loves you" (John 16:27). How sweet the moment when You told me of the love of the Spirit.

Never will I forget the place where You unveiled your glory. Like Moses, we have our clefts in the rock where we have seen the full splendor of the Godhead in the person of Christ (Exodus 33:22). David remembered the tracks of the wild goats, the land of Jordan and the Hermonites. We also remember places equal to these in blessing.

Precious Lord Jesus, give us a fresh taste of Your wondrous love to start this month. Amen.

FEBRUARY 1, EVENING

THE ONLY RESTORATION

"Without shedding of blood there is no remission."

—Hebrews 9:22

This is an unalterable truth. In all the Jewish ceremonies the only way to remove sin was with the shedding of blood. In no case, by no means, can sin be pardoned without atonement. It is obvious, then, that the only hope for me is Christ. There is no other blood shedding worth a thought as an atonement for sin. Do I believe in Him? Is the blood of His atonement truly applied to my soul?

Regardless of how moral, generous, friendly, or patriotic we are, we all equally need Him. There are no exceptions to this rule. Sin will yield to nothing less powerful than the blood of Him who is our propitiation.

What a blessing we have in this one way of pardon. Why seek another? Those who practice mere formal religion cannot understand why we rejoice that our sins are forgiven. Their works, prayers, and ceremonies give them little comfort. They should be anxious because they are neglecting the one great salvation and attempting to obtain forgiveness without the shedding of blood.

My soul, sit down and watch God's justice punish sin. All that punishment is executed on your Lord Jesus. Fall down in humble joy and kiss the dear feet of Him whose blood made your atonement.

It is foolish when we turn to our feelings for comfort. That is a habit we learned in the legal bondage of Egypt. The only restorative for a guilty conscience is the sight of Jesus suffering on the cross. "Its blood sustains its life" (Leviticus 17:14), and let us rest assured that this is the life of faith and joy and every other grace.

> Oh how sweet to view the flowing
> Of my Savior's precious blood;
> With divine assurance knowing
> He has made my peace with God.

A HISTORY LESSON

"The records are ancient."

—1 Chronicles 4:22

Yet they are not as ancient as the precious things that delight our souls. Take a moment and recount them, telling them over and over as misers count their gold.

The sovereign choice of the Father, as He elected us into eternal life before the earth was formed (Ephesians 1:4), is a matter so ancient that our minds cannot conceive a date. We were chosen prior to the foundations of the world. Everlasting love was a part of that choice, for it was not just an act of divine will but divine affection that set us apart. The Father loved us in and from the beginning (2 Thessalonians 2:13). This is a theme for daily contemplation.

The eternal purpose to redeem us from our foreseen ruin, and to cleanse, to sanctify, and at last to glorify us was of infinite age past, though it runs side by side with unchanging love and absolute sovereignty into the infinite future.

The covenant is always described as everlasting (Genesis 17:7). Jesus gave us His guarantee long before the first stars began to shine. It was in Him that the elect were ordained to eternal life (John 3:16). In the divine plan a most blessed covenant was established between the Son of God and His elect people. This will remain as the foundation for our safety until time ceases.

It is good to be knowledgeable about ancient things. It is a shame that many neglect and reject the past. If they knew more of their own sin, they would be ready to adore special grace. Tonight, let us admire and adore Jesus as we sing:

> A monument of grace,
> A sinner saved by blood;
> The streams of love I trace
> Up to the Fountain, God;
> And in His sacred bosom see
> Eternal thoughts of love to me.

FEBRUARY 2, EVENING

TOTALLY IN DEBT

"Therefore, brethren, we are debtors."

—Romans 8:12

As God's creatures we are all debtors to Him. Our debt is to obey Him with all our body, soul, and strength. But we broke His commandments and so are in great debt to His justice. We now owe an amount so vast that we can never repay it.

Christians, however, do not owe God's justice anything because Christ has paid the debt, and for this reason we owe Him much more as debtors to His grace and forgiving mercy. But we owe justice nothing because God will never accuse us of a debt already paid. Christ said, "It is finished" (John 19:30). Whatever His people owed was wiped away forever from the book of remembrance. Christ has fully, totally, completely satisfied divine justice. The account is settled. The handwriting is nailed to the cross (Colossians 2:14). The paid receipt is presented. We are no longer debtors to God's justice.

Although no longer debtors to justice, we have become far greater debtors to God. Pause and meditate a moment. What a debtor you are to divine sovereignty! How much then do you owe His love? He gave His only Son Jesus to die for you (John 3:16).

Think how much you owe His forgiving grace. After ten thousand failures, He loves you as infinitely as ever before.

Consider what you owe to His power. He raised you from your death in sin. He preserved your spiritual life. He has kept you from falling. Even with a thousand enemies against you, you have been able to keep on your way.

Consider what you owe His unchanging nature. You have changed a thousand times, but He has never changed, not even once.

You are totally in debt to every attribute of God. You owe Him everything. "I beseech you therefore brethren, by the mercies of God, that you present your bodies a living sacrifice, holy, acceptable to God, which is your reasonable service" (Romans 12:1).

FEBRUARY 3, MORNING

CLOSE TO THE SHEPHERD

"Tell me . . . where you feed your flock, where you make it to rest at noon."

—Song of Solomon 1:7

These words express the believer's longing to follow and to have present fellowship with Christ. Where do You feed Your flock? In Your house? I will go, if You are there. In private prayer? Then I will pray without ceasing. In Your Word? Then I will read it diligently. In Your commands? Then I will follow with all my heart.

Tell me where You feed the sheep. Wherever You stand as the Shepherd, there I will rest as one of your sheep. Only You can supply my needs. Away from You there is no satisfaction. My soul hungers and thirsts for the refreshment of Your presence.

Where does Your flock rest at noon? But what difference whether dawn or noon? My only rest is with You and Your flock. My soul's rest must be by grace and that is given only by You. Where is the "shadow of a great rock in a weary land" (Isaiah 32:2)? Can I rest there? I do not want worldly companions; I want to be Your companion.

Satan tells me I am unworthy, but I always was unworthy. Yet You love me. Therefore, my unworthiness cannot prevent fellowship with You. It is true that my faith is weak and that I tend to fall, but my weakness is the very reason I always need to be where You feed Your flock.

I need strength. I need to be kept safe beside still waters (Psalm 23:2). Should I leave you? There is no reason to leave, but there are a thousand reasons why I should stay.

Jesus calls me to come. If He withdraws, it is only to make me love His presence more. Now that I am sad and distressed at being away from Him, He will again lead me to that sheltered cranny where the lambs of His fold are sheltered from the burning sun (Ezekiel 34:14).

PAST AND FUTURE

"The love of the Lord."

—Hosea 3:1

Look back through your experience and think of how the Lord your God led you in the wilderness. Think about how He fed and clothed you, how He tolerated your bad manners and put up with your complaints. Think also about how you wanted to return to the fleshpots of Egypt, but how He opened the rock to supply you and feed you with manna from heaven.

Think of how His grace has been sufficient in all your troubles (2 Corinthians 12:9), and how His blood has pardoned all your sins, and how His rod and staff have comforted you (Psalm 23:4).

And after you have looked back on His love, let faith survey His future love. Christ's covenant and blood are about more than what is past. He who has loved and pardoned will never cease to love you, will never cease to pardon you. He is Alpha and He will be Omega. He is the first and He will be the last (Revelation 1:8).

Remember, even when you pass through the valley of the shadow of death evil need not be feared, for He will be with you (Psalm 23:4). When you stand in the cold flood of Jordan, do not be afraid. Death cannot separate you from His love. When you come into the mysteries of eternity there will be no need to tremble. "For I am persuaded that neither death nor life, nor angels, nor principalities, nor things present, nor things to come, nor height, nor depth, nor any other created thing shall be able to separate us from the love of God which is in Christ Jesus our Lord" (Romans 8:38,39).

Is your love now rekindled? Doesn't this make you love Jesus? Did not this journey through the unlimited scope of His love rekindle your heart and compel you to delight yourself in the Lord your God?

Surely as we meditate on "the love of the Lord," our hearts will burn within us to love Him more (Luke 24:32).

A FAST ROAD

"Your refuge from the avenger of blood."

—Joshua 20:3

In the land of Canaan, cities of refuge were placed so they could be reached from any location in less than half a day. The Word of our salvation is also close to us. Jesus is a present Savior and the way to Him is short. Merely renounce your own merit and lay hold of Jesus to be your all in all.

The roads to the cities of refuge were well maintained. Every river could be crossed by a bridge and every obstruction was removed to ensure rapid travel. Once a year the elders walked the road to see that nothing could impede the flight of those seeking refuge. Delay could mean death.

Similarly, the promises of the gospel graciously remove the stumbling blocks from the way. Wherever there are turnings or crossroads, signs are placed: To the city of refuge!

This is a picture of the road to Jesus Christ. It is not a detour around the law. It is not obeying this, that, and the other. It is a straight road: "Believe, and live." Yet it is a road so difficult that the self-righteous never walk it, but so easy that those who know themselves as sinners find the way to heaven by it.

Once the pursued murderer reached the outskirts of the city, he was safe. It was not necessary for him to reach the city walls; the suburbs were sufficient protection. Learn from this. All you need to do is touch the hem of Christ's garment and you will be made well (Matthew 9:21). If you just touch Him with "faith as a mustard seed" (Matthew 17:20), you will be safe:

> A little genuine grace ensures
> The death of all our sins.

Don't waste time. Don't linger. The avenger of blood is swift. He may be at your door this evening.

EQUALITY

"The Father has sent the Son as Savior of the World."

—1 John 4:14

This is a sweet thought. Jesus Christ came to earth with His Father's permission, authority, consent, and assistance. He was sent by the Father to be our Savior.

We easily forget that while there are distinctions as to the persons in the Trinity there are no differences in honor. Frequently we ascribe the honor of our salvation, or at least the depth of its love, more to Jesus Christ than to the Father. Yet it was the Father who sent Him (John 17:4). It was grace from His Father that enabled Jesus to speak such wonderful things and to minister the new covenant.

We who know the Father and the Son and the Holy Spirit never put one before the other in love. We see them all at Bethlehem, Gethsemane, and Calvary, equally engaged in the work of salvation.

Christian, have you put your confidence in the Man Christ Jesus? Have you placed your reliance strictly on Him? Are you united with Him? Then you are united with the God of heaven, because the Man Christ Jesus is your brother and you are linked to God the Eternal (Mark 3:35). The Ancient of Days (Daniel 7:22) is your Father and your friend. Oh the depths of love in the heart of Jehovah! God the Father equipped His Son for the great enterprise of mercy.

Meditate on this today. The Father sent Him. Contemplate it. Think about how Jesus works what the Father wills. In the wounds of the dying Savior, see the love of the great I AM. Let your every thought of Jesus be connected with the Eternal, ever-blessed God. "Yet it pleased the Lord to bruise Him" (Isaiah 53:10).

LISTEN

"At that time Jesus answered."

—Matthew 11:25

What an extraordinary way to begin this verse: "At that time Jesus answered." It is extraordinary because no one asked a question, nor was Jesus having a conversation with any human being. Yet it states, "Jesus answered and said, I thank You, Father." When you answer a question, you answer the person who is speaking to you. Who was speaking to Christ? His Father. Yet, there is no record of it.

This verse teaches that Jesus had continual fellowship with His Father and that God spoke to His heart so often that here it was not necessary to record it. It was Jesus' habit, indeed His very life, to talk with God.

Let's learn the lesson this simple text teaches. Just as Jesus was in this world so are we, and like Jesus we need silent fellowship with the Father in order to answer Him. The world will not know who we are talking to, but we will respond to that secret voice made audible to us through the Spirit of God. And we will recognize with joy that God has spoken.

Let us answer and speak to God, either to say that He is faithful and true, or to confess our sin through the conviction of the Holy Spirit, or to acknowledge His mercy, or to affirm the great truths which God the Holy Spirit has opened to our understanding.

What a privilege to have intimate fellowship with the Father of our spirits. It is a secret hidden from the world, a joy that even our closest friends cannot share. To hear the whispers of God's love our ears must be clean and ready to listen to His voice.

This very evening, may our hearts be ready to hear when God speaks. Like Jesus, may we be prepared to answer Him.

PRAYERS

"Praying always."

—Ephesians 6:18

What a multitude of prayers we have offered since we learned to pray. Our first prayer was to ask God for mercy and to blot out our sins. And He heard us.

Then there were more prayers. We prayed for sanctifying grace, for motivating and restraining grace. And we have been led to crave a fresh assurance of faith for a comforting application of the promises, for deliverance from temptations, for help in business and strength in trials. We have been compelled constantly to ask God for everything.

Child of God, you have never received anything for your soul from elsewhere. All the bread your soul has eaten came from heaven. All the water it has drunk flowed from the living rock: Christ Jesus. Your soul will never grow rich by itself; it is always dependent on daily bounty from God. And so our prayers ascend to heaven for eagerly sought, infinite, spiritual mercies.

Your needs are innumerable but the supplies are infinitely greater. Your prayers are as varied as His mercies are countless. You can say, "Bless the Lord, because He has heard the voice of my supplication" (Psalm 28:6).

Your prayers are many but so are God's answers, even when you dishonor Him by trembling and doubting. "I will sing aloud of Your mercy in the morning; for You have been my defense and refuge in the day of my trouble" (Psalm 59:16). He still hears, strengthens, and helps you in your day of trouble. Remember this, and let it fill your heart with gratitude to God, who hears our poor weak prayers.

"Bless the Lord, O my soul, and forget not all His benefits" (Psalm 103:2).

THE SWEETEST PRAYER

"Pray for one another."

—James 5:16

As an encouragement to offer intercessory prayer joyfully, remember that intercessory prayer is the sweetest prayer God ever hears, for it matches Christ's prayers.

Of all the incense that our great High Priest puts in the golden censer, there is not a single grain for Himself. His intercession is the most acceptable of all supplications, and the more our prayer is like Christ's, the sweeter to God it will be.

While petitions for ourselves will be accepted, our prayers for others will be the sweetest service we offer God. Through the precious merits of Jesus, these prayers have more of the fruit of the Spirit; more love, more faith, more kindness.

Intercessory prayer is exceedingly effective. What miracles it has worked! The Word of God abounds with its marvelous deeds. Believer, you have a mighty engine in your hand. Use it well, use it continually, use it with faith, and you will be a blessing to others.

When you have the King's ear, speak to Him about the suffering members of His body. When you are favored to draw near to His throne and when the King says, "Ask and I will give you what you want," do not let your request be only for yourself but include the many who need His aid.

If you have any grace and are not an intercessor that grace must be as small as a mustard seed. It is just enough to float your soul clear of the quicksand.

If you had a deep river of grace, you would joyfully carry to God a heavy cargo of the needs of others, and you would return with blessings from the Lord for them, blessings they might not have obtained but for your prayers:

> Oh, let my hands forget their skill,
> My tongue be silent, cold and still,
> This bounding heart forget to beat,
> If I forget the mercy seat.

FEBRUARY 6, EVENING

THE LAST MOVE

"Arise and depart."

—Micah 2:10

The hour is approaching when the final earthly message will come to us, as it comes to all: "Arise and depart." Depart from the home where you live. Depart from the city where your work. Depart from your family. Depart from your friends. Arise, take your last journey.

What do we know about that journey and the country where we are going? We have read little about it, and the Spirit has revealed some things, but we do not know much about the future realms. We know that a black and stormy river called Death must be crossed and that God promises to be with us there (Psalm 23:4).

But after death, what then? What world of wonder will unfold to our view? No traveller has ever returned to tell us. We do know enough, however, about the heavenly land to welcome our summons here with joy and gladness.

The journey of death may be dark, but we go fearlessly because God will be with us. When we walk through that gloomy valley with God, we will fear no evil.

We will leave all we have known and loved, but we are going to our Father's house where Jesus is. We are going to that royal city "which has foundations, whose builder and maker is God" (Hebrews 11:10). This will be our last move. We will live with Him whom we love, in the midst of His people, in the presence of God.

Think about heaven. It will help you press on and forget the toil of the way. This valley of tears is nothing but the path to the better land. This world of woe is only a stepping stone to a world of bliss:

> Prepare us, Lord, by grace divine,
> For Thy bright courts on high;
> Then bid our spirits rise, and join
> The chorus of the sky.

FEBRUARY 7, MORNING

THE HEAVENLY SUMMONS

"And they heard a loud voice from heaven saying to them, 'Come up here'."

—Revelation 11:12

We will not consider these words in their prophetic connection, but as an invitation from our great Forerunner to His sanctified people.

Sooner or later every believer will hear a loud voice from heaven saying, "Come up here." The saints should look forward to this with joy. There is no need to dread leaving this world to go to be with the Father. We should eagerly wait for the hour of our emancipation. Our song should be:

> My heart is with Him on His throne,
>   And ill can brook delay;
> Each moment listening for the voice,
>   'Rise up and come away'.

We are not called down to the grave but up to the skies. Our heaven-born spirits should long for their native air. But if the heavenly summons is delayed, God knows best when to call, "Come up here." We do not want our departure to be premature. Strong love makes us cry:

> O Lord of Hosts, the waves divide,
> And land us all in heaven.

But patience must do its perfect work. God ordains with accurate wisdom the most appropriate length of time for the redeemed to abide below. If there could be regret in heaven, it might be that we did not live longer on earth and do more good. Oh for more souls for my Lord and more jewels for His crown. But more jewels can be obtained only by more work. If we serve God fully and if He gives us precious seed to plant and then harvest a hundredfold, we would say that it is best for us to stay where we are.

Whether our Master will say, "Come" or "Stay," there is no difference as long as we have His presence.

FEBRUARY 7, EVENING

THE SWEETEST NAME

"You shall call His name Jesus."

—Matthew 1:21

When you love people, everything about them is precious. So precious is Jesus that everything about Him is inestimable and beyond all price. "All Your garments are scented with myrrh, and aloes, and cassia" (Psalm 45:8). David spoke as if the very garments of the Savior were so sweetened by His person that he could not help but love even them.

Certainly there is no place where that hallowed foot walked, no word those blessed lips uttered, no thought His loving Word revealed, that is not precious beyond all price.

This is also true of the names of Christ. They are sweet in the believer's ear. If we call the Husband of the Church her Bridegroom (Revelation 21:2), or her Friend (James 2:23), or the Lamb slain from the foundation of the world (Revelation 13:8), or the King of kings (Revelation 17:14), or the Prophet, or the Priest (Hebrews 3:1), every title or name of our Master, Wonderful Counselor, Mighty God, Everlasting Father, and Prince of Peace (Isaiah 9:6), is like honeycomb, full of sweetness and delicious.

But if there is one name sweeter than any another in the believer's ear it is the name Jesus. Jesus! The name of all our joys. If there is one name more charming and more precious than the others, it is that name. It is woven in the fabric of our psalms. Many of our hymns begin with it, and scarcely any that are good end without it. It is the total of all delights.

Jesus is the music that makes the bells of heaven ring. *Jesus* is a song in one word. *Jesus* is a matchless oratorio in two syllables. *Jesus* is all the hallelujahs of eternity in five letters:

> Jesus, I love Thy charming name,
> It is music to my ear.

PROVEN SALVATION

"He will save His people from their sin."

—Matthew 1:21

Many define salvation as being saved from hell and taken to heaven. That is one result of salvation, but it is not a tenth of the blessing. It is true that our Lord Jesus does redeem all His people from the wrath to come. He saves them from the fearful condemnation their sins have brought on them. But His triumph is far greater. "He will save His people from their sin." Oh, what a great deliverance from our worst foes!

Where Christ works a saving faith, He casts Satan from his throne and will no longer let him rule. Thus if sin reigns in your body, you are not a true Christian (Romans 6:2). Yes sin will be in us; it will not be totally expelled until the spirit enters glory. But sin will no longer have dominion. Sin will strive for dominion and work against the new spirit God has implanted, but sin will no longer get the upper hand and again be the absolute ruler of our nature (Romans 6:14). Christ is now our Ruler. Christ is now the Master of our heart. Sin is put down. The Lion of the tribe of Judah prevails; the dragon is cast out (Revelation 5:5).

Professing Christian, is sin subdued in you? If your life is unholy, your heart unchanged, you are not saved. If the Savior has not sanctified you, renewed you, given you a hatred of sin and a love of holiness, then you have not experienced salvation. Grace that does not make you holy is a worthless counterfeit.

Christ saves His people not in their sins, but from their sins. "Without holiness no man shall see the Lord: looking carefully lest anyone fall short of the grace of God" (Hebrews 12:14–15). "Let everyone who names the name of Christ depart from iniquity" (2 Timothy 2:19).

FEBRUARY 8, EVENING

GUIDE ME, O THOU GREAT JEHOVAH

"Therefore David inquired of the Lord."

—2 Samuel 5:23

When David made this inquiry he had just defeated the Philistines in a great victory. The Philistines had a mighty army, but with God's help David routed them.

Then the Philistines returned, but David would not fight them again until he had inquired of the Lord. Having previously defeated them, he could have said, "I will be victorious again. I have great confidence. I beat them before and I can do it again."

But not David. He had won the last battle in the strength of the Lord, and he would not fight again until he knew God was on his side. "Therefore David inquired of the Lord," and he waited until God gave him a sign.

Learn from David. Do not take a step without God. If you want to know the way, take God for your compass. If you want to steer your ship through the dark storm, put the Almighty at the wheel. You will escape many rocks if you let your heavenly Father take the helm. You will avoid many shoals and sandbars if you let His sovereign will choose and command.

A Puritan said, "If a Christian carves for himself, he will cut his own fingers." This is a great truth.

Another old divine stated, "He that goes ahead of the cloud of God's providence is on a fool's errand." We must let God's providence lead us. Should providence tarry, wait until providence arrives. If you get ahead of God you will be very happy to go back.

"I will instruct you and teach you in the way you should go. I will guide you with My eye" (Psalm 32:8). This is God's promise to you. Take all your perplexities to Him and say, "Lord what do You want me to do?"

Don't leave home this morning until you have asked that question.

TEMPTATION

"And do not lead us into temptation, but deliver us from the evil one."

—Luke 11:4

What we seek or shun in prayer we should equally pursue or avoid in our daily walk. Earnestly avoid temptation. Walk so guarded in the path of obedience that you will never tempt the devil to tempt you.

"Be sober, be vigilant; because your adversary the devil walks about like a roaring lion, seeking whom he may devour" (1 Peter 5:8). Enter not the jungle in search of the lion. Presumption is costly. This lion may cross your path or try to leap on you from the thicket, but don't hunt for him. If you meet him, even if you defeat him, it will be a tough struggle.

Our Savior, who experienced temptation, earnestly admonished His disciples to "pray that you may not enter into temptation" (Luke 22:40).

Even so, we shall be tempted. And so we pray, "Deliver us from the evil one." God has one Son without sin but no son who has not been tempted. "We are born to trouble as the sparks fly upward" (Job 5:7), and just as certain the Christian is born to temptation.

We must always be on the lookout for Satan, because like a thief he gives no warning of approach. Believers who have experienced the ways of Satan know that there are certain times when he is likely to attack, just as certain seasons of the year produce high winds. This danger causes us to be twice as watchful (2 Corinthians 2:11), and stumbling can be averted if we are prepared. Prevention is better than having to be cured. It is better to be so well-armed that the devil will not attack than to endure the perils of a fight you could have avoided, even if you won.

This evening, pray that you will not be tempted. Then pray that if you are tempted you will be delivered from the evil one.

PERILS IN PROSPERITY

"I know how to be abased, and I know how to abound."

—Philippians 4:12

There are many who know "how to be abased," but they have never learned "how to abound." When they reach the pinnacle of success they become dizzy and are ready to fall off. Christians disgrace their Lord far more in prosperity than in adversity. It is dangerous to be prosperous. The crucible of adversity is not as severe a trial as the gold pot of prosperity.

Malnutrition of the soul and neglect of spiritual things are frequently a result of the mercies and bounties of God. Yet the apostle tells us he also knew how to abound. When he had much, he knew how to use it. Abundant grace enabled him to carry the burden of abundant prosperity. It takes more than human skill to carry a brimming cup of mortal joy with a steady hand.

Paul had learned that skill, for he wrote, "In all things I have learned both to be full and to be hungry, both to abound and to suffer need" (Philippians 4:12). It is a divine lesson to learn how to be full.

Many ask for provisions to satisfy their selfishness, but fullness of food and good things often causes spiritual loss. When we have many of God's providential mercies, it often seems we have little of God's grace and even less gratitude for blessings received. When we are full and forget God we become satisfied with earth and forget heaven.

Be assured, it is harder to know how to be full than it is to know how to be hungry, so desperate is the tendency of pride and forgetfulness of God in human nature. Ask God to teach you "how to be full":

> Let not the gifts Thy love bestows,
> Estrange our hearts from Thee.

RESTORATION

"I have blotted out, like a thick cloud, your transgressions, and like a cloud, your sins. Return to Me, for I have redeemed you."

—Isaiah 44:22

"Like a cloud, your sins." Clouds have many shapes and shades and so do our transgressions. Clouds obscure the sunlight and darken the landscape. Sin hides the light of Jehovah's face and makes us sit in the shadow of death.

Sins arise from the miry places of our nature. Sins threaten us with storm and wind. Unlike some clouds, none of our sins produce gentle showers, but they deluge us with a fierce flood of destruction. Oh black clouds of sin, how can we have good weather while you remain?

Look joyfully on the act of divine mercy that blots out sin. God appears on the scene and with divine love reveals His grace by effectually removing the darkness, not by blowing it away but by blotting it out of existence.

Against the justified, no sin remains. The great transaction of the cross has eternally removed our transgressions. On Calvary's summit the great deed that put away the sins of the chosen was completely and effectually performed. "God demonstrates His own love toward us in that while we were still sinners, Christ died for us. Much more then, having been justified by His blood we shall be saved" (Romans 5:8–9).

Obey that gracious command: "Return to me." There is no reason for pardoned sinners to live at a distance from their God. If you have been forgiven, do not let a legal fear hold you back from the boldest access to our Lord. Backslider, repent. Don't stay in sin. Through the power of the Holy Spirit return to Him and enjoy that blessed fellowship.

Oh Lord, this night restore me. Amen.

FEBRUARY 10, EVENING

A PORTRAIT OF JESUS

"And they realized that they had been with Jesus."

—Acts 4:13

A Christian should bear a striking resemblance to Jesus Christ. You may have read beautiful and eloquent books on the life of Christ, but the best life of Christ is His living biography, written in the words and actions of His people.

If we are what we profess we would be such striking portraits of Jesus Christ that the world would not have to look for hours on end trying to find a resemblance. Rather, the world would immediately know we had been with Jesus and were taught by Him because our lives and daily actions would reflect Christ.

We need to be bold for Jesus Christ, never embarrassed to admit that we are His. Jesus will never disgrace us. Let us be careful that we never disgrace Him.

Imitate Him in your loving spirit. Think kindly, speak kindly, and be kind. Let the world say, "You have been with Jesus."

Imitate Jesus in His holiness. Go about doing good and do not waste precious time. Was Jesus self-denying, never looking out for His own interest? Be the same way. Was He devout? Be fervent in your prayers. Did He do His Father's will? Submit yourself to Him. Was He patient? Learn to endure.

And best of all, as the finest portrait of Jesus, forgive your enemies. Let those sublime words of your Master, "Father forgive them for they know not what they do" (Luke 23:34), always ring in your ears. Forgive as you hope to be forgiven. "See that no one renders evil for evil to anyone, but always pursue what is good" (1 Thessalonians 5:15), "for in so doing you will heap coals of fire on his head" (Romans 12:20).

Remember, to render good for evil is godly. Be godly in all your ways. By all means live so everyone will say, "You have been with Jesus."

RETURN

"You have left your first love."

—Revelation 2:4

We will never forget that best and brightest moment when we first saw the Lord and lost our burden. Then we received the roll of promise, rejoiced in full salvation, and went on our way in peace. It was springtime in the soul. Winter was over. Sinai's thunder was hushed and the lightning flashes were gone. You beheld God as reconciled, the law did not threaten vengeance, justice demanded no punishment.

Flowers appeared in our hearts. Hope, love, peace, and patience sprung from the soil. The hyacinth of repentance, the snowdrop of pure holiness, the crocus of golden faith, the daffodil of early love, all bloomed in the garden of our souls. The time for birds to sing had arrived. We rejoiced with thanksgiving. We magnified the holy name of our forgiving God.

Our prayer was, "Lord, I am thine, wholly thine, all I am, all I have I give to You. You bought me with Your blood, let me lose myself in Your service. In life and in death let me be consecrated to You."

Have you been faithful to this prayer? Your first love burned with a holy devotion to Jesus. Has it changed? Can Jesus say, "I have this against you, that you have left your first love" (Revelation 2:4)?

We have done so little for our Master's glory. Our winter has lasted far too long. We are as cold as ice when we should feel a summer's glow and bloom with sacred flowers. We give God pennies when He deserves dollars. No, not dollars; He deserves our heart's blood minted in the service of His church and His truth.

Oh Lord, should we continue this way after You have so richly blessed us? Will we be ungrateful and indifferent to Your good cause and work? Help us to return to our first love and send us a pleasant spring O Sun of Righteousness.

FEBRUARY 11, EVENING

THE SCALES OF GOD

*"For as the sufferings of Christ abound in us,
so our comfort also abounds through Christ."*

—2 Corinthians 1:5

This is a blessed balance. The Ruler of Providence has a set of scales; on one side He puts His people's trials and on the other side He puts their comforts. When the side holding trials is nearly empty the side holding comforts will be nearly empty. When the side holding trials is heavy, the side holding comforts will be just as full.

When the black clouds are thickest the light is brightest. When night falls and the storm threatens the Heavenly Captain is closest to His crew. It is a blessed thing that when we are most depressed we are lifted by great comfort of the Spirit.

Trials make more room for comfort. Great hearts are made from great troubles. The shovel of trouble digs the reservoir of comfort deeper and makes room for more comfort.

God comes in our heart and finds it full. He then begins to break our comforts and empty our heart that there may be room for His grace. The more trials the more comfort, because we have more room to receive it.

Another reason we can be happy in our trials is that God is closer to us. When the barn is full, we can live without God (Luke 12:16–21). When the bank account is bursting with gold we only need a little prayer, but take our security away and we want God. Once the idols are gone we are compelled to honor Jehovah.

"Out of the depths I have cried to You, O Lord" (Psalm 130:1). There is not a prayer as good as one that comes from the depths of a soul in deep trial and affliction. Thus trials and afflictions bring us to God, and nearness to God is happiness.

Oh troubled believer, do not worry about your heavy problems. Trials and afflictions are the heralds of great mercies.

THE PRESENT IMMANUEL

"He will give you another Helper, that He may abide with you forever."

—John 14:16

Before the coming of His Son the Great Father revealed Himself to believers of old. Abraham, Isaac, and Jacob knew God Almighty. Then Jesus came, and the ever-blessed Son in His own proper person was the delight of His people's eyes.

When the Redeemer ascended, the Holy Spirit became the head of this present dispensation, and His power was gloriously manifested on and after Pentecost. The Holy Spirit remains to this hour the present Immanuel: God with us. He dwells in and with His people, quickening, guiding, and ruling in our midst.

We cannot control His work for He is sovereign. But are we sufficiently troubled to obtain His help? Are we sufficiently watchful not to provoke Him to withdraw His aid? Without Him we can do nothing, but with His almighty energy the most extraordinary results can be produced. Everything depends on Him manifesting or concealing His power.

Do we look to Him for both our inner life and our outward service? Do we run before He calls and so act independent of His aid? We need to humble ourselves, this evening, for past neglects. We need the heavenly dew to rest on us, the sacred oil to anoint us, the heavenly flame to burn in us.

The Holy Spirit is not a temporary gift. He abides with the saints forever. Seek Him and He will be found. He is jealous, but He is also compassionate. If He leaves in anger, He tenderly returns in mercy. He does not grow weary of us but waits to be gracious:

> Sin has been hammering my heart
> Unto a hardness, void of love,
> Let supplying grace to cross his art
> Drop from above.

GREAT EXPECTATIONS

"Behold what manner of love the Father has bestowed on us, that we should be called children of God! Therefore the world does not know us, because it did not know Him." —1 John 3:1

If we consider who we were and what we feel ourselves to be even now when corruption is so powerful in us, we will be amazed that we have been adopted by God. What a great relationship! What a privilege! What care and tenderness children expect from their Father, and what love the Father has for His children. All this and more we have through Christ.

As for the temporary drawbacks of suffering with our elder brother, we accept this as an honor. "Therefore the world does not know us, because it did not know Him." We are content to be unknown with Him because we will be exalted with Him.

"Beloved, now are we children of God." That verse is easy to read but difficult to feel. Where are you this morning? Are you in the lowest depths of sorrow with sin rising in your spirit and grace trampled under foot? Remember, you do not live because of your graces or feelings. You live simply through faith in Jesus Christ. *Now,* with all these things against you; *now,* in the depths of sorrow; *now,* more in the valley than on the mountain; "Beloved, NOW are we children of God."

But you say, "Look at me, my life is not bright, my righteousness does not shine." Read the text: "It has not yet been revealed what we shall be, but we know that when He is revealed, we shall be like Him, for we shall see Him as He is."

May the Holy Spirit purify our minds. May His divine power refine our bodies. Then "we shall see Him as He is."

FREE

"There is therefore now no condemnation."

—Romans 8:1

Think about this! If you believe in Jesus you are actually and effectually cleared from all guilt. You are free from prison and there are no more chains. You are free from the bondage of the law, and free from sin. Your Savior's blood has made you free.

You have the right to approach your Father's throne (Hebrews 4:16). There is no vengeance or flaming sword to frighten you. Justice will not harm the innocent. Your spiritual disabilities are taken away.

There was a time when you could not see your Father's face but now you can. There was a time when you could not talk to Him but now you have access to Him with boldness (Hebrews 4:16). Once you feared hell but now that fear is gone. The innocent cannot be punished. If you believe in Jesus Christ you are not condemned. You have the same privileges as if you had never sinned. You are justified.

Every blessing that you would have had if you had kept the law is yours because Christ kept it for you. All the love and acceptance that your perfect obedience could have obtained from God is yours because Christ was perfectly obedient for you. Jesus has imputed all His merits to you. "For you know the grace of our Lord Jesus Christ, that though He was rich, yet for your sakes He became poor, that you through His poverty might become rich" (2 Corinthians 8:9). What a great debt of love and gratitude we owe our Savior:

> A debtor to mercy alone,
> Of covenant mercy I sing;
> Nor fear with Thy righteousness on,
> My person and offerings to bring:
> The terrors of law and of God
> With me can have nothing to do;
> My Savior's obedience and blood
> Hide all my transgressions from view.

FEBRUARY 13, EVENING

DAILY PROVISION

"And as for his provisions, there was a regular ration given him by the king, a portion for each day, all the days of his life."

—2 Kings 25:30

Jehoiachin was not sent away from the palace with enough supplies to last for months; he was given daily provisions. This is a picture of the happy position of the Lord's people. A daily portion is all that a person really wants. We do not need tomorrow's supplies because tomorrow's sun has not risen and tomorrow's needs have not yet been born. The thirst we might suffer in June does not need to be quenched in February. If we have enough for each day we will never be in need.

Enough for today is all we can enjoy. We cannot eat or drink or wear more than today's supply of food and clothing. The surplus gives us the care of storing it and the anxiety that someone might steal it. One staff aids a traveller; a bunch of staves is a heavy burden. Enough is as good as a feast and more than gluttony can enjoy. Enough is all we should expect, but a craving for more is ungratefulness. When our Father does not give you more, be content with your daily allowance.

Like Jehoiachin, we have a guaranteed daily provision, gracious and perpetual, given us by the King. How thankful we should be!

Beloved Christian, in matters of grace you need only a daily supply. You have no reserve of strength. Everyday you must seek help from above. It is a blessed assurance to know that your daily ration of renewed strength is provided through ongoing meditation, prayer, and waiting on God.

In Jesus you have everything. Enjoy your continuous allowance. You will not go hungry while the daily bread of grace is on the table of mercy.

THE MIRACLE

"She was healed immediately"

—Luke 8:47

One of the most touching and instructive of the Savior's miracles is before us in this text. The woman was ignorant in imagining that virtue flowed from Christ without His knowledge or will. She was a stranger to the generosity of Jesus. Had she only known His character she would not have gone behind His back to take a cure that He was so willing to give. Misery should place itself in the face of mercy.

If she had only known the love of Jesus she would have said, "I only need to be where He can see me, for His omniscience will tell Him my problem and His love will immediately heal me."

We admire her faith, but we wonder at her lack of knowledge. After being cured she rejoiced and trembled, thrilled with the miracle but fearful that Jesus would retract the blessing. She failed to comprehend the fullness of His love.

Nor is our view of Him as clear as it should be. May we "be able to comprehend with all the saints what is the width and length and depth and height—to know the love of Christ which passes knowledge; that you may be filled with all the fullness of God" (Ephesians 3:18–19).

This is the miracle. Her faith, though small and limited, was real faith. It immediately brought her healing. If we have faith then salvation is our present and eternal possession. If in the family of the Lord's children we are the most feeble we are still heirs through faith. No power, human or devil, can take away our salvation.

If we cannot clasp the Lord in our hands with Simeon (Luke 2:28), if we dare not lean our head on His bosom like John (John 13:23), we can still touch the hem of His garment and be made whole.

Take courage frightened one, "Your faith has saved you. Go in peace" (Luke 7:50). "Therefore, being justified by faith, we have peace with God through our Lord Jesus Christ" (Romans 5:1).

FEBRUARY 14, EVENING

GLORIFY JESUS

"To Him be the glory both now and forever."

—2 Peter 3:18

Heaven will be full of praises to Jesus. Throughout the unnumbered years of eternity, forever and ever, "to Him be the glory." "You are a priest forever according to the order of Melchizedek" (Hebrews 5:10). You are King of kings, Lord of lords, and the everlasting Father: "To Him be the glory both now and forever."

Never will His praises cease. That which was bought with blood deserves to last while immortality endures. The glory of the cross must never be eclipsed. The luster of the grave and the resurrection must never be dimmed. Jesus, You will be praised forever, as long as immortal spirits live, as long as the Father's throne endures: "To Him be glory and dominion forever and ever" (Revelation 1:6).

Believer, you are anticipating the time when you will join the saints above in ascribing all glory to Jesus. But are you glorifying Him now? In the words of the apostle, "To Him be the glory both now and forever."

Will you make the following your prayer this morning? "Lord, help me to glorify You. I am poor, help me to glorify You by being content. I am sick, help me to glorify You with patience. I have talents, help me to glorify You by using them. I have time, help me to redeem it by serving You. I have a heart, let me feel no love but Yours. I can think, let me meditate on You.

Lord, You put me in this world for something, show me what it is. Help me to work out Your purpose for my life. I cannot do much, but like the widow who gave out of her poverty I cast my time and eternity in Your treasury (Mark 12:44). I am all Yours. Take me. Enable me to glorify You in everything I do, in everything I say, and with everything I have. Amen"

A GIFT

"By which they have made You glad."

—Psalm 45:8

Who makes the Savior glad? His people, His church! But is it possible?

He makes us glad, but how can we make Him glad? By our love. Yet we confess with deep regret that our love is cold and distant. Still it is sweet to Jesus. Listen to His description of that love: "How fair is your love, my sister, my spouse! How much better than wine is your love" (Song of Solomon 4:10).

Jesus delights in you. When you lean on His bosom you not only receive joy you give Him joy. When you look on His all glorious face you not only obtain comfort you impart delight to Him. Our praises give Him joy, and it is not only the song of our lips but the melody of our heart's deep gratitude.

Our gifts please Him. He loves to see us place our time, our talents, and our possessions on His altar, not for their value but for our motives in giving. The humblest offerings of His saints are more acceptable than thousands of pieces of gold and silver.

Holiness is like frankincense and myrrh to Him. Forgive your enemy and you make Christ glad. Distribute your wealth to the poor and He rejoices. Be the channel for saving a soul, and He sees the travail of His soul. Proclaim His gospel and you are a sweet perfume to Him. Go to those who have never heard the message of salvation, lift up His cross, and you will give Him honor.

It is in your power to break the alabaster flask of costly fragrant oil and pour this precious oil of joy on His head (Matthew 26:7). Perfume your Lord with the myrrh, aloes, and cassia of your heart's praise.

Heaven, you will hear the songs of saints below.

LEARNING CONTENTMENT

"I have learned in whatever state I am, to be content."

—Philippians 4:11

Contentment does not come naturally. Covetousness, discontent, and complaining are as natural as thorns with roses. There is no need to plant thistles and brambles; they are indigenous to the earth and grow naturally. There is no need to teach people how to complain; they learn that without being taught.

But the precious things of the earth must be cultivated. If we want wheat we must prepare the soil and plant wheat. If we want flowers we must cultivate flowers for they will not grow naturally. Only in our new nature do we produce flowers, and we must be extremely careful and watchful to maintain and cultivate the grace God has sown in us.

Paul says, "I have learned in whatever state I am, to be content. I know how to be abased and I know how to abound. Everywhere and in all things I have both to be full and to be hungry, both to abound and to suffer need."

Here Paul implied that at one time he did not know how to be content. It was a painful experience for Paul to learn this great lesson. There were times when he thought he had learned it only to fail. Paul was an old, grey headed man and close to death, a poor prisoner locked in Nero's cold, damp dungeon before he could say, "I have learned in whatever state I am to be content."

We might be willing to endure Paul's infirmities and share that dungeon if we could learn contentment. But don't think for one moment you can gain contentment without learning or without discipline. Contentment is not something that comes naturally. It is like a science gradually acquired.

Stop complaining, even though it is second nature. Try to be a diligent student in the College of Contentment.

GRATITUDE TO THE HOLY SPIRIT

"Your good spirit."

—Nehemiah 9:20

Far too common is the sin of forgetting the Holy Spirit. This is foolishness and ingratitude. He deserves good treatment, for He is good, supremely good.

As God, He is good in essence. He shares in the threefold praise of "Holy, Holy, Holy" that ascends to the Triune Jehovah (Revelation 4:8). He is all purity, truth, and grace.

He is benevolent, tenderly bearing our waywardness, striving with our rebellion, awaking us from our death in sin, and training us for the skies. How generous, forgiving, and tender is this patient Spirit of God.

He originates and sustains all good. All His works are good to the highest degree. He suggests good thoughts, prompts good actions, reveals good truths, applies good promises, assists in good attainments, and leads to good results. All the spiritual good in the world originates and is sustained by Him. Heaven itself will owe the perfect character of its redeemed inhabitants to His good work.

He fulfills His office well. As Comforter, Instructor, Guide, Sanctifier, Quickener, and Intercessor He fulfills His duties well and each is for the highest good for the church of God. Those who yield to His influence become good. Those who obey His impulses do good. Those who live under His power receive good.

Let us act with gratitude toward so good a person. Let us revere Him and adore Him as God over all, blessed forever and ever. Let us use His power and understand our need of Him by waiting on Him in all of the Lord's work. Let us daily seek His aid and never grieve Him. Let us speak His praises at every opportunity.

The church will never prosper until it reverently believes in the Holy Spirit. He is good and kind. It is sad that we grieve Him by neglect and inconsideration.

MEMORIES OF A WELL

"And Isaac dwelt at Beer Lahai Roi."

—Genesis 25:11

At the well of Beer Lahai Roi, Hagar and Ishmael found life-saving water graciously revealed to them by God. Their visit was brief, similar to the visits some people pay the Lord in times of need. They cry to Him in trouble but forsake Him in prosperity. But Isaac dwelt there. Isaac made the well of the all-seeing God his constant source of supply.

The daily course of your life, the place where your soul dwells, is the true test of where you live. It was by this well in the evening that Isaac sat and meditated. Perhaps Hagar's providential visit crossed Isaac's mind. Perhaps he mulled over the well's mystical name or recalled meeting Rebecca here, endearing this place to him forever.

But above all, the fellowship he enjoyed with the living God at the well made him select this hallowed ground for his dwelling place. We need to learn to dwell in the presence of the living God. Pray to the Holy Spirit that today and everyday we may feel the presence of "Him who sees me" (Genesis 16:13).

May the Lord Jehovah be a well to us, delightful, comforting, unfailing, and springing up to eternal life. Our wineskins are cracked and dried, but the well of our Creator never fails. Happy are you who dwell at the well and have an abundant and constant supply. The Lord is a sure helper. His name is Shaddai: God All-sufficient.

Frequently we have the most delightful fellowship with Him, for through Him our souls have found their glorious Husband, the Lord Jesus. "In Him, we live, and move, and have our being" (Acts 17:28).

Glorious Lord, may we never leave You. May we stay in close fellowship at the well of the living God. Amen.

FEBRUARY 17, MORNING

JEHOVAH SHAMMAH, THE LORD IS THERE

"The Lord was there."

—Ezekiel 35:10

The princes of Edom saw the desolate country and thought it would be an easy conquest of Israel. Quite unknown to them, however, was one great difficulty: "The Lord was there." And in His presence the land was secure.

Whatever the machinations and devices of our enemies, we still have that same effectual barrier to stop their plans. The saints are God's heritage. He is in their midst and will protect His own. What a comfort this assurance is in times of trouble and spiritual conflict. We are continually opposed, yet perpetually preserved! How often Satan shoots his arrows against our faith, but our faith defies the power of hell's fiery darts. They are not only turned aside but extinguished because "the Lord is there."

It is our good works that Satan attacks. A saint never had a virtue or a grace that was not the target of hellish bullets. Whether it was bright sparkling hope, or warm fervent love, or all-enduring patience, or flaming zeal, the old enemy of everything that is good has tried to destroy it. The only reason anything virtuous or lovely survives is because "the Lord is there."

And if the Lord is with us through life we will also have confidence through death. When we come to die we will find that "the Lord is there." When the waves are most turbulent, the water cold, and the time passed away we shall touch bottom and know that it is good because our feet will stand on the Rock of Ages.

From the beginning of our Christian life to the end, the only reason we do not perish is because "the Lord is there." Only if the God of everlasting love could change and let His elect perish would the church be destroyed. But that cannot happen because it is written: Jehovah Shammah, the Lord is there.

FEBRUARY 17, EVENING

A REASON FOR TRIALS

"Show me why you contend with me."

—Job 10:2

Perhaps you are going through deep trials so the Lord can develop your graces. There are certain graces that would never be discovered were it not for your trials. Your faith never looks as grand in the summer as it does in the winter. Love is too often like a glowworm, showing little light unless surrounded by darkness. Hope is like a star, never seen in the sunshine of prosperity but only discovered in the night of adversity. Afflictions are often the black settings in which God places the jewels of His children's graces to make them shine brighter.

Perhaps it was only a short time ago that you prayed, "Lord, I fear I have no faith. Let me know what faith is." Wasn't this really a prayer for trials? For you will never know if you have faith until your faith is exercised. Count on this: God often sends trials so that we can discover our graces, but it is more than just a discovery because *real growth* in grace results from sanctified trials.

God often takes away our comforts and our privileges to make us better Christians. God's troops don't dwell in tents of luxury and ease. He trains His soldiers with forced marches and hard service. He makes them ford streams, swim rivers, climb mountains, and walk many miles carrying heavy knapsacks of sorrow.

Well, Christian, could this be the reason you are having heavy trials? Is this the reason He is contending with you?

> Trials make the promise sweet;
> Trials give new life to prayer;
> Trials bring me to His feet,
> Lay me low, and keep me there.

This life I live now, is training for the last day I spend on earth. This life I live now is training for my entry into eternity.

FEBRUARY 18, MORNING

CONFESSION

"Father, I have sinned."

—Luke 15:18

Those whom Christ has washed in His precious blood do not have to confess sin before God as before the Judge, because Christ has forever taken away all our sin. In a legal sense, unlike culprits and criminals, we no longer stand where we can be condemned, but are once and for all accepted in the beloved.

But having become children and having offended as children, we should daily go before our heavenly Father and confess our sin and acknowledge our iniquity. Nature teaches that it is the duty of sinning children to confess to their earthly father. We as Christians should do no less with our heavenly Father. We offend daily and should not rest until we have sought our Father's pardon.

Suppose that my trespasses against my Father are not immediately taken to Him to be washed in Jesus' cleansing blood. Will there be any consequences? If I have not sought forgiveness then any offenses against my Father have not been washed away, and I will soon feel distant from Him. I will doubt His love. I will tremble and be afraid to pray. I will be like the prodigal who, though still his father's child, was far away from home (Luke 15:17).

If with childlike sorrow I go to Him, confess, and stay in His presence until I know I am forgiven, then I will feel a holy love for my Father. My Christian walk will be more than restored, and I will enjoy present peace in God through Jesus Christ my Lord.

There is a great distinction between confessing sin as a criminal and confessing sin as a child to the Father, whose bosom is the place for His children's penitent confessions.

We have been cleansed once for all. "The blood of Jesus Christ . . . cleanses us from all sin" (1 John 1:7). But our feet still need washing from the defilement of our daily walk.

FEBRUARY 18, EVENING

THE PREFACE TO BLESSINGS

"Thus says the Lord God; 'I will also let the house of Israel inquire of Me to do this for them'."

—Ezekiel 36:37

Prayer is the forerunner of mercy. Turn to sacred history and you will find that rarely did a great mercy come unless there was supplication. You have found this true in your own personal experience. God has given you many unsolicited favors, but great prayer has always been the beginning of great mercy.

When you first found peace through the blood of the cross, you had been earnestly and frequently praying for God to remove your doubts and deliver you from distress. The assurance you received was the result of prayer.

When you experienced great rapturous joy, you looked on it as answered prayer. When you had great deliverance from severe troubles, when you found mighty help in great danger, you were able to say, "I sought the Lord, and He heard me, and delivered me from all my fears" (Psalm 34:4).

Prayer is the preface to blessing. Prayer goes before the blessing to become the blessing's shadow. When the sunlight of God's mercies rises on our needs, it casts the shadow of prayer far down the plain.

Or, to use another illustration, when God piles up a hill of mercies, He Himself shines behind them and casts on our spirit the shadow of prayer. By this we may rest certain that our continual pleading is the very shadow of mercy.

Prayer is connected with the blessing in order to show its value. If we always received blessings without asking, we would consider them commonplace. Prayer makes God's mercies more precious to us than diamonds. The things we ask for are precious, but we do not realize how precious until we have earnestly sought them:

> Prayer makes the darken'd cloud withdraw;
>   Prayer climbs the ladder Jacob saw;
> Gives exercise to faith and love;
>   Brings every blessing from above.

BEGIN AT HOME

"He first found his own brother Simon."

—John 1:41

Here is an excellent example of a vigorous spiritual life. As soon as Andrew found Christ he began to bring others to Jesus. I cannot believe that you have tasted the honey of the gospel if you eat it all yourself. True grace puts an end to spiritual monopoly.

Andrew first found his own brother Simon and then others. Close relationships have a strong demand on our first individual efforts. Andrew, you did well to begin with Simon. I do not doubt that there are Christians giving tracts to others who would do well to give away a tract inside their own home. You may or may not be called to evangelize the people in a given location, but you are most certainly called to evangelize your relatives and acquaintances. Let your religion begin at home. Many companies export their best products, but the Christian should not. Take special care to testify to your family about the sweet fruit of spiritual life.

When Andrew went to find his brother he never imagined how prominent Simon would become. As far as I can tell from Scripture, Simon Peter did more than ten Andrews even though Andrew brought Simon Peter to Jesus.

Your talents may be few, but you can still be the means of drawing to Christ someone who will become eminent in grace and service. Dear friend, little do you know your possibilities. You may say only a word to a child, but in that child there may be a slumbering noble heart which will stir the Christian church in future years.

Andrew had limited talent, but he found Peter and brought him to Jesus. Go and do likewise.

COMFORT

"God who comforts the downcast."

—2 Corinthians 7:6

Who can comfort us like God? And yet, if *we* go to a poor, depressed, and distressed child of God and whisper a sweet promise with choice words of comfort it is like they are deaf. They won't listen. They sit there drinking wormwood and gall. Comfort them anyway you can and all you will hear is mournful resignation. They will not sing a psalm of praise, nor a hallelujah, nor a joyful song.

But let God come to comfort His child, let Him lift up the mourner's countenance and the eye will glisten with hope. Hear him sing:

> Tis paradise, if thou art here;
> If thou depart, 'tis hell.

There may be no way you can cheer the person, but the Lord can. He is "the . . . God of all comfort" (2 Corinthians 1:3). "Is there no balm in Gilead, is there no physician there" (Jeremiah 8:22)? There is balm in God. There is no physician among the creatures, but the Creator is Jehovah Rophi. It is marvelous how one sweet word from God will make whole songs for Christians. One word from God is a piece of gold, and the Christian can hammer that golden promise out for weeks. Depressed and distressed Christian, do not sit down in despair. Go to the Comforter and ask for consolation.

You are a dry well. You know that when a pump is dry it must be primed before you can get water. So, Christian, when you are dry go to God. Ask Him to shed His joy in your heart that His "joy may remain in you and that your joy may be full" (John 15:11).

Don't go to earthly acquaintances, for you may find them like Job's comforters. First and foremost, go to your "God that comforts the downcast." You will soon say, "In the multitude of my anxieties within me, Your comforts delight my soul" (Psalm 94:19).

WATCHFUL

"Then Jesus was led up by the Spirit into the wilderness to be tempted by the devil."

—Matthew 4:1

When Satan tempts us his sparks fall on kindling, but when Satan tempted Christ his sparks fell on water. If the devil struck when there were no results, how much harder will he work on the flammable material of our hearts. Even if you become greatly sanctified by the Holy Spirit, that great dog of hell will bark at you.

In this world we expect temptation. Even seclusion will not keep us from the tempter. Jesus Christ was led away from human society and into a wilderness where He was tempted by the devil (Luke 4:1–2). Solitude has its charms and benefits, and it may even be useful in checking the lusts of the eye and the pride of life, but the devil will follow us to the loveliest of retreats.

Do you think that only the worldly-minded have dreadful and blasphemous temptations? Spiritual people also endure this, and those in the holiest position may suffer the darkest of temptations. Even the utmost consecration of spirit is no guarantee against Satanic temptations. Christ was consecrated through and through. It was His "food to do the will of Him who sent Me" (John 4:34), and yet He was tempted. Your heart may glow with a flame of love for Jesus, but the devil will still try to bring you down to Laodicean lukewarmness (Revelation 3:15–17).

If you can tell me when God will permit a Christian to lay aside the armor, I will tell you when Satan will stop tempting. Like the old knights at war, we must sleep with our helmet and breastplate buckled on. The arch-deceiver will seize our unguarded moments to make us his prey.

May the Lord keep us watchful in all seasons and give us a final escape from the jaw of the lion and the paw of the bear (1 Samuel 17:37).

FEBRUARY 20, EVENING

SEARCH THE SCRIPTURES

"For He said."

—Hebrews 8:5

If we could grasp these words by faith, we would have an all-conquering weapon. We could slay every doubt with this two-edged sword, and every fear would fall with a deadly wound when struck by the arrow from the bow of God's covenant.

The distresses of life, the pangs of death, the corruptions within, the snares without, and the temptations from beneath will seem like light afflictions when we hide under the shelter of: "for He said." Whether for delight in our solitude or for strength in our conflict, "for He said" must be our daily thought.

There is great value in searching the Scriptures. There may be a promise in the Word that exactly fits your situation, but if you are unaware of it you will never know its comfort and you will be like a prisoner in a dungeon. There may be one key on the ring that will unlock the door, but if you don't look for that key you may remain a prisoner even though freedom is possible. There may be a potent medicine for you in the great pharmacy of Scripture, but you may continue to be sick unless you examine and search the Scriptures to discover: "for He said."

In addition to reading the Bible, you need to memorize the rich promises of God. You may recall the sayings of great men or treasure the verses of renowned poets, but you should also be profound in your knowledge of the words of God. In times of great difficulty and doubt, quote the promises for comfort, help, and solutions. "For He said": let it dwell in you richly as "a fountain of water springing up into everlasting life" (John 4:14). This is the way to grow spiritually healthy, strong, and happy.

PRAYER AND STUDY

"Do you understand what you are reading?"

—Acts 8:30

If we sought to have a more intelligent understanding of the Word of God, we would be better teachers, "no longer children, tossed to and fro and carried about with every wind of doctrine" (Ephesians 4:14). The Author of the Scriptures, the Holy Spirit, is the only one who can properly enlighten us to understand the Word, and we should continually seek His teaching and His guidance in all truth.

When the prophet Daniel wanted to interpret the dream of Nebuchadnezzar, he prayed earnestly that God would reveal the secret to him (Daniel 2:18). The apostle John, in his vision at Patmos, saw a book sealed with seven seals, and "no one was found worthy to open and read the scroll, or to look at it." Because of this, John "wept much." But the book was then opened by the Lion of the tribe of Judah (Revelation 5:4–5). The tears of John, which were his liquid prayers, were for him the sacred keys that opened the closed book.

For the benefit of yourself and others, "ask that you may be filled with the knowledge of His will in all wisdom and spiritual understanding" (Colossians 1:9). Remember, prayer is your best means of study. Like Daniel, you will understand the dream and its interpretation after you seek God. Like John, you will see the seven seals of precious truth opened after you have wept much.

Stones are only broken with a hammer, and the stones' breakers must get on their knees. Use the hammer of diligence and bend the knee of prayer. Every stony doctrine in revelation that you need to understand will fly open after the exercise of prayer and faith.

You may force your way through anything with the leverage of prayer. Thoughts and reasonings are the steel wedges that give us a hold on truth. But prayer is the lever that forces open the iron chest of sacred mystery to reveal the treasure.

FEBRUARY 21, EVENING

DIVINE STRENGTH

"But his bow remained in strength, And the arms of his hands were made strong by the hands of the Mighty God of Jacob."

—Genesis 49:24

The strength that God gives is real strength. It is not boasted valor, or fictional, or a thing that ends up in smoke. It is true divine strength.

We can do nothing without the power of God. Joseph was able to resist temptation because God gave him strength (Genesis 39:12). All true strength comes from the mighty God of Jacob. Look at the way God gave strength to Joseph: "and the arms of his hands were made strong by the mighty God of Jacob."

In this text, God placed His hands on Joseph's hands and put His arms on Joseph's arms. In the same way that parents teach their children, the Lord teaches those who fear Him. He puts His arms around them. Marvelous condescension! God Almighty, Eternal and Omnipotent, stoops from His throne and places His hand on His child's hand and stretches His arm on His children's arms and makes them strong.

This strength is covenant strength. It is attributed to "the mighty God of Jacob." Now, whenever you read of the God of Jacob, remember God's covenant with Jacob. Christians, love to think about God's covenant. All the power, all the grace, all the blessings, all the mercies, all the comforts, and every other blessing we have flows to us from the well-head through the covenant.

If there were no covenant we would fail. All grace proceeds from the covenant as heat and light proceed from the sun. No angels ascend or descend except on the ladder that Jacob saw, and at the top of that ladder stood the covenant (Genesis 28:12).

Christian, it may be that the enemy has severely wounded you, but your bow still remains strong in God. Give all the glory to the covenant God of Jacob.

POWERFUL

"The Lord is slow to anger and great in power."

—Nahum 1:3

Jehovah "is slow to anger." When mercy comes into the world she drives winged horses, and the axles of her chariot wheels are red hot with speed. But when God's wrath goes forth, it is with slow footsteps because God "has no pleasure in the death of one who dies [in wickedness]" (Ezekiel 18:32).

God's rod of mercy is always out-stretched. His sword of justice is in its scabbard, held in place by that pierced hand of love which bled for our sins.

"The Lord is slow to anger" because He is "great in power." Those are truly great in power who have power over themselves. When God's own power restrains Himself, that is power indeed. The power that binds omnipotence is omnipotence surpassed.

A person with a strong mind can bear insults a long time, and only resents the wrong when a sense of right demands action. The weak mind, however, is easily irritated. The strong mind bears insults like a rock that does not move, though a thousand waves dash against it spraying their ineffective malice on its summit.

Though God marks His enemies, He holds back His anger and takes no action. If God were less divine He would long ago have sent His thunders and emptied the weapons of heaven on us with a blast of mighty fire. We would have been utterly destroyed. But the greatness of His power brings us mercy.

What is your condition tonight? Can you by humble faith look to Jesus and say, "My substitute, my rock, my trust?" Then do not be afraid of God's awesome power. You are forgiven and accepted. By faith you have fled to Christ for refuge (Hebrews 6:18), and the power of God need never again terrify you. The shield and sword of the warrior does not terrify those whom he loves. Rejoice! He who is "great in power" is your Father and your Friend.

FEBRUARY 22, EVENING

NEVER ALONE

"I will never leave you nor forsake you."

—Hebrews 13:5

No promise of God's can be privately interpreted. Whatever God has said to one saint He has said to all of them. When He opens a well for one, all may drink. A starving saint may be the reason He opens the storehouse, but all the hungry saints may also come and eat. Whether He gave the word to Abraham or to Moses, it makes no difference: He has also given it to you as a covenant seed.

There is not a high blessing too lofty, nor a wide mercy too extensive for you. Lift up your eyes and look north, south, east, and west. Everything is yours. Climb to Pisgah's peak and view the farthest limit of divine promise. All the land is yours. You can drink from every brook of living water. If the land flows with milk and honey, drink the milk, and eat the honey, for both are yours.

Boldly believe, because He has said, "I will never leave you nor forsake you." With that promise God gives you everything. There is no attribute of God that can stop working on your behalf. Is He mighty? Then He will show Himself strong on behalf of you who trust Him. Is He love? Then with lovingkindness He will have mercy. Whatever attributes constitute the character of Deity, everyone of them will be fully engaged for you.

To sum this up: there is nothing you can want; there is nothing you can ask for; there is nothing you can need in time or eternity; there is nothing living; there is nothing dying; there is nothing in this world; there is nothing in the next world; there is nothing now, nothing at the resurrection morning, nothing in heaven that is not contained in this text: "I will never leave you nor forsake you."

CROSS CARRYING

"Take up your cross and follow me."

—Mark 10:21

You cannot make your own cross, but unbelief is a master carpenter at cross-making. You do not choose your own cross, but self-will would try to be your lord and master. Your cross is prepared and appointed by divine love. Accept it cheerfully. You are to carry your cross without raising trivial objections.

This evening Jesus asks you to submit to His easy yoke (Matthew 11:30). Do not be insolent, or trample it in vain glory, or fall under it in despair, or run away from it in fear. Take up your cross as a true follower of Jesus.

Jesus was a cross-bearer. He leads the way along the path of sorrow, and you could not have a better guide! If He carried a cross, what nobler a burden could you carry? The *Via Crucis* is the way of safety. Do not be afraid to walk its thorny path.

The cross is not made of feathers or covered with velvet. It is heavy and cuts disobedient shoulders. But the cross is not made of iron, although your fears may have painted it the color of iron. It is a wooden cross, and you can carry it because the Man of Sorrows knows its weight. Take up your cross, and by the power of the Spirit of God you will soon be in love with it. Like Moses, you would not exchange the reproach of Christ for all the treasures of Egypt (Hebrews 11:26).

Remember, Jesus carried the cross, and so its fragrance is sweet. Remember, the cross will soon be exchanged for the crown. Remember the coming glory, and it will greatly lighten the present heaviness of trouble.

Before you fall asleep tonight, ask the Lord to help you submit your will to His. When you wake tomorrow, may you be able to carry your cross with a holy and submissive spirit as is appropriate for a follower of the Crucified.

FEBRUARY 23, EVENING

SHOWERS OF BLESSING

"I will cause showers to come down in their season; there shall be showers of blessing."

—Ezekiel 34:26

This is sovereign mercy: "I will cause showers to come down in their season." Is not sovereign mercy divine mercy? Who else but God can say, "I will cause showers to come down"? There is only One who can "command the clouds above and open the doors of heaven" (Psalm 78:23). There is only One who can speak to the clouds and "give rain on the earth and send water on the fields" (Job 5:10).

As rain upon the earth and showers upon the green herb, so is grace the needed gift of God. Nothing grows without rain. You can prepare the garden and sow the seed, but nothing happens until it rains. Divine blessing is like that. Your labor is worthless until God, who sends the showers, sends salvation down. Then it is plenteous grace. "I will cause the showers to come," not drops, but *showers*. So it is with grace. If God gives a blessing it is "good measure, pressed down, shaken together, and running over" (Luke 6:38).

Plenty of grace. Oh, we need plenty of grace to keep us humble, prayerful, and holy. We need plenty of grace to make us fervent, to keep us pure, and at last, to land us in heaven.

We must receive soaking showers of grace. "I will cause showers to come down in their season." What season are you in this morning? Is it the season of drought? Then that is the season for showers. Is it the season of great heaviness and black clouds? Then that is the season for showers. "As your days, so shall your strength be" (Deuteronomy 33:25).

"I will cause showers to come down." Here is a multiplied blessing. The word *showers* is plural. God will send all kinds of blessings! If He sends converting grace, He will also send comforting graces. He will send "showers of blessing."

Oh parched plant, look up today, open your leaves and flowers to receive a heavenly watering.

FEBRUARY 24, MORNING

CHASTENED, BUT NOT FORGOTTEN

"O Lord of hosts how long will you not have mercy on Jerusalem? . . . And the Lord answered the angel . . . with good and comforting words."
—Zechariah 1:12–13

What a sweet answer to an anxious question. Tonight let us rejoice in it. Zion, there are good things in store for you. Your trials and captivity will soon end. Your children will soon be freed. Patiently endure the road and in the darkness continue to trust God, for He greatly loves you.

God loves His church with a love that is beyond human imagination. He loves His church with all His infinite heart. Be of good courage. We cannot be far from prosperity when God speaks "good and comforting words." The prophet Zechariah tells us what these words are: "I am zealous for Jerusalem and for Zion with great zeal" (Zechariah 1:14).

The Lord loves His church so much that He cannot bear to see her go astray. And when she does, He does not want to see her suffer too greatly. He will not have His enemies afflict her; He is displeased with them for increasing her misery.

When God seems to leave His church, His heart is warm toward her. History shows that after God uses a rod to chasten His servants, He breaks that rod, as if He hates what causes His children pain. He feels the sting far more than His people. "As a father pities his children, so the Lord pities those who fear Him" (Psalm 103:13). God has not forgotten us because He chastens us. His reproofs are not evidence of His lack of love.

Never fear, the Lord has not forgotten you. He who counts the stars and calls them by name (Psalm 147:4) will not forget His children. He knows your complete situation. It is as if you were the only creature He ever fashioned, or the only saint He ever loved.

Come to Him and be at peace.

THE STORM

"The wrath to come."

—Matthew 3:7

It is pleasant to be in the country after a storm. Raindrops glisten like brilliant diamonds in the sun and the fresh smell of flowers is everywhere.

This is where the Christian is, going through a land where the storm has spent itself on the Savior's head. If any drops of sorrow are still falling they are from clouds of mercy, and Jesus cheers us with the assurance that these drops are not for our destruction.

It is terrible to watch a bad storm approaching. Birds fold their wings, cattle keep their heads down in terror, the sky grows black, the sun disappears, and the heavens turn angry and frown. How awful to wait for the advance of a hurricane, to wait in terrible apprehension until the wind blows furiously, tearing trees up from their roots, forcing rocks off their pedestals, and hurling down homes.

Sinner, this is where you are. Though no hot drops have yet fallen a shower of fire is coming (2 Peter 3:10). Though no deadly winds are yet howling around you, God's storm is gathering its dread artillery. The water is dammed up by mercy, but the floodgates will soon open. God's thunderbolts are in His storehouse, but the storm is coming (2 Peter 3:12). How awful will that moment be when God, robed in vengeance, marches in fury. Where, where, where, sinner, will you hide? Where will you run to?

Oh that the hand of mercy will lead you to Christ. He has freely given you the gospel. His wounded side is the rock of shelter. You need Him.

Believe in Him. Cast yourself in repentance on Him and the fury will be gone forever.

FIGHTING GOD

"But Jonah arose to flee to Tarshish from the presence of the Lord. He went down to Joppa."

—Jonah 1:3

Jonah refused to go to Nineveh to preach the Word of God. Instead he went to Joppa. There are times when God's servants fail to serve Him. But what are the consequences? What did Jonah lose by his action? He lost the presence and the enjoyment of God's love.

When we serve our Lord Jesus, God is with us even if the entire world is against us. "What then shall we say to these things? If God is for us, who can be against us?" (Romans 8:31). If God is with us, nothing else matters. When we start relying on ourselves, we are at sea without a captain. Then we bitterly cry and groan, "Oh my God, where have You gone? How could I have been as foolish to refuse to serve You? Let me return to my first love and rejoice in Your presence."

Jonah lost all peace of mind. Sin soon destroys a believer's comfort. It is the poisonous upas tree of Java, whose leaves distil deadly drops that destroy the life of joy and peace.

Jonah lost everything that could comfort him. He could not claim one promise of divine protection because he was disobedient. He could not say, "Lord, these difficulties come from serving you, so help me." Jonah was harvesting the results of his own actions.

Christian, do not play the Jonah unless you want to "sow the wind, and reap the whirlwind" (Hosea 8:7). You will find that in the long run it is easier to serve God than to follow your own wishes. Jonah lost time yet he still ended in Tarshish.

It is difficult to fight God. "It is hard for you to kick against the goads" (Acts 9:5). Yield to Him now.

FEBRUARY 25, EVENING

OBTAINING POWER

"Salvation is of the Lord."

—Jonah 2:9

S alvation is the work of the Lord. Only "He can make alive those who were dead in trespasses and sins" (Ephesians 2:1). God also maintains our soul in its spiritual life. He is both "Alpha and Omega" (Revelation 1:8). "Salvation is of the Lord."

If I am prayerful, God makes me prayerful. If I have graces they are God's gifts. If I live a consistent life, His hand leads me. I cannot keep myself in His care, only He can keep me. Whatever I have, it is only from the Lord.

Do I live a consecrated life? "It is no longer I who live, but Christ lives in me" (Galatians 2:20). Am I sanctified? I did not cleanse myself. It was God's Holy Spirit that sanctified me. Have I fled the pleasures of this world? God's chastisement sanctified me for my own good.

The great Instructor tells me, "On that day I will make them My jewels" (Malachi 3:17). My jewels were made in heavenly places.

I find in God all that I want, but in me I find nothing but sin and misery. "He only is my rock and my salvation" (Psalm 62:2).

Do I feed on the Word? There would be no food in the Word unless the Lord made it food for my soul and helped me to feed on it. Do I live on the manna that comes down from heaven? That manna is nothing but Jesus Christ incarnate, whose body and blood I eat and drink (Matthew 26:26–28). "As the branch cannot bear fruit of itself, unless it abides in the vine, neither can you, unless you abide in Me" (John 15:4). I must live in Him.

What Jonah learned in the deep ocean, may I learn this morning on my knees: "Salvation is of the Lord."

TRUE LEPROSY

"Indeed if the leprosy has covered all his body, he shall pronounce him clean."

—Leviticus 13:13

Although rather unusual, this regulation has a lot of wisdom. If the disease has covered the whole body and turned the skin white, it has run its course and been thrown off by the healthy body; it poses no further danger.

We are like lepers and so may apply the law of leprosy. When we see ourselves as lost, ruined, polluted, and totally covered with sin's defilement, when we see that we have no righteousness of our own and plead guilty before the Lord then we are cleansed by the blood of Jesus through God's grace.

Hidden, unfelt, and unconfessed sin is true leprosy. But when sin is felt, seen, and confessed it receives the death sentence, because the Lord looks with mercy on the afflicted soul.

As nothing is more deadly than self-righteousness, so nothing is more hopeful than a personal sense of sin. We have to confess that we are nothing but sin, for no confession short of this will be the complete truth. If the Holy Spirit is convincing us of sin, then acknowledging that we are sinners is not difficult.

There is great comfort in this text to truly awakened sinners. The fact that you are so discouraged is a sign and symptom leading to hope. Nakedness comes before being clothed. Digging the foundation comes first when building. A thorough personal sense of sin is one of the earliest works of grace.

Oh poor leprous sinner, utterly destitute, take hope from this text and come to Jesus, just as you are:

> For let our debts be what they may,
>   However great or small,
> As soon as we have nought to pay,
>   Our Lord forgives us all.
> 'Tis perfect poverty alone
>   That sets the soul at large;
> While we can call one mite our own,
>   We have no full discharge.

MOVING

"You have made the Lord, who is my refuge, even the Most High, your dwelling place."

—Psalm 91:9

The Israelites in the wilderness were frequently on the move. Only when the pillar stopped were the tents pitched. Then the next morning as the sun rose and the trumpet blew, the ark was picked up. Then the fiery, cloudy pillar led the people on again (Exodus 13:21–22). Into narrow valleys, up hill sides, through desert wastelands and wilderness—they hardly had time to rest until they heard the order, "Move out. This is not your final destination. On to Canaan." They never stayed long in one place, even at the welcome oases of wells and palm trees.

Their home was with their God. His cloudy pillar was their roof by day, and by night its flame was their household fire (Exodus 13:21). Yet they pressed on from place to place, changing locations, never able to settle. Nowhere could they say, "Now we are secure, here we shall dwell."

The Christian knows that God does not change. With Him there is no variation or shadow of turning (James 1:17). We may be rich today and poor tomorrow. We may be sick today and healthy tomorrow. We may be happy today and depressed tomorrow. But there is no change in our relationship with God. He loved me yesterday, He loves me today.

My unmoving mansion of rest is my blessed Lord. Even if my future is dim and my hopes are blasted, even if my joys die and rust destroys everything, I have lost nothing in God. He is "my strong refuge to which I may resort continually" (Psalm 71:3).

I am a pilgrim in this world but at home in my God. In the earth I roam, but in God I dwell in quiet peace.

EVERLASTING LOVE

"Whose goings forth are from of old, from ever-lasting."

—Micah 5:2

The Lord Jesus had "goings forth" for His people as their representative before the throne long before they appeared upon the stage of time. It was "from everlasting" that Jesus signed the agreement with His Father to pay on behalf of His people, blood for blood, suffering for suffering, agony for agony, and death for death.

It was "from everlasting" that He freely gave Himself to sweat great drops of blood, to be spit on and pierced, to be mocked, torn, and crushed beneath the pains of death. His "goings forth" as our payment were "from everlasting."

Pause and wonder. You had "goings forth" in the person of Jesus "from everlasting." Before you were born, Christ loved you, for His delights were with human beings even before there were any children. He thought often of them, and from "everlasting to everlasting" He had set His affection on them.

My soul, has He been drawing you to Him for such a long time that He will not accomplish it? Has He from everlasting been going to save me and will He lose me now? Has He carried me like a precious jewel for so long only to let me slip through His fingers now? Did He choose me before the mountains were created, before the oceans were dug, only to reject me today?

Impossible! He would not have loved me this long had He not been a changeless Lover. If He could have grown weary of me it would have happened long before now. If His love was not as deep as hell and as strong as death, He would have abandoned me long ago.

Joy above all joys, I know that I am His everlasting and inalienable inheritance, given to Him by His Father before the creation. Everlasting love will be my pillow tonight.

EXPECTATION

"For my expectation is from Him."

—Psalm 62:5

It is the privilege of every believer to claim this promise. Expect nothing from the world. Only if we look to God to supply our spiritual and material blessings will our *expectations* not be in vain.

We can draw from the bank of faith and have all our needs supplied by the riches of God's lovingkindness. This I know, I would rather have God for my banker than all the Rothchilds. My Lord never fails to honor His promise. When we bring the promises to His throne, He never sends them back unanswered. Therefore, I wait only at His door because He always opens it with the hand of boundless grace, and this morning I wait in *expectation*.

But we also have expectations beyond this life. We shall soon die, and even then our "expectation is from Him." Do we believe that when we are dying He will send angels to carry us to Him? Oh yes. We believe that when our pulse becomes faint and the heart heaves heavily, an angelic messenger will stand and look with loving eyes on us and whisper, "Spirit, come away."

As we approach the heavenly gate we expect to hear the welcome invitation, "Come, you blessed of my Father, inherit the kingdom prepared for you from the foundation of the world" (Matthew 25:34). We are expecting harps of gold and crowns of glory. Soon we expect to be among the multitude of shining ones before God's throne. We are looking forward and longing for the time when we shall be like our glorious Lord, and "We shall see Him as He is" (1 John 3:2).

If this is your "expectation," live for God. Live with the desire and resolution to glorify Him who supplies your material and spiritual blessings. Live for Him whose grace elected, redeemed, and called you. Live for Him who gives you a great expectation of coming glory.

FEBRUARY 28, MORNING

INEXHAUSTIBLE

"The bin of flour was not used up; nor did the jar of oil run dry, according to the word of the Lord, which He spoke by Elijah."

—1 Kings 17:16

See the faithfulness of divine love. This woman had daily needs. She had to feed her son and herself during a famine. Now, in addition, she had to feed the prophet Elijah. Three mouths to feed, and yet the bin of flour was never used up. She had a steady supply from God. Each day she went to the bin for her needs and the supply never diminished.

You have daily needs, and because they come so frequently you fear that one day the jar of oil will be empty. Rest assured on the Word of God that this will not happen. Each day, although it brings troubles, will also bring help. Even if you outlive Methuselah (Genesis 5:27), or your needs are as many as the sand on the seashore, God's grace and mercy will supply your needs and you will not lack.

During three long years, there was never a cloud in the sky. The stars never wept a holy tear of dew on the wicked earth. Famine, desolation, and death turned the land into a howling wilderness. Yet this woman was never hungry but joyful in abundance.

So will it be with you. You will see the sinner's hope perish, because sinners trust in their own strength. You will see the proud Pharisee's confidence tumble, because he builds his hope on sand. You will even see your own schemes blasted to death. But you will discover that "your place of defense will be the fortress of rocks; bread will be given you, your water will be sure" (Isaiah 33:16).

It is better to have God for your guardian than to own the Bank of England. You might deplete the wealth of the Indies, but the infinite riches of God you can never exhaust.

LOVINGKINDNESS

"With lovingkindness I have drawn you."

—Jeremiah 31:3

The thunders of the law and the terrors of judgment are used to bring us to Christ, but the final victory is produced by God's lovingkindness.

The prodigal returned to his father's house out of his sense of need. "When he was still a great way off, his father saw him and had compassion and ran and fell on his neck and kissed him" (Luke 15:20). The prodigal's last steps up to his father's house were enjoyed with the loving kiss warm on his cheek and the welcome of music in his ears:

> Law and terrors do but harden,
> All the while they work alone;
> But a sense of blood-bought pardon,
> Will dissolve a heart of stone.

One night the Master came to the door and knocked with the iron hand of the law. The door shook and trembled on its hinges. The sinner piled every piece of furniture against the door saying, "I will not admit this man."

The Master returned later, and, with His own hand, using especially the part softened by the penetrating nail, He knocked again, oh so softly and tenderly. This time the door did not shake; it opened, and bowed there was the once unwilling host, rejoicing in the guest.

"Come in, come in. You have knocked and moved my heart. I could not think of Your pierced hand leaving a trace of blood on my door and Your going away, homeless. 'Your head is covered with dew, Your locks with the drops of night'" (Song of Solomon 5:2). "I believe, I believe, Your love has won my heart."

In every case, lovingkindness wins. What Moses could never do with the tablets of stone, Christ does with His pierced hand. This is the doctrine of effectual calling. Have I experienced it? Can I say, "He drew me and I followed on, glad to confess that voice divine"?

THE SPIRIT WORKING

"Now we have received ... the spirit who is from God, that we might know the things that have been freely given to us by God."
—1 Corinthians 2:12

Have you received the Spirit who is from God? The necessity of the work of the Holy Spirit in the heart is clearly seen in that everything done by God the Father and God the Son is not effective until the Holy Spirit reveals it.

What effect does the doctrine of election have until the Spirit of God enters you? Election is dead in my consciousness until the Spirit of God "calls me out of darkness into His marvelous light" (1 Peter 2:9). Through that calling I see my election and know that I am called of God. I know that I have been chosen in His eternal purpose.

A covenant was made for us by the Lord Jesus Christ and His Father, but that covenant is useless until the Holy Spirit brings the blessings and opens our hearts to receive them. There hang the blessings on the nail, Jesus Christ, but we are too stunted to reach them. The Spirit of God takes the blessings down, gives them to us, and they are actually ours.

Covenant blessings are like manna in the skies far out of our reach. But the Spirit of God opens the windows of heaven and scatters the living bread around the camp of the spiritual Israel.

Christ's finished work is like wine stored in barrels. Because of unbelief we can neither pour nor drink. The Holy Spirit dips our cups into this precious wine and then we drink. But without the Spirit we are as dead in our sin as if the Father had never elected us, as dead as if the Son never paid for us with His blood.

The Holy Spirit is absolutely necessary for our well-being. Let us walk lovingly toward Him and tremble at the thought of grieving Him.

FEBRUARY 29, EVENING

THE WIND

"Awake, O north wind, and come O south! Blow upon my garden, that its spices may flow out."

—Song of Solomon 4:16

Anything is better than the dead calm of indifference. Our souls may wisely desire the north wind of trouble if that alone can draw perfume from our graces. As long as it is never said, "The Lord was not in the wind" (1 Kings 19:11), we will not shudder from the most wintry blast.

The spouse in our verse humbly submitted to the correction sent by her Beloved. She entreated Him for grace without stipulating how that grace should come. So like us, she was so utterly weary of deadness and unholy calm that she sighed for any move of God which would compel her to action. Yet she also desired the warm south wind of comfort, the smile of divine love, and the joy of the Redeemer's presence to arouse her out of listlessness. She wants either, or both, to delight her Beloved as spices from her garden.

She could not remain indifferent and neither can we. What an encouraging thought that Jesus can find comfort in our poor feeble graces. It seems too good to be true. May we pursue trial, or even death, if it will cheer Immanuel's heart. Oh that our hearts were crushed to atoms if by such bruising our wonderful Lord Jesus could be glorified. Unexercised grace is like sweet perfume slumbering in the cups of the flowers.

The wisdom of the great Husbandman overrules diverse and opposite causes to produce the one desired result. It makes both affliction and consolation draw forth the grateful aromas of faith, love, patience, hope, surrender, joy, and other fair flowers of the garden. May we by sweet experience know what this means.

PRECIOUS

"He is precious."

—1 Peter 2:7

"As all the rivers run into the sea, yet the sea is not full" (Ecclesiastes 1:7). All enjoyment centers in our Beloved. The glances of His eyes outshine the sun and the beauties of His face are fairer than the choicest flowers. No fragrance is like the breath of His mouth. Gems of the mine and pearls from the sea are worthless when compared to His preciousness.

Peter tells us that Jesus is precious, but he did not and could not describe how precious. No one can compute the value of "God's indescribable gift" (2 Corinthians 9:15). Words cannot depict the preciousness of the Lord Jesus, nor can words portray how essential He is to our satisfaction and happiness.

Believer, in the midst of plenty there is a famine if your Lord is absent. The sun may shine, but if Christ is hidden all your world is dark and it is night. Is the bright and morning star gone and there is no other star to yield a ray of light in its place?

What a howling wilderness this world is without our Lord! If we do not see Him our flowers wither, our enjoyable fruits decay, the birds stop singing, and storms overturn our hopes. All the lights of earth cannot produce daylight if the Sun of Righteousness is eclipsed. He is the soul of our soul, the light of our light, the life of our life.

Dear believer, what would you do with the temptations and cares of this world if you did not have Him? What would you do when you awaken and prepare for the day's battle if you did not have Him? What would you do at night when you arrive home exhausted and weary if there were no door of fellowship between you and Christ?

Blessed be His name. He will not leave you. His promise is sure, "I will never leave you nor forsake you" (Hebrews 13:5).

When you think what life would be like without Him, it magnifies His preciousness.

MARCH 1, EVENING

HELP FROM THE ENEMY

"But all the Israelites would go down to the Philistines to sharpen each man's plowshare, his mattock, his axe, and his sickle."

—1 Samuel 13:20

We are engaged in a great war with the Philistines of evil. Every weapon within our reach must be used. Preaching, teaching, praying, and giving—all must be brought into action and even talents that may be considered too cruel for service must be employed. Knives, axes, and picks may all be useful in slaying Philistines. Rough tools may deal hard blows, and killing need not be elegant so long as it is effective.

Each moment of time, in season or out; each fragment of ability, educated or not; each opportunity, favorable or unfavorable—all must be used because our foes are many and our forces are small.

Most of our tools require sharpening. We need quickness of perception, tact, energy, and promptness. In a word we need complete adaptation for the Lord's work. Practical common sense is a scarce commodity among Christian leaders. We might learn from our text and have the Philistines sharpen our weapons. This morning let us sharpen our zeal with the aid of the Holy Spirit.

Look at the heathen devotees and the torture they endure in the service of their idols. Are they the only ones who exhibit patience and sacrifice? Observe the prince of darkness. See how persevering he is in his endeavors, how unabashed in his attempts, how daring in his plans, how thoughtful in his plots, how energetic in everything.

The devils are united as one man in their infamous rebellion, but we believers are divided in God's service and scarcely ever work in unity.

Oh that from Satan's infernal industry we may learn to go about like good Samaritans, seeking whom we may bless!

NOTHING BUT CHRIST

"To me, who am less than the least of all the saints, this grace was given that I should preach among the Gentiles the unsearchable riches of Christ." —Ephesians 3:8

The apostle Paul knew it was a great privilege to preach the gospel. He did not consider this calling a drudgery but an intense delight. Yet while Paul was thankful for his office, he was greatly humbled by his success in it. The more a ship is loaded the lower it settles in the water.

The lazy indulge in a fond conceit of their abilities because they remain untried, but earnest laborers soon learn their weaknesses. If you seek humility, try hard work. If you want to know your nothingness, attempt a great thing for Jesus. If you want to feel how utterly powerless you are apart from the living God, attempt to proclaim the unsearchable riches of Christ. Then you will know, as you have never known before, what a weak unworthy thing you are.

Although the apostle Paul knew his weakness and confessed it, he was never perplexed about the subject of his ministry. From his first sermon to his last, Paul preached Christ and nothing but Christ. He lifted up the cross and extolled the Son of God. Follow his example in all your efforts to spread the glad tidings of salvation. Let "Christ and Him crucified," be your repeated theme (1 Corinthians 2:2).

Christians should be like lovely spring flowers that open their golden cups to heaven as if to say, "Fill us with sunbeams." But when the sun is hidden they close their cups and their heads droop. In the same manner we feel the blessed influence of Jesus, who is our sun, and we the flowers that yield to Him.

Oh to speak of nothing but Christ. This is the subject "that gives seed to the sower and bread to the eater" (Isaiah 55:10). This is the "live coal for the lips of the speaker" (Isaiah 6:7) and the master key to the heart of the hearer.

FEAR NOT, I AM WITH YOU

"I have tested you in the furnace of affliction."

—Isaiah 48:10

Tested and tried believer, there is comfort in the thought that "I have tested you in the furnace of affliction." These words fall like a gentle shower to put out the fury of the flame. Remember, heat has no power against asbestos armor. Let affliction come; God has chosen me. Let poverty knock, God is still in my house; He has chosen me. Sickness may intrude, but my balm is that God has chosen me. Whatever comes my way in this valley of tears, I know that God has chosen me.

If you require additional comfort, remember that the Son of God is with you in the furnace (Daniel 3:24–25). In your silent room there is One sitting beside you whom you love, though you have never seen Him. He makes your bed and smooths your pillow in all your afflictions. You may be poor and lonely, but the Lord of life and glory is a frequent visitor, and He loves to visit you in desolate places.

This friend stays close, and though you cannot see Him you may feel the pressure of His hand. Listen, you can hear His voice. Even in the valley of the shadow of death He says, "Fear not, for I am with you; be not dismayed, for I am your God" (Isaiah 41:10).

Do you remember that great speech of Caesar's? "Fear not, you carry Caesar and all his fortune." Fear not, Christian, Jesus is with you. His presence is both your comfort and safety in all your fiery trials. He will never leave even one saint that He has chosen for His own.

When you are in the "furnace of affliction," His sure word of promise is, "Fear not, I am with you." Today, take hold of Christ and say:

> Through floods and flames, if Jesus lead,
> I'll follow where he goes.

BLESSED SPIRIT

"He saw the Spirit of God descending like a dove."

—Matthew 3:16

Just as the Spirit of God descended on the Lord Jesus, the Head, so also the Spirit descends on the members of Christ's body. The Spirit's descending upon us is similar to the Spirit's falling on our Lord. There is often a rapidity about it that, almost as if we were caught off guard, speeds us onward and heavenward beyond all our expectations. Yet there is none of the hurry of this world about it, for the wings of the dove are as soft as they are swift.

Quietness seems essential to many spiritual works. The Lord is in the "still small voice" (1 Kings 19:12), and like the dew His grace is often distilled in silence.

The dove has always been the chosen symbol of purity, and the Holy Spirit is holiness itself. When the Spirit comes, everything that is pure, lovely, and of good report is made to abound (Philippians 4:8), and sin and uncleanness depart.

Peace reigns where the Holy Dove comes with power. He carries the olive branch to show that the waters of divine wrath have subsided.

Gentleness is a sure result of the Sacred Dove's transforming power. Hearts touched by His benign influence are meek and lowly both now and forever. The turtledove can endure wrong but cannot inflict it. We must be as "harmless as doves" (Matthew 10:16).

The dove is a perfect picture of love. Its call is full of affection, and the soul visited by the blessed Spirit abounds in love to sinners and above all to Jesus.

The "hovering of the Spirit of God over the face of the waters," first produced order and life (Genesis 1:2). Today too the Holy Spirit causes and encourages new life and light.

Blessed Spirit, as You rested on our dear Redeemer, rest on us tonight and forever. Amen

GRACE MAGNIFIED

"My grace is sufficient for you."

—2 Corinthians 12:9

If God's saints were wealthy and free from trials, we would not know the consolations of divine grace half as well as we do. When we see the homeless with no place to lay their head and yet they can say, "Still will I trust in you" (Psalm 56:3); when we see the indigent hungry but still trusting Jesus; when we see the bereaved overwhelmed with sorrow but still clinging to Christ; when we see such, what honor it reflects on the gospel! God's grace is illustrated and magnified in the poverty and trials of believers.

Saints, take courage in every discouragement. Believe "that all things work together for good to those who love God, to those who are the called according to His purpose" (Romans 8:28). Believe that out of apparent evil a real blessing will ultimately appear. Believe in your God, who will either work deliverance or most assuredly support you in your troubles. The patience of the saints proves the power of divine grace.

There is a lighthouse. On a calm night I cannot tell if the building is solid. But let the storm rage, and then I will know. So it is with the Spirit's work. If the lighthouse were not frequently battered by rough waters, I would never know if it could stand in a storm. If strong winds did not blow, I would never know if it was firm and secure. So, too, the master-works of God are those Christians who stand steadfast and unmovable in the midst of difficulties:

> Calm mid the bewildering cry,
> Confident of victory.

If you hope to glorify your God, plan on having many trials. No one can be illustrious before the Lord unless the conflicts are many. If your path is greatly tried, rejoice, because you will witness the all-sufficient grace of God.

As for His failing you, never dream of it; hate the thought. The God who has been sufficient for you until now can be trusted to the end.

MARCH 4, MORNING

MORE THAN EXPECTED

"They are abundantly satisfied with the fullness of Your house."

—Psalm 36:8

The queen of Sheba was amazed at the sumptuousness of Solomon's table. She lost all heart when she saw just a single day's provision, and she marvelled at the throng of servants who ate at the royal table (1 Kings 10:5).

But this is nothing compared to the hospitality of the God of grace! Millions of His people are fed daily. Hungry and thirsty, they bring large appetites to the banquet and everyone is satisfied. There is enough for each, enough for all, enough forever. The multitude at Jehovah's table is as countless as the stars of heaven, yet everyone has a generous share of meat.

Think how much grace one saint requires. It is so much that nothing but the Infinite could supply him for one day. Yet the Lord spreads His table not for one but for many saints, and not for one day but for many years, and not for many years only but for generation after generation.

Look at the full feasting mentioned in our text. The guests at mercy's banquet are abundantly satisfied, and not with ordinary food but with the special fullness of God's own house. This feasting is guaranteed to all "who trust in the shelter of Your wings" (Psalm 61:4).

I once thought that if I could only get a scrap of meat at God's back door of grace I would be satisfied. Then I would be like the woman who said, "Yes Lord, yet even the little dogs eat the crumbs which fall from their master's table" (Matthew 15:27). But no child of God is ever served scraps or leftovers. Like Mephibosheth, they all eat from the king's table (2 Samuel 9:13). In matters of grace, we all have Benjamin's portion (Genesis 43:34): five times more than we expected.

Although our needs are great, we are often amazed at the marvelous amount of grace God gives us to enjoy.

MARCH 4, EVENING

AWAKE

"Let us not sleep as others."

—1 Thessalonians 5:6

There are many ways for Christians to be wide awake. Let me strongly advise one method, and that is to talk about the ways of the Lord.

As Bunyan's Christian and Hopeful journeyed toward the Celestial City they said, "To prevent drowsiness in this place, let us fall into good discourse." Christian enquired, "Brother, where shall we begin?" Hopeful answered, "Where God began with us." Then Christian sang this song:

> When saints do sleepy grow, let them come hither,
> And hear how these two pilgrims talk together;
> Yea, let them learn of them, in any wise,
> Thus to keep open their drowsy slumbering eyes.
> Saints' fellowship, if it be managed well,
> Keeps them awake, and that in spite of hell.

Christians who isolate themselves and walk alone are likely to grow sleepy. Keep Christian company and you will be awake, refreshed, and encouraged to make quicker progress on the road to heaven. As you have fellowship with other believers, let the theme of your conversation be the Lord Jesus. Let your eye of faith be always looking to Him. Let your heart be full of Him. Let your lips speak His worth. Friend, live near the cross and you will not sleep.

Work with a deep sense of heaven's value. If you remember that you are going there, you will not sleep on the road. If you realize that hell is behind you and the devil is pursuing, you will not linger. Would a murderer sleep with the avenger of blood chasing him and the city of refuge ahead (Numbers 35:6)?

Christian, will you sleep while the pearly gates are open, and angels are waiting for you to join them, and a crown of gold awaits your head? Oh no, in holy fellowship continue to watch and "pray that you may not enter into temptation" (Luke 22:40).

A SWEET PRAYER

"Say to my soul, I am your salvation."

—Psalm 35:3

What does this sweet prayer teach me? It will be my prayer tonight, but first let it instruct. The text reveals that David had his doubts, or why else would he pray, "Say to my soul, I am your salvation"? Let me be comforted that I am not the only saint who has complained of a weak faith. If David doubted, I can conclude that even with my doubts I am still a Christian.

The text also reminds me that David was not content while he had fears and doubts, but he approached the mercy seat and prayed for assurance, valuing it more than much fine gold (Psalm 119:127).

I also learn that David knew where to obtain full assurance. It was to God that he cried, "Say to my soul, I am your salvation." I must be alone with God a great deal if I am to have a clear sense of Jesus' love. If my prayers cease, my eye of faith will grow dim. Much in prayer, much in heaven; slow in prayer, slow in growth.

Also, David was not satisfied until his assurance had a divine source. Lord, You say to my soul. Nothing but a divine testimony in the soul will make the true Christian content. Furthermore, David could not rest until his assurance was vividly personal. "Say to *my* soul, *I* am your salvation." Lord, if you would say this to all the saints it means nothing unless you say it to me.

Lord, I have sinned. I do not deserve Your smile. I can scarcely ask, but oh, please, say to my soul, "I am your salvation." Let me have a present, personal, infallible, and indisputable sense that I am Yours and You are mine. Amen.

BORN AGAIN

"You must be born again."

—John 3:7

Regeneration is the very basis of salvation. We must be diligent to know that we really are born again, for some think they are when they are not. Be assured that the name of a Christian is not the nature of a Christian. And being born in a Christian land or professing the Christian religion is worthless unless something more is added to it: being born again by the power of the Holy Spirit.

Being born again is so mysterious that human words cannot describe it. "The wind blows where it wishes, and you hear the sound of it, but cannot tell where it comes from and where it goes. So is everyone who is born of the spirit" (John 3:8).

Nevertheless, it is a change that is known and felt; known by works of holiness following it and felt by a gracious experience. This great birth is supernatural, and when it happens a new, infused life works in the heart, renews the soul, and affects the entire person. It does not change my name, but it renews my nature so that I am no longer the person I used to be. I become a new person in Christ Jesus.

Washing and dressing a body is totally different than making it live. We can do the former but only God can do the latter. If you have been born again your acknowledgment will be: "Oh Lord Jesus, the everlasting Father, You are my spiritual Parent. Your Spirit has breathed the breath of a new, holy, and spiritual life in me."

"You He made alive, who were dead in trespasses and sins" (Ephesians 2:1). My heavenly life is totally derived from You. "My life is hidden in Christ with God" (Colossians 3:3). "It is no longer I who live, but Christ lives in me" (Galatians 2:20).

May the Lord enable us to be certain that we are born again. To be unregenerate is to be unsaved, unpardoned, without God, and without hope.

PRIDE

"Before destruction the heart of a man is haughty."

—Proverbs 18:12

There is an old saying that "coming events cast their shadows before them." And Solomon teaches that "pride goes before destruction and a haughty spirit before a fall" (Proverbs 16:18). Pride is more infallibly the sign of destruction than the change of mercury in a barometer is a sign of rain. When people have "ridden the high horse," destruction has always overtaken them.

Let David's aching heart show you there was an eclipse in his glory when he considered his own greatness (2 Samuel 24:10). Watch Nebuchadnezzar, the mighty builder of Babylon, driven from men, crawling on the earth, eating grass like oxen. His body was wet with dew, his hair grew like eagle's feathers and his nails like bird's claws (Daniel 4:33). Pride made this boaster a beast, as once before it made an angel a devil (Isaiah 14:12). God hates "a proud look" (Proverbs 6:17). God's arrows are aimed at proud hearts.

Oh Christian, is your heart haughty this evening? Pride can get in the Christian's heart as well as in the sinner's. It can delude you into dreaming that "you are rich, have become wealthy, and have need of nothing" (Revelation 3:17). Are you glorying in your graces or your talents? Are you proud of your deeds and spiritual experiences?

If so, hear me well! Destruction is coming. Flaunting flowers of self-conceit will be pulled up by the roots. Mushroom graces wither in the burning heat. Self-sufficiency becomes straw for the manure pile.

If you forget to live at the foot of the cross in deep lowliness of spirit, God will chasten you with His rod. A destruction will wipe out your human joys and comforts; only your soul will be saved. Therefore, "He who glories, let him glory in the Lord" (2 Corinthians 10:17).

MARCH 6, EVENING

FAITH

"Have faith in God."

—Mark 11:22

Faith gives the soul feet for marching along the road of the commandments. Love can make the feet move swiftly, but faith is the foot that carries the soul. Faith oils the wheels of holy devotion and sincere godliness. Without faith the chariot has no wheels and we drag along.

With faith I can do all things. Without faith I have neither the inclination nor the power to do anything in God's service. If you want to find those who serve God best, look for those with the most faith.

A little faith will save a person but it will not do great things for God. Bunyan's character Little-faith could not fight Apollyon; it needed Christian to do that. Neither could poor Little-faith slay Giant Despair; it required Great-heart's arm to knock that monster down. Little-faith will most certainly go to heaven, but it often has to hide itself in a nut shell and it frequently loses everything but its jewels.

Little-faith says, "It is a rough road with sharp thorns and many dangers. I am afraid to go." But Great-faith boldly ventures forth remembering this promise, "your shoes shall be iron and bronze; as your days, so shall your strength be" (Deuteronomy 33:25). Little-faith stands despondent, crying at the river. But Great-faith sings, "When you pass through the waters, I will be with you; and through the rivers, they shall not overflow you" (Isaiah 43:2). Then Great-faith immediately fords the stream.

Do you want to be comforted and happy and enjoy religion? Would you have the religion of cheerfulness and not of gloom? Then have great faith in God. If you love darkness and are satisfied to live in gloom and misery then be content with a little faith. But if you love the sunshine and would sing the songs of rejoicing then earnestly seek this gift: great faith.

TRUST

"It is better to trust in the Lord, than to put confidence in man."

—Psalm 118:8

We have all been tempted to trust the things we can see rather than resting only on the invisible God. We often look to friends and associates for help and counsel and thus ruin the noble simplicity of relying on God. Tonight, are you worried about the cares of the day? If so, think about this.

You trust in Jesus for your salvation. Then why are you troubled? This is a promise: "Cast your burden on the Lord" (Psalm 55:22). "Be anxious for nothing, but in everything by prayer and supplication with thanksgiving, let your request be made know to God" (Philippians 4:6). You can trust God to handle your present problems.

If you cannot trust Him with your present problems, how can you trust Him for your soul's redemption? If you trust Him for your soul's redemption, you can rely on Him for smaller mercies. Isn't God enough to meet all your needs, or is His all-sufficiency too little for your needs? Do you want another eye beside the one that sees every secret thing? Is His heart faint? Is His arm weary? If so, seek another god.

But if He is Infinite, Omnipotent, Faithful, True, and All-wise then why run around looking for another confidence? Why rake the earth to find another foundation when this one is strong enough to bear all the weight you can ever build on? Christian, do not mix your wine with water, do not blend your gold of faith with the dross of human confidence. Wait only on God and let your expectation be from Him alone. Do not covet Jonah's plant but rest in Jonah's God (Jonah 4:6).

The sandy foundation of earthly trust is the choice of fools. "The wise man built his house on the rock and the rain descended, the flood came, and the wind blew and beat on the house; and it did not fall for it was founded on the rock" (Matthew 7:24–25).

MARCH 7, EVENING

TRIALS

"We must through many tribulations enter the kingdom of God."

—Acts 14:22

God's people have trials. It was never God's design for His people to be untried. "Behold I have refined you, but not as silver; I have tested you in the furnace of affliction" (Isaiah 48:10).

God's people were never chosen for worldly peace and merely earthly joy. Freedom from sickness and the pains of life was never guaranteed. When the Lord drew up the charter of privileges, He included chastisement among the things we should expect. Trials are part of our life. Trials were predestinated for us in God's solemn decrees and bequeathed to us in Christ's legacy. As surely as the stars are fashioned by God's hands and their orbits fixed by Him, our trials are allotted to us. He has ordained their season, their place, their intensity, and the effect they will have on us.

Not even good people should expect to escape troubles. If they do, they will be disappointed, for all their predecessors have had trials. Mark the patience of Job. Remember the faith of Abraham, who during trials became the "father of the faithful" (Galatians 3:9). Remember the biographies of the patriarchs, prophets, apostles, and martyrs. All these vessels of mercy passed through the fires of affliction. It is ordained that the cross of trouble will be engraved on every ship of mercy like the royal mark distinguishes a King's vessel.

Although tribulations walk the path with God's children we take comfort knowing that our Master has traveled it ahead of us. We have His presence and sympathy to cheer us, His grace to support us, and His example to teach us how to endure. The trials of this life will seem as nothing when we reach heaven.

MARCH 8, MORNING

TWO SIDES

"She called his name Ben-Oni [son of sorrow], but his father called him Benjamin [son of my right hand]."

—Genesis 35:18

In everything earthly there is both a bright and a dark side. Rachel was overwhelmed with the difficulty of her hard labor and death. Jacob wept over the loss of his wife but could see mercy in the birth of a child. We should remember that while we grieve over trials our faith triumphs in divine faithfulness.

Samson's lion yielded honey (Judges 14:8), and when properly considered so will our adversities. The stormy sea feeds multitudes with fish. The wild forest blooms with beautiful flowers. The stormy wind sweeps away the plague. The biting frost loosens the hard soil. Dark clouds distil bright drops. Black earth grows lovely flowers. A vein of good can be found in every mine of evil.

Sad hearts have peculiar skills in seeing only the worst in every trial. If there were only one swamp in the entire world, they would soon be up to their necks in it. If there was only one lion in the desert, they would hear it roar. There is a tinge of this wretched folly in all of us. We at times are likely to cry with Jacob, "All these things are against me" (Genesis 34:30).

Faith's way of walking, however, casts all care on the Lord and anticipates good results even from the worst calamities. Like Gideon's men, faith does not worry over the broken pitcher but rejoices that the lamp blazes brightly (Judges 7:16). Out of the rough oyster shell of difficulty, faith extracts the rare pearl of honor. From the deep ocean caves of distress, faith lifts the priceless coral of tried experience. When the flood of prosperity ebbs, faith finds treasures hidden in the sand. When the sun of delight sets, faith turns the telescope of hope on the starry promises of heaven.

When death appears, faith points to the light of resurrection beyond the grave and makes our dying Ben-Oni our living Benjamin.

MARCH 8, EVENING

SUPERLATIVE BEAUTY

"Yes, He is altogether lovely."

—Song of Solomon 5:16

The superlative beauty of Jesus is all-attracting. His beauty is not to be admired so much as it is to be loved. He is more than satisfying and fair; He is *lovely.* Surely we can fully justify the use of this golden word because He is the object of our warmest love, a love founded on the intrinsic excellence of Jesus' attraction.

Disciple of Jesus, look to your Master's lips and say, "His mouth is most sweet" (Song of Solomon 5:16). "Did not our heart burn within us while He talked with us on the road" (Luke 24:32). You worshippers of Immanuel, look up to His head of finest gold (Song of Solomon 5:11) and tell me, are His thoughts of you not precious? Is your adoration sweetened with affection as you humbly bow before His countenance?

Is there not a delightful attraction in His every feature? Is not His whole person fragrant with a rich savor of His good ointments, and so believers love Him? Is there one member of His glorious body who is not attracted, one portion of His person that is not a guiding star to our souls, one office that is not a strong cord to bind our hearts? Our love is more than a seal set on His heart of love. Our love is fastened on His arm of power. We anoint His whole person with the sweet ointment of our fervent love. His whole life we would imitate. His whole character we would duplicate.

In all others there is something missing. In Jesus there is perfection. Even the best of His saints have stained clothing and faces lined with worry wrinkles, and all earthly suns have spots and this beautiful world has its wildernesses.

We cannot love the whole of the most lovely thing, but Jesus is gold without alloy, light without darkness, glory without cloud. "Yes, He is altogether lovely."

LIVING IN HIM

"Abide in Me."

—John 15:4

Communion with Christ is a sure cure for every ill. Whether it is the wormwood of woe, or the sickness from surfeit in earthly delights, close fellowship with the Lord will take the bitterness from woe and the excessive fullness from the other.

Live near Jesus and it is only of secondary importance whether you live on the mountain top of honor or in the valley of humiliation. Live near Jesus. "You are hidden under the shadow of His wings" (Psalm 17:8), "and underneath are the everlasting arms" (Deuteronomy 33:27). Let nothing keep you from the blessed fellowship and the choice privilege of a soul wedded to *The Well-beloved*.

Do not be content to visit Him now and then, but stay in His company, for only in His presence is there comfort and safety. Jesus should not be a friend whom we call on every so often, but one whom we walk with forever.

You have a difficult road ahead. Do not leave without your Guide. You have to enter the fiery furnace, but do not unless, like Shadrach, Meshach, and Abednego, you have the Son of God for your companion (Daniel 3:24). Don't go to war until, like Joshua, you have seen the Captain of the Lord's host with his sword drawn (Joshua 5:13). You are about to meet your Esau of many temptations, but don't until, like Jacob at Jabbok's Brook, you have wrestled with an angel (Genesis 32:24).

In every case and in every condition you will need Jesus. But you will need Him most of all when the iron gates of death open to receive you. Keep close to your soul's Husband, lean your head on Him, and "drink of spiced wine of the juice of His pomegranate" (Song of Solomon 8:2). Then at last you will be found without spot, or wrinkle, or any such thing (Ephesians 5:27). Since you have lived with Him and in Him, you will abide with Him forever.

MARCH 9, EVENING

WHAT IF

"In my prosperity I said, 'I shall never be moved.'"

—Psalm 30:6

Give individuals wealth; let their ships come in loaded with rich cargo; let the winds and waves appear to serve them as their vessels cross mighty oceans; let their lands yield abundant crops; let the weather smile upon their harvests; let uninterrupted success accompany every business venture; let them stand in the community as successful executives; let them enjoy continued good health; let them with braced nerve and brilliant eye march through the world; let them live happily; let their spirit be buoyant; let them have a song perpetually on their lips; let their eyes sparkle with joy; let such an easy state occur and the natural consequence to anyone, including the finest Christian, will be presumption.

David had said, "I shall never be moved," and we are no better than David and probably not half as good. Beware of the smooth places where you are walking. But if the road is rough thank God.

If God always rocked us in the cradle of prosperity; if we were always bounced on fortune's knee; if there were no stains on the alabaster pillar; if there were no clouds in the sky; if there were no bitter drops in the wine of this life; if there were no such things we would be intoxicated with pleasure. We would dream that "we stand." And stand we would, but on a pinnacle, like the sailor asleep atop the mast, in jeopardy every moment.

We bless God for our afflictions. We thank Him for our changes. We extol His name for loss of property. We feel that if He had not chastened, we would have become too secure and self-confident. Continued prosperity is a fiery trial:

> Afflictions, though they seem severe,
> In mercy often are sent.

TROUBLE

"Man . . . is of few days, and full of trouble."

—Job 14:1

Before we fall asleep tonight, our text will help us to remember this sad fact, and it may help us keep a loose grip on earthly things. There is nothing pleasant in recalling that we are not above the arrows of adversity, but it might humble us and prevent us from boasting.

This may keep us from taking too deep a root in earth's soil, for we will soon be transplanted to the heavenly garden. Remember the frail tenure upon which we hold our transient mercies. If we remember that the trees of earth are marked for the woodman's axe, we would not be so quick to build our nests in them. We should love, but we should love with a love that expects separations and deaths. Our dear relations are only loaned to us, and the hour when we must return them to the lender's hand may be close.

This is certainly true of our material possessions. Riches seem to take wings and fly away, and our health is equally uncertain. Frail flowers of the field, do not count on blooming here forever. There is a time for weakness and sickness, when we will have to glorify God by suffering and not by our prosperity and health.

We cannot escape the sharp arrows of affliction. In our few days on earth, not one is secure from sorrow. Our life is a barrel full of bitter wine. If you think there is joy in this life, you would do better to look for honey in an ocean of brine.

Beloved, "Set your mind on things above, not on things of the earth" (Colossians 3:2). "Do not lay up for yourselves treasures on earth where moth and rust destroy, and where thieves break in and steal; but lay up for yourself treasures in heaven" (Matthew 6:19,20).

The path of trouble is the way home. Lord, make this thought a pillow for my weary head.

MARCH 10, EVENING

EXCEEDINGLY SINFUL

"Sin . . . exceedingly sinful."

—Romans 7:13

Do not take sin lightly. When you were converted your conscience was tender and you were afraid of the slightest sin. New converts have a godly fear of offending God. It is not too long, however, before the delicate blooms of these first ripe fruits are removed by the rough handling of the world. The sensitive plant of young holiness turns into a willow, pliant and easily yielding.

A Christian may grow callous so slowly that the sin which once startled no longer alarms. By degrees we become comfortable with sin. The ear that has been close to the booming cannon no longer hears slight sounds. At first even a little sin startles us, but soon we say, "Is this not a little one?" Then comes another, and then a larger, and then another, until by degrees we regard sin as just a little ill.

Then an unholy presumption follows: "We have not fallen into open sin. True, we tripped, but only a little, for we stood upright most of the time. We uttered only one unholy word, but most of our conversation has been consistent." So we down-play sin. We throw a robe over it and call it delicate names. Christians, beware thinking lightly of sin. Be careful not to fall little by little.

Sin, a *little* thing? Sin is poison! Sin is deadly! Sin, a *little* thing? "The little foxes spoil the vines" (Song of Solomon 2:15). A tiny coral insect built a rock that wrecked a navy. Enough little strokes will fell a mighty oak. Water wears away stones (Job 14:19).

Is sin a *little* thing? It covered the Redeemer's head with thorns and pierced His heart. It caused Him anguish, bitterness, and woe. If you could weigh the smallest sin on the scales of eternity, you would fly from it as from a serpent. "Abstain from every form of evil" (1 Thessalonians 5:22).

MARCH 11, MORNING

SOUGHT OUT

"You shall be called Sought Out."

—Isaiah 62:12

The surpassing grace of God is clearly seen in that we were not only sought but sought out. We seek a lost item, but this is only seeking not seeking out. The loss is more perplexing and the search more persevering when a thing is sought out.

We were mixed with mud. We were like a piece of precious gold that falls into the sewer. People scoop out a mass of the sewer's filth and inspect it carefully, stirring and raking, searching through the heap until the treasure is found.

To put it another way, we were lost in a complex maze, wandering here and there, when mercy came after us with the gospel. Mercy did not immediately find us; it had to search and to seek us out. We were hopelessly lost. We wandered like sheep in a strange country; it did not seem possible that even the Good Shepherd could track our devious roaming.

Glory to the unfailing grace; we were sought out! No gloom could hide us, no filth conceal us. We were found and brought home. Glory to infinite love; God the Holy Spirit restored us!

If the lives of some of God's people could be written about, we would be filled with holy astonishment. Strange and marvelous are the ways in which God finds His own. Blessed be His name. He never relinquishes the search until the chosen are sought out.

We are not sought out today and cast away tomorrow. Almightiness and wisdom combined makes no failures. We will be called, "Sought Out!"

That any one of us would be sought out by God is grace beyond degree. There is no reason for it other than God's own sovereign love. We can only lift our hearts in wonder and praise the Lord that tonight we wear the name: "Sought Out."

NEIGHBOR

"You shall love your neighbor."

—Matthew 5:43

Perhaps your neighbor rolls in riches and you are poor. Your little house is close to a fine mansion and occasionally you look at that great estate where banquets are held. God has given your neighbor these gifts, so do not envy such wealth. Be content with what you have if you cannot better it. Do not wish for your neighbor to be like you are. Love him, and then you will not envy him.

On the other hand perhaps you are rich and near to you reside the poor. Call them *neighbor,* and remember that you are to love them. The world may call the poor inferior, but they are not. They are far more your equal than your inferiors, for "God has made from one blood every nation of men to dwell on all the face of the earth, and has determined their preappointed times and the boundaries of their dwellings" (Acts 17:26).

It is your clothing that is better, not you. The poor one is a *person,* and what are you more than that? Make sure you love your neighbors, even if they are in rags or sunk in the depths of poverty.

You may say, "I cannot love my neighbors. Anything I do for them is returned with ingratitude and contempt." All the more room for the heroism of love. Would you be a feather bed warrior rather than bearing the rough fight of love? Those who dare the most will win the most. If your path of love is rough, tread it fearlessly. Love your neighbor through thick as well as thin, "for in so doing you will heap coals of fire on his head" (Romans 12:20).

If your neighbors are hard to please, don't seek their praise, please your Master. If they reject your love, your Master still loves you and your deed is as acceptable to Him as if it had been accepted by them.

Love your neighbor, for in doing this you are following in the footsteps of Christ.

MARCH 12, MORNING

FOUR THINGS

"To whom do you belong?"

—1 Samuel 30:13

You cannot be neutral in your beliefs. You either serve under the banner of Prince Immanuel, or you are a slave of the black prince, Satan. "Choose for yourselves this day whom you will serve" (Joshua 24:15).

Let me help you make a choice. Have you been born again? If so, you belong to Christ; but without the new birth you are not His.

Whom do you trust? Those who trust in Jesus are the sons of God.

Whose work are you doing? Whomever you serve is your lord and master.

What company do you keep? If you belong to Jesus, you will associate with those who carry their crosses.

What is your speech? Is it heavenly or earthly?

What have you learned about your Master? Servants learn much from their masters. If you have spent time with Jesus, it will be said of you as it was of Peter and John: "They realized that they had been with Jesus" (Acts 4:13).

"To whom do you belong?" Answer honestly before you go to sleep tonight. If you are not a Christian, you are in a slave's hard service. Run away from your cruel master and enter the service of the Lord of Love and you will enjoy blessedness.

If you are Christ's, let me advise you to do four things:

You belong to Jesus, obey Him. Let His word be your law. Let His wish be your will.

You belong to the Beloved, love Him. Let your heart embrace Him. Let your whole soul be filled with Him.

You belong to the Son of God, trust Him. Rest nowhere else but on Him.

You belong to the King of kings, be decided for Him. Then all will know, even without your being branded on the forehead, that you belong to Jesus Christ.

MARCH 12, EVENING

WHY ARE YOU SITTING HERE?

"Why are we sitting here until we die?"

—2 Kings 7:3

This devotional book was primarily intended for the edification of believers. But if you are unsaved my heart yearns for you, and I would say a word that may be a blessing.

Open your Bible and read this morning's text. It is the story of four lepers. Mark their situation, it was much the same as yours. If you remain where you are, without Jesus, you will perish. If you go to Jesus the worst that could happen is that you would die forgiven. "Nothing ventured, nothing won," is the old proverb. In your case the venture is not great. You can sit in sullen despair and no one will pity you when your ruin comes. But if you die after seeking mercy, you would be the object of universal sympathy were such a thing possible.

Those who refuse to look to Jesus do not escape their sins. You will perish if you do not trust Him. But you know that those who believe in Him are saved. Some of your own acquaintances have received this mercy. Why not you? The Ninevites said, "Who can tell?" (Jonah 3:9). Act on the same hope and try the Lord's mercy. To perish in sin is awful. If there were only a straw grab it, the instinct of self-preservation should lead you to stretch out your hand.

I have been talking to you on your own unbelieving ground. I would now assure you from the Lord: "I love those who love me. And those who seek me diligently will find me" (Proverbs 8:17). Jesus casts out no one who comes to Him. If you do come, you will find treasures far richer than the poor lepers gathered in Syria's deserted camp (2 Kings 7:8). May the Holy Spirit empower you to go to Jesus at once. Your belief will not be in vain.

When you are saved, tell the good news to others. Proclaim the good news everywhere.

May the Lord save you today.

THE RETURN

"So he put out his hand and took her, and drew her into the ark to himself."

—Genesis 8:9

Exhausted from her wanderings the dove returned to the ark as her only resting place. Exhausted she flies. She will drop. She will never reach the ark! But she struggles on and has just enough strength left to reach the edge of the ark. She can hardly perch on it. She is ready to drop but Noah has been looking for his dove all day and is ready to receive her. So he puts out his hand and draws "her into the ark to himself."

Mark that: he draws "her into the ark to himself." She did not fly directly into the ark. She flew as far as she could and then Noah put out his hand and pulled her in. This was an act of mercy shown to the wandering dove.

Seeking sinner, with all your sins you will be received by Christ. "Only return": those are God's two gracious words. Only return. The dove had no olive branch in her mouth. She had nothing but herself and her wanderings. But she returns and Noah pulls her in.

Fly wanderer. Fly fainting one. Fly back to the Savior. You are a dove even though you think of yourself as a black raven covered with the mud of sin.

Every moment you wait increases your misery. Your attempts to make yourself worthy for Jesus are nothing but vanity. Come just as you are.

"Return backsliding Israel" (Jeremiah 3:12). He does not say, "Return repenting Israel," (though there is doubtless such an invitation) but return *backsliding* one. With all your backslidings, return, return, return!

Jesus is waiting for You! He will stretch out His hand and pull you in, into Himself, which is your heart's true home.

HIS GRACE, NOT MY GRACES

"Let him who thinks he stands take heed lest he fall."

—1 Corinthians 10:12

It is curious that there is such a thing as being proud of grace. You may say, "I have great faith, I will not fall. Poor Little-faith may fall, but I will never fall." "I have fervent love," says another. "I will stand. There is no danger that I will go astray." You who boast of grace have little grace to boast about.

Some who boast imagine their graces can keep them. They do not know that the stream must flow constantly from the fountain head or the brook will soon be dry. If there is not a continuous stream of oil to the lamp, it may burn brightly today but tomorrow it will smoke with a noxious odor. Be careful that you do not boast about your graces. Let all your boasting and confidence be in Christ (2 Corinthians 10:17) and in His strength, "in Him who is able to keep you from stumbling" (Jude 24).

Spend much time in prayer. Spend even a greater time in holy adoration. Read the Scriptures earnestly and consistently. Watch your life carefully. Live near God. Take the best examples for your models. Let your speech be the fragrance of heaven. Let your heart be perfumed with affection for lost souls. Live so that everyone will know that you have been with Jesus.

When that happy day arrives, when He whom you love will say, "Friend, go up higher" (Luke 14:10), may it be your joy to hear, "You have fought the good fight, you have finished the race, you have kept the faith. Finally there is laid up for you a crown of righteousness" (2 Timothy 4:7–8).

Christian, with care, caution, holy fear and trembling keep the faith in Jesus alone. Let your constant prayer be, "Uphold me according to your word" (Psalm 119:116). He and He alone is able "to keep you from stumbling and to present you faultless before the presence of His glory with exceeding joy" (Jude 24).

GUARD DUTY

"I will guard my ways."

—Psalm 39:1

Fellow pilgrim, do not say, "I will go here and there and never sin." We are always in danger of sinning. The road is very muddy, and it is difficult to choose a path that will not soil our cloths. This is a world of tar, and we need to pay attention if we want to keep our hands clean. There is a robber who wants to take our jewels at every turn in the road. There is a temptation in every mercy. There is a snare in every joy. If we reach heaven, it will be by the miracle of divine grace and attributed entirely to our Father's power.

Be on your guard. The person who carries explosives should not go near a fire. Be careful that you do not enter into temptation. Even your daily activities are sharp tools, so watch how you handle them.

There is nothing in the world to foster a Christian's holiness, but there is everything to destroy it. You need to look to God to keep you. Your prayer must be, "Hold me up and I shall be safe" (Psalm 119:117).

After praying, be watchful. Guard your every thought, word, and action with holy jealousy. Do not expose yourself unnecessarily, but if called to go where the arrows are flying, "take your shield" (Ephesians 6:16). If the devil finds you unarmed, he will rejoice that his hour of triumph has come. You will not be killed, but you can be wounded. "Be sober, be vigilant, because your adversary the devil walks about like a roaring lion, seeking whom he may devour" (1 Peter 5:8). Therefore, be careful, and watch, and pray.

May the Holy Spirit guide us in all our ways, so that we will always please our Lord.

THE ANOINTING

"Be strong in the grace that is in Christ Jesus."

—2 Timothy 2:1

Christ is grace beyond measure. Like a reservoir that empties itself through water pipes, Christ empties His grace into His people. "Of His fullness we have all received, and grace for grace" (John 1:16). "Grace and truth came through Jesus Christ" (John 1:17). He gives grace out of His infinite mercies. He stands as an infinite fountain, always supplying grace to the empty pitchers and thirsty lips that come to Him.

Like a tree bearing sweet fruit, not to remain on the branches but to be picked by all who are hungry, Christ bears grace to pardon, to cleanse, to preserve, to strengthen, to enlighten, to quicken, or to restore. And it is free. There is no cost. It is generously offered to all people.

The blood pumps from the heart, but it belongs equally to every part of the body. Likewise the influence of grace is the inheritance of every saint. We all receive the same saving and sustaining grace.

This is the reason for the sweet fellowship between Christ and His church. Christ is the head on which the oil was first poured, and this same oil runs to the hems of the garments. The poorest saint has anointing from the same costly oil that fell on the head, Christ.

The sap of grace flows from the stem to the branch, and the stem is sustained by the same nourishment that feeds the branch; thus we have true fellowship. As we daily receive grace and recognize it as coming from Jesus, He has fellowship with us, and we enjoy the pleasure of fellowship with Him.

Make daily use of your riches in the covenant.

HALF HEARTED

"He did it with all his heart. So he prospered."

—2 Chronicles 31:21

This is not unusual. It is a general rule that those who work with all their heart prosper. Those who go to their labor half-heartedly are almost certain to fail. The only harvest God gives the lazy is weeds. He does not send wealth to those who refuse to dig for hidden treasure. If you want to prosper, be diligent in business.

It is the same in christianity. If you would prosper in your work for Jesus, let His work come from all your heart. Put as much effort, energy, heartiness, and earnestness into His service as you do into your career.

The Holy Spirit helps our infirmities, but He does not encourage laziness. He desires active believers. The people most useful to the church of Jesus Christ are those who work with all their hearts. Who are the most successful Sunday School teachers? The most talented? No! The most successful are those whose hearts are on fire. They see their Lord riding forth in the majesty of His salvation, and their whole heart is seen in their endurance.

At first there may be a failure, but the devoted worker carries on with a whole heart that exclaims, "It is the Lord's work, and it must be done. My Lord has called me to do it and in His strength I will accomplish it."

Are you serving your Master with all your heart today? Remember the earnestness of Jesus! How wholeheartedly He worked! He could honestly say, "The zeal for your house has eaten Me up" (Psalm 69:9). The night that "His sweat became like great drops of blood falling down to the ground" (Luke 22:44), He carried a great burden on those blessed shoulders. When He poured out His heart, it was not a weak effort, for He was making salvation for His people.

How can we be half-hearted in His cause?

FELLOW PILGRIM

"I am a stranger with you."

—Psalm 39:12

Yes, Lord, a stranger *with* You but not *to* You. All my natural alienation from You has been removed by grace. I walk with You through this sinful world as a pilgrim in a foreign country.

You are a stranger, Lord, in Your own world. Humanity forgets You and dishonors You. It sets up new laws and alien customs and does not know You. Yes, God, Your dear Son "came to His own, and His own did not receive Him" (John 1:11). "He was in the world, and the world was made through Him, and the world did not know Him" (John 1:10). Never was a foreigner so speckled a bird (Jeremiah 12:9) among the inhabitants of any land as Your beloved Son was among His mother's people. It is no wonder that I who live for Jesus should be unknown and a stranger here.

Lord, I would not be a citizen where Jesus is an alien. Your pierced hand has untied the cords that had bound my soul to earth, and now I am a stranger in this land. My speech seems to these Babylonians among whom I live as an outlandish tongue. My manners are singular. My actions are strange.

But there is pleasure in being a stranger with You, for You are my fellow sufferer, my fellow pilgrim. It is a great joy to walk in this blessed fellowship! "My heart burns within me while He talks with me on the road" (Luke 24:32). And though I am a sojourner, I am more blest than those who sit on thrones and far more at home than those who live in mansions:

> To me remains nor place, nor time:
> My country is in every clime;
> I can be calm and free from care
> On any shore, since God is there.
> While place we seek, or place we shun,
> The soul finds happiness in none;
> But with a God to guide our way,
> 'Tis equal joy to go or stay.

KEEP ME BACK

"Keep back Your servant also from presumptuous sins."

—Psalm 19:13

This was the prayer of "the man after God's own heart" (1 Samuel 13:14). If holy David needed to pray this way, then how necessary is this prayer for babes in grace. It is as if David said, "Keep me back, or I will rush headlong into sin." Our evil nature, like an ill-tempered horse, is likely to run away. May the grace of God hold the bridle so that we will not rush into mischief. What sins would the best of us commit were it not for the checks the Lord sets on us in providence and grace.

The psalmist's prayer is directed against the worst form of sin, that which is deliberate and willful. The apostle Paul solemnly warns the saints against the most loathsome sins. "Therefore put to death your members which are on the earth; fornication, uncleanness, passion, evil desire, and covetousness, which is idolatry" (Colossians 3:5).

Do the saints need these warnings? Indeed we do. The whitest robes, unless their purity is preserved by divine grace, will be defiled with filthy spots.

Experienced Christians, don't boast in your experience. You will trip if you look away from "Him who is able to keep you from stumbling, and [who will] present you faultless before the presence of His glory" (Jude 24). You who fervently love the Lord, who have a faith that is constant and a hope that is bright, do not say that you will never sin. Instead, cry, "Do not lead us into temptation" (Matthew 6:13).

There is enough kindling in the best of hearts to light a fire that will burn to the lowest hell if God does not extinguish the sparks as they fall. Who would have dreamed that righteous Lot (2 Peter 2:7) would be found drunk and committing uncleanness (Genesis 19:33)?

Hazael said, "Is your servant a dog that he should do this gross thing?" (2 Kings 8:13). We are likely to ask the same self-righteous question. May infinite wisdom cure us of the madness of self-confidence.

MARCH 16, EVENING

POVERTY

"Remember the poor."

—Galatians 2:10

W hy does God allow so many of His children to be poor? He could make us all rich. He could lay bags of gold at our door. He could send us a large annual income. He could scatter around our homes an abundance of provisions just as He made quail lie in heaps around the camp of Israel (Exodus 16:13) and rained bread from heaven to feed them (Exodus 16:4).

There is no reason for us to be poor, except that He sees it as best. "The cattle on a thousand hills are His" (Psalm 50:10). He could supply them to us. He could make the richest, the greatest, and the mightiest bring all their power and riches to our feet.

But He does not choose to do this. He allows some of us to be poor and others of us to languish in privation and obscurity. Why? There are many reasons. One is to give those who are blessed with much an opportunity to show their love for Jesus. If all their needs were met, they would lose the sweet privilege of exhibiting their love by not ministering in giving to Christ's poorer sisters and brothers.

We show our love when we sing of Him and when we pray to Him, but God has ordained that we should prove our love by our actions. If we truly love Christ we will care for those whom He loves. Those who are cherished by Him, will be cherished by us.

It is more than a duty; it is a privilege to help the poor of the Lord's flock. Remember the words of Jesus, "Assuredly, I say to you, inasmuch as you did it to one of the least of these My brethren, you did it to Me" (Matthew 25:40). Surely this assurance is motivation enough to lead us to help others with a willing hand and a loving heart.

Remember that what we do for His people is graciously accepted by Christ as if it were done to Him.

PEACEMAKERS

"Blessed are the peacemakers, for they shall be called sons of God."

—Matthew 5:9

This is the seventh beatitude, and seven was the number of perfection among the Hebrews. Perhaps the Savior placed the peacemaker seventh on the list because the peacemaker most closely resembles the perfect man Christ Jesus. If you want perfect blessedness, so far as it can be enjoyed on earth, become a peacemaker.

There is a significance in the position of this text. The verse which precedes it speaks of the blessedness of "the pure in heart, for they shall see God." It is well to understand that our wisdom is to be "first pure, then peaceful" (James 3:17). Our peace is never to be a compact with sin or toleration with evil. We must set ourselves like steel against everything that is contrary to God and His holiness. Once purity is established in our hearts we can proceed to peace.

The verse that follows our text is also appropriately placed. Regardless of how peaceful we may be, in this world we will be misrepresented and misunderstood. Even the Prince of Peace by His very peacefulness brought fire on the earth. Although He loved mankind and did no harm, "He was despised and rejected by men, a man of sorrows and acquainted with grief" (Isaiah 53:3).

Peaceful one, don't be surprised when you meet with enemies for the beatitudes continue with, "Blessed are those who are persecuted for righteousness' sake, for theirs is the kingdom of heaven." The peacemakers are more than blessed, they are encircled with blessings.

Lord, give us grace to climb to this seventh beatitude! Purify our minds that we may be first pure, then peaceful. Fortify our souls that our peace may not make us cowards when for Your sake we are persecuted.

MARCH 17, EVENING

ONE FAMILY

"For you are all sons of God through faith in Christ Jesus."

—Galatians 3:26

The fatherhood of God is common to all His children. Oh Little-faith, you have often said, "I wish I had the courage of Great-heart, that I could wield a great sword and be as valiant. But I stumble on every straw, and a shadow makes me afraid."

Listen, Little-faith. Great-heart is God's child and so are you. Great-heart is not one particle more God's child than you are. Peter and Paul, the most highly favored apostles, were of the family of the Most High, and so are you. The weakest Christian is as much a child of God as the strongest believer:

> This covenant stands secure,
>   Though earth's old pillars bow;
> The strong, the feeble, and the weak,
>   Are one in Jesus now.

All the names are in the same family register. One may have more grace, but God our heavenly Father has the same tender heart. One may do more mighty works, and bring more glory to his Father, but the least in the kingdom of heaven is as much the child of God as the greatest. Let this comfort and cheer you as you draw near to God and say, "Father."

Although we are comforted by knowing this, let us not be content with a weak faith. Like the apostles, let us ask "to be strengthened in the faith" (Acts 16:5). Regardless of how feeble our faith is, if it is real faith in Christ we will reach heaven though it will not much honor the Master here or give us an abundance of joy and peace on this pilgrimage.

If you want to live for Christ's glory and be happy in His service seek to be completely filled with the Spirit. "There is no fear in love; but perfect love casts out fear" (1 John 4:18).

LOVE BEYOND MEASURE

"As the Father loved Me; I also have loved you."

—John 15:9

Jesus loves His people the same way the Father loves the Son, and that love is without a beginning. "Yes, I have loved you with an everlasting love" (Jeremiah 31:3).

You can trace the beginning of human affection and easily find the beginning of your love for Christ, but His love to us is a stream whose source is hidden in eternity. God the Father loves Jesus changelessly. Christian, be comforted because there is no change in Jesus Christ's love to those who rest in Him.

Yesterday on the mountain you said, "He loves me." Today you are in the valley of humiliation, but He loves you just the same. On the hill you heard His sweet voice speaking of love. Now on the rough sea, when all His waves and billows wash over you, His heart is still faithful to His ancient choice. The Father loves the Son without end, and the Son loves His people without end.

Saint, do not fear loosing the silver cord (Ecclesiastes 12:6), for His love will never cease. Rest assured that Christ will go with you even down to the grave. And up from the grave He will be your guide to heaven.

Moreover, the Father loves the Son without measure, and that same unmeasurable love is bestowed on His chosen ones by the Son. Christ's entire heart is dedicated to His people. He "loved me and gave Himself for me" (Galatians 2:20). His is a love "which passes knowledge" (Ephesians 3:19).

We have an eternal Savior, a precious Savior who loves us beyond measure, without change, without beginning, without end, just as the Father loves the Son. There is much food here for those who know how to digest it.

May the Holy Spirit lead us and then our "souls shall be satisfied as with marrow and fatness" (Psalm 63:5).

MARCH 18, EVENING

FAITH

"Strengthened in faith."

—Romans 4:20

Christian, take good care of your faith. Remember, faith is the only way you can obtain blessings. If we want blessings from God, only faith can bring them down.

Prayer cannot draw down answers from God's throne unless it is the earnest prayer of a believer. Faith is the angelic messenger between the soul and the Lord Jesus in glory. Let that angel be withdrawn and we can neither send up prayers nor receive answers.

Faith is the telegraph wire that links earth and heaven, and on it God's messages of love move quickly. "It shall come to pass that before they call I will answer; and while they are still speaking I will hear" (Isaiah 65:24). If that wire of faith is broken, we are unable to receive the promise.

Am I in trouble? I can obtain help by faith. Am I beaten up by the enemy? By faith my soul runs into the dear Refuge. But take faith away and in vain I call to God, for then there is no road between my soul and heaven. Even in the deepest winter faith is the road on which the horses of prayer travel, but if that road is blocked how can we communicate with the Great King?

Faith links me with divinity. Faith clothes me with the power of God. Faith engages on my side the omnipotence of Jehovah. Faith ensures every attribute of God in my defense. Faith helps me defy the hosts of hell. Faith makes me march triumphant over the necks of my enemies.

Without faith, how can I receive anything from the Lord? "But let him ask in faith, with no doubting, for he who doubts is like a wave of the sea driven and tossed by the wind" (James 1:6). Christian, with faith you can win all things but without it you can obtain nothing. Jesus said, "If you can believe, all things are possible to him who believes" (Mark 9:23).

MARCH 19, MORNING

FOOD IN ABUNDANCE

"And she ate and was satisfied, and kept some back."

—Ruth 2:14

Whenever we are privileged to eat the bread Jesus gives we are like Ruth, satisfied with a full and pleasant banquet. When Jesus is the host, no guest leaves hungry. Our mind is satisfied with the precious truth Christ reveals.

Our heart is content with Jesus, the "altogether lovely" object of affection (Song of Solomon 5:16). Our hope is satisfied, for "whom have I in heaven but You?" (Psalm 73:25). Our desire is fulfilled, for what more could we wish than "to gain Christ and be found in Him" (Philippians 3:8–9)?

Jesus fills our consciences with perfect peace, our judgements with the certainty of His teaching, our memory with the recollections of what He has done, and our imaginations with the prospects of what He is yet to do.

As Ruth was "satisfied and kept some back," so it is with us. We have had deep drinks and thought we could take in all of Christ, but we consumed only a small portion. We have sat at the table of the Lord's love and said, "Nothing but the infinite can ever satisfy. I am such a sinner that only infinite merit can wash my sins away." But our sins were removed and there was merit to spare. We have had our hunger relieved at the feast of sacred love and found a wealth of spiritual meat remaining.

There are pleasing things in the Word of God that we have yet to enjoy. We feel like the disciples to whom Jesus said, "I still have many things to say to you, but you cannot bear them now" (John 16:12). Yes, there is unrealized grace. There are places of fellowship nearer Christ that have not been reached and heights of communion which our feet have not climbed. At every banquet of love there are many baskets of leftovers (Matthew 14:20, 15:37). Let us magnify the generosity of our glorious Boaz (Ruth 2:14).

MARCH 19, EVENING

BELOVED

"My beloved."

—Songs of Solomon 2:8

This is the golden name the ancient church sometimes gave to the Anointed of the Lord. "The time of singing has come, and the voice of the turtledove is heard in the land" (Song of Solomon 2:12). "My beloved is mine and I am His. He feeds his flock among the lilies" (Song of Solomon 2:16).

In this song of songs she calls Him that delightful name, "My beloved." Even during the long winter when idolatry withered the garden of the Lord, the prophets found space to lay aside the burden of the Lord to say with Isaiah, "Now let me sing to my Well-beloved a song of my beloved regarding His vineyard" (Isaiah 5:1).

At this time He had not been made flesh, He had not dwelt among us, His face had not been seen by the saints, and no one had beheld His glory. Still He was the consolation of Israel, the hope and joy of all the chosen, the beloved of our soul, precious beyond price, and "the chief among ten thousand" (Song of Solomon 5:10).

The church so loves Jesus and so claims Him as her beloved that the apostle Paul defies the whole universe to separate the church from the love of Christ. "Who shall separate us from the love of Christ? Shall tribulation, or distress, or persecution, or famine, or nakedness, or peril or sword? As it is written; 'For Your sake we are killed all day long: we are accounted as sheep for the slaughter.' Yet in all these things we are more than conquerors through Him who loved us" (Romans 8:35–37):

> My sole possession is Thy love;
>   In earth beneath, or heaven above,
> I have no other store;
>   And though with fervent suit I pray,
> And importune Thee day by day,
>   I ask Thee nothing more.

THE EXAMPLE FOR HUSBANDS

"Husbands, love your wives, just as Christ also loved the church."

—Ephesians 5:25

What a golden example Christ gives His disciples! The life of Jesus is an exact transcript of perfect virtue. He, and He alone is both the model and the teacher of holiness. Under no circumstances should we be content until we reflect the grace that was in Him.

The Christian husband is to look on the portrait of Christ Jesus and paint according to that copy. The true Christian husband ought to be to his wife as Christ is to His church. The love of a husband is special.

The Lord Jesus cherishes the church and places on her a distinct affection that sets her above the rest of mankind. "I pray for them. I do not pray for the world but for those whom You have given Me" (John 17:9). The elect church is the favorite of heaven, the treasure of Christ, the crown on His head, the bracelet on His arm, the breastplate around His heart, and the very center of His love.

A husband should love his wife with a constant love because this is the way Jesus loves His church. Jesus does not vary in His affection. He may change His demonstration of that affection but the affection is always constant.

A husband should love his wife with an enduring love. "Nothing shall be able to separate us from the love of God which is in Christ Jesus our Lord" (Romans 8:39).

A true husband loves his wife with a hearty, fervent, and intense love: not with just mere words.

Ah, beloved, what else could Christ have done to prove His love? Jesus has a delightful love for His spouse, and He treasures her affection, and delights in her with pleasant satisfaction.

Believer, you marvel at Jesus' love. You admire it. But are you emulating it? In your marital relationship is the rule and measure: "just as Christ loved the church"?

MARCH 20, EVENING

ALONE

"You will be scattered each to his own, and will leave Me alone."

—John 16:32

Few had fellowship with the sorrows of Gethsemane. Most of the disciples were not sufficiently advanced in grace to be admitted into "the agony" (Luke 22:44). Occupied with the passover feast at their own homes, these disciples represent those who live according to the letter of the law but are mere babies in the spirit of the gospel.

Twelve, no eleven, were privileged to enter Gethsemane to see this great sight, and out of the eleven, eight were left at a distance. The eight had fellowship, but not the intimate kind where only a few are admitted. Only three could approach the veil of our Lord's mysterious sorrow (Matthew 26:36), yet behind that veil even these three were not admitted. They stayed a stone's throw away (Luke 22:41). Jesus must tread the winepress alone (Isaiah 63:3).

Peter and the two sons of Zebedee represent the few eminent, experienced saints who may be called "fathers." These three men, having done business on great waters, can to some degree measure the huge Atlantic waves of their Redeemer's passion.

For their strengthening and for the good of others, some saints are given special and tremendous conflicts that permit them to enter the inner circle and hear the pleadings of the suffering High Priest. They have fellowship with Him and "rejoice to the extent that [they] partake of Christ's sufferings . . ." (1 Peter 4:13).

Yet even these cannot penetrate the secret places of the Savior's agony. "Thine unknown sufferings" is the remarkable expression of the Greek liturgy. There was an inner chamber in our Master's grief. Shut out from human knowledge and fellowship, Jesus is left alone and more than ever becomes an "indescribable gift" (2 Corinthians 9:15). Isaac Watts is correct when he sings:

> And all the unknown joys he gives,
> Were bought with agonies unknown.

INEFFECTIVENESS

"Can you bind the clusters of the Pleiades, or loosen the belt of Orion?"

—Job 38:31

If we are ever inclined to boast about our abilities, the magnificence of nature will quickly show how puny we are. We cannot move the smallest of the twinkling stars or extinguish one sunbeam. We speak of power, but the heavens laugh at us. When Pleiades shines in the spring we cannot influence it: when Orion reigns in winter we cannot ease the cold chill. The seasons revolve according to divine appointment, and the entire human race cannot change it. Lord, "what is man that You are mindful of him" (Psalm 8:4)?

In the spiritual, as in the natural, man's power is limited. When the Holy Spirit sheds His delight in the soul, none can disturb that. All the cunning and malice of this world is ineffectual to stop the life-giving power of the Comforter. When He stoops to visit and revive a church, the most obstinate enemies cannot thwart the good work. They may ridicule it, but they can no more stop it than they can prevent spring from coming. When God wills, so it must be.

On the other hand, if the Lord in sovereignty or justice shackles a person in soul bondage, no one can give them liberty. He alone can remove the winter of spiritual death from an individual or a nation. He loosens the bands of Orion. No one else can. Oh that He would perform this miracle tonight.

Lord, end my winter and let my spring begin. I cannot raise my soul from death and insensibility. "With men, this is impossible, but with God all things are possible" (Matthew 19:26). I need heavenly influences, the clear shining of Your love, the beams of Your grace, the light of Your countenance. These are the Pleiades to me. I suffer greatly from sin and temptation. This is my winter, my terrible Orion. Lord, work wonders in me and for me. Amen.

MARCH 21, EVENING

THE PRAYER

"He went a little farther and fell on His face and prayed, saying, 'O My Father, if it is possible let this cup pass from Me; nevertheless, not as I will, but as You will.'" —Matthew 26:39

There are several things to be learned from our Savior's prayer during His hour of great trial.

It was a lonely prayer. Believer, in times of trials you need to be alone in prayer. Family prayer, social prayer, and prayer in the church is precious but not sufficient. It is in your private devotions, where only God hears you, that the best beaten spices will smoke in your offering "to the Lord as a soothing aroma" (Genesis 8:21).

It was a humble prayer. Luke says He knelt (Luke 22:41) but Matthew says He fell on His face. Humble servant of the great Master, where is your place before God? Humility gives you a good foothold in prayer, and there is no hope of succeeding with God without it.

It was a family prayer. Jesus prayed, "O My Father," and you will find these words a great strength in times of trial. You have no rights as a subject of the King; you forfeited them by treason. But nothing can relinquish your birthright to the Father's protection. Do not be afraid to say, "Oh my Father, hear my cry."

It was a persevering prayer. Jesus prayed three times. Keep praying until you prevail. Be like the widow who sought justice by coming so frequently that she wearied the judge (Luke 18:5). Continue in prayer and watch in prayer with thanksgiving.

Finally, it was a prayer of surrender. "Nevertheless, not as I will, but as You will." Yield, and God yields. Let it be as God wills, for He determines what is best. Be content to leave your prayer in His hands. He knows when to give, how to give, what to give, and what to withhold. So plead earnestly and persistently, but with humility and submission. You will surely prevail.

LET THEM GO

"Father, I desire that they also whom You gave Me may be with Me where I am."

—John 17:24

O h death, why do you touch the tree where the weary seek shade and rest? Why do you snatch away the fruitful trees? If you must use your axe, use it on the trees that yield no fruit. We might even thank you for that. But why do you cut down the good cedars of Lebanon? Spare the righteous; do not use your axe.

But no, death takes the best of our friends. The most generous, the most prayerful, the most holy, and the most devoted must die. Why? Because of Jesus' prevailing prayer: "Father, I desire that they also whom You gave me may be with Me where I am." It is this prayer that bears our loved ones on wings to heaven. Every time a believer leaves this earth for paradise it is an answer to Christ's prayer.

A good old Puritan remarked, "Many times Jesus and His people pull against one another in prayer. You bend your knee in prayer and say, 'Father, I desire that Your saints be with me where I am.' But Christ says, 'Father, I desire that they may be where *I* am.'" Thus the disciple is at cross-purposes with the Lord. The loved one cannot be in both places.

Now what prayer would you choose to have answered? If the King were to step from His throne and say, "Here are two supplicants praying in opposition to each other, which prayer should be answered?" I am sure that even in agony you would say, "Jesus, not my will but Yours."

You would give up your prayer for your loved one's life if you realized that Christ is praying in the opposite direction. "Father, I desire that they also whom You gave Me may be with Me where I am."

Lord, You shall have them. By faith we let them go.

MARCH 22, EVENING

GREAT DROPS OF BLOOD

"His sweat became like great drops of blood falling down to the ground."

—Luke 22:44

The mental pressure from our Lord's agony forced the pores of His body to sweat great drops of blood. What a tremendous weight of sin crushed the Savior! What a demonstration of the mighty power of His love!

Isaac Ambrose observed that the sap which flows from the uncut tree is always the best. This precious tree yielded sweet spices when it was wounded by whips and pierced by nails. But it produced its finest spices preceding that, when there was no whip, no nail, no physical wound.

Christ suffered willingly. Without being lanced His blood flowed freely. No need for a surgeon to use a scalpel; His blood flowed spontaneously. No need for Moses to cry, "Spring up, O well" (Numbers 21:17). Of itself His blood flows in crimson torrents.

When people suffer greatly, apparently the blood rushes to their heart. Their face becomes pale and frequently they faint. The blood has gone inward as if to nourish the inner being. But look at our Savior. He is so utterly oblivious of self, that instead of His agony driving His blood to His heart to nourish Himself, it flows outward to minister to us. The agony of Christ, as His blood is poured out on the ground, pictures the fullness of the offering He made for us.

Can you perceive the intensity of His suffering? Will you hear its voice as it speaks? "You have not yet resisted to bloodshed, striving against sin" (Hebrews 12:4).

Let the great Apostle and High Priest be our example. Sweat blood if you have to, rather than yield to the great tempter of your soul.

TALKING STONES

"I tell you that if these should keep silent, the stones would immediately cry out."

—Luke 19:40

Could stones really cry out? Indeed they could if He who freed the vocal cords of mutes also told the stones to lift their voices. And if they spoke, what a great testimony of praise it would be to the wisdom and the authority of Christ, who created them by the word of His power. Should we not then speak highly of Him who made us anew? "For I say to you that God is able to raise up children to Abraham from these stones" (Matthew 3:9).

The old rocks could tell of chaos and order. They could talk about God's handiwork in the successive stages of creation's drama. Then why can't we talk about God's decrees, or about His great work in ancient times, or about all that He has done for His church in days past?

If stones were to speak they could tell of their breaker, how he took them from the quarry and made them suitable for the temple. Then why can't we tell of the glorious Breaker, who broke our hearts with the hammer of His Word in order to build us into His temple?

If the stones could cry out they would magnify the builder who polished and fitted them to be suitable for a palace. Then why can't we tell of our Architect and Builder who has placed us in the temple of the living God?

If the stones could cry out they might have a long, long, story to tell about being a memorial, for many times in Scripture a great stone was dedicated as a memorial to the Lord for divine help received. We also can testify of stones of help and pillars of remembrance.

And though the broken stones of the law cry out against us, Christ, who rolled the stone away from His tomb, intercedes for us. Stones might well cry out, but we will not let them. We will silence their noise with our song. We will sing a sacred song and bless the majesty of the Most High. We will glorify Him whom Jacob called, "the Shepherd, the Stone of Israel" (Genesis 49:24).

MARCH 23, EVENING

HEARD

"He was heard because of His godly fear."

—Hebrews 5:7

There is nothing worse than being utterly forsaken. "See," said Satan to Jesus, "You haven't a friend anywhere. Your Father doesn't love You. He will not send an angel from His courts to help You. All heaven is alienated from You. You are alone."

"Even the close friends of Your sweet counsel are worth nothing. Son of Mary, look at Your brother James and Your beloved disciple John and Your bold apostle Peter. Cowards! They sleep while You suffer. You have no friends in heaven or earth.

"All hell is against you. I have stirred my infernal den. I have sent messages throughout all regions summoning every prince of darkness to attack You. We will spare no arrows. We will use all our infernal might to overwhelm You, and what can You do? You are alone."

It is possible that this was the temptation of Jesus because the appearance of an angel to strengthen Him removed that fear. "He was heard because of His godly fear." He was not alone, heaven was with Him. But before that this may be the reason He came to His disciples three times (Matthew 26:43). As Hart put it:

> Backwards and forwards thrice He ran,
> As if He sought some help from man.

Jesus would see if it was really true that all had forsaken Him. He found them asleep (Matthew 26:43). Perhaps He took some minor comfort from the thought that they were sleeping not from disloyalty but from sorrow. "The spirit indeed is willing, but the flesh is weak" (Matthew 26:41).

At any rate, "He was heard because of His godly fear." Jesus was heard in His deepest anguish. Rejoice, you too will be heard.

JOY

"In that hour Jesus rejoiced in the Spirit."

—Luke 10:21

The Savior was "a Man of Sorrows" (Isaiah 53:3). Yet every thinking mind has discovered that down deep in His soul Jesus carried an inexhaustible treasury of refined and heavenly joy. No one ever had a deeper, purer, more abiding peace than our Lord Jesus Christ.

"You have loved righteousness and hated lawlessness; therefore God, Your God, has anointed You with the oil of gladness more than Your companions" (Hebrews 1:9). His great compassion gave Him the deepest possible delight because compassion brings joy.

There were several remarkable times when this joy was poured out. "In that hour Jesus rejoiced in the spirit and said, 'I thank You, Father, Lord of heaven and earth'" (Luke 10:21). Even when it was night, Christ had His songs. Although His face was marred and His countenance had lost the luster of earthly happiness He was radiant with the matchless splendor of unparalleled satisfaction as He thought of the reward.

"I will declare Your name to My brethren; in the midst of the assembly I will praise You" (Psalm 22:22). In this verse, the Lord Jesus is a blessed picture of His church on earth, where she expects to walk with her Lord along a thorny road. Through much tribulation she is forcing her way to the crown. Carrying the cross is the church's duty, to be scorned as an alien is her position.

Yet the church has a deep well of joy for her children. There is wine, oil, and corn hidden in the midst of the New Jerusalem that sustains and nourishes the saints of God, and occasionally, as in our Savior's case, there is a season of intense delight. "There is a river whose streams shall make glad the city of God" (Psalm 46:4).

Exiles though we are, we rejoice in our King. Yes, in Him we rejoice exceedingly and in His name we set up our banners.

MARCH 24, EVENING

BETRAYED

"Are you betraying the Son of Man with a kiss?"

—Luke 22:48

"The kisses of an enemy are deceitful" (Proverbs 27:6). We need to be on guard when the world puts on a loving face. For just as the world betrayed our Master, it will betray us with a kiss.

Whenever people are about to stab Christianity they often profess a great reverence for it. Beware of the sleek-faced hypocrisy that is the armorbearer of heresy and infidelity. Be aware of how deceptive the unrighteous are and be "wise as a serpents" (Matthew 10:16), in order to detect and avoid the plans of the enemy.

The young man without understanding was led astray by the kiss of a strange woman (Proverbs 7:13). May we be graciously instructed today so that the "flattering lips" of the world will not affect us (Proverbs 7:21). Holy Spirit, do not let us be betrayed with a kiss!

What if I should be guilty of the same accursed sin as Judas? I have been baptized in the name of the Lord Jesus. I am a member of His visible church. I take communion. All of these are kisses of my lips. Am I sincere? If not, I am a base traitor.

Do I live in the world as carelessly as unbelievers and yet profess to follow Jesus? If so, then I expose my belief to ridicule and cause people to speak evil of the holy name by which I am called. Surely if I act inconsistently I am a Judas, and "it would have been good for that man if he had never been born" (Mark 14:21).

Oh Lord, make me sincere and true. Preserve me from every false way. Never let me betray my Savior. I love you Jesus, and though I often grieve You my desire is to be faithful to death. Amen.

Oh God, forbid that I would be a high soaring professing Christian and then fall into the lake of fire (Revelation 20:10) because I betrayed my Master with a kiss. Amen.

A SWEET NAME

"The Son of Man."

—John 3:13

Our Master frequently used this title, "The Son of Man." He could have spoken of Himself as "Wonderful, Counselor, Mighty God, Everlasting Father, Prince of Peace" (Isaiah 9:6). Oh, the lowliness of Jesus! He calls Himself "the Son of Man." Let us learn from our Savior to never seek great titles or proud degrees.

There is, however, an even dearer thought. Jesus loved and honored humanity so much that He chooses "the Son of Man" as His favorite name. In displaying this name, it is as if He pins medals of honor on the chest of humanity, proclaiming the love of God to the seed of Abraham. Son of Man—whenever used, it beams a halo around the head of Adam's children.

Perhaps there is a more precious thought still. Jesus Christ called Himself the Son of Man to express His oneness and sympathy with His people. This reminds us that we may approach Him without fear. We may take all our grief and trouble to Him because He knows them from His own experience. Because He Himself suffered as the Son of Man, He is able to strengthen and comfort us. All hail blessed Jesus!

Throughout eternity Jesus will use that sweet name to acknowledge that He is our brother. What a precious reminder of His grace, His humility, and His love!

> Oh, see how Jesus trusts Himself
>   Unto our childish love,
> As though by His free ways with us
>   Our earnestness to prove!
> His sacred name a common word
>   On earth He loves to hear;
> There is no majesty in Him
>   Which love may not come near.

PROTECTED

"Jesus answered, 'I have told you that I am He. Therefore, if you seek Me, let these go their way.'"

—John 18:8

Even in His hour of trial Jesus cared for His sheep. He submitted to the enemy, but He also interposed a word of power to free His disciples. But as to Himself, He was "as a sheep before its shearers . . . He opened not His mouth" (Isaiah 53:7). For His disciples, however, He speaks with Almighty energy. This is love—constant, self-forgetting, faithful love.

There is much more here than at first appears. Have we not the very soul and spirit of the atonement in these words? The Good Shepherd gives His life for the sheep (John 10:11), and pleads that they must therefore go free. This Pledge is guaranteed, and justice demands that those for whom He is a substitute should go their way. In the middle of Egypt's bondage His voice rings as a word of power: "Let My people go" (Exodus 5:1).

Out of the slavery of sin and Satan the redeemed must come. In every cell of the Dungeon of Despair the sound is echoed, "Let these go their way." Satan hears the well-known voice and lifts his foot from the neck of the fallen. Death hears it and the grave opens to let the dead rise.

Our way is progress, holiness, triumph, and glory and none shall dare hold us. No starving lion will be in our way, no ravenous beast will attack. The deer of the morning has drawn the cruel hunters from the rest of the herd, and now the timid doe and the fawn may graze in perfect peace among the lilies of His love.

The thundercloud has burst over the Cross of Calvary, and thus the pilgrims of Zion will never be killed with bolts of vengeance. Come, rejoice in the protection your Redeemer has secured for you. Bless His name today and everyday.

WHEN HE COMES

"When He comes in the glory of His Father with the holy angels."

—Mark 8:38

If you have shared in Jesus' shame you will share in the glory that will surround Him when He again appears. Beloved one, are you with Christ Jesus? Is there a vital union that knits you to Him? Then today you share His shame. You have taken up His cross. You bear His reproach. But rejoice, for you will be with Him when the cross is exchanged for the crown.

Examine yourself this evening. If you are not with Him in regeneration, then you will not be with Him when He comes in glory. Unless you have fellowship with Him now, you will never understand the bright happy period when the King will come with all His holy angels.

Oh my friend, if you are indeed His beloved you will not be far from Him. If His friends and His neighbors are called to see His glory, what will it be like if you are married to Him? Will you be distant? Though it will be a day of judgment, you will not be far from the heart that admitted angels into intimacy and has now admitted you into union with Him.

Did He not say, "I will betroth you to Me forever; Yes, I will betroth you to Me in righteousness and justice, in lovingkindness and mercy" (Hosea 2:19)? His own lips have said, "I am married to you" (Jeremiah 3:14).

If the angels, who are only friends and neighbors, will be with Him, then it is abundantly clear: "You shall no longer be forsaken! Nor shall your land any more be termed Desolate, but you shall be called My delight and your land Married" (Isaiah 62:4).

This is a morning star of hope. It is exceedingly brilliant. May it light up your darkest and most desolate experience.

FORSAKEN

"Then all the disciples forsook Him and fled."

—Matthew 26:56

He never deserted them, but at the beginning of His suffering they fled in cowardly fear. This is just one example of the frailty of all believers. At best we are but sheep and run when the wolf appears. The apostles had been warned of the danger, and they promised to die rather than forsake their Master. Yet they were suddenly seized with panic and fled.

It may be that today I decide to live totally for my Lord. If I then imagine that I will be perfectly faithful, let me watch out. The same evil heart of unbelief may make me run away like the apostles. It is one thing to promise and quite another thing to perform. It would have been to their eternal honor to have stayed at Jesus' side. If they fled from the honor, will I be any different? Where else could they have been as safe? Their Master could have called for more than twelve legions of angels (Matthew 26:53). They fled their true safety. Oh God, may I not also play the fool.

Divine grace can make the coward brave. Smoking flax can flame like fire on the altar when the Lord wills it (Isaiah 42:3). These very apostles who were as timid as rabbits grew to be as bold as lions after the Spirit descended on them. The Holy Spirit can make my cowardly spirit brave to confess my Lord and to witness for His truth.

What anguish must have filled the Savior as He saw His friends so faithless. This was one bitter ingredient in His cup. That cup is now drained dry, and may I not put another drop in it. If I forsake my Lord, I will crucify Him again and put Him to open shame (Hebrews 6:6).

Keep me, Oh blessed Spirit, from so shameful a deed.

A SMALL THING

"And she said, 'Yes Lord, yet even the little dogs eat the crumbs which fall from their master's table.'"

—Matthew 15:27

This woman gained great comfort in her misery by thinking great thoughts of Christ. The Master had been talking about the children's bread. Jesus, the Master of the table of grace, is so generous that there is an abundance of bread on His table, an abundance so great that crumbs may be left on the floor for the dogs.

This woman knew Jesus' table was full and that all she needed was a crumb. Remember, she wanted to have a devil cast out of her daughter and this was important to her (Matthew 15:22). Her esteem of Christ was so high that she said, "It is nothing to Him, it is but a crumb for Christ to give." This is the royal road to comfort. Great thoughts of your sin will drive you to despair. Great thoughts of Christ will pilot you to the haven of peace.

My sins are many, but it is nothing for Jesus to take them all away. The weight of my guilt presses me down like a giant's foot crushing a worm, but it is nothing more than a grain of dust to Jesus. "Christ has redeemed us from the curse of the law, having became a curse for us for it is written, ('Cursed is everyone who hangs on a tree')" (Galatians 3:13).

It will be but a small thing for Him to give me full forgiveness, though it will be an infinite blessing for me to receive it. This woman opens her soul's mouth wide, expecting great things from Jesus, and He fills her with His love.

My friend, do the same. She held on to Christ. She even drew arguments out of His hard words. She believed great things of Him and she overcame.

Her case is an example of prevailing faith. If we would conquer, we must imitate her tactics.

THIS IS LOVE

"The love of Christ which passes knowledge."

—Ephesians 3:19

The love of Christ in its sweetness, its fullness, and its greatness surpasses all human comprehension. What language can describe His matchless and unparalleled love toward the children of men? It is so vast and boundless that, like a bird skimming the water but not diving to the depths, words only touch the surface while love beyond measure lies below. A poet says it well:

O love, thou fathomless abyss!

The love of Christ is indeed measureless and fathomless. Before we can have any idea of the love of Jesus, we must understand His previous glory in the height of its majesty and His incarnation in all the depths of its shame.

Who can tell of the majesty of Christ? When He was enthroned in the highest heavens He was very God of very God. "All things were made through Him and without Him nothing was made that was made" (John 1:3). His almighty arm upholds the planets (Colossians 1:17). The praises of cherubim and seraphim perpetually surrounded Him. The full chorus of hallelujahs of the universe flow unceasingly to the foot of His throne. He reigns supreme above all His creatures. He is God over all, blessed forever.

Who can tell His height of glory then? Who can tell how low He descended? To be a man was something, to be a man of sorrows was far more. To bleed, and suffer, and die was much for the Son of God. To suffer unparalleled agony, to endure a death of shame and desertion by His Father, this is a depth of condescending love that the most brilliant of minds utterly fails to comprehend. This is love, love that "passes knowledge."

Oh let this love fill our hearts with adoring gratitude and lead us to practical revelation of its power.

A SWEET AROMA

"I will accept you as a sweet aroma."

—Ezekiel 20:41

The merits of our great Redeemer are a sweet aroma to the Most High. Whether we speak of the active or passive righteousness of Christ, the fragrances are equal.

There was a sweet perfume in His active life as He honored the law of God. He made every precept glitter like a precious jewel in the pure setting of His own person.

The same fragrance was evident in His passive obedience. Without complaint He submitted to and endured hunger and thirst and cold and nakedness. He sweat great drops of blood, gave His back to those who struck Him, gave His face to those that plucked out His hair, and was nailed to the cruel wood to suffer the wrath of God on our behalf. These things are precious to the Most High.

Because of what Jesus has done—His dying, His substitutionary sufferings, His vicarious obedience—the Lord our God accepts us. What preciousness there is in Him to make up for our lack of preciousness. What a sweet aroma to put away our bitterness. What a cleansing in His blood to take away sin like ours. What a glory in His righteousness to make such unacceptable creatures accepted in the Beloved!

How sure and unchanging our acceptance is because it is in Him. Never doubt your acceptance in Jesus. You cannot be accepted by God without Christ, but once you have received His merit you cannot be rejected even with all your doubts, fears, and sins.

Jehovah's gracious eye never looks on you in anger when He looks at you through Christ, for then He sees no sin. Though you still struggle with sin, you are always accepted in Christ, always blessed, and always dear to the Father's heart.

So sing, and as you see the smoking incense of the merit of the Savior rising before the sapphire throne let the incense of your praise rise.

MARCH 28, EVENING

JEWELS

"Though He was a Son, yet He learned obedience by the things which He suffered."

—Hebrews 5:8

We are told that the Captain of our salvation was made perfect through suffering. Therefore, we who are sinful and far from perfect should not question when we are called to suffer. Shall the head be crowned with thorns, and the other members of the body be pampered on the dainty lap of luxury? Must Christ pass through seas of His own blood to win the crown and we walk to heaven in silver slippers? No, our Master's experience teaches that suffering is necessary to the true-born child of God.

There is, however, a comforting thought in our text. The fact of Christ's "being made perfect through suffering" means He can have complete sympathy with us. "For we do not have a High Priest who cannot sympathize with our weaknesses, but was in all points tempted as we are, yet without sin" (Hebrews 4:15). In this empathy of Christ we find sustaining power.

One of the early martyrs said, "I can bear it all, for Jesus suffered, and He suffers in me now. He sympathizes with me, and this makes me strong."

Believer, hold on to this thought in times of agony. Let the thought of Jesus strengthen you as you follow in His steps. May you find pleasant support and fellowship in His sympathy.

Remember, to suffer is an honorable thing, but to suffer for Christ is glorious. The apostle Paul rejoiced that he was counted worthy to suffer for Christ. "For I consider that the sufferings of this present time are not worthy to be compared with the glory which shall be revealed to us" (Romans 8:18).

The jewels of a Christian are afflictions. The regalia of God's anointed kings are their troubles, sorrows, and griefs. Do not shun this honor. Grief exalts us. Trouble lifts us. "If we endure, we shall also reign with Him" (2 Timothy 2:12).

MARCH 29, MORNING

UNANSWERED, NOT UNHEARD

"I called Him, but He gave me no answer."

—Song of Solomon 5:6

Prayer sometimes lingers like a petitioner at the gate who waits for the King to come and give a blessing. When He has given a servant great faith, the Lord has been known to test it by long delays. He has permitted His servant's voice to echo as if the prayer never reached the ceiling. It is as if the prayer knocked at the golden gate but the gates remained closed as if rusted shut. Like Jeremiah we may cry, "You have covered Yourself with a cloud, that prayer should not pass through" (Lamentations 3:44).

True saints have waited patiently without an answer, not because they were unaccepted but because it pleased Him who is Sovereign and who gives "according to His good pleasure" (Ephesians 1:9). If it pleases Him to let us wait, shall He not do as He wills with His own? Beggars must not be choosers as to time, place, or form.

We must be careful not to think that delays in prayer are denials. God's bills will be paid on time. We cannot permit Satan to shake our confidence in the God of truth by pointing to unanswered prayers. Unanswered petitions are heard. God keeps a file for our prayers. They are not blown away by the wind; they are treasured in the King's archives where every prayer is recorded.

Tested believer, listen to His promise: "You number my wanderings. Put my tears in Your bottle; Are they not in Your book?" (Psalm 56:8). Someday He will appear and have you take off the sackcloth and ashes of long waiting, and then He will give you the scarlet and fine linen of full completion.

NUMBERED

"He was numbered with the transgressors."

—Isaiah 53:12

Why did Jesus come to this earth to suffer for sinners? This wonderful condescension was justified by many powerful reasons.

By His coming, "we have an Advocate with the Father, Jesus Christ the righteous" (1 John 2:1). In some court trials there is an identification of the attorney with the client so that in the eyes of the law they are one. When the repentant sinner is brought to the bar of justice, Jesus appears and answers the accusations. He points to His side, His hands, and His feet and challenges Justice to bring anything against this sinner. He pleads His blood so triumphantly that the Judge proclaims, "Deliver him from going down to the Pit, I have found a ransom" (Job 33:24).

Our Lord Jesus was numbered with the transgressors to draw our hearts to Him. We may come boldly and confess our guilt. He who is numbered with us cannot condemn us.

He was holy and written among the holy. We were guilty and numbered with the guilty. He transferred His good name to this dark indictment and our bad names were taken off the indictment and written on the roll of acceptance. Jesus has taken our lives of misery and sin in exchange for His wealth, His righteousness, and His blood. Everything that He has is given to us.

Rejoice believer, we are united with Him who was numbered among the transgressors. "Therefore, if anyone is in Christ he is a new creation; old things have passed away; behold all things have become new" (2 Corinthians 5:17). Prove you are truly saved by being numbered with those who are a new creation in Him.

RESTORED

"Let us search out and examine our ways, and turn back to the Lord."

—Lamentations 3:40

The spouse who fondly loves her absent husband longs for his return; a protracted separation from her companion is a semi-death to her spirit: and so it is with those who love the Savior, they must see His face, they must have fellowship with Him.

A reproaching glance or an uplifted finger will trouble obedient, loving children who do not want to offend their parents. Beloved, it was once so with you. A text of Scripture, a threatening, a touch of the rod of affliction, and you went to the Father's feet and cried, "Show me why You contend with me" (Job 10:2).

Is it still that way with you? Or are you content to follow Jesus at a distance? Can you imagine not walking with Christ? Does this thought trouble you? Can you endure having your beloved Lord walk away from you because you are walking contrary to Him? Have your sins separated you from God? Is your heart at rest?

Oh let me affectionately warn you. It is a serious thing when we can be content without the present enjoyment of the Savior's face. Let us understand what an evil thing this is, to have little love for our Savior, little joy in our precious Jesus, little fellowship with the Beloved. Hold a true Lent in your soul as you sorrow over the hardness of your heart.

Remember where you first received salvation. Go immediately to the cross. There and there only can your spirit be revived no matter how hard, how insensible, or how dead you have become. Go again in the rags, poverty, and defilement of your natural condition. Clasp the cross, look in those languid eyes, bathe in the fountain filled with blood, for this will bring back your first love. This will restore the simplicity of your faith and the tenderness of your heart.

MARCH 30, EVENING

HIS SUFFERING

"And by His stripes we are healed."

—Isaiah 53:5

Pilate delivered our Lord to the lictors to be scourged and crucified (Mark 15:15). The Roman scourge was a most dreadful instrument of torture. It was made from the sinew of oxen with interwoven sharp bones. Every time the lash fell, these pieces of bone inflicted terrible lacerations as the flesh was torn from the victim's body. Jesus had been beaten earlier, but this torture by the Roman lictors was the most severe of His flagellations. My soul, stand here and weep over His poor stricken body.

Believer in Jesus, can you gaze on Him without tears as He stands before you as the mirror of agonizing love? He is as beautiful as the lily of innocence, and as red as the rose with the crimson of His own blood. As we feel the sure and blessed healing His stripes have accomplished, our hearts melt with love and grief. If ever we have loved You, Lord Jesus, it is now:

> See how the patient Jesus stands,
> Insulted in His lowest case!
> Sinners have bound the Almighty's hands,
> And spit in their Creator's face.
>
> With thorns His temples gor'd and gash'd
> Send streams of blood from every part;
> His back with knotted scourges lash'd
> But sharper scourges tear His heart.

Pray to our Beloved to print the image of His suffering on your heart today. Then this evening, return to commune with Him and express the sorrow that your sin cost Him so great a price.

WATCHING

"Now Rizpah . . . from the beginning of harvest . . . did not allow the birds of the air to rest on them by day nor the beasts of the field by night."
—2 Samuel 21:10

If the love of a woman for the bodies of her slain sons could make her prolong this mournful vigil, should we grow tired of considering the sufferings of our blessed Lord?

As she drove away the birds of prey, we should drive from our minds those worldly and sinful thoughts that defile us. Away, you birds of evil wing! Leave the sacrifice alone!

She stayed there, lonely and unsheltered, during the heat of summer, the dew of the night, and the dampness of rain. Sleep would not come to her weeping eyes even though her heart was heavy to slumber. How very much she loved her children.

Should Rizpah be faithful and we run at the first trial or inconvenience? Are we such cowards that we cannot suffer with our Lord? This woman even chased away wild animals. Are we ready to encounter every foe for Jesus' sake?

Her children were slain by others and she wept and watched. What should we do, we who by our sins have crucified our Lord? Our obligations are boundless, our love should be fervent, our repentance complete. To watch with Jesus is our business, to protect His honor our occupation, to stay by His cross our comfort.

Those ghastly corpses might well have frightened Rizpah especially at night. But in our Lord, at whose cross we sit, there is nothing revolting, everything is attractive. Never was living beauty so enchanting as in the dying Savior.

Jesus, we will stand by You. We ask that You graciously unveil Yourself to us. Then we will not sit underneath sackcloth but in a royal pavilion.

MARCH 31, EVENING

THE KISS

"Let him kiss me with the kisses of his mouth."

—Song of Solomon 1:2

For several days we have been meditating on the Savior's passion and we will linger here a little longer.

As we begin a new month, may we seek our Lord with the same desires that glowed in the heart of the elect spouse. She immediately leaps to Him. There are no opening words. She doesn't even mention His name. Instantaneously she is in the heart of her theme and she speaks of Him who was the only him in the world to her.

Her love is bold! It was much condescension that permitted the weeping penitent to anoint His feet with fragrant oil (Luke 7:38); it was rich love that allowed the gentle Mary to sit at His feet and learn of Him (Luke 10:39); but here, love is strong and fervent and aspires to much higher admiration and more intimate fellowship with Him.

Esther trembled in the presence of Ahasuerus (Esther 4:16). But here the spouse of the Beloved feels the joyful liberty of perfect love and knows no fear. If we have received the same free spirit, this joyful, fearless, and perfect love is also ours.

Believers, enjoy the affection of Jesus' love, represented in our text by kisses. The kiss of reconciliation we enjoyed at our conversion was as sweet as honey. The kiss of acceptance is still warm on our brow, for we know that He accepted us through His rich grace. And we desire the kiss of daily, present fellowship day after day, until we finally receive the kiss of consummation in heaven.

Faith is our walk. Fellowship is our rest.

Faith is the road. Communion with Jesus is the well from which we pilgrims drinks.

Oh lover of our souls, do not be a stranger to us. Let the lips of Your blessing meet the lips of our asking. Let the lips of Your fullness touch the lips of our need. Amen.

APRIL 1, MORNING

IT IS TIME

"It is time to seek the Lord."

—Hosea 10:12

The month of April is said to derive its name from the latin verb *aperio,* meaning "to open." All the buds and blossoms are now opening for we have arrived at the flowering time of the year.

Reader, if you are not saved, may your heart be awakened by nature to receive the Lord. Every blossoming flower warns you that it is time to seek the Lord. Let your heart bud and bloom with holy love for Jesus.

Are you young and strong? Then I plead with you to give your vigor to the Lord. It was my unspeakable happiness to be called in early youth, and I praise the Lord everyday for it. Salvation is priceless, let it come when it may; But, oh, an early salvation has double value because you may die before you reach the prime of life.

"It is time to seek the Lord." You who feel the first sign of decay should quicken your pace. That hollow cough and that feverish flush are warnings. Do not delay. It is indeed "time to seek the Lord."

Do I observe a little grey mingled with your once luxurious curls? The years are rapidly passing; death is swiftly approaching. Let this return of spring awaken you to set your house in order.

Dear reader, if you are elderly, let me plead and implore you to delay no longer. There is a day of grace now; be thankful for that. But it is a limited season, and it grows shorter with every tick of the clock.

Here in your quiet room, on the first night of another month, I speak to you as best I can by paper and ink. As God's servant, from my innermost soul, I give you this warning, "It is time to seek the Lord."

Do not ignore this. It may be your last call from destruction. It may be the final syllable from the lips of grace.

APRIL 1, EVENING

SILENCE

"He answered him not one word."

—Matthew 27:14

Jesus was never slow to speak when He could bless others, but He would not say one word for Himself. "No man ever spoke like this man" (John 7:46), and no man was ever silent like Him.

Was this singular silence a manifestation of His perfect self-sacrifice? Did it prove that He would not speak a word to prevent His crucifixion? A crucifixion which He dedicated as an offering for us.

Had He so totally surrendered that He would not intervene on His own behalf but was willing to be bound and slain as a sacrifice, without struggle, without complaint? Was this silence a type of the defenselessness of sin? Nothing can be said to justify or excuse human guilt, thus He who bore its whole weight stood speechless before His judge.

Is long-suffering silence the best reply to a denying world? Calm endurance answers some questions infinitely more conclusively than the loftiest eloquence. The best apologists for Christianity in the early days were often its martyrs. The anvil breaks a lot of hammers by quietly bearing their blows.

The silent Lamb of God furnished us with a grand example of wisdom. Where every word was an occasion for new blasphemy, He added no fuel to the flames of sin. The ambiguous and the false, the unworthy and the mean, will soon overthrow and discredit themselves. Thus truth can afford to be quiet and finds silence to be its wisdom.

Evidently our Lord, by His silence, fulfilled a remarkable prophecy. A long defense would have been contrary to Isaiah's prophecy: "He was led as a lamb to the slaughter. And as a sheep before its shearers is silent. So He opened not His mouth" (Isaiah 53:7). His silence conclusively proved that He was the true Lamb of God. As the true Lamb we honor Him this morning.

Be with us Jesus, and in the silence of our heart let us hear the voice of Your love. Amen.

APRIL 2, MORNING

THAT DAY

"He shall see His seed, He shall prolong His days, and the pleasure of the Lord shall prosper in His hand."

—Isaiah 53:10

Pray for a speedy fulfillment of this promise. Prayer is easy work when our desires are grounded and anchored in God's own promise. How can He that gave the word refuse to keep it? Constant truthfulness cannot disgrace itself by a lie. Eternal faithfulness cannot degrade itself by neglect. God must bless His Son. His covenant binds Him to it. What the Spirit prompts us to ask Jesus for is the same thing that God decrees to give Him.

Whenever you are praying for the kingdom of Christ, let your eyes behold the dawning of the blessed day that is fast approaching, when the Crucified One will receive His coronation in the place where He was rejected (Revelation 21:5).

Have courage, you who prayerfully work for Christ with only the smallest of successes. It won't always be this way. Better times are coming. Your eyes cannot see the blissful future, but borrow the telescope of faith, wipe the misty breath of your doubts from the glass, and look through it to see the coming glory.

Reader, is this your frequent prayer? Remember, the same Christ who tells us to say, "Give us this day our daily bread" (Matthew 6:11), also gives us this petition, "Hallowed be Your name, Your kingdom come. Your will be done on earth as it is in heaven" (Matthew 6:10).

Do not pray only about your own sins, your own wants, your own imperfections, your own trials. Let your prayers climb the starry ladder; and as you approach the blood-sprinkled mercy seat, offer this prayer continually: "Lord, extend the kingdom of Your dear Son." Such a prayer fervently presented will elevate the spirit of all your devotions.

But remember, prove the sincerity of your prayer by working to promote the Lord's glory.

SCAPEGOAT

"They took Jesus and led Him away."

—John 19:16

Jesus had been in agony all night. He had spent the early morning at the hall of Caiaphas. He had been rushed from Caiaphas to Pilate, from Pilate to Herod, and then back to Pilate. He had little strength left. Neither food nor drink was given to Him. They wanted His blood. They led Him out to die, loaded with the cross. Oh sorrowful procession! Oh my soul, weep.

What can we learn as we see our blessed Lord led away? Can we see the truth foreshadowed by the scapegoat (Leviticus 16:10)? The high priest put both hands on the head of the scapegoat, confessed the sins of the people, and asked God that those sins be taken from the people and laid on the goat. Then the goat was led into the wilderness to symbolize the carrying away of the sins of the people.

We see Jesus brought before the priests and rulers and pronounced guilty. God Himself imputes our sins to Him. "The Lord has laid on Him the iniquity of us all" (Isaiah 53:6). "He made Him who knew no sin to be sin for us" (2 Corinthians 5:21). We see the great Scapegoat, the substitute for our guilt, being led away. He carries on His shoulders our sin, represented by the cross.

Beloved, can you feel assured that He carried your sin? As you look at the cross on His shoulders, does it represent your sin? There is one way to tell. Have you laid your hands on His head, confessed your sin, and then trusted in Him? If so, your sin no longer lies on you. It has been transferred by blessed imputation to Christ. He carries it on His shoulder as a load heavier than the cross.

Do not let this picture vanish until you have rejoiced in your own deliverance and adored the loving Redeemer on whom your iniquities were laid and carried away.

APRIL 3, MORNING

CONFESSION

"All we like sheep have gone astray: we have turned, every one, to his own way: and the Lord has laid on Him the iniquity of us all."

—Isaiah 53:6

Here is a confession of sin common to all the elect people of God. We have all fallen, and from the first saint who entered heaven, to the last who will enter, our common chorus is, "All we like sheep have gone astray."

This unanimous confession is special and particular. "We have turned, everyone, to his own way." There is a distinctive sinfulness about every individual. Each of us has some special aggravation.

While genuine repentance naturally associates us with other penitents, it also produces a kind of loneliness. "We have turned, everyone, to his own way," is a confession that each one has sinned uniquely, or sinned with an intensity that could not be perceived in others.

This confession is unreserved. There is not a word to detract from its force, not a syllable of excuse. The confession gives up all claims of self-righteousness. It is the declaration of the consciously guilty; guilty with aggravations, guilty without excuse. We stand with our weapons of rebellion broken in pieces and cry, "All we like sheep have gone astray; we have turned, everyone, to his own way."

Yet there are no hopelessly distressing moans with this confession, because the next sentence makes it almost a song: "The Lord has laid on Him the iniquity of us all." This phrase is the most grievous in our text; yet it overflows with comfort.

Isn't it amazing that where misery was concentrated, mercy reigned. Where sorrow reached a climax, weary souls find rest. The Savior bruised is the healer of bruised hearts. The lowest repentance gives way to assured confidence by gazing at Christ on the cross.

RIGHTEOUS

"For He made Him who knew no sin to be sin for us that we might become the righteousness of God in Him."

—2 Corinthians 5:21

Sorrowing Christian, why are you weeping? Are you grieving over your iniquity? Look to your perfect Lord and remember that you are complete in Him.

In God's sight you are as perfect as if you had never sinned. No, it is better than that, for the Lord of Righteousness has put His divine garment on you. And so you are more than righteous; you have the righteousness of God (1 Corinthians 1:30).

You who are sorrowing over inbred sin and wickedness, remember, none of your sins can condemn you in Christ (Romans 8:1). You have learned to hate sin, but learn this also: Sin is not yours; it was laid on Christ's head. Your standing is not in yourself; it is in Christ. Your acceptance is not in yourself; it is in your Lord. You are as accepted by God today as you will be when you stand before His throne, free from all this life's corruption.

Oh, I urge you, remember this precious thought: perfection in Christ! You are complete in Him. With your Savior's garment on, you are holy as the Holy One.

"Who is he who condemns? It is Christ who died, and furthermore is also risen, who is even at the right hand of God, who also makes intercession for us" (Romans 8:34).

Christian, rejoice. You are accepted in the beloved, so what do you have to fear? Smile, and live near your Master in the suburbs of the Celestial City. Soon, when your time comes, you will go to where Jesus sits, and you will reign at His right hand, just as "when He had by Himself purged our sins, He sat down at the right hand of the Majesty on high" (Hebrews 1:3).

And all this because our divine Lord "who knew no sin was made sin for us that we might become the righteousness of God in Him."

THE MOUNTAINTOP

"Come, and let us go up to the mountain of the Lord."

—Isaiah 2:3

It is exceedingly beneficial to rise above this present evil world to something nobler and better. "The cares of this world and the deceitfulness of riches choke the word" (Matthew 13:22) and are also apt to choke everything good within us. We grow fretful and depressed, or perhaps proud and worldly. It is good to cut down these thorns and briers, because heavenly seed sown among them is not likely to yield a harvest.

Where can we find a better sickle with which to cut them down than in our fellowship with God and the heavenly things of the kingdom?

In the valleys of a mountainous country many of the inhabitants are deformed. They have a sickly appearance because the atmosphere is charged with miasma. But up in the mountains the people are robust. They breathe clear fresh air as it blows from the virgin snows of the summits. It would be good for the valley dwellers to leave their homes in the marshes and inhale the bracing air of the hills.

It is to such a climb that I invite you this evening. May the spirit of God assist you to leave the mists of fear, the fevers of anxiety, and all the ills that gather in this valley of earth and to ascend the mountains of anticipated joy and blessing.

May God the Holy Spirit cut the cords that keep us here and help us to climb. Too often we sit like eagles chained to a rock. But unlike the eagles, we love our chain. May God grant us grace that, if we cannot escape from the chain of the flesh, we may escape the chain of the spirit.

May our souls, like Abraham, attain the mountaintop and there commune with the Most High.

APRIL 4, EVENING

OUR CROSS

"On him they laid the cross that he might bear it after Jesus."

—Luke 23:26

Simon's carrying the cross is a picture of the church's responsibility throughout all generations. After Jesus, the church is the cross-bearer.

Mark this, Christian: Jesus did not suffer to exclude you from suffering. He bears a cross, not for you to escape it, but that you may endure it. Christ saves you from sin but not from sorrow. Remember that and expect to suffer (John 16:33).

But here is comfort. In our case, as in Simon's, it is not our cross but Christ's cross that we carry. When you are harassed for holiness, when your faith brings cruel mockings, remember that it is not your cross, but it is Christ's cross. How delightful it is to carry the cross of our Lord Jesus!

You carry the cross after Him, and you have blessed company, because your path is marked with the footprints of your Lord. The marks of His blood-red shoulders are on that heavy burden. It is His cross and He walks before you as a shepherd walks before his sheep. Jesus said, "If anyone desires to come after Me, let him deny himself, and take up his cross daily and follow Me" (Luke 9:23).

And remember this, although Simon had to carry the cross for just a little while, it brought him lasting honor. The cross we carry is only for a little while, at most, and then we will receive the crown of glory.

We should love the cross, and instead of cringing from it welcome it. "For our light affliction which is but for a moment is working for us a far more exceeding and eternal weight of glory" (2 Corinthians 4:17). "The things which are seen are temporary, but the things which are not seen are eternal" (2 Corinthians 4:18).

HUMILITY

"Before honor is humility."

—Proverbs 15:33

The humiliation of your soul always brings a positive blessing. If we empty our hearts of self God will fill them with His love. If you desire closer communion with Christ remember the words of the Lord: "But on this one will I look; on him who is poor and of a contrite spirit and who trembles at My word" (Isaiah 66:2).

Stoop, if you would climb to heaven. You must grow downward in order to grow upward. Humble souls have the sweetest fellowship with heaven. God will deny no blessing to a thoroughly humbled spirit. "Blessed are the poor in spirit, for theirs is the kingdom of heaven" (Matthew 5:3). All the riches and treasures of God's whole storehouse will be deeded as a gift to the soul that is humble enough to receive it and humble enough not to grow proud because of it.

God blesses us to the fullest measure and extremity of what we can handle. If you do not get a blessing it is because it is not safe for you to have one. If our heavenly Father were to let your unhumbled spirit win a victory in His holy war, you would pilfer the crown for yourself. Then when you met a new enemy you would fall a victim to it. You are kept low for your own safety.

When a person is sincerely humble and never ventures to touch a grain of praise there is scarcely any limit to what God will do. Humility makes one ready to be blessed by the God of all grace. Humility makes one fit to deal efficiently with everyone.

True humility is a flower that will beautify any garden. True humility is a sauce to season and improve every dish of life. Whether it be prayer or praise, whether it be work or suffering, the genuine salt of humility cannot be used to excess.

APRIL 5, EVENING

OUTSIDE

"Therefore let us go forth to Him, outside the camp, bearing His reproach."

—Hebrews 13:13

Jesus, bearing His cross, went forth to suffer outside the gate. The Christian's reason for leaving the camp of the world's sin and religion is not because we want to be alone but because Jesus did it. The disciples must follow their Master.

Christ is not of the world (John 8:23). His life and his testimony were a constant protest against conformity with the world. His affection for people was overflowing, but still He was separate from sinners.

In the same way, Christ's people must "go forth to Him." They must take their position "outside the camp" as witness bearers for the truth. They must be prepared to walk the straight and narrow path. They must have bold, unflinching, lion-like hearts, loving Christ first and His truth next and both beyond all the world.

Jesus would have His people "go forth outside the camp" for their own sanctification. You cannot grow in grace when you conform to the world. The life of separation may be a path of sorrow, but it is the highway of safety. The separated life may cost you many sorrows, everyday may be a battle, but it is a happy life.

No joy can excel that of the soldier of Christ. Jesus reveals Himself graciously and gives such sweet refreshment that the warrior feels more calm and peace in daily strife than sinners in their hours of rest.

The highway of holiness is the highway of fellowship with Jesus. We will win the crown if we are enabled by divine grace to follow Christ "outside the gate."

The crown of glory will follow the cross of separation. A moment's shame will be well compensated by eternal honor. A little time of witnessing will seem nothing when "we shall always be with the Lord" (1 Thessalonians 4:17).

TOTAL

"In the name of the Lord I will destroy them."

—Psalm 118:12

Our Lord Jesus by His death did not purchase just a part of you, but all of you. He contemplated in His sacrifice our total sanctification—spirit, soul, and body. This is the triple kingdom where He is to reign without a rival.

The newborn nature that God gives the regenerate must assert the rights of the Lord Jesus Christ. My soul, as a child of God, you must conquer every unblessed area. You must subdue all your powers and passion to the silver scepter of Jesus' gracious reign. Never be satisfied until He who is King by purchase becomes King by coronation.

Sin no longer has ownership in any part of you. We fight a good and lawful battle when we seek, in the name of God, to drive sin out. Oh my body, you are a member of Christ. Can I tolerate your subjection to the prince of darkness? Oh my soul, Christ has suffered for your sins and redeemed you with His most precious blood. Can I permit your memory to become a storehouse of evil or your passion to be a firebrand of iniquity? Can I surrender my judgment to be perverted by error? Can I let my will be led in chains of iniquity? No! My soul, you are Christ's. Sin has no right to you.

Christian, be courageous. Do not be depressed as though your spiritual enemies could never be destroyed. You are able to overcome them, but not in your own strength, for your weakest spiritual enemy is too much for you alone. You, however, can and will overcome them through the blood of the Lamb.

Do not ask, "How can I dispossess them, for they are greater and more powerful than I am?" Go to the strong for strength. Wait humbly on God and the mighty God of Jacob will surely come to the rescue, and you will sing victory through His grace.

THE DISMAL LIST

"How long, O you sons of men, will you turn my glory to shame?"

—Psalm 4:2

An instructive writer has compiled a dismal list of honors that the blinded people of Israel awarded their long-expected King.

1. They gave Him a *procession of honor* in which Roman legionaries, Jewish priests, and ordinary men and women marched as He Himself carried His cross. This triumph the world awarded to Him who overthrew earth's dreadful foes. Derisive shouts were His only acclamation and cruel taunts His only song of praise.

2. They presented Him with the *wine of honor,* but not the gold cup of fine wine. Rather, they offered Him the criminal's stupefying death-drink, which He refused. Later when He cried, "I thirst, . . . they filled a sponge with sour wine, put it on hyssop and put it to His mouth" (John 19:28–29). Oh what wretched, detestable inhospitality to the King's Son!

3. He was provided with an *honor guard,* which showed their esteem by gambling for His garments. The bodyguard of the adored One of heaven was a quartet of brutal gamblers.

4. A *throne of honor* was found for Him on the bloody tree. No comfortable place of rest would rebels give our sovereign Lord. The cross was the full expression of the world's feeling toward Him. "There," they seemed to say, "Thou Son of God, this is the manner that God Himself would be treated if we could reach Him."

5. The *title of honor* was nominally "King of the Jews." But that blinded nation distinctly repudiated the title. In reality, by their choice of Barabbas (John 18:40), they called Him "King of thieves." And they put Jesus in the place of lowest shame, between two thieves. His glory was turned to shame by the sons of men.

But His glory will yet gladden the eyes of saints and angels world without end.

APRIL 7, MORNING

CONFESSION

"Deliver me from the guilt of bloodshed, O God, The God of my salvation. And my tongue shall sing aloud of Your righteousness."

—Psalm 51:14

In this solemn confession, David names his sin. He does not call it manslaughter, indiscretion, or an unfortunate accident to an honorable man. David calls it what it is, bloodshed. David did not personally kill Bathsheba's husband, but he planned it (2 Samuel 11:15). Before the Lord, David was a murderer.

Learn in confession to be honest with God. Do not give fair names to foul sins. Though you call them what you will, sin will smell no sweeter. What God sees your sins to be, you must feel them to be; and with openness of heart, acknowledge their true character.

David was evidently depressed with the heinousness of his sin. It is easy to use words, but it is difficult to feel their meaning. The fifty-first Psalm is a photograph of a broken spirit. No matter how excellent our words, if our hearts are not conscious of the hell sin deserves and if our spirits are not broken we cannot expect to find forgiveness.

Our text is an earnest prayer addressed to the God of salvation. It is His prerogative to forgive. It is His very name and agency to save those who seek His face. Better still, the text calls Him the God of *my* salvation. Yes, blessed be His name, even while I am going to Him through Jesus' blood, I can rejoice in the God of my salvation.

The psalmist ends with a praiseworthy vow. If God will deliver him, he will sing. No, more than sing, David will "sing aloud." Who can sing quietly about this great mercy?

But look at the subject of the song: "Your righteousness." We will sing of the finished work of the precious Savior, and the one who knows the most of forgiving love will sing the loudest.

WRATH

"For if they do these things in the green wood, what will be done in the dry?"

—Luke 23:31

The following interpretation of Jesus' question is full of teaching: "If I, the innocent substitute for sinners, suffered like this, what will happen to the sinners—the dry tree—when they fall into the hands of an angry God?" When God saw Jesus in the sinner's place, He did not spare Him (Romans 8:32), and when God finds the unregenerate without Christ, neither will He spare them.

Sinner, Jesus was led away by His enemies (Matthew 27:31), and you too will be dragged away by fiends to the place appointed for you. Jesus was deserted by God, and if He was deserted (who was a sinner only by our sins being imputed to Him), how much more will you be?

"Eli, Eli, lama sabachthani?" What an awful shriek (Matthew 27:46)! But what will be your cry when you say, "Oh God! Oh God! Why have You forsaken me?" And the answer comes back, "I will laugh at your calamity; I will mock when your terror comes" (Proverbs 1:26).

If God spared not His own Son (Romans 8:32), how much less will He spare you! What whips of burning wire will be yours when conscience smacks with all its terrors. You rich, you merry, you self-righteous sinners; who would stand in your place if God should say, "Awake O sword against the one that rejected Me. Strike them, and let them feel the sting forever"?

Jesus was spit on (Matthew 26:67). Sinner what will your shame be? We cannot put in one word all the sorrows that fell on the head of Jesus who died for us. Therefore, I cannot tell you what streams, what oceans of grief, will roll over your spirit if you die without Christ.

You may die later, you may die now. By the agonies of Christ, by His wounds and by His blood, do not bring on yourself the wrath to come! Trust in the Son of God and you will never die (John 3:16)!

APRIL 8, MORNING

TRIUMPH

"I will fear no evil for You are with me."

—Psalm 23:4

Notice how the Holy Spirit can cause the Christian to thrive regardless of outward circumstances. We have a bright light that shines in us when all is dark. We are firm, happy, calm, and peaceful when the world shakes and the pillars of earth are removed.

Even death with all its terrible influences, has no power to stop the music in a Christian's heart. Instead that music becomes sweeter, clearer, and more heavenly. The last kind act of death is to let our earthly song melt into the heavenly chorus and to turn our temporary joy into eternal happiness. Have confidence in the blessed Spirit's power to comfort.

Dear reader, do you fear poverty? Do not worry about it. The divine Spirit can give you a prosperity greater than the wealthy have in their earthly abundance. You do not know the joys that will grow for you around the house where grace will plant the roses of contentment.

Are you conscious of a growing bodily weakness? Do you expect to suffer long nights of deterioration and days of pain? Do not be sad! That bed can become a throne. It may be that every pain shooting through your body is a refining fire to consume your dross, a beam of glory to light up the secret parts of your soul.

Are your eyes growing weak? Jesus will be your light.

Is your hearing failing? Jesus' name will be your soul's best music and His presence your delight.

Socrates use to say, "Philosophers can be happy without music." Christians can be happier than philosophers when all the outward reasons to rejoice are gone.

In You, my God, my heart will triumph, come what may! By Your power, Oh blessed Spirit, my heart will be exceeding glad even if every earthly thing should fail me. Amen.

APRIL 8, EVENING

GRATITUDE

"And a great multitude of the people followed Him, and women who also mourned and lamented Him."

—Luke 23:27

In the crowd that hounded the Redeemer to His doom were some gracious souls. Their bitter anguish was expressed with wailing and weeping, good music to accompany that march of sorrow.

When my soul's imagination sees the Savior bearing His cross to Calvary, I join the godly women and weep. Indeed, there is a case for grief that lies deeper than those mourning women thought.

They weep about innocence being mistreated, goodness being persecuted, love bleeding, and meekness about to die. But in my heart there is a deeper and more distressing reason to mourn. My sins were the scourges that lacerated those blessed shoulders. My sins crowned with thorns that bleeding brow. My sins cried, "Crucify Him! Crucify Him!" My sins laid the cross on His gracious shoulders.

Jesus being led to die is sorrow enough for one eternity, but my having been His murderer is more, infinitely more grief than one poor fountain of tears can express.

It is not hard to guess why those women loved Him and wept, but they had no greater reasons for love and grief than my heart has. Nain's widow saw her son raised from the dead (Luke 7:15), but I have been raised in newness of life. Peter's mother-in-law was cured of a fever (Mark 1:30), but I was cured of the greater plague of sin. Mary and Martha were blessed with His visits (Luke 10:38), but He dwells in me. His mother gave birth, but He is formed in me as the hope of glory (Colossians 1:27).

I have a debt as great as these holy women. Let me equal them in gratitude or sorrow:

> Love and grief my heart dividing,
>   With my tears His feet I'll bathe—
> Constant still in heart abiding,
>   Weep for Him who died to save.

YOUR GOODNESS

"Your gentleness has made me great."

—Psalm 18:35

This text may be translated, "Your goodness has made me great." David ascribed his greatness to the goodness of God, not to himself.

"Your providence" is another translation. Providence is nothing more than goodness in action. Goodness is the bud, and providence is the flower. Or goodness is the seed, and providence is the harvest.

Some translate this verse, "Your help," which is another word for providence. Providence is the firm ally of the saints and aids them in the service of their Lord.

Another translation is, "Your humility has made me great." "Your condescension," therefore might serve as a comprehensive reading, combining all the thoughts mentioned. God making Himself little is the cause of our being made great. We are so little that if God were to manifest His greatness without His condescension we would be trampled under His feet. But God, who must stoop to view the skies and bend to see what angels do, turns His eye even lower and looks to the insignificant and repentant and makes them great.

The Septuagint translates this, "Your discipline"— Your fatherly correction—"has made me great." The Chaldee paraphrase reads, "Your word has increased me." Still the idea is the same.

David ascribes all his own greatness to the condescending goodness of his Father in heaven. May this sentiment be echoed in our hearts this evening as we cast our crowns at Jesus' feet and cry, "Your gentleness has made me great."

How marvelous is our experience of God's gentleness. How gentle His corrections. How gently His patience. How gentle His teachings. How gently He draws us to Him.

Believer, meditate on this theme. Let gratitude wake you. Let humility be deepened. Let love be quickened before you fall asleep tonight.

APRIL 9, EVENING

AT THE CROSS

"The place called Calvary."

—Luke 23:33

The hill of comfort is the hill of Calvary. The house of consolation is built with the wood of the cross. The temple of heavenly blessing is founded on the split rock, riven by the spear that pierced His side. No scene in sacred history ever cheered the soul like Calvary's tragedy:

Is it not strange, the darkest hour
    That ever dawned on sinful earth,
Should touch the heart with softer power,
    For comfort, than an angel's mirth?
That to the Cross the mourner's eye should turn,
    Sooner than where the stars of Bethlehem burn?

Light now shines from the midday-midnight surrounding Golgotha, and every flower of the field blooms sweetly beneath the shadow of that once accursed tree. In that place of thirst, grace has dug a fountain that forever gushes with waters pure as crystal, each drop capable of alleviating the problems of mankind.

You who have had your seasons of trials will confess that it was not at Mt. Olivet, nor the hill of Sinai, nor on Tabor where you found comfort. Rather, it was Gethsemane, Gabbatha, and Golgotha that comforted you. The bitter herbs of Gethsemane have often taken away the bitters of your life. The whip of Gabbatha has often scourged away your cares. The groans of Calvary have put all other groans to flight. It is Calvary that produces extraordinary and rich comforts.

We would never have known Christ's love in all its height and depth if He had not died. We could never have guessed the Father's deep affection if He had not given His Son to die. The common mercies we enjoy all sing of love, just like the sea shell that we put to our ear whispers of the ocean. Yet if we desire to hear the ocean itself we must not look at everyday blessings but at the transactions of the crucifixion.

If you want to know love, go to Calvary and see the Man of sorrows die.

APRIL 10, MORNING

AN ANGEL

"For there stood by me this night an angel of the God to whom I belong and whom I serve."

—Acts 27:23

The storm and the darkness, coupled with the imminent risk of shipwreck, made the vessel's crew fearful and anxious. One man alone remained calm and reassured the others. Paul was the one with enough courage to say, "Take heart men." There were veteran Roman legionaries on board and brave old mariners, yet their poor Jewish prisoner was braver than all of them.

Paul had a secret friend who gave him courage. The Lord Jesus sent a heavenly messenger with words of consolation to His faithful servant. Thus Paul radiated confidence and spoke as if he were relaxing at home.

If we fear the Lord, we may expect timely intervention when our trial is at its worst. Angels are not kept from us by storms or hindered by darkness. It is not beneath seraphs to visit the poorest of the heavenly family. If angels' visits are few and far between at ordinary times, their visits will be frequent during our nights of storms and tossings.

Friends may leave us when we are under pressure, but our meetings with the inhabitants of the angelic world will increase. The strength of their love words, brought from the throne via Jacob's ladder, will enable us to be strong and to do great deeds.

Dear reader, is this an hour of trial? Then ask for special help. Jesus is the angel of the covenant, and if you earnestly seek His presence, it will not be denied.

Some have had the angel of God stand by them in a night of storm. When anchors would not hold and shipwreck was near, they remember the comfort which that presence brought:

> O angel of my God, be near,
>   Amid the darkness hush my fear:
> Loud roars the wild tempestuous sea,
>   Thy presence, Lord, shall comfort me.

POURED WATER

"I am poured out like water, and all My bones are out of joint."

—Psalm 22:14

Was there ever a sadder spectacle of sorrow! In soul and body, our Lord felt Himself to be as weak as water poured out. Placing the cross in its socket had violently shaken Him, strained all His ligaments, put His every nerve on edge, and dislocated all His bones.

Burdened with His own weight, the majestic sufferer felt the strain increasing every moment of those six long hours. His sense of faintness and general weakness were overpowering. In His own consciousness He became nothing but a mass of misery and fainting sickness.

When Daniel saw the great vision, he described his sensations: "No strength remained in me; for my vigor was turned to frailty in me and I retained no strength" (Daniel 10:8). How much weaker was our greater Prophet when He saw the dread vision of the wrath of God and felt it in His own soul!

To us, the sensations that our Lord endured would have been insupportable, and kind unconsciousness would have come to our rescue. But in His case He was wounded and *felt* the sword; He drained the cup and *tasted* every drop.

As we kneel before our ascended Savior's throne, remember the way in which He prepared a throne of grace for us. Let us in spirit drink of His cup that we may be strengthened for our hour of heaviness, whenever it comes.

In His natural body every part suffered, but from this grief and woe His body came out uninjured to glory and power. Likewise in His spiritual body, every member must also suffer, but we will come through the furnace. The fire has no power; the hairs of our head will not be singed, our garments will not be affected, and even the smell of fire will not be on us (Daniel 3:27).

PAIN AND SIN

"Look on my affliction and my pain. And forgive all my sins."

—Psalm 25:18

It is well when prayers about our sorrow are linked with pleas concerning our sins; when being under God's hand, we are not totally occupied with our pain, but also remember our offenses against God.

It is well to take both sorrow and sin to the same place. It was to God that David carried his sorrow. It was to God that David confessed his sin. This being the case, we must take our sorrows to God, even our little sorrows, because "the very hairs of your head are all numbered" (Matthew 10:30). Your great sorrows you may commit to Him, because He "has measured the waters in the hollow of His hand" (Isaiah 40:12). Go to Him, whatever your present trouble, and you will find Him able and willing to lift your sorrow.

But we must also take our *sins* to God. We must carry them to the cross that the blood may fall on them to purge away their guilt and destroy their defiling power.

The special lesson of the text is this: In the proper spirit, we are to go to the Lord with our sorrows and with our sins. All that David asks concerning his sorrow is, "Look on my affliction and my pain." But the next petition is vastly more explicit, definite, decided, and plain: "Forgive all my sins."

Many sufferers would have said, "Remove my affliction and my pain, and look at my sins." Not David; he cries, "Lord, as for my affliction and my pain, I will not dictate to Your wisdom. Lord, look at them, I will leave them to You. I would be delighted to have my pain removed, but do as You will. As for my sins, Lord, I know what I want done with them. I must have them forgiven. I cannot endure the weight of their curse for another moment."

A Christian considers sorrow lighter than sin. We can endure continuing trouble, but we must not support the burden of transgressions.

APRIL 11, EVENING

DEPRESSED

"My heart is like wax; it has melted within Me."

—Psalm 22:14

Our blessed Lord experienced a terrible sinking and melting of soul. "The spirit of a man will sustain him in sickness, but who can bear a broken spirit?" (Proverbs 18:14). Deep depression is the most painful of trials. More than any other time, we need God when depression melts our hearts.

Believer, come near the cross this morning. Humbly adore the King of glory who was once brought far lower in mental distress and inward anguish than any of us ever will be. Note His fitness to be our faithful High Priest. "He Himself took our infirmities and bore our sicknesses" (Matthew 8:17).

Especially let those of you whose sadness relates to the withdrawal of a sense of their Father's love enter into a close, intimate fellowship with Jesus. Do not despair, since our Master has passed through this dark room.

Our souls may sometimes hunger and thirst in agony to see the light of the Lord's countenance. At times like that, remember the sweet sympathy of our great High Priest. Our drops of sorrow will soon be forgotten in the ocean of His griefs. Then how high should our love rise!

Strong and deep love of Jesus, come in like the sea at high tide. Cover all my powers, drown all my sins, wash away all my cares, lift up my earth-bound soul and float it to my Lord's feet.

There let me die, a poor broken shell, washed up by His love, having no virtue or value of my own. Only this I venture: to whisper to Him that if He will put His ear to me, He will hear within my heart the faint echoes of the vast waves of His own love, love that has brought me where I delight to be: at His feet forever.

GARDENS

"The King's Garden."

—Nehemiah 3:15

When Nehemiah mentioned the King's garden, it brought to my mind the paradise the King of kings prepared for Adam. Sin utterly ruined that delightful place and drove the children of men to work the ground that now produces thorns and briers (Genesis 3:17–18).

My soul, remember the fall, because it was your fall. Weep because the Lord of love was so shamefully treated by the human race of which you are a member. Look how dragons and demons dwell on this fair earth that was once a garden of delight.

There is another King's garden that the King waters with His bloody sweat—Gethsemane (Luke 22:44). Here the bitter herbs are sweeter to renewed souls than Eden's luscious fruits. In this garden the mischief of the serpent in the first garden was undone. Here the curse was lifted from earth and carried by the woman's promised seed. My soul, think of the agony and the passion.

Go to the garden of the olive press and view your great Redeemer rescuing you from your lost estate. This garden of gardens is where the soul may see both the guilt of sin and the power of love, two sights that surpass all others.

Is there no other King's garden? Yes, my heart, you are His garden, or you should be. Do the flowers flourish? Do choice fruits appear? Does the King walk here and rest? Let me make sure that the plants are trimmed and watered and the little foxes that spoil the vines are captured (Song of Solomon 2:15). Come, Lord, and let the heavenly wind "blow upon my garden that its spices may flow out" (Song of Solomon 4:16).

Nor must I forget the King's garden of the church. Oh Lord, send Your church prosperity. Rebuild her walls, nourish her plants, ripen her fruit, and from the huge wilderness reclaim the barren waste and make it "a King's garden."

APRIL 12, EVENING

A BUNDLE OF MYRRH

"A bundle of myrrh is my beloved to me."

—Song of Solomon 1:13

Myrrh often represents Jesus because myrrh is precious, perfumed, and pleasant: it also heals, preserves, and disinfects and is connected with sacrifice. But why is He compared to "a bundle of myrrh?"

First, for abundance. He is a full supply. He is not a drop, or a shoot, or a single flower. He is a whole bundle. There is enough in Christ to meet all my needs. May I not be slow to avail myself of Him.

Second, our well-beloved is compared to a bundle of myrrh for fullness and variety. "In Him dwells all the fullness of the Godhead bodily" (Colossians 2:9). Everything we need is in Him. As you look at His different characters you will see a marvelous variety: Prophet, Priest, King, Husband, Friend, Shepherd. Consider His life, death, resurrection, ascension, second coming. View His virtue, gentleness, courage, self-denial, love, faithfulness, truth, and righteousness. Everywhere He is a bundle of preciousness.

He is also a bundle of myrrh for preservation, not loose myrrh dropped and stepped on, but myrrh tied up or stored in a jewelry case. We value Him as our greatest treasure. We prize His words and His ordinances. We keep our thoughts and knowledge of Him under lock and key, lest the devil would steal anything from us.

Moreover, Jesus is a bundle of myrrh for uniqueness. This symbol suggests the idea of distinguished, discriminating grace. "Just as He chose us in Him before the foundation of the world" (Ephesians 1:4), He was set apart for His own. He gives His perfume only to those who have fellowship with Him.

Oh blessed are the people whom the Lord has admitted into His secrets and for whom He sets Himself apart! Oh choice and happy are those who can say, "A bundle of myrrh is my beloved to me."

LEAN HEAVILY

"Then he shall put his hand on the head of the burnt offering and it will be accepted on his behalf to make atonement for him."

—Leviticus 1:4

Our Lord's being made "sin for us" (2 Corinthians 5:21) is seen in the Old Testament transfer of sin to the bullock. The hand on the bullock's head was not a light touch. The original word means to lean heavily, as in the expression, "Your wrath lies heavy upon me" (Psalm 88:7). Surely this is the very essence and nature of faith. A faith that not only brings us in contact with the great Substitute, but teaches us to lean heavily on Him with all the burdens of our guilt.

Jehovah places on the Substitute's head all the offenses of His covenant people. Then each chosen one is brought personally to ratify this solemn covenant act, by grace and faith to lay their hands on the head "of the Lamb slain from the foundation of the world" (Revelation 13:8).

Believer, do you remember that rapturous day when you first realized pardon through Jesus the sin-bearer? Can you make a glad confession and join with the writer in saying, "My soul recalls the day of deliverance with delight. Loaded with guilt and full of fears, I saw my Savior as my Substitute, and I laid my hand on Him. How timid at first, but courage grew and confidence was confirmed until I leaned my soul entirely on Him. Now it is my unceasing joy to know that my sins are no longer imputed to me but are laid on Him."

Blessed discovery! Eternal solace of a grateful heart!

> My numerous sins transferred to Him,
>   Shall never more be found,
> Lost in His blood's atoning stream,
>   Where every crime is drowned!

RIDICULE

"And those who see Me ridicule Me: they shoot out the lip, they shake the head."

—Psalm 22:7

Mockery was a major ingredient in our Lord's sorrow. Judas mocked Him in the garden. The chief priests and scribes laughed Him to scorn. Herod thought Him nothing. The servants and the soldiers jeered and brutally insulted Him. Pilate and the guards ridiculed His royalty. On the tree all sorts of horrid jests and hideous taunts were hurled at Him.

Ridicule is always hard to bear, but when we are in intense pain it is so heartless and cruel that it cuts to the quick. Imagine the Savior crucified, racked with anguish beyond mortal imagination. Then picture that multitude mocking in bitter contempt of one poor suffering victim.

Surely there must have been something more in the crucified One than they could see. Why else would this large crowd unanimously show such contempt? Was this not evil itself confessing, at the very moment of its greatest apparent triumph, that it could do nothing more than mock the victorious goodness which was reigning on the cross?

Oh Jesus, despised and rejected, how could You die for people who treated You so badly? This is love amazing, love divine; yes this is love beyond degree.

We too despised You in our unregenerate days. And even since our new birth we have often placed the world high in our hearts, even though You bled to heal our wounds, and You died to give us life.

Oh that we could put You on a glorious high throne in everyone's heart. We would sing Your praises over land and sea until all would universally adore as once they did unanimously reject:

Thy creatures wrong Thee, O Thou sovereign Good!
Thou art not loved, because not understood:
This grieves me most, that vain pursuits beguile
Ungrateful men, regardless of Thy smile.

APRIL 14, MORNING

It Is Well

"Say to the righteous that it shall be well with them."

—Isaiah 3:10

It is always well with the righteous. If our text had said, "Say to the righteous that it shall be well with them in their prosperity," we would be thankful for wealth. But prosperity is an hour of peril as well as a gift from heaven. Or if it had been written, "It is well with them under persecution," we would have been thankful for this assurance because persecution is hard to endure.

But when time is not mentioned, all times are included. God's "shalls" must always be understood in the largest expanse of time. From the beginning to the end of the year, from the first evening shadows until the day star shines, in all conditions and under all circumstances, it shall be well with the righteous.

It is so well with the righteous that we could not imagine it to be better. We are well fed, feeding on the flesh and blood of Jesus. We are well clothed, wearing the imputed righteousness of Christ. We are well housed, dwelling in God. We are well married, our soul is knit in bonds of marriage to Christ. We are well provided for, having the Lord as our Shepherd. We are well endowed, with heaven as our inheritance. It is well with the righteous, well on divine authority. The mouth of God speaks this comforting assurance to us.

Oh beloved, if God declares that all is well, then ten thousand devils may declare it harmful, but we laugh them to scorn. Blessed be God for a faith that enables us to believe God when the creatures contradict Him. The Word says that at all times it is well with the righteous.

Beloved, if you cannot see it, let God's word assure you. Believe it on divine authority. Believe it with more confidence than if your eyes and your feelings told you.

Whom God blesses is blessed indeed. What His lips declare is truth sure and steadfast.

FORSAKEN

"My God, My God, why have You forsaken Me?"

—Psalm 22:1

Here is the Savior in the depth of sorrow. No other place shows the grief of Christ like Calvary, and no other moment at Calvary is so full of agony as that in which His cry cuts the air, "My God, My God, why have You forsaken Me?"

At that moment extreme physical weakness was united with acute mental torture from the shame and ignominy through which He had passed. He suffered spiritual agony surpassing all expression when His Father's presence departed. This was the black midnight of His horror, and He descended into the abyss of suffering.

No one can grasp the full meaning of these words. Some of us think at times we could cry, "My God, My God, why have You forsaken me?" There are seasons when the brightness of our Father's smile is eclipsed by clouds and darkness. But remember, God never forsakes us. It is only a seeming forsaking, but in Christ's case it was a real forsaking.

We grieve at a little withdrawal of our Father's love. But who can measure the depth of the agony it caused Jesus at the real turning away of God's face from His Son?

In our case our cry is often dictated by unbelief. In His case it was the utterance of a dreadful fact. God had really turned away from Him for a season.

Oh poor, distressed soul, who once lived in the sunshine of God's face but now you are in darkness, remember that He has not really forsaken you. God in the clouds is as much our God as when He shines in all the lustre of His grace.

If the thought that He has forsaken you causes agony, what anguish was the Savior's when He exclaimed, "My God, My God, why have You forsaken Me?"

LIFTED

" And bear them up forever."

God's people need bearing up. We are very heavy. We have no wings. We need divine grace to mount on wings "covered with silver and feathers of yellow gold" (Psalm 68:13).

By nature sparks fly up, but sinful souls fall down. Oh Lord, "bear them up forever," said David. Here he feels other souls should be lifted as well as his own. When you ask this blessing for yourself, do not forget others.

There are three ways God's people need to be lifted up. They need to be elevated in character. Lift them up, Oh Lord. Do not permit them to be like the world's people! The world lies in the grasp of the wicked one; lift them out of it. The world's people are looking for silver and gold, seeking their own pleasures and the gratification of their lusts.

Lord, lift Your people above all this. Keep them from being "muckrakers," as John Bunyan called the ones who were always scraping after gold! Set their hearts on the risen Lord and the heavenly heritage.

Believers need to be lifted up to flourish in conflict. If they seem to fall in battle, Oh Lord be pleased to give them the victory. If the foot of the foe is on their necks only for a moment, help them to grasp the sword of the Spirit and eventually win the battle.

Lord, bear up Your children's spirits in the day of conflict. Do not let them sit in the dust mourning forever. Do not permit the adversary to disturb and worry them. If they have been persecuted like Hannah (1 Samuel 1:14), let them sing of the mercy of a delivering God.

Let us also ask our Lord to bear them up at the end, bear them up by taking them home. Lord, lift their bodies from the grave and raise their souls to Your eternal kingdom in glory.

THE PRECIOUS BLOOD

"The precious blood of Christ."

—1 Peter 1:19

Standing at the foot of the cross we see His hands, feet, and side spilling crimson streams of precious blood. This blood is precious because it redeems and atones. It atones for the sins of Christ's people. It redeems us from being under the law. It reconciles us to God. It makes us one with Him.

Christ's blood is precious in its cleansing power. "The blood of Jesus Christ, His Son, cleanses us from all sins" (1 John 1:7). "Though your sins are like scarlet, they shall be as white as snow" (Isaiah 1:18). Through Jesus' blood there is not a spot left on any believer. No wrinkle or any such thing remains. Oh precious blood that makes us clean. Oh precious blood that removes the stains of abundant iniquity. Oh precious blood that permits us to stand accepted in the Beloved, even when we have rebelled against our God.

The blood of Christ is precious in its preserving power. We are safe from the destroying angel under the sprinkled blood (Exodus 11:5). Remember, when God sees the blood, we are spared. This is comfort when the eye of faith is dim, because God's eye never changes.

The blood of Christ is precious because it sanctifies. The same blood that justifies by taking away sin also awakens the new nature and leads us to subdue sin and to follow the commands of God. There is no motive for holiness as great as that which streamed from Jesus' veins.

Precious, unspeakably precious, is this blood, because it has overcoming power. It is written, "They overcame him by the blood of the lamb" (Revelation 12:11). We who fight with the precious blood of Jesus on our side fight with a weapon that can never be defeated.

The blood of Jesus! Sin dies at its presence. Death ceases to be death. Heaven's gates open. The blood of Jesus! We will march on, conquering and to conquer, as long as we trust its power!

APRIL 16, MORNING

STEADY HANDS

"And his hands were steady until the going down of the sun."

—Exodus 17:12

So mighty was the prayer of Moses that everything depended on it. The petitions of Moses troubled the enemy more than the fighting of Joshua. Yet both were needed.

In our soul's conflict, force and fervor, decision and devotion, and valor and vehemence must join forces. You must wrestle with your sin, but the major part of the wrestling must be done alone in private with God.

Prayer holds up the token of the covenant before the Lord. The rod was the emblem of God's working with Moses, the symbol of God's government in Israel. Learn, pleading saint, to hold up the promise and the oath of God before Him. The Lord cannot deny His own declarations. Hold up the rod of promise, and you will have what you desire.

When Moses grew weary, his friends assisted him. When your prayers weaken, let faith support one hand and holy hope uplift the other. Prayer seated on the stone of Israel, the rock of our salvation, will persevere and prevail.

Beware of weak devotion. If Moses felt it, who can escape? It is easier to fight sin in public than to pray against it in private. Joshua never grew weary fighting, but Moses grew weary praying. The more spiritual an exercise, the more difficult it is for flesh and blood to maintain it.

Let us cry for special strength. May the spirit of God, who helps our infirmities, enable us to continue with our hands steady "until the going down of the sun." May the Spirit help us until the evening of life is over, until we come to the rising of a better sun in the land where prayer is swallowed up in praise.

APRIL 16, EVENING

SPRINKLED BLOOD

"To the blood of sprinkling that speaks better things than that of Abel."

—Hebrews 12:24

Have you come to the blood of sprinkling? My question is not, have you come to a knowledge of doctrine, to an observance of ceremonies, or to a certain form of experience. My question is, have you come to the blood of Jesus? The blood of Jesus is the life of all vital godliness.

If you have truly come to Jesus, we know how you came: The Holy Spirit sweetly brought you to the blood of sprinkling, with no merits of your own. Guilty, lost, and helpless, you came to take that blood, and that blood alone, as your everlasting hope.

You came to the cross of Christ with a trembling, aching heart. You heard that precious sound, the voice of the blood of Jesus. The dropping of His blood is the music of heaven to the penitent of earth.

We are full of sin, yet the Savior asks us to lift our eyes to Him. As we gaze on His streaming wounds, each falling drop of blood cries, "It is finished. I have made an end of sin. I have brought everlasting righteousness." This is the sweet language of the precious blood of Jesus.

If you have ever come to the blood of sprinkling, you will feel a need to come daily. Those who do not desire to wash in that fountain everyday have never washed in it. It is the believers' joy and privilege that the fountain is still open.

Past experiences are doubtful as food for Christians. Only a daily coming to Christ can give joy and comfort.

This morning, let us sprinkle our doorpost with blood and then feast on the Lamb, fully assured that the destroying angel must pass us by (Exodus 12:13).

ONE WISH

"We wish to see Jesus."

—John 12:21

The world seeks satisfaction in earthly comfort, enjoyment and riches, while a sinner under conviction seeks only a Savior. "Oh that I knew where I might find Him" (Job 23:3). When persons are truly awakened to guilt, you could pour the gold of India at their feet and the response would be, "Take it away. We want only to find Him."

It is a blessed thing when we bring all our wishes to focus on one central object. When we have fifty different objectives, our heart resembles a pool of stagnant water slowly spreading into a marsh breeding miasma and disease. But when all our aspirations are brought into one channel, the heart becomes like a river of pure water, running swiftly to fertilize the fields.

Blessed are those who have one objective, even if it has not been realized, provided that objective is Jesus Christ. If Jesus is the soul's desire, it is a blessed sign of divine work.

These people will never be content with mere ordinances. They will say, "I want Christ. I must have Him. Mere ordinances are of no use to me. I want Him. While I am dying of thirst you offer me the empty pitcher; give me water or I die. Jesus is my soul's desire. I wish to see Jesus!"

Dear reader, is this your condition? Have you only one wish and that is Christ? Then you are not far from the kingdom of heaven.

Is your only wish to be washed from all your sins in Jesus' blood? Can you really say, "I would give up everything if I could only feel that I have an interest in Christ?"

Then despite all your fears, be of good cheer. The Lord loves you. You will soon be able to "stand fast therefore in the liberty by which Christ has made you free" (Galatians 5:1).

APRIL 17, EVENING

THE SCARLET CORD

"She bound the scarlet cord in the window."

—Joshua 2:21

Rahab's life depended on the promise of the spies (Joshua 2:14). She looked on these spies as representatives of the God of Israel. Her faith was simple and firm, and it showed her obedience. Tying a scarlet cord in a window was a trivial act, but she dared not run the risk of omitting it.

Listen, my soul, there is a lesson here. Have you paid attention to the Lord's will, even to the commands that seem non-essential? Have you participated in believers' baptism and the Lord's Supper? If these are neglected, there is disobedience in your heart. Be blameless in all things, even in tying a scarlet cord, if that is a command.

This act of Rahab offers a solemn lesson. Have I implicitly trusted in the precious blood of Jesus? Have I tied the scarlet cord so tight in my window that my trust can never be removed? Or do I look out at the Dead Sea of my sins, or the Jerusalem of my hopes, without seeing the blood and all things in connection with its blessed power?

The passer-by can see the scarlet cord if it hangs from the window. It will be well for me if my life makes the power of the atonement conspicuous to all. What is there to be ashamed of? Let men or devils gaze if they will, the blood is my triumph and my song.

My soul, there is one who will see that scarlet cord even when your faith is so weak that you cannot see it. Jehovah, the Avenger, will see it and pass over you.

Jericho's walls fell flat. Rahab's house was on the wall and yet it stood unmoved (Joshua 6:17). My nature is built in the wall of humanity, and yet, when destruction strikes, I shall be secure.

My soul, tie the scarlet cord in the window and rest in peace.

HE WILL DO WHAT HE SAID

"For You said, 'I will surely treat you well.'"

—Genesis 32:12

When Jacob was on the other side of the Jabbok brook, Esau was coming to meet him with armed men. Jacob earnestly sought God's protection. He reasoned and pleaded, "For You said, 'I will surely treat you well.'" Oh the force of that plea! He was holding God to His word: "You said."

God's faithfulness is a splendid horn of the altar to grasp, but His promises are even mightier as they hold you securely. "For You said, 'I will surely treat you well.'"

"Indeed, let God be true but every man a liar" (Romans 3:4). Will He be true? Will He keep His word? Will every word of His lips stand fast and be fulfilled?

Solomon's prayer of dedication at the temple contained this same mighty plea. "Now I pray, O God of Israel, let your word come true which You have spoken to Your servant David my father" (1 Kings 8:22,26).

When a promissory note is given, a promise is made to pay at the due date. God never dishonors His bills. The credit of the Most High never was impeached, and it never will be. God is punctual to the moment. God is never early, but He is never late.

Thoroughly search God's word, and compare it with the experience of God's people. You will find the two totally agree. Many an old saint has said with Joshua, "Not one thing has failed of all the good things which the Lord your God spoke concerning you. All have come to pass for you; not one word of them has failed" (Joshua 23:14).

If you have a divine promise, you need not plead with an "if." The Lord will certainly fulfill the promise or else He would not have given it to you. God does not give you His words merely to quiet you for awhile and then later put you off. When God speaks, it is because He will do what He has said.

APRIL 18, EVENING

NOW SEEN

"Then behold, the veil of the temple was torn in two from top to bottom."

—Matthew 27:51

Tearing this strong, thick veil from top to bottom was a mighty miracle. But it was not intended merely as a display of power, for much may be learned from it.

The old law of ordinances ended when Jesus died, and the sacrifices were finished. All was fulfilled in Him, and therefore the temple, where ordinances and sacrifices occurred, was marked with an evident manifestation of decay.

The tearing of the veil revealed the hidden things of the old dispensation. The mercy seat could now be seen and the glory of God gleamed above it. By the death of Jesus we now have a clear revelation of God. Life and immortality are brought to light and things that were hidden from the foundation of the world are manifested in Him.

The annual ceremony of atonement was thus abolished. The place of the symbolic ritual was broken up because the atoning blood sprinkled once a year within the veil had now been offered once for all by the great High Priest. The blood of bullocks or lambs was no longer needed because Jesus had shed His blood. Access to God had been opened up, and this access is the privilege of every believer in Christ Jesus.

It is not a small rip through which we can only peek at the mercy seat. No, the tear reaches from the top to the bottom. "Therefore, brethren having boldness to enter the Holiest by the blood of Jesus, by a new and living way which He consecrated for us, through the veil, that is, His flesh" (Hebrews 10:19).

The opening of the Holy of Holies by our Lord's expiring cry is a type of the opening of the gates of paradise to all the saints. Our bleeding Lord has the key to heaven. "He who opens and no one shuts, and shuts and no one opens" (Revelation 3:7).

Let us enter with Him into the heavenly places and sit at His right hand (Matthew 22:44).

APRIL 19, MORNING

AMEN

"The Amen."

—Revelation 3:14

The word *Amen* solemnly confirms that which went before. Jesus is the great Confirmer. Forever and unchanging is "the Amen" in all His promises.

Sinner, I would comfort you with this reflection. Jesus Christ said, "Come to Me, all you who labor and are heavy laden, and I will give you rest" (Matthew 11:28). If you come to Him, He will say "Amen" to this promise in your soul. His promise is true. "A bruised reed He will not break" (Matthew 12:20). Oh you poor, broken and bruised heart, if you come to Him He will say "Amen" to you. He will be as true to your soul as He has been with countless others in years past.

Christian, this should be comforting to you. There has never been a word that left the Savior's lips which He has ever retracted. "Heaven and earth will pass away but My words will by no means pass away" (Matthew 24:35). If you grasp just half a promise, you will find it to be true.

Jesus is Yes and Amen in all His offices. He was a Priest to pardon and cleanse, and He is still Amen as Priest. He was a King to rule and reign and to defend His people with His mighty arm, and He is still Amen as King.

He was a Prophet of old, telling of good things to come. His lips are still most sweet and still drop with honey. He is still Amen as Prophet. He is Amen as to His righteousness. His sacred robe will remain beautiful and glorious even when nature finally decays.

He is Amen in every single title He bears. He is your Husband never seeking a divorce, your Friend closer than a brother, your Shepherd in death's dark valley, your Help and your Deliverer, your Castle and your High Tower. He is the Horn of your strength, your confidence, your joy, your all in all. Yes, your Amen in all.

APRIL 19, EVENING

WITH HIM

"That through death He might destroy him who had the power of death, that is, the devil."

—Hebrews 2:14

Child of God, death has lost its sting because the devil's power over it has been destroyed. Stop being afraid to die. Ask grace from God the Holy Spirit that through an intimate knowledge and a firm belief in your Redeemer's death you may be strengthened for that final hour.

Living near the cross of Calvary you may think of death with pleasure and welcome it with intense delight because it is sweet to die in the Lord. It is a covenant blessing to sleep in Jesus. Death is no longer banishment but a return from exile. It is a home-going to the many mansions where loved ones already dwell.

The distance between glorified spirits in heaven and militant saints on earth seems great, but it is not. We are not far from home, a moment will bring us there. How long is the voyage? How many wearying winds must beat on the sail before it will be folded in the port of peace? How long will the soul be tossed on the waves before it comes to that sea where there are no storms?

Listen to the answer. "Absent from the body . . . present with the Lord" (2 Corinthians 5:8). Your ship has just departed, but it is already home. To that storm-tossed ship on the Lake of Galilee, Jesus said, "Peace be still" (Mark 4:39), "and immediately the boat reached the shore" (John 6:21). Do not think there is a long period between the moment of death and the eternity of glory. When the eyes close on earth they open in heaven.

Child of God, there is nothing to fear in dying. Through the death of your Lord "death is swallowed up in victory. O death where is your sting?" (1 Corinthians 15:54–55).

Death is but a Jacob's ladder whose foot is in the dark grave but whose top reaches everlasting glory.

THE BATTLE

"Fight the Lord's battles."

—1 Samuel 18:17

God's elect on earth are fighting on the earth, supported by Jesus Christ the Captain of their salvation (Hebrews 2:10). Jesus assures us, "Lo I am with you always, even to the end of the age" (Matthew 28:20).

Pay attention to the shouts of war! Let the people of God close ranks. Let no one's heart fail. It is true that right now the battle is turned against us, and unless the Lord Jesus lifts His sword we do not know what will become of the church of God in this land.

But be of good courage. We greatly need a bold voice and a strong hand to preach and publish the old gospel for which martyrs bled and confessors died. The Savior, by His Spirit, is still on the earth. Let this comfort us. He is in the midst of the fight and thus the battle is never in doubt. As the conflict rages, what sweet satisfaction to know that the Lord Jesus, our great Intercessor, is prevalently pleading for His people!

Oh anxious one, do not look at the battle below, for then you will be covered with smoke and your clothes will be rolled in blood. Lift your eyes to where the Savior lives and pleads, for while He intercedes the cause of God is safe.

Let us fight as if all depends on us, but let us look up and know that all depends on Him.

By the lilies of Christian purity, by the roses of the Savior's atonement, we charge you who are lovers of Jesus to fight valiantly in the Holy War for truth and righteousness. Fight for the kingdom and the crown jewels of your Master.

Onward, "for all shall know that the Lord does not save with sword and spear; for the battle is the Lord's" (1 Samuel 17:47).

APRIL 20, EVENING

JOY UNSPEAKABLE

"I know that my Redeemer lives."

—Job 19:25

The core of Job's comfort lies in that little word *my,* my Redeemer, and in the fact that the Redeemer lives.

Oh to get hold of a living Christ! I must have a part in Christ before I can enjoy Him. Gold in the mine is of no value to me. It is gold in my pocket that will allow me to purchase bread. A redeemer who does not redeem me, an avenger who will never stand up for my blood, is of no avail. Do not rest until by faith you can say, "Yes, I cast myself on my living Lord and He is mine."

You may hold Him with a feeble hand and consider it presumption to say, "He lives as my Redeemer." Yet remember, if you have faith no larger than a grain of mustard seed that entitles you to say it.

But there is another word in our text that expresses Job's strong confidence: "I know." To say, "I hope so, I trust so," is comfortable. There are thousands in the fold of Jesus who barely get much further, but to reach the essence of consolation you must be able to say, "I know."

Ifs, buts, and perhaps are murderers of peace and comfort. Doubts are dreary things in time of sorrow. If I have any suspicion that Christ is not mine, there is vinegar mixed with the gall of death. But if I know that Jesus lives for me then darkness is not dark and even the night is light (Psalm 139:12). Surely if Job, in those ages before the coming and advent of Christ, could say, "I know," then we should be as positive.

God forbid that our positiveness should be presumption. Let us make sure that our evidence is right, lest we build on an ungrounded hope. And then let us not be satisfied with the mere foundation, for it is from the upper rooms that we have the best view.

The living Redeemer, truly mine, is joy unspeakable.

INDESTRUCTIBLE

"Who is even at the right hand of God."

—Romans 8:34

He who was once despised and rejected now occupies the highest position of the beloved and honored Son. The right hand of God is the place of majesty and favor.

Our Lord Jesus is His people's representative. When He died for them, they had rest; when He rose again for them, they had liberty; when He sat down at His Father's right hand, they had favor, honor, and dignity. The raising and elevation of Christ is the elevation, the acceptance, the enshrining, and the glorifying of all His people because He is their head and representative.

This sitting at the right hand of God, then, is to be viewed as the acceptance of the person of the Guarantee, the reception of the Representative, and therefore the acceptance of our souls. This is our sure freedom from condemnation. "Who is he who condemns?" (Romans 8:34). Who can condemn those who are in Jesus at the right hand of God?

The right hand is the place of power. Christ at the right hand of God has all power in heaven and on earth. "All authority has been given to Me in heaven and on earth" (Matthew 28:18). Who can fight against the people who have such power vested in their Captain?

Oh my soul, what can destroy you if Omnipotence is your helper? If the protection of the Almighty covers you, what weapon can harm you? If Jesus is your all-prevailing King and has placed your enemies underneath His feet, if sin, death, and hell are vanquished by Him, and if you are represented in Him, then there is no way you can be destroyed.

Jesu's tremendous name puts all our foes to flight:
Jesus, the meek, the angry Lamb, a Lion is in fight.
By all hell's host withstood; we all hell's host
  o'erthrow;
And conquering them, through Jesu's blood
  We still to conquer go.

APRIL 21, EVENING

EXALTED

"Him God has exalted."

Jesus our Lord, once crucified, dead, and buried now sits on the throne of glory. The highest place heaven offers is His by undisputed right. He is exalted at the Father's right hand. As Jehovah He has eminent glories that finite creatures cannot share. But the honors that Jesus wears in heaven as Mediator are the heritage of all the saints.

It is delightful to reflect how close Christ's union is with His people. We are actually one with Him. We are members of His body. His exaltation is our exaltation. He will allow us to sit with Him on His throne just as He has overcome and "sat down at the right hand of the Majesty on high" (Hebrews 1:3).

He has a crown (Revelation 4:4) and He gives us crowns (James 1:12; 1 Peter 5:4). He has a throne (Revelation 4:2), but He does not keep if for Himself. On His right hand there must be His queen, arrayed in gold from Ophir (Psalm 45:9). He cannot be glorified without His bride (Revelation 21:9).

Believer, look to Jesus. Let the eye of your faith behold Him with many crowns on His head (Revelation 19:12). Remember, "it has not yet been revealed what we shall be, but we know that when He is revealed we shall be like Him, for we shall see Him as He is" (1 John 3:2).

You will not be as great as He is. You will not be divine. But you will, in a measure, share the same honors and enjoy the same happiness that He possesses. So be content to live unknown and to walk your weary way through the fields of poverty or up the hills of affliction. One day you will reign with Christ because He has "made us kings and priests to our God" (Revelation 5:10).

What a wonderful thought for the children of God. Christ is our glorious representative in heaven. Soon He will come and take us to be with Him, to see His glory and to share His joy.

APRIL 22, MORNING

NO FEAR

"You shall not be afraid of the terror by night."

—Psalm 91:5

What is the terror by night? It may be the cry of fire, the noise of thieves, a frightened imagination, or the shriek of sudden sickness or death.

We live in a world of death and sorrow. We can expect terror both at night and at high noon. This should not trouble us, for regardless of the terror the promise is that the believer shall not be afraid.

Why should we? God our Father is here, and He will be here through all the lonely hours. He is an almighty Watcher, a sleepless Guardian, a faithful Friend (Psalm 121:3–4). Nothing can happen unless He permits it. Even hell itself is under His control. Darkness is not dark to Him (Psalm 139:12). He has promised to be a "wall of fire" around His people (Zachariah 2:5), and who can break through such a barrier?

Sinners should be afraid. There is an angry God above them, a guilty conscience in them, and a yawning hell underneath them.

But we who rest in Jesus are saved from all of this through His rich mercy. If we give way to foolish fears we dishonor our Lord and lead others to doubt the reality of godliness. We ought to be afraid of being afraid, lest we grieve the Holy Spirit. Away with dismal foreboding and groundless apprehensions. God has not forgotten to be gracious, nor has He withdrawn His tender mercies.

It may be night in the soul, but there is no need to fear. The God of love does not change. Children of light may walk in darkness but they are not lost. No, they prove their adoption by trusting in their heavenly Father, which is something hypocrites cannot do.

> Though the night be dark and dreary,
>   Darkness cannot hide from Thee;
> Thou art He, who, never weary,
>   Watches where Thy people be.

APRIL 22, EVENING

MORE THAN CONQUERORS

"Yet in all these things we are more than conquerors through Him who loves us."

—Romans 8:37

We go to Christ for forgiveness and then too often look to the law for power to fight our sins. Thus Paul rebukes us, "O foolish Galatians! Who has bewitched you that you should not obey the truth? . . . This only I want to learn from you. Did you receive the Spirit by the works of the law or by the hearing of faith. Are you so foolish? Having begun in the Spirit are you now being made perfect by the flesh?" (Galatians 3:1–2).

Take your sins to Christ's cross. There the old nature can be crucified, for we are crucified with Him (Galatians 2:20). The only weapon to fight sin is the spear that pierced Jesus' side. Let me illustrate. You want to overcome an angry temper, but it is possible that you never tried the right way, going to Jesus with it. Ask yourself, how did I receive salvation? You answer, I came to Jesus just as I was and I trusted Him to save me. So, too, you must kill your angry temper. You must go to the cross and say, "Lord I trust you to deliver me from my angry temper."

Are you covetous? Do you feel the world entangling you? You may struggle against this evil as long as you please, but you will never be delivered from it in any way but by the blood of Jesus. Take it to Christ. Tell Him, "Lord I have trusted You. Your name is called Jesus because You save Your people from their sins. Lord, this is one of my sins. Save me from it."

Your prayers, your repentance, and all your tears, all of them together are worth nothing apart from Him. "None but Jesus can do helpless sinners good" or helpless saints either. "In all these things we are more than conquerors through Him who loved us."

Our laurels must be grown among His olives in Gethsemane.

APRIL 23, MORNING

SCARS

"Behold, in the midst of the throne . . . stood a Lamb as though it had been slain."

—Revelation 5:6

Why should our exalted Lord appear in glory with His wounds?

The wounds of Jesus are His glories, His jewels, and His sacred ornaments. In the eye of the believer Jesus is beautiful because He is white and red, white with innocence and red with His own blood. We see Him as the lily of matchless purity and as the rose crimsoned with His own blood.

Christ is lovely on Olivet and Tabor and by the sea, but there was never such a matchless Christ as He that hung on the cross. There we see all His beauties perfected, all His attributes developed, all His love drawn out, all His character expressed. Beloved, the wounds of Jesus are more beautiful than all the splendor and pomp of kings. His thorny crown is greater than an imperial diadem.

Jesus wears the appearance of a slain Lamb as His royal robes. In these robes He wooed and redeemed our souls by His complete atonement. These wounds are more than ornaments; they are trophies of His love and victory. He has divided His victory with the strong. He has redeemed a great multitude that no one can number and His scars are the memorial of that fight.

If Christ loves to retain the thought of His sufferings for His people, how precious should His wounds be to us.

> Behold, how every wound of His
> A precious balm distills,
> Which heals the scars that sin had made,
> And cures all mortal ills.
> These wounds are mouths that preach His grace;
> The ensigns of His love;
> The seals of our expected bliss
> In paradise above.

APRIL 23, EVENING

COVENANT

"And because of all this we make a sure covenant."

—Nehemiah 9:38

There are many occasions in our experience when we may properly, and with great benefit, renew our covenant with God. Like Hezekiah, we have recovered from sickness and have had years added to our lives (2 Kings 20:6). After any deliverance from trouble, when our joys bloom again, let us visit the foot of the cross and renew our consecration. This should be especially true after we have sinned and grieved the Holy Spirit or brought dishonor on the cause of God. It is then we need to look to that blood that can makes us whiter than snow, and again offer ourselves to the Lord.

Our troubles confirm our dedication to God and so should our prosperity. When we have occasions that deserve to be called "crowning mercies," when surely He has crowned us with blessings, we should also crown our God. Bring all the jewels of the divine regalia that have been stored in the jewel closet of our hearts and let God sit on the throne of our love arrayed in royal apparel.

If we could learn to profit by our prosperity, we would not need as much adversity. If we could gather from God's blessings all the good it might confer on us, we would not have to feel the rod as often.

Have we received a blessing we did not expect? Has the Lord put our feet in a large room? Can we sing of mercies multiplied? Then this is the day to put our hands on the horns of the altar and say, "Bind me here, my God. Bind me here with cords for ever."

Because we need fulfillment of new promises from God, let us offer renewed prayers that our old vows may not be dishonored. This morning, make a sure covenant with Him and express gratitude for His pains.

SPRINGTIME

"The flowers appear on the earth; the time of singing has come, and the voice of the turtledove is heard in our land."

—Song of Solomon 2:12

Spring is wonderful. The long dreary winter helps us to appreciate its pleasant warmth, and the promise of summer enhances its delights.

After periods of depression it is delightful to see the light of the Sun of Righteousness. Our slumbering graces rise from their lethargy like the crocus and daffodil from their beds of earth. Our hearts are made happy with delicious notes of gratitude that are far more melodious than the warbling of birds; and their comforting assurances of peace are infinitely more delightful than the sound of the turtledove.

This is the time for the soul to seek communion with her Beloved. She must rise from natural depravity and leave her old associations.

If we do not hoist the sail when the breeze is favorable we are to blame. Times of refreshing should not pass without action. When Jesus visits us in tenderness and pleads with us to arise, can we be so base as to refuse His request? He has risen that He may draw us after Him. By His Holy Spirit we are revived so that in newness of life we can ascend into the heavenlies and have fellowship with Him.

Let our winter suffice for coldness and indifference. Lord create a spring in us, let our sap flow with vigor and our branches blossom.

Oh Lord, if it is not springtime in my chilly heart, I ask You to make it so. I am tired of living at a distance from You. This long, dreary winter, when will You end it? Come Holy Spirit, renew my soul! Make me alive! Restore me. Have mercy on me. This very night I earnestly ask You to have pity on Your servant. Send me a happy revival of spiritual life. Amen

APRIL 24, EVENING

HE CALLS

"Rise up my love, my fair one, and come away."

—Song of Solomon 2:10

I hear the voice of my Beloved. He speaks to me! Fair weather is smiling on the face of the earth, and he does not want me spiritually asleep while nature is awaking from winter's rest. He calls me to "rise up," for I have been sleeping too long in earthy clay pots.

He is risen, and I am risen in Him. Why then should I sleep in the dust? From lesser loves, desires, pursuits, and aspirations I would rise toward Him. He calls me "my love" and considers me beautiful. This is a good reason for rising.

He calls me to "come away" from everything selfish, grovelling, worldly, and sinful. Yes, He even calls me from the outwardly religious world that does not know Him and has no affinity to the mystery of the higher life.

He calls me to "come away," and there is no harsh sound in His voice. What is there, then, to hold me in this wilderness of foolishness and sin? Oh my Lord, if only I could come, but I am caught in thorns and cannot escape. If it were possible I would have neither eyes, nor ears, nor heart for sin.

You call saying, "Come away." This is a melodious call. To come to You is to come home from exile. To come to You is to come to land from a raging storm. To come to You is to come to rest after long labor. To come to You is to come to the goal of my desires and the summit of my wishes.

But Lord, how can a stone rise, or how can a lump of clay come away from the horrible pit?

Oh raise me, draw me to You. Your grace can do it. Send Your Holy Spirit to kindle the sacred flame of love in my heart, and I will rise until I leave life and time behind me, and indeed come away.

THE GUEST

*"If anyone hears My voice and opens the door,
I will come in to him and dine with him and he
with Me."*

—Revelation 3:20

What is your desire this evening? Is it set on heavenly things? Do you long to enjoy the high doctrine of eternal love? Do you desire liberty in intimate fellowship with God? Do you aspire "to comprehend with all the saints what is the width and length and depth and height—to know the love of Christ which passes all knowledge" (Ephesians 3:18–19)?

If so, then draw near to Jesus. You must see Him clearly as precious and complete. You must view His work, His position, and His person. If you understand Christ, you will receive an anointing from the Holy One, an anointing from Him who knows all things.

Do you say, "Oh that He would dwell in me. If only He would make my heart His dwelling place forever"? Then open the door, beloved, and He will come in. He has been knocking for the sole purpose of dining with you. He will dine with you, because you have the house and He has the provisions. He could not dine with you if the desire were not in your heart. Nor could you entertain Him, for you are the one with the empty kitchen and He has the provisions.

Fling open the door of your soul, and He will come in with the love you long to feel. He will come with the joy that your poor depressed spirit needs. He will bring peace where you have none. He will come with His decanters of wine and sweet apples of love. He will cheer you until you have no other sickness but that of "love overpowering, love divine."

Only open the door to Him. Drive out His enemies. Give Him the keys to your heart, and He will live there forever.

What wondrous love that brings such a guest to dwell in such a heart.

REMEMBRANCE

"Do this in remembrance of Me."

—1 Corinthians 11:24

This text indicates that Christians may forget Christ! There would be no need for this loving exhortation if there was not a fearful supposition that our memories might prove treacherous. This is not an unfounded supposition. It is often confirmed in our experience as a lamentable fact.

It seems almost impossible that those who have been redeemed by the blood of the Lamb and loved with an everlasting love (Jeremiah 31:3) could forget their gracious Savior. But if this is startling to the ear, it is only too apparent to the eye to deny the crime.

Forget Him who never forgot us? Forget Him who gave His blood for our sins? Forget Him who loved us even to death? Is this possible? Yes, it is not only possible, but it is too sadly a fault with all of us that we treat Him like a visitor who has come only for an evening. He whom we should make the permanent resident of our memories is only a visitor. The cross, where memory should linger and forgetfulness should be an unknown intruder, is desecrated by the feet of forgetfulness.

Does your conscience say this is true? Do you find yourself forgetting Jesus? Some creature steals your heart and you become unmindful of Him on whom your affection ought to be set. Some earthly business engrosses your attention when you should fix your eyes steadily on the cross.

It is the incessant turmoil of the world and the constant attraction of earthly things that takes our soul from Christ. Our memories preserve a poisonous weed that causes the rose of Sharon to wither.

Let us find a heavenly forget-me-not and wrap it around our heart for Jesus our Beloved. And whatever else we forget, let us hold fast to Him.

PERSECUTION

"I die daily," said the apostle (1 Corinthians 15:31), and this was the life of the early Christians. Wherever they went, death was at hand. Today we are not called to pass through such fearful persecution, but if we were, the Lord would give us grace to bear the test.

For many of us the tests of the Christian life are not so terrible outwardly, but they are still likely to overcome us. To bear the sneer of the world is inconsequential. But to bear the test of its flattery, its soft words, its oily speeches, its groveling, and its hypocrisy is far more difficult.

Our danger is that we grow rich, become proud, and give ourselves to the evil world's fashions and so lose our faith. If riches are not the trial, worldly cares are every bit as mischievous.

If we cannot be torn to pieces by the roaring lion, we may be hugged to death by the bear. The devil little cares which it is, as long as it destroys our love for Christ and our confidence in Him.

I fear that the Christian church is more likely to lose integrity in these soft and silken days than in rougher times. We must be alert, for we walk the enchanted ground, and we will fall asleep unless our faith in Jesus is a reality and our love to Jesus a vehement flame.

Many in these days of easy profession are more likely to be weeds than wheat. Hypocrites with beautiful masks are not true-born children of the living God.

Christian, do not think that this is a time when you can dispense with watchfulness or holy devotion. You need these things more than ever.

May God the eternal Spirit display His omnipotence in you, so that you may say in all the soft and the rough things, "We are more than conquerors through Him who loved us" (Romans 8:37).

APRIL 26, EVENING

THE SOURCE

"God, our own God, shall bless us."

—Psalm 67:6

It is strange how little we use the spiritual blessings God gives us. But even stranger is how little we make use of God. Although He is "our own God," we ask very little of Him.

How seldom we ask His counsel. How often we go about our business without seeking His guidance! How constantly we strive in our troubles to carry our burdens instead of casting them on the Lord, instead of asking Him to sustain us.

This is not because we may not, for the Lord seems to say, "I am yours, come and make use of me. Come freely to my store, and the more often you come the more welcome you are." It is our own fault if we do not utilize the riches of our God.

Since you have such a friend and He invites you, take from Him every day. Never want while you have God to go to. Never fear or faint while you have God to help you. Go to His treasures and take whatever you need; there is all that you could want. Learn the divine skill of making God all things to you. He can supply you with everything, or better yet, He can be everything.

Let me urge you to make use of God. Make use of Him in prayer. Go to Him often because He is your God. Do not fail to use this privilege. Fly to Him. Tell Him your needs.

If some dark providence has clouded you, use God as a sun, and if a strong enemy is attacking, find in Jehovah a shield (Psalm 84:11). He is both a sun and a shield to His people. If you have lost your way in the mazes of life, use Him as a guide. He promises, "I will instruct you and teach you in the way you should go; I will guide you with My eye" (Psalm 32:8).

Whatever you are, wherever you are, remember that God is what you want, where you want, and everything you want.

APRIL 27, MORNING

ALL HAIL THE KING

"The Lord is King forever and ever."

—Psalm 10:16

Jesus Christ is no despot claiming divine right. He is really and truly the Lord's anointed! "For it pleased the Father that in Him all the fullness should dwell" (Colossians 1:19). God has given Him all power and all authority. As the Son of man, He is head over all things to His church. He reigns over heaven and earth and hell with the keys of life and death (Revelation 1:18).

Certain princes have delighted to call themselves kings by popular will, and certainly our Lord Jesus Christ is this to His church. If we could vote whether or not He should be King in the church, every believing heart would crown Him.

Oh that we could crown Him more gloriously than we do! We should count no expense wasted that would glorify Christ. Suffering would be pleasure and loss would be gain if we could surround His brow with brighter crowns and make Him more glorious in the eyes of men and angels.

Yes, He shall reign. Long live the King! All hail to You, King Jesus! Go forth, you who love your Lord. Bow at His feet. Carpet His way with the lilies of your love and the roses of your gratitude:

> Bring forth the royal diadem,
> And crown Him, Lord of all.

Yet more than this, the Lord is King in Zion by right of conquest. He has taken and carried by storm the hearts of His people. He has slain their enemies, who held them in cruel bondage.

In the Red Sea of His blood, our Redeemer has drowned the Pharaoh of our sins. He has delivered us from the iron yoke and heavy curse of the law. We are His portion.

All hail King Jesus! We gladly accept Your reign. Rule in our hearts forever, Oh wonderful Prince of Peace.

APRIL 27, EVENING

FEASTING YOUR FAITH

"Remember the word to your servant, upon which You have caused me to hope."

—Psalm 119:49

Whatever your special need, there is a promise in the Bible for you.

Are you weak and feeble because your way is rough and you are weary? Here is a promise: "He gives power to the weak" (Isaiah 40:29). When you read this promise, take it back to the great Promiser and ask Him to fulfill His own word.

Are you seeking Christ and thirsting for closer fellowship with Him? This promise shines like a star: "Blessed are those who hunger and thirst for righteousness, for they shall be filled" (Matthew 5:6). Take that promise to the throne frequently. Do not request anything else, but go to God over and over again saying, "Lord, You have said it. Do as You have said."

Are you distressed because of sin and burdened with a heavy load of iniquities? Listen to these words: "I, even I, am He who blots out your transgressions . . . and I will not remember your sins" (Isaiah 43:25). You have no merit of your own. There is no reason why He should pardon you. But plead His written promises and He will perform them.

Are you afraid that you will not be able to hold on until the end? Is that your condition? Then take this word of grace to the throne and claim it: "For the mountains shall depart and the hills be removed, but My kindness shall not depart from you" (Isaiah 54:10).

If you have lost the sweet sense of the Savior's presence and if you are seeking Him with a sorrowful heart, remember these promises: "Return to Me and I will return to you" (Malachi 3:7); "For a mere moment I have forsaken you. But with great mercies I will gather you" (Isaiah 54:7).

Feast your faith on God's own word. Whatever your fears, whatever your needs, go to the Bank of Faith with your Father's promise and say, "Remember the word to Your servant, upon which You have caused me to hope."

APRIL 28, MORNING

ANY EXCEPTIONS?

"For all the houses of Israel are impudent and hard hearted."

—Ezekiel 3:7

Are there any exceptions? No, and if this is a description of the favored nation—if the best are this bad—then what must the worst be?

Come, my heart, consider your part in this universal accusation. As you consider it, feel the shame because you may be guilty.

The first charge is impudence, a self-reliance and lack of holy shame, as well as a boldness to do evil. Before my conversion, I could sin and feel no constraint. I could hear of my guilt and remain arrogant. I could confess my iniquity and manifest no inward humiliation. For a sinner to go to God's house and pretend to pray and praise is brazenness of the worst kind.

Since the day of my new birth, I have doubted my Lord to His face, murmured unblushingly in His presence, worshipped Him in a slovenly manner and sinned without regret. If my forehead were not so ironclad and harder than flint I would have far more holy fear and deeper repentance of spirit. Woe to me, I am one of the impudent house of Israel.

The second charge is hardheartedness, and I plead guilty. Once I had a heart of stone and though through grace I now have a new heart, much of my bullheadedness remains. I am not as moved by Jesus' death as I should be. I am not moved enough by the ruin of lives, the wickedness of the times, the chastisement of my heavenly Father, and my own failures.

Oh that my heart would thoroughly melt when I think of my Savior's suffering and death. Would to God I were rid of the millstone within me, this hateful body of death.

But blessed be the name of the Lord for the disease is not incurable. The Savior's precious blood is the universal antidote. And me, even me, it will effectually soften, until my heart melts like wax before the fire.

APRIL 28, EVENING

DAYS OF DARKNESS

"You are my hope in the day of doom."

—Jeremiah 17:17

The path of the Christian is not always bright with sunshine. There are times of darkness and storm. True, it is written about wisdom that "her ways are ways of pleasantness" (Proverbs 3:17). And it is a great truth that our faith will give happiness below as well as bliss above. The Word tells us that "the path of the just is like the shining sun that shines ever brighter unto the perfect day" (Proverbs 4:18). But at certain periods clouds cover the believer's sun, and we walk in darkness and see no light.

There are many who have rejoiced in the presence of God for a season. They basked in sunshine in the early stages of their Christian experience. They walked along the green pastures beside still waters (Psalm 23:2). Then suddenly they found the glorious sky clouded. Instead of the Land of Goshen (Genesis 45:10), they had to walk the sandy desert. In the place of sweet waters, they found troubled, bitter streams.

Then they say, "Surely if I were a child of God this would not happen." Oh do not say that, those of you who are walking in darkness, for the best of God's saints must drink the wormwood. The dearest of His children must bear the cross. No believer has enjoyed perpetual prosperity. No believer can always keep his harp from the willows (Psalm 137:2).

Perhaps the Lord allotted you a smooth and unclouded path because you were weak and timid. He tempered the wind to the shorn lamb. But now that you are stronger in the spiritual life, you must enter the riper and rougher experience of God's full-grown children.

We need winds and storms to exercise our faith, to tear off the rotten branches of self dependence, and to ground us more firmly in Christ.

The day of evil reveals the value of our glorious hope.

BEYOND COMPREHENSION

"The Lord takes pleasure in His people."

—Psalm 149:4

The love of Jesus to us is comprehensive. There is no part of His people's lives that He ignores. Every aspect of our lives is important to Him.

Believer, He not only thinks of you as immortal, but He knows that you are also mortal. Do not doubt or deny this, because "the very hairs of your head are all numbered" (Matthew 10:30); and "the steps of a good man are ordered by the Lord and He delights in his way" (Psalm 37:23).

It would be sad if this mantle of love did not totally cover us. What harm would befall if part of our lives were not under our gracious Lord's inspection and care. Believer, rest assured that Jesus cares about every aspect of your daily life. His tender love is so great that you may ask His help in everything. In all your afflictions, He is afflicted. "As a father pities his children, the Lord pities those who fear Him. He knows our frame: He remembers that we are dust" (Psalm 103:14). He not only understands His people, He also comprehends their diverse and innumerable concerns.

Christian, do you think you can measure the love of Christ? Think what His love has brought you: justification, adoption, sanctification, eternal life! The riches of His goodness are unsearchable. Oh that you were "able to comprehend with all the saints what is the width and length and depth and height—to know the love of Christ which passes knowledge" (Ephesians 3:19).

Shall this great love have only half of our hearts? Shall it have a cold love in return? Shall Jesus' marvelous lovingkindness and tender care have a faint response and a late acknowledgment?

Oh my soul, tune your harp to a glad song of thanksgiving! Go to sleep rejoicing. You are not a desolate wanderer. You are a beloved child, watched over, cared for, supplied, and defended by the Lord.

APRIL 29, EVENING

COMPLAINERS

"And all the children of Israel complained."

—Numbers 14:2

There are Christians who complain today just as they did in the camp of Israel. There are those who, when the rod falls, cry out against discipline. They ask, "Why am I afflicted? What have I done to be chastened?" A word with you, my complaining friend.

Why should you complain about being chastened by your heavenly Father? Should He treat you better than you deserve? Think what a rebel you were, but He pardoned you! Surely, if in His wisdom He sees fit to chasten, you should not complain. After all, you are not afflicted as much as your sins deserve. Think about the sin in your heart and you will no longer wonder why a rod is needed to drive it out.

Weigh yourself and look at how much dross is mingled with gold. Do you think the fire is too hot to purge away so much dross? Does your proud rebellious spirit prove that your heart is not thoroughly sanctified? Are your complaints contrary to the holy submissive nature of God's children? Is the correction unnecessary?

If you complain about the chastening, remember that it will go hard with complainers. God always chastises His children twice if they do not bear the first stroke patiently. But remember this, "He does not afflict willingly, nor grieve the children of men" (Lamentations 3:33).

All His corrections are sent in love to purify you and to draw you closer to Him. Surely it will help you to bear the chastening with submissiveness if you are able to recognize your Father's hand in it. "For whom the Lord loves He chastens, and scourges every son whom He receives. If you endure chastening, God deals with you as with sons" (Hebrews 12:6).

Don't complain. Some of those who complained were destroyed by the destroyer (Numbers 14:29).

APRIL 30, MORNING

GOD'S THOUGHTS

"How precious also are your thoughts to me, O God!"

—Psalm 139:17

Divine infinite knowledge gives no comfort to the ungodly, but to the child of God it overflows with consolation. God is always thinking about us. He never turns His mind from us. We are always before His eyes (Isaiah 49:16).

This is precisely the way we want it. It would be dreadful to exist for a moment without being observed by our heavenly Father. His thoughts are always tender, loving, wise, prudent and far-reaching. His thoughts bring countless benefits.

The Lord did always think about His people; hence their election and the covenant of grace that secures their salvation. He always thinks of them; hence their final perseverance by which they will be brought safely to their final rest.

In all our wanderings, the watchfulness of the Eternal Watcher is evermore fixed on us. We never roam beyond the Shepherd's eye (Psalm 139:7). In our sorrows He observes us incessantly; not an ache escapes Him. In our toils He marks all our weariness and writes about the struggles of His faithful ones in His book (Psalm 87:6). The thoughts of the Lord encompass us in all our paths and penetrate our innermost being. Not a nerve or tissue, not a valve or vessel of our bodies is uncared for. All the littles of our little world are watched over by our great God.

Dear reader, is this precious to you? Then hold on to it. Never be led astray by those philosophical fools who preach an impersonal God and talk of self-existent, self-governing matter. The Lord lives and thinks about us. This is a truth far too precious to have someone steal.

The written word of royalty is valued so highly that those who have it consider their fortunes made. But how much greater to be thought of by the King of kings! If the Lord thinks about us then all is well and we may rejoice evermore.

APRIL 30, EVENING

BEAUTIFUL FLOWERS AND HERBS

"His cheeks are like a bed of spices, banks of scented herbs."

—Song of Solomon 5:13

The month of flowers has arrived. March winds and April showers have done their work. The earth is full of beauty. Come my soul, put on your best clothes and gather a bouquet of heavenly thoughts.

You know where the bed of spices is. Many times you have smelled the perfume of the scented herbs. Go to your Beloved and find love and joy in Him.

That cheek so cruelly beaten with a rod, so often moist with sympathetic tears and then defiled with spittle; that cheek as it smiles with mercy is a sweet fragrance to my heart. Oh Lord Jesus, You did not hide Your face from shame and pain; therefore, I will take great delight in praising You.

Your cheeks were furrowed by the plow of grief and made crimson with blood from Your thorn-crowned temple. These marks of boundless love attract my soul far more than banks of scented herbs.

If I cannot see all of Your face, I want to see Your cheek. The slightest glimpse of You is exceedingly refreshing to my spiritual sense and gives me great delight.

In Jesus I find not only fragrance but a bank of heavenly scented herbs. I find not one flower but all kinds of beautiful flowers. He is my rose and my lily, my violet and my cluster of henna.

When He is with me it is May all year round, and my soul washes her happy face in the morning dew of His grace, and I find solace in the birds who are singing His promises.

Precious Lord Jesus, let me know the blessedness that dwells in permanent, unbroken fellowship with You. I am poor and worthless, yet you stoop to kiss my cheek. Oh let me kiss You with the kisses of my lips.

BLESSED ROSE

"I am the rose of Sharon."

—Song of Solomon 2:1

Whatever beauty there is in the material world, Jesus Christ far exceeds that in the spiritual world. The rose is considered the most beautiful of flowers, but Jesus is infinitely more beautiful in the garden of the soul than all the roses of earth. He is first as the fairest among ten thousand (Song of Solomon 5:10). He is the sun; all others are stars. The heavens and the day are dark when compared with Him, for the King in His beauty outshines all.

"I am the rose of Sharon." This was the best and rarest of roses. Jesus is more than a rose. Jesus is "the rose of Sharon"—the best of the best. He is positively lovely and superlatively the loveliest.

There is variety in His appeal. The rose is delightful to look at, and its fragrance is both pleasant and refreshing. Each of the spiritual senses of the soul—tasting, feeling, hearing, seeing, and smelling—find appropriate fulfillment in Jesus.

Even the recollection of His love is sweet. Take the rose of Sharon, pull off its leaves, save them in the jar of memory. You will find that the fragrance of each leaf fills the house with perfume long afterward.

Christ satisfies the highest taste of the most educated. An amateur in perfumes will be quite satisfied with the rose, but when our souls arrive at the highest degree of true taste, we will be content only with Christ. No, we will also be better able to appreciate Him.

Heaven possesses nothing that excels the rose of Sharon. What emblem can possibly describe His beauty? Human speech and earth-born things fail. All of earth's choicest charms commingled only feebly picture His abounding preciousness.

Blessed rose, bloom in my heart forever.

LEFT IN THE WORLD

"I do not pray that You should take them out of the world."

—John 17:15

In God's own time, there is a sweet and blessed event coming to all believers, and that is going home to be with Jesus. In a few more years, the Lord's soldiers, those fighting the good fight of faith, will cease the battle and hear, "Well done, good and faithful servant, . . . enter into the joy of your Lord" (Matthew 25:21).

Christ prays for His people to be with Him in His glory (John 17:24), but He does not pray that they be taken from this world immediately.

Yet frequently the weary pilgrim prays, "Oh, that I had wings like a dove! I would fly away and be at rest" (Psalm 55:6). But this is not how Christ prays. He asks that we be kept from the evil one (John 17:15), but He never asks that we be admitted to glory until the time is right.

Christians may want to die when they have troubles. Ask them why and they may tell you, "Because we would rather be with the Lord." I am afraid it is not because they want to be with the Lord so much as they want to get rid of their troubles! When there are no trials, they do not seem to have the same wish to die.

It is quite right to desire to depart if we can have the same spirit about it that Paul did, because to be with Christ is far better (2 Corinthians 5:6–8). But the desire to escape from trouble may be a selfish one.

Glorify God with your life here for as long as He pleases, even if you are in the middle of toils, conflict, and suffering.

Let Him say when it is enough.

THE EPITAPH

"These all died in faith."

—Hebrews 11:13

This is the epitaph of those blessed saints who fell asleep before the coming of our Lord. It is immaterial how they died, whether from old age or violence. The only thing worth noting is that they died in faith.

They died in faith because they lived in faith. Faith was their comfort, their guide, their motive, their support. Thus they died in spiritual grace, ending their life-song with the same beautiful melody Jesus had first given them.

They did not die resting in their accomplishments and achievements. They clung to the first way of acceptance with God and held on to the way of faith until the end. Faith is as precious to die by as to live by.

Dying in faith has a distinct reference to the past. They believed the promises and were assured that their sins were blotted out through the mercy of God.

Dying in faith has to do with the present. These saints were confident of their acceptance with God. They enjoyed the beams of His love and rested in His faithfulness.

Dying in faith looks to the future. They fell asleep affirming that the Messiah would surely come "and . . . stand at last on the earth" (Job 19:25), and that "the dead will be raised incorruptible, and we shall be changed" (1 Corinthians 15:52). To them the pains of death were the pangs of birth to a better state.

Take courage as you read this epitaph. Your road of grace is that of faith. "We walk by faith, not by sight" (2 Corinthians 5:7). Your road is not sight because sight rarely cheers us. This same path has been the way of the brightest and the best. Happy are you if it is yours.

This evening look again to Jesus, "the author and finisher of our faith" (Hebrews 12:2). Thank Him for giving you the same faith as these souls now have in glory.

MAY 2, EVENING

A TROUBLING PROMISE

"In the world you will have tribulation."

—John 16:33

Have you ever wondered why we have this promise?

Look up at your pure and holy heavenly Father. Do you know that one day you will be like Him? Will you easily be conformed to His image, or will it require much refining in the furnace of affliction? Will it be easy to get rid of your corruptions and be made perfect as your Father in heaven is perfect?

Next, Christian, look down. Do you know the foe that is under your feet? You were once a servant of Satan and no king willingly loses his subjects. Do you think Satan will leave you alone? No, he will always be "your adversary the devil walking about like a roaring lion, seeking whom he may devour" (1 Peter 5:8). Christian, expect trouble when you look down.

Now look around. Where are you? You are in an enemy's country. This world is not your home. You are a stranger and a pilgrim. This world is not your friend. If this world is your friend, then you are not God's friend, for "a friend of the world makes himself an enemy of God" (James 4:4).

Be assured that you will find the enemy everywhere. When you walk, expect an ambush at every turn. Even when you are sleeping, you are resting on the battlefield. The trials of earth are most difficult.

Finally, look within. Look in your heart, and observe the sin and self that is there. If you had no devil to tempt you, no enemies to fight you, no world to ensnare you, you would still find your heart full of enough evil to trouble you. "The heart is deceitful above all things and desperately wicked" (Jeremiah 17:9).

Expect trouble, but do not worry about it. God is with you to help and strengthen. He has promised, "I will be with him in trouble; I will deliver him and honor him" (Psalm 91:15).

MAY 3, MORNING

UNUSED HELP

"A very present help."

—Psalm 46:1

Covenant blessings are not only to be looked at, they are to be appropriated. Even our Lord Jesus is given to us for our present use.

Believer, you do not use Christ as you should. When you are in trouble, why don't you tell Him about your grief? He has a sympathizing heart and He can comfort and strengthen you. Unfortunately you are going to all your friends except your best Friend; you are telling your plight to everyone, except the Lord.

Are you burdened with this day's sins? Here is a fountain filled with blood. Use it saint, use it.

Has a sense of guilt come over you? The pardoning grace of Jesus can be proved again and again. Come to Him at once for cleansing.

Do you deplore your weakness? He is your strength. Lean on Him.

Do you feel naked? Come, put on the robe of Jesus' righteousness. Don't just look at it, wear it. Strip off your righteousness and your fears, and put on His white linen robe. It was meant to be worn.

Do you feel sick? Pull the night bell of prayer, call on the Beloved Physician, and He will give a cordial to revive you.

You are poor, but you have a wealthy Father. Go and ask Him to give from His abundance. After all, He has promised that we are "heirs—heirs of God and joint heirs with Christ" (Romans 8:17).

There is nothing Christ dislikes more than for His people to make a show-thing of Him and not use Him. He loves to be employed by us. The more burdens we put on His shoulders, the more precious He will be:

> Let us be simple with Him, then,
>   Not backward, stiff, or cold,
> As though our Bethlehem could be
>   What Sinai was of old.

MAY 3, EVENING

FALSE GODS

"Will a man make gods for himself which are not gods?"

—Jeremiah 16:20

One great besetting sin of ancient Israel was idolatry, and spiritual Israel is plagued with the same folly. Remphan's star (Acts 7:43) no longer shines, women no longer weep for Zabbud (Ezra 8:14), but Mammon (Luke 16:13) still intrudes with his golden calf, and the shrines of pride are not forsaken. Self in various forms struggles to subdue the chosen ones, and the flesh sets up its altars wherever there is space.

Favorite children are often the cause of much sin in believers. The Lord is grieved when He sees us spoiling them excessively. Children can live to be a curse to us as great as Absalom was to David, or they can be taken from us to leave our homes desolate. If Christians want to grow thorns to stuff their sleepless pillows, let them indulge their children.

This is a great question: "Will a man make gods . . . which are not gods?" The objects of our foolish loves are doubtful blessings. The comfort they yield is dangerous, and the help they give in time of trouble is little indeed. Why then are we so bewitched with foolishness?

We pity the heathen who adores a god of stone, and yet we worship a god of gold. Where is the vast superiority between a god of flesh and one of wood?

The principle, the sin, and the folly is the same, except that in our case the crime is more aggravated because we have more light. The heathen bows to a false deity, but the heathen has never known the true God.

We commit two evils: we forsake the living God, and we turn to idols (Jeremiah 2:13; 5:7). May the Lord purge us from this terrible iniquity!

> The dearest idol I have known,
>   Whatever that idol be;
> Help me to tear it from thy throne,
>   And worship only thee.

MAY 4, MORNING

ROYALTY

"Having been born again, not of corruptible seed but incorruptible."

—1 Peter 1:23

In 1 Peter 1:22, Peter earnestly exhorts the scattered saints to "love one another fervently with a pure heart." Wisely, he does not base his argument on law, nature, or philosophy but on the high and divine nature God has planted in His people. Just as some judicious tutor of princes might strive to develop a kingly spirit and dignified behavior in his pupils, Peter looks on God's children as heirs of glory, a royal priesthood, a holy nation, princes of the blood royal, descendants of the King of kings, and earth's truest and oldest aristocracy (1 Peter 2:9).

Peter says to them, "See that you love one another: because of your noble birth; because you are born of incorruptible seed; because your lineage descends from God, the Creator of all things; because of your immortal destiny, for you will never pass away even though the glory of the flesh will fade and its existence will cease." It would be well if, in the spirit of humility, we would recognize the true dignity of our regenerated nature and live up to it.

What are Christians? Compared with a king, we add priestly sanctity to royal dignity. The king's royalty often lies only in the crown, but with Christians it is infused in our innermost nature. Through the new birth we are as much above humanity as a human is above the beast that perishes. Surely in all our dealings we should conduct ourselves not as the lost, but as the chosen, distinguished by sovereign grace. We "are a chosen generation, a royal priesthood, a holy nation, His own special people" (1 Peter 2:9). We cannot grovel in the dirt as others, or live like the world's citizens.

Oh believers in Christ, let the dignity of your nature and the brightness of your prospects constrain you to cling to holiness and to avoid every appearance of evil.

A DISTINCTIVE FAVOR

"I will be their God, and they shall be My people."

—2 Corinthians 6:16

What a lovable title: "My people."

What an encouraging revelation: "Their God."

What meaning is expressed in those two words "my people"! Here is our specialness. The whole world is God's. The heavens and even the heaven of heavens is the Lord's, and He also reigns among the children of men. But of those He has chosen, of those He has purchased, He says what He does not say to others, "My people." In these words there is the idea of proprietorship. In a special way "the Lord's portion is His people; Jacob is the place of His inheritance" (Deuteronomy 32:9).

All the nations on earth are His. The whole world is in His power. Yet His chosen people are exclusively His possession. He has purchased them with His own blood (Acts 20:28). He has brought them close to Himself (James 4:8). He has inscribed them on the palms of His hands (Isaiah 49:16). And thus He loves them with an everlasting love (Jeremiah 31:3).

Dear friend, can you by faith see yourself in this group? Can you look to heaven and say, "My Lord and my God?" (John 20:28). He is mine by that lovable relationship which entitles me to call Him Father; mine by that hallowed fellowship in which I delight, when He manifests Himself to me.

Can you read the Book of Inspiration and find your salvation assured? Can you read your title written in precious blood? Can you by humble faith hold Jesus' garments and say, "My Christ?"

If you can, then God calls you and others like you, "My people." If God is your God and Christ is your Christ, the Lord has given you a special, distinctive favor. You are the object of His choice, accepted in the beloved Son.

WISDOM

*"He who heeds the word wisely will find good.
And whoever trusts in the Lord, happy is he."*

—Proverbs 16:20

Wisdom is true strength. Wisely handling the matters of life gives the richest enjoyment and presents the noblest occupation for our powers. Thus through wisdom we find good in the fullest sense. Without wisdom we are like wild donkeys running here and there wasting strength and energy.

Wisdom is the compass by which we steer across the trackless waste of life. Without it we are a derelict vessel at the mercy of winds and waves.

We must be prudent in a world like this, or we will find no good. We will be betrayed by unnumbered afflictions. The pilgrims will badly wound their feet among the briers of life unless they pick their steps with utmost caution. We, who are in a wilderness infested with robbers, must handle matters wisely if we would have a safe journey.

If, trained by the Great Teacher, we follow where He leads, we will find good even in this dark abode. There are celestial fruits to be gathered this side of Eden's arbor and songs of paradise to be sung in the groves of earth.

But can we find wisdom? Many have dreamed of it but never possessed it. Where shall we learn it?

Listen to the voice of the Lord, for He has declared the secret. He has revealed where true wisdom lies. The answer is in our text: "Whoever trusts in the Lord, happy is he."

The true way to handle a matter wisely is to trust in the Lord. This is the sure clue to the most intricate complexities of life. Follow it and find eternal bliss. You who trust in the Lord have a diploma for wisdom granted by inspiration. Happy are you now, and happier will you be above.

Lord in this beautiful evening, walk with me in the garden and teach me the wisdom of faith. Amen.

A DWELLING PLACE

"We abide in Him."

—1 John 4:13

D o you want a home for your soul? You ask, "How much does it cost?" The price is something less than proud human nature would like to pay. It is "without money and without price" (Isaiah 55:1).

Ah, you would like to pay a respectable rent. You would love to do something to win Christ. Then you cannot have this house, for it is without price.

Will you take my Master's house on a lease for all eternity, with nothing to pay for it, nothing but the daily ground rent of loving and serving Him forever? Will you take Jesus and dwell in Him?

This house is furnished. It is filled with more riches than you will spend as long as you live. In it you can have intimate communion with Christ and feast on His love. Here are tables well-stored with food to live on forever.

In this house when you are weary, you find rest with Jesus, and from this house you see heaven.

Do you want this house? "Ah, I would like to have the house, but may I?" Yes. Here is the key: "Come to Jesus."

But you say, "My appearance is too shabby for such a house." Never mind that, there are fine cloths inside. If you feel guilty and condemned, come. Although the house is too good for you, Christ will make you good enough for the house. He will wash and cleanse you, and then you will be able to say, "I dwell in Him."

Believer, you are blessed to have this dwelling place. You are greatly privileged to have this strong habitation in which you are forever safe. "Dwelling in Him," you have not only a perfect and secure house but an everlasting one.

When this world will have dissolved like a dream, our house will live and will stand more imperishable than marble, more solid than granite. It will be as self-existent as God, for it is God Himself. Remember, "We abide in Him."

LINGERING

"All the days of my hard service I will wait."

—Job 14:14

Our short visit on earth will make heaven more heavenly. Nothing makes rest so pleasant as work. Nothing renders security so enjoyable as being in harm's way.

The bitter taste of earth will give relish to the new wine that sparkles in the golden bowls of glory. Our battered armor and our scars will make the victory more illustrious when we are welcomed to the heavenly seats of those who have overcome the world. We could not have full fellowship with Christ if we did not temporarily live below.

Jesus was baptized with a baptism of suffering on earth. We must be baptized with the same suffering if we would share His kingdom. Fellowship with Christ is so honorable that the worst sorrow of earth is a small price for gaining it.

Another reason for lingering here is for the good of others. We would not want to enter heaven until our work here is finished. It may be that we are still ordained to minister light to souls blinded in the wilderness of sin.

Our prolonged stay here is for God's glory. A tried and tested saint, like a well-cut diamond, glitters greatly in the King's crown. Nothing reflects honor like a protracted and severe trial that ends in triumphant endurance. We are God's workers and He will be glorified by our afflictions. It is for the honor of Jesus that we endure the trials of our faith with sacred joy.

Let all surrender their wishes to the glory of Jesus and feel, "If my lying in the dust would elevate my Lord by so much as an inch, let me still lie among the plant pots of earth. If to live on earth forever would make my Lord more glorious, it would be my heaven to be shut out of heaven."

Our time is fixed and settled by eternal decree. Do not be anxious. Wait patiently until the gates of pearl open.

MAY 6, EVENING

OUR BELOVED PHYSICIAN

"Great multitudes followed Him, and He healed them all."

—Matthew 12:15

What a mass of hideous sickness Jesus must have seen. Yet He was not disgusted but patiently healed them all. What a variety of evils He must have seen. What sickening ulcers and festering sores. Yet He was prepared for every type of evil and was victorious over its every form. Let the arrows fly from any angle, He quenches their fiery power.

The heat of fever, the cold of fluid buildup, the lethargy of paralysis, the rage of madness, the filth of leprosy, the darkness of blindness: All knew the power of His word and fled at His command. In every corner of the field, He triumphed over evil and received honor from the delivered captives. He came, He saw, and He conquered everywhere.

He is the same this morning. Whatever my case may be, the beloved Physician can heal me. Whatever the state of others whom I remember in prayer, I have hope in Jesus that they will be healed. My child, my friend, or my dearest one, I have hope for each and all when I remember the healing power of my Lord.

In my own situation, however severe my struggle with sin and infirmities, I too may be of good cheer. He who on earth walked the hospitals still dispenses His grace and works wonders among His children. Let me earnestly go to Him at once.

Let me praise Him this morning as I remember how He wrought His spiritual cures. He took on Himself our sicknesses. "By His stripes we are healed" (Isaiah 53:5). The church on earth is full of souls healed by our beloved Physician. The inhabitants of heaven confess that "He healed them all."

Come then and spread the virtue of His grace. Let it be "an everlasting sign that shall not be cut off" (Isaiah 55:13).

OUR GREAT PHYSICIAN

"Jesus said to him, 'Rise, take up your bed and walk'."

—John 5:8

Like many others, this ailing man had been waiting for a miracle. Wearily he watched the pool, but no angel came. He waited for years because he thought this was the only way. Little did he realize there was One close by who could heal instantly.

Today, many are in the same plight. They wait for some singular emotion, some remarkable impression or celestial vision. They wait in vain. They watch for nothing. Suppose that even in a few cases remarkable signs are seen. These are rare, and none have a right to expect them. None, especially those who have infirmities, could get to the water even if an angel came.

It is a sad reflection that tens of thousands are now waiting for healing through the use of methods, ordinances, vows, and resolutions. They are waiting in vain, utterly in vain. And as they wait, these poor souls forget the ever-present Savior who asks them to look to Him and be saved. He could heal them at once, but they prefer to wait for an angel and a miracle.

Trusting Jesus is the sure way to every blessing. He is worthy of the most implicit confidence, but unbelief makes them prefer the cold porches of Bethesda to the warmth of His love.

Oh that the Lord would turn His eye on the multitudes who are this way tonight. May He forgive their disregard of His divine power. He calls them with that sweet constraining voice to rise up from their beds of despair and, in the energy of faith, to take up their beds and walk.

Oh Lord, hear our prayer for all who are sick at this calm hour of sunset. Before the day breaks, may they look to You and live.

MAY 7, EVENING

WHO HEALED YOU?

"But the one that was healed did not know who it was."

—John 5:13

Years pass quickly for the healthy and happy. But those thirty-eight years of disease must have dragged long and weary in the life of this poor ailing man.

When Jesus healed him as he lay at the pool of Bethesda, he was immediately aware of the change. So too is the sinner immediately conscious of change when, after weeks and months of paralysis, despair and weariness, the Lord Jesus speaks the word of power that brings joy and peace to all who believe. Immediately there is a consciousness of the change because evil has been removed. The new imparted life is too remarkable to be possessed and remain inoperative. The change is too marvelous not to be perceived.

Yet the poor man at Bethesda was ignorant of the *author* of his cure. He did not know the sacredness of Jesus, or the offices Jesus sustained, or the errands that brought Him among people.

Much ignorance of Jesus may remain in hearts that have felt the power of His blood. We must not hastily condemn their lack of knowledge, but where we can see a faith that saves the soul, we must believe that salvation has been granted.

The Holy Spirit makes sinners penitent long before He makes them spiritual. Those who believe what they know will soon know more clearly what they believe. Ignorance is, however, an evil. This poor man was questioned by the Pharisees and was unable to cope with them.

It is good to answer those who deny, but we cannot unless we know and understand the Lord Jesus. The cure of this man's ignorance, however, soon followed the cure of his infirmity. He was visited by the Lord in the temple, and after that gracious manifestation, he testified "that it was Jesus who had made him well" (John 5:15).

Lord, if You have saved me, show Yourself that I may declare You to the world.

MAY 8, MORNING

THE PLURALITY OF GOD

"Now acquaint yourself with Him and be at peace."

—Job 22:21

If we want to acquaint ourselves with God and be at peace, we need to know Him as He is revealed in Scripture. We must know Him not only in the unity of His essence and subsistence, but also in the plurality of His persons. God said, "Let us make man in Our image" (Genesis 1:26). Let you and I not be content until we know something about that "us."

Endeavor to know the Father. Bury your head in His neck with deep repentance. Confess that you are not worthy to be called His child. Receive the kiss of His love. Let the token of His eternal faithfulness be a ring on your finger. Sit at His table and let your heart be merry in His grace.

Also seek to know the Son of God, who is the brightness of His Father's glory. The Son, with unspeakable condescension of grace, became man for our sakes. Know Him in the singular complexity of His nature, for He is both eternal God and suffering finite man. Follow Him as He walks the waters with the tread of deity. See Him as He sits on the well in the weariness of humanity. Do not be satisfied until you know a great deal about Jesus Christ, your Friend, your Brother, your Husband, and your all.

Do not forget the Holy Spirit. Obtain an understanding of His nature, character, attributes, and works. Look at the Spirit of God, who "hovered over the face of the waters" (Genesis 1:2) and brought order from chaos. This same Spirit now visits the chaos of your soul and creates the order of holiness. See Him as the Lord and giver of spiritual life, the Illuminator, the Instructor, the Comforter, and the Sanctifier. See Him as He descends on the head of Jesus (Matthew 3:16) and then rests on you who are as the skirts of His garments (Psalm 133:2).

An intelligent, scriptural, and experimental belief in the Trinity-in-Unity is yours if you truly know God; and this knowledge brings peace.

MAY 8, EVENING

EVERY BLESSING

"Who has blessed us with every spiritual blessing."

—Ephesians 1:3

Christ gives His people all the goodness of the past, the present, and the future. In the mysterious ages of the past, the Lord Jesus was His Father's first elect. He shares His election with us because we were chosen in Him before the foundation of the world. "Come you blessed of My Father, inherit the kingdom prepared for you from the foundation of the world" (Matthew 25:34).

From all eternity Jesus is the "only begotten Son" (John 3:16). By adoption and regeneration, He has elevated us "to become children of God, to those who believe in His name" (John 1:12). In the everlasting settlements of predestinating wisdom and omnipotent decree, the eye of the Lord Jesus is always on us. We may rest assured that in the span of destiny there is nothing against the interests of His redeemed.

The marvelous incarnation of the God of heaven is ours. The bloody sweat, the scourge, and the cross are ours forever. Whatever blissful results flow from perfect obedience, finished atonement, resurrection, ascension, or intercession, all are ours by His gift.

His dominion over principalities and powers and His absolute majesty in heaven are employed for the benefit of those who trust in Him. Our "names are written in heaven" (Luke 10:20), and "He lives to make intercession" for us (Hebrews 7:25). God "raised Him from the dead and seated Him at His right hand in the heavenly places, far above all principality and power and might and dominion and every name that is named not only in this age but also in that which is to come. And He put all things under His feet" (Ephesians 1:20–22).

His high status is as much ours as was His abasement. Jesus, who entered the depths of woe and death for us, does not withdraw His gift now that He is enthroned in the highest heavens.

CLOSE COMMUNION

*"Come, my beloved, let us go forth to the field . . .
let us see if the vine has budded."*

—Song of Solomon 7:11,12

The church was ready to begin a difficult task and needed her Lord's company. She does not say, "I will go," but "let us go." It is blessed when Jesus is at our side!

It is the business of God's people to be trimmers of God's vines. Like our first parents, we have been put in the garden of the Lord to be useful, so let us go forth to the field.

Observe that when the church is in her right mind she wants joyful communion with Christ in all her labors. Some imagine that they cannot serve Christ actively and still have fellowship with Him. They are mistaken. Without a doubt it is easy to waste the inward life on outward exercises and complain with the spouse, "They made me the keeper of the vineyards, but my own vineyard I have not kept" (Song of Solomon 1:6). But there is no reason why this should be the case, except through our own folly and neglect of Jesus.

A believer may even do nothing and grow quite as lifeless in spiritual things as those who are busy for Christ but neglect Him. Mary was not praised for sitting still but for sitting at Jesus' feet (Luke 10:42). Even so, Christians are not to be praised for neglecting duties under the pretense of having secret fellowship with Jesus. It is not sitting, but sitting at Jesus' feet that is commendable.

Do not think that activity itself is evil. It can be a great blessing and a means of grace. Paul called it a grace given to him to be allowed to preach (Galatians 1:16), and every form of Christian service may become a personal blessing.

Those who have the most fellowship with Christ are not recluses or hermits with time to spare. They are indefatigable laborers who are working for Jesus. As they labor He is by their side. Remember, then, in anything we have to do for Jesus, we can do it and should do it in close communion with Him.

MAY 9, EVENING

RISEN

"But now Christ is risen from the dead."

—1 Corinthians 15:20

All of Christianity rests on the fact that Christ is risen from the dead, because, "if Christ is not risen then our preaching is empty and your faith is also empty," and "you are still in your sins" (1 Corinthians 15:14,17).

The divinity of Christ finds its proof in His resurrection. He was "declared to be the Son of God with power according to the spirit of holiness by the resurrection from the dead" (Romans 1:4). It would be reasonable to doubt His deity if He had not risen.

Moreover, Christ's sovereignty over all depends on His resurrection. "For to this end Christ died and rose and lived again that He might be Lord of both the dead and the living" (Romans 14:9).

Our justification, that choice blessing of the covenant, is linked with Christ's triumph over death and the grave. "He was delivered up because of our offenses and was raised because of our justification" (Romans 4:25).

Even our regeneration is connected with His resurrection. "His abundant mercy has begotten us again to a living hope through the resurrection of Jesus Christ from the dead" (1 Peter 1:3).

Our ultimate resurrection rests in Christ's rising. "If the Spirit of Him who raised Jesus from the dead dwells in you, He who raised Christ from the dead will also give life in your bodies through His Spirit who dwells in you" (Romans 8:11).

If Christ did not rise, then we will not rise. But if He is risen, then they who are asleep in Christ have not perished, and in their flesh they will surely see God.

Thus the silver thread of resurrection runs through all the believer's blessings. From regeneration to eternal glory it binds them together.

This glorious fact is established beyond a doubt, and we can rejoice in it. Now is Christ risen from the dead.

MAY 10, MORNING

MY TESTIMONY

"The only begotten of the Father, full of grace and truth."

—John 1:14

Believer, you can testify that Christ is the only begotten of the Father and the first begotten of the dead.

He is divine to me even if to the rest of the world He is human. What He has done for me, only God could do. He has subdued my stubborn will, melted an unyielding heart, opened gates of brass, and snapped bars of iron.

He has turned my sorrow into laughter and my desolation into joy. He has led my captivity captive (Ephesians 4:8) and made my heart "rejoice with joy inexpressible and full of glory" (1 Peter 1:8). Let others think as they will, to me He must be the only begotten of the Father. Blessed be His name.

He is full of grace. If He had not been, I would never have been saved. He drew me even when I struggled to escape His grace. When at last I came trembling like a condemned culprit to the mercy seat, He said, "Your many sins are forgiven, be of good cheer."

He is full of truth. His promises are true. Not one has ever failed me. I tell you a servant never had a master such as mine. Never did anyone have a brother like Him. Never did a spouse have such a husband as Christ has been to my soul. Never did a sinner have a better Savior. Never did a mourner have a better comforter than Christ has been to my spirit. I want no one else.

In life, He is my life. In death, He will be the death of death. In poverty, Christ is my riches. In sickness, He makes my bed. In darkness, He is my star. In brightness, He is my sun. He is the manna of my wilderness camp, the new corn of my Canaan.

Jesus is all grace and no wrath, all truth and no falsehood. He is infinitely full of truth and grace.

My soul, this evening with all your might bless the only begotten.

MAY 10, EVENING

ALWAYS WITH US

"I am with you always."

—Matthew 28:20

It is good that there is One who never changes and who is always with us. It is good that there is one stable rock in the waves of the sea of life.

Oh my soul, do not set your affections on rusting, moth-eaten, decaying treasures. Set your heart on Him who is always faithful (Matthew 6:19–21). Do not build your house on the moving quicksand of a deceitful world. Build your hopes on the Rock that will stand immovably secure in high winds, heavy rains, and roaring floods (Matthew 7:24).

Place your treasure in the only secure cabinet. Store your jewels where you can never lose them. Put them all in Jesus Christ. Set all your affection on Him. Place all your hope in His merit. Deposit all your trust in His effectual blood. Put your joy in His presence. Then you will laugh at loss and defy destruction.

Never forget that all the flowers in the world's garden will fade and that the day is coming when nothing will be left but the black, cold earth. Death's black extinguisher will soon put out your candle.

Oh how sweet to have sunlight when the candle is gone! The dark flood must soon roll between you and all you have. Wrap around your heart Him who will never leave you. Trust Him who will go with you through the black and surging current of death's stream. He will land you safely on the celestial shore and make you sit with Him in heavenly places (Hebrews 1:13).

Oh afflicted and sorrowing one, tell your secrets to the "friend who sticks closer than a brother" (Proverbs 18:24). Trust all your concerns to Him who can never be taken from you, who will never leave you (Hebrews 13:5), and who will never let you leave Him (John 10:28–29). This friend is the Lord Jesus Christ, who is "the same yesterday, today and forever" (Hebrews 13:8).

"I am with you always" is enough for my soul to live on. All others can forsake me if they wish.

COURAGE

"Only be strong and very courageous."

—Joshua 1:7

God's tender love for His servants makes Him concerned about our inner feelings. He desires us to be of good courage.

Some think it a small matter for believers to be troubled with doubts and fears. God does not. Our text indicates that our Master does not want us entangled in fear. He wants us free from cares and doubts. Our Master is more concerned with our unbelief than we are.

When depressed, we are victims of a terrible sickness. Let us not trifle with this disease. Take it immediately to our beloved Physician. Our Lord does not want us to remain sad. It was a law of King Ahasuerus that no one could enter the king's court dressed in mourning (Esther 1:1). This is not the law of the King of kings. We may come sorrowing, but He puts "the garment of praise for the spirit of heaviness" on us (Isaiah 61:3).

Christians should be courageous. We glorify the Lord when we endure trials in an heroic manner. If we are fearful and fainthearted, we dishonor our God. Besides, it is a bad example. This disease of doubtfulness and discouragement is an epidemic that could spread among the Lord's flock. One downcast believer can make twenty souls sad.

If you do not keep your courage, Satan will be too much for you. Let your spirit be joyful in God your Savior. "The joy of the Lord is your strength" (Nehemiah 8:10), and no fiend of hell can make progress against you. Moreover, labor is easy to those of cheerful spirit. Success waits on cheerfulness. The ones who toil while rejoicing in God, and believing with all their hearts have success guaranteed.

If you sow in hope, you will reap in joy. Therefore, dear reader, only be strong and very courageous.

REVEALED

"And will manifest myself to him."

—John 14:21

The Lord Jesus gives special revelations of Himself to His people. The Scriptures declare this (Galatians 1:12), and many of God's children can testify to its truth from their experience. They have received special manifestations of their Lord and Savior Jesus Christ.

The biographies of famous saints recount instances of Jesus speaking in a very special manner and unfolding the wonders of His person. These experiences so saturated them with happiness that they thought they were in heaven. They were not, of course, but they were certainly on its threshold; for when Jesus reveals Himself, it is heaven on earth. It is paradise in embryo. It is bliss begun.

The revelation of Christ produces holy influences on the believer. One effect of this will be humility. If a person says, "I had a supernatural experience, therefore I am superior," that individual did not have communion with Jesus. "He regards the lowly, but the proud He knows from afar" (Psalm 138:6). Jesus does not need to come near the proud to know them, and He will never visit them in love.

Another effect will be happiness. "In Your presence is fullness of joy. At Your right hand are pleasures evermore" (Psalm 16:11).

Holiness will certainly follow. The person who has no holiness has never had the manifestation of which our text speaks. Some allege a great revelation, but believe no one until you see their walk matching their words. "Do not be deceived, God is not mocked; for whatever a man sows, that he will also reap" (Galatians 6:7). God will not bestow His favor on the wicked. While He will not cast away a perfect person, He will not respect an evil doer.

There are thus three effects from being near Jesus: humility, happiness, and holiness. May God give you all three this morning.

MAY 12, MORNING

MOVING

"Do not fear to go down to Egypt, for I will make of you a great nation there. 'I will go down with you to Egypt, and I will also surely bring you up again'." —Genesis 46:3-4

Jacob must have shuddered at the thought of leaving the land of his father's sojourn to go and live among heathen strangers. It would be a new scene and likely a trying one. Yet the way appeared to be ordained by God and Jacob resolved to go.

This is frequently the position of believers; they are called to new dangers and trials. When this occurs, imitate Jacob by offering sacrifices of prayer to God and seeking His direction. Do not take a step until you have waited on the Lord for His blessing. Then you will have Jacob's companion as your friend and helper.

What blessed assurance to know the Lord is with us in all our ways and that He condescends to go down with us in our humiliation and banishment. Even if we have to cross the ocean, our Father's love to us will beam like the sun in its strength. We cannot hesitate to go where Jehovah promises His presence. Even the valley of death grows bright with the radiance of this assurance.

Believer, march with faith in God and you will have Jacob's promise. You will be brought up again from the troubles of life or the chambers of death. Jacob's seed came out of Egypt in due time, and you will pass unharmed through the trials of life and the terror of death.

Exercise Jacob's confidence. "Fear not" is both the Lord's command and His divine encouragement to those who at His leading are launching on new seas.

The divine presence and preservation forbids even one unbelieving fear. Without our God we should be afraid to move. But when He sends us, it is dangerous to linger.

Go forward and do not fear.

MAY 12, EVENING

THE MORNING

"Weeping may endure for a night, but joy comes in the morning."

—Psalm 30:5

C hristian, if you are in a night of trial, think about tomorrow. Cheer your heart with the thought of the coming of your Lord and be patient for:

> Lo! He comes with clouds descending.

Be patient! The Vinekeeper waits until His harvest is ready to reap. Be patient! You know He said, "Behold, I am coming quickly and My reward is with Me to give to everyone according to his work" (Revelation 22:12).

If this morning is your low point, remember:

> A few more rolling suns, at most,
> Will land thee on fair Canaan's coast.

Today your head may be crowned with thorny troubles, but before long you will wear a starry crown. Your hand may be filled with cares, but it will soon sweep the harp strings of heaven. Your garments may be soiled with dust, but by and by they will be white. Wait a little longer. Your trials and troubles will seem as nothing when you look back. Looking at them here, they may seem immense, but when you get to heaven you will:

> With transporting joys recount,
> The labors of our feet.

Our trials will then seem light and momentary afflictions. Press on boldly. If the night has never been so dark, still the morning is coming. This is more than those who are shut up in the darkness of hell can say.

Do you know what it is to live on the future, to live on expectation, to live on heaven? Believer, you have a sure and a comforting hope. It may be dark now, but it will soon be light. It may be all trial now, but it will soon be all happiness.

What difference does it make if weeping may endure for a night, because joy comes in the morning!

WEALTH

"You are my portion, O Lord."

—Psalm 119:57

Look at your possessions and compare them with others. Some people own large farms. They are rich and their harvests produce a golden increase. But what are such harvests when compared with God, who is the God of harvests? What are bursting barns compared with Him, who feeds you with the bread of heaven?

Some people have large urban real estate holdings. Their wealth is abundant and flows in streams until they become a reservoir of gold. But what is gold when compared with God? You could not live on gold, and your spiritual life could not be sustained by it. Put gold on a troubled conscience and it cannot soothe the pangs. Apply gold to a despondent heart and it cannot stop a solitary groan or grief. Even if you are poor you have your God, and in Him you have more than gold or riches could ever buy.

Some have their wealth in what people love best, applause and fame. But ask yourself, is God more to you than that? What if thousands cheered you, would this prepare you to cross the Jordan? No, for there are griefs in life that applause can never alleviate, and there is a deep need during a dying hour that no riches can meet.

But when God is your portion, you have more than all else put together. In Him every need is met, whether in life or in death. With God you are rich indeed, for He will supply your need, comfort your heart, alleviate your grief, guide your steps, be with you in the dark valley, and take you home to enjoy Him forever.

"I have enough," says Esau, and this is the best thing that one of the world can say.

"I have all things," Jacob replies, but this is a note too high for carnal minds.

MAY 13, EVENING

HEIRS

"Joint heirs with Christ."

—Romans 8:17

The boundless realms of His Father's universe are Christ's by prescriptive right. As "heir of all things" (Hebrews 1:2), He is the sole proprietor of the vast creation of God. Our text grants believers the deed of "joint heirs with Christ," and our Lord has ratified that with His chosen people.

The golden streets of paradise, the pearly gates, the river of life, the transcendent bliss, and the unspeakable glory are given to us for an everlasting possession. All that Jesus has He shares with His people. He even places the crown royal on the head of His church, appointing her a kingdom and calling her "a chosen generation, a royal priesthood, a holy nation" (1 Peter 2:9).

Jesus removed His crown that we might have a glorious coronation. He would not sit on His own throne until He had procured a place for all who overcome by His blood. Crown the head and the whole body shares the honor.

This is the reward for every Christian conqueror. Christ's throne, crown, scepter, palace, treasure, robe, and heritage are yours. Christ considers His happiness complete when His people share it with Him. "The glory which You gave Me, I have given them" (John 17:22). "These things I have spoken to you that My joy may remain in you and that your joy may be full" (John 15:11).

The smiles of His Father are all the sweeter to Jesus because His people share in them. The honors of His kingdom are all the more pleasing to Jesus because His people will be with Him in glory. His conquests are more valuable because by them His people overcome. He delights in His throne because on it there is a place for them. His joy is more delightful because He calls them to enter into it.

MAY 14, MORNING

THE SHEPHERD

"He will gather the lambs with His arm, and carry them in His bosom."

—Isaiah 40:11

Who is the subject of such gracious words? The Good Shepherd. Why does He carry the lambs in His bosom? Because He is tender, and any weakness immediately melts His heart.

The sighs, the innocence, and the feebleness of the little ones draw His compassion. It is His duty, as a faithful High Priest, to consider the weak. He purchased them with His blood. They are His property. He must and will care for those for whom He paid so great a price.

He is responsible for each lamb, bound by covenant pledges not to lose one. Moreover, they are all a part of His glory and reward.

How can we understand the expression, "He will carry them?" Sometimes He carries the lambs by not allowing them to endure heavy trials. Providence deals tenderly. Often lambs are carried by being filled with an unusual sense of love, so they can bear up and stand fast. Though their knowledge may not be deep, they have great sweetness in what they do know.

Frequently He carries the lambs by giving them a simple faith that takes the promise just as it stands and runs with trust in every trouble straight to Jesus. This simplicity of faith gives an unusual degree of confidence that carries them above the world.

He also carries them in His bosom, and this is boundless affection. Would He lift them to His bosom if He did not love them? This is tender nearness; they could not be nearer. This is hallowed familiarity. There are precious love-passages between Christ and His weak ones. Here is perfect safety. In His bosom who can hurt them? They must hurt the Shepherd first.

This is perfect rest and sweetest comfort. Surely we are not sufficiently sensitive to the infinite tenderness of Jesus!

MAY 14, EVENING

JUSTIFICATION

"Everyone who believes is justified."

—Acts 13:39

The believer in Christ receives the gift of justification, a fruit of faith produced not in the future, but right now. Justification is the result of faith, and it is given the moment you accept Christ as your all in all.

Those in heaven, who stand before the throne of God this morning, are justified, but so are we. We are as clearly justified as those who walk the streets of glory and sing melodious praises with celestial harps.

The thief on the cross was justified the moment he turned the eye of faith to Jesus. Paul, after years of service, was not justified any more than the thief who had no opportunity to serve.

Today we are accepted in the Beloved. *Today* we are absolved from sin. *Today* we are acquitted at the bar of God. What a soul-transporting thought!

There are some clusters of Eshcol's vine (Deuteronomy 1:24) that we will not be able to pick until we enter heaven, but this vine also runs over the wall to us now. Unlike the corn that cannot be eaten until we cross the Jordan, justification is manna in the wilderness, a portion of our daily nutriment supplied by God.

We are now, even now, pardoned. Even now our sins are put away. Even now we stand in the sight of God accepted as though we had never been guilty. "There is therefore now no condemnation to those who are in Christ Jesus" (Romans 8:1).

Even now (1 John 3:2) there is not a sin in the Book of God against one of His people. "Who shall bring a charge against God's elect?" (Romans 8:33). There is not a speck, spot, stain, wrinkle, or any such thing remaining on any believer in the matter of justification in the sight of the Judge of all the earth.

Let this privilege wake us to present duty. While life lasts, let us spend and be spent for our precious Lord Jesus.

MAY 15, MORNING

PERFECTED

"Made perfect."

—Hebrews 12:23

There are two kinds of perfection the Christian needs: the perfection of justification in the person of Jesus, and the perfection of sanctification worked by the Holy Spirit.

At present, corruption remains in the heart of the regenerate, as experience teaches. Within us are lusts and evil imaginations. But I rejoice to know that the day is coming when God will finish the work He has begun. He will present my soul perfect in Christ and perfect through the Spirit, without spot, blemish, or any such thing.

Can it be true that this poor sinful heart of mine is to become holy even as God is holy? Can it be that this spirit which often cries, "O wretched man that I am! Who will deliver me from this body of death?" (Romans 7:24) shall be rid of sin and death. Can it be that someday nothing evil will pester my ears or disturb my peace? Oh, happy hour! Hurry!

When I cross the Jordan, the work of sanctification will be finished, and not until that moment shall I even claim perfection. Then my spirit will have its last baptism in the Holy Spirit's fire. I think I want to die just to receive that last and final purification which will usher me into heaven.

In heaven there will not be an angel purer than I. With a double sense I will be able to say "I am clean through the blood of Jesus and through the work of the Spirit." Oh how we should extol the power of the Holy Spirit in making us worthy to stand before our Father in heaven.

Yet do not let the hope of perfection in heaven make you content with imperfection now. If this occurs, your hope is not genuine. A good hope is a purifying thing. The work of grace must dwell in you now or it cannot be perfected then.

Let us pray to be filled with the Spirit, that we may bring forth increasingly the fruits of righteousness.

MAY 15, EVENING

BLESSED

"Who gives us richly all things to enjoy."

—1 Timothy 6:17

Our Lord Jesus is always giving. Not for one solitary moment does He withdraw His hand. As long as there is a vessel of grace not full to the brim, the oil will flow.

He is a sun ever shining. He is manna always falling. He is a rock in the desert sending out streams of life from His smitten side. The rain of His grace is always dropping. The river of His bounty is always flowing. The well of His love is continually overflowing. As the King can never die His grace can never fail.

Daily we pick His fruit. Daily His branches bend down to our hands with a fresh supply of mercy. There are seven feast days in His weeks and as many banquets in His years, each day and each year of our life in Him is a feast. Everyone returns from His door blessed. Everyone leaves His table satisfied. "Through the Lord's mercies we are not consumed, because His compassions fail not, they are new every morning. Great is Your faithfulness" (Lamentations 3:22–23).

Who can know the number of His blessings or recount the list of His generosity? Every sand that drops from the glass of time is but a late follower of a myriad of mercies. The wings of our hours are covered with the silver of His kindness and the yellow gold of His affection. From the mountain of eternity, the river of time carries the golden sands of His favor to us. The countless stars are only a standard bearer of a more innumerable host of blessings.

How can my soul extol Him who daily loads us with benefits and crowns us with loving kindness and tender mercy (Psalm 103:4)? Oh that my praise could be as ceaseless as His bounty!

Oh miserable tongue, how can you be silent? Wake up and praise Him. "Awake lute and harp. I will awaken the dawn. I will praise You, O Lord" (Psalm 108:2).

FILLED DITCHES

"And he said, 'thus says the Lord; "Make this valley full of ditches." For thus says the Lord; "You shall not see wind; yet the valley shall be filled with water . . .".'" —2 Kings 3:16,17

The armies of the three kings were dying of thirst and God was about to send water. With the words of our text the prophet Elisha announced this coming blessing.

This case was one of human helplessness. These valiant men could not produce a drop of water from either the skies or the wells of earth. Often the people of the Lord are at their wits end. They see their helplessness and learn experientially where their help is to be found.

Still the people were to prepare, while believing for a divine blessing. They were to dig ditches that would hold the precious liquid.

The church by her various agencies, efforts, and prayers must make herself ready to be blessed. The church must make the pools; the Lord will fill them. This must be done in faith, with a full assurance that the blessing is about to descend.

Then came the blessing. The rain did not pour from the clouds as in Elijah's case, but the pools were filled in a silent and mysterious manner. The Lord has His own sovereign methods of action. God is not tied to method and time, as we are. God does as He pleases. It is ours, thankfully, to receive from Him but not to dictate to Him.

Note the remarkable abundance of the supply: there was enough for the need of all. So, too, with the gospel blessing all the needs of the congregation and the entire church will be met by divine power in answer to prayer. Above all, victory will be speedily given to the armies of the Lord.

What am I doing for Jesus? What trenches am I digging?

Oh Lord, make me ready to receive the blessing You are so willing to give. Amen.

IMITATING CHRIST

"Walk just as He walked."

—1 John 2:6

Why should Christians imitate Christ? They should do it for their own sake. If they want a healthy state of soul, if they want to escape sin sickness, if they want to enjoy the vigor of growing grace; for their own happiness, let Jesus be their model.

If they want to drink the wines of the lees, well refined (Isaiah 25:6), if they want holy and happy communion with Jesus, if they want to be lifted above the cares and troubles of this world, let them walk as He walked. There is nothing that can assist you to walk rapidly toward heaven like wearing the image of Jesus on your heart.

It is when, by the power of the Holy Spirit, you are enabled to walk with Jesus in His very footsteps that you are the happiest. You know with certainty that you are a child of God. Peter was both unsafe and uneasy away from Jesus.

Strive to be like Jesus for Christianity's sake. Ah poor Christianity, you have been shot at by cruel foes, but you have not been as badly wounded by your foes as you have been by your friends. Who wounded the fair hand of godliness? Was it not the professing Christian who used the dagger of hypocrisy? The wolf dressed in sheep's clothing enters the fold and worries the flock more than the lion outside. There is no weapon as deadly as a Judas kiss. Inconsistent believers injure the gospel more than the sneering critic or the infidel.

Imitate Christ's example. Christian, do you love your Savior? Is His name precious? Is His cause dear? Do you want the kingdoms of this world to become His? Is it your desire that He should be glorified? Are you longing for souls to be won to Him? Then imitate Jesus! Imitate His example.

Be "an epistle of Christ, known and read by all men" (2 Corinthians 3:2).

SERVANTS

"You are my servant, I have chosen you."

—Isaiah 41:9

If we have received the grace of God in our hearts, its practical effect has been to make us God's servants. Now we may be unfaithful servants, and we certainly are unprofitable ones; but blessed be His name, we are His servants. We wear His clothes. We eat at His table. We obey His commands.

We were once the servants of sin. But He who made us free has taken us into His family and taught us obedience to His will. We do not serve our Master perfectly, but we would if we could. As it is, we hear God's voice saying, "You are My servant," and we answer with David, "O Lord, truly I am Your servant . . . You have loosed my bonds" (Psalm 116:16).

The Lord calls us, however, not only to be His servants but His chosen ones. He says, "I have chosen you." We did not choose Him; He chose us. We were not always God's servants; it was sovereign grace that changed us. The eye of sovereignty singled us out and the voice of unchanging grace declared, "Yes, I have loved you with an everlasting love" (Jeremiah 31:3).

Long before time or space was created, God wrote on His heart the names of His elect people and predestinated them to be conformed to the image of His Son. He ordained them heirs of all the fullness of His love, His grace, and His glory. What great comfort!

Do you think the Lord has loved us this long only to throw us away? He knew how stiff-necked we would be. He understood that our hearts were evil. Yet He made the choice. Our Savior is not a fickle lover. He does not love for awhile because of some gleam of beauty from His church's eye, and then afterward cast her off because of her unfaithfulness. No, He married the church in eternity past, and it is written that, "He hates divorce" (Malachi 2:16).

The eternal choice is a bond upon *our* gratitude and upon *His* faithfulness.

MAY 17, EVENING

FULLNESS

"In Him dwells all the fullness of the Godhead bodily; and you are complete in Him."

—Colossians 2:9–10

All the attributes of Christ as God and man are at our disposal. "All the fullness of the Godhead"; whatever that marvelous term may comprehend, is ours to make us complete.

He cannot endow us with the attributes of deity, yet He has done all that can be done for us. He has made even His divine power and Godhead subservient to our salvation. His omnipotence, omniscience, omnipresence, immutability, and infallibility are all combined for our defense.

Arise, believer, look at your Lord Jesus hitching His divine Godhead to the chariot of salvation! How vast His grace. How firm His faithfulness. How unswerving His immutability. How infinite His power. How limitless His knowledge. All these are the foundation of salvation. All are covenanted to us as our perpetual inheritance.

Every drop of the fathomless love of the Savior's heart is ours. Every sinew in the arm of His might, every jewel in the crown of His majesty, as well as the immensity of divine knowledge and the sternness of divine justice; all are ours. All will be employed for us.

The whole of Christ in His adorable character as the Son of God is given to us richly to enjoy. His wisdom is our direction. His knowledge is our instruction. His power is our protection. His justice is our guarantee. His love is our comfort. His mercy is our solace. His immutability is our trust. He makes no reserve. He opens the recesses of the Mount of God and invites us to dig in its mines for the hidden treasures. "All, all, all are yours," He says. "Be satisfied with favor, be full of the goodness of the Lord."

How wonderful to see Jesus in this light and to call on Him with assured confidence that in seeking His love or power all we need to do is ask for what He has already faithfully promised.

MAY 18, MORNING

AFTER

"Afterward."

—Hebrews 12:11

Christians are happy after their trials. No calm is deeper than the one that follows a storm. We all rejoice in the sun after the rain.

Victory banquets are for combat veterans only. After killing the lion, they eat the honey. After climbing the Hill Difficulty, they rest in the arbor. After walking the Valley of Humiliation, after fighting Apollyon (Revelation 9:11), the shining one appears to them with a healing branch from the tree of life.

Our sorrows, like the passing keels of vessels on the sea, leave a silver line of holy light behind them "afterwards." It is a sweet, deep and wonderful peace that follows the horrible turmoil which once reigned in our tormented, guilty souls.

See, then, the happy condition of Christians! We have the best things last, and in the world the worst things first. But even our worst things here often follow good things, for harsh plowing yields a joyful harvest. Even now we grow rich by our losses, rise by our falls, live by dying, and become full by being emptied.

If grievous affliction yields so much peaceful fruit in this life, what will be the full vintage of joy afterward in heaven? If our dark nights are as bright as the world's days, what will our days be like then? If our starlight is more splendid than the sun here, what must sunlight be like there? If we can sing in a dungeon, how sweetly will we sing in heaven? If we can praise the Lord in the fire, how gloriously will we extol Him before the eternal throne? If evil is good to us now, what will be the overflowing goodness of God to us then?

Oh blessed "afterwards!" Who would not be a Christian? Who would not carry the cross for the crown? But we need patience. Our rest is not today, nor our triumph for the present, but "afterward." Wait, oh soul, "let patience have its perfect work that you may be perfect and complete, lacking nothing" (James 1:4).

THE RULERS

"I have seen servants on horses, while princes walk on the ground like servants."

—Ecclesiastes 10:7

Upstarts frequently usurp the highest places while the truly great linger in obscurity.

Even though He is the Prince of the kings of the earth, when our Lord was on earth, He walked the footpath of weariness and service as the Servant of servants. So do not be surprised if His followers, who are princes of the blood, are looked on and treated as inferior and contemptible.

This world is upside down, thus the first are last and the last are first. See how the sinful sons of Satan (John 8:44) arrogantly dominate this earth. What a high horse they ride. How they show their power. Haman is in the court, while Mordecai sits at the gate (Esther 2:21). David wanders on the mountain, while Saul reigns in state (1 Samuel 21:10). Elijah is complaining in the cave, while Jezebel is boasting in the palace (1 Kings 19:2). Yet who would want to trade places with these proud rebels?

On the other hand, who would envy the despised saints? When the wheel turns, those who are the lowest rise and the highest sink. Have patience, believer, eternity will correct all the wrongs of time.

Do not fall into the error of letting your passions and carnal appetites ride in triumph, while your nobler powers crawl in the dust. Grace must reign as a prince and make the members of Christ's body instruments of righteousness.

The Holy Spirit loves order. He therefore sets our powers and faculties in place. He gives the highest room to those spiritual faculties that link us with the great King. Let us not disturb the divine arrangement but ask for grace to keep our bodies under control and to bring them into subjection.

We were not born again to allow our passions to rule. We were newly created to reign in Christ Jesus over the triple kingdom of our spirit, soul, and body, and all for the glory of God the Father.

MAY 19, MORNING

UNANSWERED PRAYER

"He prayed that he might die."

—1 Kings 19:4

This is remarkable. The man who was never to die, the man for whom God had an infinitely better plan, the man who would be carried to heaven in a chariot of fire, the man who would be translated and never see death (2 Kings 2:11); this man would pray, "It is enough! Now Lord, take my life for I am no better than my fathers" (1 Kings 19:4).

This is a memorable proof that God does not always answer prayer the way we want Him to. He gave Elijah something far better that he asked for, and thus God really heard and answered him.

Isn't it strange that Elijah the lion-hearted would be so depressed by Jezebel's threat that he would ask to die? How kind was our heavenly Father not to take his depressed servant at his word. There is a limit to the doctrine of the prayer of faith.

We do not expect that God will give us everything we ask for. We know that sometimes we ask and do not receive because we ask in error. If we ask for that which is not promised, if we run counter to the spirit the Lord would have us cultivate, if we ask contrary to His will or the decrees of His providence, if we ask merely for the gratification of our own comfort without an eye to His glory, if we ask such things we cannot expect to receive an answer.

When we ask in faith without doubting and do not receive the precise thing asked for, we will still receive an equivalent and more. As someone remarked, "If the Lord does not pay in silver, He will pay in gold, and if He does not pay in gold, He will pay in diamonds."

If He does not give you precisely what you ask for, He will give you what is tantamount, and you will greatly rejoice when you receive it.

Dear reader, be much in prayer and make this evening a season of earnest intercession, but be careful what you ask for.

THE BLESSING OF HIS LOVE

"Marvelous loving kindness."

—Psalm 17:7

When we give our hearts with our offerings, we give well. Unfortunately we often fail. But the gifts from our Lord and our Master are always given with the love of His heart.

He does not send us the cold meat and broken pieces from the table of His luxury. He dips our morsels in His own dish and seasons our provisions with the spices of His fragrant affections. When He puts the golden emblems of His grace in our palms, He accompanies the gift with such a warm pressure on our hands that His manner of giving is as precious as the gift.

When He comes to our homes on His errands of kindness, He does not act as some harsh visitor. He sits by our side, not despising our poverty or blaming our weakness. He speaks with smiles. Golden sentences drop from His gracious lips. He embraces us with affection. If He gives only a penny, the way He gives would turn it to gold. As it is, the costly gifts are set in a golden basket by His pleasant countenance. It is impossible to doubt the sincerity of His love, because there is a bleeding heart stamped on the face of all His generous acts.

He gives liberally. There is not one hint that we are a burden to Him, not one cold look for His poor pensioners. He rejoices in His mercy and presses us to His bosom while He pours out His life for us. There is a fragrance in His perfume that only His heart could produce. There is a sweetness in His honeycomb that has the very essence of His soul's affection mingled with it.

May we continually taste and know the blessing of His love.

GENTLE CORDS

"I drew them with gentle cords. With bands of love."

—Hosea 11:4

Our heavenly Father often draws us with the gentle cords of His love. Yet we respond slowly to His gentle impulses.

We have not reached Abraham's confidence if we have not left our worldly cares with God (Genesis 15:6). We are like Martha, worried and troubled about many things (Luke 10:41). Our meager faith brings leanness to our souls. We do not open our mouths wide, even though God has promised to fill them.

This evening, does He draw you to trust Him? Can you hear Him say, "Come My child and trust Me. The veil is torn, so enter My presence and boldly approach the throne of My grace. I am worthy of your fullest confidence, so cast your cares on Me. Shake off the dust of your cares and put on your beautiful garments of joy." Even though He calls with tones of love to His blessed comforting grace, we will not come.

At another time He may call us to closer communion with Him. We have been sitting on the doorstep of God's house and He asks us into the banquet hall to dine with Him. But we might decline the honor.

There are secret rooms not yet open to us. Jesus invites us to enter, but we refuse. Shame on our cold hearts. We are poor as lovers of our sweet Lord Jesus. We are not fit to be His servants, much less His bride. Yet He exalts us to be bone of His bone and flesh of His flesh, to be married to Him by a glorious marriage covenant.

This is love, but it is love that takes no denial. If we do not obey the gentle drawings of His love, He will send affliction to drive us closer. He will have us closer to Him. What foolish children we are to refuse those bands of love and thus bring on our backs that scourge of small cords that Jesus knows how to use.

MAY 20, EVENING

DREARY "IFS"

"If indeed you have tasted that the Lord is gracious."

—1 Peter 2:3

If—this is not a matter to be taken for granted. If—there is a probability that some may not have tasted that the Lord is gracious. If—this is not a general but a special mercy. If these things are so, we need to inquire if we know the grace of God by inward experience for every spiritual favor is a matter for heart-searching.

There must be earnest and prayerful inquiry. No one ought to be content with an "if" when it comes to tasting that the Lord is gracious. Even if a jealous and holy distrust of self gives rise to the question, to *continue* in such doubt would be evil.

We must not rest without a desperate struggle to clasp the Savior in the arms of faith and say, "I know whom I have believed and am persuaded that He is able to keep what I have committed to Him until that Day" (2 Timothy 1:12). Believer, do not rest until you have a full assurance of your interest in Jesus. Let nothing satisfy until the infallible witness of the Holy Spirit assures you that you are a child of God.

Do not trifle here. Let no "perhaps," or "I doubt," or "if," or "maybe" satisfy your soul. Build on eternal truths, truly build on them. Get the sure mercies of David, and get them surely. Cast your anchor within the veil and ensure that your soul is linked to the anchor by a cable that will not break.

Advance beyond these dreary "ifs." Live no more in the wilderness of doubt and fear. Cross the Jordan of distrust and enter the Canaan of peace where the land flows with milk and honey.

GRAIN

"There is grain in Egypt."

—Genesis 42:2

Famine pinched all the nations, and it seemed inevitable that Jacob and his family would suffer. But the God of providence, who never forgets the objects of electing love, had grain stored in Egypt. God had given the Egyptians warnings of the coming famine through Joseph, who led them to store grain in the years of plenty. Jacob never expected deliverance from Egypt.

Believer, though all things are apparently against you, rest assured that God has made a reservation on your behalf. In the roll of your grief there is a saving clause. Somehow He will deliver you. Somewhere He will provide for you. Your rescue may come from a very unexpected source, but help will assuredly come, and you will magnify the name of the Lord.

If men do not feed you, ravens may (1 Kings 17:4). If earth does not yield wheat, heaven may drop manna (Exodus 16:15). Therefore, be of good courage. Rest quietly in the Lord who can make the sun rise in the west if He pleases. He can make the source of your distress the channel of your delight.

The corn in Egypt was in the hands of the beloved Joseph. He opened and closed the warehouses at will. The riches of providence are all in the absolute power of our Lord Jesus, who will dispense them liberally to His people. Joseph was abundantly ready to supply his own family. Jesus is unceasing in His faithful care of His children.

Our business is to go after the help which is provided. We must not sit still in despondency. Prayer will carry us into the presence of our royal Brother. Once before His throne, we have only to ask to have. His stores are not exhausted; there is plenty of grain. His heart is not hard; He will give us the grain.

Lord, forgive our unbelief. This evening may we draw from Your fullness and receive grace for grace. Amen.

MAY 21, EVENING

TRIALS

"He led them forth by the right way."

—Psalm 107:7

The changing scene often leads the anxious believer to ask, "Why is this happening to me?" I look for light, but there is only darkness. I look for peace, but all I see is trouble. Lord, You have hid Your face and I am troubled. Just yesterday "I could read my title clear to mansions in the sky," but today my eyes are dim, and my hopes are clouded. Yesterday I could climb to Pisgah's top (Numbers 21:20), view the landscape, and rejoice in my future inheritance. Today my spirit has no hope or joy, only much fear and distress.

Is this part of God's plan for me? Can this be the way God would bring me to heaven? Yes, oh yes. The eclipse of your faith, the darkness of your mind, the loss of your hope—all these things are part of God's method of preparing you for the great inheritance you will soon receive.

These trials strengthen and test your faith. They are waves that wash you further up the rock. They are winds that move your ship swiftly toward the desired haven. In the words of David, "He guides them to their desired haven" (Psalm 107:30).

By honor and by dishonor, by evil report and by good report, by plenty and by poverty, by joy and by distress, by persecution and by peace—by all of these things the life of your soul is maintained and you are helped on your way.

Believer, your sorrows are part of God's plan. They are essential. "We must through many tribulations enter the kingdom of God" (Acts 14:22). Learn then "to count it all joy when you fall into various trials" (James 1:2):

> O let my trembling soul be still,
> And wait Thy wise, Thy holy will!
> I cannot, Lord, Thy purpose see,
> Yet all is well since ruled by Thee.

ALTOGETHER LOVELY

"Behold, You are handsome, my beloved."

—Song of Solomon 1:16

Our Beloved is most handsome from every point of view. Our various experiences are given to us by our heavenly Father to furnish us with fresh views of the loveliness of Jesus. How pleasant are our trials when they give us a clearer view of Jesus.

We have seen Him from the top of Amana, from the top of Shenir and Hermon (Song of Solomon 4:8). He has shone on us as the sun at noon. But we have also seen Him "from the lion's den and from the mountains of the leopards" (Song of Solomon 4:8), and He has lost none of His loveliness.

From the languishing sick bed or even from the edge of the grave, we have turned our eyes to our soul's spouse, and He has never been anything but handsome.

Many of His saints have looked on Him from the gloom of dungeons and through the red flames of the stake. Yet they never uttered a bad word about Him but died extolling His surpassing charms. What a noble and pleasant occupation, to gaze forever on our sweet Lord Jesus.

It is an unspeakable delight to see the Savior in all His offices and discover Him matchless in each, to shift the kaleidoscope, as it were, and find fresh combinations of matchless grace.

In the manger and in eternity, on the cross and on His throne, in the garden and in His kingdom, among thieves or in the midst of cherubim, He is altogether lovely. Carefully examine every little act of His life and every trait of His character and you will find Him as lovely in the minute as in the majestic.

Judge Him as you will, you cannot criticize Him. Weigh Him as you please, you will find a full measure. Eternity will not discover the shadow of a spot in our Beloved. Rather as ages revolve, His glories will shine with inconceivable splendor, and His unutterable loveliness will more and more ravish all celestial minds.

MAY 22, EVENING

PERFECTING

"The Lord will perfect that which concerns me."

—Psalm 138:8

The confidence David expresses is divine confidence. He does not say, "I have grace enough to perfect me," or "my faith is so steady that it will not stagger," or "my love is so warm that it will never grow cold," or "my resolution is so firm that nothing can move it." No, David's dependence was on the Lord alone.

If we indulge in any confidence that is not grounded on the Rock of ages it will fall and cover us with ruin, sorrow, and confusion. Time will unravel all that nature spins, to the eternal confusion of those who are wrapped up in it.

The Psalmist was wise; he rested on nothing except the Lord's work. It is the Lord who has begun the good inner work in us. It is the Lord who carries it on. If He does not finish it, it never will be completed. If there is one stitch in our celestial righteous garment that we inserted, then we are lost. But the Lord who began it will complete it (Philippians 1:6). He has done it all, must do it all, and will do it all. Our confidence must not be in what we have done, nor in what we have resolved to do, but entirely in what the Lord will do.

Unbelief insinuates, "You will never be able to stand. Look at the evil in your heart. Remember the sinful pleasures and temptations of the world? You will certainly be allured by them and led astray."

Ah, yes, we would indeed perish if left to our own strength. If alone we had to navigate our frail vessels over so rough a sea, we would give up in despair. But thanks be to God, He will perfect that which concerns us and bring us to the desired haven.

We can never be too confident when we confide only in Him and never be too concerned to have that trust.

GIFTS

"You have bought me no sweet cane with money."

—Isaiah 43:24

Worshippers at the temple often brought presents of sweet perfume to be burned on God's altar. But Israel, in times of backsliding, was selfish and made few offerings to the Lord. This was evidence of their cold heart toward God and His house.

Reader, does this ever happen to you? Can the complaint in our text occasionally, if not frequently, be brought against you? Those who are poor in pocket but rich in faith will be accepted even if their gifts are small. But, my poor reader, do you give in fair proportion to the Lord, or is the widow's mite kept back from the sacred treasury (Mark 12:42)?

Wealthy believers should be thankful for the money entrusted to them, but they should never forget their larger responsibility, "for everyone to whom much is given, much will be required" (Luke 12:48). So, my wealthy reader, are you aware of your obligations? Are you giving to the Lord according to the benefits received?

Jesus gave His blood for us. What should we give Him? We, and all that we have, are His. He has purchased us, so can we act as if we were our own? Oh for more consecration! Oh for more love!

Blessed Jesus, how good of You to accept our sweet cane bought with money. Nothing is too costly for a tribute to Your unrivalled love. Yet You receive with favor the smallest sincere token of our affection. You accept our poor forget-me-nots as precious, even though they are only a bunch of wild flowers. May we never grow stingy toward You. From this hour may we never hear You complain of us because we withheld our gifts of love. Amen.

We will "honor the Lord with our possessions and with the first fruits of all our increase" (Proverbs 3:9). Then we will confess, "All things come from you and of Your own have we given You" (1 Chronicles 29:14).

MAY 23, EVENING

HEARD

"Blessed be God, who has not turned away my prayer."

—Psalm 66:20

If we honestly look at our prayers, we will be amazed that God ever answered them. There may be some who, like the Pharisee, think their prayers are worthy of acceptance (Luke 18:11). True Christians, however, weep over their prayers and desire to pray more earnestly.

Remember how cold your prayers have been, when in your prayer closet you should have wrestled like Jacob (Genesis 32:24). Instead, your petitions were weak and few and far removed from that humble, believing, persevering faith that cries, "I will not let You go unless You bless me" (Genesis 32:26). Wonder of wonders that God heard our cold prayers and not only heard, but answered them.

Reflect on how infrequently you have prayed. Only in trouble have you gone to the mercy seat. Then when deliverance has come you slide back to your old prayerless habits.

Despite this, God has continued to bless you. When you neglected the mercy seat God did not desert you, but in the bright light of the Shekinah God has always been visible between the wings of the cherubim, where He promised to meet and speak with us (Exodus 25:22).

It is marvelous that the Lord would consider and answer those intermittent spasms of importunity which come and go with our needs. What a God! He hears the prayers of those who come to Him when they have pressing needs even though they neglect Him when they have received a mercy. He answers those who approach Him when they are forced to come even though they forget to address Him when mercies are plentiful and sorrows are few. Let His gracious kindness in hearing such prayers touch our hearts.

From this morning on may we be found "praying always with all prayer and supplication in the Spirit, being watchful to this end with all perseverance and supplication for all the saints" (Ephesians 6:18).

CONDUCT

"Only let your conduct be worthy of the gospel of Christ."

—Philippians 1:27

The Greek word for conduct means more than conversation; it signifies the actions, the manner of life, and the privileges of citizenship. Thus we are commanded to let our actions, as citizens of the New Jerusalem, be worthy of the gospel of Christ.

What sort of conduct is this? In the first place, because the gospel is very simple, Christians should be simple and plain in their habits. There should be simplicity in our manner, our speech, our dress, and our behavior. Such is the very soul of beauty.

The gospel is preeminently true. It is gold without dross. A Christian's life is lusterless and valueless without the jewel of truth.

The gospel is fearless. It boldly proclaims the truth whether it is accepted or not. We must be equally faithful and unflinching. But the gospel is also gentle. Mark this spirit in its Founder: "a bruised reed He will not break" (Isaiah 42:3). Some believers are sharper than a thorn hedge. This is not like Jesus. Let us win others by the gentleness of our words and acts.

The gospel is loving. It is the message of God's love for and to a lost and fallen race. One of Christ's last commands to His disciples was, "Love one another" (John 15:17). We need more real love and unity among the saints and more tender compassion toward the souls of the worst and vilest.

We must never forget that the gospel of Christ is holy. It never excuses sin. It pardons it, but only through atonement.

Our life is to resemble the gospel in all of this. We must shun not only the grosser vices but anything that hinders our perfect conformity to Christ. For His sake, for our own sake, and for the sake of others, we must strive day by day to let our conduct agree more with His gospel.

MAY 24, EVENING

DO NOT FORSAKE ME

"Do not forsake me, O Lord."

—Psalm 38:21

We frequently pray that God will not forsake us in our hour of trials and tests. We need, however, to use this prayer all the time. There is not a moment in our life that we can do without His constant upholding. Whether in light or in darkness, in fellowship or in temptation, we need to pray, "Do not forsake me, O Lord." "Hold me up and I shall be safe" (Psalm 119:117). A little child learning to walk needs the hand of it's mother. The ship without a captain drifts from its course. We cannot make it without continued aid from above.

This morning pray, "Do not forsake me, O Lord." Father do not forsake Your child, lest I fall by the hand of the enemy. Shepherd, do not forsake Your lamb, or I will wander from the safety of the fold. Great Vineyard Keeper, do not leave your plant, or I will wither and die. "Do not forsake me, O Lord," now, or at any moment of my life.

Do not forsake me in my joys, lest they fully engage my heart. Do not forsake me in my sorrow, lest I murmur against You. Do not forsake me during repentance, lest I lose the hope of pardon and fall into despair. Do not forsake me in the day of my strongest faith, lest my faith degenerate into presumption.

Do not forsake me. Without You I am weak; with You I am strong. Do not forsake me. My path is dangerous and full of snares. I desperately need Your guidance.

The hen does not forsake her chickens. Cover me with Your feathers, and under Your wings I will take refuge" (Psalm 91:4). "Be not far from me. Trouble is near and there is none to help" (Psalm 22:11). "Do not leave me nor forsake me, O God of my salvation" (Psalm 27:9).

TELL IT

"So they rose up that very hour and returned to Jerusalem . . . and they told about the things that had happened on the road and how He was known to them." —Luke 24:33–35

When the two disciples reached Emmaus and were having dinner, the mysterious stranger who had expounded Scripture to them "took bread, blessed and broke it and gave it to them. Then their eyes were opened and they knew Him and He vanished from their sight" (Luke 24:31), despite their insisting that He stay with them.

Now, much later, their love was both a light and wings for their feet. They forgot the darkness, their weariness was gone, and immediately they returned the more than seven miles to tell the great news that the Lord was risen and appeared to them. They reached the Christians in Jerusalem, they were received by a burst of joyful news before they could tell their own story.

These early Christians were on fire. They spoke of Christ's resurrection and proclaimed what they knew of their Lord. Their experiences became common property.

This evening, let their example impress us deeply. We too must bear witness concerning Jesus. John's account at the garden tomb was supplemented by Peter's, and Mary gave additional information. Combined, we have the full testimony. We each have special gifts and distinct manifestations, but the one object God has is to perfect the complete body of Christ. Therefore, we must bring our spiritual possessions, lay them at the apostles' feet, and distribute all that God has given.

Keep back no part of His precious truth. Speak what you know, and testify of what you have seen. Do not let work, darkness, or the unbelief of friends weigh one moment on the scale. Up! March to the place of duty, and there tell what great things God has shown you.

ANXIOUS

"Cast your burden on the Lord, and He shall sustain you."

—Psalm 55:22

Concern, even with legitimate things, if carried to excess, is sin. The precept to avoid anxious concern is frequently taught by our Savior and reiterated by the apostles. If neglected, it produces transgression.

The very essence of anxiety is to imagine that we are wiser than God. We thrust ourselves in His place. We do what He has undertaken to do for us. We believe that what we need, He will forget. We try to carry our weary burdens and act as if He were unable or unwilling to take them.

This disobedience of His plain precept, this unbelief in His Word, this presumption on His providence; this is all sinful. Yet more than this, anxious concern often leads to acts of sin.

We who cannot leave our affairs in God's hands, we who insist on carrying our own burdens, are likely to be tempted to use the wrong methods of help. This leads to forsaking God as our counselor and resorting to human wisdom. "They have forsaken Me, the fountain of living waters, and hewn themselves cisterns—broken cisterns that can hold no water" (Jeremiah 2:13).

Anxiety makes us doubt God's lovingkindness. Anxiety makes our love for Him grow cold. We distrust and grieve the Spirit of God. Our prayers become hindered. Our consistent example becomes marred. Our lives become self-seeking. Lack of confidence in God leads us to wander far from Him.

Through simple faith in His promise, cast each burden on Him. Be "anxious for nothing" (Philippians 4:6). He undertakes to care for us. This will keep us close to Him and give us strength in great trials.

"You will keep him in perfect peace whose mind is stayed on You, because he trusts in You" (Isaiah 26:3).

ENDURE

"Continue in the faith."

—Acts 14:22

Perseverance is the badge of a true saint. The Christian life is both a beginning and a continuation in the ways of God as long as life lasts.

Napoleon said, "Conquest has made me what I am, and conquest must maintain me." It is the same with a Christian. Under God, dear saint in the Lord, conquest has made you what you are and conquest must sustain you. Your motto must be, "Excelsior." Only a true conqueror will continue until war's trumpet is silenced. Then the conqueror will be crowned.

Therefore, perseverance is the target of our spiritual enemies. The world does not object to your being a Christian for awhile, just as long as you cease your pilgrimage and settle down to buy and sell in Vanity Fair.

The flesh also seeks to ensnare and prevent you from pressing on to glory. It tempts, "it is weary work being a pilgrim. Come, give it up. Am I always to be humiliated? Give me at least a furlough from this ongoing warfare."

Satan, too, will make fierce attacks on your perseverance. It will be the target for his arrows. He will try to hinder. He will insinuate that your perseverance is no good and that you need a rest. He will try to make you weary of suffering. He will whisper, "Curse God and die" (Job 2:9). He will attack your steadfastness. "What is the good of being so zealous? Be quiet like the rest. Sleep as others do."

He will assail your doctrinal position. "Why do you hold to these denominational creeds? Sensible people are getting more liberal. They are removing the old landmarks. Fall in with the times."

Wear your shield, Christian. Close your armor and cry mightily to God that, by His Spirit, you will endure to the end.

MAY 26, EVENING

AT THE KING'S TABLE

"So Mephibosheth dwelt in Jerusalem, for he ate continually at the king's table. And he was lame in both his feet."

—2 Samuel 9:13

Mephibosheth contributed little to the prestige of the royal table. Yet he had a constant place there because King David could see in Mephibosheth's face the features of the beloved Jonathan.

Like Mephibosheth, we may cry to the King of Glory, "What is Your servant, that You should look upon such a dead dog as I?" (2 Samuel 9:8). But still our Lord loves us because He sees in our appearance the remembrance of His dearly beloved Jesus.

The Lord's people are precious to Him for Jesus' sake. The love which the Father has for His only begotten is so great that God raises Jesus' lowly brothers and sisters from poverty and banishment to royal companions of noble rank and regal advantage.

Our imperfection does not rob us of our privileges. Lameness does not disbar us from being heirs of heaven: The cripple is as much a child of God as if he could run like Asahel (2 Samuel 2:18). Our claim to heaven does not go limp, even though our bodies may. The king's table is a noble hiding place for lame legs. At the gospel feast, we learn to glory in infirmities because the power of Christ rests on us.

Yet grievous disability may mar the character of the best-loved saints. Here is one who dines with David, yet who is so lame in both feet that he cannot leave with the king when David flees the city (2 Samuel 15:14).

Saints whose faith is weak and whose knowledge of God is limited are great losers. They are exposed to many enemies and cannot follow the king. This disease (for it is a disease) is caused by falls. Bad nursing in spiritual infancy often causes converts to fall into depression from which they never recover, while in other cases sin breaks bones.

Lord, help the lame to leap like deer, and satisfy all Your people with the bread of Your table. Amen.

SELF-ESTEEM

"What is your servant that you should look upon such a dead dog as I?"

—2 Samuel 9:8

If Mephibosheth was so humbled by David's kindness, what should we be like in the presence of our gracious Lord? The more grace we have, the less highly we will think of ourselves, for grace, like light, reveals our impurity.

Eminent saints have scarcely known what to compare themselves to, and their sense of unworthiness has been clear and keen. "I am," said holy Rutherford, "a dry and withered branch, a piece of dead carcass, dry bones, and not able to step over straw." In another place he stated that except for rare occasions, he was as sinful as Judas the betrayer, and Cain the murderer.

The lowest objects in nature appear to the humble mind to have a preference above itself, because these low objects have never contracted sin. A dog may be greedy, fierce, or filthy, but it has no conscience to violate, no Holy Spirit to resist. A dog may be worthless, but with a little kindness, it will love its owner and be faithful to death.

The term "dead dog" is the most expressive of all terms of contempt. But it is none too strong to express the self-abhorrence of instructed believers. It is not mock modesty; they mean what they say. They have weighed themselves in the balance of the sanctuary and found out the foolishness of their nature.

At best, we are but animated dust. But viewed as sinners we are monsters. What a wonder that the Lord Jesus should set His heart's love on the likes of us.

Even though we are only dust and ashes, we must and we will "magnify the exceeding greatness of His grace." Oh heaven and earth, break forth in a song! Give all the glory, honor and praise to our sweet Lord Jesus.

GLORIFIED REST

"Whom He predestined, these He also called; whom He called, these He also He also justified and whom He justified, these He also glorified."
—Romans 8:30

This is a precious truth, believer. You may be poor, or suffering, or unknown. Take encouragement by reviewing your calling. There are excellent benefits that flow from being called by God, including the blessing in our morning text.

As surely as you are God's child today, all of your trials will soon end. You will be rich. Wait awhile, your weary head will soon wear the crown of glory, your work-worn hands will hold the palm branch of victory.

Don't worry about your troubles. Rejoice! Before long you will be where "there shall be no more death, nor sorrow, nor crying. There shall be no more pain" (Revelation 21:4). The chariots of fire are at your door, and in a moment they will carry you to the glorified (2 Kings 6:17). The everlasting song is almost on your lips. The doors of heaven are open for you. You will enter into His rest.

If He has called you, nothing can separate you from His love. Distress cannot sever the bond. The fire of persecution cannot burn the link. The hammer of hell cannot break the chain. You are secure.

The voice that first called you will call you again from earth to heaven, from the dark gloom of death to immortality's unuttered splendor. Rest assured, the heart of Him who justified you beats with infinite love for you. You soon will be with the glorified. You are waiting here only to be made ready for your inheritance. When that is done, the wings of angels will carry you away to the mount of peace, joy and blessedness where you will rest forever and ever:

> Far from a world of grief and sin,
> With God eternally shut in.

RECOLLECTIONS

"This I recall to mind, therefore I have hope."

—Lamentations 3:21

Memory is often the slave of depression. Depressed minds remember every dark foreboding of the past and dwell on every gloomy part of the present. Thus memory in sackcloth is a cup of gall and wormwood.

This depression, however, is not necessary, because wisdom can readily transform memory into a comforting angel. Memory can be trained to bring a wealth of hope. It does not have to wear a crown of iron. It may encircle the head with a tiara of gold.

This was Jeremiah's experience. In the verse before our text, memory brought him to deep depression: "My soul still remembers and sinks within me" (Lamentations 3:20). But as our text shows, this same memory restored him to hope and comfort: "This I recall to my mind, therefore I have hope." Like a two-edged sword, his trained memory killed his pride with one edge and then slew his depression with the other.

It is a general principle that if we exercise our memories wisely we might, even in our darkest depression, strike a match that immediately lights a comforting lamp. There is no need for God to create a new thing on earth to restore believers' joy. All we need to do is prayerfully rake the ashes of the past, and we will find light for the present. If we turn to the Book of Truth and the throne of grace, our candles will shine again.

It is ours to remember the lovingkindness of the Lord and to recall His deeds of grace. Let us open the volume of recollections that is so richly illuminated with memories of mercy, and we will soon be happy.

Memory may be, as Coleridge calls it, "the bosom spring of joy." When the Divine Comforter bends it to His service, memory may be chief among earthly comforts.

MAY 28, EVENING

ABHORRING SIN

"You . . . hate wickedness."

—Psalm 45:7

"Be angry and do not sin" (Ephesians 4:26). There can hardly be any goodness in us if we are not angry at sin. If we love the truth, we hate every false way.

Our Lord Jesus hated it when temptation came. Three times it assailed Him in different forms, but He always met it with, "Get behind Me, Satan" (Matthew 16:23).

Jesus hated sin in others. He showed this in tears of pity more than in words of rebuke. Yet what language could be more severe, more Elijah-like, than the words, "Woe to you, scribes and Pharisees, hypocrites! For you devour widow's houses, and for a pretense make long prayers" (Matthew 23:14).

Jesus hated wickedness so much that He bled to wound it to the heart. He died that it might die. He was buried that He might bury it in His tomb. He rose that He might forever trample it beneath His feet.

Christ is in the Gospel, and that Gospel is opposed to wickedness in every shape. Wickedness arrays itself in beautiful cloths and even imitates the language of holiness. The precepts of Jesus, however, like His famous scourge of small cords, chases it out of the temple (Matthew 21:12). He will not tolerate it in the church.

In the heart where Jesus reigns, what war there is between Christ and Belial (2 Corinthians 6:15). When our Redeemer comes to be our Judge, those thundering words, "Depart from Me, you cursed" (Matthew 25:41) are His life's teaching concerning sin, which is manifested in His abhorrence of iniquity.

As warm as His love for sinners, His hatred of sin is hotter. As perfect as His righteousness, so complete will be the destruction of every form of wickedness.

Glorious champion of right and destroyer of wrong, for this cause "therefore God, Your God has anointed You with the oil of gladness more than Your companions" (Hebrews 1:9).

REBUILDING JERICHO

"Cursed be the man before the Lord who rises up and builds this city Jericho."

—Joshua 6:26

Whoever would rebuild Jericho would be cursed. Whoever would restore a human made form of religion will be equally cursed. In our fathers' day this gigantic religious system fell by the power of their faith, the perseverance of their efforts, and the blast of their gospel trumpets.

Today there are some who would rebuild that cursed man made system on its old foundations. Oh Lord, please stop their unrighteous endeavors and pull down every stone they build. It would be serious business with us to be thoroughly purged of every error that has a tendency to develop religion by works, rather than by faith.

When we have made a clean sweep at home, we should seek in every way to oppose its all-too-rapid spread abroad in both the church and in the world. This can be done in secret by fervent prayer and in public with explicit testimony. We must warn with judicious boldness those who are inclined to error. We must instruct the young in gospel truth. We must aid in spreading the light more thoroughly through the land, for darkness hates light.

Are we doing all we can for Jesus and the gospel? If not, our negligence plays into the hands of Satan. What are we doing to spread the Bible? Are we promoting good, sound gospel writings? Luther once said, "the devil hates goose quills," and with good reason. Writers, by the Holy Spirit's blessing, have done Satan's kingdom much damage. If the thousands who will read this short word will do all they can to hinder the rebuilding of this accursed Jericho, the Lord's glory will speed among the lost.

Reader, what can you do? What will you do?

MAY 29, EVENING

CATCHING LITTLE FOXES

"Catch us the foxes, the little foxes that spoil the vines."

—Song of Solomon 2:15

Little thorns can cause much suffering. Little clouds can hide the sun. Little foxes spoil the vines. Little sins do mischief to tender hearts. Little sins burrow in the soul so that Christ will not fellowship with us.

A great sin cannot destroy a Christian. A little sin can make a Christian miserable. Jesus will not walk with a Christian unless every known sin is driven out. He says, "If you keep My commandments, you will abide in My love, just as I have kept My Father's commandments and abide in His love" (John 15:10).

Some Christians seldom enjoy their Savior's presence. Why? Surely it is an affliction for a tender child to be separated from the Savior. Are you a child of God? Are you satisfied with not seeing your Father's face? Are you the spouse of Christ? Are you content without His company? If so, you have fallen into a sad state.

Ask this question. What has driven Christ from you? He hides His face behind the wall of your sins. That wall may be built from little pebbles as easily as from great stones. The sea is made of drops, and rocks are made of grains. The sea that divides you from Christ is made of accumulated drops of your little sins. The rock which has almost wrecked your ship may have been made by the living coral of daily little sins.

If you would live with Christ, if you would walk with Christ, if you would see Christ, if you would have fellowship with Christ, then pay attention to "the little foxes that spoil the vines, for our vines have tender grapes."

Jesus invites you to go with Him and capture the little foxes. Like Samson (Judges 15:4), He will surely catch the foxes. Go hunting with Him.

SLAVES OF SIN

"That we should no longer be slaves of sin."

—Romans 6:6

Christian, keep away from sin, for it has already cost you enough. Burned child, will you play again with fire? When you have been between the jaws of the lion will you step in his den a second time? Have you had enough of the old serpent? Did he poison you once? Will you play in the snake's hole a second time?

Do not be so insane or so foolish! Did sin ever give you any real pleasure? Did you ever find any solid satisfaction in it? If you did and that makes you happy, go back to wearing chains.

Sin never did give you what it promised. Sin only deluded you with lies. Do not get snared a second time by the old fowler. Be free. Let the memory of your bondage prevent you from entering the trap again. Sin is contrary to the design of eternal love. Do not run against the purposes of your Lord.

Another thought should restrain you from sin. Christians can never sin cheaply. There is a heavy price to pay for iniquity. Transgression destroys peace of mind, obscures fellowship with Jesus, hinders prayer, and brings darkness to the soul. Do not be the slave of sin. "The way of the unfaithful is hard" (Proverbs 13:15).

There is a higher argument. Each time you serve sin, you have "crucified again the Son of God and put Him to open shame" (Hebrews 6:6). Can you bear that?

If you have fallen in sin today, it may be that the Master has sent this admonition to bring you back. Turn to Jesus again. He has not forgotten His love for you. His grace is still the same. Come with weeping and repentance to His footstool, and once more you will be received in His heart. He will set your feet on a rock and establish your steps (Psalm 40:2).

MAY 30, EVENING

CROSSING THE KIDRON

"The king himself also crossed over the Brook Kidron."

—2 Samuel 15:23

David and his sorrowing company passed that gloomy brook while fleeing from his traitorous son. The man after God's own heart (1 Samuel 13:14) was not exempt from trouble. David's life was full of difficulty. He was both the Lord's anointed and the Lord's afflicted.

Why then should we expect to escape trouble? At sorrow's gates even the most virtuous of our faith have waited with ashes on their heads. Why then should we complain as if some strange thing has happened to us (1 Peter 4:12)?

The King of kings Himself was not favored with a more cheerful or royal road. He too passed over the filthy ditch of Kidron, in which the sludge from Jerusalem flowed. God had one Son without sin, but not a single child without the rod. It is a great joy for believers that Jesus "was in all points tempted as we are" (Hebrews 4:15).

What is your Kidron this morning? Is it a faithless friend, a sad bereavement, a slanderous reproach, a dark fear? The King has passed over all of these before you. Is it pain, poverty, persecution, contempt? Over each of these, the King has gone before us. "In all their affliction He was afflicted" (Isaiah 63:9).

The idea that trials will not come must be banished at once. He who is the Head of all saints knows by experience the grief that we think is unique to us.

Despite the trials, troubles and difficulties, David later returned in triumph to his city. Similarly, David's Lord rose victorious from the grave, so let us then be of good courage, for through Him we also will win the day. We will draw water out of the wells of salvation, even though for a short time we have to pass the noxious streams of sin and sorrow.

Courage, soldiers of the Cross. Our King triumphed after crossing Kidron. So will you.

MAY 31, MORNING

GRAND AND GLORIOUS PHYSICIAN

"Who heals all your diseases."

—Psalm 103:3

It is a humbling statement that we are all, more or less, suffering under the disease of sin. But what a comfort to know that we have a great Physician who is both willing and able to heal.

Think of Jesus for awhile this evening. His cures are rapid: There is life in a look at Him (John 3:14). His cures are radical: He strikes at the center of the disease. His cures are sure and certain: He never fails, and the disease never returns. There is no relapse when Christ heals. There is no fear that His patients will be merely patched up. He makes new creatures of us. He gives us a new heart and puts a right spirit in us.

He is highly skilled in all diseases. Physicians generally have a specialty. Although they may know a little about almost all our pains and ills, there is generally one disease they have studied more than others.

Jesus Christ is thoroughly acquainted with the whole of human nature. He is as much at home with one sinner as with another. He has never met an out-of-the-way case that was difficult. Though He has dealt with extraordinary complications of strange diseases, with one glance He knows how to treat the patient. He is the only universal doctor and His medicine is the only true universal remedy. Whatever your spiritual malady, apply at once to the Divine Physician.

There is no heartbreak that Jesus cannot heal. "The blood of Jesus Christ His Son cleanses us from all sin" (1 John 1:7). We have only to think of the multitudes who have been delivered from all sorts of diseases through the power and virtue of His touch.

Joyfully place yourself in His hands. Trust Him, and sin will die. Love Him, and grace will live. Wait for Him, and grace will be strengthened. See Him as He is, and grace will be perfected forever.

DAY AND NIGHT

"So the evening and the morning were the first day."

—Genesis 1:5

Is this how it was in the beginning? Did light and darkness divide time in the first day? Little wonder, then, that my circumstances change from the sunshine of prosperity to the midnight of adversity. It will not always be high noon in my soul. At times, I must expect to mourn the loss of former joys and seek my Beloved in the night.

I am not alone in this, for all the Lord's beloved ones had to sing the mingled song of judgment and mercy, of trial and deliverance, of sorrow and delight. It is one of the arrangements of Divine providence that day and night will not cease in the spiritual or natural creation until we reach the land where "there shall be no night" (Revelation 22:5). What our heavenly Father ordains is wise and good.

What then, my soul, is best for you to do? First, learn to be content with this divine order. As Job said, "Shall we indeed accept good from God, and shall we not accept adversity?" (Job 2:10).

Next, rejoice in the morning and evening. Praise the Lord for the sun of joy when it rises and for the gloom of evening as it falls. There is beauty both in sunrise and sunset. Sing of it, and glorify the Lord. Sing like the nightingale, pour out your notes at all hours.

Believe that the night is as useful as the day. The dew of grace falls heavily in the night of sorrow. The stars of promise shine gloriously in the darkness of grief.

Continue serving day and night. If during the day, the watchword be *work;* at night exchange it for *watch.* Every hour has its duty. Continue working for your Lord until He suddenly appears in His glory.

My soul, your evening of old age and death is drawing near. Do not fear. It is part of the day, and your Lord will shelter you all the day long (Deuteronomy 33:12).

DESERTS TO GARDENS

"He will make her wilderness like Eden."

—Isaiah 51:3

I think I see a howling wilderness, a great and terrible desert like the Sahara, and I perceive nothing pleasant. I am wearied with a vision of hot, arid sand, strewn with thousands of bleached skeletons.

These wretched people expired in anguish, having lost their way in this pitiless waste. What an appalling and horrible sight! It is a boundless sand sea without oasis, a depressing grave-yard of a forsaken race.

But suddenly I see a plant of renown springing from the scorching sand. It grows and buds, and the bud expands. It is a rose, and at its side is a lily. And miracle of miracles, as the fragrance of those flowers is diffused, the wilderness is transformed into a fruitful field. It blossoms exceedingly and radiates the glory of Lebanon, the excellency of Carmel and Sharon (Isaiah 35:2).

Do not call it the Sahara, call it Paradise. It is no longer the valley of death, for where the skeletons lay bleaching in the sun, resurrection is proclaimed, and the dead spring up, a mighty army full of life immortal.

Jesus is that renowned plant, and His presence makes all things new.

Nor is the wonder any less in each individual's salvation. I see you, dear reader, cast out, an infant, unclothed, unwashed, defiled with your own blood, left for the wild animals (Ezekiel 16:6).

But a jewel has been thrown in your heart by a divine hand, and for its sake you have been pitied and cared for by divine providence. You are washed and cleansed from your defilement. You are adopted into heaven's family. The fair seal of love is on your head. The ring of faithfulness is on your hand. You are now a prince unto God, even though at one time you were an orphan, cast away.

Treasure this matchless power and grace that changes deserts into gardens and makes the empty heart sing for joy.

JUNE 1, EVENING

THE INNER FIGHT

"For the flesh lusts against the Spirit, and the Spirit against the flesh."

—Galatians 5:17

In every believer's heart there is a constant struggle between the old and new natures. The old nature is still active and loses no opportunity to employ its deadly weapons against newborn grace.

On the other hand, the new nature is always watching to resist and destroy its enemy. Grace within us will employ prayer, faith, hope, and love to cast out evil. Grace puts on the whole armor of God . . . and wrestles earnestly (Ephesians 6:11).

These two opposing natures will never cease their struggle as long as we are in this world. In *Pilgrim's Progress,* the battle of Christian with Apollyon lasted three hours, but Christian's battle with himself lasted from the Wicket Gate to the river Jordan.

The enemy is so securely entrenched that it can never be totally driven out while we are in this body. But even though we are often harassed, and at times in bruising conflict, we have an Almighty helper, even Jesus, the Captain of our salvation. He is always with us. He assures us that "in all these things we are more than conquerors through Him who loved us" (Romans 8:37). With His assistance, the new-born nature is more than a match for its inner foes.

What adversary are you fighting today? Is Satan, or the world, or the flesh fighting against you? Do not be discouraged or frightened. Fight on. God is with you. Jehovah Nissi is your banner. Jehovah Rophi is the healer of your wounds.

Do not fear, for you will overcome in Him. Who can defeat Omnipotence? Fight on, "looking unto Jesus, the author and finisher of our faith" (Hebrews 12:2). Though the conflict is long and demanding, sweet will be the victory, glorious the promised reward:

> From strength to strength go on;
> Wrestle, and fight, and pray,
> Tread all the powers of darkness down,
> And win the well-fought day.

MY TEACHER, MY MASTER

"Good teacher."

—Matthew 19:16

If the young man in our text used this title in speaking to our Lord, how should I address Him? He is indeed my teaching Master and my ruling Master. I delight to run His errands and sit at His feet. I am both His servant and His disciple.

If He should ask me why I call Him "good," I have a ready answer, "No one is good but One, that is God" (Matthew 19:17). But then Jesus is God, and all the goodness of Deity shines forth in Him.

In all my experience I have found Him good, and all the good I have comes to me through Him. He was good to me when I was dead in sin, raising me by His Spirit's power; and He has been good to me in all my needs, trials, struggles, and sorrows.

There could never be a better Master. His service is freedom. His rule is love. I wish I were one thousandth as good a servant.

When He teaches me as my Rabbi, He is also unspeakably good. His doctrine is divine. His manner is condescending. His spirit is gentle. No error is mixed with His instruction—it is pure golden truth. His teaching leads to goodness, sanctification, and edification.

Angels find Him a good Master and delight to pay their honor at His footstool. The ancient saints also discovered Him to be a good Master. They rejoiced and sang, "I am Your servant, Oh Lord!" My own humble testimony is equally the same.

I will witness to my friends and neighbors. Possibly they will be led by my testimony to seek my Lord Jesus as their teacher and master.

If only they would! They would never be sorry. If once they take His easy yoke, they will find His service so royal that they will enlist forever.

STATUS

"These were the potters and those who dwell at plants and hedges; there they dwelt with the king for his work."

—1 Chronicles 4:23

Pottery making and gardening were not prestigious trades, but the king needed potters. Therefore the potters were in royal service, even if their medium was only clay.

You may be engaged in the most menial part of the Lord's work, but it is a great privilege to do anything for the King. Stick to your calling, and know that "though you lie down among the saddlebags, you will be like the wings of a dove covered with silver and her feathers with yellow gold" (Psalm 68:13).

The text tells about those who cultivated plants and hedges. It was back-breaking work. The laborers may have wanted to live in the city with its life, society, and culture. But they stayed in the country because they were doing the king's work. The place where we live is fixed, and we are not to leave on a whim or impulse. We must serve the Lord where we are by being a blessing to those around us.

Those potters and gardeners had a royal commission, for they dwelt "with the king," though they were among the hedges, plants, and clay.

No lawful place or lowly task can keep us from communion with our divine Lord. Even if you visit or work in slums or jails, the King goes with you. In all works of faith, count on Jesus' fellowship. When you are in His work, you can count on having His smile.

You unknown workers who labor for your Lord among the dirt and wretchedness of the lowest of the low, be of good cheer. Jewels have been found in rubbish piles. Clay pots have been filled with heavenly treasure. Weeds have been transformed into precious flowers.

Live with the King to do His work, and when He writes His chronicles, your name will be lovingly recorded.

JUNE 3, MORNING

AT THE CROSS

"He humbled Himself."

—Philippians 2:8

Jesus is the great teacher of lowliness. Every day we need to learn this from Him. See the Master taking a towel and washing His disciples feet (John 13:5). Follower of Christ, will you humble yourself? When you see Him as the Servant of servants, how can you be proud?

Our text is the epitome of His biography: "He humbled Himself." On earth He was always stripping off one robe of honor and then another, until, finally naked, He was fastened to the cross. There He emptied His innermost self, pouring out His life-blood for all. Then they laid Him penniless in a borrowed grave. How low our dear Redeemer was brought!

How then can we be proud? Stand at the foot of the cross and count the purple drops by which you have been cleansed. See the thorn-crown. Mark His scourged shoulders gushing crimson. See His hands and feet roughly nailed. He is mocked and scorned. The bitterness, the pangs, and the throes of inward grief show in His body. Hear the chilling shriek, "My God, My God, why have You forsaken Me?" (Matthew 27:45).

If you do not fall prostrate before that cross, you have never seen it. If you are not humbled in the presence of Jesus, you do not know Him. You are so lost that nothing can save you but the sacrifice of God's only begotten (John 3:16).

Think of the cross: As Jesus stooped for you, bow in lowliness at His feet.

A sense of Christ's amazing love to us tends to humble us even more than a consciousness of our own guilt. This evening, may the Lord bring us in contemplation to Calvary. There our position will no longer be that of pompous pride, but we will take the humble place of people who love much because much has been forgiven them.

Pride cannot live beneath the cross. Let us sit there and learn, then rise and put our lesson into practice.

JUNE 3, EVENING

KINDNESS AND LOVE

"The kindness and love of God our Savior."

—Titus 3:4

It is sweet to see the Savior communing with His beloved people. There is nothing more delightful than being led by the divine Spirit to this fertile field of happiness.

Consider the history of the Redeemer's love to you. A thousand enthralling acts of affection come to mind, and each act weaves your heart to Christ. Thoughts and emotions intertwine to secure your renewed soul to Jesus.

When we meditate on this amazing love and behold our all-glorious Savior endowing His church with all His ancient wealth, our souls may well faint with joy. Who can endure this weight of love? Even a partial sense that the Holy Spirit gives is sometimes more than the soul can contain. How rapturous it would be to see it completely.

When the soul understands how to discern all the Savior's gifts and has the wisdom to estimate and the time to mediate on them, we will commune with Jesus in a sweeter fellowship.

Who can imagine the pleasantness of this fellowship? It must be that "eye has not seen, nor ear heard, nor [has it] entered into the heart of man the things which God has prepared for those who love Him" (1 Corinthians 2:9). Oh to burst open the door of our Joseph's granaries and see the bounty He has stored for us—this will overwhelm us with love.

By faith we see as "in a mirror dimly" (1 Corinthians 13:12) the reflected image of His boundless treasures. But when we will actually see the heavenly things with our own eyes, how deep will be the stream of fellowship where our souls will bathe! Until then, our loudest sonnets will be reserved for our loving benefactor, Jesus Christ our Lord.

His love is very pleasant to me, surpassing the love of women (2 Samuel 1:26).

GLORIOUS JESUS

"Received up in glory."

—1 Timothy 3:16

On this earth our beloved Lord was humiliated and wounded. "He was despised and rejected by men, a man of sorrows and acquainted with grief" (Isaiah 53:3). He whose brightness is like the morning wore a sackcloth of sorrow for His daily clothes. Shame was his coat. Reproach was His robe.

But on that bloody tree He triumphed over all the powers of darkness. Our faith beholds our King returning from "Edom with dyed garments from Bozrah. This One who is glorious in His apparel. Travelling in the greatness of His strength . . ." (Isaiah 63:1).

How glorious must He have been in the eyes of seraphs when "He was taken up and a cloud received Him" (Acts 1:9). He now wears that glory, the glory He had with God from the beginning, plus another glory above all: the glory He earned in His fight against sin, death, and hell.

As Victor, He wears the illustrious crown, and a new sweeter song swells on high. Listen to it! "Worthy is the lamb who was slain . . . and has redeemed us to God by [His] blood" (Revelation 5:9,12).

He wears the glory of the Intercessor who can never fail; the Prince who can never be defeated; the Conqueror who has vanquished every foe; the Lord who has the heart's allegiance of every subject. Jesus wears all the glory that the magnificence of heaven can bestow and that ten thousand times ten thousand angels can minister to Him. You cannot, by the wildest stretch of imagination, conceive His exceeding greatness.

Yet there is a further revelation of His glory, for He will descend from heaven in great power with all the holy angels. "To him who overcomes I will grant to sit with Me on My throne" (Revelation 3:21). The splendor of that glory! It will overjoy our hearts. Eternity will sound His praise. "Your throne, O God, is forever and ever" (Psalm 45:6).

Reader, is He glorious in your sight this evening?

JUNE 4, EVENING

SHUT IN

"The Lord shut him in."

—Genesis 7:16

Noah was shut in, away from all the world, by the hand of divine love. The door of electing purpose is placed between us and the world of the wicked one. We are not of this world, just as our Lord Jesus was not of this world (John 8:23). We cannot participate in the sin, the frivolity, and the pursuits of the multitude. We cannot play in the streets of Vanity Fair with the children of darkness. Our heavenly Father has shut us in, as Noah was shut in with God.

"Come into the ark," was the Lord's invitation (Genesis 7:1). Here God showed that He intended to dwell in the ark with His servant and his family. Likewise, all the chosen dwell in God and God in them. Blessed are the people who dwell in the same circle that contains God in the Trinity of His persons, Father, Son, and Spirit.

Never be careless about the gracious call which says, "Come, my people. Enter your closet and shut the door. Hide for a moment until the trial is past." Noah was so shut in that evil could not reach him. The floods only lifted him toward heaven, and the winds only blew him on his way.

Outside the ark all was in ruin, but inside there was rest and peace. Outside of Christ we perish, but in Christ there is perfect safety.

Noah was so shut in that he could not even desire to come out. Those who are in Christ are in Him forever. They will never go out again. Eternal faithfulness has shut them in. Infernal malice cannot drag them out. The Prince of David "opens and no one shuts and shuts and no one opens" (Revelation 3:7).

In the last days, He will rise up and shut the door. It will be useless for mere professors to knock and cry, "Lord, Lord, open to us," for His answer will be, "I do not know you" (Matthew 25:11–12).

Lord, shut me in by Your grace. Amen.

DISTINGUISHING MARKS

"He who does not love does not know God."

—1 John 4:8

The distinguishing mark of a Christian is confidence in the love of Christ.

First, faith sets a seal on the believer, enabling the soul to say with the apostle, "The Son of God who loved me and gave Himself for me" (Galatians 2:20). Then love gives the countersign, stamping the heart with gratitude and love to Jesus: "we love Him because He first loved us" (1 John 4:19).

During that grand, heroic period when Christianity began, believers wore this double mark clearly for all to see. They were people who knew the love of Christ, and they rested on that love as one leans on a solid staff.

But their love toward the Lord was not a quiet emotion hidden in the secret chamber of their hearts. Nor did they speak or sing of it only in their private assemblies, when they met on the first day of the week.

Christ Jesus, the crucified, was their passion, their vehement and all-consuming energy. It was as if He were visible in all their actions, conversations, and even in the look in their eyes. Love to Jesus was a flame that fed on the core and heart of their being. Its force burned through to the outer person and shone there for all to see. Zeal for the glory of King Jesus was the seal and mark of all genuine Christians.

Because of their dependence on Christ's love, they dared much. Because of their love for Christ, they did much.

It is the same today. The children of God are ruled in their innermost powers by love; "the love of Christ compels us" (2 Corinthians 5:14). We rejoice that divine love is set on us. We feel it in our hearts as it is placed there by the Holy Spirit. We love the Savior fervently with a pure heart.

My reader, do you love Him? Before you go to sleep tonight, honestly answer this important question.

JUNE 5, EVENING

VILE

"Behold, I am vile."

—Job 40:4

One encouraging word to you, poor lost sinner. You think you cannot come to God because you are vile, yet there is not a saint living on earth who has not felt vile. If Job, Isaiah, and Paul had to admit they were vile, you should not be ashamed to confess the same.

If divine grace does not eradicate all sin from the believer, how do you hope to do it yourself? If God loves His people while they are vile, do you think your vileness will prevent His loving you? Believe on Jesus, you outcast of the world's society! Jesus calls you, just as you are:

> Not the righteous, not the righteous;
> Sinners, Jesus came to call.

Even now, say, "You died for sinners, and I am a sinner. Lord Jesus, sprinkle Your blood on me." If you will confess your sin, you will find pardon. If you will say with all your heart, "I am vile, wash me," you will be washed now. The Holy Spirit will enable you to cry from your heart:

> Just as I am, without one plea
> But that Thy blood was shed for me,
> And that Thou bidd'st me come to Thee,
> O Lamb of God, I come!

If this was your plea, you will rise from reading this morning's devotion with all your sins pardoned. Although you woke up this morning with every sin you ever committed on your head, you will rest tonight accepted in the Beloved. Though once degraded with the rags of sin, you will be adorned with a robe of righteousness as white as the angels.

"Now," mark it, "now is the acceptable time . . . now is the day of salvation" (2 Corinthians 6:2). "But to him who . . . believes on Him who justifies the ungodly, his faith is accounted for righteousness" (Romans 4:5).

Oh! May the Holy Spirit give you saving faith in Him who receives even the vilest.

JUNE 6, MORNING

PRIVILEGE AND RESPONSIBILITY

"Are they Israelites? So am I."

—2 Corinthians 11:22

In our text we have a personal claim that needs proof. The apostle knew that his claim was indisputable, but there are many who have no right to the title and yet claim to belong to the Israel of God.

If we confidently declare that we too are Israelites, let us say it only after we have searched our hearts in the presence of God. If we can give proof that we are following Jesus, if we can say from the heart that we trust Him wholly, trust Him only, trust Him simply, trust Him now, and trust Him forever, then we are saints of God and all their enjoyments are our possessions.

We may be the very least in Israel, "less than the least of all the saints" (Ephesians 3:8), yet the mercies of God belong to us as saints. We may say, "Are they Israelites? So am I." Every promise is mine. Every grace is mine. And every glory will be mine. The claim, rightfully made, will yield untold comfort.

When God's people are rejoicing that they are His, what happiness for me to say, "So am I." When they speak of being pardoned, justified, and accepted in the Beloved, what joy for me to respond, "Through the grace of God, so am I."

But this claim not only has its enjoyment and privileges, it also has conditions and duties. We must share with God's people in cloud as well as in sunshine. When we hear them spoken of with contempt and ridicule for being Christians, we must come boldly forward and say, "So am I."

When we see them working for Christ, giving their time, their talent, their whole heart to Jesus, we must be able to say, "So do I."

Let us prove our gratitude by our devotion. Let us live as those who, having claimed the privilege, are willing to take the responsibility.

HATE EVIL

"You who love the Lord, hate evil."

—Psalm 97:10

You have good reason to hate evil. Consider the harm it has already caused. What a world of mischief sin has brought to your heart. Sin blinded you from the beauty of the Savior. Sin made you deaf to the Redeemer's tender invitations. Sin took your feet into the way of death. Sin poisoned the very fountain of your being. Sins stained your heart and made it "deceitful above all things and desperately wicked" (Jeremiah 17:9).

Oh what a creature you were when evil had done its utmost, before divine grace interposed! You were an heir of wrath. You ran to do evil. All of us were like this. Paul reminds us that "such were some of you, but you were washed, but you were sanctified, but you were justified in the name of the Lord Jesus and by the Spirit of our God" (1 Corinthians 6:11).

We have good reason for hating evil when we look back and trace its deadly workings. The mischief evil did was so great that our souls would have been lost if omnipotent love had not interfered to redeem us.

Even now evil is an active enemy, ever waiting to hurt and to drag us to destruction. Therefore, "hate evil," unless you want trouble. If you want thorns in your path and nettles in your death pillow, then do not hate evil. But if you want to live a happy life and die a peaceful death, walk in the ways of holiness. Hate evil until the end. If you truly love your Savior and would honor Him, then "hate evil."

We know of no cure for the love of evil in a Christian quite like abundant fellowship with the Lord Jesus. Dwell with Him and it is impossible to be at peace with sin:

> Order my footsteps by Thy word,
> And make my heart sincere;
> Let sin have no dominion, Lord,
> But keep my conscience clear.

ZEAL

"Be zealous."

—Revelation 3:19

If you want to see souls converted; if you want to hear the cry, "The kingdoms of this world have become the kingdoms of our Lord" (Revelation 11:15); if you want to place crowns on the Savior's head; if you want to lift His throne high, then be filled with zeal.

In God's plan, the method for the world's conversion is through the zeal of the church. Every grace shall do exploits, but zeal will be first. Prudence, knowledge, patience, and courage will follow, but zeal must lead the way.

It is not the extent of your knowledge, though that is useful; it is not the extent of your talent, though that is not to be despised—it is your zeal that will do great exploits.

This zeal is the fruit of the Holy Spirit, and it draws vital force from the continued operations of the Spirit. If our inner life dwindles, if our heart beats slowly before God, we will suffer apathy. But if we are strong and vigorous within, then we will feel a loving anxiety to see God's kingdom come, and His will be done on earth as it is in heaven (Matthew 6:10).

A deep sense of gratitude nourishes Christian zeal. Look at the pit from where you were dug, and you will find abundant reason to work to exhaustion for God.

Zeal is also stimulated by thoughts of our eternal future. Zeal looks with tearful eyes to the flames of hell and cannot sleep. Zeal looks with anxious gaze to the glories of heaven and awakens. Zeal feels the time is short compared with the work to be done. Thus zeal devotes all that it has to the cause of its Lord.

Zeal is constantly strengthened by remembering Christ's example. Jesus was clothed with zeal. Let us prove that we are His disciples by manifesting the same spirit of zeal.

WARRIORS

"Many fell dead, because the war was God's."

—1 Chronicles 5:22

Warrior, fighting under the banner of the Lord Jesus, read this verse with holy joy. If the war is God's, the victory is sure. As it was in the days of old, it is the same today.

The sons of Reuben, the Gadites, and half of the tribe of Manasseh could muster only less than forty-five thousand troops, but in the war with the Hagarites, they killed one hundred thousand. "They cried out to God in the battle. He heeded their prayer because they put their trust in Him" (1 Chronicles 5:18–20).

It is our duty to go in Jehovah's name, for even if we are only a handful, the Lord of Hosts is with us as our Captain.

They were armed with shields, bows, and swords, but they did not place their trust in these weapons. We too must use all the appropriate tools, but our confidence must rest in the Lord alone. "You, O Lord are a shield for me" (Psalm 3:3). The great reason for their extraordinary success was that the "war was God's."

Beloved, in fighting sin without and within, with doctrinal or practical error, with spiritual wickedness in high or low places, with devils or their allies, you are waging Jehovah's war. Unless Jehovah can be conquered, you need never fear defeat. Do not worry when facing superior numbers. Do not recoil from large difficulties or seeming impossibilities. Do not flinch from wounds or death. Strike with the two-edged sword of the Spirit, and the slain will lie in heaps.

The battle is the Lord's, and He will deliver His enemies into our hands. Enter the conflict with steadfast foot, strong hand, dauntless heart, and flaming zeal. The hosts of evil will fly like chaff before the gale:

Stand up! stand up for Jesus!

THE RIGHT QUESTION

"Now you shall see whether what I say will happen to you or not."

—Numbers 11:23

God made a promise to Moses that He would feed all of Israel with meat for a whole month (Numbers 11:20). Yet Moses, caught in a moment of unbelief, is at a loss to know how the promise can be fulfilled.

Moses looked to the creature instead of the Creator. Does the Creator expect the creature to fulfill His promises? No. God who makes the promise fulfills it with His own unaided omnipotence. If He speaks, it is done, and done by Him. God's promises do not depend for their fulfillment on the cooperation of the puny strength of humanity.

Even though we perceive Moses's mistake, we sometimes do the same thing. God has promised to supply our needs, but we look to the creature to fulfill what God has promised. Then, perceiving the creature to be weak and feeble, we indulge unbelief.

Why do we do this? Do we go to Alpine peaks for summer heat? Do we journey to the North Pole for sun-ripened fruit? These would be as foolish as looking to the weak for strength or to the creature to do the Creator's work.

Let us put the question on the right footing. The ground of faith is not the sufficiency of the visible means for fulfilling the promise, but the all-sufficiency of the invisible God. He will most certainly do what He has said. If we still mistrust after seeing that the responsibility lies with the Lord and not with the creature, then God's question comes home mightily, "Has the Lord's arm been shortened?" (Numbers 11:23).

May it happen in His mercy that, if this question is asked, our souls will hear the blessed declaration of our text, "Now you shall see whether what I say will happen to you or not."

JUNE 8, EVENING

LIFE'S SONG

"The Lord has done great things for us and we are glad."

—Psalm 126:3

Some Christians are inclined to look on the dark side of everything and to dwell more on what they have gone through than on what God has done for them. Ask their impression of the Christian life, and you hear about conflicts, afflictions, depressing adversities, and the sinfulness of their hearts. They scarcely mention the mercy and the help of God.

A healthy Christian will joyously say with David, "He also brought me up out of a horrible pit. Out of the miry clay. And set my feet upon a rock, and established my steps. He has put a new song in my mouth—Praise to our God" (Psalm 40:2–3). "You have done great things; O God, who is like You?" (Psalm 71:19).

It is true that we endure trials, but it is equally true that we are delivered from them. It is true that we have sin, but it is just as true that we have an all-sufficient Savior who overcame sin to deliver us from sin's dominion.

We cannot deny that we have been in the Slough of Despond and crept through the Valley of Humiliation. It would, however, be wicked to forget that we have been brought through them safely and that we have learned from the experiences. We have not remained there, because our Almighty Helper and Leader has "brought us out to rich fulfillment" (Psalm 66:12).

The deeper our troubles the louder our thanks will be to God, who has led and preserved us. Grief cannot mar the melody of our praise. Grief is merely the bass line of our life's song: "The Lord has done great things for us, and we are glad."

SEARCH

"Search the Scriptures."

—John 5:39

The Greek word for search signifies a strict, close, diligent, and curious search, like a search for gold, or a hunt for game. Do not be content with reading a chapter or two superficially, but, with the light of the Spirit, diligently seek the hidden meaning of the Word.

Holy Scripture requires searching, for much of it can be learned only by careful study. There is milk for babies, but there is also meat for adults. The rabbis wisely say, "A mountain of matter hangs on every word." Tertullian exclaims, "I adore the fullness of the Scriptures."

There is no profit in skimming the Book of God. We must dig and mine the Word until we obtain the hidden treasure. The door of the Word can only be opened with the key of diligence. The Scriptures must be searched. They are the writings of God. They bear the divine stamp and seal. Who would dare treat them lightly? Those who despise Scripture despise its Author.

The Word of God will richly reward its searchers. God is not asking us to sift a mountain of chaff for an occasional grain of wheat. The Bible is pure grain. All we have to do is open the silo door and find it.

Scripture grows on the student. It is full of surprises. Under the teaching of the Holy Spirit the Scripture glows with the splendor of revelation. It resembles a vast temple paved with rubies, emeralds, and all kinds of gems. There is no merchandise like the merchandise of scriptural truth.

Lastly, the Scriptures reveal Jesus. "These are they which testify of Me" (John 5:39). No more powerful motive can be urged on Bible readers.

Those who find Jesus find life, heaven, and all things. Happy are you who, searching your Bible, discover the Savior.

WHY AM I STILL HERE?

"We live to the Lord."

—Romans 14:8

If God had willed it, each of us might have entered heaven at the moment of conversion. It was not absolutely necessary for our preparation for immortality to tarry here. It is possible to be taken to heaven and to partake of the inheritance of the saints, even if one just came to a saving faith in Jesus.

It is true, though, that sanctification is a long and continuous process. We will not be perfected until we lay aside our bodies and enter glory. Nevertheless, had the Lord willed it, He might have changed us from imperfection to perfection and taken us to heaven at once.

Why then are we here? Would God keep His children out of paradise a moment longer than necessary? Why is the army of the living God still on the battlefield when one charge might give them the victory? Why are His children running here and there through a maze, when a solitary word from His lips would bring them to the center of their hopes in heaven?

The answer is that we are left here to "live to the Lord" and to bring others to know His love. We remain on earth to scatter good seed, to plow untilled ground, to preach salvation. We are here as "the salt of the earth" to be a blessing to the world (Matthew 5:13). We are here to glorify Christ in our daily lives. We are here as workers for Him and as workers together with Him (1 Corinthians 3:9). Make sure this is your work. Live earnest, useful, and holy lives to the praise of the glory of His grace.

Meanwhile, long to be with Him, and daily sing:

> My heart is with Him on His throne,
>   And ill can brook delay;
> Each moment listening for the voice,
>   'Rise up, and come away'.

REFLECTION

"These are they which testify of Me."

—John 5:39

Jesus Christ is the Alpha and the Omega, the First and the Last (Revelation 1:11). He is the constant theme of the Bible, from the first to the last page.

At the creation we see Jesus as one of the sacred Trinity (John 1:1–3). We glimpse Him in the promise of the woman's seed. We see Him typified in Noah's ark. We walk with Abraham as he sees the Messiah's day. We dwell in the tents of Isaac and Jacob, who are feeding on the gracious promise. We hear the venerable Israel talking of Shiloh. In the numerous types of the law, we find the Redeemer abundantly foreshadowed.

Prophets and kings, priests and preachers, all look one way: they stand as the cherubs did over the ark, desiring to look in and read the mystery of God's great propitiation.

In the New Testament, our Lord is even more apparent as the one pervading subject. It is not an ingot found here and there, or gold dust thinly scattered: It is a floor of solid gold. The whole substance of the New Testament is Jesus Christ crucified. Even the closing sentence is jewelled with the Redeemer's name. Always read Scripture in this light.

Consider the Word to be a mirror in which Christ looks down from heaven. We see His face reflected "in a mirror dimly" (1 Corinthians 13:12), but also in such glory as to prepare us to see Him face to face.

Perfumed by His love, this volume contains Jesus' letters to us. These pages are the garments of our King, and they smell of myrrh, aloe, and cassia.

Scripture is the royal chariot in which Jesus rides. It is the swaddling bands of the holy child Jesus. Unroll them and you find your Savior.

The quintessence of the Word of God is Christ.

JUNE 10, EVENING

AN EXOTIC FLOWER

"We love Him because He first loved us."

—1 John 4:19

The only light ever reflected on this planet comes from the sun, and there is no true love for Jesus that does not come from the Lord Jesus Himself. It is from this overflowing fountain of infinite love that our love to God is returned. It is a great and certain truth that "we love Him because He first loved us."

Anyone may have cold admiration when studying the works of God. Warm love, however, can be kindled in the heart only by God's Spirit. What a wonder that people like us could ever be brought to love Jesus. How marvelous that when we had rebelled against Him, He could display amazing love and draw us back.

No, there would never have been a grain of love toward God unless it was sown in us by the sweet seed of His love. Love in us, then, has for its parent the love of God, which has been poured out in our hearts by the Holy Spirit (Romans 5:5). After it is divinely born, it must be divinely nourished. Love is exotic. It is not a plant that will flourish naturally in human soil. It must be watered from above. Love for Jesus is a delicate flower, and, if the only nourishment it receives is from the rock of our hearts, it will soon wither. As love comes from heaven, it must feed on heavenly bread. It cannot exist in the wilderness unless it is fed by manna from on high. Love must feed on love.

The very soul and life of our love to God is His love to us.

> I love thee, Lord, but with no love of mine,
>   For I have none to give;
> I love thee, Lord; but all the love is thine,
>   For by thy love I live.
> I am as nothing, and rejoice to be
>   Emptied, and lost, and swallowed up in thee.

DESTROYED

"There He broke the arrows of the bow, the shield and sword of battle."

—Psalm 76:3

Our Redeemer's glorious cry, "It is finished" (John 19:30), was the death knell for all the adversaries of His people. It was the "breaking of the arrows of the bow, [and] the shield and sword of battle."

The hero of Golgotha, using His cross as an anvil and His anguish as a hammer, broke bundle after bundle of our sins. He broke the poison "arrows of the bow," trampling every indictment and destroying every accusation.

What glorious blows the mighty Breaker gives with a hammer far stronger than Thor's fabled weapon! The diabolical darts fly to fragments and the infernal shields are broken like potters' vessels!

From its sheath of hellish workmanship, He draws the dread sword of satanic power and snaps it across His knee as one would break dry kindling to throw in a fire.

Beloved, no sin of a believer can now be an arrow to wound. No condemnation can now be a sword to kill. The punishment of our sin was borne by Christ. A full atonement was made for all our iniquities by our blessed Substitute and Surety.

Who can accuse you? Who can condemn? Christ has died. Christ has risen again. Jesus has emptied the arrows of hell. Christ has quenched every fiery dart. Christ has broken off the head of every arrow of wrath. The ground is strewn with the splinters and artifacts of hell's weapons. They are visible only to remind us of our former danger and our great deliverance.

Sin no longer has dominion over us. Jesus has made an end of it. He has put it away forever. Enemy, your destructions have come to a perpetual end.

"Talk of all His wondrous works! Glory in His holy name. Let the hearts of those rejoice who seek the Lord. Remember His marvelous works which He has done" (Psalm 105:2–5).

JUNE 11, EVENING

SELF JUDGMENT

"You have been weighed in the balances and found wanting."

—Daniel 5:27

We frequently need to weigh ourselves on the scale of God's Word.

It is a holy exercise to read one of David's psalms and to meditate on each verse and ask, "Can I say this? Have I felt like David? Has my heart ever been broken because of sin as David's heart was when he wrote the penitential psalms? Has my soul been as full of true confidence in God in times of difficulty as his was when he sang of God's mercies in the cave of Adullam or in the holds of Engedi? Do I take the cup of salvation and call on the name of the Lord?"

Then turn to the life of Christ, and as you read, ask yourself if you are conformed to His likeness. Try to assess if you have the meekness, the humility, and the loving spirit that He always inculcated and displayed.

Then go to the epistles. Have you ever cried out with the apostle, "O wretched man that I am! Who will deliver me from this body of death?" (Romans 7:24). Have you ever felt Paul's self-abasement? Have you ever seemed to be the chief of sinners and less than the least of all the saints? Have you known anything of his devotion? Could you join him in saying, "For me to live is Christ, and to die is gain" (Philippians 1:21)?

If we read God's word as to test our spiritual condition we will have good reason to pray frequently, "Lord, I feel I have never been here. Oh bring me here. Give me the true repentance I just read about. Give me real faith. Give me a warmer zeal. Inflame me with more fervent love. Grant me the grace of meekness. Make me more like Jesus. Let me not be found wanting when weighed in the balances of the sanctuary, for fear I would be found wanting in the scales of judgment. Amen."

"For if we would judge ourselves we would not be judged" (1 Corinthians 11:31).

SAVED AND CALLED

"Who has saved us and called us with a holy calling."

—2 Timothy 1:9

The apostle writes in the perfect tense when he says, "Who has saved us." Believers in Christ Jesus are saved. They are not looked on as people in a hopeful state who may ultimately be saved; they are saved already.

Salvation is not a blessing to be enjoyed on the death bed, or to be sung about in a future state. Salvation is to be obtained, received, promised, and enjoyed now.

The Christian is perfectly saved in God's purpose. God has ordained salvation and that purpose is complete. You are saved because the price has been paid. "It is finished" was the cry of the Savior just before He died (John 19:30). The believer is perfectly saved in his covenant Head. Just as we fell in Adam, we live in Christ.

This complete salvation is accompanied by a holy calling. Those the Savior called on the cross are in due time effectually called to holiness by the power of God the Holy Spirit. Thus they leave their sins and endeavor to be like Christ. They choose holiness, not out of compulsion, but from the impulse of a new nature that leads them to rejoice in holiness as naturally as they formerly delighted in sin.

God did not call us because we were holy. He called us that we might be holy. Holiness is the beauty produced by His workmanship. The excellencies we see in a believer are as much the work of God as the atonement itself. Thus the fullness of the grace of God is brought out.

Salvation must be of grace, because the Lord is the author of it. What motive but grace could move Him to save the guilty? Salvation must be of grace, because the Lord works in such a manner that our righteousness is forever excluded.

This is the believer's privilege—a present salvation. This is the believer's calling—a holy life.

TAKE FREELY

"Whoever desires, let him take the water of life freely."

—Revelation 22:17

Jesus says, "Take the water of life freely." He wants no payment or preparation. He seeks no recommendation from our virtuous emotions. If you are willing, you are invited. Come!

You have no belief and no repentance, but come to Him and he will give them to you. Come just as you are. Take freely, without money and without price (Isaiah 55:1). He gives Himself to the needy.

Drinking fountains are valuable and we can hardly imagine anyone so foolish as to stand at one and cry, "I cannot drink because I do not have any money in my pocket." However poor you may be, there is the fountain, and you may drink. Thirsty pedestrians, whether dressed in work clothes or formal attire, do not need permission to drink from it. The generosity of some good people put the refreshing water there, and we drink it with no questions asked.

Perhaps the only people who go thirsty through streets where there are drinking fountains are certain ladies and gentlemen in their carriages, who, though very thirsty, would not think of being so unsophisticated as to get out to drink. To drink at a common fountain is beneath them, and so they ride by with parched lips.

Oh how many there are who are rich in their own good works and will not come to Christ. They say, "I will not be saved in the same way as the prostitute or the penniless. What! Go to heaven the same way as a garbage collector. Is there no path to glory but the path which led the thief? I will not be saved that way." Such people remain thirsty, without living water.

But "Let him who thirsts come. Whoever desires, let him take the water of life freely."

TO PRAY AND NOT TO PRAY

"Remove falsehood and lies far from me."
—Proverbs 30:8
"O my God, be not far from me."
—Psalm 38:21

Here we have two great lessons: what to earnestly pray against and what to earnestly pray for.

The happiest state of a Christian is the holiest state. Just as the most heat is nearest to the sun, the most happiness is nearest to Christ. Christians do not enjoy comfort when their eyes are fixed on falsehood. There is no satisfaction unless the soul is awakened to the ways of God. The world may find happiness elsewhere, but we cannot.

I do not blame the ungodly for rushing to pleasure. Why should I? Let them have their fill. That is all they have to enjoy. A converted wife who despaired for her husband's salvation was always very kind to him. She said, "I fear this is the only world in which he will be happy. Therefore, I have made up my mind to make him as happy as I can in it."

Christians, however, must seek their delights in a sphere higher than the insipid frivolities or sinful enjoyments of this world, for vain pursuits are dangerous to those who have been born again.

There was a philosopher who, while looking up at the stars, fell into a pit. But how deeply do they fall who look down! Their fall is fatal. Christians are not safe when the soul is lazy and God is far away. We are always safe as to our standing in Christ, but we are not safe with relying on past experiences in holiness and fellowship.

Satan rarely attacks believers who live near God. It is when we depart from God that we become spiritually starved and feed on falsehoods. Then the devil discovers our weakness and attacks. Satan may occasionally stand foot to foot with the child of God who is active in his Master's service, but such a battle is generally short.

The one who slips while going down to the Valley of Humiliation invites Apollyon (Revelation 9:11) to assail.

Oh for grace to walk humbly with our God!

JUNE 13, EVENING

HOLINESS AND DELIGHT

"Delight yourself also in the Lord, and He shall give you the desires of your heart."

—Psalm 37:4

These words must seem surprising to those who are strangers of vital godliness, but to the sincere believer it is a recognized truth. The life of a believer is described in our text as a delight in God. This verse certifies that true religion overflows with happiness and joy.

Ungodly people and mere professors of Christianity never look on their faith as joyful. To them it is dull service, duty, and necessity but never delight or pleasure. If they come to church at all, it is either for gain or because they dare not do otherwise. The thought of *delight* in religion is so strange to most people that no two words in their language are further apart than *holiness* and *delight*.

Believers who know Christ understand that *delight* and *faith* are so blessedly united that the gates of hell cannot prevail to separate them. Those who love God with all their hearts find that His ways are ways of pleasantness and all His paths are peace (Proverbs 3:17). The saints discover such joys, such brimful delights, and such overflowing blessedness in their Lord that, instead of serving Him from habit, they would follow Him anywhere, even if all the world cast out His name as evil.

We do not fear God because of any compulsion. Our faith is not chained. Our profession is not bondage. We are not dragged into holiness or driven to duty. No, our holiness is our pleasure. Our hope is our happiness. Our duty is our delight. Delight and true religion are as allied as root and flower, as indivisible as truth and certainty. They are two precious jewels glittering side by side in a setting of gold:

> Tis when we taste Thy love,
> Our joys divinely grow,
> Unspeakable like those above,
> And heaven begins below.

JUNE 14, MORNING

THE SHAME OF SIN

"O Lord, to us belongs shame . . . because we have sinned against You."

—Daniel 9:8

A deep sense and a clear sight of the gravity of sin and the punishment it deserves should make us lie prostrate before God's throne.

As Christians, what a tragedy that we have sinned. We are blessed, yet we are ungrateful. We are privileged beyond most, yet we have not produced fruit. Even those saints who have long been engaged in Christian warfare are embarrassed to look on their past.

As for the days before we were regenerated, may they be forgiven and forgotten. Since then, although we have not sinned as before, we have sinned against light and against love, light that penetrated our minds and love that made us rejoice. Oh the atrocity of the sin of a pardoned soul.

An unpardoned sinner sins cheaply compared with the sin of God's own elect. But look at David. Though many will talk of his sin, I ask you to look at his repentance. Hear his broken bones as each one moans its distressing confession (Psalm 51:8). Mark his tears as they fall (Psalm 6:6). Hear his deep sighs accompanying the soft music of his harp (Psalm 31:10).

If we have sinned, let us seek the spirit of penitence. Look at Peter! We speak a great deal about Peter denying his Master. But remember this, "Peter went out and wept bitterly" (Luke 22:62). Have we no denials of our Lord to lament with our tears? Our sins, before and after conversion, would consign us to the place of inextinguishable fire were it not for sovereign mercy that snatched us like brands from the burning.

My soul, bow under a sense of your natural sinfulness and worship your God. Admire the grace that saves you, the mercy that spares you, and the love that pardons you.

JUNE 14, EVENING

LAUGHTER

"And Sarah said, 'God has made me laugh, and all who hear will laugh with me'."

—Genesis 21:6

It was far beyond the power of nature, even contrary to its laws, that old Sarah could have a son.

It is beyond all ordinary rules that I, a poor, helpless, undone sinner, could find grace to carry in my soul the indwelling Spirit of the Lord Jesus. But I—who once despaired because my nature was as dry, withered, barren, and accursed as a howling wilderness—have been made to bring forth fruit unto holiness.

My mouth is filled with joyous laughter because of the singular, surprising grace I received from the Lord. I found Jesus, the promised seed, and He is mine forever. This morning, I lift up psalms of triumph to the Lord who remembers me. "My heart rejoices in the Lord. My strength is exalted in the Lord. I smile at my enemies, because I rejoice in Your salvation" (1 Samuel 2:1).

I want everyone who has heard of my great deliverance from hell and my most blessed visitation from on high to laugh for joy with me. I want to surprise my family with my abundant peace. I want to delight my friends with my ever-increasing happiness. I want to edify the church with my grateful testimony. I even want to impress the world with the cheerfulness of my daily conversation.

Bunyan tells us that Mercy laughed in her sleep. No wonder, she dreamed of Jesus. My joy will equal Mercy's as long as my Beloved is the theme of my daily thoughts.

The Lord Jesus is a deep sea of joy, and my soul will dive in and be swallowed up in the delights of His society.

Sarah looked on her Isaac and laughed, and all her friends laughed with her.

You, my soul, look on your Jesus and "rejoice with joy inexpressible and full of glory" (1 Peter 1:8).

THE ROSE AND THE LILY

"He who opens and no one shuts."

—Revelation 3:7

Jesus is the keeper of the gates of paradise. In front of every believer He opens a door that no one, human or devil, can close. What joy to find that faith in Him is the golden key to the everlasting doors. My soul, are you carrying this key in your pocket? Or are you trusting in some deceitful locksmith who will fail you in the end?

Listen to this preacher's parable and remember it. The great King prepared a banquet. He proclaimed to all the world that no one could enter unless they brought the fairest flower that blooms. People came to the palace gates by the thousands, and each one brought a flower they considered the queen of the garden. But some carried the deadly nightshade of superstition, or the flaunting poppies of false religion, or the hemlock of self-righteousness. These were not precious to the King, and the bearers were not let in.

My soul, have you gathered the rose of Sharon and the lily of the valley (Song of Solomon 2:1)? If so, when you come to heaven's gate all you need to do is show this choicest of flowers and the gates will open. With the rose of Sharon in your hand, you will find the way to the throne of God. Heaven has nothing that excels this rose's beauty, and out of all the flowers that bloom in paradise, none can rival the lily of the valley.

My soul, by faith get Calvary's blood-red rose in your hand. Wear it, and by communion preserve it, and by daily watchfulness make it your all in all. You will be blessed beyond all bliss and happy beyond all dreams.

Jesus, be mine forever. Be my God, my heaven, my all. Amen.

THE PROMISE

"And I give them eternal life and they shall never perish."

—John 10:28

There is no room for unbelief in a Christian's life. If a child of God mistrusts His love, His truth, His faithfulness, it displeases our Father. We should not grieve Him by doubting His upholding grace.

Christian, it is contrary to every promise in God's precious Word that we could be forgotten or left to perish. He is truth who said, "Can a woman forget her nursing child and not have compassion on the son of her womb? Surely they may forget. Yet I will not forget you. See, I have inscribed you on the palms of My hands" (Isaiah 49:15–16).

There is great value in the promise, "For the mountains shall depart and the hills be removed. But My kindness shall not depart from you, nor shall My covenant of peace be removed says the Lord, who has mercy on you" (Isaiah 54:10).

Hear the truth of Christ's words: "My sheep hear My voice, and I know them and they follow Me. And I give them eternal life and they shall never perish, neither shall anyone snatch them out of My hand. My Father, who has given them to Me, is greater than all and no one is able to snatch them out of My Father's hand" (John 10:27,29).

There would not be a doctrine of grace if one child of God perished. Where is the veracity of God, His honor, His power, His grace, His covenant, His oath, if just one who trusted in Christ was lost?

Banish those unbelieving fears that dishonor God. Arise, shake off the dust, and put on your beautiful garments. Remember it is sin to doubt His Word. He has promised that you will never perish. Let the eternal life in you rejoice with confidence:

> The gospel bears my spirit up:
> A faithful and unchanging God
> Lays the foundation for my hope,
> In oaths, and promises, and blood.

EXPOSITORY OF A VERSE

"The Lord is my light and my salvation; Whom shall I fear? The Lord is the strength of my life; Of whom shall I be afraid?"

—Psalm 27:1

That "the Lord is my light and my salvation" is personal. He is *my* light and *my* salvation, and of this I am so assured that I declare it boldly.

At salvation, divine light is poured into the soul. Where there is not enough light to reveal our darkness and to make us long for the Lord Jesus, there is no evidence of salvation.

After conversion, God is our joy, comfort, guide, teacher, and in every sense our light. He is the light within, the light around, the light reflected from us, and the light revealed to us. Note that it is not merely that the Lord gives light, but that He is light; not that He only gives salvation, but that He is salvation.

We who by faith have laid hold on God have all the covenant blessings in our possession. Our text is put in the form of a question, "Whom shall I fear?" This is a rhetorical question. The powers of darkness are not to be feared because the Lord, our light, destroyed them. The damnation of hell is not to be dreaded because the Lord is our salvation. This confidence does not rest on human strength but on the omnipotent power of "I AM" (Exodus 3:14).

That "the Lord is the strength of my life" is the third glowing phrase. It shows that the writer's hope was fastened with three cords that could not be broken. We may well indeed accumulate terms of praise where the Lord has lavished deeds of grace. Our life derives all its strength from God. If He makes us strong, all the machinations of the adversary can not make us weak.

"Of whom shall I be afraid?" This bold question looks into the future as well as to the present. And the answer is, "If God is for us, who can be against us" (Romans 8:31), either now or in time to come?

A REMARKABLE PRAYER

"Help, Lord."

—Psalm 12:1

This prayer is remarkable. It is short, timely, abounding, and suggestive.

David mourns the shortage of godly people and lifts his heart in supplication. When the creatures fail us, we fly to the Creator. David evidently felt his own weakness, or he would not have cried for help. At the same time, he honestly intended to exert himself, because the word *help* is inapplicable where we do nothing.

There is directness, clearness of perception, and distinctness of utterance in this two-word petition. More is said here than in many rambling outpourings. The Psalmist runs straight to God with a well-considered prayer. David knows what he is seeking and where to seek it. Lord, teach us to pray in the same blessed manner.

This prayer can be said frequently. In providential afflictions it is suitable for the tried believer who finds all other helpers failing. Students in doctrinal difficulty may obtain aid by lifting up the cry of "Help, Lord," to the Holy Spirit, who is the great teacher. Spiritual warriors in inner conflict may send to the throne for reinforcements with this request. Workers in heavenly labor may use it to obtain grace in time of need. Seeking sinners in doubt and alarm may offer the same weighty supplication. In fact, in every case, time, and place, this prayer will serve needy souls. "Help, Lord," is a prayer for the living and the dying, the suffering or the working, the rejoicing or the sorrowing. In Him our help is found. Do not be slow to cry to Him.

The answer to this prayer is certain when sincerely offered through Jesus. The Lord's character assures us that He will not leave His people. God's relationship to us as Father and Husband guarantee His aid. His gift of Jesus is a pledge of every good thing. His promise stands, "Fear not, I will help you" (Isaiah 41:13).

WELL DIGGING

"Then Israel sang this song: 'Spring up, O well! All of you sing to it."

—Numbers 21:17

The wilderness well of Beer was famous because it was the subject of a promise. That was the well where the Lord said to Moses, "Gather the people together, and I will give them water" (Numbers 21:16). When the people needed water, it was promised by their gracious God. When we need fresh supplies of heavenly grace, the covenant Lord has pledged to give us all we require.

The well was the cause of a song. Before the water gushed out, cheerful faith prompted the people to sing. As they saw the crystal fountain bubbling up, the music grew more joyous. In the same way, we who believe the promise of God should rejoice in the prospect of divine revival. As we experience it, our holy joy should overflow.

Are you thirsty? Do not murmur: Sing. Spiritual thirst is bitter, but you do not have to remain thirsty, for the promise indicates a well nearby. Look for it.

The well was also the center of prayer: "Spring up, O well." We must ask for what God has promised. If we fail to ask, we have neither the desire nor the faith to receive the promise.

This evening, let us ask that the Scripture we have read and our devotional exercise will not be an empty formality, but a channel of grace to our souls. Oh that God the Holy Spirit would work in us with all His mighty power, filling us with all the fullness of God.

Finally, the well was the object of effort. "The well the leaders sank, dug by the nation's nobles, by the lawgiver, with their staves" (Numbers 21:18). The Lord wants us obtaining grace actively. Our staves are poorly adapted for digging in the sand, but we must use them to the best of our ability. Prayer must not be neglected. The Lord will give us His grace. Seek Him in whom are fresh springs.

YOUR REDEEMER

"Your Redeemer."

Jesus the Redeemer is ours forever. All the offices of Christ are held on our behalf. He is our King, our Priest, and our Prophet. Whenever we read a new title of the Redeemer, let us appropriate Him as ours under that name. The Shepherd's staff, the Father's rod, the Captain's sword, the Priest's miter, the Prince's scepter, and the Prophet's mantle are all ours. Everything Jesus has He will employ for our exaltation, and all His prerogatives will be exercised for our defence. His fullness is our unfailing, inexhaustible treasure house.

The humanity He took on is also ours in all its perfection. Our gracious Lord gives us the spotless virtue of His stainless character, the meritorious mastery of a devoted life, and the reward He procured by obedient submission and incessant service. He makes His spotless garments our covering beauty. The glittering virtues of His character become our ornaments and jewels. The superhuman meekness of His death is our boast and glory.

He bequeaths His manger so we can learn how God came down to earth. His cross teaches how we may go to God. All His thoughts, emotions, actions, utterances, miracles, and intercessions were for us.

He walked the road of sorrow on our behalf. His heavenly legacy is the result of His life's labors. He is ours. He is not embarrassed to be acknowledged as "our Lord Jesus Christ," even though He is the blessed and only Potentate, the King of kings and the Lord of lords. Christ everywhere and everyway is our Christ forever and ever.

"Your Maker is your husband. The Lord of host is His name" (Isaiah 54:5). Oh my soul, this morning, by the power of the Holy Spirit, call Him, *your* Redeemer.

THE MASTER'S GARDEN

"I have come to my garden, my sister, my spouse."

—Song of Solomon 5:1

The believer's heart is Christ's garden. He bought it with His precious blood, and He enters to claim it as His own.

A garden implies separation, for it is not the open common, nor a wilderness. It is walled around or hedged in. Oh that we could see that wall between the church and the world made broader and stronger. It makes me sad to hear Christians say, "Well, there is no harm in this or in that." Sometimes we try to be as accommodating to the world as possible. Grace has run low in the soul that raises the question of how far it may go in conforming to the world.

A garden is a place of beauty. It far surpasses wild, uncultivated land. The genuine Christian must seek to be more excellent in life than even the best moralist, because Christ's garden should produce the best flowers. Even the best is poor when compared with what Christ deserves. Do not put Him off with withering and dwarf plants. The rarest, richest, and choicest lilies and roses should bloom in the heart Jesus calls His own.

The garden is a place of growth. We are not to remain undeveloped, always mere buds but no blossoms. We should "grow in the grace and knowledge of our Lord and Savior Jesus Christ" (2 Peter 3:18). Growth should be rapid where Jesus is the vineyard keeper and the Holy Spirit is the dew from above.

A garden is a place of retreat. The Lord would have us reserve our souls as a place where He can come. Oh that Christians would keep their hearts for Christ alone. Like Martha, we often worry and trouble ourselves with much serving so that we do not have room for Christ, and thus we fail to sit at His feet (Luke 10:41).

This evening, may the Lord grant you the sweet showers of His grace to water His garden.

COME HOLY SPIRIT

"And they were all filled with the Holy Spirit."

—Acts 2:4

Rich would be our blessings today if we were filled with the Holy Spirit. The effect of this sacred filling is impossible to overestimate. Life, comfort, light, purity, power, peace, and many other precious blessings are inseparable from the Spirit's benevolent presence.

As sacred oil, He anoints believers and sets them apart to the priesthood of saints. He gives grace to execute duties. As the true purifying water, He cleanses and sanctifies believers from the power of sin and works the Lord's good pleasure in them. As the light, He shows people their lost condition and reveals the Lord Jesus to them. He guides believers in the way of righteousness. Enlightened by His pure celestial ray, they are no longer in darkness but are in the light of the Lord.

As fire, He both purges our dross and sets our consecrated nature ablaze. He is the sacrificial flame that enables us to offer our entire soul as a living sacrifice. As heavenly dew, He removes our barrenness and fertilizes our lives. Oh that He would drop on us at this early hour! Such morning dew would be a sweet beginning for this day.

As the dove, with wings of peaceful love, He grieves over His church and over the souls of believers. As a Comforter, He dispels the cares and doubts that mar the peace of His beloved ones. He descends on the chosen as He did on the Lord in the Jordan (John 1:32). "For as many as are led by the Spirit of God, these are sons of God, . . . by whom we cry out, Abba Father" (Romans 8:14–15).

As the wind, He brings the breath of life. "The wind blows where it wishes" (John 3:8), performing the quickening operations by which the spiritual creation is animated and sustained.

Would to God that we might feel His presence this day and every day.

JUNE 19, MORNING

SHADOWS

"My beloved is mine . . . . Until the day breaks and the shadows flee away. Turn, my beloved, and be like a gazelle or a young stag upon the mountains of Bether." —Song of Solomon 2:16–17

Surely if there is a happy verse in the Bible, this is it: "My beloved is mine and I am His." It is so peaceful, so full of assurance, so running over with happiness and contentment that it might well have been written by the same hand that penned the twenty-third Psalm.

Yet these verses are not entirely sunlit. There is a cloud in the sky that casts a shadow over the scene. Listen: "Until the day breaks and the shadows flee away."

There is also that word about the "mountains of Bether," or "mountains of division." To our love, anything with division is bitter.

Beloved, this may be your present state of mind. You do not doubt your salvation. You know Christ is yours, but you are not feasting with Him. You understand your vital interest in Him. There is no doubt that you are His and He is yours, but His left hand is not under your head and His right hand does not embrace you (Song of Solomon 8:3).

A shade of sadness is cast over your heart, perhaps by affliction, or by the temporary absence of your Lord, but even so you exclaim, "I am His." You are forced to go to your knees and pray, "Until the day breaks and the shadows flee away."

Where is He? The answer comes that He feeds among the lilies. If we would find Christ, we must have fellowship with His people. We must come to the ordinances with His saints.

Oh for an evening glimpse of Him! Oh to have dinner with Him tonight.

SIFTING

"For surely I will command, and will sift the house of Israel among all nations, as grain is sifted in a sieve; yet not the smallest grain shall fall to the ground." —Amos 9:9

Every sifting comes by divine command and permission. Satan must ask before he can lay a finger on Job (Job 1:12).

Our sifting is the direct work of heaven. The text says, "I will command, and will sift the house of Israel." Satan, like a drudge, may hold the sieve, hoping to destroy the grain, but the overruling hand of the Master purifies the grain by the very process that the enemy intended to be destructive.

Precious—but much sifted—grain on the Lord's floor, take comfort in this blessed fact: The Lord directs both sifting and sieve to His glory and your eternal good.

The Lord Jesus will surely use the fan to divide the precious from the vile. The pile on the barn floor is not clean food; the winnowing process must continue. In the sieve, true weight alone has power. Husks and chaff have no substance and will blow away in the wind. Only solid grain will remain.

Observe the complete safety of the Lord's wheat. The least grain has a promise of preservation. God sifts, and it is a stern and terrible work. He sifts us in all places, "among all nations." He sifts in the most efficient manner, "as grain is sifted in a sieve." Yet, not the smallest, the lightest, or the most shrivelled grain falls to the ground.

Every individual believer is precious in the sight of the Lord. A shepherd would not lose one sheep. A jeweler would not lose one diamond. A mother would not lose one child. The Lord will not lose one of His redeemed.

Regardless of how insignificant we are, if we are the Lord's, let us rejoice for we are preserved in Christ Jesus.

HURRY

"They immediately left their nets and followed Him."

—Mark 1:18

When Simon and Andrew heard the call of Jesus they immediately obeyed. If we would immediately practice what we hear in teaching and read in good books, we would be spiritually enriched. You will not lose your loaf of bread if you eat it. You cannot be deprived of the benefit of a doctrine that you practice.

Most readers and hearers purpose to make changes, but unfortunately their resolution is a blossom that never buds and never produces fruit. They wait, they waver, and they forget. Like ponds that freeze at night, they thaw during the day only to be frozen again. That fatal *tomorrow* is blood red with the murder of proposed resolutions. It is the slaughterhouse of the innocent.

We are concerned that this book of devotions will produce fruit. So we pray that readers will not be readers only, but will use these devotions in daily practice. The practice of truth is the most profitable reading of all. Should you be impressed with any duty while perusing these pages, hurry and do it before the holy glow departs. Leave your nets and go do your Master's work. Do not give the devil a place by your delay. Hurry while opportunity and desire are in happy conjunction. Do not be caught in your own nets. Break the meshes of worldliness and go where glory calls you.

Happy is the writer whose readers resolve to carry out a book's teachings. That author's harvest will be a hundredfold, and his Master will have great honor. Would to God that such a reward be given these brief meditations and hurried hints.

Grant it, Oh Lord, to your servant. Amen.

MY WONDERFUL LORD

"You are fairer than the sons of men."

—Psalm 45:2

The entire person of Jesus is one gem. His total life is one impression of the seal. He is altogether complete, not only in His several parts, but also as a gracious all-glorious whole.

His character is not a mass of beautiful colors mixed with confusion. He is not a heap of precious stones laid carelessly on one another. He is a picture of beauty and a breastplate of glory. In Him, all good things are in their proper place and assist in adorning each other. Not one feature in His glorious person attracts attention at the expense of another. He is perfect and altogether lovely.

Oh Jesus! Your power, Your grace, Your justice, Your tenderness, Your truth, Your majesty, and Your immutability make up a God-man that neither heaven nor earth have seen elsewhere.

Your infancy, Your eternity, Your sufferings, Your triumphs, Your death, and Your immortality are all woven in one gorgeous and seamless tapestry. You are music without discord. You are many, but not divided. You are all things, yet not diversity. As all the colors blend into one resplendent rainbow, all the glories of heaven and earth meet in You. They unite so wondrously that there is none like You.

If all the most excellent virtues were bound in one bundle, they could not rival You. You are the mirror of all perfection. You have been anointed with the holy oil of myrrh and cassia that God has reserved for You alone. Your fragrance is holy perfume unequalled and unmatched: Each spice is fragrant but the compound is truly divine.

> Oh, sacred symmetry! oh, rare connection
> Of many perfects, to make one perfection!
> Oh, heavenly music, where all parts do meet
> In one sweet strain, to make one perfect sweet!

THE BASICS

"The solid foundation of God stands."

—2 Timothy 2:19

This is the foundation of our faith, that "God was in Christ reconciling the world to Himself, not imputing their trespasses to them" (2 Corinthians 5:19).

The great facts on which genuine faith rely are these: "The Word became flesh and dwelt among us" (John 1:14); "Christ also suffered once for sins, the just for the unjust, that He might bring us to God" (1 Peter 3:18); "Who Himself bore our sins in His own body on the tree" (1 Peter 2:24); "the chastisement for our peace was upon Him and by His stripes we are healed" (Isaiah 53:5). In one word, the great pillar of the Christian's hope is *substitution*.

The vicarious sacrifice of Christ is for the guilty, Christ being made sin for us that we might be made the righteousness of God in Him (2 Corinthians 5:21). Christ offered up a true and proper removal of guilt and a substitutionary sacrifice for as many as the Father gave Him, for as many as are known to God by name, for as many as are recognized in their own hearts by trusting in Jesus; this is the cardinal fact of the gospel.

If this foundation were removed, what could we do? But it stands as firm as God's throne. We know it. We rest on it. We meditate on it. We proclaim it. We want to be actuated and moved by gratitude for it in every part of our life and conversation.

Direct attacks are frequently made on the doctrine of the atonement because the world cannot bear substitution. It gnashes its teeth at the thought of the Lamb of God bearing its sin. But we who know by experience the preciousness of this truth will unceasingly proclaim it with confidence. We will not dilute it, change it, or fritter it away.

It will still be Christ, a positive substitute, bearing human guilt and suffering in our place. We cannot—we dare not—give it up, because it is our life. We believe that "the solid foundation of God stands."

JUNE 21, EVENING

BUILDING

"Yes, He shall build the temple of the Lord. He shall bear the glory."

—Zechariah 6:13

Christ is the builder of His spiritual temple, and He has built it on the mountains of His unchanging affection, His omnipotent grace, and His infallible truth.

As David prepared the material for Solomon's temple (1 Chronicles 22:14), the Lord is preparing material for His temple. There are the cedars of Lebanon, but they are not framed for the building. They are not cut down and shaped into planks whose beautiful odor will gladden the courts of the Lord's house in Paradise.

There are the rough stones still in the quarry, which must be cut and squared. This is Christ's own work. Each individual believer is being prepared, polished, and made ready for their place in the temple by Christ's own hands. Afflictions cannot sanctify unless they are used by Him. Our prayers and efforts cannot make us ready for heaven unless Jesus creates our hearts anew.

In the building of Solomon's temple, "no hammer, or chisel or any iron tool was heard in the temple while it was being built" (1 Kings 6:7). All the material was delivered cut to size, perfectly ready for the exact spot it was to occupy.

In the temple Jesus is building, the preparation is done on earth. When we reach heaven, there will be no sanctifying us there, no squaring with affliction, no polishing with suffering. Christ will make us suitable here. When He has completed it, we will be carried by a loving hand across the stream of death and brought to the heavenly Jerusalem. There we will be eternal pillars in the temple of our Lord:

> Beneath His eye and care,
> The edifice shall rise,
> Majestic, strong, and fair,
> And shine above the skies.

JUNE 22, MORNING

UNSHAKEN

"That the things which cannot be shaken may remain."

—Hebrews 12:27

We have many things that can be shaken. There is nothing solid or stable under the rolling skies. Change is written on everything. Yet we have certain "things which cannot be shaken." This evening I invite you to think about them, that if all the things that could be shaken were taken away, you may find real comfort in the things that remain.

Whatever your losses have been or may be, you still enjoy present salvation. You are standing at the foot of His cross, trusting alone in the merit of Jesus' precious blood. No rise or fall of the market can interfere with your salvation. No bank failure, no decline in business or bankruptcies, can shake that. You are a child of God, God is your Father, and no change of circumstances can rob you of that. If losses bring poverty and strip you bare, "let not your heart be troubled" (John 14:1). You can still say, "He is my Father," and that "in His house are many mansions" (John 14:2).

You have another permanent blessing, the love of Jesus Christ. He who is God and Man loves you with the strength of His affectionate nature, and nothing can affect that. "Though the fig tree may not blossom, nor fruit be on the vines. Though the labor of the olive may fail and the fields yield no food. Though the flock may be cut off from the fold and there be no herd in the stalls—Yet I will rejoice in the Lord. I will joy in the God of my salvation" (Habakkuk 3:17–18).

Our best portion and richest heritage cannot be lost. Whatever the trial, do not be cast down by what happens in this poor fleeting state of time. Our hope is above the sky. We can be as calm as the summer's ocean as we see the wreck of all earthly things, because we rejoice in the God of our salvation.

HALF BAKED

"Ephraim is a cake unturned."

A cake unturned is half-baked, and so was Ephraim. In many respects he was untouched by divine grace. Although there was some partial obedience, there was a lot of rebellion.

My soul, is this the case with you? Are you thorough in the things of God? Has grace touched the very center of your being? Can you feel its divine operation in your life, your actions, your words, and your thoughts? To be sanctified in spirit, soul, and body should be your aim and prayer.

Although sanctification may not now be perfected in you, it must be evident in all your actions for there cannot be the appearance of holiness in one place and sin reigning in another. If this is the case, you are a half-baked cake.

A cake not turned is soon burned. Although you cannot have too much true religion, there are some who seem burned black with bigoted zeal. Others are charred to a cinder with a vain Pharisaic ostentation of those religious performances that fit their disposition. An assumed appearance of superior sanctity frequently accompanies a total absence of all vital godliness. Those saints in public are devils in private. They deal in flour by day and in soot by night. The cake burned on one side is mere dough on the other.

If this is I, Oh Lord, turn me. Turn my unsanctified side to the fire of Your love. Let me feel the sacred glow. Let my burned side cool while I learn my weakness and that I need the heat from Your heavenly flame.

Do not let me be "a double-minded man, unstable in all [his] ways" (James 1:8). Let me be entirely under the powerful influence of reigning grace. If I am left as an unturned cake and am not on both sides the subject of Your grace, I will be consumed forever in everlasting burnings. Amen.

ADOPTED BY HEAVEN

"Waiting for the adoption."

—Romans 8:23

In this world the saints are God's children, but the world can discover this only by certain moral characteristics, for our adoption is not yet manifested or openly declared.

Among the Romans, a child might be adopted and privately kept for a long time. But there was a second public adoption in which the child was brought before the constituted authorities. The child's clothing was removed and the adopting father dressed the child in a manner appropriate to the family status.

"Beloved, now we are the children of God; and it has not yet been revealed what we shall be" (1 John 3:2). We are not dressed in the clothing that is appropriate for a member of the royal family of heaven. We are wearing in this flesh and blood what we wore as the children of Adam. But we know that "when He is revealed, we shall be like Him, for we shall see Him as He is" (1 John 3:2).

Can you imagine a child taken from the lowest ranks of society and adopted by a Roman senator? That child might say, "I long for the day when I will be publicly adopted. Then I will leave these common cloths and wear senatorial robes." That child is happy in what has been given and eagerly awaits the fullness of what has been promised.

This is how it is with us. We are waiting to put on our proper clothes. We are young nobles and have not yet worn our crowns. We are young brides eagerly awaiting the marriage day. Our very happiness makes us groan for more. Our joy, like a swollen spring, longs to well up like an Icelandic geyser, leaping to the skies. Our joy heaves and groans within our spirit for want of space to manifest itself to the world.

INSIDE INFORMATION

"A certain woman . . . said to Him, 'Blessed is the womb that bore You, and the breasts which nursed You!' But He said, ' . . . blessed are those who hear the word of God and keep it'." —Luke 11:27-28

It is fondly imagined by some that it must have been a special privilege to have been the mother of our Lord. They supposed that Mary had the benefit of looking into His heart in a way that we could not hope to do. There may be some plausibility in this supposition, but not as much as some may think.

We do not know if Mary knew more than others. What she did know she did well to hide in her heart (Luke 2:19). From anything we read in the Evangelists, it does not appear that she was instructed better than any other disciple. Nevertheless, all that she knew, we also may discover. Do you wonder why I say this?

"The secret of the Lord is with those who fear Him. And He will show them His covenant" (Psalm 25:14). Remember the Master's words: "No longer do I call you servants, for a servant does not know what his master is doing; but I have called you friends, for all things that I heard from My Father I have made known to you" (John 15:15).

Our blessed divine revealer of secrets tells us His heart. He holds back nothing that would be of benefit. His own assurance is, "If it were not so I would have told you" (John 14:2).

This morning He reveals Himself to us, but not to the world. We may not shout, "Blessed is the womb that bore You," but we will bless God that, having heard the Word and kept it, we have as true a communion with the Savior as the Virgin had. We have as true an acquaintance with the secrets of His heart as she can be supposed to have obtained. Happy is the soul to be so privileged.

CONSCIENCE

"Shadrach, Meshach, and Abednego answered and said . . . But let it be known to you, O king, that we do not serve your gods.'"

—Daniel 3:16,18

This narrative of courage and marvelous deliverance of the three holy children, or rather three holy champions, is designed to uphold truth in the teeth of tyranny or the jaws of death.

Let young Christians especially learn from the champions' example. In matters of faith in religion and uprightness in business, never sacrifice your conscience. Lose all rather than lose your integrity. When everything else is gone, hold on to a clear conscience. It is the rarest jewel that can adorn a mortal.

Do not be guided by the will-o'-the wisp policy. Be led by the pole star of divine authority. Follow the right regardless of the hazards. When you see no advantage, "walk by faith, not by sight" (2 Corinthians 5:7).

Do God the honor of trusting Him when it comes to loss because of principle. See if He will be your debtor. See if He will prove that even in this life "godliness with contentment is great gain" (1 Timothy 6:6). "Seek first the kingdom of God and His righteousness and all these things shall be added to you" (Matthew 6:33).

Should it happen that, in the providence of God, you are a loser because of your conscience, you will find the Lord repays not with the silver of earthly prosperity, but with the gold of spiritual joy.

Remember, our lives do not consist in the abundance of what we possess. An innocent spirit, a heart void of offense, and the favor and smile of God are greater than the riches of the mines of Ophir or the commerce of Tyre.

"Better is a dinner of herbs where love is, than a fatted calf with hatred" (Proverbs 15:17). An ounce of the heart's contentment is worth a ton of gold.

CLIMBING THE MOUNTAIN

"Get up into the high mountain."

—Isaiah 40:9

Our knowledge of Christ is similar to climbing one of the Welsh mountains. At the base you see very little. The mountain appears to be only half as high as it really is. Confined in a valley, you see only the rippling brooks as they descend to the stream at the foot of the mountain.

As you climb the first rising knoll, the valley lengthens and widens beneath you. Go higher, and you see the countryside for four or five miles. You are delighted with the widening view.

Climb higher and the scene enlarges. When you reach the summit and look east, west, north, and south, you see almost all of England. Yonder is a forest in some distant county, perhaps two hundred miles away. Far off is the sea and the masts of the ships in a busy port. Over there is a shining river. In the distance are the smoking chimneys of a manufacturing town. This panorama pleases and delights you. You could not have imagined that so much could be seen at this elevation.

The Christian life is similar. When we first believe in Christ, we see only a little of Him, but the higher we climb the more we discover of His beauties. Who has ever reached the summit? Who has been "able to comprehend with all the saints what is the width and length and depth and height—to know the love of Christ which passes knowledge" (Ephesians 3:19)?

Paul, as an old grey-haired man shivering in a Roman dungeon, could say with greater emphasis than we, "I know whom I have believed" (2 Timothy 1:12). Each of Paul's experiences had been similar to climbing a hill. Each trial was like the ascension of another summit. In his death he would gain the mountain top, where he would see the whole of the faithfulness and love of Him to whom he had committed his soul.

Dear friend, "get up into the high mountain."

ASSURANCE

"The dove found no resting place for the sole of her foot."

—Genesis 8:9

Reader, can you find rest outside the ark, Christ Jesus? Then your religion is vain. Are you satisfied with anything less than a conscious knowledge of your affiliation and share in Christ? Then woe to you. If you profess to be a Christian and yet find full satisfaction in worldly pleasures and pursuits, your profession is false.

If your soul can stretch at rest in a bed long enough and under covers wide enough in the chambers of sin, then you are a hypocrite. You are far from good thoughts of Christ or any perception of His preciousness.

If, on the other hand, you feel you could indulge in sin without punishment, yet that indulging would be punishment in itself; if you could have the whole world and live in it forever, and that would be misery; then be of good courage because God—your God—is what your soul craves, and you are a child of God.

With all your sins and imperfections be comforted, knowing that if your soul has no rest in sin, you are not a sinner. If you are still crying after and craving after something better, then Christ has not forgotten you, because you have not forgotten Him.

Believers cannot do without their Lord. Words are inadequate to express their thoughts of Him. We cannot live on the sand of the wilderness; we want the manna that drops from on high. Our easily broken earthenware bottles of creature confidence cannot yield a drop of moisture. We drink of the rock that follows us and that rock is Christ.

When you feed on Him, your soul can sing, "He satisfies my mouth with good things, so that my youth is renewed like the eagle's" (Psalm 103:5).

If you do not have Him, your overflowing wine vats and well filled barns cannot give satisfaction. You can only commiserate over them in the words of wisdom, "Vanity of vanities, all is vanity" (Ecclesiastes 1:2).

JUNE 25, EVENING

AWFUL GRANDEUR

"Have you become like us?"

—Isaiah 14:10

What will be the apostate's doom when they stand before God? How will they endure that voice, "Depart from Me, you cursed, into everlasting fire" (Matthew 25:41). What will be their shame on the last great day when, before the assembled multitudes, these apostates will be unmasked?

See the sinners who never professed Christ rising from their beds of fire and pointing to the apostates. "There they are," says one. "Will they preach the gospel in hell?" "There," says another, "he rebuked me and he was a hypocrite." "Ah," says another, "Here comes a church going member who boasted of having everlasting life. Look at him now!" No greater eagerness will ever be seen among Satanic tormentors than that day when the devils drag the hypocritical souls down to perdition.

Bunyan pictured this with awe-full poetic grandeur when he wrote of the backway to hell: "Seven devils bound the wretch with nine cords and dragged him from the road to heaven, where he had professed to walk, and thrust him through the back door into hell."

Professors of Christ, watch out for that back way to hell. "Examine yourselves as to whether you are in Christ. Test yourselves. Do you not know yourself, that Christ is in you? (2 Corinthians 13:5).

It is the easiest thing in the world to give a lenient verdict when you are to be tried. But be just and true. Be just to all, but rigorous to yourself. Remember, if you do not build on the rock, the house will have a great fall.

May the Lord give you sincerity, constancy, and firmness. In no day, however evil, may you turn aside.

ESCAPING CORRUPTION

"Having escaped the corruption that is in the world through lust."

—2 Peter 1:4

Banish forever any thoughts of indulging the flesh if you want to live in the power of your risen Lord. It is evil for the believer, who is alive in Christ, to dwell in the corruption of sin.

"Why do you seek the living among the dead?" the angel asked Magdalene (Luke 24:5). Should the living dwell in the tomb? Should divine life be enclosed in the burial vault of fleshly lusts? How can we partake of the cup of the Lord and still drink the cup of sin?

Believers, surely you are delivered from open lusts and sins, but have you also escaped the secret and delusive bait of the satanic fowler? Have you deserted the lust of pride? Have you avoided idleness? Have you departed carnal security? Are you daily seeking to live above worldliness, the pride of life, and ensnaring selfishness?

Remember, this is why you have been enriched with the treasures of God. If you are indeed the chosen of God and beloved by Him, do not permit all the lavish treasure of grace to be wasted. Follow after holiness, which is the Christian's crown and glory.

An unholy church is useless to the world. It is of no value. It is an abomination. It is hell's laughter and heaven's abhorrence. The worst evils that have ever come on the world have been brought by an unholy church.

Oh Christian, the vows of God are on you. You are God's priest: Walk according to your position. You are God's royalty: Reign over your lusts. You are God's chosen: Do not associate with the sin of this world.

Heaven is your portion, so live like a heavenly spirit. Prove that you have true faith in Jesus. There cannot be faith in the heart unless there is holiness in the life:

> Lord, I desire to live as one
> Who bears a blood-bought name,
> As one who fears but grieving Thee,
> And knows no other shame.

JUNE 26, EVENING

SEPARATION

"Only you shall not go very far away."

—Exodus 8:28

This is a crafty word from the lips of the archtyrant, Pharaoh. If the Israelite slaves want to leave Egypt, they cannot go far. Pharaoh wants them close enough to feel the terror of his arms and to be observed by his spies.

Like Pharaoh, the world despite its clamor for diversity, does not love the nonconformity to its ways and dissent from them, by those who follow Christ. It would have us be more tolerant and not be severe. Death to the world and burial with Christ are experiences the carnal mind treats with ridicule. Thus the ordinance of separation is almost universally neglected and scorned.

Worldly wisdom recommends the path of compromise and moderation. According to this carnal policy, purity is desirable but we are warned about being too precise. Truth, of course, is to be followed, but error should not be severely denounced.

"Yes," says the world, "be spiritually minded by all means, but do not deny yourself a little happy society, an occasional 'blow out' and a wild Christmas party. What is the point of being against something when it is fashionable and everybody does it?"

Multitudes of professing Christians, to their eternal ruin, yield to this terrible, cunning advice. If we would totally follow the Lord, we must go to the wilderness of separation and leave the Egypt of the carnal world behind. Leave its maxims, leave its pleasures, and leave its religion. Go where the Lord calls His sanctified ones.

When the town is on fire, our house cannot be too far from the flames. When the plague sweeps the land, we too are in danger. The further one is from a viper the better, and the further from worldly conformity the better.

To all true believers, let the trumpet call be sounded. "Come out from among them and be separate" (2 Corinthians 6:17).

YOUR CALLING

"Let each one remain in the same calling in which he was called."

—1 Corinthians 7:20

Some people have the foolish notion that the only way they can live for God is to become a minister or a missionary. Think of how many would be shut out from any opportunity of magnifying the Most High if this were the case. Beloved, it is not the office, it is earnestness. It is not the position, it is grace that enables us to glorify God.

God is surely glorified at the shoemaker's table, where the godly worker plies the awl and sings of the Savior's love. God may be glorified here more than in many cathedrals where official religion performs its scant duties.

The name of Jesus is glorified by the poor, uneducated teamster driving a team of horses and blessing God. Speaking to fellow laborers by the roadside, the teamster glorifies Jesus as much as Boanerges thundering the gospel around the country. God is glorified as we serve Him in our proper vocations.

Take care, dear reader, that you do not forsake the path of duty by leaving your occupation. Take care that you do not dishonor your profession while in it. Think little of yourself, but do not think little of your calling. Every lawful trade may be sanctified by the gospel to the noblest ends.

Turn to the Bible and you will find the most menial forms of labor connected either with the most daring deeds of faith or with people whose lives have been illustrious for holiness.

Do not be discontent with your calling. Whatever God has made your position or your work (Psalm 75:6-7), stay there unless you are positive that God calls you to something else.

Let your first duty be to glorify God to the utmost of your power. Fill your present sphere with His praise. If He wants you to move, He will show you.

This evening, set aside false ambition. Embrace peaceful content.

JUNE 27, EVENING

EYES ON JESUS

"Looking unto Jesus."

—Hebrews 12:2

It is the work of the Holy Spirit to turn our eyes from self to Jesus. Satan's work is just the opposite. Satan insinuates, "Your sins are too great for pardon. You have no faith. You do not repent enough. You will never be able to continue to the end. You do not have the joy of God's children. You have only a weak grip on Jesus." These are thoughts about self, and we will never find comfort or assurance if we look to them.

The Holy Spirit turns our eyes entirely away from self. When He tells us that we are nothing, He tells us that Christ is all in all. Remember, it is not your hold on Christ, but Christ Himself that saves. It is not your joy in Christ, but Christ Himself that saves. It is not even your faith in Christ, though that is the instrument; it is Christ's blood and merits. Do not even look at your hand that is grasping Christ: look to Christ Himself. Do not look to your hope either, but to Jesus, the source of your hope. Do not look to your faith, but to Jesus, the author and finisher of your faith (Hebrews 12:2).

We will never find happiness by looking at *our* prayers, works, or feelings. It is who Jesus is, not what we are, that gives the soul rest.

If we want to overcome Satan and have peace with God, we must be "looking to Jesus." Simply keep your eye on Him. Let His death, His suffering, His merits, His glories, and His intercession be fresh on your mind. When you wake in the morning, look to Him. When you lie down at night, look to Him. Do not let your hopes or fears come between you and Jesus. Follow after Him. He will never fail you:

> My hope is built on nothing less
>   Than Jesu's blood and righteousness:
> I dare not trust the sweetest frame,
>   But wholly lean on Jesu's name.

CHRIST MUST BE EVERYTHING

"But Aaron's rod swallowed up their rods."

—Exodus 7:12

This incident is instructive of the sure victory of divine handiwork over all opposition. Whenever a divine principle is formed in the heart, even though the devil may fashion a counterfeit and produce a swarm of opponents, it will swallow up all its foes.

If God's grace takes possession of a person, the world's magicians may throw down all their cunning and poisonous rods, but Aaron's rod will swallow them up.

The sweet attractions of the cross will woo and win the heart. Those who once lived only for this deceitful earth now have their eyes on the upper spheres, and with wings they mount to celestial heights. When grace has won the day, the sinner seeks the world to come.

This may also be observed in the life of the believer. What multitudes of foes our faith has met! The devil threw down our host of old sins, and they turned to serpents. Ah, but the cross of Jesus destroyed them all. Faith in Christ makes quick work of sin.

Then the devil launched another host of serpents in the form of worldly trials, temptations, and unbelief. But faith in Jesus overcame them. The same absorbing principle shines in the faithful service of God! With an enthusiastic love for Jesus, difficulties are overcome, sacrifices become pleasure, sufferings are honors.

Unfortunately, there are many who profess this religion but do not have it. The Christianity they have will not pass this test. Examine yourself, my reader, on this point. Aaron's rod proved its heaven-given power. Is your Christianity proving itself?

If Christ is anything, He must be everything.

Do not rest until love and faith in Jesus is the master passion of your soul.

ASLEEP IN JESUS

"God will bring with Him those who sleep in Jesus."

—1 Thessalonians 4:14

Do not imagine that the soul sleeps in insensibility. "Today you will be with Me in Paradise" is the whisper of Christ to every dying saint (Luke 23:43). They "sleep in Jesus," but their souls are before the throne of God praising Him day and night. They sing hallelujahs to Him who washed their sins in His blood (Revelation 19:6).

The body sleeps in its lonely bed of earth beneath the grass. The idea connected with this sleep is *rest*. Sleep makes each night a Sabbath rest from the day's work. Sleep shuts the door of the soul and orders all intruders to wait. The toilworn believer quietly sleeps like a weary child slumbering on its mother's breast.

Happy are those who die in the Lord. They rest from labor, and their works follow them (Revelation 14:13). Their quiet rest will never be broken until God rouses them to their full reward. Guarded by angels and curtained by eternal mysteries, the inheritors of glory sleep on until the fullness of time will bring the fullness of redemption.

What an awakening they will have! They were laid in their last resting place weary and worn, but that is not how they will rise. They went to their rest with deeply furrowed brows and wasted features, but they will wake in beauty and glory. The shrivelled seed, so destitute of form and beauty, rises from the dust a beautiful flower. The winter of the grave gives way to the spring of redemption and the summer of glory.

Blessed is death for Christians, since through it the divine power disrobes us of these work clothes and dresses us in the wedding garment of incorruption. Blessed are those who "sleep in Jesus."

KEEP US

". . . God withdrew from him, in order to test him, that He might know what was in his heart."

—2 Chronicles 32:31

Hezekiah had much pride. Self-righteousness had crept in because he thought he was great. His carnal security resulted in the grace of God being withdrawn for a period of time. This accounts for his folly with the Babylonians.

If the grace of God should leave the best Christian, how careful should we, the worst transgressors, be. If left to your own devices, you who are the warmest for Christ would cool to sickening Laodicean lukewarmness (Revelation 3:16); you who are sound in the faith would be white with the leprosy of false doctrine; you who now walk with integrity would reel and stagger with the drunkenness of evil passions.

Like the moon, we borrow our light. Bright as we become when grace shines on us, we are darkness itself when the Sun of Righteousness withdraws. Therefore, cry to God that He will never leave. Plead, "Do not take Your Holy Spirit from me" (Psalm 51:11).

Have You not said, "I, the Lord, keep it. I water it every moment: lest any hurt it. I keep it night and day" (Isaiah 27:3)?

Lord, keep us everywhere. Keep us in the valley when we murmur against Your humbling hand. Keep us on the mountain so we are not prideful that You have lifted us. Keep us in youth when our passions are strong. Keep us in old age when we become conceited with our wisdom. Keep us when we come to die, lest at the end we would deny You. Keep us in living, keep us in dying, keep us in working, keep us in suffering, keep us in fighting, keep us in resting, keep us in everything and everywhere because in every way we need You, Oh our God! Amen.

JUNE 29, EVENING

LIBERALITY

"And the glory which You gave me I have given them."

—John 17:22

Behold the superlative liberality of the Lord Jesus, for He has given us His all. Though a tithe of His possessions would make a universe of angels rich beyond all thought, He was not content until He had given us all that He had.

It would have been surprising grace even if He had allowed us to eat the crumbs of His bounty under the table of His mercy. But Jesus does nothing halfway, and so He makes us sit and share in the feast.

Had He given us only a small pension from His royal treasury, we still would have cause to love Him eternally. But He wants His bride as rich as He is, and so He will not have a glory or a grace that we will not share. He has not been content with less than making us joint heirs with Him (Romans 8:17).

He has emptied all His estate into the treasury of the church. He has all things in common with His redeemed. There is not one room in His house where He will keep the key from His people. He gives them complete liberty to take all that He has. He loves them to make free use of His treasury and appropriate as much as they can carry. The boundless fullness of His all-sufficiency is as free to the believer as the air we breathe.

Christ has put the wine bottle of His love to believers's lips and told us to drink forever. We are welcome to drain it, but it cannot be exhausted. We are told to drink abundantly, it is all our own. What greater proof of fellowship can heaven or earth offer?

> When I stand before the throne
> Dressed in beauty not my own;
> When I see Thee as Thou art,
> Love Thee with unsinning heart;
> Then, Lord, shall I fully know—
> Not till then—how much I owe.

NOTHING TOO HARD

"Ah, Lord God! Behold, You have made the heavens and the earth by Your great power and out stretched arm. There is nothing too hard for You." —Jeremiah 32:17

At this time the Chaldeans had surrounded Jerusalem. Sword, famine, and pestilence had desolated the land. Yet Jeremiah was commanded by God to purchase a field and have the deed of transfer legally sealed and witnessed.

This was a strange purchase for a rational man. Prudence could not justify it, for there was little probability that the buyer would ever enjoy it. But Jeremiah made the purchase because God had told him to.

Jeremiah's reasoning ran like this: Lord God, You can make this field useful to me. You can rid it of oppressors. You can make me sit under my vine and my fig tree and enjoy it. "You have made the heavens and the earth by your great power and out stretched arm. There is nothing too hard for You."

This confidence gave such a majestic authority to the early saints that they dared to do what God commanded. Whether it was Noah building a ship on dry land, Abraham offering up his only son, Moses despising the treasures of Egypt, or Joshua besieging Jericho for seven days with only ram's horns for weapons; they all acted on God's commands, even when it seemed contrary to reason. As a result of their obedience, the Lord gave them rich rewards.

Would to God we had in the Christianity of these modern times a more potent infusion of this heroic faith. If we would venture more on the naked promise of God, we would enter a world of wonders where today we are strangers.

Let Jeremiah's confidence be ours; nothing is too hard for the God that created the heavens and the earth.

EVERFLOWING

"In both summer and winter it shall occur."

—Zechariah 14:8

The streams of living water that flow from Jerusalem are not dried up by the parching heat of summer, nor are they frozen by the cold winds of blustering winter.

Rejoice, Oh my soul that you are here to testify of the faithfulness of the Lord. The seasons change, and you change; but the Lord is always the same. The streams of His love to you are as deep, as broad, and as full as ever.

The heat of business is worrisome, and scorching trials make me need the cooling influences of the river of His grace. I may go anytime and drink from the inexhaustible fountain that flows in both summer and winter. The upper springs are never insufficient, and, blessed be the name of the Lord, the lower springs cannot fail either.

Elijah found the brook Cherith dried up (1 Kings (17:7), but Jehovah was still the same God of providence. Job said his brothers were like deceitful brooks (Job 6:15), but he discovered that God was an overflowing river of consolation.

The Nile is the great confidence of Egypt, but its banks are variable. Our Lord, however, is always the same. Cyrus captured the city of Babylon by changing the course of the Euphrates. But no power, human or infernal, can divert the currents of divine grace. Ancient river beds are dry and desolate, but the streams that have their source on the mountain of divine sovereignty and infinite love will always be full and overflowing. Generations melt away, but the course of grace is unaltered. The river of God may sing with greater truth than the brook in the poem:

> Men may come, and men may go,
> But I go on forever.

Happy are you, my soul, to be led beside these still waters.

SPEAK, MY LORD

"The sound of the Lord God, walking in the garden in the cool of the day."

—Genesis 3:8

Now that the cool of the day has arrived, rest and listen to the voice of God. He is always ready to speak whenever you are prepared to listen. If there is any slowness in communication, it is not on His part. He stands at the door and knocks. If anyone hears His voice and opens the door, He will come in (Revelation 3:20).

What is the condition of my heart? I hope it is well trimmed, watered, and producing fruit for Him. If not, He will reprove me, but I still pray for Him to come. There is nothing that can bring my heart to a perfect condition like the presence of the Sun of Righteousness, who brings healing in His wings (Malachi 4:2).

Come, Oh Lord, my God: My soul earnestly invites you. I eagerly await you. Come, Oh Lord Jesus, my well-beloved. Plant fresh flowers in me like the ones that bloom in Your matchless character. Come, Oh my Father, the Vinekeeper. Deal with me in Your tenderness and wisdom. Come, Oh Holy Spirit, moisten my whole nature like the herbs covered with the evening dew.

Oh that God would speak to me. "Speak, for Your servant hears" (1 Samuel 3:10). Oh that He would walk with me. I am ready to give my heart and mind to Him. Every other thought is hushed.

I am asking only for what He delights to give. I am sure that He will condescend to have fellowship with me because He has given His Holy Spirit to live with me forever.

Sweet is the cool twilight. Every star seems like the eye of heaven and the cool wind is like the breath of celestial love.

My Father, my elder Brother, my sweet Comforter, speak now in loving kindness. You have opened my ear and I am not rebellious. Amen.

A REJOICING HEART

"Our heart shall rejoice in Him."

—Psalm 33:21

Blessed is the fact that Christians can rejoice in deep distress. Trouble may surround them, but still they sing. And like many birds, they sing best in cages. Waves may roll over them, but their souls rise to the surface, and they see the light of God's countenance. Christians have a buoyancy that keeps their heads above water and helps them to sing in the storms.

To whom should the glory be given for this? To Jesus, of course; it is all by Jesus. Trouble does not bring consolation to believers. It is the presence of the Son of God with them in the fiery furnace that fills their hearts with joy.

They are sick and suffering, but Jesus visits them and makes their bed. They are dying, the cold chilly waters of Jordan gather, but Jesus puts His arms around them and cries, "Fear not, beloved. To die is to be blessed. The waters of death for you have their source in heaven. They are not bitter, they are sweet as nectar, because they flow from the throne of God."

As the departing saints wade through the stream, as the surge gathers around them, as heart and flesh fail, the same voice sounds, "Fear not, for I am with you. Be not dismayed, for I am your God" (Isaiah 41:10).

As the saints near the borders of the infinite unknown, and are almost afraid to enter the realm of shadows, Jesus says, "Do not fear, little flock, for it is your Father's good pleasure to give you the kingdom" (Luke 12:32).

Thus strengthened and consoled, believers are not afraid to die. They are willing to depart, because they have seen Jesus as the Morning Star, and they long to gaze on Him as the sun in its strength.

Tonight, the presence of Jesus is all the heaven we desire. Jesus is:

> The glory of our brightest days;
> The comfort of our nights.

DO NOT BE SILENT

"To You I will cry, O Lord my Rock; do not be silent to me, lest I become like those who go down to the pit."

—Psalm 28:1

A cry is the natural expression of sorrow and a suitable utterance when all other methods of appeal fail. The cry, however, must be directed to God alone, for cries to others are often wasted pleas. When we consider the readiness of the Lord to hear and His ability to help, we have good reason to direct our appeals to the God of our salvation. It will be useless to call to the rocks in the day of judgment, but our Rock answers our cries.

"Do not be silent to me." A person limited to reading written prayers, may be content not to have prayers answered, but genuine supplicants must have answers. These are not satisfied with results that only calm the mind or subdue the will; they must receive actual replies from heaven or they cannot rest. And they want those replies at once, for they dread even a moment of God's silence. God's voice is often so terrible that it shakes the wilderness, but His silence is equally full of awe.

When God is close, do not be silent. Cry with greater earnestness. When your notes grow shrill with eagerness and grief, He will not deny you a hearing. What a dreadful situation you would be in if God were to become forever silent. If God were silent to you, "you would become like those who go down to the pit." Deprived of the God who answers prayer, you would be in a more pitiable plight than the dead in the grave. It would not be long before you would sink to the same level as the lost in hell.

We must have answers to prayer. Ours is an urgent case of dire necessity. Surely the Lord will speak peace to our agitated minds. He never can find it in His heart to permit His own elect to perish.

JULY 2, EVENING

WELL FED

"The ugly and gaunt cows ate up the seven fine looking and fat cows."

—Genesis 41:4

Pharaoh's dream has too often been my experience. Days of laziness have destroyed all that I achieved in times of zealous industry. My seasons of coldness have frozen the pleasant glow of periods of passionate enthusiasm. My fits of worldliness have thrown me back from spiritual gains.

I need to be aware of lean prayers, lean duties, and lean experiences. These will eat the fat of my comfort and peace. If I neglect prayer for long, I stand to lose all the spirituality I have attained. If I do not draw fresh supplies from heaven, the old corn in my granary is soon consumed by the famine raging in my soul.

When the caterpillars of indifference, the cutworms of worldliness, and the moths of self-indulgence leave my heart desolate and my soul languishing, my former fruitfulness and growth in grace avails little or nothing.

I should be concerned not to have any days of lean flesh or ill-favored hours! If everyday I journeyed toward the goal, I would soon reach it. But backsliding leaves me far from the prize of my high calling and robs me of the advances that I have already made.

The only way my days can be as the fine looking and fat cows is to feed them in the right meadow, to spend them with the Lord in His service, in His company, in His fear, and in His way.

Why should every year not be richer than the last in love, usefulness, and joy; for I am nearer the celestial hills, I have more experience with my Lord, and I should be more like Him?

Oh Lord, keep me far from the curse of leanness of soul (Psalm 106:15). Let me not have to cry, "My leanness, my leanness, woe to me" (Isaiah 24:16)!

I am well fed and well nourished in Your house, and I praise Your name.

SUFFERING

"If we endure, we shall also reign with Him."

—2 Timothy 2:12

Do not imagine that you are enduring for Christ if you are not in Christ. Beloved friend, are you trusting in Jesus only? If not, whatever you may be enduring on earth, you are not enduring with Christ. You have no hope of reigning with Him in heaven.

Neither are we to conclude that all a Christian endures is suffering with Christ. It is essential that we be called by God to suffer. If we are rash and imprudent and run to positions that neither providence or grace has prepared, we need to question if we are sinning rather than communing in suffering with Jesus.

If you let passion replace judgment and self-will reign instead of Scriptural authority, you are fighting the Lord's battle with the devil's weapons. Don't be surprised if you cut your fingers.

When trouble comes as the result of sin, do not think that you are suffering with Christ. When Miriam spoke evil of Moses and became leprous, she was not suffering for God (Numbers 12:10). Suffering that God accepts must have God's glory as its purpose. If I suffer to earn a reputation or to win applause, I will get no reward other than that of the hypocrite (Matthew 6:1).

Search to see if you are truly suffering with Jesus. If so, what is such "light affliction" compared to reigning with Him (2 Corinthians 4:17)? It is blessed to be in the furnace with Christ, such an honor to stand in the pillory with Him, that if there were no future reward, we could count ourselves happy in this honor.

But when the compensation is eternal and infinitely more than we had any right to expect will we not take up the cross with eagerness and go on our way rejoicing?

SANCTIFICATION

"Sanctify them by Your truth. Your word is truth."

—John 17:17

Sanctification begins with regeneration as the Spirit of God infuses that new and living principle by which we become a new creation in Christ Jesus (2 Corinthians 5:17).

This work begins the new birth (John 3:3) and is carried on in two ways; by mortification, which subdues and keeps the lust of the flesh under control; and by vivification, which transforms the life God has put in us into a well of water springing up to everlasting life.

This process is carried on every day by *perseverance,* through which the Christian is preserved and continues in grace and abounds in good works, to the praise and glory of God. It culminates, or is perfected, in *glory.* The soul, after being thoroughly purged, is caught up to dwell with holy beings at the right hand of the Majesty on high.

The Spirit of God is the author of this sanctification, but there is a visible agency that must not be forgotten. "Sanctify them," said Jesus, "by Your truth. Your word is truth." Many passages of Scripture prove that the instrument of sanctification is the Word of God.

The Spirit of God brings the precepts and doctrines of truth to our minds and applies them with power. These are heard in the ear, received in the heart, and work in us the will to do God's pleasure. The truth is the sanctifier. If we do not hear or read the truth, we will not grow in sanctification. We progress in sound living only as far as we progress in sound understanding. "Your word is a lamp to my feet and a light to my path" (Psalm 119:105).

Do not say that error is a matter of mere opinion. No one indulges an error of judgment without sooner or later tolerating that error in practice. Hold fast to the truth, and you will be sanctified by the Spirit of God.

INNER PURITY

"He who has clean hands and a pure heart, who has not lifted up his soul to an idol, nor sworn deceitfully."

—Psalm 24:4

The practice of holiness is a precious mark of grace. I fear many have perverted the doctrine of justification by faith to the point that good works are treated with contempt. If so, they will receive everlasting contempt at the last great day.

If our hands are not clean, let us wash them in Jesus' precious blood and then lift pure hands to God. Clean hands will not suffice unless they are connected to a pure heart. True religion is a heart work. We may wash the outside of a cup as long as we please, but if the inside is filthy, we are filthy altogether in God's sight.

Our hearts are more truly ourselves than our hands. Our very life lies within the inner nature; thus the imperative need for purity within. "Blessed are the pure in heart, for they shall see God" (Matthew 5:8). All others are blind bats.

The saint born for heaven "has not lifted up his soul to an idol." All of us have joys by which our souls are lifted. Sinners lift theirs in empty, carnal delights, but saints love more substantial things. Like Jehoshaphat, the saints are lifted up in the ways of the Lord (1 Kings 22:43).

If you are content with husks, you will be counted with the swine. Does the world satisfy you? Then you have your reward. Make sure you enjoy it. There will be no other joys.

Saints are also people of honor and do not swear deceitfully. Their word is their only oath, but that is better than the oaths of twenty sinners. False speaking will shut anyone out of heaven. A liar will not enter God's house regardless of professions or works.

Reader, does this text condemn you, or do you hope to ascend to the hill of the Lord?

SUPER SAINTS

"Called to be saints."

—Romans 1:7

It appears to me that we often regard the apostolic saints as if they were saints in a manner more special than other children of God. All are saints whom God has called by His grace and sanctified by His Spirit. Yet we tend to look on the apostles as extraordinary beings, scarcely subject to the same weakness and temptations that we encounter.

In doing this we forget the great truth that the nearer one lives to God, the more intensely one mourns over evil in the heart. Also, the more our Master honors us in His service the more the flesh tempts us.

Had we seen the apostle Paul, we would have thought him remarkably like the rest of the chosen family. Had we talked with him, we would have found that his experience and ours were much the same. Paul was more faithful, more holy, and more deeply taught, but he endured the same trials that we do.

Look not then on the ancient saints as exempt from infirmities or sin. Do not regard them with mystic reverence that almost makes us idolaters. Their holiness is attainable. We are "called to be saints" by the same voice which summoned them to their higher vocation. It is our duty to force our way into the inner circle of saintship.

If these saints were superior to us in their attainments, and they certainly were, let us follow their example and emulate their enthusiasm and holiness. We have the same light. The same grace is accessible to us. Do not be satisfied until you have equalled them in heavenly character.

They lived with Jesus, and they lived for Jesus; therefore, they grew like Jesus. Let us live by the same Spirit and our saintship will soon be apparent.

AWAY WITH DOUBTS

"Trust in the Lord forever, for in the Lord Jehovah is everlasting strength."

—Isaiah 26:4

Since you have such a God to trust, rest on Him with all your weight. Resolutely drive out all unbelief. Endeavor to get rid of doubts and fears that mar your comfort. There is no excuse for fear when God is the foundation of your trust.

Loving parents would be deeply hurt if their children did not trust them. How ungenerous, how unkind our conduct, when we put so little confidence in our heavenly Father, for He has never failed us, and He never will.

It would be good if doubting unbelief was driven from the household of God. But I fear old unbelief is as nimble now as when the psalmist asked, "Has His mercy ceased forever? Has His promise failed for evermore?" (Psalm 77:8).

David said of Goliath's sword, "There is none like it" (1 Samuel 21:9). He had used it once in his youthful victory, and it proved to be made of the right metal. Therefore he praised it afterwards.

We should speak well of our God. "Know this day, and consider it in your heart, that the Lord Himself is God in heaven above and on the earth beneath, there is no other" (Deuteronomy 4:39). "To whom then will you liken Me. Or to whom shall I be equal?" Says the Holy One (Isaiah 40:25).

Rather than allowing doubts to live in our heart, we should take the whole detestable crew and execute them at the brook as Elijah did the prophets of Baal (1 Kings 18:40). We have been in many trials, but we have never been where we could not find in God all that we needed.

Be encouraged. Trust in the Lord forever. Rest assured that His everlasting strength will be as it has been: your support and sustenance.

JULY 5, EVENING

SECURE

"Whoever listens to me will dwell safely, and will be secure, without fear of evil."

—Proverbs 1:33

Divine love is conspicuous when it shines in the midst of judgment. Beautiful is the lone star that smiles through a break in the thunder clouds. Bright is the oasis that blooms in the desert. But brighter and fairer is God's love in the midst of wrath.

When the Israelites provoked the Most High by their continued idolatry, God punished them by withholding both dew and rain which brought a great famine in the land (1 Kings 17:1). Although God did this, He still cared for His chosen. If all the brooks were dry, there would be one reserved for Elijah (1 Kings 17:3), and when that brook failed, God still provided (1 Kings 17:16). God had a remnant according to the election of grace. His one hundred prophets were hidden, fifty to a cave (1 Kings 18:4). They were fed from King Ahab's table by the faithful, God-fearing steward, Obadiah.

It may be inferred that God's people are safe come what may. Let earthquakes shake the earth, let the planets themselves be split, even amid the wreck of worlds, the believer will be as secure as in the calmest hour of rest. If God does not save His people under heaven, He will save them in heaven. If the world becomes too hot to hold them, heaven will be the place of their reception and their safety.

Be confident when you hear of wars and rumors of wars. Do not let global agitation distress you. Whatever happens on this earth, you will be secure under Jehovah's broad wing. Trust in His promises. Rest in His faithfulness. Laugh at the blackest future. There is nothing dreadful for you in it.

Your only concern should be to show the world the blessedness of listening to the voice of wisdom.

THE PRICE

"How many are my iniquities and sins?"

—Job 13:23

Have you ever seriously considered how great the sin of God's people is? Think how heinous your own transgressions are and you will realize that sins here and there tower up like an alp. Your iniquities are heaped on each other, adding difficulty to difficulty, like the old fable of the giants who piled mountain on mountain.

What an aggregate of sin there is in just one of God's most sanctified children. Multiply that by the multitude of the redeemed, "a great multitude which no one could number" (Revelation 7:9), and you have some conception of the great mass of the guilt of the people for whom Jesus shed His blood.

We see a more adequate idea of sin's magnitude when we contemplate the great remedy provided: the blood of Jesus Christ, God's only and well-beloved Son. God's Son! Angels cast their crowns before Him! All the choral symphonies of heaven surround His glorious throne. God over all. God blessed forever. Amen.

Yet He takes the form of a servant and is scourged, pierced, bruised, torn, and finally slain, because nothing but the blood of the incarnate Son of God could make atonement for our offenses. No human mind can estimate the infinite value of the divine sacrifice!

As great as the sin of God's people is, the atonement that takes it away is immeasurably greater. Thus even when sin rolls like a black flood and memories of the past are bitter, the believer can stand before the blazing throne of the great and holy God and cry, "Who is he who condemns? It is Christ who died and furthermore is also risen" (Romans 8:34).

While the recollection of sin fills us with shame and sorrow, we use it as a reflector to show the brightness of mercy. Guilt is the dark night in which the fair star of divine love shines with serene splendor.

JULY 6, EVENING

PRAY FOR US

"Brethren, pray for us."

—1 Thessalonians 5:25

We reserve this one morning to remind our readers to pray for the ministers of the gospel. We implore every Christian to keep the fervent request of this text, which was first uttered by the apostle and is now repeated by us.

Believers, our work is solemnly momentous. It involves prosperity or grief to thousands. We are on God's eternal business, and our word is life unto life, or death unto death. A heavy responsibility rests on us. It will be no small mercy if at the last we are found innocent of the blood of all people (Ezekiel 33:9).

As officers in Christ's army, we are the special target of the hostility of both sinners and devils. They watch for us to stumble and work to pull us down. Our sacred calling involves temptations you will never experience. Above all, it often draws us from a personal enjoyment of the truth to a ministerial and official consideration of it.

We meet with difficult cases, and our wits are often frayed. We observe sad backsliding, and our hearts are wounded. We see millions perish, and our spirits sink. We also want to assist you by our preaching. We desire to be a blessing to your children. We long to be useful to saint and sinner. Therefore, dear friends, intercede for us with God. Miserable we are if we miss the aid of your prayers. Happy we will be if we live in your supplications.

You do not look to us but to the Master for spiritual blessings. Yet how many times has He given you those blessings through us? Pray then, again and again, that we may be the earthen vessels in which the Lord puts the treasure of the gospel (2 Corinthians 4:7).

We, the whole company of missionaries, ministers, city missionaries, and Bible students do in the name of Jesus implore you, "BRETHREN, PRAY FOR US."

LIVE

*"When I passed by you and saw you strug-
gling, . . . I said to you, . . . live."*

—Ezekiel 16:6

Saved one, gratefully consider our text's mandate
of mercy. Note that this positive command of God
is majestic. In our text is a sinner expecting nothing but wrath. But the eternal Lord, passing by in His
glory, looks, pauses, and then pronounces the solitary
but royal word, "Live." Who but God could give life
with a single syllable?

But this fiat has many aspects. When God commands "Live," here is judicial life. The sinner is ready
to be condemned, but the mighty One says, "Live,"
and the sinner rises pardoned and absolved.

Here also, is spiritual life. We did not know Jesus:
Our eyes could not see Christ, our ears could not hear
His voice, but Jehovah said, "Live," and we who were
dead in trespasses and sins were made alive (Ephesians
2:1).

It also includes glorified life, which is the perfection
of spiritual life. "Yes, I said to you, Live," and that
word rolls on through all the years of time until death
comes. In the midst of the shadows of death, the Lord's
cry is still heard: "Live." On resurrection morning that
same word will be echoed by the archangel: "Live."
And holy spirits will rise to heaven, to be blest forever
in the glory of their God by the power of the word:
"Live."

This is an irresistible mandate. Saul of Tarsus was
on the road to Damascus to arrest certain saints. But
a voice was heard from heaven, a light brighter than
the sun was seen, and Saul cried, "What shall I do
Lord? (Acts 22:10).

"Live" is a mandate of free grace. When sinners are
saved, it is only and solely because God will do it to
magnify His free, unpurchased, unsought grace. Christian, see your position. You are a debtor to grace. Show
your gratitude by living an earnest, Christ-like life.

UNDERSTANDING FAITH

"Please tell me where your great strength lies."

—Judges 16:6

Where does faith find its strength? It is found in the food that it feeds on, for faith studies what the promise is: an emanation of divine grace, an overflowing of the great heart of God. Faith says, "My God has given this promise in love and grace. Therefore, it is quite certain that His Word will be fulfilled."

Then faith thinks, "Who gave this promise? Who is the author?" Then faith remembers that it is from God, who cannot lie—God omnipotent, God immutable. Therefore the promise must be fulfilled, and faith advances in this firm conviction.

Faith remembers why the promise was given: for God's glory. Faith feels perfectly sure that God's glory is safe, that God will never stain His own throne or mar the lustre of His crown. Therefore the promise will stand.

Then faith also considers the amazing work of Christ as clear proof of the Father's intention to fulfill His word. "He who did not spare His own Son, but delivered Him up for us all, how shall He not with Him also freely give us all things?" (Romans 8:32).

Faith looks back to the battles that have strengthened and to the victories that have given courage, and it remembers that God has never failed. No, not even once. Faith recollects times of great peril when deliverance came, or hours of dreadful need when strength was found. Faith cries that it will never be led to think that God can change and leave His servant now. "Thus far the Lord has helped us" (1 Samuel 7:12), and He will continue to help.

Faith views each promise in its connection with the promise giver, and because it does, it can say with assurance, "Surely goodness and mercy shall follow me all the days of my life" (Psalm 23:6).

A TEACHING FAITH

"Lead me in Your truth and teach me. For You are the God of my salvation; on You I wait all the day."

—Psalm 25:5

When trembling believers begin to walk in the way of the Lord, they ask to be led like children upheld by their parents' hands, and they crave to be further instructed in the alphabet of truth.

Experimental teaching is the burden of this prayer. David knew much, but he felt some ignorance and wanted to remain in the Lord's school. Four times in two verses he applies for a scholarship in the college of grace.

It would be well for many believers if, instead of following their own devices and cutting new paths of thought, they would enquire about the good old ways of God's own truth and ask the Holy Spirit to give them a sanctified understanding and a teachable spirit.

"For you are the God of my salvation." The Three-in-One Jehovah is the Author and Perfecter of salvation. Reader, is He the God of your salvation? Do you find in the Father's election, in the Son's atonement, and in the Spirit's awakening all the grounds of your eternal hope? If so, you may use this as an argument to obtain further blessings. If the Lord has ordained to save you, surely He will not refuse to instruct you. It is a happy thing when we can address the Lord with David's confidence. It gives great power in prayer and comfort in trials.

"On You I wait all the day." Patience is the daughter of faith. We cheerfully wait when we are certain we will not wait in vain. It is our duty and our privilege to wait on the Lord in service, in trust, in worship, and in expectancy all the days of our life. Then our faith will be tested and true, a faith that will bear continuous trials.

We will not grow weary of waiting on God when we remember how long and how graciously He once waited for us.

MEMORIES

"Forget not all His benefits."

—Psalm 103:2

I t is a delight and a blessing to recall how God has worked in the lives of ancient saints; to observe His goodness in delivering them, His mercy in pardoning them, and His faithfulness in keeping His covenant with them.

But of even more interest and blessing is a review of God's hand in our own lives. At the very least, we should look on our history as being as full of God, as full of His goodness and truth, as much a proof of His faithfulness and veracity as the lives of any of the saints who have gone before.

We do our Lord an injustice when we assume that it was only in those early days He worked His mighty acts and revealed His strength; when we assume that He does not perform miracles or assist the saints who are on the earth today. Evaluate your own life and you will discover blessings that not only renewed you but brought glory to your God.

Has God worked in your life? Have you passed through the rivers supported by the divine presence? Have you walked through fires unharmed (Isaiah 43:2)? Have you choice evidence of His blessings? Has the God who gave Solomon the desire of his heart listened to you and answered your requests (2 Chronicles 1:10)? The God of lavish bounty of whom David sang, "Who satisfies your mouth with good things" (Psalm 103:5)—has He satisfied you with more than your heart could wish? Has He made you lie down in green pastures? Has He led you beside still waters (Psalm 23:2)?

Surely God's goodness is the same to us as it was to the saints of old. Let us, then, weave His mercies into a song. Let us take the pure gold of thankfulness and the jewels of praise and make them into another crown for Jesus. Let our souls make music as sweet and as exhilarating as came from David's harp. Let us praise the Lord whose goodness and mercy is forever.

LIGHT AND DARKNESS

"And God divided the light from the darkness."

—Genesis 1:4

There are two principles at work within a believer. In our natural condition there was only one principle, darkness, but now light has entered, and the two principles disagree. Listen to the apostle Paul: "For I delight in the law of God according to the inward man. But I see another law in my members, warring against the law of my mind, and bringing me into captivity to the law of sin which is in my members" (Romans 7:23).

How does this occur? Darkness, by itself, is quiet and undisturbed, but when the Lord sends in light, there is a conflict for the one opposes the other.

And if there is a division within the Christian, there is certain to be a division without. As soon as the Lord gives the believer light, we separate from the darkness of mere worldly religion and outward ceremony, for nothing short of the gospel of Christ will now satisfy us. We secede from worldly society and frivolous amusements to seek the company of the saints: "We know that we have passed from death to life, because we love the brethren" (1 John 3:14).

Light gathers to light and darkness to darkness. What God has divided, let us never try to reunite. Just as Christ bore His reproach, let us come out from the ungodly and be His chosen people. He was holy, harmless, undefiled, and separate from sinners. We too should be nonconformists to the world. We must dissent from all sin and be distinguished from the rest of humanity by our likeness to our Master.

FELLOW CITIZENS

"Fellow citizens with the saints."

—Ephesians 2:19

What does it mean to be a fellow citizen with the saints? It means that we are under heaven's government and Christ the King of heaven reigns in our hearts. It means our daily prayer is, "Your will be done on earth as it is in heaven" (Matthew 6:10). The proclamations issued from the throne of glory are freely received by us, and the decrees of the Great King are cheerfully obeyed.

As citizens of the New Jerusalem, we share heaven's honors. The glory of the beatified saints belongs to us, because we are already children of God, already royalty of the blood imperial. Already we wear the spotless robe of Jesus' righteousness. Already we have angels for our servants, saints for our companions, Christ for our brother, God for our Father, and a crown of immortality for our reward.

As citizens, we have common rights to all the property of heaven. The gates of pearl and the walls of chrysolite are ours (Revelation 21:21). The azure light of the city that does not need lamps or sunlight is ours. The river of the water of life and the twelve types of fruit that grow on the trees along its banks are ours (Revelation 22:1–2). There is nothing in heaven that does not belong to us. "Things present, or things to come," are all ours (Romans 8:38).

As citizens of heaven, we enjoy its delights. Do those who are there rejoice over sinners who repent and prodigals who return (Luke 15:7)? So do we. Do they chant the glories of triumphant grace (Revelation 4:8)? We do the same. Do they cast their crowns at Jesus's feet (Revelation 4:10)? Whatever honor we have, we cast there too. Are they warmed by His smile? It is no less sweet to us. Do they look forward to His second coming (Revelation 22:20)? We also look and long for His appearing.

Citizen of heaven, let your walk and actions be consistent with your high dignity.

EVENING AND MORNING

"The evening and the morning were the first day."

—Genesis 1:5

The evening was darkness and the morning was light, but the two together are called by the name that is given to the light alone! This is somewhat remarkable, and it has an exact analogy in spiritual experience. In every believer there is darkness and light. Yet we are not called sinners, even though there is sin in us. We are called saints because we possess some holiness.

This is a great comfort to those who ask, "Can I be a child of God if there is so much darkness in me?" Yes, like the day, you take your name from the morning, not the evening. You are spoken of in the Word of God as if you were perfectly holy. Even though there is darkness in you, you are called the child of light and day (1 Thessalonians 5:5). You are named after your predominating quality in the sight of God.

Observe that the evening comes first. Naturally we are darkness first in order of time, and the gloom is often first in our mournful apprehension, driving us to cry in deep humiliation, "God be merciful to me, a sinner."

The morning is placed second. It dawns when grace overcomes nature. It is a blessed adage of John Bunyan, "That which is last, lasts forever." That which is first yields, in good season, to the last. Nothing comes after the last. Although you are naturally darkness, when you become light in the Lord there is no evening. "Your sun shall no longer go down" (Isaiah 60:20).

The first day in this life is an evening and a morning. But the second day, when we will be with God forever, is a day with no evening. There will only be one sacred, high, and eternal noon.

BEING ESTABLISHED

"After you have suffered a while, perfect, establish, strengthen and settle you."

—1 Peter 5:10

You have seen the arch of heaven as it spans the plain. It colors are glorious. Its hues are rare. It is beautiful; but it passes away and is gone. The gorgeous colors give way to fleecy clouds and the sky is no longer brilliant with the tints of heaven. It is not lasting. How can it be? Even a glorious show comprised of transitory sunbeams and passing raindrops cannot last.

The graces of Christian character must not be like the rainbow's transitory beauty. Quite the opposite. Christian character must be established, settled, and lasting.

Believer, endeavor to make sure that every good thing you have will last. May your character not be written on sand, but inscribed on the rock! May your faith not be a baseless fabric of vision but built of material that will endure when the awful fire consumes the hypocrite's wood, hay, and straw (1 Corinthians 3:12).

May you be rooted and grounded in love (Ephesians 3:17). May your convictions be deep, your love real, your desires earnest. May your life be so settled and established that all the blasts of hell and all the storms of earth will never be able to remove you.

Notice how this blessing of being established in the faith is obtained. The apostle points us to suffering—"After you have suffered a while." We will not be deeply rooted unless rough winds pass over us. The gnarled roots of the oak tree and those strange twisted branches tell of the many storms that have swept over it.

The Christian is made strong and firmly rooted by all the trials and storms of life. Do not fear the tempestuous wind of trials. Take comfort. Believe that in their rough discipline God is fulfilling our text in you.

INSTRUCT YOUR CHILDREN

*"Tell your children about it. Let your children
tell their children. And their children another
generation."*

—Joel 1:3

By God's grace, in this simple way, a living testimony for truth will always be kept alive. The beloved of the Lord are to hand down their witness for the gospel and the covenant. This is our first duty.

We are to begin at home. It is a bad preacher who does not commence a ministry at home. The heathen are to be sought, the highways and the hedges are to be searched, but home has first claim. Do not reverse the order of the Lord's arrangements.

Teaching our children is a personal duty. We cannot delegate it to Sunday School teachers or other friendly aids. They can assist, but this sacred obligation is primarily ours, and proxies and sponsors are unbiblical substitutes. Mothers and fathers must, like Abraham, teach their households the fear of the Lord (Genesis 17:23).

Parental teaching is a natural duty (Proverbs 22:6). Who is more able to look after a child's well-being than the parents? If you neglect the instruction of your children, you are worse than a brute.

A family's religious instruction is necessary for the nation, the family, and the church. By a thousand plots, false teachings are advancing. One of the most effective methods for resisting its inroads, however, is almost neglected; namely, the instruction of children in the faith. Would that parents wake up to its importance.

It is a pleasant duty to talk about Jesus to our sons and daughters, and through it God saves the children by the parent's prayers and admonitions.

May every household in which this volume will come honor the Lord and receive His smile.

JULY 11, EVENING

GOD IN THREE PERSONS

"Sanctified by God the Father."/"Sanctified in Christ Jesus."/"In sanctification of the Spirit."

—Jude 1; 1 Corinthians 1:2; 1 Peter 1:2

Mark well the union of the three divine Persons in their gracious acts. A believer who makes a preference in the Persons of the Trinity is foolish. A believer who chooses Jesus as the embodiment of everything lovely and gracious but sees the Father as severely just and destitute of kindness is wrong. Equally wrong is the one who exalts the decrees of the Father and the atonement of the Son to the depreciation of the work of the Spirit.

In deeds of grace, none of the Persons of the Trinity act separately. They are as united in their deeds as in their essence. In their love toward the chosen, they are one, and in their actions they are undivided.

Especially note this unity and equity in the matter of sanctification. We may without mistake speak of sanctification as the work of the Spirit, but let us be cautious not to view it as if the Father and the Son have no part in it. It is correct to speak of sanctification as the work of the Father, of the Son, and of the Spirit. Jehovah said, "Let us make man in Our image, according to Our likeness" (Genesis 1:26). Thus, "We are His workmanship, created in Christ Jesus for good works, which God prepared before hand that we should walk in them" (Ephesians 2:10).

See the value the triune God sets on real holiness, since all three Persons in the Trinity work together to produce "a glorious church not having spot or wrinkle or any such thing" (Ephesians 5:27).

Believer, as a follower of Christ, set a high value on holiness, on purity of life and godliness of conversation. Value the blood of Christ as the foundation of your hope. Never speak disparagingly of the work of the Spirit.

This morning, live so as to manifest the work of the triune God.

HEAVEN

"His heavenly kingdom."

—2 Timothy 4:18

Heaven, the city of the great King, is a place of active service. Ransomed spirits serve Him day and night in His temple, never ceasing to fulfill the good pleasure of their King. They always rest from cares in ease and freedom, but never rest in the sense of inactivity and idleness.

Jerusalem the golden is the place of communion with all the people of God. We will sit with Abraham, Isaac, and Jacob in eternal fellowship. We will have high conversation with the noble host of the elect. We will all reign with Him who by His love and potent arm brought us home. We will not sing solos, but in choirs we will praise our king.

Heaven is the place of victory realized. Whenever you have achieved a victory over lust, whenever, after a hard struggle, you have laid temptation dead at your feet, you have in that hour a foretaste of the joy that awaits you eternally when the Lord treads Satan under your feet. You will find "in all these things we are more than conquerors through Him who loved us" (Romans 8:37).

Paradise is also the place of security. When you enjoy the full assurance of faith on earth, you have the pledge of that glorious security which will be yours when you are a perfect citizen of the heavenly Jerusalem. Oh my sweet home Jerusalem, the happy harbor of my soul!

Thanks, even now, to Him whose love has taught me to long for home. But when I possess it in eternity, my thanks will be even louder:

> My soul has tasted of the grapes,
>   And now it longs to go
> Where my dear Lord His vineyard keeps
>   And all the clusters grow.
> Upon the true and living vine
>   My famished soul would feast,
> And banquet on the fruit divine,
>   An everlasting guest.

ANGER

"Then God said to Jonah, 'Is it right for you to be angry'?"

—Jonah 4:9

Anger is not necessarily sinful, although it does have a tendency to run wild, and we should quickly question its character by asking, "Is it right for me to be angry?" Perhaps we might answer, "Yes."

We do well when we are angry with sin. Sin is a wrong against our good and gracious God, and it is a wrong against ourselves, because it shows our foolishness after so much divine instruction. Sin is a loathsome and hateful thing, and a renewed heart cannot patiently endure it. If you are not angry at transgression, you will sin. God is angry with the wicked. It is written in His Word. "You who love the Lord hate evil" (Psalm 97:10).

Far more frequently, however, our anger is not commendable or justifiable, and then we must say "No" to it. Why should we be annoyed with children, disturbed with employees, and irritated with friends? Does this anger honor our Christian profession or glorify God? Is it not the old evil heart seeking to regain dominion? We should resist with all the strength of our newborn nature.

Many Christians give way to their tempers as if it were impossible to resist. Remember this, we must be conquerors in every point or we will not be crowned. If we cannot control our tempers, how has grace transformed us? Someone once told Mr. Jay that grace was often grafted on a crab apple stump. "Yes," said he, "but the fruit will not be crabs."

Do not make natural infirmity an excuse for sin. Fly to the cross and pray that God will crucify your temper. Ask Him to renew you in His own image of gentleness and meekness.

FOR US

"When I cry out to You, then my enemies will turn back; this I know, because God is for me."

—Psalm 56:9

It is impossible for human words to express the full meaning of this delightful phrase, "God is for me." He was for us, before the worlds were made. He was for us, or He would not have given His well-beloved Son. He was for us when He struck His Only Begotten and laid the full weight of His wrath on Him. Even then God was for us, though He was against Him. He was for us, when we were ruined in the fall. Even then He was for us, despite our rebellious actions. He was for us, when, with a high hand, we defied Him. He was for us, or He would not have brought us humbly to seek Him.

He has been for us, in all our struggles. We have been summoned to encounter hosts of dangers, and we have been assailed by temptations from without and within. How could we have remained unharmed to this hour if He had not been for us?

He is for us with all the infinity of His being, with all the omnipotence of His love, with all the infallibility of His wisdom. Arrayed in His divine, eternal attributes, He is for us forever, even when yonder blue skies will be rolled up like a worn-out garment.

Because He is for us, our prayers will always ensure His help. "This I know," said David, "When I cry out to You. Then my enemies will turn back." This is no uncertain hope in God. This is a well-grounded assurance.

I too will direct my prayer to You. I will look with assurance for the answer. It will come. My enemies will be defeated because God is for me.

Believer, how blessed to have the King of kings on your side. You are safe with such a Protector! "If God is for us, who can be against us?" (Romans 8:31).

JULY 13, EVENING

WITHOUT HUMAN HELP

"If you use your tool on it, you have profaned it."

—Exodus 20:25

God's altar was to be built of unhewn stones, that no trace of human skill or labor might be seen on it.

Human wisdom, however, trims and arranges the doctrines of the cross into an artificial system that is more congenial to the depraved tastes of the fallen nature. But instead of improving the gospel, carnal wisdom contaminates it and invents another gospel that is not the truth of God. Any alteration or amendment to the Lord's own Word defiles it.

The proud heart is eager to have a part in the justification of its soul. Its own preparations for Christ are dreamed of, humblings and repentings are trusted, good works are celebrated, natural ability is flaunted, and by every means that heart attempts to place human tools on the divine altar. It would be well if sinners remembered that, instead of perfecting the Savior's work, their carnal confidences pollute and dishonor it.

The Lord alone must be exalted in the work of atonement. Not a single mark of a human chisel or hammer will be allowed. There is an inherent blasphemy in attempting to add to what Christ Jesus, in His dying moments, declared to be finished. There is a sacrilege in trying to improve that which the Lord Jehovah finds perfect.

Trembling sinner, put your tools away and fall on your knees in humble supplication. Accept the Lord Jesus alone to be the altar of your atonement. Rest in Him alone. Take warning from this morning's text as to what doctrines you believe. There is among Christians far too much inclination to square and reconcile to human understanding the truths of revelation. This is a form of irreverence and unbelief. Strive against it. Receive the truth as it is found in the Word.

Rejoice that the doctrines of the Word are unhewed stones, stones that are the only suitable material to build an altar for the Lord.

JULY 14, MORNING

SEEKING

"As the first day of the week began to dawn, Mary Magdalene and the other Mary came to see the tomb."

—Matthew 28:1

Let us learn from Mary Magdalene how to obtain fellowship with the Lord Jesus. Mary sought the Savior early in the morning. If you think you can wait for Christ and have fellowship with Him in the distant future, you never will have fellowship, for the heart fitted for communion is a hungering and a thirsting heart.

Mary sought Him with great boldness. The other disciples trembled and fled, but she stood at the tomb. If you want Christ, seek Him boldly. Let nothing hold you back. Defy the world. Press on where others flee.

Mary sought Christ faithfully. She stood at the tomb. Some find it hard to stand by a living Savior. She stood by a dead one. Let us seek Christ this way, by clinging to the very least thing that has to do with Him, and so remain faithful when others would forsake Him.

She sought Jesus earnestly: She stood weeping (John 20:11). Those teardrops were a prayer that captured the Savior and made Him appear. If you desire Jesus's presence, weep to get it! If you cannot be happy unless He comes and says, "You are My beloved," you will soon hear His voice.

She sought only the Savior. She didn't care about angels. She turned her back on them. Her search was only for her Lord. If Christ is your one and only love, if your heart has cast out all rivals, you will soon have the comfort of His presence. Mary Magdalene sought intensely because she loved greatly.

May we have the same intensity of affection. May our heart, like Mary's, be full of Christ. May our love, like her's, be satisfied with nothing short of Jesus.

Oh Lord, reveal Yourself to us this evening. Amen.

PRIVATE PRAYER

"A fire shall always be burning on the altar; it shall never go out."

—Leviticus 6:13

Keep the altar of your private prayers burning. Since it is here that the sanctuary and family altars borrow their fire, let us keep the fire of private prayer burning. Secret devotion is the essence, evidence, and barometer of Christianity. Burn the fat of your sacrifices here. Let your closeted prayer seasons be regular, frequent, and undisturbed. "The effective fervent prayer of a righteous man avails much" (James 5:16).

Have you nothing to pray for? Let me suggest these: the church, a ministry, your own soul, your children, relatives, neighbors, your country, and the cause of God and truth throughout the world.

Examine yourself on this important matter. Do you engage in lukewarm private devotions? "Because you are lukewarm, and neither cold nor hot, I will vomit you out of My mouth" (Revelation 3:16). Do the chariot wheels drag heavily? If so, be alarmed at this sign of decay. Go with weeping and ask for the Spirit of grace and supplication. Set aside a special time for extraordinary prayer. If the fire should be smothered beneath the ashes of worldly conformity, it will dim the fire on the family altar and lessen your influence in the church and world.

Our text applies to the golden altar of the heart. God loves to see the hearts of His people glowing toward Him. Let us give God our hearts blazing with love for Him. May we seek His grace in such abundance that the fire will never be quenched. Many foes will attempt to extinguish it, but if the unseen hand pours the sacred oil, the fire will blaze brighter and higher. Use texts of Scripture as fuel, for each verse is a live coal. But above all, spend much time alone with Jesus.

ONE WORD

"He appeared first to Mary Magdalene."

—Mark 16:9

Jesus may have "appeared first to Mary Magdalene" not only because of her persevering seeking and deep love for Him, but also because she was a special trophy of Christ's delivering power. Learn from this: Greatness of sin before conversion does not hinder one from being especially favored with special fellowship.

Mary Magdalene left all to become a constant attendant to the Savior. He was her first and chief object. Many who were on Christ's side did not take up Christ's cross as she did. She spent her substance in relieving His needs. If we would see Christ, let us serve Him closely.

Tell me which Christians sit most often under the banner of His love and drink the deepest from the cup of communion. I am sure it is those who give the most, who serve the best, and who stay the closest to His bleeding heart.

Notice how Christ revealed Himself to this sorrowing one, by a single word, "Mary" (John 20:16). Just one word from His voice and she knew Him. Her heart showed her allegiance by one word, for her heart was too full to say more. That one word was most fitting for the occasion because it implies obedience. She said, "Master."

There is no state of mind in which this confession of allegiance will be cold. When your spirit glows most with the heavenly fire you will say, "I am Your servant. You have set me free." If you can say, "Master," if you feel that His will is your will, then you stand in a happy and holy place.

He had to have said, "Mary," or she could not have said, "Rabboni." See then, from all this, how Christ honors those who honor Him. See how our love draws our Beloved. See how just one word of His turns weeping to rejoicing.

His presence makes the heart's sunshine.

JULY 15, EVENING

DEPENDENT

"So they gathered it [manna] every morning."

—Exodus 16:21

Work to maintain a sense of total dependence on the Lord's good will and pleasure for the continuance of your richest enjoyments. Never try to live on old manna. Never seek help in Egypt. Everything must come from Jesus, or you will be ruined forever. Old anointing will not suffice. Your head must have fresh oil poured on it from the golden horn of the sanctuary or it will cease from its glory.

Today you may be on the summit with God. Only He who has put you there can keep you there. If He does not, you will sink more rapidly than you can imagine. Your mountain stands firm only while He keeps it in place.

If He hides His face, you will soon be troubled. If the Savior chooses, He can instantly darken any window through which you see the light of heaven. Joshua commanded the sun to stand still (Joshua 10:12), but Jesus can shroud it in total darkness. He can withdraw the joy of your heart, the light of your eyes, and the strength of your life. Your comforts are in His hands. At His will those comforts can flee. We need to feel and recognize this moment-by-moment dependence on Him.

He permits us to pray only for daily bread (Matthew 6:11) and promises only that "as [our] days, so shall [our] strength be" (Deuteronomy 33:25). But is it not best for us that we go often to His throne to be reminded of His love? How rich the grace He continually supplies. How blessed that He does not stop supplying because of our ingratitude. The golden shower never ceases. The cloud of blessing lingers over where we live.

Oh Lord Jesus, we bow at Your feet, conscious of our utter inability to do anything without You. In every favor that we are privileged to receive, we adore Your blessed name and acknowledge Your unexhausted love. Amen.

JULY 16, MORNING

FINDING COMFORT

"You will arise and have mercy on Zion; for the time to favor her. Yes, the set time, has come. For Your servants take pleasure in her stones, and show favor to her dust." —Psalm 102:13–14

Selfish people in trouble are exceedingly hard to comfort, because their springs of comfort lie entirely within, and when they are sad, their springs are dry.

Generous people who are full of Christian philanthropy have other springs from which to supply themselves with comfort. They can go to God and find abundant help, and they discover reasons for consolation in things relating to the world, the nation, and above all, the church.

David in this Psalm was exceedingly sorrowful. He wrote, "I am like an owl of the desert. I lie awake, and am like a sparrow alone on the housetop" (Psalm 102:7). The only way David could find comfort was in the conviction that God would have mercy on Zion and that Zion would eventually prosper. Regardless of how low his feelings were, David knew Zion would rise. Christian, learn comfort from God's gracious dealings with the church. That which is precious to your Master should be precious to you.

If your way is dark, your heart should be happy with the triumphs of His cross and the spread of His truth. Your personal troubles will be forgotten while you look not only on what God has done and is doing for Zion, but on the glorious things He is yet to do for His church.

Whenever you are sad or depressed, forget yourself and your little concerns and seek the welfare and prosperity of Zion. When you are on your knees, do not limit your petitions to the narrow circle of your own difficulties. Send out prayers of longing for the church's prosperity. "Pray for the peace of Jerusalem" (Psalm 122:6), and your soul will be refreshed.

JULY 16, EVENING

ARE YOU ELECTED?

"Knowing, beloved brethren, your election by God."

—1 Thessalonians 1:4

Many want to know if they are elected before they look to Christ. The only way this question will be answered, however, is by looking to Jesus.

Do you feel that you are a lost and guilty sinner? Go straight to the cross of Christ and tell Jesus what you have read in the Bible: "The one who comes to Me I will by no means cast out" (John 6:37). Tell Him that God, through the apostle, has said, "This is a faithful saying and worthy of all acceptance, that Christ Jesus came into the world to save sinners, of whom I am chief" (1 Timothy 1:15).

Look to Jesus and believe on Him, and you will have proof of your election. As surely as you believe, you are elected. If you will give yourself wholly to Christ and trust Him, then you are one of God's chosen.

But if you stop and say, "I first want to know if I am elected," you will never know. Go to Jesus just as you are. Forget the curious inquiry about election. Go straight to Christ and hide in His wounds. Then you will know election. The assurance of the Holy Spirit will be given, and you will be able to say, "I know whom I have believed and am persuaded that He is able to keep what I have committed to Him until that Day" (2 Timothy 1:12).

Christ was at the everlasting council. He can tell you whether you were chosen or not. There is no other way to find out. Put your trust in Him and His answer will be, "Yes, I have loved you with an everlasting love; therefore with lovingkindness I have drawn you" (Jeremiah 31:3).

There will be no doubt about His having chosen you when you have chosen Him.

Sons we are through God's election,
Who in Jesus Christ believe.

JULY 17, MORNING

NO PRISONERS

"Do not let one of them escape."

—1 Kings 18:40

The prophet Elijah's prayer had been answered. Fire came down from heaven and consumed the sacrifice in the presence of all the people. Elijah then ordered the Israelites to capture the priests of Baal. He sternly cried, "Do not let one of them escape. So they seized them and Elijah brought them down to the Brook Kishon and executed them there" (1 Kings 18:40).

Our sins are likewise doomed; not one of them is to be preserved. Even our darling sins must die. Do not spare them. Strike, though they are as precious as an Isaac. Strike, because God struck at sin when it was laid on His own Son. With stern and unflinching purpose, let us condemn to death the sins that are the idols of our hearts.

You ask how to accomplish this? Jesus will be your power. You were given grace to overcome sin in the covenant. You have strength to win the victory in the crusade against inward lusts, because Christ Jesus has promised to be with you even to the end.

If you would triumph over darkness, enter the presence of the Sun of Righteousness. No place is as well-adapted for the discovery of sin or for the recovery from its power and guilt, as the immediate presence of God. When Job's eye of faith rested on God, he abhorred sin and repented in dust and ashes (Job 42:6).

When even the fine gold of the Christian often becomes dim, we need the sacred fire to consume the dross. Fly to God, "for our God is a consuming fire" (Hebrews 12:29) who consumes not our spirit, but our sins.

Let the goodness of God excite in us a sacred jealousy and a holy revenge against iniquities that are hateful in His sight. "Now go and attack Amalek and utterly destroy all they have" (1 Samuel 15:3). Do not let one sin escape.

JULY 17, EVENING

THE LAST

"They shall break camp last with their standards."

—Numbers 2:31

When the armies of Israel were marching, the camp of Dan brought up the rear. Though the Danites were last their position in the march was unimportant because they were part of the nation. The entire nation followed the same fiery, cloudy pillar. They all ate the same manna and drank from the same spiritual rock. They all journeyed to the same inheritance.

Come, my heart, cheer up, even if you are last and least. It is your privilege to be in the army and to share with those who lead. Someone has to be last in honor and esteem. Someone has to do the menial work for Jesus. Why not me? In a poor village, among peasantry, or in a back street among the degraded, I will work and "break camp last with my standard."

The Danites today occupy a very useful place. Stragglers have to be picked up and lost property has to be gathered. Fiery spirits may dash forward over new paths to learn fresh truth and win more souls, but a more conservative spirit may be engaged in reminding the church of her ancient faith and restoring her fainting children. Every position has duties. The slowly moving children of God may find their position to be a great blessing to the entire host.

The rear guard is a place of danger. There are foes behind and foes ahead. Attacks may come from any quarter. We read that Amalek attacked Israel and slew some of the rear guard (Exodus 17:8).

Experienced Christians will find much work for their weapons. They need to aid those doubting, desponding, and wavering souls who are lacking in faith, knowledge, and joy. These must have help. It is the business of the well-taught saint to carry the standard of the last.

My soul, tenderly watch and help those who are last.

ORDER

"They do not push one another; every one marches in his own column."

—Joel 2:8

"The locusts have no king. Yet they all advance in ranks" (Proverbs 30:27). Their number is legion, yet they do not crowd each other and throw their columns into confusion. This remarkable fact shows how thoroughly the Lord has infused the spirit of order into His universe. The smallest animated creatures are controlled as much as the rolling planets or the seraphic messengers.

It would be wise for believers to be ruled by the same influence in their spiritual life. In Christian graces no one should usurp the sphere of another. Affection must not smother honesty, courage must not elbow weakness, modesty must not jostle energy, and patience must not slaughter resolution.

One duty must not interfere with another. Public usefulness must not injure private holiness. Church work must not push family worship into a corner. It is evil to offer God one duty stained with the blood of another. Each is beautiful in its season, but only in its season.

It was to the Pharisee that Jesus said, "These you ought to have done without leaving the others undone" (Luke 11:42). The same rule applies to our personal positions. We must know our place, take it, and keep it. We must minister as the Spirit gives us ability and not intrude on another believer's domain.

Our Lord Jesus taught us not to covet the high places. "For he who is least among you all will be great" (Luke 9:48). Let it be far from us to be envious spirits. Let us feel the force of the Master's command and obey by keeping rank with the rest of the host.

Tonight, let us make sure that we are keeping the unity of the Spirit in the bond of peace (Ephesians 4:3). Let our prayer be that in all the churches of the Lord Jesus peace and order will prevail.

JULY 18, EVENING

GOD'S GLORY IN THE STORM

"The Lord our God has shown us His glory."

—Deuteronomy 5:24

God's great design in all His works is the manifestation of His own glory. But how can God's glory be manifested to such fallen creatures as us? Our eye is not single. We always have a side glance toward our own honor and too high an estimate of our own powers, and thus we are not qualified to behold the glory of the Lord.

It is clear that self must get out of the way so there can be room for God to be exalted. This is why He often brings us trials and difficulties, that, being conscious of our folly and weakness, when deliverance comes, we will have been fitted to behold the majesty of God.

If your life is an even, smooth path, you will see little of the Lord's glory. You will have no occasion to cry out to Him and be filled with His revelation. If you navigate only little streams and shallow creeks, you will know nothing about the God of storms. "Those who go down to the sea in ships. Who do business on great waters. They see the works of the Lord and His wonders in the deep" (Psalm 107:23–24).

It is in the huge Atlantic waves of bereavement, poverty, temptation, and reproach that we learn the power of Jehovah, because we feel the littleness of our ability. Thank God if you have been led along a rough road. This is what has given you experience in God's greatness and lovingkindness. Your troubles have enriched you with a wealth of knowledge that could not be gained by any other means. Like Moses, your trials have been the cleft of the rock where Jehovah placed you to see His glory as it passed (Exodus 33:22).

Praise God that you have not been left to the darkness and ignorance of continued prosperity. The great fight of affliction has prepared you for the manifestation of His glory, in His wonderful dealings with you.

WEAK THINGS

"A bruised reed He will not break, and smoking flax He will not quench."

—Matthew 12:20

What is weaker than a bruised reed? Let a wild duck light on it and it snaps. Let a foot brush against it, and it is bruised and broken. Every breeze that blows across the river moves it back and forth. You can conceive of nothing more frail or brittle, nothing whose existence is in more jeopardy, than a bruised reed.

Look at a smoking flax. What is it? There is a spark, but it is almost smothered. An infant's breath could blow it out. Nothing has a more precarious existence than its flame.

These are weak things. Yet Matthew says of them, "A bruised reed [Jesus] will not break, and smoking flax He will not quench."

Some of God's children are made strong to do mighty works for Him. God has His Samsons who can pull up the gates of Gaza and carry them to the hill top (Judges 16:3). God has a few of the mightiest who are lion-like, but the majority of His people are a weak, trembling race. They are like starlings, frightened at every passer by. They are a fearful little flock.

If temptation comes, they are caught like birds in a snare. If trials threaten, they are ready to faint. Their frail boat is tossed to and fro by every wave. They drift like a sea gull on the crest of the billows. Weak things, without strength, without wisdom, without foresight.

Weak as they are, and because they are so weak, the promise of our text is special to them. This is grace and graciousness! This is love and lovingkindness! It opens the compassion of Jesus, so gentle, tender, considerate!

We need never cringe from His touch. We need never fear a harsh word from Him. Although He might chide us for weakness, He will not rebuke us. Bruised reeds receive no blows from Him, the smoking flax no dampening frowns.

JULY 19, EVENING

GUARANTEED HEIR

"The guarantee of our inheritance."

—Ephesians 1:14

What light, what joy, what consolation, and what delight is experienced by those who feed on Jesus alone. Yet we know that what we have of Christ's preciousness in this life is imperfect at best. As an old writer said, "Tis but a taste!"

"You have tasted that the Lord is gracious" (1 Peter 2:3), but you do not know just how good and how gracious. All you know is that His sweetness makes you long for more. "We also who have the firstfruits of the Spirit, even we ourselves, groan within ourselves, eagerly waiting for the adoption, the redemption of our body" (Romans 8:23).

Here in this world we are like Israel in the wilderness, who had just one cluster from Eshcol (Deuteronomy 1:25); but there in our inheritance we will be in the vineyard. Here we see the manna falling like small seeds; but there we will eat the bread of heaven and the old corn of the kingdom.

We are only beginners in spiritual education. We have learned the letters of the alphabet but cannot as yet read words, much less put a sentence together. As an old puritan said, "He that has been in heaven but five minutes knows more than the general assembly of divines on earth."

We may have unfilled needs and wants here, but soon every wish will be satisfied there. All our powers will find the sweetest employment in that eternal world of joy. Oh Christian, wait just a few years. In a little time you will be rid of all your trials and troubles. Your eyes now diffused with tears will weep no longer. You will gaze in indescribable rapture on the splendor of Him who sits on the throne. More than that, you will sit on His throne. The triumph of His glory will be shared by you. His crown, His joy, and His paradise will be yours.

You will be a joint heir with Him who is the heir of all things.

A DIVINE QUESTION

"And now why take the road to Egypt, to drink the waters of Sihor?

—Jeremiah 2:18

By numerous miracles, by abundant mercies, by strange deliverance, Jehovah had proven to be worthy of Israel's trust. God had protected them with a hedge, yet they broke it down (Psalm 80:12). They abandoned the true and living God to follow after false gods.

The Lord frequently reproved them for this infatuation. Our text contains but one instance of God earnestly reasoning with them. This text may be translated, "Why do you wander so far and leave your own cool stream? Why do you forsake Jerusalem to go to Noph and to Tahapanes? Why are you so strangely set on mischief? Why can't you be content with the good and the healthy? Why do you follow after that which is evil and deceitful?"

Is this not a word of reason and warning to the Christian? True believer, called by grace and washed in the precious blood of Jesus, you have tasted better than the muddy rivers of this world's pleasure. You have had fellowship with Christ. You have had the joy of seeing Jesus and leaning your head on His bosom.

Can the trifles, the songs, the honors, and the laughter of this world satisfy you after that? You have eaten the bread of angels. Can you now live on husks? Good Rutherford once said, "I have tasted of Christ's own manna, and it has put my mouth out of taste for the stale bread of this world's joys."

I think it should be the same with you. If you are wandering after the waters of Egypt, return quickly to the one living fountain. The waters of Sihor may be sweet to the Egyptians, but it will be bitter to you.

"Why take the road to Egypt?" Jesus asks you this question this evening. How will you answer Him?

JULY 20, EVENING

ENEMY IMPOSSIBILITIES

"The daughter of Jerusalem has shaken her head behind your back."

—Isaiah 37:22

Reassured by the word of the Lord, the trembling citizens of Zion grew bold and shook their heads at Sennacherib's boastful threats (Isaiah 36:1). Strong faith enables the servants of God to look with calm contempt on their most arrogant foes.

We know that our enemies are attempting impossibilities. They seek to destroy the eternal life that cannot die while Jesus lives. They seek to overthrow the citadel against which "the gates of Hades shall not prevail" (Matthew 16:18). "It is hard for [them] to kick against the goads" (Acts 9:5), yet they rush against Jehovah to their hurt.

We know their weakness. What are they but human? And what is a human but a worm (Psalm 22:6)? They roar and foam like waves of the sea, frothing out their shame. When the Lord arises, they will fly as chaff before the wind and be consumed as kindling. They are utterly powerless to damage the cause of God. The weakest soldier in Zion's ranks can laugh them to scorn.

Above all, we know that the Most High is with us. Where are His enemies? "Woe to him who strives with his Maker! Let the potsherd strive with the potsherds of the earth! Shall the clay say to him who forms it, 'What are you making'?" (Isaiah 45:9). "You shall break them with a rod of iron; You shall dash them to pieces like a potter's vessel" (Psalm 2:9).

Banish all fears! The kingdom is safe in the King's hands. Shout for joy! "Our God reigns" (Isaiah 52:7)! His foes will "be trampled down under Him as straw is trampled down for the refuse heap" (Isaiah 25:10):

> As true as God's own word is true;
> Nor earth, nor hell, with all their crew,
>   Against us shall prevail.
> A jest, and by-word, are they grown;
> God *is* with us, we *are* His own,
>   Our victory cannot fail.

ANSWER THIS

"Why do I go mourning?"

—Psalm 42:9

Can you answer this question, believer? Can you find any reason why you are mourning instead of rejoicing? Why do you yield to gloomy anticipations? Who told you the night would never end in day? Who told you the sea of circumstances would ebb until there would be nothing left but miles of mud and horrible poverty? Who told you that the winter of your discontent would proceed from frost to frost, from snow, and ice, and hail to deeper and heavier tempests of despair?

Don't you know that day follows night, that high tide comes after low tide, that spring and summer succeed to winter? Hope! Hope because God does not fail. God loves you in the midst of all this. Mountains are as real when they are hidden by night as in the day. God's love is as true to you now as it was in your brightest moments. The Father does not always chasten. Your Lord hates the rod as much as you do. He uses it for a reason that should make you willing to receive it: It works for your lasting good.

You will yet climb Jacob's ladder with the angels and see Him who sits at the top: your covenant God. You will, amid the splendor of eternity, forget the trials of time, or remember them only to bless the God who led you through them for your lasting good.

Come, sing in the midst of trials. Rejoice, even as you pass through the furnace. Make the wilderness bloom like the rose. Cause the desert to ring with your exalting joys. These light afflictions will soon be over. Then you will be forever with the Lord. Your happiness will never end:

> Faint not nor fear, His arms are near,
> He changeth not, and thou art dear;
> Only believe and thou shall see,
> That Christ is all in all to thee.

THE BRIDE

"I am married to you."

—Jeremiah 3:14

Jesus Christ is joined to His people in marriage union. In love He embraced His church, long before she fell under the yoke of bondage. Full of affection He toiled, like Jacob for Rachel, until the full amount of her purchase price had been paid (Genesis 29;27).

Having sought her by His Spirit and brought her to know and love Him, He awaits the glorious hour when she will "be glad and rejoice and give him glory, for the marriage of the Lamb has come and His wife has made herself ready" (Revelation 19:7). "Blessed are those who are called to the marriage supper of the Lamb" (Revelation 19:9).

The glorious Bridegroom has not presented His church before the Majesty of heaven. The church has not entered the enjoyment of her dignities as His wife and queen. The church is still wandering in a world of woe. But even now she is the bride, the spouse of Jesus, and she is precious in His sight, written on His hands and united with His person.

On earth, He offers the church all the affectionate appointments of His love. He makes rich provisions for her needs. He pays all her debts. He allows her to assume His name and to share in all His wealth. Death severs the marital tie between the most loving couples, but it cannot divide the links of this immortal marriage.

In heaven, "they neither marry nor are given in marriage, but are like angels of God" (Matthew 22:30). But there is one marvelous exception to this rule. In heaven, Christ and His church will celebrate their joyous marriage.

Surpassing all human union is that mystical cleaving to the church, for which Christ left His Father and became one flesh with His church.

JULY 22, MORNING

BEHOLD THE MAN

"Behold the Man!"

—John 19:5

I f there is one place where our Lord Jesus most fully became the joy and comfort of His people it is where He plunged deepest into the depths of woe.

Come, gracious souls, behold the Man in the garden of Gethsemane. Behold His heart so brimming with love that He cannot hold it in, yet so full of sorrow that it must be vented. Behold the bloody sweat as it distills from every pore of His body and falls to the ground.

Behold the Man as soldiers drive nails into His hands and feet. Look up, repenting sinners, and see the sorrowful image of your suffering Lord. Mark Him, as ruby drops glisten on His crown of thorns and adorn it with priceless gems.

Behold the Man when all His bones are out of joint, and He is poured out like water and brought to the dust of death. God has forsaken Him; hell surrounds Him.

Behold, and see. Was there ever sorrow like His sorrow? You who pass by, stop and draw near. Look on this spectacle of grief. It is unique and unparalleled, a wonder to men and angels, and a prodigy unmatched.

Behold the King of Misery, the Emperor of Woe, the one who had no equal or rival in agonies! Gaze on Him, all you who mourn. If there is no consolation in a crucified Christ, there is no joy in earth or heaven. If in the ransom price of His blood there is no hope, then there is no pleasure at the right hand of God.

We have only to sit at the foot of the cross to be less troubled about our doubts and woes. We have only to see His sorrows to be ashamed to mention our sorrows. We have only to look at His wounds to heal our own.

If we are to live holy lives, it must be by the contemplation of His death. If we would rise to dignity, it must be by considering His humiliation and His sorrow.

JULY 22, EVENING

EVEN YOU

"Even you were as one of them."

—Obadiah 1:11

Jacob expected some brotherly kindness from Edom in a time of difficulty, but Edom joined forces with Jacob's enemies.

Special emphasis in our text is placed on the word *you,* as when Caesar cried to Brutus, "and *you* Brutus?" A bad action may be all the worse because of the individual who committed it. When *we* sin, we who are the chosen favorites of heaven, we sin with an emphasis. Ours is a crying offence because we are so uniquely favored.

If an angel should lay a hand on us when we are doing evil, no rebuke other than this question is needed, "*You?* What are you doing?" Much forgiven, much delivered, much instructed, much enriched, and much blessed we are. Shall we then dare do evil? God forbid!

A few minutes of confession may be beneficial this morning. Have you never been wicked? At an evening party certain people laughed at uncleanness and the joke was not offensive to you. "Even you were as one of them." When hard words were spoken concerning the ways of God, you were bashfully silent and to the onlookers, "Even you were as one of them." When the worldly were cheating in the market, perhaps "Even you were as one of them." When they unrighteously pursued an unrighteous profit, perhaps you were equally greedy. Is there any difference between you and them?

Be honest with yourself. Make sure that you are a new creature in Christ Jesus. When you have this assurance, walk jealously lest any could again say, "Even you were as one of them."

You do not want to share their eternal doom. Why do you want to be like them here? Do not follow them, lest you come to their ruin. Side with the afflicted people of God and not with the world.

CLEANSES

"The blood of Jesus Christ His Son cleanses us from all sin."

—1 John 1:7

"Cleanses," says our text, not "shall cleanse." There are multitudes who have a dying hope they may be pardoned. Yet how infinitely better it is to have cleansing now rather than to depend on the bare possibility of forgiveness at death.

Some imagine that a sense of pardon is obtainable only after many years of Christian experience. But forgiveness of sin is a present blessing, a privilege for today, a joy for this hour. The moment a sinner trusts Jesus, complete forgiveness occurs.

Our text is written in the present tense to indicate *continuance*. The blood *cleansed* yesterday, it *cleanses* today, and it will *cleanse* tomorrow. Christian, it will always be this way until you cross the river. Every hour you may come to this fountain because it still cleanses.

Note the completeness of the cleansing. "The blood of Jesus Christ His Son cleanses us from *all* sin." Reader, I cannot tell you the exceeding sweetness of this word, but I pray to God the Holy Spirit to give you a taste of it. Many are our sins against God, but whether the bill is small or large, the same receipt discharges one as well as the other. The blood of Jesus Christ is as blessed and divine a payment for the transgressions of blaspheming Peter as for the shortcomings of loving John. Our iniquity is gone, gone at once, and gone forever!

Blessed completeness! What a sweet theme to dwell on as one goes to sleep:

> Sins against a holy God;
> Sins against His righteous laws;
> Sins against His love, His blood;
> Sins against His name and cause;
> Sins immense as is the sea—
> From them all He cleanses me.

JULY 23, EVENING

STAND

"Stand still and see the salvation of the Lord."

—Exodus 14:13

These words are God's command to believers when they are reduced to great distress and brought to extraordinary difficulties. They cannot retreat. They cannot go forward. They are shut up on the right hand and on the left. What can they do? The Master's word to them is, "Stand still."

At times like this, it is good to listen only to the Master, for other and evil advisers come with their suggestions. Despair whispers, "Lie down and die. Give it all up." But God would have us to be of cheerful courage, and even in our worst times He would have us rejoice in His love and faithfulness.

Cowardice says, "Retreat. Go back to the world's way of action. You cannot play the Christian's part. It is too difficult. Relinquish your principles." Regardless of how much Satan may urge, you cannot follow this course if you are a child of God, because His divine command tells you to go from strength to strength. And you will! Neither death nor hell can turn you from your course. If for a while you are called to stand still, it is only to renew your strength for some greater advance.

Haste cries, "Do something. Wake up. Waiting is sheer idleness." And thus we may be led to do something now, instead of looking to the Lord, who will not only do something but everything.

Presumption boasts, "If the sea is in front of you, march into it and expect a miracle." But Faith does not listen to Despair, nor to Cowardice, nor to Haste or Presumption. Faith hears God say, "Stand still." Remain upright and ready for action, expect further orders, but cheerfully and patiently wait on the directing voice. It will not be long until God will say to you as distinctly as He spoke to Moses, "Go forward."

A GREAT CAMP

"His camp is very great."

—Joel 2:11

Consider the mightiness of the Lord, who is your glory and defence. He is a man of war, Jehovah is His name. All the forces of heaven are at His call. Legions wait at His door. Cherubim and seraphim, watchers and holy ones, principalities and powers; all are attentive to His will. If our eyes were not blinded by the ophthalmia of the flesh, we would see horses and chariots of fire surrounding the Lord's beloved (2 Kings 6:17).

All the powers of nature are subject to the absolute control of the Creator. Stormy wind and tempest, lightning and rain, snow and hail, soft dew and cheering sunshine; all come and go at His decree. He binds the cluster of the Pleiades and loosens the belt of Orion (Job 38:31).

Earth, sea, air, and the places under the earth are the barracks for Jehovah's great armies. Space is His camp ground. Light is His banner. Flame is His sword. When He goes to war, famine ravages the land, pestilence smites the nations, hurricanes sweep the sea, tornadoes shake the mountains and earthquakes make the solid world tremble.

As for animate creatures, they are all under His dominion. From the great fish that swallowed the prophet (Jonah 1:17), to swarms of flies, that plagued the field of Zoan (Psalm 78:45), all are His servants. His camp is very great.

My soul, see that you are at peace with this mighty King. Even more, enlist under His banner. To fight against Him is madness. To serve Him is glory. Jesus, Immanuel, God with us is ready to receive recruits for the army of the Lord. If you are not enlisted, go to Him before you go to sleep. Beg to be accepted through His merits.

If you are His already, as I hope I am, a soldier of the cross, be of good courage. The enemy is powerless compared with your Lord, whose camp is very great.

JULY 24, EVENING

FLEE

"He had left his garment in her hand and fled outside."

—Genesis 39:13

In contending with certain sins, the only way to be victorious is to run from them. The ancient naturalists wrote much of the legendary serpent, the basilisk, whose eyes fascinated its victims and made them easy prey. Those who would be safe from acts of evil must run from them. A covenant must be made with our eyes not even to look on the cause of temptation. Such sins only need a spark to begin and a blaze follows.

Who would willingly enter the leper's prison and sleep amid its horrible corruption? Only someone who desired to become leprous. If the mariners knew how to avoid a storm, they would rather do anything than run the risk of weathering it. Cautious pilots have no desire to sail close to sandbars or see if they can touch a rock without springing a leak. Their aim is to keep in the middle of a safe channel.

This day I may be exposed to great peril. Give me the serpent's wisdom to avoid it (Matthew 10:16). The wings of a dove may be of more use to me today than the jaws of a lion. I may look like an apparent loser by declining evil company, but I had better leave my coat than lose my character. It is not necessary for me to be rich, but it is imperative for me to be pure. No ties of friendship, no chains of beauty, no flashes of talent, and no shafts of ridicule must turn me from the wise resolve to flee sin.

The devil I am to resist, and he will flee (James 4:7). But the lusts of the flesh I must flee, or they will surely overcome me.

Oh God of holiness, preserve Your Josephs that Vanity Fair may not bewitch them with vile suggestions. May the horrible trinity of the world, the flesh, and the devil never overcome us! Amen.

THE WORK OF ADVERSITY

"In their affliction they will earnestly seek Me."

—Hosea 5:15

Losses and adversities are frequently the method the great Shepherd uses to fetch home His wandering sheep. Like fierce dogs, they worry the wanderers back to the fold. Often Christians become obedient to the Lord's will through shortness of bread and hard labor.

When rich and increased in goods, many Christians carry their heads loftily and speak boastfully. Like David, they flatter themselves, saying, "Now in my prosperity . . . I shall never be moved . . . my mountain stands strong" (Psalm 30:7).

When Christians grow wealthy or have good reputations, excellent health, and happy families, they often include Mr. Carnal Security at their dinner tables. If they are true children of God, there is a rod waiting for them. Wait. You may see their substance melt away as a dream. There goes a portion of their estate; how quickly the acres change hands. That debt, that dishonored bill; how fast the losses roll in. Where will it end?

When these embarrassments occur one after another, it is a blessed sign of divine life if Christians become distressed about their backsliding and return to God. Blessed are the waves that wash the sailor on the rock of salvation. Losses in business are often sanctified to the soul's enrichment.

If chosen souls will not come to the Lord full handed, they will come empty handed. If God in His grace finds no other means of making us honor Him, He will cast us into the deep. If we fail to honor Him on the pinnacle of riches, He will bring us to the valley of poverty.

Do not faint, heir of sorrow, when you are thus rebuked. Recognize the loving hand that chastens and say, "I will arise and go to my father" (Luke 15:18).

DILIGENCE

"Giving all diligence, add to your faith virtue, to virtue knowledge, to knowledge self-control, to self-control perseverance, to perseverance godliness." —2 Peter 1:5–6

If you want to enjoy the eminent grace of being fully assured of faith, then under the blessed influence and assistance of the Holy Spirit do what the Scripture tells you: "give diligence." Be sure that your faith is the right kind, that it is not mere belief of doctrine, but a simple faith that depends on Christ, and on Christ alone.

Give diligent heed to your courage. Plead with God to give you a lion's courage, that with a consciousness for right you may go boldly forward.

Study the Scriptures to get knowledge, for the knowledge of doctrine will tend to confirm faith. Try to understand God's Word. "Let the word of Christ dwell in you richly" (Colossians 3:16).

When you have done this, add self-control. Pay attention to your body and have self-control without. Pay attention to your soul and have self-control within. Get self-control of lip, life, heart, and thought.

Then add to this, with the help of the Holy Spirit, patience. Ask Him to give you patience that endures affliction; patience that, when tried, you shall come forth as gold; patience so that you will not murmur or be depressed in affliction.

When that grace is won, seek godliness. Godliness is something more than religion. Make God's glory your object in life. Live in His sight. Dwell close to Him. Then when you have godliness, add brotherly love. Have a love for all the saints and then add a charity that opens it arms with an intense love for their souls.

When you are adorned with these jewels, you will know by the clearest evidence your calling and election is sure.

PRINCES

"That He may seat him with princes."

—Psalm 113:8

Our spiritual privileges are of the highest order. "With princes," is the place of select society. Truly our fellowship is with the Father and His Son Jesus Christ" (1 John 1:3).

Speaking of select society, there is none like this! "You are a chosen generation, a royal priesthood, a holy nation. His own special people" (1 Peter 2:9). We have come "to the general assembly and church of the first born who are registered in heaven" (Hebrews 12:23).

Saints are admitted to the throne room. Princes enter when common people must stand at a distance. The child of God has free access to the inner courts of heaven. "For through Him we both have access by one Spirit to the Father" (Ephesians 2:18). "Let us therefore come boldly to the throne of grace" (Hebrews 4:16).

Among princes there is abundant wealth. But what is the abundance of princes compared with the riches of believers? "All things are yours, and you are Christ's, and Christ is God's" (1 Corinthians 3:23). "He who did not spare His own Son, but delivered Him up for us all, how shall He not with Him also freely give us all things?" (Romans 8:32).

Princes have distinctive power. Princes of heaven's empire have great influence. They wield a scepter in their domains. They sit on Jesus' throne, for they "shall reign forever and ever" (Revelation 22:5) over the united kingdom of time and eternity.

Princes have special honor. We may look down on all earth-born dignity from the eminence where grace has placed us. What is human grandeur compared to this? He "raised us up together, and made us sit together in the heavenly places in Christ Jesus" (Ephesians 2:6). We share the honor of Christ. Compared to this, earthly splendors are not worth a thought.

Union with the Lord is a coronet of beauty outshining all the blaze of imperial pomp.

PROMISES

"Exceedingly great and precious promises."

—2 Peter 1:4

If you want to experience the preciousness of the promises, if you want to enjoy them in your heart, spend much time meditating on them. Promises are like grapes in the wine press; squeeze them and juice will flow. Thinking about these hallowed words will often be the prelude to their fulfillment.

While you are reflecting on them, the favor you are seeking will come. Many a Christian who has thirsted for the promise has found its blessing gently distilling in their soul, and they rejoice that they were led to place the promise near their heart.

Besides meditating on the promises, seek to receive them as the very words of God. Say to your soul, "If I were dealing with an individual's promise, I would carefully consider the ability and the character of the person who had covenanted with me." It is the same with the promises of God. My eye must not be so fixed on the greatness of the mercy, for that may stagger me. Let my eye be fixed on the greatness of the Promiser, for that will cheer me. My soul, it is God, your God. The God who cannot lie, this God speaks to you now.

This Word of His that you are considering is as true as His existence. He is a God unchangeable. He has not altered the things that He has spoken. He has not called back one single consolatory sentence. Nor can He fail in wisdom as to the time when He will bestow the favor. He knows when it is best to give and when it is better to withhold.

Since this is the word of a God so true, so unchanging, so powerful, and so wise, I will, I must, believe the promise.

If we meditate on the promises and consider the Promiser, we will experience their sweetnesses and obtain their fulfillments.

PARDONED

"Who shall bring a charge against God's elect?"

—Romans 8:33

Most blessed challenge! Impossible to answer! Every sin of the elect was laid on the great Champion of our salvation and was carried away by the atonement. There is no sin in God's book against His people. They are justified in Christ forever.

When the guilt of sin was taken away, the punishment of sin was removed. For the Christian there is no blow from God's angry hand; no, not so much as a single frown of punitive justice. The believer may be chastised by his Father, but God the Judge has nothing to say to the Christian except, "I have absolved you. You are acquitted."

For the Christian there is no penal death in this world, much less any second death. We are completely free of all punishment as well as the guilt of sin. Even the power of sin is removed. It may stand in our way and agitate us, but sin is a conquered foe to every soul in Jesus.

We can overcome every sin as long as we rely on God. Those who wear the white robe in heaven overcame through the blood of the Lamb (Revelation 7:13), and we may do the same. No lust is too mighty, no besetting sin too strongly entrenched. We can overcome through the power of Christ. Christian believe it, your sin is a condemned thing. It may kick and struggle, but it is doomed to die. God has written condemnation across it. Christ has crucified it. Go now and mortify it.

May the Lord help you to live to His praise, for sin with all its guilt, shame, and fear is gone:

> Here's pardon for transgressions past,
> It matters not how black their cast;
> And, O my soul, with wonder view,
> For sins to come here's pardon too.

FOOLISH

"I was so foolish and ignorant. I was like a beast before You."

—Psalm 73:22

This is the confession of the man after God's own heart. In telling us about his inner life, David writes, "I was so foolish and ignorant." Here the word *foolish* means more than it normally signifies. In an earlier verse David wrote, "I was envious of the boastful when I saw the prosperity of the wicked" (Psalm 73:3). This shows that David's intended folly was sinful. David puts himself down as being envious, so envious that he was foolish and ignorant.

It was a sinful folly, that is a folly which could not be excused by frailty but was condemned because of its perverseness and wilful ignorance. David was envious of the present prosperity of the ungodly because he forgot the dreadful end awaiting the sinner.

Are we better than David, that we should call ourselves wise? Do we profess to have attained perfection, or to have been so chastened that the rod has taken the wilfulness completely out of us? Ah, this is pride indeed. If David was foolish, how foolish are we in our own esteem?

Look back, believer. Think how you doubted God when He had been faithful. Think of your foolish cry, "Not so, my Father," when He afflicted you to give you a larger blessing. Think of the many times you have misread His providence, misinterpreted His dispensation, and groaned, "All these things are against me," when they were working together for your good (Romans 8:28).

Let us remember how often we have chosen sin because of its pleasure, when that pleasure was a root of bitterness to us. Surely if we know our own hearts, we must plead guilty to sinful folly. We must be conscious of this foolishness. We must make David's resolve our own, "You will guide me with Your counsel" Psalm 73:24.

DOING GOOD

"Went about doing good."

—Acts 10:38

These few words are an exquisite miniature of the Lord Jesus Christ. Not many touches, but they are the strokes of a master's pencil. Of the Savior, and only of the Savior, is this true in the fullest, broadest, and most unqualified sense: He "went about doing good."

From this description it is evident that He personally did good. The evangelists tell us that He touched the leper with His finger and anointed the eyes of the blind. In cases where He was asked to speak the word from a distance, He usually went directly to the sick bed and worked the cure in person.

The lesson to us is that if we would do good we must do it personally. Give donations with your own hand and with a kind look or word that will enhance the value of the gift. Speak to friends about their soul with a loving appeal that will have more influence than a whole library of tracts.

Our Lord's method of doing good was His incessant activity. He did not only the good close at hand, but He also "went about" on errands of mercy. In all of Judea there was scarcely a village or hamlet that was not gladdened by the sight of Him. How this reproves the creeping, loitering manner in which many Christians serve the Lord. "Let us not grow weary in doing good, for in due season we shall reap if we do not lose heart" (Galatians 6:9).

Our text implies that Jesus Christ went out of His way to do good. He was never deterred by danger or difficulty. He sought the objects of His gracious intentions. So must we. If old plans do not work, let us try new ones, because fresh experiments sometimes achieve more than regular methods.

The practical application of this may be summed up by the words, "He has left an example that we should follow" (1 Peter 2:21).

JULY 28, EVENING

NEVERTHELESS

"Nevertheless I am continually with You."

—Psalm 73:23

Nevertheless: notwithstanding all the foolishness and ignorance that David had been confessing to God, by not one atom less was it true and certain that David was still saved and accepted by God.

The blessing of being constantly in God's presence was undoubtedly his. David was fully conscious of his own lost estate and the deceitfulness and vileness of his nature. Yet David, by a glorious outburst of faith sings, "Nevertheless I am continually with You."

Believer, you are forced to confess and acknowledge with Asaph, "Nevertheless, since I belong to Christ I am continually with God!" You are continually on His mind. He is always thinking of you for your own good (Isaiah 49:15–16). You are continually before His eye, and His eye never sleeps but perpetually watches over you (Psalm 121:3). You are continually in His hand, so that none can snatch you away (John 10:28). You are continually on His heart, worn there as a memorial, just as the priest bore the names of the twelve tribes on his heart (Exodus 39:14).

You always think of me, Oh God. The heart of Your love yearns towards me. You are always making providence work for my good. You have "set me as a seal upon Your heart, as a seal upon your arm. Your love is strong as death, . . . many waters cannot quench love, nor can the floods drown it" (Song of Solomon 8:6,7).

Surprising grace! You see me in Christ. Though in myself abhorred, You see me wearing Christ's righteous garments and washed in His blood. Thus I stand accepted in Your presence. I am continually in Your favor, "continually with You." This is comfort for the tried and afflicted soul who is pestered by the tempest within. Look at the calm without.

Nevertheless. Oh say it in your heart and receive the peace it gives. "*Nevertheless* I am continually with You."

THOSE THE FATHER GIVES

"All that the Father gives Me will come to Me."

—John 6:37

This declaration involves the doctrine of election; there are some whom the Father gave to Christ. This also involves the doctrine of effectual calling; those who are given must and will come. Regardless of how they attempt to fight, they will be brought out of darkness into God's marvelous light (1 Peter 2:9).

Our text also teaches the indispensable necessity of faith. Even those who are given to Christ are not saved unless they come to Jesus. They must come by that door, for there is no other way to heaven but by the door, Christ Jesus. All that the Father gives to the Redeemer must come to Him. None can come to heaven unless they come to Christ.

Oh the power and majesty that rests in the words will come. *He does not say that they have the power to come, or that they may come if they wish, but that they* will come. The Lord Jesus by His messengers, His Word, and His Spirit sweetly and graciously compels people to come, that they may eat at His marriage feast. He does this, not by any violation of free human agency, but by the power of His grace.

I may exercise power over another's will, yet that one may be perfectly free because the constraint is exercised according to the laws of the human mind. Jehovah Jesus knows how, with irresistible arguments addressed to the understanding, with mighty reasons appealing to affections, with the influence of His Holy Spirit on all the powers and passions of the soul, to bring the person to God. The whole individual, once so rebellious, now yields cheerfully to His government, subdued by sovereign love.

But how shall those be known whom God has chosen? Those that willingly and joyfully accept Christ, that come to Him with simple and unaffected faith, who rest on Him for all their salvation and all their desire; this is how they shall be known.

Reader, have you come to Jesus this way?

JULY 29, EVENING

HIS WONDERFUL LOOK

"And when he thought about it, he wept."

—Mark 14:72

Some have speculated that as long as Peter lived, his tears flowed whenever he remembered denying his Lord. This may have been true, for Peter's sin was very great, but grace had been perfectly applied.

The same experience is common to all who are redeemed. Like Peter, we remember our boastful promise, "Lord, I am ready to go with You, both to prison and to death" (Luke 22:33). We eat our own words with bitter herbs of repentance when we think of what we vowed to be and then what we have become. We may weep whole showers of grief.

Peter thought about denying his Lord. He thought about the place where he did it, the little reasons that led him to such a heinous sin, the oaths and blasphemies uttered as he sought to confirm his lie, and the dreadful hardness of heart that drove him to do so again and yet again.

When we are reminded of our sins and exceeding sinfulness, can we remain detached and stubborn? Will we make our houses a Bochim and cry to the Lord for renewed assurance of pardoning love (Judges 2:4–5)? May we never take a dry-eyed look at sin, for fear that we would have a tongue parched in the flames of hell.

Peter also thought about his Master's look of love. The Lord followed the rooster's warning with an admonitory look of sorrow, pity, and love (Luke 22:61). That glance was never out of Peter's mind while he lived. It was far more effectual than ten thousand sermons without the Spirit. The penitent apostle would be sure to weep when he recollected the Savior's full forgiveness, which restored him to his former place. To think that we have offended so kind and good a Lord is more than sufficient reason for being continual weepers.

Lord, strike our rocky hearts and make the waters flow. Amen.

SECURITY

"The one who comes to Me I will by no means cast out."

—John 6:37

No limit is set on the duration of this promise. It does not say, "I will not cast out a sinner the first time," but, "I will by no means cast out." The original reads, "I will not, not cast out," or, "I will never, never cast out." The text means that Christ will not at first reject a believer; and since He will not do it at first, He will not do it at the last.

Suppose the believer sins after coming? "If anyone sins, we have an Advocate with the Father, Jesus Christ the righteous" (1 John 2:1).

Suppose that believer backslides? "I will heal their backsliding. I will love them freely, for my anger has turned away from him" (Hosea 14:4).

But believers may fall under temptation. "God is faithful, who will not allow you to be tempted beyond what you are able, but with the temptation will also make the way of escape that you may be able to bear it" (1 Corinthians 10:13).

But believers may sin as David did. Yes, but God will do for them the same that David requested. "Purge me with hyssop and I shall be clean. Wash me and I shall be whiter than snow. Blot out all my iniquities" (Psalm 51:7,9).

"And I give them [My sheep] eternal life, and they shall never perish, neither shall anyone snatch them out of My Father's hand" (John 10:28). What do you say to this, trembling and feeble mind? Is not this a precious mercy? When you come to Christ, He does not treat you well for a little while and then send you away. He will receive you and make you His bride, and you will be His forever. "For you did not receive the spirit of bondage again to fear, but you received the Spirit of adoption by whom we cry out, Abba, Father" (Romans 8:15).

Oh the grace in these words, "The one who comes to me, I will by no means cast out."

JULY 30, EVENING

FELLOWSHIP

"I in them."

—John 17:23

If this is the union that exists between our souls and the person of our Lord, deep and broad is the channel of our communion. It is not a narrow pipe through which a thread-like stream may flow. It is a channel of amazing depth and breadth. Along its glorious length, a ponderous volume of living water rushes.

He has set before us an open door (John 10:9); let us not be slow to enter. This city of communion has many pearly gates. Each gate is wide open; we may enter assured of our welcome. If there was one small opening through which we could talk with Jesus, it would be a high privilege to have a word of fellowship through this narrow space. But how much more blessed to have so large an entrance.

Had the Lord Jesus been far away, with many a stormy sea between, we would have longed to send a messenger to Him, carrying our love and bringing tidings back from His Father's house. But see His kindness; He has built His house next to ours. No even more, He takes lodging with us and dwells in our poor humble hearts for perpetual fellowship. Oh how foolish we must be if we do not live in habitual fellowship with Him.

When the road is long, dangerous, and difficult, friends seldom meet each other. But when they live together, shall Jonathan forget David? When her husband is traveling, a wife may go many days without holding a conversation with him. But she would never have to be separated if he was in the house with her.

Believer, sit at His banquet of wine. Seek the Lord for He is near. Embrace Him for He is your Brother. Hold Him fast for He is your Husband. Press Him to your heart, He is your own flesh.

JULY 31, MORNING

PRAISE

"These are the singers . . . . they were employed in that work day and night."

—1 Chronicles 9:33

It was organized so that the sacred chant never ceased in the temple. Singers were always praising the Lord because His mercy endures forever. Mercy did not cease, either by day or night; therefore, the music never hushed its holy ministry.

My heart, there is a lesson sweetly taught in the ceaseless song of Zion's temple. You are a constant debtor; see that your gratitude, like love, never fails. God's praise is constant in heaven, your final dwelling place, so learn to practice the eternal hallelujah here.

Around the earth the sun scatters its light. Its beams awaken grateful believers to the tune of their morning hymn. By this, perpetual praise is kept up at all hours, covering our globe in a mantle of thanksgiving with a golden belt of song.

The Lord always deserves to be praised for who He is, for His works of creation and providence, for His goodness towards His creatures, and especially for all the marvelous blessings that flow from the transcendent act of redemption.

It is always beneficial to praise the Lord. It cheers the day and brightens the night. It lightens toil and softens sorrow. Over earthly gladness it sheds a sanctifying radiance that makes it less liable to blind us with its glare.

Do we have something to sing about at this moment? Can we weave a song out of past deliverance, or present joys, or future hopes? Each yields summer fruit. The hay is housed, the golden grain invites the sickle, and the sun lingers to shine on a fruitful earth. The interval of shade is shortened so that we may lengthen the hours of devout worship.

By the love of Jesus, let us be stirred to close the day with a psalm of sanctified gladness.

SWEET PROMISES

"Let me go to the field, and glean heads of grain."

—Ruth 2:2

Downcast and troubled Christian, come and glean this morning in the broad field of promise. Here are abundant and precious promises that meet your needs exactly.

Take this one. "A bruised reed He will not break, and smoking flax He will not quench" (Isaiah 42:3). Does this meet your need? Here is a reed, helpless, insignificant, and weak. It is a bruised reed, out of which no music can come. It is weaker than weakness itself. Yet He will not break it.

Perhaps you are like the smoking flax, out of which no light or warmth can come. But He will not quench you. He will blow with His sweet breath of mercy until He fans you into a flame.

Would you glean another ear? "Come to Me, all you who labor and are heavy laden, and I will give you rest" (Matthew 11:28). What soft words! Your heart is tender and the Master knows it. He speaks gently to you. Will you obey and come to Him now?

Take another ear of corn. "Fear not, you worm Jacob . . . I will help you says the Lord and your Redeemer, the Holy One of Israel" (Isaiah 41:14). How can you fear with such wonderful assurance?

You may gather ten thousand golden ears like these! "I have blotted out, like a thick cloud, your transgressions, and like a cloud your sin" (Isaiah 44:22). Or this, "Though your sins are like scarlet, they shall be as white as snow. Though they are red like crimson, they shall be as wool" (Isaiah 1:18). Or this, "The spirit and the bride say, come! And let him who hears say, come! And let him who thirsts come. Whoever desires, let him take the water of life freely" (Revelation 22:17).

Our Master's field is full and rich. The precious promises lie in front of you. Gather them. Make them your own. Grasp these sweet promises. Thresh them by mediation. Feed on them with joy.

AUGUST 1, MORNING

HARVEST TIME

"You crown the year with Your goodness."

—Psalm 65:11

All year long, every hour of every day, God is richly blessing. Whether we are asleep or awake, His mercy waits on us.

The sun may leave us a legacy of darkness, but our God never ceases to shine on His children with His beams of love. Like a river, His lovingkindness is always flowing with a fullness as inexhaustible as His own nature. Like the atmosphere that surrounds the earth and supports life, the benevolence of God surrounds all His creatures: "In Him we live and move and have our being" (Acts 17:28).

The sun on summer days gladdens us with beams more warm and bright than at other times. Rivers at certain seasons are swollen by the rain. The atmosphere itself is sometimes filled with fresh, bracing, or balmy influences. The mercy of God also has its golden hours, its days of overflowing, when the Lord magnifies His grace before His children.

The joyous days of harvest are a special season of excessive favor. Prior to autumn, all was merely expectation and hope. It is in the glory of autumn that the ripe gifts of providence are abundantly bestowed. Autumn is the mellow season of realization. Great is the joy of harvest. Happy are the reapers who fill their arms with the liberality of heaven.

The Psalmist tell us that the harvest is the crowning of the year (Psalm 65:9ff). Surely these crowning mercies call for crowning thanksgiving! Let us have inward emotions of gratitude. Let our hearts be warmed. Let our spirits remember, meditate, and think on this goodness of the Lord.

Let us praise Him with our lips, and laud and magnify His name, from whose bounty all this goodness flows. Then let us glorify God by yielding our gifts to His cause.

A practical proof of our gratitude is a special thank-offering to the Lord of the harvest.

AUGUST 1, EVENING

LIVING STONES

"Who works all things according to the counsel of His will."

—Ephesians 1:11

O ur belief in God's wisdom supposes and necessitates that He has a settled purpose and a plan in the work of salvation.

What would creation have been without His design? Is there a fish in the sea or a bird in the air whose formation was left to chance? No. In every bone, muscle, sinew, gland, and blood vessel, you can see the presence of God working everything according to the design of His infinite wisdom.

Could God be present in creation, ruling over all, and not be present in grace? Shall the new creation have the fickle genius of free will to preside over it when divine counsel rules the old creation? Look at Providence. Not a sparrow "falls to the ground apart from your Father's will. The very hairs of your head are all numbered" (Matthew 10:30). God weighs the mountains of our grief in scales and the hills of our tribulation in balances.

Could there be a God in providence and not in grace? Could the shell be ordained by wisdom and the kernel be left to blind chance? No. He knows the end from the beginning (Isaiah 46:10).

He sees in the end's appointed place not merely the cornerstone laid by the blood of His dear Son (Mark 12:10), but also the ordained position of each chosen stone taken from the quarry of nature and polished by His grace. He sees the final building from corner to cornice, from base to roof, from foundation to pinnacle. He has a clear knowledge of every stone that will be laid in its prepared space and how vast the edifice will be. When the top stone is placed we will shout, "Grace! Grace! unto it" (Zechariah 4:7).

At the end it will be seen clearly that in every chosen vessel of mercy, Jehovah did as He willed with His own. It will be evident that in every part of the work of grace, He accomplished His purpose and glorified His name.

AUGUST 2, MORNING

THE GLEANER

"So she gleaned in the field until evening."

—Ruth 2:17

Let me learn from Ruth the gleaner. As she gathered ears of corn, so must I go to the fields of prayer and meditation. Hearing the word, may I gather spiritual food.

Ruth gathers her portion ear by ear. As her gains are little by little, so must I be content to search for single truths. Every ear helps to make a bundle, and every gospel lesson assists in making us wise to salvation.

Ruth keeps her eyes open. If she stumbles, she may have less to carry home at the end of the day. I too must be watchful. I fear I have already lost much. Oh that I may properly estimate my opportunities and glean with greater diligence.

Ruth stops for all she finds, and so must I. High spirits criticize and object, but lowly minds glean and receive benefit. A humble heart is a great help in profitably hearing the gospel. The engrafted, soul-saving Word is received only in meekness (James 1:21). A stiff back makes a bad gleaner. Down, master pride! You are a vile robber not to be endured for a moment.

What Ruth gathers she holds. If she dropped one ear to find another, the result of her day's work would be scant. She is as careful to retain as to obtain, and at last her gains are great.

How often I forget everything I hear. The second truth pushes the first out of my head. My reading and hearing end in much ado about nothing! Do I feel the importance of storing truth? A hungry belly makes the gleaner wise. If there is no corn in her hand, there will be no bread on her table. She labors under the sense of necessity, and thus her walk is nimble and her grasp is firm.

I have a greater need. Lord, help me to feel it. May it urge me to glean in fields that yield so bountiful a reward to diligence.

AUGUST 2, EVENING

THE LIGHT

"The lamb is its light."

—Revelation 21:23

Quietly contemplate the Lamb as the light of heaven. Light in Scripture is the emblem of joy; and the joy of the saints in heaven is found in the fact that Jesus chose us, loved us, bought us, cleansed us, robed us, kept us, and glorified us. We are here entirely through the Lord Jesus. Each one of these thoughts is like a cluster of the grapes of Eshcol:

Light is the cause of beauty. You cannot see beauty when the light is gone. Without light no radiance flashes from the sapphire, no peaceful ray from the pearl. All the beauty of the saints above comes from Jesus. Like planets, they reflect the light of the Sun of Righteousness. They live as beams proceeding from the central orb. If He withdrew, they must die. If His glory were veiled, their glory must expire.

Light is also the emblem of knowledge. In heaven our knowledge will be perfect, and the Lord Jesus will be the fountain of it. Dark providence, never understood here, will become plain in the light of the Lamb. Oh what unfolding there will be! What glorifying of the God of love!

Light also manifests. In this world "it has not yet been revealed what we shall be" (1 John 3:2). God's people are a hidden people. But when Christ receives His people in heaven, He will touch them with His love and change them into the image of His manifested glory.

They were poor and wretched, but what a transformation! They were stained with sin, but with one touch of His finger, they are as bright as the sun, as clear as crystal. Oh what a manifestation! All this proceeds from the exalted Lamb.

Whatever there may be of radiant splendor, Jesus will be the center and soul of it. Oh to be present to see Him in His own light! The King of kings. The Lord of lords.

BE THERE

"But as He went."

—Luke 8:42

Jesus was on His way to Jairus' home to raise the ruler's daughter from the dead. Jesus, however, is so overflowing in goodness that along the way He does another miracle. While this rod of Aaron bears the blossom of an unaccomplished wonder (Numbers 17:5), it yields the ripe almonds of a perfect work of mercy.

It is enough if we have one purpose and accomplish it. It would be imprudent to expend unnecessary energy along the way. Hurrying to the rescue of a drowning friend, we cannot afford to exhaust our strength on someone else in danger. It is enough for a tree to yield one type of fruit. It is enough for us to fulfill our own special calling.

Our Master, however, knows no limit of power or boundary. He is so full of grace that His path, like the sun that shines, is radiant with lovingkindness everywhere. He is a swift arrow of love that not only reaches its ordained target, but perfumes the air it flies through. Virtue is always going out of Jesus, like sweet perfume from flowers or water from a sparkling fountain. What a delightful encouragement this truth gives.

If our Lord is ready to heal the sick and bless the needy then, my soul, do not be slow to draw close to Him. Let Him smile on you. Do not be slow to ask, for He abundantly gives. Pay serious attention to His Word. Let Jesus speak through it to your heart.

Where He is to be found, be there. Obtain His blessing. When He is present to heal, He can heal you. Surely He is present even now. He always comes to hearts that need Him. Do you need Him? Ah, He knows how much.

Son of David, turn Your eye, look on the distress that is here. Make Your servant whole. Amen.

KNOWLEDGE

"The people who know their God will be strong."

—Daniel 11:32

Every believer understands that knowing God is the highest and best form of knowledge. This knowledge is spiritual and it strengthens our faith. Believers are constantly spoken of in Scripture as people who are enlightened and taught by the Lord. They are said to "have an anointing from the Holy One" (1 John 2:20). It is the Spirit's work to lead them into all truth, to increase and foster their faith.

Knowledge strengthens love as well as faith. Knowledge opens the door through which we see our Savior. Knowledge paints the portrait of Jesus, and when we see that portrait, we love Him. We cannot love a Christ we do not know. If we know only a little of what He has done for us and what He is doing now, we can love Him only a little. The more we know Him, the more we will love Him.

Knowledge also strengthens hope. How can we hope for something if we do not know it exists? Hope may be the telescope, but until we receive instructions our ignorance stands in front of the glass and we see nothing. Knowledge removes the interposing object, then when we look through the bright optic glass we discern the glory to be revealed and anticipate it with joyous confidence.

Knowledge supplies reasons for patience. How can we have patience unless we know something of the sympathy of Christ and understand the good that comes out of the correction our heavenly Father sends?

Nor is there one single grace of the Christian that, under God, will not be fostered and perfected by knowledge. How important then to grow not only in grace, but also in the "knowledge of our Lord Jesus Christ" (2 Peter 1:8).

BLIGHT

"I struck you with blight and mildew and hail in all the labors of your hands."

—Haggai 2:17

Hail is destructive to a standing crop. Hail breaks and beats the precious grain into the ground. We ought to be grateful when the harvest is spared from this terrible ruin. Let us offer the Lord our thanksgiving.

Even more to be feared are those mysterious crop destroyers such as fungus, parasitic fungi, and mildew. These turn the grain to a mass of soot, or decompose it, or dry up the grain; and all is beyond human control. The farmer is compelled to cry, "This is the finger of God."

Were it not for the goodness of God, the rider on the black horse would soon scatter famine over the land (Revelation 6:5). Infinite mercy spares the food, but in view of the active agents that are always present to destroy the harvest, we are wisely taught to pray, "Give us this day our daily bread" (Matthew 6:11). The curse is all around us. We have constant need of God's blessing. When blight and mildew come, they are chastisement from heaven. We must learn to bear the rod and Him that appointed it.

Spiritual mildew is a common evil. When our work is most promising, this blight appears. We hope for many conversions, but instead find general apathy, abounding worldliness, or cruel hardness of heart. There may not be open sin in those for whom we labor, but there is a deficiency of sincerity and decision that sadly disappoints our desires.

We learn from this about our dependence on the Lord and the need to pray that no blight will fall on our work. Spiritual pride or laziness will soon bring the dreadful evil that only the Lord of the harvest can remove. Mildew may even attack our hearts and shrivel our prayers and devotions. May it please the great Vine-keeper to avert so serious a calamity.

Shine, blessed Sun of Righteousness, and drive the blight away.

AUGUST 4, EVENING

GOOD OUT OF EVIL

"We know that all things work together for good to those who love God."

—Romans 8:28

There are some points on which believers are absolutely certain. We know, for instance, that God is in the vessel even when it rocks the most. We believe an invisible hand is always on the world's tiller, that wherever providence may drift, Jehovah steers.

This reassuring knowledge prepares us for everything. We look over the raging waters and see the spirit of Jesus walking on the waves. We hear His voice, "Be of good cheer! It is I; do not be afraid" (Matthew 14:27).

We know that God is always wise. We are confident that there can be no accidents and no mistakes. Nothing can occur without His permission. If we lose all we have, it is better to lose than to have, if God so wills. The worst calamity is the wisest and the kindest thing that could happen to us if God ordains it.

"We know that all things work together for good to those who love God." This is not just a theory. It is a fact. Everything has worked for my good. The poisonous drugs mixed in correct proportions have worked their cure. The sharp cuts of the scalpel have taken away the diseased growth to facilitate healing. Every past event in my life has produced divine and blessed results. I believe that God rules all, that He governs wisely, and that He brings good out of evil. My heart is assured, and I calmly meet each trial as it comes.

Believers in the spirit of true submission can pray, "Send me what You will, my God, just so long as it comes from You. You never gave a harmful portion from Your table to any of Your children."

> Say not my soul, "From whence can God
> relieve my care?"
> Remember that Omnipotence has servants
> everywhere.
> His method is sublime, His heart
> profoundly kind,
> God never is before His time, and never is
> behind.

AUGUST 5, MORNING

CAN WE ESCAPE THE CRUCIBLE?

"Shall your brethren go to war while you sit here?"

—Numbers 32:6

Family membership has obligations. The Reubenites and Gadites would have been most unbrotherly had they claimed their part of the conquered land and then let the rest of Israel fight alone for their share.

We have received much through the efforts and sufferings of the saints in years passed. If we do not make some return to the church of Christ by giving our best energies, then we are unworthy to be enrolled in her ranks. Others are combating the errors of the age, or excavating the perishing from the ruins of the fall. If we fold our hands in idleness we need to be warned, lest the curse of Meroz fall on us (Judges 5:23).

The Master of the vineyard says, "Why have you been standing here idle all day?" (Matthew 20:6). Personal service to Jesus is the duty of all. The work of devoted missionaries and fervent ministers shame us if we sit in idleness. Shrinking from trial is the temptation of those who are at ease in Zion. If possible, they would escape the cross and yet wear the crown.

To them the question of this evening's meditation is applicable. If the most precious are tried in the fire, can we escape the crucible? If the diamond must be ground on the wheel, can we be made perfect without suffering? Why should we be treated better than our Lord? The firstborn felt the rod, why not the younger children?

It is cowardly for a soldier of the cross to choose a downy pillow and a silk couch. Wiser by far are those who, resigned to divine will, grow by the energy of grace. They learn to gather lilies at the foot of the cross. Like Samson, they find honey in the lion (Judges 14:8).

QUESTIONS FOR THE WATCHMAN

"Watchman, what of the night?"

—Isaiah 21:11

We have enemies. Errors are a numerous horde, and a new one appears every hour. What heresy should I guard against? Sin creeps from its lurking places when darkness reigns. I must climb the watchtower and watch with prayer.

Our heavenly Protector foresees all the attacks that are about to be made on us. He prays that our faith will not fail when we are sifted as wheat (Luke 22:31). Oh gracious Watchman, continue to forewarn us about our foes, and for Zion's sake, do not hold Your peace.

"Watchman, what of the night?" What weather is coming for the church? Are the clouds lowering, or is it clear? We must care for the church of God with anxious love. With infidelity threatening, let us observe the signs of the times and prepare for conflict.

"Watchman, what of the night?" What stars are visible? What precious promises suit our present situation? You sound the alarm, also give us the consolation. Christ, the pole star, is ever fixed in His place, and all the stars are secure in the right hand of their Lord.

Watchman, when is the morning coming? The bridegroom tarries. Are there no signs of His coming as the Sun of Righteousness? Has not the morning star risen as the pledge of day? When, then, will the day dawn and the shadows flee away (Song of Solomon 2:17)?

Oh Jesus, if You do not come in person for your waiting church today, come in Spirit to my sighing heart and make it sing for joy.

> Now all the earth is bright and glad
>   With the fresh morn;
> But all my heart is cold, and dark and sad:
>   Sun of the soul, let me behold Thy dawn!
>   Come, Jesus, Lord,
> O quickly come, according to Thy word.

FILLED WITH HIS GLORY

"Let the whole earth be filled with His glory. Amen and amen."

—Psalm 72:19

This is a large petition. To intercede for an entire city requires a stretch of faith. There are times when prayer for an individual is enough to stagger us, but how far-reaching was the psalmist's dying intercession! How comprehensive! How sublime! "Let the whole earth be filled with His glory!"

It does not exempt a single country, however crushed by the foot of superstition. It does not exclude a single nation, however barbarous. For the jungle as well as the city, for all climates and races, this prayer is uttered. The whole circle of the earth is encompassed, and no child of Adam is omitted.

We must be about our Master's business, or we cannot honestly offer this prayer. The petition is not asked with a sincere heart unless we endeavor, God helping us, to extend the kingdom of our Master. Yet there are some who neglect both to pray and to work.

Turn your eyes to Calvary. See the Lord of Life nailed to a cross. His head, hands, and feet are bleeding. Can you look on this miracle of miracles, the death of the Son of God, and not feel a marvelous adoration that language can never express?

When you feel the blood applied to your conscience, when you know that He has blotted out your sins, you are not appreciative unless you fall to your knees and cry, "Let the whole earth be filled with His glory. Amen, and amen."

Can you bow before the Crucified in loving homage and not wish to see your Monarch as master of the world? Shame on you if you pretend to love your Prince and do not desire to see Him as the universal ruler. Your holiness is worthless unless it leads you to wish that the same mercy extended to you may bless the whole world.

Lord, it is harvest time. Put Your sickle in and reap.

OUR LOVE

"Rightly do they love You."

—Song of Solomon 1:4

Believers love Jesus with an affection deeper than they dare give to any other being. Believers would sooner lose father and mother than part with Christ. Believers hold all earthly comfort with loose hands, but they carry Jesus locked in their hearts. They voluntarily deny themselves for His sake, but they will not be driven to deny Him. It is an inadequate love for God that the fire of persecution can dry. The true believer's love is a deeper stream than this.

People have worked to divide the faithful from their Master, but their attempts have been fruitless in every age. Neither crowns of honor nor frowns of anger can untie this Gordian knot. This is no ordinary attachment that the world's power can dissolve. Neither man nor devil have found a key that opens this lock. Never has the craft of Satan been weaker than when he has exercised it in an attempt to break apart two divinely welded hearts.

It is written, and nothing can blot out this sentence, "Rightly do they love You." The intensity of our love is not so much to be judged by what it appears to be as by what we long for. It is our daily lament that we cannot love Him enough. Would that our hearts were capable of holding more and reaching further. Like Samuel Rutherford, we sigh and cry, "Oh, for as much love as would go round about the earth and over heaven—yea, the heaven of heavens, and ten thousand worlds—that I might let all out upon fair, fair, only fair Christ."

Our longest reach is but one stretch of love, and our affection is but a drop in a bucket compared with His love. But measure our love by our intentions and it is high indeed. Oh, that in one great gathering we could give all the love in all hearts to Him who is altogether lovely.

ALTHOUGH SATAN HINDERS

"Satan hindered us."

—1 Thessalonians 2:18

Since the first hour when goodness came in conflict with evil, Satan has hindered. From all points of the compass, all along the line of battle, in the front and in the rear, and at dawn and at midnight, Satan has hindered.

If we work in the field, he seeks to break the plow. If we build the wall, he works to throw down the stones. If we would serve God in suffering or conflict, Satan tries to hinder us.

He first hindered us when we were coming to Jesus Christ. We had fierce conflicts with Satan when we first looked to the cross and lived. Now that we are saved, he endeavors to hinder the completeness of our personal character.

You may be congratulating yourself, saying, "I have hitherto walked consistently; no one can challenge my integrity." Beware of boasting, for your virtue will be tested. Satan will direct his engines against that very virtue for which you are the most known. If you have been a firm believer, it won't be long until your faith is attacked. If you have been as meek as Moses, expect to be tempted to speak unadvisedly. The birds peck at the ripest fruit and wild boars dash their tusks at the choicest vines.

Satan is sure to hinder when we are devoted in prayer. He checks our petitions and weakens our faith, that, if possible, we may miss a blessing.

Satan is also vigilant in obstructing Christian effort. There was never a revival of Christianity without a revival of his opposition. As soon as Ezra and Nehemiah began to build the wall, Sanballat and Tobiah were stirred up to hinder them (Nehemiah 2:19).

What then? We are not alarmed because Satan hinders us, for this is proof that we are on the Lord's side, doing the Lord's work. In His strength we will win the victory and triumph over our adversary.

AUGUST 7, EVENING

THE SPIDER'S WEB

"They . . . weave the spider's web."

—Isaiah 59:5

Look at the spider's web, which is designed to catch its prey. It is a suggestive picture of the hypocrite's religion. The spider grows fat on flies and the Pharisee has a reward.

Foolish people are easily trapped by the loud professions of pretenders, and even the more judicious cannot always escape. Philip baptized Simon the sorcerer (Acts 8:13), whose deceitful declaration of faith was soon exploded by Peter's stern rebuke. Reputation, praise, advancement, and other flies are the small game hypocrites take in their nets.

A spider's web is a marvel of skill. Look at it and admire the cunning hunter's wiles. Is not a deceiver's religion equally fascinating? How do they make barefaced lies appear to be the truth? How do they make tinsel answer so well the purpose of gold?

A spider's web comes from within the spider. The bee gathers her wax from the flowers, but the spider sucks no flowers and yet spins material to any length. In the same way, hypocrites find trust and hope in themselves. Their anchor was forged on their own anvil, their cable twisted by their own hands. They lay their own foundations and cut pillars for their own houses, refusing to be debtors to the sovereign grace of God.

A spider's web is frail. It is no match for a broom. Hypocrites need no heavy artillery to blow their hopes to pieces; a mere puff of wind will suffice. Hypocritical cobwebs will come down when the broom of destruction sweeps.

This reminds me that these cobwebs are not to be tolerated in the Lord's house. He will see that they—and those who spin them—will be destroyed forever.

Oh my soul, rest on something better than a spider's web. Make the Lord Jesus your eternal hiding place.

ALL THINGS ARE POSSIBLE

"All things are possible to him who believes"

—Mark 9:23

Many professing Christians are always doubting and fearing. They forlornly think that this is the necessary state of believers. But this is a mistake, for "All things are possible" to the one who believes. It is possible to live so that a doubt or fear will be only a bird flitting across the soul, but never lingering.

When you read of the high and sweet fellowship enjoyed by favored saints, you may sigh and murmur in the chamber of your heart, "Alas, this is not for me." Oh climber, if you have faith, you will stand on the sunny pinnacle of the temple, because "all things are possible to him who believes."

You hear of exploits that holy people have done for Jesus: how much they enjoyed Him, how much they have been like Him, how they have endured great persecutions for His sake. You may say, "Ah, as for me, I am but a worm. I can never attain to this."

There is nothing these saints were that you may not be. There is no elevation of grace, no attainment of spirituality, no clearness of assurance, no post of duty that is not open to you, if you believe.

Put aside your sackcloth and ashes. Rise to the dignity of your true position. You are little in Israel because this is what you want. It is not proper for a child of the King to grovel in the dust. Ascend! The golden throne of assurance is waiting! The crown of fellowship with Jesus is ready to be worn. Wrap yourself in scarlet and fine linen. Eat sumptuously every day. If you believe, you may eat the choicest wheat and drink wine (Deuteronomy 32:14).

Gather golden sheaves of grace, for they await you in the fields of faith. "All things are possible to him who believes."

AUGUST 8, EVENING

THE CITY

"The city had no need of the sun or the moon to shine in it."

—Revelation 21:23

Yonder in the better world, the inhabitants are independent of all creature comforts. They have no need of clothes; their white robes never wear out or become dirty. They do not need medicine to heal diseases, for "the inhabitants will not say, 'I am sick'" (Isaiah 33:24). They do not need sleep to rest their frames; they do not rest day or night but unceasingly praise Him (Revelation 4:8).

They do not need social relationships to minister comfort. What happiness they may derive from companionship is not essential to their bliss. Their Lord's society is enough for their greatest desire.

They do not need teachers. Doubtlessly they commune with one another concerning the things of God, but they do not require this for instruction, because "they shall all be taught by God" (John 6:45).

Ours are the alms at the king's gate, but there they feast at the King's table. Here we lean on friendly arms; there they lean on their Beloved and on Him alone. Here we must have the help of our companions; there they find all they want in Christ Jesus. Here we have meat that spoils and clothing that wears out; there they find everything in God. Here we use the bucket to fetch water from the well; there they drink from the fountain head and put their lips to the living water. Here the angels bring us blessings; there we will not need messengers. They do not need Gabriel to bring love notes from God; they see Him face to face.

Oh what a blessed time that will be! We will have risen above every cause and will rest on the bare arm of God. What a glorious hour when God, and not His creatures, when the Lord, and not His works, will be our daily joy. Our soul will then have attained perfect bliss.

A MIRACLE OF GRACE

"He appeared first to Mary Magdalene, out of whom He had cast seven demons."

—Mark 16:9

Mary of Magdala was the victim of a fearful evil, for she had been possessed by not one devil, but seven. These dreadful inmates caused much pain and pollution to the poor frame in which they had found a lodging. Hers was a hopeless, horrible case. She could not help herself, and no human assistance could avail.

But Jesus passed her way. Unsought, and probably even resisted by the poor demoniac, He uttered the word of power, and Mary of Magdala became a trophy of the healing power of Jesus. All seven demons left her, never to return. They were forcibly ejected by the Lord of all.

What blessed deliverance! What happy change! From delirium to delight, from despair to peace, from hell to heaven! Immediately she became a constant follower of Jesus, catching His every word, following His winding steps, sharing His toilsome life. She became His generous helper and was first among that group of healed and grateful women who ministered to Him from their substance.

When Jesus was lifted up in crucifixion, Mary shared His shame. We find her first looking from a distance, then drawing near to the foot of the cross. She could not die on the cross with Jesus, but she stood as close as she could. When His blessed body was taken down, she watched to see how and where it was placed.

She was the faithful and watchful believer, last at the tomb where Jesus slept, first at the grave when He arose. Her holy faithfulness made her a favored beholder of her beloved Rabboni. Jesus called her by name and made her His messenger of good news to the trembling disciples and Peter.

Grace found her a maniac and made her a minister. Grace cast out devils and she saw angels. Grace delivered her from Satan and united her forever to the Lord Jesus.

Dear Lord, may I also be such a miracle of grace. Amen.

CHRIST IS

"Christ who is our life."

—Colossians 3:4

Paul's marvelous, rich expression indicates that Christ is the source of our life: "You He made alive, who were dead in trespasses and sins" (Ephesians 2:1). That same voice which brought Lazarus out of the tomb (John 11:43) also raises us to newness of life.

Christ is now the substance of our spiritual life. It is by His life that we live. He is in us as the hope of glory, the springs of our actions, the central thought that moves every other thought.

Christ is the sustenance of our life. What can the Christian feed on but Jesus' flesh and blood? "This is the bread which comes down from heaven, that one may eat of it and not die" (John 6:50). Oh way worn pilgrims in this wilderness of sin, you will never get food to satisfy the hunger of your spirit, unless you find it in Him.

Christ is the solace of our life. All our true joys come from Him. In times of trouble, His presence is our consolation. There is nothing worth living for but Him. His lovingkindness is better than life (Psalm 63:3)!

Christ is the object of our life. As the ship speeds toward the port, believers hasten to the haven of their Savior. As the arrow flies to the target, the Christian flies towards perfecting fellowship with Christ Jesus. As soldiers fight for their regiment and are crowned in its victory, the believer contends for Christ and obtains triumph out of the Master's triumph.

Christ is the example of our life. Where this life is within us there will be—there must be—the same developments without. If we live in close fellowship with the Lord Jesus, we will grow like Him. We will see Him as our Divine copy. We will seek to walk in His footsteps until He becomes the crown of our life in glory.

Oh, how safe, how honored, how happy are Christians, since Christ is their life.

POWER TO FORGIVE

"The Son of Man has power on earth to forgive sins."

—Matthew 9:6

This is one of our great Physician's mightiest works: He has the power to forgive sin! While He lived below, before the ransom had been paid, before the blood had been literally sprinkled on the mercy seat, He had power to forgive sin.

Now that He has died, He still has that power. What power must dwell in Him who, to the final penny, faithfully discharged the debts of His people. He has boundless power now that He has finished transgression and made an end of sin.

If you doubt it, see Him rising from the dead! Behold Him in ascending splendor raised to the right hand of God (Acts 2:33). Hear Him pleading before the eternal Father, pointing to His wounds, urging the merit of His sacred passion. What power to forgive!

"He ascended on high . . . And gave gifts to men" (Ephesians 4:8). "Him God has exalted to His right hand to be Prince and Savior . . . to forgive sins" (Acts 5:31). The most crimson sins are removed by the crimson of His blood.

At this moment, dear reader, whatever your sinfulness, know that Christ has power to pardon you and millions like you. He has nothing else to do to win your pardon. All the atoning work is done. He can, in answer to your tears, forgive your sins this evening and make you aware of it. He can breathe into your soul this very moment "the peace of God, which surpasses all understanding" (Philippians 4:7).

Do you believe this? I trust you do believe. May you experience now the power of Jesus to forgive sin! Waste no time in applying to the Physician of souls. Hasten to Him with words like these:

> Jesus! Master! hear my cry;
> Save me, heal me with a word;
> Fainting at Thy feet I lie,
> Thou my whispered plaint hast heard.

MONTHS PAST

"Oh, that I were as in months past."

—Job 29:2

Numbers of Christians view the past with pleasure, but the present with dissatisfaction. They look back on the days when they communed with the Lord as the sweetest and best they have ever known. The present, however, is clad in mourning garments of gloom and dreariness.

Once they lived near Jesus, but now they have wandered from Him. All they can say is, "Oh, that I were as in months past." They complain of having lost their present peace of mind, or their enjoyment in grace, or their tender conscience, or their zeal for God's glory.

The causes of this mournful condition are many. It may arise through neglect of prayer, which is the beginning of spiritual decline.

Or it may be the result of idolatry, the heart being occupied with something beside God, or affections being set on earthly rather than heavenly things. A jealous God will not be content with a divided heart. He must be loved first and best. He will withdraw the sunshine of His presence from a cold, wandering heart.

Or the cause may be found in self-confidence and self-righteousness. When pride is busy in the heart, self is exalted, instead of lying low at the foot of the cross.

Christian, if you are not as you were in months past, do not rest satisfied. Go at once to seek your Master, and tell Him about your sad state. Ask for His grace and strength to help you walk closer with Him. Humble yourself before Him, and He will lift you up once again to enjoy the light of His countenance.

Do not sit down to sigh and lament. While the beloved Physician lives, there is hope. No, more than hope, there is a certainty of recovery.

EVERLASTING CONSOLATION

"Everlasting consolation."

—2 Thessalonians 2:16

*C*onsolation. There is music in that word. Like David's harp, it charms away the evil spirit of depression.

It was a distinguished honor for Barnabas to be called "the son of consolation" (Acts 4:36), but it is also one of the illustrious names of one greater than Barnabas. The Lord Jesus is "the consolation of Israel" (Luke 2:25). "Everlasting consolation," here is the cream of all, for the eternity of comfort is the crown and glory of it.

What is this "everlasting consolation?" It includes a sense of pardoned sin. A Christian receives the witness of the Spirit that God has "blotted out, like a thick cloud your transgressions, and like a cloud your sins" (Isaiah 44:22). If sin is pardoned, this is "everlasting consolation."

Next the Lord gives His people an abiding sense of acceptance in Christ. Christians know that God looks on them as standing in union with Jesus. This is "everlasting consolation."

Let sickness prostrate us; we have seen hundreds of believers as happy in the weakness of disease as they would have been in the strength of hale and blooming health. Let death's arrow pierce us to the heart and our comfort does not die. We have often heard the songs of saints rejoicing because the living love of God was shed abroad in their hearts in dying moments. Yes, a sense of acceptance in the Beloved is an "everlasting consolation."

Christians have a conviction of their security. God has promised to save those who trust in Christ. The Christian does trust in Christ and believes that God will be as good as His word and that salvation is assured. We are safe by virtue of being bound up in the person and the work of Jesus.

OUR GOD REIGNS

"The Lord reigns; let the earth rejoice."

—Psalm 97:1

There is no cause for despair so long as this blessed sentence is true. On earth the Lord's power controls the rage of the wicked as readily as it does the rage of the sea. His love refreshes the poor with mercy as easily as it does the earth with showers. His majesty gleams in flashes of fire amid the tempest's horror. The glory of the Lord is seen in its grandeur in the fall of empires and the crash of thrones. In all our conflicts and tribulations, we may behold the hand of the divine King:

> God is God; He sees and hears
> All our troubles, all our tears.
> Soul, forget not, 'mid thy pains,
> God o'er all forever reigns.

In hell, evil spirits acknowledge with misery His undoubted supremacy. When evil is permitted to roam, it is with a chain on its heel, the bit in its mouth, and the hook in its jaw. Death's darts are under the Lord's lock. The grave's prisons have divine power for their warden. The terrible vengeance of the Judge of all the earth makes fiends cower and tremble like dogs in the kennel, fearing the hunter's whip:

> Fear not death, nor Satan's thrusts,
> God defends who in Him trusts.

In heaven no one doubts the sovereignty of the King Eternal. All fall on their faces to honor Him. Angels are His messengers. The redeemed are His favorites. All delight to serve Him day and night. May we soon reach the city of the great King!

> For this life's long night of sadness
> He will give us peace and gladness.
> Soul, remember, in thy pains,
> God o'er all forever reigns.

THE RAINBOW

"The rainbow shall be seen in the cloud."

—Genesis 9:14

The rainbow, the symbol of the covenant with Noah, is typical of our Lord Jesus, who is the Lord's witness to the people. When may we expect to see the token of the covenant? The rainbow is only to be seen painted on a cloud.

When the sinner's conscience is dark with clouds, when past sins are mourned and lamented before God, then Jesus Christ is revealed as the covenant rainbow, displaying all the glorious hues of the divine character and symbol of peace.

When trials and tests surround believers, it is sweet to see the person of our Lord Jesus Christ, to see Him bleeding, living, rising, and pleading for us. God's rainbow is hung over the cloud of our sins, sorrows, and trials to prophesy our deliverance.

Nor can a cloud alone make a rainbow. There must be the crystal drops to reflect the light of the sun. So our sorrows must not only threaten, they must really fall. There would not have been a Christ for us if the vengeance of God had been merely a threatening cloud. Punishment must fall in terrible drops. Until there is real anguish in the sinners' conscience, there is no Christ for them. Until the chastisement becomes grievous, they cannot see Jesus.

But there must also be a sun. Clouds and raindrops do not make rainbows unless the sun shines. Beloved, our God, who is as the sun to us, always shines. We do not always see Him, for clouds may hide His face. But no matter what drops may be falling, or what clouds may be threatening, if He shines, there will be a rainbow at once.

It is said that when we see the rainbow, the shower is over. When Christ comes, our troubles disappear. When we see Jesus, our sins vanish, our doubts and fears subside. When Jesus walks the waters of the sea, how profound the calm.

AUGUST 12, EVENING

CEDARS

"The cedars of Lebanon which He planted."

—Psalm 104:16

Lebanon's cedars are emblematic of the Christian, for they owe their planting entirely to the Lord. This is true also of every child of God. We are neither man-planted nor self-planted, but God-planted. The mysterious hand of the divine Spirit dropped the living seed in a heart that He had prepared. True heirs of heaven acknowledge the great Vinekeeper as their planter.

The cedars of Lebanon are not dependent on man for watering. They stand on the lofty rock and are not moistened by human irrigation. Our heavenly Father supplies them. Thus it is with Christians who have learned to live by faith. They are independent of man, even in temporal things. For their continued maintenance, they look to the Lord their God, and to Him alone. The dew of heaven is their portion. The God of heaven is their fountain.

The cedars of Lebanon are not protected by any mortal power. They owe nothing to man for their preservation from stormy wind and tempest. They are God's trees, kept and preserved by Him alone. It is precisely the same with the Christian. We are not hot-house plants, sheltered from temptation. We stand exposed, with no shelter or protection, except the broad wings of the eternal God, who always covers the cedars that He planted.

Like cedars, believers are full of sap. They have vitality enough to be ever green, even in winter's snows.

Lastly, the flourishing and majestic condition of the cedar is to the praise of God only. The Lord, even the Lord alone, has been everything to the cedars. As David sweetly puts it, "Praise the Lord . . . fruitful trees and all cedars" (Psalm 148:9). In the believer there is nothing that can magnify man. We are planted, nourished, and protected by the Lord's own hand. To Him let all the glory be ascribed.

GOD REMEMBERS

"And I will remember My covenant."

—Genesis 9:15

Mark the form of this promise. God does not say, "When you look on the rainbow, when you remember My covenant, then I will not destroy the earth." No, it is gloriously put, not on our fickle and frail memory, but on God's infinite and lasting memory. "The rainbow shall be in the cloud, and I will look on it to remember the everlasting covenant" (Genesis 9:16).

It is not my remembering God, it is God's remembering me that is the ground for my safety. It is not my laying hold of His covenant, but His covenant's laying hold on me. Glory be to God, the whole of the bulwark of salvation is secured by divine power.

Even the remembrance of the covenant is not left to our memories. We might forget, but our Lord cannot forget the saints whom He has inscribed on the palms of His hands (Isaiah 49:16). It is with us as it was with Israel in Egypt. The blood was on the lintel and the two door posts, but the Lord did not say, "When you see the blood I will pass over you," but, "When I see the blood I will pass over you" (Exodus 12:23).

Looking to Jesus brings me joy and peace, but it also secures my salvation. It is impossible for God to look at Christ, our bleeding Surety, and be angry with us for sins already punished in Him. No, it is not left with us even to be saved by remembering the covenant. There is no blend of material here, not a single thread of the creature mars the fabric. It is not of man, neither by man, but of the Lord alone.

We should remember the covenant, and through divine grace we will remember it. But the hinge of our safety does not hang there; it is God's remembering us, not our remembering Him. Thus the covenant is everlasting.

CHEERFUL HOLINESS

"For You Lord, have made me glad through Your work."

—Psalm 92:4

Do you believe that your sins are forgiven and that Christ has made a full atonement for them? Then you should be a joyful Christian. You should live above the common trials and troubles of this world!

Since your sin is forgiven, can it matter what happens to you now? Luther said, "Smite, Lord, smite, for my sin is forgiven; if You have but forgiven me, smite as hard as You will." In a similar spirit you may say, "Send sickness, poverty, losses, crosses, persecution. Send what You will, You have forgiven me and my soul is glad."

Christian, if you are saved, be glad, grateful, and loving. Cling to the cross that took your sin away. Serve Him who served you. "I beseech you therefore, brethren, by the mercies of God, that you present your bodies a living sacrifice, holy, acceptable to God, which is your reasonable service" (Romans 12:1).

Do not let your zeal evaporate in the vapor of some little song. Show your love in expressive expressions. Love the believers in Him who loved you (Romans 12:10). If there is a Mephibosheth who is lame or in need, help him for Jonathan's sake (2 Samuel 9:3ff). Where there are poor tried believers, weep with them; carry their cross for the sake of Him who wept for you and carried your sins.

Since you are forgiven freely (Romans 8:32), for Christ's sake go and tell others the joyful news of pardoning mercy. Do not be content to keep this unspeakable blessing for yourself alone. Preach the story of the cross. Holy gladness and holy boldness will make you a good preacher, and all the world will be your pulpit.

Cheerful holiness is the most forcible of sermons, but the Lord must give it. Seek it this morning before you go into the world. When you rejoice in the Lord's work, there is no need to be afraid of being too glad.

AUGUST 14, MORNING

HE KNOWS

"I know their sorrows."

—Exodus 3:7

God's children are cheered as they sing, "This my father knows." They are comforted to know that their dear Friend and tender soul-husband knows all about them.

He is the *Physician,* and if He knows all, there is no need for the patient to know. Hush, my silly, fluttering heart, prying, peeping, and suspecting! What you do not know now, you will know in heaven. Meanwhile Jesus, the beloved Physician, knows your soul in adversity. Why do you need an analysis of all the medicine or a list of all the symptoms? This is the Physician's work and not mine. If He writes the prescription in letters I cannot read, I will not be uneasy. I will rely on His unfailing skill to make everything clear in the final result, regardless of how mysterious it seems.

He is the *Master,* and thus we are to obey and not judge. "A servant does not know what his master is doing" (John 15:15). Shall the architect explain all the plans to every laborer on the job? The vase on the wheel cannot guess the shape of its pattern; if the potter understands, what matters the ignorance of the clay? My Lord must not be cross-examined any more by one so ignorant as me.

He is the *Head,* and thus all understanding centers there. What judgment has an arm? What comprehension has a foot? All the power to know is found in the head. Why should each member of the body have a brain of its own when the head fulfills every intellectual duty? In this believers must rest their comfort in sickness, not that they can see the end, but that Jesus knows all.

Sweet Lord, be our eye and soul. Let us be content to know only what You choose to reveal. Amen.

MEDITATION

"Isaac went out to meditate in the field in the evening."

—Genesis 24:63

This occupation is admirable. If those who spend so many hours in idle company, light reading, and useless pastimes could learn wisdom, they would find more interest and profit in meditation than the foolishness that currently charms them.

If we were alone with God more often, we would know more, live nearer to Him, and grow in grace. Meditation chews the cud that extracts the real nutriment from the mental food gathered elsewhere. When Jesus is the theme, meditation is sweet. Isaac found Rebecca while meditating (Genesis 24:63), and many others have found their best beloved there.

The choice of place was admirable. The field is a study, with texts for thought all around. From the cedar to the hyssop, from the soaring eagle to the chirping grasshopper, from the blue expanse of heaven to a drop of dew, everything is full of teaching.

When the eye is divinely opened, that teaching flashes on the mind far more vividly than from books. Our little rooms are neither so healthy, so suggestive, so agreeable, or so inspiring as the fields. Count nothing common or unclean there. When you feel that all created things point to their Maker, the field immediately becomes sacred.

Admirable was the time. Sunset, as it draws a veil over the day, is like the repose of the soul when earthborn cares yield to the joys of heavenly communion. The glory of the setting sun excites our wonder. The solemnness of approaching night awakens our awe.

If the business of this day will permit, it would be good to spend an hour walking in the field at evening. If not, the Lord is also in the city, and He will meet you in your bedroom or in the crowded street. Let your heart go to meet Him.

A TENDER, A RENEWED HEART

"I will . . . give you a heart of flesh."

—Ezekiel 36:26

A heart of flesh is known by its sensitivity to sin. To indulge a foul imagination or to allow a wild desire to tarry for a moment is quite enough to make a heart of flesh grieve before the Lord. A heart of stone calls a great iniquity nothing. A heart of flesh is grief-stricken by any iniquity.

A heart of flesh is tender to God's will. My Lord Self-will is a great blusterer. It is hard to subject him to God's will. But when my heart is flesh, my will quivers like an aspen leaf in every breath of heaven. It bows like a willow in every breeze of God's Spirit.

The natural will is cold, hard iron and cannot be hammered into shape. The renewed will, like molten metal, is soon molded by the hand of grace.

In the fleshy heart there is tenderness of affection. The hard heart does not love the Redeemer. The renewed heart burns with affection toward Him. The hard heart is selfish and coldly demands, "Why should I weep for sin? Why should I love the Lord?" But the heart of flesh says, "Lord, You know that I love You. Help me to love You more!"

Many are the privileges of this renewed heart:

> Tis here the Spirit dwells,
> 'Tis here that Jesus rests.

The renewed heart is fitted to receive every spiritual blessing, and every blessing comes to it. It is prepared to yield every heavenly fruit to the honor and praise of God; therefore, the Lord delights in it.

A tender heart is the best defence against sin and the best preparation for heaven. A renewed heart stands on its watchtower looking for the coming of the Lord Jesus.

Have you a tender heart of flesh?

No Glory

"Give unto the Lord the glory due to His name."

—Psalm 29:2

God's glory is the result of His nature and His acts. He is glorious in His character. There is such an abundance of everything that is holy, good, and lovely in God that He must be glorious. The actions that flow from His character are also glorious. While He intends that they should manifest His goodness, mercy, and justice, He is equally concerned that the glory associated with them should be given only to Him.

There is nothing in which we can glory. Who makes one different from another? What do we have that we did not receive from the God of all grace? Then how careful should we be to walk humbly before the Lord. The moment we glorify ourselves, we become the rival of the Most High.

Shall the insect of an hour glorify itself against the sun that warmed it into life? Shall a fragment of a vase exalt itself above the artist who fashioned it on the wheel? Shall the dust of the desert strive with the whirlwind? Shall the drops of the ocean struggle with the tempest? "Give unto the Lord, Oh you mighty ones, give unto the Lord the glory due to His name."

Yet it is one of the hardest struggles of the Christian life to learn: "Not unto us, O Lord, not unto us, but to Your name give glory" (Psalm 115:1). This lesson God is always teaching, at times by the most painful discipline. Let Christians begin to boast, "I can do all things," without adding "through Christ who strengthens me" (Philippians 4:13), and before long they will groan, "I can do nothing."

When we do anything for the Lord and He is pleased to accept our work, let us lay our crowns at His feet and exclaim, "Not I, but the grace of God which was with me!"

FIRSTFRUITS

"We also, who have the firstfruits of the Spirit."

—Romans 8:23

Present possession is declared in our text. At this present moment we have the firstfruits of the Spirit. We have repentance, that gem of the first water; faith, that priceless pearl; hope, the heavenly emerald; love, the glorious ruby. We are already made "new creations in Christ Jesus" (2 Corinthians 5:17) through the effectual working of God the Holy Spirit.

"Firstfruit" is so called because it comes first. As the wave sheaf was the first of the harvest, so spiritual life and all the graces that adorn it are the first operation of the Spirit of God in our souls.

The firstfruits were the pledge of the harvest. As soon as the Israelites plucked the first handful of ripe ears, they looked forward with glad anticipation to the time when the wagon would creak because it was loaded with grain. When God gives us the pure and good work of the Holy Spirit, it is a prognosis of the coming glory.

The firstfruits were always holy to the Lord, and so our new nature, with all its powers, is a consecrated thing. The new life is not ours in the sense that we should ascribe its excellence to our merits. It is Christ's image and creation, ordained for His glory.

But the firstfruits were not the harvest, and the work of the Spirit is not the consummation: The perfection is yet to come. We must not boast that we have attained. The wave sheaf is not all the produce of the year. We must "hunger and thirst for righteousness" (Matthew 5:6).

Dear reader, this evening open your mouth wide, and God will fill it. Let the blessing of your present possession of His Spirit excite a sacred gluttony in you for more grace. Groan within for a higher degree of consecration. Your Lord will grant it. He "is able to do exceedingly abundantly above all that we ask or think" (Ephesians 3:20).

AUGUST 16, EVENING

MERCY

"The mercy of God."

—Psalm 52:8

Meditate a little on the mercy of the Lord, for it is a tender mercy. With a gentle, loving touch, He heals the broken heart. He is as gracious in the manner of His mercy as in the matter of it.

It is a great mercy. There is nothing little in God, and His mercy is like Him: infinite. His mercy is so great that it forgives great sins of great sinners after great lengths of time. His mercy gives great favors and great privileges. It raises us to great enjoyments in the great heaven of the great God.

It is an undeserved mercy. Indeed, all true mercy is undeserved, for deserved mercy is a misnomer for justice. Sinners had no right to kind consideration from the Most High. If they were delivered from wrath, sovereign love alone has found a cause, because there was none in sinners.

It is a rich mercy. Some things are great but have little power. This mercy is medicine to your drooping spirits, a golden ointment to your bleeding wounds, a heavenly bandage to your broken bones, a royal chariot for your weary feet, a bosom of love for your trembling heart.

It is a manifold mercy. As Bunyan says, "All the flowers in God's garden are double." There is no single mercy. You may think you have only one mercy, but you will find it to be a whole cluster of mercies.

It is an abounding mercy. Millions have received it. It is an unfailing mercy. It will never leave you. If mercy is your friend, mercy will be with you in temptation to keep you from yielding to sin. Mercy will be with you in trouble to prevent you from sinking. Mercy will be with you in living to be the light and life of your support. Mercy will be with you in dying, and it will be the joy of your soul when earthly comforts are ebbing fast.

LIMITS

"This sickness is not unto death."

—John 11:4

From our Lord's words we learn that there is a limit to sickness. This ultimate end of this sickness was controlled. Lazarus might pass through death, but death was not to be the ultimatum of his sickness (John 11:44).

In all sickness, the Lord says to the waves of pain, "You shall go this far, but no further." His fixed purpose is not the destruction, but the instruction of His people. Wisdom hangs the thermometer that regulates the furnace's heat.

The limit is encouraging in its comprehensiveness. The God of providence has limited the time, manner, intensity, repetition, and effects of all our sicknesses. Each throb of pain is decreed. Each sleepless hour is predestinated. Each relapse is ordained. Each depression of spirit is foreknown. Each sanctifying result is eternally purposed. Nothing great or small escapes the ordaining hand of Him who numbers the hairs of our head (Matthew 10:30).

The limit is wisely adjusted to our strength, to the end designed, and to the grace apportioned. His affliction of us is not haphazard; the weight of every stroke of the rod is accurately measured. He who makes no mistakes in balancing the clouds and allocating the heavens commits no errors in measuring out the ingredients that compose the medicine of souls. We cannot suffer too much, or be relieved too late.

The limit is tenderly appointed. "He does not afflict willingly, nor grieve the children of men" (Lamentations 3:33). A mother's heart cries, "Spare my child." But no mother is more compassionate than our gracious God. When we consider how hard we are to control, it is a wonder that we are not driven with a sharper bit.

This thought is full of consolation. He who has fixed the bounds of our habitation has also fixed the bounds of our tribulation.

AUGUST 17, EVENING

APOSTATES

"Stranger's have come into the sanctuaries of the Lord's house."

—Jeremiah 51:51

The faces of the Lord's people were covered with shame because it was a terrible thing for individuals to intrude into the Holy Place reserved for the priests.

Everywhere around us we see this same tragedy. Many ungodly people are now being educated to enter the ministry. What a crying sin! How fearful that the ministry is offered to the unconverted and that among the more enlightened churches of our land there is such a laxity of discipline. If you who read this devotion will take this matter before the Lord Jesus today, He will interfere and avert the evil that is about to come on His church.

To adulterate the church is to pollute a well, to pour water on fire, to sow a fertile field with stones. May we have the grace to maintain the purity of the church. The church must be an assembly of believers, not an unsaved, unconverted community.

Our zeal must, however, begin at home. Let us examine our right to eat at the Lord's table. Let us ensure that we have our wedding garments on, lest we be the intruders in the Lord's sanctuaries. "Many are called, but few are chosen" (Matthew 20:16). The way is narrow and the gate is straight (Matthew 7:13–14).

Oh for grace to come to Jesus with the faith of God's elect. He who struck Uzzah for touching the ark (2 Samuel 6:7) is very jealous of His ordinances. As a true believer I may approach them freely. As an alien I must not touch them lest I die.

Heart-searching is the duty of all who are baptized or who come to the Lord's table. "Search me, O God, and know my heart; try me and know my anxieties; and see if there is any wicked way in me. And lead me in the way everlasting" (Psalm 139:23).

GREAT GRACE

"Then they gave Him wine mingled with myrrh to drink, but He did not take it."

—Mark 15:23

This is a golden truth. The Savior did not put the wine mixed with myrrh to His lips.

On the heights of heaven, the Son of God stood of old and looked down on our globe. He measured the long descent to the utmost depths of human misery. He realized the total of all the agonies that expiation would require. He solemnly determined that to offer a sufficient atoning sacrifice He must go from the highest to the lowest, from the throne of highest glory to the cross of deepest woes.

This myrrhed cup, with its tranquilizing influence, would reduce the utmost limit of His misery. Thus He refused it. He would not stop short of all that He had undertaken to suffer for His people.

In times of grief, many have sought relief that would have been injurious. Have you ever eagerly prayed for relief from suffering, only to have Providence take the love of your life with a single blow? Christian, if it had been said to you, "If you desire it, that loved one of yours will live, but God will be dishonored," could you have said, "Your will be done?"

It is sweet to be able to say, "My Lord, if I can honor You more by suffering, if the loss of all my earthly goods will bring You glory, then let me suffer. I refuse comfort if it does not honor You."

Oh that we would walk more in the footsteps of our Lord, cheerfully enduring each trial for His sake. Promptly and willingly putting away thoughts of self and comfort when it would interfere with finishing the work He has given us to do.

Great grace is needed, but great grace is provided.

SAVIOR, LIKE A SHEPHERD

"He shall stand and feed His flock in the strength of the Lord."

—Micah 5:4

Christ's reign in His church is that of a Shepherd-King. He has supremacy, but it is that of a wise and tender shepherd over his needy and loving flock. He commands and receives obedience, but it is the willing obedience of sheep well cared for. It is obedience rendered joyfully to a beloved Shepherd, whose voice the sheep know so well. He rules by the force of love and the energy of goodness.

His reign is practical in its character, for "He shall stand and feed." The great Head of the church is actively engaged in providing for His people. He does not sit on the throne of an empty empire. He does not hold a scepter without wielding it. He stands and feeds. The expression *feed* in the original Greek means "to shepherd," to do everything expected of a shepherd: guide, watch, preserve, restore, and tend, as well as feed.

His reign is continual in duration. It is not that "He shall feed now and then, and then leave His position." It is not that "He will one day grant a revival and the next day leave His church barren." His eyes never slumber. His hands never rest. His heart never ceases to beat with love. His shoulders are never weary of carrying His people's burdens.

His reign is effectually powerful in its action, for "He shall feed in the strength of Jehovah." Wherever Christ is, there is God. Whatever Christ does is the act of the Most High. It is a joyful truth to consider that He who stands today representing the interests of His people is very God of very God, to whom every knee will bow (Philippians 2:10).

Happy are we who belong to such a Shepherd, whose humanity communes with us and whose divinity protects us. Let us worship and bow before Him as the people of His pasture.

CAPTURED?

"Pull me out of the net which they have secretly laid for me, for You are my strength."

—Psalm 31:4

Our spiritual foes are of the serpent's brood and seek to ensnare us subtly. The prayer in our text supposes the possibility of believers being caught like a bird.

So skillfully does the fowler work that simple ones are soon caught. The text asks that the captive may be delivered out of Satan's nets. This is a proper prayer and will be answered. Eternal love can rescue the saint from the jaws of the lion and the belly of hell. It may require a sharp pull to save a soul from the net of temptation, it may require a mighty pull to extricate a saint from the snares of malicious cunning, but the Lord is equal to every emergency. The most skillfully placed nets of the hunter can never hold His chosen ones.

Woe to those who are clever at net laying. Those who tempt others will be destroyed.

"You are my strength." What inexpressible sweetness is found in these four words! How joyfully we may encounter toil and how cheerfully we may endure suffering when we lay hold of celestial strength. Divine power will tear apart the work of our enemies, confound their politics, and frustrate their knavish tricks.

Happy are we who have such matchless might on our side. Our own strength would be of little help in the nets of the cunning, but the Lord's strength is always available. We have but to invoke it to find it. If we are depending alone on the strength of the mighty God of Israel, we may use our holy reliance as a plea in supplication:

> Lord, evermore Thy face we seek:
> Tempted we are, and poor, and weak;
> Keep us with lowly hearts, and meek.
> Let us not fall. Let us not fall.

AUGUST 19, EVENING

DAVID'S EXPERIENCES

"The sweet psalmist of Israel."

—2 Samuel 23:1

Among all the saints recorded in Scripture, David possesses experiences of the most striking, varied, and instructive kind. In his history we find unique trials and temptations, and thus David is greatly suggestive as a type of our Lord.

David also experienced the trials and sorrows common to many people. Kings have their troubles, and David wore a crown; the peasant has cares, and David handled a shepherd's crook; the wanderer has many hardships, and David lived in the caves of Engedi; the captain has his difficulties, and David found the sons of Zeruiah too hard for him. The psalmist was also tried by his friends, and Ahithophel, his counselor, forsook him: "Even my own familiar friend in whom I trusted, who ate my bread, has lifted up his heel against me" (Psalm 41:9).

His worst foes were in his own home. His children were his greatest affliction. The temptations of poverty and wealth, honor and reproach, and health and weakness all tried him. Temptations from without disturbed his peace and temptations from within marred his joy. David no sooner escaped from one trial than he had another. As soon as he emerged from one season of despondency and alarm, he was again brought to the lowest depths. All God's waves and billows rolled over him.

This is probably the reason why David's psalms are so universally the delight of experienced Christians. Whatever their frame of mind, whether ecstacy or depression, David has exactly described their emotions. He was an able master of the human heart, because he was educated in the best of all schools, the school of heart-felt personal experience.

As we are instructed in the same school, as we mature in grace and in years, we increasingly appreciate David's Psalms. They are green pastures. Let David's experiences cheer and counsel you today.

AUGUST 20, MORNING

THE WALL

"They fortified Jerusalem as far as the broad wall."

—Nehemiah 3:8

Well fortified cities have broad walls, and in her zenith Jerusalem was no exception. The new Jerusalem must be surrounded and preserved by a broad wall of nonconformity to the world and separation from the world's customs and spirit.

The tendency these days is to break down the holy barrier and blur the distinction between the church and the world. Christians are no longer strict and Puritanical. Questionable literature is read by all. Frivolous pastimes are indulged in. A general laxity threatens to deprive the Lord's peculiar people of those sacred singularities that separate them from sinners. It will be an ill day for the church and the world when the proposed merger will be complete. Then another deluge of wrath will be ushered in.

Beloved reader, make this your goal. In heart, in word, in dress, and in action, maintain the broad wall. Remember "that friendship with the world is enmity with God" (James 4:4).

The broad wall offered a pleasant place for the inhabitants of Jerusalem to walk. Here, they had a commanding view of the surrounding country. This reminds us of the Lord's exceeding broad commandments. We walk at liberty in communion with Jesus, overlooking the scenes of earth and looking out toward the glories of heaven. Separated from the world and denying ourselves all ungodliness and fleshly lusts we are, nevertheless, not in prison or within narrow bounds. No, we walk at liberty, because we keep His precepts.

Come, reader, this evening walk with God in His statues. As friend met friend on the city wall, meet your God in the way of holy prayer and meditation. The bulwarks of salvation are yours to walk on. You are free citizens of the royal city, the metropolis of the universe.

GIVING

"He who waters will also be watered himself."

—Proverbs 11:25

Our text teaches a great lesson: To get, we must give; to accumulate, we must scatter; to be happy, we must make others happy; to be spiritually vigorous, we must seek the spiritual good of others. By watering others, we are watered.

How? Our efforts to be useful bring out our powers for usefulness. We have latent talents and dormant faculties that are brought to light by exercise. Our strength for laboring is hidden even from ourselves until we venture to fight the Lord's battles or attempt to climb the mountains of difficulty. We do not know what tender sympathies we possess until we try to dry the widow's tears and soothe the orphan's grief.

We often find that in attempting to teach others, we gain instruction. What gracious lessons some of us have learned at sick beds. We went to teach the Scriptures but came away blushing that we knew so little. In conversations with poor saints, we are taught the way of God more perfectly and obtain a deeper insight into divine truth. Watering others makes us humble. We discover how much the penniless saint may outstrip us in knowledge. Great grace is found where we had not looked.

Our own comfort is also increased by working for others. We endeavor to cheer them and the consolation gladdens our hearts. Like the two men in the snow, one rubbed the other's limbs to keep him from dying, and in so doing he kept his own blood circulating and saved his own life.

The poor widow of Zarephath (Luke 4:26) gave out of her scanty supply to the prophet, and from that day she never again knew what need was.

"Give and it will be given to you; good measure, pressed down, shaken together and running over" (Luke 6:38).

NOT IN VAIN

"I did not say to the seed of Jacob, seek Me in vain."

—Isaiah 45:19

We may gain much solace by considering what God has not said. What He has said is inexpressibly full of comfort and delight. What He has not said is scarcely less rich in consolation. It was what God did not say that preserved the kingdom of Israel in the days of Jeroboam, the son of Joash. "The Lord did not say that He would blot out the name of Israel from under heaven" (2 Kings 14:27).

Our text assures that God will answer prayer, because He "did not say to the seed of Jacob, seek Me in vain." You who write bitter things against yourselves should remember that. Let your doubts and fears say what they will, if God has not cut you off from mercy, there is no room for despair. Even the voice of conscience is of little weight if it is not seconded by the voice of God.

What God has said, tremble at! But do not let your vain imagination overwhelm you with despondency and sinful despair. Many have the suspicion that there may be something in God's decree that shuts them out from hope. But our text is a complete refutation to that fear, for no true seeker can be decreed to wrath. "I have not spoken in secret, in a dark place of the earth. I did not say to the seed of Jacob, 'Seek Me in vain'." God has clearly revealed that He will hear the prayer of those who call on Him. He has so firmly, so truthfully, so righteously spoken, that there can be no room for doubt.

He does not reveal His mind in unintelligible words, but He speaks plainly and positively. "Ask and you will receive" (John 16:24). Trembling one, believe this sure truth: prayer must and will be heard. Never, even in the secrets of eternity, has the Lord ever said, "Seek Me in vain."

LOVESICK

"I charge you, O daughters of Jerusalem, if you find my beloved, that you tell him I am lovesick."

—Song of Solomon 5:8

This is the language of believers craving fellowship with Jesus. They are lovesick for their Lord. Gracious souls are never perfectly at ease unless they are close to Christ. When they are away from Him, they lose their peace. The nearer to Him, the nearer to the perfect calm of heaven. The nearer to Him, the fuller the heart, and not just in peace, but in life, vigor, and joy.

What the sun is to the day, what the moon is to the night, what the dew is to the flower, Jesus Christ is to us. What bread is to the hungry, what clothing is to the naked, what the shadow of a great rock is to the traveller in a weary land, this is what Jesus Christ is to us.

Therefore, if we are not consciously one with Him, it is little wonder that our spirits cry in the words of the Song, "If you find my beloved, that you tell him I am lovesick." This earnest longing after Jesus has a blessing attached to it. "Blessed are those who hunger and thirst for righteousness, for they shall be filled" (Matthew 5:6). Supremely blessed are they who thirst after the Righteous One. Blessed is that hunger since it comes from God.

If I do not have the blessedness of being filled, I seek the same blessedness in its sweet bud, hungering in emptiness and eagerness until I am filled with Christ. If I am not full of Jesus, it will be next door to heaven to hunger and thirst after Him. There is a sacredness about that hunger, for it sparkles among the beatitudes of our Lord. But the blessing involves a promise. These hungry ones *shall be filled* with what they desire.

If Christ causes us to long after Him, He will certainly satisfy those longings. When He comes, as come He will, oh how sweet it will be.

UNSEARCHABLE

"The unsearchable riches of Christ."

—Ephesians 3:8

My Master has riches beyond the count of arithmetic, the measure of reason, the dream of imagination, or the eloquence of words. His riches are unsearchable! You may look, study, and ponder with monumental thought, but Jesus is a Savior greater than you can ever imagine.

My Lord is more ready to pardon than you are to sin, more able to forgive than you are to transgress. My Master is more willing to supply your needs than you are to confess them.

My Master has riches of happiness to bestow on you now. He can make you lie down in green pastures; He can lead you beside the still waters (Psalm 23:2). There is no music like His music, when He is the Shepherd and you are the sheep lying at His feet. There is no love like His; neither heaven nor earth can match it. To know Christ and to be found in Him, oh, this is life, this is joy! "A feast of choice pieces, a feast of wines on the lees, of fat things full of marrow, of well refined wines on the lees" (Isaiah 25:6).

My Master does not treat His servants crudely. He gives to them as a king gives to kings. He gives them two heavens, a heaven below in serving Him here and a heaven above in delighting in Him forever.

On the way to heaven, He will give you all you need. Your place of defense will be the fortress of rocks. Bread will be given, and your water will be sure (Isaiah 33:16). But it is there, *there,* where you will hear the song of those who triumph, the shout of those who feast. *There* you will view the glorious and beloved One face to face.

The unsearchable riches of Christ! This is the tune for both the minstrels of earth and the harpers of heaven.

Lord, teach us more and more of Jesus, and we will tell the good news to others. Amen.

No Tears

"The voice of weeping shall no longer be heard."

—Isaiah 65:19

The glorified no longer weep, because all causes of grief are gone. There are no broken friendships or blighted prospects in heaven. Poverty, famine, peril, persecution, and slander are unknown there; no pain distresses, no thought of death or bereavement saddens. They weep no more because they are perfectly sanctified.

No evil heart of unbelief prompts them to depart from the living God. They are without fault before His throne. They are fully conformed to His image. They weep no more because all fear of change is past.

They know they are eternally secure. Sin is shut out, and they are shut in a city that will never be attacked. They bask in a sun that will never set and drink from a river that will never run dry. They pick fruit from a tree that will never wither. Countless cycles may revolve, but eternity will not be exhausted; and while eternity endures, their immortality and blessedness will coexist with it. They are forever with the Lord.

They weep no more because every desire is fulfilled. They cannot wish for anything, because they are completely satisfied. Eye, ear, heart, hand, judgment, imagination, hope, desire, and will are all fully satisfied.

Imperfect as our present ideas are of the things that God has prepared for them that love Him, we do know this by the revelation of the Spirit. The saints above are supremely blessed. The joy of Christ, which is an infinite fullness of delight, is in them. They bathe in the bottomless, shoreless sea of infinite blessing.

This same joyful rest will soon be ours, and it may not be long. Soon the weeping willow will be exchanged for the palm branch of victory. Sorrow's dewdrops will be transformed into the pearls of everlasting bliss.

"Therefore comfort one another with these words" (1 Thessalonians 4:18).

FAITH AND LOVE

"That Christ may dwell in your hearts through faith."

—Ephesians 3:17

It is desirable beyond measure that we, as believers, have the person of Jesus constantly before us. This will inflame our love and increase our knowledge of Him.

I would to God that my readers were all diligent scholars in Jesus' college, students of Corpus Christi, the body of Christ, resolved to attain a good degree in the learning of the cross.

To have Jesus ever near, the heart must be full of Him, welling up with His love, even running over. Thus the apostle prays "that Christ may dwell in your hearts." See how Paul wants Jesus close to him. You cannot get a subject closer than having it in your heart.

"That Christ may dwell." Not that He may be a casual visitor, but that Jesus may become the Lord and Tenant of your innermost being and never leave. Observe the words: "dwell in your heart." Not in your thoughts alone, but in your affections. Not merely in your mind's meditations, but in the heart's emotions.

Let us love Christ, not with a love that flames up and then dies out in a few embers, but with a constant flame fed by sacred fuel, like the altar fire that never went out.

This can only be accomplished by faith. Faith must be strong, or love will not be fervent. The root of the flower must be healthy, or the bloom will not be beautiful. Faith is the lily's root; love is the lily's bloom.

Reader, Jesus cannot be your heart's continual love unless you have a firm grip on Him by your heart's faith. Therefore pray that you may always trust Christ in order to always love Him.

If your love is cold, your faith is wilting.

THE BREAKER

"The one who breaks open will come up before them."

—Micah 2:13

Because Jesus has gone before us, things are different. He has conquered every foe that obstructed the way. Cheer up faint-hearted warrior. Not only has Christ traveled the road, He has also slain your enemies.

Do you dread sin? He has nailed it to His cross. Do you fear death? He has been the death of death. Are you afraid of hell? He has barred it from coming against any of His children. Believers will never see the gulf of perdition.

Whatever foes may face the Christian, Christ has already overcome them. There are lions, but their teeth are broken. There are serpents, but their fangs are extracted. There are rivers, but they are bridged or fordable. There are flames, but we wear that matchless garment which renders us invulnerable to fire.

The sword that has been forged against us is already blunted. The instruments of the enemy's war have already lost their edge. God has taken away, in the person of Christ, all the power of anything that can hurt us.

Well then, the army may safely march on. You may go joyously along your journey, for all your enemies are conquered, beaten, and vanquished. All you need to do is divide the spoils.

You will still engage in combat, but your fight is with a vanquished foe. His head is broken. He may attempt to injure you, but his strength is not sufficient. Your victory will be easy. Your treasure will be beyond counting:

> Proclaim aloud the Savior's fame,
> Who bears *the Breaker's* wondrous name;
> Sweet name; and it becomes Him well,
> Who breaks down earth, sin, death, and hell.

MISCHIEF

"If fire breaks out and catches in thorns, so that stacked grain, standing grain, or the field is consumed, he who kindled the fire shall surely make restitution." —Exodus 22:6

But what restitution can one make who starts the fires of error or lasciviousness and sets souls ablaze with the fire of hell? Their guilt is beyond estimate. The results are irrevocable.

If such an offender is forgiven, what grief will it cause in retrospect, since this mischief cannot be undone. A bad example may kindle a flame that years of amended character cannot quench. Burning the grain is bad enough, but how much worse to destroy the soul!

It may be useful to reflect if we have been guilty of this offense, or to enquire if we presently have evil in us that has a tendency to damage the souls of our relatives, friends, or neighbors.

The fire of strife is a terrible evil when it breaks out in a Christian church where converts were multiplied and God was glorified. Jealousy and envy do the devil's work. Where the golden grain was being housed to reward the toil of a Boaz (Ruth 2:1), the fire of enmity comes in and leaves little behind but smoke and a heap of blackness.

Woe to those who offend. May it never be us. Although we cannot make restitution, we will certainly be the chief sufferers if we are the chief offenders. Those who feed the fire deserve censure, but the one who kindles it is most to blame.

Discord usually takes first hold of the thorns and is nurtured by the hypocrites and mere professors of Christianity. Then away it goes among the righteous, blown by the winds of hell, and no one knows where it will end.

Oh Lord, giver of peace, make us peacemakers. Never let us aid and abet strife, or even unintentionally cause the least division among Your people. Amen.

THE SENSES OF FAITH

"His fruit was sweet to my taste."

—Song of Solomon 2:3

Faith in the Scripture is an emblem of all the senses.

It is sight: "Look unto me and be saved" (Isaiah 45:22). It is hearing: "Hear and your soul shall live" (Isaiah 55:3). It is smelling: "All Your garments are scented with myrrh and aloes and cassia" (Psalm 45:8). "Your name is ointment poured forth" (Song of Solomon 1:3).

Faith is spiritual touch. By faith the woman "came from behind and touched the hem of His garment" (Matthew 9:20). Faith is equally spiritual taste. "How sweet are Your words to my taste. Sweeter than honey to my mouth" (Psalm 119:103). Jesus said, "Unless you eat the flesh of the Son of Man and drink His blood, you have no life in you" (John 6:53). This *taste* is faith in one of its highest operations.

One of the first performances of faith is hearing. We hear the voice of God, not with the outward ear alone but with the inner ear. We hear God's Word, and we believe it to be true. This is the *hearing* of faith.

Then our mind looks on the truth as it is presented, and we understand it. We perceive its meaning. This is the *seeing* of faith. Next we discover its preciousness. We begin to admire it and find it fragrant. This is the *smell* of faith. Then we appropriate the mercies that are prepared for us in Christ. This is the *touch* of faith. Then follows the enjoyments: peace, delight, communion. This is the *taste* of faith.

Anyone of these acts of faith manifests saving faith. To hear Christ's voice as the sure voice of God in the soul will save us. But what really gives true enjoyment is the aspect of faith where Christ, by holy taste, is received and made the sweet and precious food of our souls.

Then we sit "down in His shade with great delight" and find "His fruit sweet to [the] taste" (Song of Solomon 2:3).

FREE TO ENJOY HIM

"If you believe with all your heart, you may."

—Acts 8:37

These words may answer your questions concerning the ordinances. Perhaps you say, "I am afraid to be baptized. It is such a solemn thing to be buried in baptism, in which I am also raised with Him (Colossians 2:12). And I do not feel at liberty to come to the Master's table. I am afraid of eating and drinking judgment, not discerning the Lord's body" (1 Corinthians 11:29).

Trembler, Jesus has given you liberty. Do not be afraid. If strangers come to your home they stand at the door or wait in the hall. They would never dream of intruding without an invitation. But your children roam freely about the house.

When the Holy Spirit has given you the spirit of adoption (Romans 8:15), you may come to Christian ordinances without fear. The same rule applies to the Christian's inward privileges. You may think that you are not allowed to "rejoice with joy inexpressible and full of glory" (1 Peter 1:8). But if you get inside Christ's door or sit at the bottom of His table, you will be content. You will not have fewer privileges than the great, for God makes no distinctions in how He loves His children. A child is a child to Him. He will not make you a hired servant. You will feast on the fatted calf and have music and dancing as if you never went astray.

When Jesus comes into the heart, He issues a general decree to be glad in the Lord. Chains are not worn in the court of King Jesus. Our admission to full privileges may be gradual, but it is sure.

Perhaps you are saying, "I wish I could enjoy the promise and walk at liberty in my Lord's commands." His response: "If you believe with all your heart, you may." Take the chains off your neck, captive. Jesus makes you free.

THE NEW COVENANT

"He has commanded His covenant forever."

—Psalm 111:9

The Lord's people delight in the covenant. It is a never-failing source of comfort as the Holy Spirit leads them to the banqueting house and waves the banner of love over them (Song of Solomon 2:4). They delight to contemplate the antiquity of the covenant. They remember that before the day star knew its place, or planets knew their orbit, the interests of the saints were made secure in Christ Jesus.

It is particularly pleasing to remember the sureness of the covenant while meditating on "the sure mercies of David" (Isaiah 55:3). They delight to celebrate it as signed, sealed, ratified, and in all things ordered well. It often makes their hearts dilate with joy to think of its immutability. It is a covenant that neither time or eternity, nor life or death will ever be able to violate, for it is a covenant as old as eternity and as everlasting as the Rock of Ages.

They also rejoice to feast on the fullness of this covenant. God is their portion, Christ their companion, the Spirit their Comforter, earth their lodge, and heaven their home.

They see in the covenant an inheritance reserved for every soul who possesses an interest in its ancient and eternal deed of gifts. Their eyes sparkle when they see it as a treasure trove in the Bible. How their souls are glad when they see in the last will and testament of their divine kinsman the inheritance that was willed to them.

It is especially the pleasure of God's people to contemplate the graciousness of the new covenant. They see that the law was made void because it was a covenant of human works and merit. But the new covenant is enduring because grace is the basis, grace the condition, grace the species, grace the bulwark, grace the foundation, and grace the top stone.

The covenant is a treasury of wealth, a granary of food, a fountain of life, a storehouse of salvation, a charter of peace, and a haven of joy.

GLORY THAT ATTRACTS

"When they saw Him, all the people were greatly amazed, and running to Him, greeted Him."

—Mark 9:15

What a great difference between Moses and Jesus. When the prophet of Horeb had been forty days on the mountain, he experienced a kind of transfiguration. His face shone with exceeding brightness. He had to put a veil over his face, because the people could not endure to look on Moses's glory (Exodus 34:29:ff).

Our Savior had been transfigured with a glory greater than had Moses. Yet the people were not blinded by the blaze of His countenance. Rather, "they were greatly amazed, and running to Him, greeted Him."

The glory of the law repels. The greater glory of Jesus attracts. Jesus is holy and just, yet blended with His purity there is so much truth and grace that sinners run to Him, amazed at His goodness and fascinated by His love. They greet Him, become His disciples, and take Him as their Lord and Master.

Reader, it may be that you are blinded by the dazzling brightness of the law of God. You feel its claims on your conscience, but you cannot obey it in your life. Not that you find fault with the law; on the contrary, you find that it commands your highest esteem. Yet it does not draw you to God. Rather, it hardens your heart, and you are verging on desperation.

Dear heart, turn your eyes from Moses and look to Jesus. See His flowing wounds and His head crowned with thorns. He is the Son of God, and He is greater than Moses. He is also the Lord of love and more tender than the lawgiver. He bore the wrath of God and in His death revealed more of God's justice than Sinai on fire.

Look, sinner, to the bleeding Savior. Feel the attraction of His love, and fly to His arms and be saved.

UNBELIEF

"How long will these people reject Me."

—Numbers 14:11

Strive with all diligence to keep out that monster unbelief. It so dishonors Christ that He will withdraw His presence if we insult Him with it. Unbelief is a weed whose seeds can never entirely be extracted from the soil, but we must aim at its root with zeal and perseverance. Among hateful things, unbelief is the most abhorred. Its injurious nature is so venomous that those who even listen to it are hurt.

In your case, believer, unbelief is wicked because the past mercies of your Lord increase your guilt. When you distrust the Lord Jesus you may as well cry, "Behold, I am weighed down by you, as a cart full of sheaves is weighed down" (Amos 2:13). This is crowning His head with thorns of the sharpest kind.

It is cruel for a well-beloved wife to mistrust a kind and faithful husband. The sin is needless, foolish, and unwarranted. Jesus has never given the slightest ground for suspicion. It is hard to doubt those whose conduct is uniformly affectionate and true. Jesus is the Son of the Highest and has unbounded wealth. It is shameful to doubt Omnipotence and distrust all-sufficiency.

If the cattle on a thousand hills will suffice for our most hungry feeding, surely the storehouses of heaven will not be emptied by our eating. If Christ were only a cistern, we might soon exhaust His fullness. But who can drain a fountain? Myriads of spirits have drawn their supplies from Him, and not one has murmured at the scanty resources.

Away, then, with the traitor unbelief. Its only errand is to cut the bonds of fellowship and make us mourn our absent Savior. Bunyan tells us that unbelief has "as many lives as a cat." If so, let us kill one now and continue the work until the entire nine are gone.

Away with you, traitor, my heart abhors you.

THE CHOICE TREASURE

"Into Your hand I commit my spirit; You have redeemed me, O Lord God of truth."

—Psalm 31:5

These words have been frequently used by saints in their hour of departure. We may profitably consider them this evening. The object of the faithful saint's concern in life and death is not the body or the estate, but the spirit. This is the choice treasure, and if it is safe, all is well.

What is this mortal state compared with the soul? The believer commits the soul to the hand of God, for the soul came from Him, is His own, and He has sustained it. He is therefore able to keep it, and it is fitting that He should receive it at the end. All things are safe in Jehovah's hands. What we entrust to the Lord will be secure, both now and in that day of days toward which we are rapidly traveling.

It is peaceful living and glorious dying to rest in the care of heaven. At all times we should commit our all to Jesus' faithful hand. Then, although life may hang by a thread and adversities may multiply as the sands of the sea, our soul will dwell at ease and delight in quiet resting places.

"You have redeemed me, O Lord God of truth." Redemption is a solid basis for confidence. David did not know Calvary as we do, but temporal redemption cheered him and eternal redemption will sweetly console us. Past deliverances are strong pleas for present assistance. What the Lord has done, He will do again. He does not change. He is faithful to His promises and gracious to His saints. He will not turn away from His people:

> Thou mayst chasten and correct,
>   But Thou never canst neglect;
> Since the ransom price is paid,
>   On Thy love my hope is stay'd.

OIL

"Oil for the light."

—Exodus 25:6

My soul, you need oil. Your lamp cannot burn without it. You have no oil well springing up in your human nature. You must go and buy oil from those who sell it, or like the foolish virgins you will cry, "Our lamps are going out" (Matthew 25:8).

Even the most consecrated lamps could give no light without oil. Even those that glowed in the tabernacle needed oil. Although no rough winds blew on them, they required trimming. Your need is equally as great. Under the most delightful of circumstances, you cannot give light for another hour, unless you receive the fresh oil of grace.

Only one oil could be used in the Lord's service, and it was not petroleum or fish oil or that extracted from nuts. One oil, and only one oil was selected: the finest olive oil.

Pretended grace from natural goodness, fancied grace from priestly hands, or imaginary grace from ceremonies can never serve the true saint of God. We know that the Lord will not be pleased even with rivers of such oil. We go to the olive press of Gethsemane and draw our supply from Him who was crushed. The oil of gospel grace is pure, and the light that burns from it is clear and bright.

Our churches are the Savior's golden candelabra. If we are to be lights in this dark world, we must have great quantities of holy oil. Let us pray that our ministers and our churches may never lack oil for light.

Truth, holiness, joy, knowledge, and love are all beams of sacred light, but we cannot give light unless in private we receive oil from God the Holy Spirit.

BARREN NO LONGER

"Sing, O barren."

—Isaiah 54:1

Though we have brought some fruit to Christ, there are times when we feel barren. Prayer is lifeless, love is cold, faith is weak, and each grace in the garden of our heart is like a languishing, drooping flower in the hot sun. We need a refreshing shower.

In this condition, what can we do? Our text supplies the answer. "Sing, O barren, . . . break forth into singing and cry aloud." But what can I sing about? I cannot talk about the present, and even the past looks bleak. Ah, I can sing of Jesus Christ. I can talk of visits the Redeemer has made to me. I can magnify His great love, when He came from the heights of heaven for His people's redemption.

I will go to the cross again. Come, my heavily-laden soul. You once lost your burden there; go to Calvary again. Perhaps the cross that gave you life will give you fruitfulness.

What is my barrenness but the platform for His fruit-creating power? What is my desolation but the black velvet setting for the sapphire of His everlasting love? I will go to Him in poverty, I will go in helplessness, I will go in all my shame and backsliding. I will tell Him that I am still His child, and with confidence in His faithful heart, even I, the barren one, will sing.

Sing, believer, it will cheer your heart and the hearts of other desolate ones. Sing on, for now that you are really ashamed of being barren, you will soon be fruitful. Now that God has made you loath to be without fruit, He will cover you with clusters.

The experience of barrenness is painful, but the Lord's visitations are delightful. A sense of our own poverty drives us to Christ, and that is where we need to be. In Him our fruit is found.

MERCY

"Have mercy upon me, O God."

—Psalm 51:1

When Dr. William Carey was suffering from a dangerous illness, he was asked, "If this sickness proves fatal, what passage would you select as the text for your funeral sermon?"

He replied, "Oh, I feel that such a poor, sinful creature is unworthy to have anything said about him. But if a funeral sermon must be preached, let it be from these words. 'Have mercy upon me, O God, according to Your lovingkindness; according to the multitude of Your tender mercies, blot out my transgressions'."

In the same spirit of humility, he directed in his will that the following inscription and nothing more should be cut on his gravestone:

> WILLIAM CAREY, BORN AUGUST 17th, 1761
> DIED—
> A wretched, poor, and helpless worm
> On Thy kind arms I fall.

Only on the footing of free grace can the most experienced and most honored of saints approach God. The greatest are conscious that, at best, they are only human. Empty boats float high, but heavily loaded vessels are low in the water. Mere professors of Christ can boast, but true children of God cry for mercy.

We need the Lord to have mercy on our good works, our prayers, our preaching, our charity, and even our holiest things. The blood was not only sprinkled on the doorpost of Israel's dwelling houses, but also on the sanctuary, the mercy seat, and the altar. Because as sin intrudes into our holiest things, the blood of Jesus is needed to purify them from defilement.

If mercy is needed for our duties, what can be said about our sins? It is sweet to remember that inexhaustible mercy is waiting to be gracious, to restore our backsliding and make our broken bones rejoice!

CAREFUL WALKING

"All the days of his separation he shall eat nothing that is produced by the grapevine from seed to skin."

—Numbers 6:4

Nazarites had taken vows, and among them was one that barred them from drinking wine. To ensure that they did not violate this vow, they were forbidden to drink the vinegar of wine or strong liquors. To make the rule even clearer, they were not to touch unfermented juice or eat either fresh or dried grapes. To secure the integrity of the vow, they were not allowed anything that had to do with the vine. They were to avoid all appearance of evil.

Surely this is a lesson to the Lord's separated ones, teaching us to come away from sin in every form, to avoid not merely its grosser shapes, but even its similarity and spirit. Such strict walking is despised these days, but rest assured, dear reader, it is both the safest and the happiest walk. Those who yield a point or two to the world are in fearful peril. Those who eat the grapes of Sodom will soon drink the wine of Gomorrah.

A little crevice in the sea bank in Holland lets in the sea and the gap speedily widens until a province floods. Worldly conformity, in any degree, is a snare to the soul and makes it more and more liable to presumptuous sins.

The Nazarite who drank grape juice could not be totally sure if fermentation had begun. Consequently he could not be certain that his vow was intact. The yielding Christian's conscience must feel that the inward monitor is in doubt. Things doubtful we need not doubt; they are wrong for us (Romans 14:23). Things tempting must not be dallied with; flee from them with speed. Better to be sneered at as a Puritan than despised as a hypocrite.

Careful walking may involve much self-denial, but it has pleasures that are more than a sufficient reward.

WAITING

"Wait on the Lord."

—Psalm 27:14

It may seem an easy thing to wait, but it is a posture that takes years for the Christian soldier to learn. Marching and quick marching are easier than standing still. There are hours of perplexity when the most willing spirit, anxiously desiring to serve the Lord, does not know what to do. We are thrown into commotion. What can we do? Fly back like a coward? Turn to the right in fear, or rush forward in presumption?

No, simply wait, but wait in prayer. Call on God and spread the case before Him. Tell Him your difficulty and plead His promise of aid. In the dilemmas of life, it is sweet to be as humble as a child and to wait with simplicity of soul. It will be well when you feel and know your own folly, and are heartily willing to be guided by the will of God.

Wait in faith. Express your total confidence in Him. Unfaithful, untrusting waiting is an insult to the Lord. Believe that if He keeps you waiting until midnight, He will still come at the right time.

Wait in quiet patience. Do not rebel because you are under affliction, but bless God for it. Never murmur as the children of Israel did against Moses. Never wish you could go back to the world.

Simply, with your whole heart, without any self-will, say to your covenant God, "Lord, not my will, but your will. I do not know what to do. I am brought to the brink. I will wait until You divide the flood or drive back my foes. I will wait if You will keep me. My heart is fixed on You alone. Oh God, my spirit waits for You in the full conviction that 'You have been a shelter for me, a strong tower from the enemy. I will abide in Your tabernacle forever; I will trust in the shelter of Your wings'" (Psalm 61:3,4). Amen.

AUGUST 30, MORNING

BELOVED PHYSICIAN

"Heal me, O Lord, and I shall be healed."
—Jeremiah 17:14
"I have seen his ways and will heal him."
—Isaiah 57:18

It is the sole prerogative of God to remove spiritual disease. Natural disease may be instrumentally healed by physicians, but even then the ultimate honor is to be given to God. It is God who gives virtue to medicine and power to the human frame to cast off disease.

As for spiritual sickness, this remains for the great Physician alone to heal. He claims it as His prerogative. "I kill and I make alive; I wound and I heal" (Deuteronomy 32:39). One of the Lord's choice titles is Jehovah-Rophi: the Lord that heals you. I will "heal you of your wounds" (Jeremiah 30:17) is a promise that could not come from the lips of men or women, but only from the mouth of the eternal God. On this account the psalmist cried to the Lord, "O Lord heal me, for my bones are troubled" (Psalm 6:2). "Heal my soul for I have sinned against You" (Psalm 41:4).

The godly also praise the Lord saying, "He heals all your diseases" (Psalm 103:3). He who made us can restore us. He who created our nature can make it new again. What a transcendent comfort that in the person of Jesus "dwells all the fullness of the Godhead bodily" (Colossians 2:9).

Whatever your disease, the great Physician can heal you. If He is God, there is no limit to His power. Come with the blind eye of darkened understanding; come with the limping foot of wasted energy; come with the maimed hand of weak faith; come with the fever of an angry temper; come with the chill of shivering despondency. Come just as you are. He who is God can heal you.

No one can restrain the healing virtue that proceeds from Jesus our Lord. All His patients have been cured in the past and will be cured in the future.

You can be among them, my friend, if you will but rest in Him this evening.

AUGUST 30, EVENING

TRUST

"On My arm they will trust."

—Isaiah 51:5

In seasons of severe trial, there is nothing on earth for Christians to trust in. They are compelled to cast themselves on God alone. When our vessel is beached on its side and no human deliverance is available, we must simply and entirely trust in the providence and care of God. It is a happy storm that wrecks us on this rock. Oh blessed hurricane that drives the soul to God and God alone!

Sometimes there is no getting at God because of the multitude of our friends. But when we are so friendless, so poor, or so helpless that we have nowhere else to turn, we can fly to our Father's arms and be blessedly held there. When troubles are so burdensome and pressing that we cannot tell them to anyone but our God, let us be thankful for them. We will learn more of our Lord during difficulty and loss than at any other time.

Oh, tempest-tossed believer, it is a happy trouble that drives you to your Father. Now that you have only your God to trust, see to it that you put your full confidence in Him. Do not dishonor your Lord and Master with unworthy doubts and fears. Be strong in faith and give glory to God. Show the world that your God is worth ten thousand worlds. Show the rich how rich you are in poverty when the Lord God is your helper. Show the strong how strong you are in weakness, when underneath you are the everlasting arms (Deuteronomy 33:27).

Now is the time for feats of faith; be strong and very courageous (Joshua 1:7). The Lord your God will certainly—as surely as He built the heavens and the earth—glorify Himself in your weakness and magnify His might in the midst of your distress.

May the Holy Spirit give you rest in Jesus this closing day of the month.

WALKING IN THE LIGHT

"If we walk in the light as He is in the light."

—1 John 1:7

"As He is in the light." Can we ever reach this? Will we ever be able to walk in the light as clearly as He whom we call, "Our Father"? Will we ever be able to walk in the light as He of whom it is written, "God is light and in Him is no darkness at all" (1 John 1:5)?

Certainly this is the model. Our Savior said, "You shall be perfect, just as your Father in heaven is perfect" (Matthew 5:48). Although we may feel that we can never rival the perfection of God, yet we are to seek after it. We are never to be satisfied until we attain it.

What is meant by the expression that the Christian is to walk in the light as God is in the light? I believe it infers *likeness,* although not to the same degree. We are as truly in the light, as heartily in the light, as sincerely in the light, as honestly in the light, but we are not there in the same measure as God.

I cannot stare at the sun; it is too bright for my eyes. But I can walk in the light of the sun. Although I cannot attain the perfection of purity and truth that belongs to the Lord of hosts, yet I can set the Lord always before me, and I can strive with the help of the indwelling Spirit to conform to His image.

That famous old commentator, John Trapp, said, "We may be in the light as God is in the light for quality, but not for equality." We are to have the same light, and to have it as God has it. As for equality with God in his holiness and purity, however, that must be left until we cross the Jordan and enter the perfection of the Most High.

Remember, the blessing of sacred fellowship and perfect cleansing are combined with walking in the light.

AUGUST 31, EVENING

GUIDANCE

"You will guide me with Your counsel, and afterward receive me to glory."

—Psalm 73:24

The psalmist felt a need for divine guidance. He had discovered the foolishness of his heart and feared it would lead him astray. He resolved that God's counsel should guide him.

A sense of our own folly is a great step toward being wise when it leads us to rely on the wisdom of God. The blind one leans on a friend's arm and reaches home safely. We lean on divine guidance, assured that, though we cannot see, it is always safe to trust the all-seeing God.

In our text, "You will" is a blessed expression of confidence. The psalmist was sure that the Lord would guide, and this is a word for you too, believer. Rest on it. Be assured that God will be your counselor and friend: "I will instruct you and teach you in the way you should go: I will guide you with My eye" (Psalm 32:8). In His written Word, you have this assurance partly fulfilled, for Holy Scripture is His counsel to you.

A sailor is lost without a compass. A Christian is lost without the Bible. Scripture is an errorless chart or map on which every shoal is described and all the channels, from the quicksand of destruction to the haven of salvation, are marked and mapped by One who knows the way. Blessed are You, Oh God, that we may trust You to guide us now and guide us even to the end.

After guidance through life, the psalmist anticipates a divine reception: "and afterward receive me to glory." What a thought! God will receive you to glory—You!—wandering, erring, straying. He will bring you safe at last to glory. This is your promise. Live on it today.

Should life's perplexities surround you, go straight to the throne in the strength of this text.

SIMPLY TRUSTING

"Trust in Him at all times."

—Psalm 62:8

Faith is as much the rule of our passing life as it is of our spiritual life. We should have faith in God for earthly affairs as well as for heavenly business. It is only as we learn to trust God to supply all our daily needs that we can live above the world.

We are not to be idle. This would show that we do not trust God but the devil, who is the father of idleness. We are not to be reckless or rash, which is to trust in chance and not the living God, who is a God of purpose and order. Acting in prudence and uprightness, we are to rely simply and entirely on the Lord.

Let me commend to you a life of trusting in God for your earthly affairs. If you trust in Him, you will not be compelled to mourn because you used sinful means to grow rich. Serve God with integrity. If you do not achieve worldly success, at least you will not have sin on your conscience.

Trusting God, you will not be guilty of self-contradiction. Those who trust in the winds sail this way today, that way tomorrow, and another way the next day. But those who trust in the Lord are like a motor-powered vessel. They cut through the waves, defy the winds, and make one bright silvery straight track to the destined haven.

Live by biblical principles. Never bow to the varying customs of worldly wisdom. Walk a path of integrity. Show that you are invincibly strong in the strength that confidence in God alone confers. Thus you will be delivered from anxious cares. You will not be troubled with evil news. Your heart will be fixed, trusting in the Lord.

How pleasant to float along the stream of providence! There is no more blessed way of living than to live a life of dependence upon a covenant-keeping God. We have no cares, for He cares for us; we have no troubles, because we cast our burdens upon the Lord (1 Peter 5:7).

SEPTEMBER 1, EVENING

MY PHYSICIAN

"But Simon's wife's mother lay sick with a fever, and they told Him about her at once."

—Mark 1:30

This is an interesting little look into the home of an apostolic fisherman. We immediately see that household joys and cares are not a hindrance to the full work of the ministry. As a matter of fact, they furnish an opportunity for personally witnessing the Lord's gracious work on one's own family. They may even instruct the teacher better than any other earthly disciple could. True Christianity and household life go well together.

Peter's house was probably a poor fisherman's hut. Yet the Lord of Glory entered it, lodged there, and worked a miracle in it. If this book is being read this morning in an humble dwelling, let this fact encourage the residents to seek the company of King Jesus, who is more often in little huts than in rich palaces.

Jesus is looking around your room now. He is waiting to be gracious. Sickness had entered Simon's house. Fever in a deadly form had prostrated his mother-in-law. When Jesus came, they told Him of her affliction and He hastened to the patient's bed.

Is there any sickness in your home this morning? You will find Jesus is the best physician. Go to Him. Tell Him all about the problem. Immediately lay the case before Him. It concerns one of His people, therefore it is not trivial to Him. Observe that immediately the Savior restored the sick woman. No one can heal like Jesus.

We may not be sure that the Lord will at once remove all disease from those we love. We do know, however, that believing prayer for the sick is often followed by restoration (James 5:15).

If the person is not healed, we must bow to Him who determines life and death. The tender heart of Jesus waits to hear our griefs. Let us pour them into His patient ear.

SEPTEMBER 2, MORNING

MIRACLES, SIGNS AND WONDERS

"Unless you people see signs and wonders you will by no means believe."

—John 4:48

Craving for miracles was a symptom of the sick minds in our Lord's day. These people refused solid nourishment and sought mere marvels. They had no interest in the gospel they desperately needed. The miracles, which Jesus did not always choose to give, is what they eagerly demanded.

Today many must see signs and wonders or they will not believe. Some have said in their heart, "I must feel deep horror of soul, or I will never believe in Jesus." But what if you never feel it? Probably you never will. Will you go to hell out of spite because God treated you differently? Another may say, "If I had a dream, or if I could feel a sudden tingle of I know not what, then I would believe."

Thus you undeserving mortals dream that my Lord is to be dictated to by you! You who are beggars at His gate asking for mercy, you want to write the rules and regulations as to how He will give that mercy. Do you think He will submit to this? My Master is generous, but He has a right royal heart. He rejects all demands and maintains His sovereignty of action.

If this is your case, my dear reader, why do you crave signs and wonders? Is not the gospel its own sign and wonder? Is not this the miracle of miracles: "God so loved the world that He gave His only begotten Son, that whoever believes in Him should not perish but have everlasting life" (John 3:16)?

Surely these precious words, "Whoever desires, let him take the water of life freely" (Revelation 22:17), and the solemn promise, "The one who comes to Me I will by no means cast out" (John 6:37), are better than signs and wonders!

A truthful Savior ought to be believed. He is truth itself. Why do you ask proof of the veracity of One who cannot lie?

SEPTEMBER 2, EVENING

NO IFS OR BUTS

"Tell me, O you whom I love."

—Song of Solomon 1:7

It is well to be able to say of the Lord Jesus, without any "if" or "but," that it is "You whom I love." Many say they hope they love Him, or they trust they love Him, yet only those with a shallow and poor experience will be content with this relationship. Christians should give no rest to their spirit until they are certain about this vital matter.

We should not be satisfied with a superficial hope that Jesus loves us or with a blind trust that we love Him. The old saints did not generally speak with "buts, ifs, hopes, and trusts" in this matter. They spoke positively and plainly. "I know whom I have believed," said Paul (2 Timothy 1:12). "I know that my Redeemer lives," said Job (Job 19:25).

Get positive knowledge of your love of Jesus. Do not be satisfied until you can speak of your faith in Him as a reality. Be sure, by receiving the witness of the Holy Spirit and by having His seal on your soul by faith. True love for Christ is always the work of the Holy Spirit. It can be worked in the heart only by Him. He is the efficient cause of it.

The logical reason we love Jesus is found in Jesus Himself, for He first loved us" (1 John 4:19). Why do I love Jesus? Because He "gave Himself for me" (Galatians 2:20). I have life through His death and peace through His blood. "Though He was rich, yet for your sakes He became poor" (2 Corinthians 8:9).

Why do we love Jesus? Because of His excellence. We are filled with a sense of His beauty, an admiration of His charms, and a consciousness of His infinite perfection. His goodness, greatness, and loveliness combine in one resplendent ray to enchant the soul until we exclaim, "Yes, He is altogether lovely" (Song of Solomon 5:16).

Blessed love! This love binds the heart with chains softer than silk, yet stronger than steel.

THE REASON FOR TRIALS

"The Lord tests the righteous."

—Psalm 11:5

"All events are under the control of Providence. Consequently, all the trials of our outward life are traceable to the great First Cause. Out of the golden gate of God's purposes the armies of trial march, clad in iron armor and armed with the weapons of war.

All providences are doors to trials. Even our mercies, like roses, have their thorns. One may drown in seas of prosperity as well as in rivers of affliction. Our mountains are not too high and our valleys are not too low for temptations. Trials lurk on every road. Everywhere, above and beneath, we are beset and surrounded with danger.

Yet no shower falls unpermitted from the threatening cloud. Every raindrop has its orders before it falls. The trials that come from God are sent to prove and strengthen our graces. They illustrate the power of divine grace to test the genuineness of our virtues and add to their energy.

Our Lord, in His infinite wisdom and superabundant love, sets so high a value on His people's faith that He will not screen them from those trials which strengthen faith. You would never have possessed the precious faith that now supports you if the trial of your faith had not been like fire. You are a tree that never would have rooted so deep if the wind had not rocked you back and forth.

Worldly ease is a great foe of faith. It loosens the joints of holy valor. It snaps the sinews of sacred courage. The balloon never rises until the cords are cut. It is affliction that does this sharp service for believing souls. While the wheat sleeps comfortably in the husk, it is useless as food. It must be threshed out of its resting place before its value can be known.

Thus it is well that Jehovah sends trials to the righteous, for it causes them to grow rich in the things of the Lord.

SEPTEMBER 3, EVENING

HIS TOUCH

"I am willing; be cleansed."

—Mark 1:41

Primeval darkness heard the Almighty command, "Let there be light; and there was light" (Genesis 1:3). The Word of the Lord Jesus is equal in majesty to that ancient word of power. Redemption, like Creation, has its word of might. Jesus speaks and it is done.

Leprosy would not yield to human remedies, but it fled at the Lord's, "I am willing." The disease showed no sign of remission, and nature did not contribute to its abatement; but the Word of Jesus immediately healed the leper.

Sinner, you are in a plight more miserable than the leper. Follow the leper's example and go to Jesus. Implore Him. Kneel before Him and say, "If You are willing, You can make me clean" (Mark 1:40). Exercise what little faith you have. You do not have to say more than, "Lord, if You are willing, You can make me clean." There is no need to doubt the result of the supplication. Jesus heals all who come. Jesus casts out none who come to Him.

In reading the narrative surrounding our morning's text, we notice that Jesus touched the leper. This unclean person had broken the regulations of the ceremonial law and pushed his way into the house. But far from reprimanding him, Jesus broke through the law in order to meet him. Jesus cleansed the leper and in that touch became Levitically defiled (Leviticus 13:46). In the same manner Jesus Christ, who knew no sin, "was made sin for us that we might be made the righteousness of God in Him" (2 Corinthians 5:21).

Sinners should go to Jesus and believe in the power of His blessed substitutionary work and learn of His gracious touch. That hand which multiplied loaves, which saved sinking Peter, which upholds afflicted saints, which crowns believers—that same hand will touch every seeking sinner today, and in a moment it will make them clean. The love of Jesus is the source of salvation. He loves, He looks, He touches us, and *we live*.

SEPTEMBER 4, MORNING

WEIGHTS AND MEASURES

"You shall have honest scales, honest weights, an honest ephah, and an honest hin."

—Leviticus 19:36

Scales, weights, and measures were to be governed by the standard of justice. Surely Christians should not need to reminded of this in their business. There are, however, other scales that weigh moral and spiritual things, and these often need to be examined. Let us call in the weights and measures inspector this evening.

The balances in which we weigh our own and other people's characters, are they accurate? Do we turn *our* ounces of goodness into pounds but other people's gallons of excellences into pints? Christian, check your weights and measures.

The scales in which we measure our trials and troubles, are they according to standard? Paul, who suffered more than we, called his afflictions light (2 Corinthians 4:17). Wait! Surely something is wrong with the scales! We must correct this, lest we get reported to the court above for unjust dealings.

Those weights with which we measure our doctrinal beliefs, are they fair? The doctrines of grace should have the same weight with us as the precepts of the Word, no more and no less. With many, however, one scale or the other is unfairly weighted. It is a grand matter to give honest measure in truth.

The measures in which we estimate our obligations and responsibilities look rather small. When a rich person gives no more to the cause of God than the poor contributes, is that an "honest ephah and a honest hin?" When ministers are half starved, is that honest dealings? When the poor are despised and the ungodly wealthy are held in admiration, is that balance?

Reader, I might lengthen the list, but I prefer to leave it as your evening's work to find and destroy all unrighteous balances, weights, and measures.

GOOD SOLDIERS

"Woe is me, that I dwell in Meshech, that I dwell among the tents of Kedar!"

—Psalm 120:5

As a Christian, you have to live in the midst of an ungodly world. It is useless to cry, "Woe is me." Jesus did not pray for you to be taken out of the world (John 17:15), and what He did not pray for, you do not need.

It is better to meet difficulty in the Lord's strength and glorify Him in that difficulty. The enemy is ever on the watch to detect inconsistency in your conduct. Therefore be holy, and remember that the eyes of all are on you. More is expected of you than others. Strive to give no occasion for blame. Let your goodness be the only fault they can discover. Like Daniel, compel them to say, "We shall not find any charge against this Daniel unless we find it against him concerning the law of his God" (Daniel 6:5).

Seek also to be useful as well as consistent. Perhaps you think, "If I were in a better position I might serve the Lord's cause, but I cannot do any good where I am." But the more crooked the people are where you live, the more you are needed to help set them straight. If they are quite perverse, the more need you have to turn their proud hearts to the truth. The physician should be where the sick are. The soldier, to win honor, must be in the hottest battle.

When weary of the strife and sin that meets you, remember that all the saints have endured similar trials. They were not carried on feather beds to heaven, and you must not expect to travel more easily than they did. They hazarded their lives to the death, and you will not be crowned until you also have endured hardness as a good soldier of Jesus Christ (2 Timothy 2:3).

Therefore, "Watch, stand fast in the faith, be brave, be strong" (1 Corinthians 16:13).

CURIOUS

"Have you entered the springs of the sea?"

—Job 38:16

Some things in nature must remain a mystery even to the most intelligent and enterprising investigators. Human knowledge has boundaries beyond which it cannot pass. Universal knowledge is for God alone.

If this is true in things that can be seen, I may rest assured that it is even more so in matters spiritual and eternal. Why then have I been torturing my mind with speculations as to destiny and will, fixed fate, and human responsibility? I cannot comprehend these deep and hidden truths. It would be easier to find the depths from which the old ocean drew her watery stores.

Why am I so curious to know the reason of my Lord's providence, the motive of His actions, and the design of His visitations? Will I ever be able to clasp the sun in my fist or hold the universe in my palm? Yet these are as a drop in a bucket compared with the Lord my God. Let me not strive to understand the infinite, but spend my strength in love.

What I cannot gain by intellect I can possess by affection. Let that suffice. I cannot penetrate the heart of the sea, but I can enjoy the healthful breezes that sweep over its surface. I can sail over its blue waves with favorable winds.

If I could enter the springs of the sea, the feat would serve no useful purpose either to myself or others. It would not save the sinking vessel, or give the drowned mariner back to his weeping wife and children. Neither would solving deep mysteries avail me one iota. The least love to God and the simplest act of obedience to Him are better than the profoundest scientific knowledge.

My Lord, I leave the infinite to You. I pray that You will keep me away from a love for the tree of knowledge and give me a great love for the tree of life. Amen.

LIGHTS

"In the midst of a crooked and perverse generation, among whom you shine as lights in the world."

—Philippians 2:15

We use lights to make things apparent. Christians should so shine that a person could not live among them for a week without knowing the gospel. Our conversations should be such that all who are around us will clearly perceive who owns us and whom we serve. The image of Jesus should be reflected in our daily actions.

Lights are also intended for guidance. We are to help those around us who are in the dark. We are to hold forth the Word of Life. We are to point sinners to the Savior and the weary to a divine resting place. People sometimes read their Bibles and fail to understand its meaning. We should be ready, like Philip, to instruct the inquirer in the meaning of God's Word, the plan of salvation, and the godly life (Acts 8:30).

Lights are also used for warnings. On our rocks and shoals a lighthouse is sure to be erected. Christians should know that there are many false lights everywhere and that the true light is needed. Wreckers for Satan are always tempting the ungodly to sin in the name of pleasure. They hoist a false light. It is our responsibility to raise the true light on every dangerous rock. We must point out every sin and tell what that sin leads to, so that we may be innocent of the sinner's blood.

Lights also have a cheering influence, and so do Christians. A Christian should be a comforter with kind words and sympathy. We should carry sunshine wherever we go and diffuse happiness around us:

> Gracious Spirit dwell with me;
> I myself would gracious be,
> And with words that help and heal
> Would thy life in mine reveal,
> And with actions bold and meek
> Would for Christ my Savior speak.

SEPTEMBER 6, MORNING

JUDGE YOURSELF

"If you are led by the Spirit, you are not under the law."

—Galatians 5:18

If we look at our character and position from a legal point of view, we will only despair when we come to the end of our reckoning. But if we are wise we will despair at the beginning. If we are to be judged on the footing of the law, there is no one living who is justified. How blessed to know that we dwell in the domain of grace and not law.

When thinking of my state before God, the question is not, "Am I perfect before the law?" The question is, "Am I perfect in Christ Jesus?" That is a very different matter. I do not need to ask, "Am I naturally without sin?" I must ask, "Have I been washed in the fountain that was opened for sin and uncleanness?" It is not, "Am I in myself pleasing to God?" But "Am I accepted in the Beloved?"

Christians who view the evidence from the top of Sinai grow alarmed concerning salvation. It is far better if they read their title by the light of Calvary. Their faith has unbelief in it and is not able to save them. Thus they must consider and rely only on the object of their faith, Jesus Christ, for there is no failure in Him, and therefore they will be safe.

My hope is dimmed by my anxious cares about present things. How can I be accepted? If I had considered the basis of my hope, I would have seen that the promise of God stands sure. Thus whatever my doubts, His oath and promise never fail.

Ah, believer, it is always safer to be led by the Spirit into gospel liberty than to wear legal chains. Judge yourself by what Christ is rather than what you are. Satan will try to mar your peace by reminding you of your sinfulness and imperfections. You can meet his accusations only by faithfully adhering to the gospel and refusing to wear the yoke of bondage.

SEPTEMBER 6, EVENING

METHODS

". . . they could not come near Him because of the crowd, they uncovered the roof where He was. So when they had broken through they let down the bed on which the paralytic was lying."—Mark 2:4

Faith is full of inventions. The house was packed, and a crowd blocked the door, but faith found a way to reach the Lord and place the paralytic before Him.

If we cannot get sinners to Jesus by ordinary methods, we must use extraordinary ones. It seems, according to Luke 5:19, that the roof was made of tiles which had to be removed. This would make some noise, kick up dust, and cause some danger to those below. But when the case is urgent, we must not mind running risks and disturbing property. Jesus was there to heal, so let the tiles be removed. Faith ventured everything so that the poor paralytic's sins would be forgiven.

Oh, that we had a daring faith! This morning, can we seek it for ourselves and our fellow workers? Can we try today to perform some gallant act for the love of souls and the glory of our Lord? While the world invents new products and genius serves all the purposes of human desire, can faith not invent some new method and by it reach the outcasts who lie perishing?

It was the presence of Jesus that excited victorious courage in the four stretcher bearers. Is the Lord among us? Have we seen His face this morning? Have we felt His healing power? If so, then through door, through window, or through roof break through all impediments and work to bring souls to Jesus. All methods are good when faith and love are truly set on winning souls. If hunger for bread can break through stone walls, surely hunger for souls is not to be hindered.

Oh Lord, make us quick to suggest methods of reaching Your sin-sick ones. Make us bold to carry out the plan regardless of the danger. Amen.

THE CRUEL SEA

"There is trouble on the sea; it cannot be quiet."

—Jeremiah 49:23

We have no idea what sorrow may be on the sea this evening. Far away, a hurricane may be seeking the lives of sailors. Hear the wind of death howl among the ropes of the rigging. Listen to the timbers creak and strain as the waves beat like battering rams on the hull! God help you, drenched and wearied ones! My prayer goes up to the great Lord of sea and land that He will make the storm a calm and bring you safely to your harbor (Psalm 107:29–30).

How often the boisterous sea swallows up ships and sends thousands of bodies to lie where pearls are deep. The sorrow of death upon the sea is echoed in the long wail of widows and orphans, and the salt of the sea is in the eyes of many mothers and wives. Remorseless billows, you have devoured the love of women and the support of their households.

What a resurrection there will be from the caverns of the deep when the sea gives up the dead (Revelation 20:13)! Until then, there will be sorrow on the sea. As if in sympathy with the woes of earth, the sea is forever fretting along a thousand shores. Hear her wailing with a sorrowful cry like her own birds, booming with a hollow crash of unrest, raving with uproarious discontent, chafing with a hoarse wrath, or jangling with the voices of ten thousand murmuring pebbles.

The roar of the sea may be joyous to a rejoicing spirit, but to the children of its sorrow the wide, wide ocean is even more forlorn than the wide, wide world. This is not our rest. The restless billows tell us that. There is a land where there is no more sea (Revelation 21:1), and our faces are steadfastly set toward it. We are going to the place the Lord told us about. Until then, we cast our sorrows on the Lord who walked the sea of old. Our Lord makes a way for His people through the depths of the sea.

SEPTEMBER 7, EVENING

DEVELOPING FRUIT

"Your fruit is found in me."

—Hosea 14:8

Our fruit comes from God, through our union with Christ. The fruit of the branch is directly traceable to the root. Sever the connection, and the branch dies, and no fruit is produced. But through our union with Christ, we bring forth fruit. Every bunch of grapes started in the root, passed through the stem, flowed through the sap vessels, and fashioned itself externally into fruit.

In a similar manner, every good work was first in Christ before it was brought forth in us. Christian, prize your precious union to Christ, for it is the source of all fruitfulness. If you were not joined to Jesus Christ, you would be a barren branch.

Our fruit also comes from God's providence. When the dew drops fall from heaven, when the clouds look down from on high and are about to distill their liquid treasure, when the bright sun swells the berries of the cluster, then each heaven sent gift may whisper to the tree, "From me your fruit comes."

The fruit owes much to the root, which is essential to fruitfulness, but it also owes much to external influences. How much we owe to God's providential grace! He provides us constantly with life, teaching, consolation, strength, or whatever else we need. Whatever we have or are, we owe to Him.

Finally, our fruit comes from God's wise cultivation of His vineyard. The gardener's sharp knife promotes fruitfulness by thinning clusters and cutting off superfluous shoots. So it is Christian, with the pruning the Lord gives you. "I am the true vine, and My Father is the vine dresser. Every branch in Me that does not bear fruit He takes away; and every branch that bears fruit He prunes that it may bear more fruit" (John 15:1–2).

Since our God is the author of our spiritual graces, let us give Him all the glory of our salvation.

SEPTEMBER 8, MORNING

ALIVE IN CHRIST

"The exceeding greatness of His power toward us who believe, according to the working of His mighty power which He worked in Christ when He raised Him from the dead."—Ephesians 1:19,20

In the resurrection of Christ, as in our salvation, only His mighty divine power was used. What then can we say to those who think conversion was worked by their free will? When we see the dead rise from the grave by their own power, then we may expect the ungodly to turn to Christ by their own free will. It is not through the word preached or the word read; all awakening proceeds from the Holy Spirit.

This power is irresistible. All the soldiers and even the high priest could not keep the body of Christ in the tomb. Death could not hold Jesus in its bonds. This is the same irresistible power put into believers when they are raised to newness of life. No sin, no corruption, no devils in hell, or sinner on earth can stop the hand of God's grace when it intends to convert a soul. If God omnipotently says, "You shall," the sinner cannot say, "I will not."

Observe that the power which raised Christ from the dead was glorious. It reflected honor on God but worked dismay in the hosts of evil. There is great glory to God in the conversion of every sinner.

It was everlasting power. We, being raised from the dead, do not go back to our dead works or to our old corruptions, but we live to God. "Because I live, you will live also" (John 14:19). "For you died, and your life is hidden with Christ in God" (Colossians 3:3). "Just as Christ was raised from the dead by the glory of the Father, even so we also should walk in newness of life" (Romans 6:4).

And mark the connection in our text of the new life to Jesus. The same power that raised the Head works life in the members. What a blessing to be made alive together with Christ!

UNCOMMON EXPERIENCES

"I will answer you, and show you great and mighty things, which you do not know."

—Jeremiah 33:3

There are various translations of these words. One version renders it, "I will show you great and fortified things." Another says, "great and reserved things."

All the developments of spiritual life are not alike. Yes, there are the common frames and feelings of repentance, faith, joy, and hope, and all of these are enjoyed by the entire family of believers. But there is also a realm of rapture, communion, and conscious union with Christ that is far from common. There are heights in experiential knowledge of the things of God that the eagle's eye of discernment and philosophic thought have never seen. There are great, mighty, fortified, reserved, and special things in the Christian experience.

We do not have the high privilege of John to lean on Jesus' bosom (John 13:23), or of Paul to be caught up into the third heaven (2 Corinthians 12:2). God alone can take us there, but the chariot in which He takes us, and the fiery steeds that drag the chariot are prevailing prayers. Prevailing prayer is victorious over the God of mercy: "In his strength he struggled with God. Yes, he struggled with the Angel and prevailed. He wept, and sought favor from Him. He found Him in Bethel. And there He spoke to us" (Hosea 12:4).

Prevailing prayer enables us to cover heaven with clouds of blessing and earth with floods of mercy. Prevailing prayer carries the Christian aloft to Pisgah and shows us the inheritance reserved. It elevates us to Tabor and transfigures us until we are like our Lord.

If you want to reach something higher than ordinary grovelling experiences, look to the Rock that is higher than you (Psalm 61:2). Gaze with the eye of faith through the window of urgent prayer. When you open the window on your side, it will not be bolted on the other.

SEPTEMBER 9, MORNING

EQUALITY

"Around the throne were twenty-four thrones, and on the thrones I saw twenty-four elders sitting, clothed in white robes."

—Revelation 4:4

These representatives of the saints in heaven are placed "around the throne." In the passage where Solomon sings of the king at his table (Song of Solomon 1:12), some translate it "a round table." From this, some expositors, without straining the text, have said, "There is an equality among the saints." The idea is conveyed by the equal nearness to God of the twenty-four elders.

The condition of glorified spirits in heaven is nearness to Christ, clear vision of His glory, open access to His court, and familiar fellowship with Him. In this respect, there is no difference between one saint and another. All the people of God—apostles, martyrs, ministers, or private and obscure Christians—will all be seated near the throne.

There they will gaze on their exalted Lord and be satisfied with His love. They will all be near Christ, all ravished with His love, all eating and drinking at the same table with Him. All equally loved as His favorites and friends, even if not all equally rewarded as servants.

Let believers on earth imitate the saints in heaven in nearness to Christ. Let us on earth be as the elders are in heaven, sitting around the throne. May Christ be the object of our thoughts and the center of our lives.

Lord Jesus, draw us nearer to you. Say to us, "Abide in Me, and I in you" (John 15:4). Permit us to sing, "His left hand is under my head, and His right hand embraces me" (Song of Solomon 2:6). Amen.

> O lift me higher, nearer Thee,
> And as I rise more pure and meet,
> O let my soul's humility
> Make me lie lower at Thy feet:
> Less trusting self, the more I prove
> The blessed comfort of Thy love.

SEPTEMBER 9, EVENING

THE MOUNTAIN TOP

"And He went up on the mountain and called to Him those He Himself wanted. And they came to Him."

—Mark 3:13

Here was sovereignty. Impatient spirits may fret and fume because they are not called to the highest places in ministry, but let us rejoice that Jesus calls "those He Himself wanted." If He calls us to be doorkeepers, let us cheerfully bless Him for His grace in permitting us to do anything in His service.

The call of Christ's servants comes from above. Jesus stands on the mountain, forever above the world in holiness, earnestness, love, and power. Those He calls must go up the mountain. They must seek to rise to His level by living in constant communion with Him. They may not be able to ascend to classic honors, or attain scholastic eminence; but like Moses, they must go up the mountain of God. They must have familiar fellowship with the unseen God. If not, they will never be fully qualified to proclaim the gospel of peace.

Jesus went alone to have high fellowship with the Father. If we are to be a blessing, we must do the same. Little wonder the apostles were clothed with power when they came down from the mountain where Jesus was. This morning, we must endeavor to climb the mount of communion, for there we may be ordained to the life work for which we are set apart.

Let us not look on a human face today until we have first seen Jesus. Time spent with Him is repaid with blessed interest. We too will cast out devils and work wonders if we go to the world with the divine energy that Christ alone can give. It is useless to fight the Lord's battle until we are armed with heavenly weapons.

We must see Jesus. This is essential. At the mercy seat we will linger until He manifests Himself. Until we can truthfully say, "We were with Him in the holy mountain."

EVENING WOLVES

"Evening wolves."

—Habakkuk 1:8

While writing this book, the expression "evening wolves" recurred so frequently that, in order to be rid of its constant insistence, I determined to give it a page. The evening wolf, infuriated by a day of hunger, was fiercer and more ravenous than it would have been in the morning.

This furious creature represents our doubts and fears after a hard day of distractions, perhaps losses in business or taunting from fellow workers. How thoughts howl in our ears! "Where is your God?" How voracious and greedy are these thoughts! They swallow all suggestions of comfort and remain as hungry as ever. Great Shepherd, slay these evening wolves and invite your sheep to lie down in green pastures, undisturbed by insatiable unbelief.

The fiends of hell are like evening wolves. When the flock of Christ is in a cloudy and dark day and its sun seems to be going down, these fiends hasten to tear and devour. They will scarcely attack a Christian in the daylight of faith; but in the gloom of a soul's conflict they strike. Oh You who laid down Your life for the sheep, preserve them from the fangs of the wolf.

False teachers, who craftily and industriously hunt for the precious life and devour believers by falsehoods, are as dangerous and detestable as evening wolves. Darkness is their element, deceit their character, and destruction their end (2 Peter 2:1). We are in great danger when they wear sheep's clothing (Matthew 7:15). Blessed are you who are kept from them, because thousands are made the prey of the grievous wolves that enter the fold of the church.

What a wonder of grace when fierce persecutors are converted. Then the wolf dwells with the lamb, and people with cruel, ungovernable dispositions become gentle and teachable.

Oh Lord, convert false teachers and persecutors. This is our evening prayer. Amen.

A SEPARATED LIFE

"Be separate."

—2 Corinthians 6:17

Christians, while in the world, are not to be of the world. The great object of our lives is to be distinguished from the world. "For to me, to live is Christ" (Philippians 1:21). "Whether you eat, or drink, or whatever you do, do all to the glory of God" (1 Corinthians 10:31).

Store up treasurers in heaven. "Do not lay up for yourself treasures on earth, where moth and rust destroy and where thieves break in and steal" (Matthew 6:19). You may strive to be rich, but make it your ambition to "be rich in good works" (1 Timothy 6:18). You may have pleasure, but when you are happy speak "to one another in psalms and hymns and spiritual songs, singing and making melody in your heart to the Lord" (Ephesians 5:19).

In your spirit, as well as in your aim, you should differ from the world. Wait humbly before God. Always be conscious of His presence. Delight in communion with Him. Seek to know His will. This will prove that you are of the heavenly race.

You should be separate from the world in your actions. If a thing is right, though you lose by it, it must be done. If it is wrong, though you would gain by it, you must scorn the sin for your Master's sake.

"Have no fellowship with the unfruitful works of darkness, but rather expose them" (Ephesians 5:11). "Walk worthy of the calling with which you were called" (Ephesians 4:1). Christian, you are a child of the King. Keep unspotted from the world. Do not soil the fingers that will soon sweep celestial strings. Do not let the eyes become windows of lust, they will soon see the King in His beauty. Do not defile those feet in miry places, they will soon walk the golden streets. Do not let your heart be filled with pride and bitterness, it will soon be filled with heaven and overflow with ecstatic joy.

SEPTEMBER 11, MORNING

WALKING CAREFULLY

"Lead me, O Lord, in Your righteousness because of my enemies."

—Psalm 5:8

Very bitter is the enmity of the world against the people of Christ. The world will forgive a thousand faults in others, but it will magnify the most trivial offence in the followers of Jesus.

Instead of regretting this, let us turn it to our advantage. Since so many are watching for us to stumble, let it be an incentive to walk carefully before God. If we live carelessly, the lynx-eyed world will soon see it. With its hundred tongues it will spread the story, exaggerated and emblazoned by the zeal of slander. It will shout triumphantly, "Aha! See how those Christians act! All of them are hypocrites." Thus will much damage be done to the cause of Christ, and much insult offered to His name.

The cross of Christ is offence enough to the world (Galatians 5:11). Let us be careful not to add any offence of our own. The cross is "to the Jews a stumbling block and to the Greeks foolishness" (1 Corinthians 1:23). Let us be careful not to add our own folly to the scorn with which the world derides the gospel. How jealous should we be of ourselves! How rigid with our consciences! In the presence of adversaries who misrepresent our best deeds and impugn our motives, we need to be circumspect!

Pilgrims travel as suspects through Vanity Fair. Not only are we under surveillance; there are more spies than we thought. Espionage is everywhere. If we fall, we may sooner expect generosity from a wolf, or mercy from a fiend, than anything like patience from those who spice their infidelity to God with scandals against His people.

Oh Lord, always lead us, lest our enemies trip us! Amen.

SACRED JEALOUSY

"God is jealous."

—Nahum 1:2

Believer, your Lord is jealous of your love. Did He choose you? He cannot bear that you would choose another. Did He buy you with His own blood? He cannot endure that you would think you are your own, or that you belong to this world. He loved you with such a love that He would not stop in heaven without you. He would sooner die than you should perish. He cannot endure anything standing between your heart's love and Him.

He is jealous of your trust. He will not permit you to trust in an arm of flesh. He cannot bear that you should hew broken cisterns, which hold no water, and forsake the fountain of living waters (Jeremiah 2:13).

When we lean on Him, He is glad. But when we transfer our dependence to another, when we rely on our wisdom or that of a friend, or worst of all, when we trust in any works of our own, He is displeased and will chasten us to bring us back to Him.

He is also jealous of our company. There should be no one with whom we converse so much as with Jesus. To abide in Him only, this is true love. To commune with the world, to find sufficient solace in our carnal comforts, this is grievous to our jealous Lord. He wants us to abide in Him and enjoy His constant fellowship. Many of the trials He sends are to wean our hearts from the creature and fix them more closely on Him.

Let this jealousy, which should keep us near Christ, also comfort us. If He loves so much as to care about our love, we may be sure that nothing will harm us, for He will protect us from all our enemies.

May we have grace today to keep our hearts in sacred purity for our Beloved alone. May we with sacred jealousy shut our eyes to all the fascinations of the world!

VICTORIOUS FAITH

"I will sing of mercy and justice."

—Psalm 101:1

Faith triumphs in trial. When reason is thrust in the inner prison with its feet held firmly in the stocks, faith makes the dungeon walls ring with music. "I will sing of mercy and justice. To You, O Lord, I will sing praises." Faith pulls the black mask from the face of trouble and discovers the angel. Faith looks up at the cloud and sees:

> It is big with mercy and shall break
> In blessings on her head.

There is reason to sing even in the judgments of God, because the trial is not so heavy as it might have been, and the trouble is not so severe as we deserved. Neither is our affliction as crushing as the burden that some others have carried.

Faith sees in the worst sorrow that there is nothing punishing. There is not a drop of God's wrath in it. The worst sorrow is sent in love. Faith discerns love gleaming like a jewel on the breast of an angry God. Faith says, "This is a badge of honor, for the child must feel the rod." Faith then sings of the sweet result of sorrows that work for our spiritual good. No, even more, faith says, "Our light affliction, which is but for a moment, is working for us a far more exceeding and eternal weight of glory" (2 Corinthians 4:17).

So faith rides the black horse (Zechariah 6:6), conquering and to conquer, trampling down carnal reason and fleshly sense, chanting notes of victory in the thickest fight:

> All I meet I find assists me
>   In my path to heavenly joy:
> Where, though trials now attend me,
>   Trials never more annoy.
> Blest there with a weight of glory,
>   Still the path I'll never forget,
> But, exulting, cry, it led me
>   To my blessed Savior's seat.

SEPTEMBER 12, EVENING

WELL DIGGERS

"As they pass through the Valley of Baca, they make it a spring; the rain also covers it with pools."

—Psalm 84:6

Our text teaches that the work of one individual may often prove valuable to another.

We read books that are full of consolation and dropping with honey. Ah, we think, this author has been here before and dug this well for us. Books like *Night of Weeping, Midnight Harmonies, Eternal Day, A Crook in the Lot,* and *Comfort for Mourners* are wells dug by pilgrims and still quite useful to us.

We notice this in the Psalms. "Why are you cast down, O my soul?" (Psalm 42:5). Travelers have been delighted to see footprints on a barren shore. Christians love to see the guideposts of pilgrims, while passing through this vale of tears.

The pilgrims dug the well, but strangely it fills from the top instead of the bottom. We use the methods, but the blessing does not spring from methods and ordinances. We dig the well, but heaven fills it with rain. "The horse is prepared for the day of battle, but deliverance is of the Lord" (Proverbs 21:31). The rain fills the pools, so that the springs become useful as reservoirs. The labor is not lost, but yet it does not supersede divine help.

Grace may well be compared to rain for its purity, for its refreshing and vivifying influence, for its coming alone from above, and for the sovereignty with which it is given or withheld.

May our readers have showers of blessings. May the wells that they have dug be filled with water! Oh, what are methods and ordinances without the smile of heaven! "They are like clouds and wind without rain" (Proverbs 25:14) and dried up pools (Isaiah 42:15).

Oh God of love, open the windows of heaven and pour out a blessing! Amen.

SEPTEMBER 13, MORNING

CHRIST RECEIVES SINNERS

"This Man receives sinners."

—Luke 15:2

Observe the condescension here. This Man, who towers above all others, who is holy, harmless, undefiled, and separate from sinners—this Man receives sinners. This Man, who is none other than the eternal God before whom angels veil their faces—this Man receives sinners. It needs an angel's tongue to describe this mighty love.

That any of us would be willing to seek the lost is nothing special. But that He, the offended God, against whom the transgression has been committed, would take the form of a servant, bear the sins of many, and should then be willing to receive the vilest of the vile, this is marvelous!

"This Man receives sinners," not for them to remain sinners, but He receives them to pardon their sins. He receives them to justify them, to cleanse their hearts with His purifying Word, to preserve their souls by the indwelling of the Holy Spirit, and to enable them to serve, praise, and have fellowship with Him.

He takes sinners from the garbage heap and wears them as jewels in His crown (Malachi 3:17). He plucks them as firebrands from the burning (Amos 4:11). He preserves them as costly monuments of His mercy.

None are as precious in Jesus' sight as the sinners for whom He died. When Jesus receives sinners, it is not with a roadside reception, where He charitably entertains them as stranded travelers. No, He opens the golden gates of His royal heart to receives sinners. He admits the humble penitent into a personal union as a member of His body, of His flesh and of His bones. There was never a reception like this!

Even this evening He is still receiving sinners. Would to God sinners would receive Him.

OUR ADMIRAL

"And other little boats were also with Him."

—Mark 4:36

Jesus was the Lord High Admiral of the sea that night, and His presence preserved the entire convoy.

It is well to sail with Jesus, even in a small boat. When we sail in Christ's company, we may not be guaranteed fair weather, for great storms tossed the vessel that carried our Lord. We must not expect to find the sea less boisterous around our little boat. If we go with Jesus, we must be content to fare as He fares. When the waves are rough to Him, they will be rough to us.

It is by tempest and tossing that we will reach land, as He did before us. When the storm swept over Galilee's dark lake, all hearts feared shipwreck. When all human help was useless, the slumbering Savior arose and with a word transformed the riot of waves into the deep quiet of calm. Then all the little vessels were at rest.

Jesus is the star of the sea. Though there be sorrow on the sea, when Jesus is on it there is also joy. May our hearts make Jesus the anchor, the rudder, the lighthouse, the life boat, and even the harbor.

His church is His flagship. Let us watch her movements and cheer her officers with our presence. The Lord High Admiral is her great attraction. Let her follow in His wake, mark His signals, steer by His chart, and never fear while He is within calling distance. Not one ship in the convoy will be wrecked. The great Admiral will steer every vessel safely to the desired haven.

This morning, let us by faith slip our cables off the dock for another day's cruise and sail with Jesus. Winds and waves may not spare us, but they will obey Him. Therefore, whatever squalls may occur without, faith will feel a blessed calm within.

He is ever in the center of the weather beaten company. Let us rejoice in Him. His vessel has reached the haven and so will ours.

SEPTEMBER 14, MORNING

THE PENITENT

"I acknowledge my sin to You, and my iniquity I have not hidden. I said, 'I will confess my transgression to the Lord.' And You forgave the iniquity of my sin." —Psalm 32:5

David's grief for sin was bitter. Its effects were visible on his body. "My bones grew old" (Psalm 32:3). "My vitality was turned into the drought of summer" (Psalm 32:4). David could not find a remedy until he made a full confession before the throne of heavenly grace.

He tells us that during the time he kept silent his heart became more and more filled with grief. Like a mountain spring whose outlet is blocked, his soul was swollen with torrents of sorrow. He made excuses and tried to divert his thoughts, but it was all to no purpose. Like a festering sore, his anguish gathered. He would not use the lance of confession and his spirit was tormented until it knew no rest.

At last it came to him. He must return to God in humble penitence or die. He hastened to the mercy seat and there unrolled the volume of his iniquities before the all-seeing One. He acknowledged his evil ways in the language of the fifty-first and other penitential Psalms.

Having done this, a work so simple and yet so difficult because of pride, he immediately received the token of divine forgiveness, "that the bones You have broken may rejoice" (Psalm 51:8). David rose from his knees singing the blessedness of one whose transgressions are forgiven.

See the value of a confession produced by grace. Mercy is freely given, not because the repentance and confession deserve mercy, but for Christ's sake.

Blessed be God. There is always healing for the broken heart. The fountain is always flowing to cleanse our sins. Truly, Oh God, You are a God "ready to pardon" (Nehemiah 9:17). Therefore will we acknowledge our iniquities.

BAD NEWS

"He will not be afraid of evil tidings."

—Psalm 112:7

Christian, you should not dread the arrival of evil tidings. If you are distressed by them, what about people who do not know God, who have never proved His faithfulness? It is no wonder that they are bowed down with alarm and cowed with fear.

You are of another spirit. You have been begotten to a living hope (1 Peter 1:3). Your heart lives in heaven and not on earthly things. Now if you are as distracted by evil tidings as others, what is the value of grace that you profess to have received? Where is the dignity of that new nature you claim to possess?

If you are filled with alarm, you will doubtless be led into sins common to unbelievers in difficult circumstances. The ungodly, when they are overtaken by evil news, rebel against God. They murmur and think that God deals harshly with them. Will you fall in the same sin? Will you provoke the Lord as they do?

The unconverted often run to the wrong things in order to escape difficulties. You will do the same if your mind yields to the present pressure. Trust in the Lord and wait patiently for Him. Your wisest course is to do as Moses did at the Red Sea. "Stand still and see the salvation of the Lord" (Exodus 14:13).

If you give way to fear when you hear evil tidings, you will be unable to meet trouble in a calm composure that sustains under adversity. How can you glorify God if you play the coward? Saints have often sung God's high praises in the fires. Your doubting and desponding, as if you had nothing to help you, will not magnify the Most High.

Take courage. Rely in sure confidence on the faithfulness of your covenant God. "Let not your heart be troubled, neither let it be afraid" (John 14:27).

NEARNESS

"A people near to Him."

—Psalm 148:14

The dispensation of the old covenant brought distance. When God appeared to His servant Moses, He said, "Do not draw near this place. Take your sandals off your feet" (Exodus 3:5). When He manifested Himself on Mount Sinai to His chosen and separated people, one of His first commands was, "Set bounds around the mountain" (Exodus 19:23).

In sacred worship at the tabernacle and the temple, the thought of distance to God was always prominent. Most of the people did not even enter the outer court. Only the priest was permitted into the inner court, while in the innermost place, the holy of holies, only the high priest entered and just once a year.

In those early ages, it was as if the Lord taught that sin was so utterly loathsome that sinners would be treated as lepers and left outside the camp. When God drew near, the Israelites felt the width of their separation from a holy God.

When the gospel came, we were placed on quite another footing. The word "Go" was exchanged for "Come." Distance gave way to closeness. "But now in Christ Jesus you who once were far off have been brought near by the blood of Christ" (Ephesians 2:13).

Incarnate Deity has no wall of fire around it. "Come to Me, all you who labor and are heavy laden, and I will give you rest" (Matthew 11:28) is the joyful proclamation of God in human flesh. He does not heal the leper from a distance, but "stretched out His hand and touched him, and said to him, 'I am willing; be cleansed'" (Mark 1:41).

What a state of safety and privilege this nearness to God through Jesus is! Yet this will be followed by a dispensation of greater nearness, when it will be said, "The tabernacle of God is with men, and He will dwell with them" (Revelation 21:3). "Surely I am coming quickly. Amen. Even so, come quickly Lord Jesus" (Revelation 22:20).

SEPTEMBER 15, EVENING

PARTAKERS OF THE DIVINE NATURE

"Partakers of the divine nature."

—2 Peter 1:4

Partakers of the divine nature do not become God. The essence of Deity is not participated in by the creature. A gulf is fixed between the intrinsic nature of the creature and the Creator.

The first man, Adam, was made in the image of God (Genesis 1:26). We, by the renewal of the Holy Spirit, are in a diviner sense made in the image of the Most High, and are "partakers of the divine nature."

We are, by grace, made like God. "God is love" (1 John 4:8). We become love: "Everyone who loves is born of God" (1 John 4:7). God is truth (Psalm 31:5). We become truth, and we love what is true. "The Lord is good" (Psalm 100:5). He makes us good by His grace, and we become the pure in heart who shall see God (Matthew 5:8). We become "partakers of the divine nature" in a high sense, in as lofty a sense as can be conceived, short of our being absolutely divine.

Do we become members of the body of the divine person of Christ? Yes, the same blood that flows in the head flows in the hand. The same life that quickens Christ quickens His people. "For you died, and your life is hidden with Christ in God" (Colossians 3:3). As if this were not enough, we are married to Christ (Revelation 19:7). He has betrothed us in righteousness and faithfulness, and we are joined to the Lord in one spirit.

Marvelous mystery! Who can understand it? One with Jesus! We are one with Him as the branch is one with the vine. We are a part of the Lord, our Savior and Redeemer!

While we rejoice in this, remember, those who are made "partakers of the divine nature" will manifest their high and holy relationship in their association with others. It will be evident from their daily walk and conversation that they have escaped the corruption that is in the world through lust (2 Peter 1:4). Oh for more divine holiness of life!

SEPTEMBER 16, MORNING

THE FAITHFUL SEA

"Am I a sea, or a sea serpent, that you set a guard over me?"

—Job 7:12

This was a strange question for Job to ask the Lord. Job felt too insignificant to be so strictly watched and chastened. He hoped that he was not so unruly as to need such restraining. Yet this enquiry was natural enough from one surrounded with such insupportable miseries.

It is true that we are not the sea, but we are even more troublesome and unruly! The sea obediently respects its boundary, and though that is only a belt of sand, it does not leap over the limit (Jeremiah 5:22–23). Mighty as the ocean is, it hears and respects the divine command even while raging with tempest.

Self-will, however, defies heaven and oppresses earth with its rebellious rage. The sea, obedient to the moon, ebbs and flows in both passive and active obedience with ceaseless regularity. We, however, are restless beyond our sphere. We sleep when duty calls and are indolent when we should be active. We will neither come nor go at the divine command. We prefer to do what we should not and leave undone that which is required.

Every drop in the ocean, every beaded bubble, every yeasty foam flake, every shell and every pebble feels the power of law and yields or moves at once. Oh that our nature were but one thousandth part as much conformed to the will of God!

We call the sea fickle and false, but how unchangeable it is. Since our fathers' days, and the time long before them, the sea is where it was, beating on the same cliffs to the same tune. We know where to find it. It does not forsake its bed, and its ceaseless boom does not change. But where is vain, fickle humanity? Can we guess what folly will next seduce us from obedience? We need more watching than the billowy sea because we are far more rebellious.

Lord, rule us for Your own glory. Amen.

SEPTEMBER 16, EVENING

PRAYING FOR CHILDREN

"Bring him to Me."

—Mark 9:19

Despairing, the disappointed father turned from the disciples to their Master. His son was in the worst possible condition, and all help had failed. But when the parent in faith obeyed the Lord Jesus' word, "Bring him to Me," the suffering child was delivered from the evil one.

Children are a precious gift from God, but much anxiety comes with them. They may be a great joy or a great bitterness. They may be filled with the Spirit of God or possessed with the spirit of evil. In all cases, the Word of God gives one method for curing their ills: Bring them to Jesus.

Our cries for our children should precede the cries that announce their actual birth in this world of sin. Oh for more agonizing prayer while they are still babies. In the days of their youth, we may see sad signs of that dumb and deaf spirit which will neither pray nor hear the voice of God. But Jesus still commands, "Bring them to Me."

When they are grown, they may wallow in sin and foam with enmity against God. Then, when our hearts are breaking, we should remember the great Physician's words, "Bring them to Me." We should cease to pray for them only when they cease to breathe. No case is hopeless while they live, because Jesus lives. Sin is there, so let our prayers begin to attack it.

Sometimes the Lord causes His people to be driven in a corner, that they may know firsthand how necessary He is. Ungodly children, when they show us our own helplessness against the depravity of their hearts, drive us to flee to the strong for strength. This is a great blessing.

Whatever your morning's need may be, let it, like a strong current, carry you to the ocean of divine love. Jesus can remove sorrow. He delights to comfort. Hasten to Him while He waits to meet with you.

AN ENCOURAGING WORD

"Encourage him."

—Deuteronomy 1:38

God uses His people to encourage one another. He did not say to an angel, "Gabriel, My servant Joshua is about to lead My people to Canaan. Go and encourage him." God never works needless miracles. If His purposes can be accomplished by ordinary means, He will not use a miraculous agency.

Gabriel was not half as qualified for the work as Moses. A friend's sympathy is more precious than an angelic ambassador. The angel knows the Master's bidding better than the people's testings and trials. An angel has never experienced the hardness of the road, or seen the fiery serpents, or experienced leading a stiff-necked multitude in the wilderness as Moses had done.

We should be glad that God usually encourages us through others. It forms a bond of Christian love. Being mutually dependent fuses us more completely into one family.

Believer, take our text as God's message to you. Work to help others. Especially strive to encourage them. Talk cheerfully to the young, anxious enquirer. Lovingly try to remove stumbling blocks. When you find a spark of grace in the heart, kneel down and blow it into a flame.

Leave the new believers to discover the roughness of the road by degrees. But tell them about the strength that dwells in God, the sureness of the promises, and the charms of communion with Christ. Aim to comfort the sorrowful and to energize the depressed. Speak a word in season to the weary, and encourage the fearful to go on their way with gladness.

God encourages as He points to the heaven He has prepared for you. The Spirit encourages as He works in you the desire to do God's will and pleasure.

Imitate divine wisdom. Encourage others.

SEPTEMBER 17, EVENING

TWO VITAL POINTS

"If we live in the Spirit, let us also walk in the Spirit."

—Galatians 5:25

The two most vital and important points to Christians in their holy lives are the life and the walk of faith. If we properly understand these, we are not far from being a master in Christian experience.

You will never find true faith without finding true godliness. You will never discover a truly holy life that does not have for its root a living faith on the righteousness of Christ. Woe to those who seek one without the other.

There are some who try to cultivate faith and forget holiness. They may be very high in orthodoxy, but they will be deep in condemnation if they hold the truth in unrighteousness. Then there are others who have strained after holiness of life, only to have denied the faith. They are like the Pharisees of whom the Master said, "You are like whitewashed tombs which indeed appear beautiful outwardly, but inside are full of dead bones and all uncleanness" (Matthew 23:27).

We must have faith, for this is the foundation. We must have holiness, for this is the superstructure. Do not seek a holy life without faith, for that would be to erect a house that cannot offer permanent shelter because it has no foundation on a rock.

Let faith and life be put together, and like the two abutments of an arch, they will make our holiness enduring. Like light and heat streaming from the same sun, both are full of blessing. Like the two pillars of the temple, both are for glory and beauty. They are two streams from the fountain of grace, two lamps lit with holy fire, two olive trees watered by heavenly care.

Oh Lord, today, give us life within, and it will outwardly reveal itself to Your glory. Amen.

SEPTEMBER 18, MORNING

OUR LEADER

"And they follow Me."

—John 10:27

We should follow our Lord as unhesitatingly as sheep follow their shepherd. He has a right to lead us wherever He pleases, for we are "bought with a price" (1 Corinthians 7:23). Let us recognize the rights of redeeming blood.

The soldier follows the captain. The servant obeys the master. How much more should we follow our Redeemer, who purchased us "with His own blood" (Acts 20:28)? We are not true to our profession of being Christians if we question the bidding of our Leader and Commander.

Submission is our duty. Raising trivial objections is our folly. Often our Lord could say to us, as He did to Peter, "What is that to you? You follow Me" (John 21:22). Wherever Jesus leads, He goes before us. If we do not know where to go, we know with whom we go. With such a companion, who can dread the perils of the road? The journey may be long, but His everlasting arms will carry us to the end.

We should follow Christ in simplicity and faith, because the paths in which He leads us all end in glory and immortality. It is true that they may not be smooth paths. They may be covered with sharp, flinty trials, but they lead to "the city which has foundations, whose builder and maker is God" (Hebrews 11:10). "All the paths of the Lord are mercy and truth to such as keep His covenant and His testimonies" (Psalm 25:10).

Let us put full trust in our Leader. Come what may, prosperity or adversity, sickness or health, popularity or contempt, we know that His purpose will be worked out and that His purpose is pure and unmingled good to every heir of mercy.

We will find it sweet to go up the bleak side of the hill with Christ. When rain and snow blow, His dear love will make us far more blessed than those who sit at home and warm their hands at the world's fire.

Jesus, draw us, and we will run after You. Amen.

SEPTEMBER 18, EVENING

LIBERTY AND FREEDOM IN CHRIST

"In the liberty by which Christ has made us free."

—Galatians 5:1

Here is a choice passage, believer: "When you pass through the waters, I will be with you" (Isaiah 43:2). You are free to claim that promise. Here is another: "The mountains shall depart and the hills be removed, but My kindness shall not depart from you" (Isaiah 54:10). You are free to claim that promise. You are a welcome guest at the table of the promises.

Scripture is a never failing treasury, filled with the boundless stores of grace. Scripture is the bank of heaven. You may draw from it as much as you please, without interference or hindrance. If you come in faith, there is not a promise in the Word that will be withheld.

In the depths of trials, let this freedom comfort you. In the midst of distress, let it cheer you. When sorrows surround you, let it be your solace. This is your Father's token of love and you are free to use it.

It is our privilege to have free access to our heavenly Father. Whatever our desires, our difficulties, or our needs, we are at liberty to tell Him everything. It does not matter how much we may have sinned, we may ask and expect pardon. It does not matter how poor we are, we may plead His promise that He will provide all needful things.

We have permission to approach His throne at all times (Hebrews 4:16). In midnight's darkest hour, or in high noon's most burning heat, exercise your right, believer, and live up to your privilege. You are free to all that is treasured in Christ.

It does not matter what you need. There is fullness of supply in Christ, and it is there for you. Oh what a freedom is yours! Freedom from condemnation, freedom to the promises, freedom to the throne of grace, and at last freedom to enter heaven!

SEPTEMBER 19, MORNING

PLEADING

"For this child I prayed."

Devout souls delight to look on mercies they have obtained in answer to supplication. Answered prayers reveal God's special love. When we can name our blessings, they will be as precious to us as Hannah's child, Samuel ("asked of God"), was to her. Peninnah had many children (1 Samuel 1:2), but they came as a common blessing, unsought in prayer. Hannah's one heaven-given child was far more precious because he was the fruit of earnest pleading.

How sweet was that water to Samson when God split the hollow place in answer to his prayer (Judges 15:19). Quassin (an intensely bitter amaroid) turns water bitter, but prayer puts a sweetness in the water.

Did we pray for the conversion of our children? When they are saved, how doubly sweet to see in them our petitions fulfilled. Better to rejoice over them as the fruit of our pleading than as the fruit of our bodies.

Have we sought the Lord for some choice spiritual gift? When it comes, it will be wrapped in the gold cloth of God's faithfulness and truth, and it will be doubly precious.

Have we petitioned for success in the Lord's work? How joyful is the prosperity that comes flying on the wings of prayer. It is always best to receive blessings by the door of prayer, for then they are blessings indeed and not temptations. Even when the answer does not come immediately, the blessings grow all the richer because of the delay.

That which we gain by prayer we should dedicate to God, just as Hannah dedicated Samuel. The gift came from heaven, let it return to heaven. Prayer brought it, and gratitude sang over it, let devotion consecrate it.

Dear reader, is prayer your rest or your weariness? Which?

SEPTEMBER 19, EVENING

PRACTICAL HARMONY

"The sword of the Lord and of Gideon."

—Judges 7:20

Gideon ordered his men to do two things. "He put a trumpet into every man's hand, with empty pitchers, and torches inside the pitchers" (Judges 7:16). "They blew the trumpets and broke the pitchers that were in their hands. They held the torches in their left hands and the trumpets in their right hands for blowing—and they cried, 'The sword of the Lord and of Gideon'" (Judges 7:19–20).

This is precisely what all Christians must do. First, they must shine, perhaps by breaking the pitcher that conceals their light, or by throwing aside the basket that has been hiding their candles. "Let your light so shine before men, that they may see your good works and glorify your Father in heaven" (Matthew 5:16).

Then there must be sound, the blowing of the trumpet. There must be activities for ingathering sinners by proclaiming Christ crucified. Christians must take the gospel to them, carry it to their door, place it in their way. Let them not escape it. Blow a trumpet in their ear. Remember the true war cry of the church is Gideon's watchword, "The sword of the Lord and of Gideon!"

God must do it, for it is His work, but we are not to sit idle. If we only cry, "The sword of the Lord," we will be guilty of idle presumption. If we only shout, "The sword of Gideon," we manifest idolatrous reliance on the arm of flesh. We must blend the two in practical harmony. "The sword of the Lord and of Gideon."

We can do nothing by ourselves. We can do everything with the help of God. Therefore, in His name, let us determine to serve with a flaming torch of holy example and with trumpet tones of earnest declaration and testimony. God will be with us. Midian will be put to confusion (Judges 8:28), and the Lord of hosts will reign forever and ever.

EVENING OPPORTUNITIES

"In the evening do not withhold Your hand."

—Ecclesiastes 11:6

Opportunities are plentiful in the evening. People return from work, and the zealous soul winner finds time to talk to them about the love of Jesus. Do I have any evening work to do for Jesus? If not, let me begin immediately. Sinners are perishing for lack of knowledge, and if I loiter, I may find my clothes crimson with the blood of souls.

Jesus gave both of His hands to the nails. How can I keep back one of mine from His blessed work? Night and day He toiled and prayed for me. How can I give a single hour to pamper my flesh with luxurious ease? Idle heart, stretch out your hands and work, or lift them up in prayer. Heaven and hell are real. Let me be real and this evening sow good seed for the Lord my God.

The evening of life also has its callings. Life is so short that a morning of vigor and an evening of decay is all there is. To some it seems long, but a couple of dollars is a large sum of money to a poor person. Life is so brief that we cannot afford to lose a day.

It has been well said that if a great king brought an immense heap of gold and told us to take as much of it as we could count in a day, we would make a long day of it. We would begin early in the morning, and continue until late at night. But to win souls is far nobler, so why do we withdraw from it?

Some are spared to live a long evening of green old age. If this will be my case, let me use the talents I still retain and to the last hour serve my blessed and faithful Lord. By His grace I will die in harness and lay down my charge only when I lay down my body.

Age may instruct the young, cheer the faint, and encourage the depressed. If evening has less vigorous heat, it should have more calm wisdom.

REASONS TO REJOICE

"I will rejoice over them to do them good."

—Jeremiah 32:41

The delight God has in His saints is heart warming to us, for we cannot see any reason why the Lord would take pleasure in us, and we do not take delight in ourselves. We often groan about being burdened. We are conscious of our sinfulness. We deplore our unfaithfulness. And we fear that God's people cannot take much delight in us because they perceive our imperfections and follies, and because they lament our infirmities rather than admire our graces.

Yet we love to dwell on this transcendent truth, this glorious mystery, that "as the bridegroom rejoices over the bride, so shall your God rejoice over you" (Isaiah 62:5). We do not read in the Bible that God delights in cloud-capped mountains or sparkling stars. We read that He "rejoices in His inhabited world and delights in the sons of men" (Proverbs 8:31).

We do not even find it written that angels give Him delight. Nor does He say, concerning cherubim and seraphim, "You shall be called Hephzibah . . . for the Lord delights in you" (Isaiah 62:4). But He says all this to poor fallen creatures like you and me. We who are debased and depraved by sin, but saved, exalted, and glorified by His grace. In strong language He expresses His delight in His people!

Who could have conceived the eternal One bursting into song? Yet it is written, "He will rejoice over you with gladness. He will quiet you with His love. He will rejoice over you with singing" (Zephaniah 3:17).

When He looked on the world He created, He said, "It was good" (Genesis 1:25). But when He looks on those who are the purchase of Jesus' blood, His own chosen ones, it seems as if the great heart of the Infinite overflowed in divine exclamations of joy.

We should utter grateful responses to such a marvelous declaration of His love by singing, "I will rejoice in Your salvation" (Psalm 9:14).

SEPTEMBER 21, MORNING

ASSURED OF HEAVEN

"Do not gather my soul with sinners."

—Psalm 26:9

David prayed this out of fear. Something must have whispered to him, "Perhaps you may be gathered with the wicked." That fear, although marred by unbelief, springs from holy concern arising from remembering past sins.

Even the pardoned will enquire, "What if at the end my sins are remembered and I am left off the roll of the saved?" We recall our unfruitfulness: so little grace, love, and holiness. And when we look to the future, we see our weakness, and the temptations which beset us, and we fear that we may fall.

A sense of sin, present evil, and prevailing corruption compels us to pray in fear and trembling, "Do not gather my soul with sinners." Reader, if you have prayed this prayer, if your character is described in this Psalm, do not fear that you will be gathered with sinners.

Do you have David's two virtues, the outward walking in integrity and the inward trusting in the Lord? Are you resting on Christ's sacrifice? Can you surround the altar of God with humble hope? If so, rest assured that you never will be gathered with the wicked.

The gathering at the judgment will be like this. "First gather together the tares and bind them in bundles to burn them, but gather the wheat into my barn" (Matthew 13:30). If you are like God's people, you will be with God's people. You cannot be gathered with the wicked for you are dearly bought. Redeemed by the blood of Christ, you are His forever, and where He is there His people must be.

You are loved too much to be thrown away with reprobates. Shall one dear to Christ perish? Impossible! Hell cannot hold you! Heaven claims you! Trust in your Surety. Do not fear!

BE HAPPY

"Let Israel rejoice in their Maker."

—Psalm 149:2

Be happy, believer, but take care that your happiness has its foundation in the Lord. You have much to rejoice about. You can sing with David, "God my exceeding joy" (Psalm 43:4). Be glad that the Lord reigns, that Jehovah is King! Rejoice that He sits on the throne and rules all things!

Every attribute of God should be a fresh ray in the sunlight of our happiness. That He is wise should make us glad, for then we know our own foolishness. That He is mighty should cause us to rejoice, for we tremble at our weaknesses! That He is everlasting should always be the theme of our joy, knowing how we wither as the grass. That He is unchanging should perpetually yield a song, since we change every hour.

He is full of grace. He overflows with grace. Grace is the covenant He has given to us. It is ours to cleanse us, ours to keep us, ours to sanctify us, ours to perfect us, ours to bring us to glory. All this should make us glad in Him.

Gladness in God is like a deep river, and we have only touched its banks. We know little of its clear, sweet, heavenly streams. Onward the depth is greater and the current more powerful in its joy.

The Christian delights not only in what God is, but also in all that God has done. The Psalms show that God's people thought much about God's actions and had a song concerning each one. So let God's people rehearse the deeds of the Lord! Let them tell of His mighty acts and "sing to the Lord for He has triumphed gloriously" (Exodus 15:1)!

Let us not cease singing. As new mercies flow, our gladness in the Lord's loving acts and grace should make us thankful. Let us be glad and rejoice in the Lord our God.

A PRAYER FOR THE OVERWHELMED

"When my heart is overwhelmed; lead me to the rock that is higher than I."

—Psalm 61:2

Most of us know what it is to be overwhelmed, to be an empty dish turned upside down, to be submerged and thrown on our side like a vessel mastered by the storm.

Discoveries of inward corruption will do this if the Lord permits the great deep of our depravity to be troubled and to cast up mud and dirt. Disappointments and heartbreak are also overwhelming when billow after billow rolls over us, and like a broken shell, we are hurled to and fro in the surf.

Blessed be God, for at times like this we are not without an all-sufficient comfort (2 Corinthians 1:4). Our God is the harbor of weather-beaten sails, the hospice of forlorn pilgrims.

He is higher than we are. His mercy is higher than our sins. His love is higher than our thoughts. It is pitiful to see people trust in something lower than themselves, but our confidence is fixed on an exceeding high and glorious Lord. He is a Rock and does not change. He is a high rock because the storm that overwhelms us rolls far beneath His feet. He is not disturbed by the storm but rules it at His will.

If we get under the shelter of this lofty Rock we may defy the hurricane. All is calm under the lee of that towering cliff. And when our troubled minds are confused, we need a pilot to guide us to this divine shelter. Hence the prayer of the text.

Oh Lord, our God, by Your Holy Spirit teach us the way of faith. Lead us to Your rest. The wind blows us out to sea, the helm answers not to our puny hand. You alone can steer us over the bar and between the sunken rocks to the fair haven. How dependent we are on You. We need You to bring us to You, to be wisely directed and steered to safety and peace. This is Your gift to us, and Yours alone. Tonight, be pleased to deal well with Your servants. Amen.

ACCEPTED IN THE BELOVED

"Accepted in the beloved."

—Ephesians 1:6

What a privilege! It includes our justification before God, but the term *accepted* in the Greek means more than that. It signifies that we are the objects of divine delight. How marvelous that we worms and mortal sinners should be the object of divine love. But it is only because we are "accepted in the beloved."

Some Christians base their acceptance only on what they feel. When their spirits are lively and their hopes are bright, they think God accepts them because they feel so high, so heavenly minded, so above the earth! But when their souls cleave to the dust, they are the victims of a fear that they are no longer accepted. How much happier they would be and how much more they would honor the Savior if they knew that their high joys do not exalt them and their low despondencies do not depress them in their Father's sight. They stand accepted in One who never changes, in the One who is always the beloved of God, in the One who is always perfect, in the One who is always without spot or wrinkle.

Rejoice, believer, you are "accepted in the beloved." When you look within and say, "Nothing is acceptable," try looking at Christ and see that in Him everything is acceptable to God. Do your sins trouble you? God has cast your sins in the depths of the sea (Micah 7:19). You are accepted in the Righteous One.

You have to fight corruption and wrestle with temptation, but know that you are already accepted in Him who has overcome the powers of evil. When the devil tempts you, be of good cheer for he cannot destroy you because you are accepted in Him who has broken Satan's head.

Know with full assurance your glorious standing. Even souls already glorified and accepted in heaven "in the beloved" are not more accepted than you.

THE MISPLACED IF

"Jesus said to him, 'If you can believe.'"

—Mark 9:23

A certain man had a son with a mute spirit (Mark 9:17). The father, having seen the futile endeavors of the disciples to heal his child, had little or no faith. When the father approached Jesus he said, "But if you can do anything have compassion on us and help us" (Mark 9:22).

Now there was an *if* in his question, but the trembling father put it in the wrong place. Jesus Christ, without commanding him to retract his *if,* kindly places it in its legitimate position, saying, "If you can believe, all things are possible to him who believes" (Mark 9:23). By this, the man's trust was strengthened, and he prayed with tears, "Lord, I believe, help my unbelief" (Mark 9:24). Instantly Jesus spoke the word, and the devil was cast out with an injunction never to return (Mark 9:25).

There is a lesson here. We, like this man, often see an *if* somewhere, but we blunder by putting it in the wrong place. *If* Jesus can help me. *If* He can give me grace to overcome temptation. *If* He can give me pardon. *If* He can make me successful.

No, *if* you can believe, He both can and will answer your prayer. *If* you confidently trust, just as all things are possible to Christ, all things will be possible to you. Faith stands in God's power and is clothed in God's majesty. It wears royal robes and rides the King's horse, for it is grace which the King delights to honor.

Faith, covered with the glorious might of the all-working Spirit, becomes, in the omnipotence of God, mighty to dare and to endure. "With men this is impossible, but with God all things are possible" (Matthew 19:26). My soul, can you believe your Lord tonight?

SEPTEMBER 23, EVENING

ASKING FOR HELP

"For I was ashamed to request of the king an escort . . . because we had spoken . . . saying, 'The hand of our God is upon all those for good who seek Him . . .'."   —Ezra 8:22

A convoy of soldiers would have been desirable for these pilgrims, but a holy shame-facedness would not allow Ezra to ask for one. He feared that the heathen king would think his profession of faith in God was mere hypocrisy, or that the king would imagine the God of Israel was unable to preserve His own. Ezra would not lean on the arm of flesh; therefore, the caravan set out with no visible protection. But they were protected, guarded by Him who is the sword and shield of His people.

It is to be feared that few believers feel this holy jealousy for God. Even those who walk by faith occasionally mar the lustre of their lives by craving human aid. It is a most blessed thing not to have props but to stand on the Rock of Ages, upheld by the Lord alone.

Would any believers seek endowments for their church if they remembered that the Lord is dishonored by their asking for worldly aid? It is as if the Lord could not supply the needs for His own cause. Would we hastily run to friends and relatives if we remembered that the Lord is magnified by our implicit reliance on His solitary arm?

Should we ask for help? Assuredly. But our fault seldom lies in neglecting to ask. Far more frequently it springs out of foolishly believing in worldly assistance rather than believing in God. Few neglect the creature's arm, and many sin by making too much of it.

Learn, dear reader, to glorify the Lord by not asking, if your asking would dishonor the name of God.

AN OXYMORON

"I sleep, but my heart is awake."

—Song of Solomon 5:2

Paradoxes abound in the Christian experience, and here is one. The spouse in our text was asleep, yet she was awake. The two points here are a mournful sleepiness and a hopeful wakefulness.

"I sleep." Through the sin that dwells in us we may become lax in holy duties, slothful in religious exercises, dull in spiritual joys, and altogether lethargic and careless. This is a shameful and dangerous condition for one in whom the quickening Spirit dwells. It is high time for us to shake off the bands of sloth. It is to be feared that many believers are losing their strength as Samson lost his locks, by sleeping on the lap of carnal security (Judges 16:19).

With a perishing world around us, to sleep is cruel. With eternity so close, it is madness. Yet none of us are as awake as we should be. A few thunder claps would do us all good and unless we wake up, we will have them in the form of catastrophe, personal bereavements, and other losses. Oh that we may leave the bed of fleshly ease and go forth with flaming torches to meet the coming Bridegroom (Matthew 25:6).

My heart is awake. This is a happy sign. Life is not extinct, though it is sadly smothered. When our renewed heart struggles against our natural heaviness, we should be grateful to sovereign grace for keeping a little vitality in the body of this death.

Jesus will hear, help and visit our hearts, for the voice of the wakeful heart is really the voice of our Beloved saying, "Open to me." Holy zeal will surely unlock the door:

> Oh lovely attitude! He stands
> With melting heart and laden hands;
> My soul forsakes her every sin,
> And lets the heavenly stranger in.

SEPTEMBER 24, EVENING

WHAT CHRIST HAS DONE

"Just, and the justifier of the one who has faith in Jesus."

—Romans 3:26

"Therefore having been justified by faith, we have peace with God through our Lord Jesus Christ" (Romans 5:1). Conscience accuses no longer because judgment now decides for sinners instead of against them. Memory with deep sorrow looks back on past sins with no dread of any penalty, for Christ has paid the debt of His people and received the divine receipt. Unless God could be so unjust as to demand double payment for one debt, no soul for whom Jesus died as a substitute can ever be cast into hell.

It seems to be one of the principles of our enlightened nature to believe that God is just. At first, this brings us terror, but it is marvelous that this same belief later becomes a pillar of our confidence and peace. If God is just, then I, a sinner without a substitute, must be punished. But then Jesus stands in my place and is punished for me. Now if God is just, then I, a sinner standing in Christ, can never be punished.

God must change His nature before one soul for whom Jesus was a substitute can ever be punished. God must change His nature before one soul for whom Jesus was a substitute can ever suffer the lash of the law. Jesus, having taken the place of the believer, having given a full equivalent to divine wrath, causes the believer to shout with glorious triumph, "Who shall bring a charge against God's elect? It is God who justifies. Who is he who condemns? It is Christ who died and furthermore is also risen" (Romans 8:33–34).

My hope does not live because I am not a sinner, but because I am a sinner for whom Christ died. My trust is not that I am holy, but that He is my righteousness. My faith does not rest on what I am or shall be, or feel, or know. My faith rests in who Christ is, in what He has done, and in what He is now doing for me.

CHRIST OUR WISDOM

"Who became for us wisdom."

—1 Corinthians 1:30

Humanity seeks rest, and by nature does not seek it from the Lord Jesus Christ. Educated people, even when converted, tend to look on the simplicities of the cross of Christ with little reverence or love. They are snared in the old net that trapped the Grecians and tended to mix philosophy with revelation (Acts 17:18). The temptation of the highly educated is to depart from the simple truth of Christ crucified and invent a more intellectual doctrine.

This thinking led some early Christian churches into Gnosticism and bewitched them with all sorts of heresies. This is the root of several non-Christian religions and other false beliefs which in days gone by were so fashionable, and even today ensnare some Christians.

Whoever you are, good reader, and whatever your education, if you are the Lord's, be assured you will find no rest in philosophizing divinity. You may receive the dogma of one great thinker, or the dream of another profound reasoner, but what the chaff is to the wheat these are to the pure Word of God. Only in Christ Jesus is "hidden all the treasures of wisdom and knowledge" (Colossians 2:3).

All attempts on the part of Christians to be syncretists or eclectics must fail. True heirs of heaven must come back to the grand and simple reality that makes the plowboy's eye flash with joy and gladdens the heart of the pious pauper: "Jesus Christ came into the world to save sinners" (1 Timothy 1:15).

"The fear of the Lord is the beginning of wisdom; a good understanding have all those who do His commandments. His praise endures forever" (Psalm 111:10).

MYRTLE TREES

"The myrtle trees in the hollow."

—Zechariah 1:8

The vision in this chapter describes the condition of Israel in Zechariah's day. The interpretation describes the church of God as we find it in today's world.

The church is compared to a myrtle grove flourishing in a valley. It is hidden, unobserved, asking no honor, and attracting no attention from the casual observer. The church, like her head, has a glory, but it is concealed from carnal eyes because the time of her splendor has not arrived.

The idea of tranquil security is also suggested. The myrtle grove in the valley is peaceful even though a storm sweeps over the mountain's summit. Tempests spend their force on the craggy peaks of the Alps, but down in the hollow there flows "a river whose streams shall make glad the city of God" (Psalm 46:4). The myrtles flourish by these waters, unshaken by the impetuous wind.

Great is the inward tranquility of God's church. Even when opposed and persecuted she has a peace that Jesus gives. But it is not as the world gives (John 14:27). It is the peace of God which surpasses all understanding, and it will guard our hearts and minds through Christ Jesus (Philippians 4:7).

The metaphor clearly pictures the peaceful, perpetual growth of the saints. The myrtle does not shed its leaves. It is always green. The church, even in the worst of times, still has the flourishing verdure of grace, and she often exhibits it most when the winters are hardest. She prospers greatly when her adversities are severe.

Thus the text hints at victory. The myrtle is the emblem of peace and a significant token of triumph. The church is victorious. "We are more than conquerors through Him who loved us" (Romans 8:37). Living in peace, the saints fall asleep in the arms of victory.

THOUGHTS ON DYING

"Wail, O cypress, for the cedar has fallen."

—Zechariah 11:2

When the crash of a falling oak is heard, it is a sign that the lumber harvesters are in the forest and that every tree may tremble, because tomorrow the sharp edge of the axe may find them. We are all like trees marked for the axe. The fall of one should remind us that, whether we are as great as the cedar or as humble as a fir, the appointed hour is fast approaching.

I trust that by frequently hearing of death we do not become callous to it. May we never be like the birds in the steeple who build their nests when the bells are tolling and sleep quietly when the funeral peals are ringing. May we regard death as the most weighty of all events, and may we be sobered by its approach.

It ill-behooves us to play while our eternal destiny hangs on a thread. The sword is out of its scabbard; let us not trifle. It is polished and sharp; let us not play with it. Those who do not prepare for death are more than ordinary fools; they are mad. When the voice of God is heard among the trees of the garden, let fig tree and sycamore, elm and cedar, hear the sound.

Be ready, servant of Christ; your Master comes quickly (Revelation 3:11), when an ungodly world least expects Him. See to it that you are faithful in His work, because a grave will soon be dug for you. Be ready, parents. See that your children are raised in the fear of God, for they must soon be orphans. Be ready, business leaders, for the days of your terrestrial service will soon end, and you will be called to give account for the deeds done in the body.

May we all prepare for the tribunal of the great King with a care that shall be rewarded with the gracious commendation, "Well done good and faithful servant" (Matthew 25:21).

SEPTEMBER 26, EVENING

WHO IS LIKE YOU?

"Happy are you, O Israel! Who is like you, a people saved by the Lord."

—Deuteronomy 33:29

Those who affirm that Christianity makes people miserable and wretched are utter strangers to it. Christianity exalts us. It makes us children of God.

Do you suppose that God will give all the happiness to His enemies and reserve all the mourning for His own family? Will His foes have laughter and joy while His children inherit sorrow and wretchedness? Will the sinner, who has no part in Christ, be rich and happy, while we go mourning as if we were penniless beggars?

No, we will "know what is the hope of His calling, what are the riches of the glory of His inheritance in the saints" (Ephesians 1:18). We have "not received the spirit of bondage again to fear, but we have received the Spirit of adoption by whom we cry out, 'Abba Father'" (Romans 8:15).

The rod of chastisement must rest on us, but it works the peaceable fruit of righteousness (Hebrews 12:11). With the aid of the divine Comforter, the saved of the Lord will "rejoice in Your salvation" (Psalm 9:14).

We are married to Christ (Revelation 19:7). Will our great Bridegroom permit His spouse to linger in grief? Our hearts are knit to Him (Colossians 2:2). We are His members (1 Corinthians 6:15). Though we may suffer as our Head once suffered, we are "blessed with every spiritual blessing in the heavenly places in Christ" (Ephesians 1:3).

We have the guarantee of our inheritance in the comforts of the Spirit. We have a foretaste of our portion. There are streaks of the light of joy to announce our eternal sunrise. Our riches are beyond the sea. Our city lies on the other side of the river, and its gleams of glory cheer our hearts and urge us on. Truly it is said of us, "Happy are you, O Israel! Who is like you, a people saved by the Lord."

My Testimony

"My Beloved put His hand by the latch of the door, and my heart yearned for Him."

—Song of Solomon 5:4

Knocking was not enough. My heart was too sleepy, too cold, and too ungrateful to get up and open the door. But the touch of His effectual grace woke me.

Oh, the long-suffering of my Beloved, to linger when He found Himself shut out and me asleep on my bed of sloth! Oh, the greatness of His patience, to knock and knock again, asking me to open the door (Revelation 3:20). How could I have refused Him? Blessed indeed is the hand that lifts the latch and turns the key. Now I see that nothing but my Lord's power can save a naughty mass of wickedness like me.

Ordinances fail. Even the gospel had no effect until His hand was stretched out. Now I perceive that His hand is good and everything else is unsuccessful. He can open when nothing else will. Blessed be His name. I feel His gracious presence even now. Well may my heart be moved for Him when I think of all that He has suffered for me, and of my ungenerous return.

I have allowed my affections to wander. I have set up rivals. I have grieved Him. To the sweetest and dearest of all I have been unfaithful. Oh, my cruel sins, my cruel self! What can I do? Tears are a poor show of repentance. My whole heart boils with indignation at myself. Wretch that I am. I treat my Lord, my All-in-All, my exceeding great joy, as though He were a stranger.

Jesus, you freely forgive, but this is not enough to prevent my unfaithfulness in the future. Kiss away these tears and purge my heart, bind it to You so that I will never wander again.

MY HEAVENLY FATHER
WATCHES OVER ME

"The Lord looks from heaven, He sees all the sons of men."
—Psalm 33:13

Perhaps no figure of speech represents God in a more gracious light than when He is spoken of as stooping from His throne and coming down from heaven to attend to the needs and woes of humanity. We love Him who, when Sodom and Gomorrah were full of iniquity, would not destroy those cities until He had personally visited them (Genesis 18:26).

We cannot help pouring out our hearts in affection to our Lord, who inclines His ear from the highest glory (Psalm 78:1) and puts it to the lip of the dying sinner, whose failing heart longs for reconciliation.

How can we not love Him when we know that the very hairs of our heads are all numbered (Matthew 10:30), or that He knows our paths and the ways we walk (Psalm 142:3), or that He instructs and teaches us in the way we should go (Psalm 32:8)? Especially is this great truth brought near to our hearts when we recall how attentive He is, not merely to our temporal interests but to our spiritual concerns also.

Though leagues of distance lie between the finite creature and the infinite Creator, there are links that unite. When you weep, God sees it. "As a father pities his children, so the Lord pities those who fear Him" (Psalm 103:13). Your sigh moves the heart of Jehovah. Your whisper inclines His ear. Your prayer stays His hand. Your faith moves His arm to help.

Do not think that God sits on high ignoring you. Remember, however poor and needy you may be, the Lord thinks upon you (Psalm 40:17). "The eyes of the Lord run to and from throughout the whole earth, to show Himself strong on behalf of those whose heart is loyal to Him" (2 Chronicles 16:9).

SEPTEMBER 28, MORNING

ANSWERED PRAYER

"And seven times he said, 'Go again'."

—1 Kings 18:43

Success is certain when the Lord promises it. Although you may have pleaded for months without any evidence of an answer, the Lord hears when you are earnest about a matter that concerns His glory.

The prophet in our text, on the top of Carmel, continued to wrestle with God and never for a moment feared that he would not be heard. Six times the servant returned without the answer, but on each occasion the only words Elijah spoke were, "Go again."

We must not dream of unbelief, but hold to our faith. Faith sends expectant hope to look from Carmel's peak. If nothing is seen, faith sends again and again. Far from being crushed by repeated disappointments faith becomes animated to plead more fervently. Faith is humbled, but not abashed. Its groans become deeper, its sighs more vehement, but faith never relaxes its hold or stays its hand.

It would be more agreeable to flesh and blood to have a speedy answer. But believing souls have learned to be submissive. They find it good to wait for, as well as wait on, the Lord. Delayed answers often set the heart searching, which may lead to needed contrition and spiritual reformation. The greatest danger is that we would become impatient and miss the blessing. Reader, do not fall into that sin. Continue in prayer and watching.

At last a little cloud was seen (1 Kings 18:44), the sure forerunner of torrents of rain. Even so with you, the token for good shall surely be given. You will rise as a prevailing prince to enjoy the mercy you have sought.

"Elijah was a man with a nature like ours" (James 5:17). His power with God did not lie in his own merit. If his believing prayer availed so much, why not yours? Plead the precious blood. "The effective, fervent prayer of a righteous man avails much" (James 5:16). "You do not have because you do not ask" (James 4:2).

SEPTEMBER 28, EVENING

THE LEPER

"Indeed if the leprosy covers all the skin of the one who has the sore, he shall pronounce him clean."

—Leviticus 13:13

This is a strange regulation. Yet there is wisdom in it and this morning it may be well for us to see the typical application of so singular a rule. We are lepers and the law of the leper is applicable. When we see ourselves as altogether lost, ruined, and covered with the defilement of sin; when we disclaim all self-righteousness and plead guilty before the Lord, then we are clean through the blood of Jesus and the grace of God.

Hidden, unfelt, and unconfessed iniquity is true leprosy. But when sin is seen, felt, and confessed, it receives its death blow. Then the Lord looks with eyes of mercy on the afflicted soul. As nothing is more deadly than self-righteousness, so nothing is more hopeful than contrition.

We must confess that we are nothing but sin. No confession short of this will be the whole truth. If the Holy Spirit is at work, convincing us of sin, there will be no difficulty about making such an acknowledgment; it will spring spontaneously from our lips.

What comfort does the text offer to those under a deep sense of sin? Sin mourned and confessed will never keep us from the Lord Jesus. "The one who comes to Me I will by no means cast out" (John 6:37).

Though as dishonest as the thief, though as unchaste as a harlot,though as fierce as Saul of Tarsus, though as cruel as Manasseh, though as rebellious as the prodigal, the great heart of love will look on those who feel they have no worth. Sinners will be pronounced clean when they trust in Jesus crucified. Poor heavy laden sinner, come to Him:

> Come needy, come guilty, come loathsome
>   and bare;
> You can't come too filthy—come just as
>   you are."

SEPTEMBER 29, MORNING

HELD

"I found the one I loved. I held him and would not let him go."

—Song of Solomon 3:4

Does Christ receive us when we come to Him despite our past sinfulness? Does He ever chide us for having tried all other refuges first? Is there none like Him on earth? Is He the best of all the good, the fairest of all the fair? Then let us praise Him!

Daughters of Jerusalem, extol Him with tambourine and harp! Down with your idols. Up with the Lord Jesus. Let the standards of pomp and pride be trampled under foot, but let the cross of Jesus be lifted up. A throne of ivory for our King Solomon. Let Him be set on high forever. Let my soul sit at His foot stool, kiss His feet, and wash them with my tears.

How precious is Christ! How can it be that I have thought so little of Him? How can I go to others for joy and comfort when He is so full, so rich, and so satisfying?

Fellow believer, make a covenant with your heart that you will never depart from Him, then ask your Lord to ratify it. Ask Him to make you like a signet ring (Haggai 2:23) on His finger and a bracelet on His arm.

I would live in Christ's heart. I would eternally abide there. "Even the sparrow has found a home, and the swallow a nest for herself, where she may lay her young—even Your altars, O Lord of hosts, my King and my God" (Psalm 84:3). I too would make my nest, my home, in You. May I nestle close to You, Oh Jesus, my true and only rest:

> When my precious Lord I find,
> All my ardent passions glow;
> Him with cords of love I bind,
> Hold and will not let Him go.

SEPTEMBER 29, EVENING

SINGING PRAISES

"Sing out the honor of His name; make His praise glorious."

—Psalm 66:2

Praising God is not optional. Praise is God's most righteous prerogative. Every Christian is obligated to praise God.

It is true that we have no authoritative red-lettered instruction for daily praise and no commandment prescribing certain hours of song and thanksgiving. But the law written on our hearts teaches that it is right to praise God. And this unwritten mandate comes with as much force as if it had been recorded on tables of stone and handed to us from the top of thundering Sinai. Yes, it is the Christian's duty and pleasure to praise God, but more than that, it is the absolute obligation of our lives.

You who are always mourning, do you think that you can discharge your duties to your God without songs of praise? You are bound by the bonds of His love to bless His name as long as you live. His praise shall continually be in your mouth (Psalm 34:1). You are blessed in order to bless Him. "This people I have formed for Myself; they shall declare My praise" (Isaiah 43:21).

If you do not praise God, you are failing to produce the fruit the Divine Vinekeeper has a right to expect. Do not hang your harps on the willows (Psalm 137:2). Take them down and strive with a grateful heart to bring forth its loudest music. Arise and sing His praise.

With every morning's dawn, lift your notes of thanksgiving, and with every setting sun, sing your song. Cover the earth with your praise. Surround it with an atmosphere of melody, and God will hear from heaven and accept your music:

> Even so I love Thee, and will love,
> And in Thy praise will sing,
> Because Thou art my loving God,
> And my redeeming King.

SEPTEMBER 30, MORNING

DEAD SERMONS, DEAD PRAYERS

" A living dog is better than a dead lion."

—Ecclesiastes 9:4

Life is precious. Even its humblest form is superior to death. This is especially true in spiritual things, for it is better to be the least in the kingdom of heaven than the greatest outside of it. The lowest degree of grace is superior to the noblest development of an unregenerate nature.

When the Holy Spirit implants divine life in the soul there comes a precious deposit that the refinements of education cannot equal. The thief on the cross excels Caesar on his throne. Lazarus among the dogs is better than Cicero among the senators. The most unlettered Christian is in the sight of God superior to Plato.

Life is the badge of nobility in the realm of spiritual things. People without life are only coarser or finer specimens of the same lifeless material. They need to be revived because they are dead in trespasses and sins.

A living, loving gospel sermon, even unlearned in content and uncouth in style, is better than the finest discourse devoid of unction and power. A living dog keeps better watch than a dead lion. The poorest spiritual preacher is infinitely preferred over the exquisite orator who has no wisdom, but words and no energy, but sound.

The same is true with our prayers. If we are alive in them through the Holy Spirit they are acceptable to God through Jesus Christ, even if we consider them worthless. We would be like dead lions by giving a grand performance in which our hearts were absent. It is putrefying in the sight of the living God.

Oh for living groans, living sighs, and living despondencies rather than lifeless songs and dead calms. Better anything than death, even the snarling of the dog of hell will at least keep us awake, but dead faith and dead profession is the greatest curse we can have.

Lord, revive us.

SEPTEMBER 30, EVENING

PLEASANT FRUIT

"And at our gates are pleasant fruit, all manner, new and old. Which I have laid up for you, my beloved."

—Song of Solomon 7:13

Our hearts have "pleasant fruit, all manner, new and old, which we have laid up for our beloved." During this rich autumn season let us observe our harvest. We have new fruit. We desire to feel new life, new joy, new gratitude. We want to make and fulfill new resolutions.

But we also have some old fruit. There is our first love, which is a choice fruit that Jesus delights in. There is our first faith, which brought us from nothing to possessing all things. There is our first joy, when we came to know the Lord. Let us revive our old fruit.

We also have our old memories of God's promises. How faithful God has been! "Great is Your faithfulness" (Lamentations 3:23). In sickness, how softly He made our bed. "The Lord will strengthen him on his bed of illness; You will sustain him on his sick bed" (Psalm 41:3). In deep waters, how firmly He held us up. "When you pass through the waters I will be with you, And through the rivers they shall not overflow you" (Isaiah 43:2). In the flaming furnace, how graciously He delivered us. "When you walk through the fire you shall not be burned; nor shall the flame scorch you" (Isaiah 43:2). Old fruit, indeed! We have much fruit, for His mercies have been more than the hairs of our head.

This morning, we have both old and new fruit. But this is the point: they are all stored up for Jesus. The best and most acceptable fruit are those in which only Jesus is glorified and we take no credit. Let our fruit be only for our Beloved and not for the world.

Jesus, we will lock the garden door so that no one will rob what is Yours. Everything is Yours, and Yours only, Oh Jesus, our Beloved.

GRACE AND GLORY

"The Lord will give grace and glory."

—Psalm 84:11

Jehovah is generous, and He enjoys giving. His gifts are precious beyond measure and as freely given as the light of the sun.

He gives grace to His elect because He wills it. He gives grace to His redeemed because of His covenant. He gives grace to His called because of His promise. He gives grace to believers because they seek it. He gives grace to sinners because they need it.

He gives grace abundantly, seasonably, constantly, readily, and sovereignly. Grace in all forms He freely gives to His people. He generously pours out to us the grace that comforts, preserves, sanctifies, directs, instructs, and assists.

Sickness may come, but the Lord will give grace. Poverty may happen, but grace will be furnished. Death must come, but grace will light a candle in the darkest hour. As another year rolls around and the leaves begin to fall how blessed to enjoy this unfailing promise, "The Lord will give grace."

In this verse the little conjunction *and* is a diamond rivet that ties the present to the future. Grace and glory always go together. God has married them, and no one can separate these words. The Lord will never deny a soul glory after He has freely given His grace. Indeed glory is nothing more than grace in Sunday dress, grace in full bloom, grace like autumn fruit, is mellow and perfect.

No one can tell how soon we will have glory. It may be that before this month is over we will see the Holy City. Whether the interval is short or long, we will be glorified soon.

The glory of heaven, the glory of eternity, the glory of Jesus, the glory of the Father: all this the Lord will surely give to His chosen. What a wonderful promise from a faithful God.

THE HOPE OF HEAVEN

"Because of the hope which is laid up for you in heaven."

—Colossians 1:5

Our hope in Christ for the future is the mainspring and mainstay of our joy here. It will enliven our hearts to think about heaven, because everything we could possibly desire is there. Here we are weary and toil-worn, but in the land of rest fatigue will be banished forever and sweat will never moisten our brow.

To you who are weary and exhausted, the word *rest* is full of heaven. Here we are always struggling. We are so tempted within and so attacked by foes without that we have little or no peace. But in heaven we will enjoy the victory, for the banner will be waved in triumph and the sword will be put away. We will hear our Captain say, "Well done, good and faithful servant" (Matthew 25:21).

We have suffered sorrow after sorrow, but we are going to the land of the immortal, where death is unknown. "And God will wipe away every tear from their eyes, there shall be no more death, nor sorrow, nor crying. There shall be no more pain for the former things have passed away" (Revelation 21:4).

Here sin is an ongoing grief, but there we will be perfectly holy. "There shall by no means enter it anything that defiles, or causes an abomination or a lie, but only those who are written in the Lamb's book of Life" (Revelation 21:27). Through the Spirit of God the hope of heaven is the most powerful force for producing virtue in us. It is a fountain of joyous effort, it is the cornerstone of cheerful holiness.

The person who has this hope goes to work with vigor, "for the joy of the Lord is your strength" (Nehemiah 8:10). You fight temptation with intensity, for the hope of heaven "quenches all the fiery darts of the wicked one" (Ephesians 6:16). You can work without a present reward because you look for a reward in the world to come.

OCTOBER 2, MORNING

GREATLY LOVED

"A man greatly beloved."

—Daniel 10:11

Child of God, do you hesitate to appropriate this title? Has unbelief made you forget that you are greatly loved? You must have been greatly loved to have been bought "with the precious blood of Christ, as of a lamb without blemish and without spot" (1 Peter 1:19). When God sacrificed His only begotten Son, you were greatly loved.

You lived in sin and indulged in it. You have to be greatly loved for God to have been so patient with you. You were called by grace, led to the Savior, and made a child of God and heir of heaven. All this proves a very great and abounding love.

Since that time, whether your path has been rough with troubles or smooth with mercies, you have total proof that you are greatly loved, for if the Lord has chastened you, it has not been in anger; and if He has made you poor, in grace He has made you rich. The more unworthy you feel, the more evidence you have that nothing but unspeakable love could have given you the Lord Jesus. The less self-esteem you feel, the clearer the display of God's abounding love in choosing you, calling you, and making you an heir of heaven.

Since there is such love between God and us, let us live in the influence and pleasantness of it. Let us use the privilege of our position. Let us not approach our Lord as though we were strangers, or as if He were unwilling to hear us, for we are greatly loved by our loving Father. "He who did not spare His own Son, but delivered Him up for us all, how shall He not with Him also freely give us all things" (Romans 8:32)?

Come boldly, believer, for despite Satan's whisperings and your own doubting heart, you are greatly loved. Meditate on the exceeding greatness and faithfulness of divine love this evening, and go to bed in peace.

OCTOBER 2, EVENING

ANGELS

"Are they not all ministering spirits sent forth to minister for those who will inherit salvation?"

—Hebrews 1:14

Angels are the unseen attendants of the saints of God. "He shall give His angels charge over you, To keep you in all your ways. In their hands they shall bear you up, Lest you dash your foot against a stone" (Psalm 91:11–12). The angels' loyalty to their Lord leads them to take a deep interest in the children of His love. "There is joy in the presence of the angels of God over one sinner who repents" (Luke 15:10).

In biblical times the children of God were blessed with the visible appearance of angels. Today, heaven is still open and the angels of God, although unseen by us, ascend and descend on the Son of Man to visit His heirs of salvation. Seraphim still fly with live coals from the altar to touch the lips of God's children (Isaiah 6:6). If our eyes could be opened, we would see that "the mountain was full of horses and chariots of fire" (2 Kings 6:17).

An innumerable company of angels watch and protect God's royal children. Spenser's line is not poetic fiction when he writes:

How oft do they with golden pinions cleave
The flitting skies, like flying pursuivant
Against foul fiends to aid us militant!

The chosen are elevated to high dignity when the angels of heaven become our willing servants. We are well defended, since all the twenty-thousand chariots of God are armed for our deliverance (Psalm 68:17).

To whom do we owe all this? Let the Lord Jesus Christ be forever endeared to us, for through Him we "are raised up and made to sit together in the heavenly places in Christ Jesus" (Ephesians 2:6). "The angel of the Lord encamps all around those that fear Him, And delivers them" (Psalm 34:7).

All hail Jesus! The great Angel of Jehovah's presence. To You we offer our morning praise.

OCTOBER 3, MORNING

TEMPTATION

"For in that He Himself has suffered, being tempted, He is able to aid those who are tempted."

—Hebrews 2:18

This is a common thought, and yet it tastes like nectar to the weary: Jesus was tempted as I am. You have heard that truth many times, but have you grasped it? He was tempted with the same sins into which we fall.

Do not disassociate Jesus from your humanity. It is a dark room you are going through, but Jesus went through it before you. It is a difficult fight you are waging, but Jesus stood foot to foot with the same enemy. Be of good cheer, Christ has carried the burden, and the blood-stained footsteps of the King of glory can be seen ahead of you on the road you are traveling.

But there is something even sweeter, for Jesus was tempted and yet never sinned. Therefore it is not needful that I should sin, for Jesus was a man. If He endured these temptations and did not sin, then in His power His children may also cease from sin.

New believers often think that temptation itself is a sin. They are mistaken. There is no sin in being tempted; there is sin only in yielding to temptation. This is a comfort even for the severely tempted. This is added encouragement if you remember that the Lord Jesus, though tempted, gloriously triumphed and overcame. The Head has triumphed and the members share in the victory.

Fears are needless. Christ is with us. Christ is our defense. Our place of safety is close to the Savior. Perhaps we are being tempted just so that it will drive us closer to Him. Blessed is any storm that drives us closer to our Savior's love. Blessed are any wounds that make us seek the beloved Physician.

Tempted one, come to your tempted Savior, for He sympathizes with your weaknesses (Hebrews 4:15).

OCTOBER 3, EVENING

EVENING LIGHT

"But at evening time it shall happen that it will be light."

—Zechariah 14:7

Frequently we look ominously at growing old. We forget that "at evening . . . it will be light." Old age for many saints is the best time of life. A milder air fans the sailor's face as the shore of immortality nears. Fewer waves agitate the sea, and quiet reigns deep, still, and somber. From the altar of age, the flashes of youthful fire are gone, but the true flame of earnest feeling remains.

These pilgrims have reached the land Beulah, that delightful country whose days are as the days of heaven on earth (Isaiah 62:4). Angels visit it, celestial breezes blow over it, flowers of paradise grow in it, and heavenly music fills the air. It is like Eden. Some dwell here for years, while others come to it just a few hours before their departure.

The setting sun looks larger than it does at midday, and a glorious splendor tints all the clouds that surround it. Pain cannot break the calm of the pleasant twilight of age. "My strength is made perfect in weakness" (2 Corinthians 12:9). The ripe fruit of choice experience has been gathered for the rare meal of life's evening, and the soul prepares for rest.

The Lord's people will also enjoy light in the hour of death. Unbelief laments, "The shadows fall, night is coming, existence is ending." But faith cries, "No, the night may be far spent, but the true day is about to dawn. Light is come, the light of immortality, the light of the Father's countenance. Soul, get ready to move. The angels are waiting to escort you. Farewell, beloved one, you are gone."

Now it is light. The pearly gates are open, the streets shine in the jasper light. We cover our eyes, but you see the unseen. Farewell believer. You have light, while for us, it is still only evening time.

MY ADVOCATE

"If anyone sins, we have an Advocate with the Father. Jesus Christ the righteous."

—1 John 2:1

"If anyone sins, we have an Advocate." Yes, even if we sin we still have Him. John does not say, "If anyone sins he has forfeited his Advocate," but, sinners though we are, "we have an Advocate."

All the sin that a believer ever did, or may do, cannot destroy our relationship with the Lord Jesus Christ. And He is the Advocate we need. *Jesus* is the name of the one who delights to save. "You will call His name Jesus for He will save His people from their sins" (Matthew 1:21). His sweet name implies His victory.

Christ is a name meaning "the anointed," which reveals His authority to plead. *Christ* has a right to plead because He is the Father's own appointed advocate and elected priest. If God has given help to One that is mighty to save, we can put our troubles where God has given help. He is Christ and He is authorized. He is Christ and He is qualified. The anointing has fully prepared Him for His work. He can plead and move the heart of God. What words of tenderness, what sentences of persuasion, the anointed one will use when He stands to plead for me.

One more word of His name remains: "Jesus Christ *the Righteous*." This is not only about His character, but also His plea. It is His character, and if the Righteous One is my Advocate, then my cause is good. It is His plea, for He meets the charge of unrighteousness against me with the plea that He is righteous. He declares Himself my substitute. He puts His obedience against my unrighteousness.

My soul, you have a friend well-qualified to be your Advocate. He can only succeed. Leave it entirely in His hands.

WHAT A MEAL!

"So he arose, and ate and drank; and he went in the strength of that food forty days and forty nights."

—1 Kings 19:8

All the strength our gracious God supplies is to be used for His service and not for willfulness or boasting. When the prophet Elijah "slept under a broom tree, suddenly an angel touched him, and said to him, 'Arise and eat.' Then he looked, and there by his head was a cake baked on coals and a jar of water" (1 Kings 19:5–6).

Elijah was not so refined that he would take only a gourmet lunch. He was commissioned to travel for forty days and forty nights to Horeb, the mountain of God (1 Kings 19:8).

When the Master invited the disciples to come and eat breakfast, He said to Peter, "Feed my sheep," and then, "Follow Me" (John 21:12–19). And so it is with us; we eat the bread of heaven to give us strength in our Master's service. We come to the passover and eat the lamb with a belt on our waist, sandals on our feet, and the staff in our hand, ready to start as soon as we have satisfied our hunger (Exodus 12:11).

Some Christians like to live *on* Christ but not *for* Christ. Earth should be a preparation for heaven, and heaven is the place where saints feast and work. They sit at the table of our Lord and serve Him day and night in His temple. They eat heavenly food and perform perfect service.

Believer, in the strength you gain daily from Christ, work for Him. You are not to hold the precious grains of truth like wheat buried with an Egyptian mummy. You need to grow the wheat.

Why does the Lord give both rain and gentle sunshine? It is to help the fruit of the earth yield food. In the same way the Lord feeds and refreshes our souls, that we may have renewed strength to promote His glory.

SALVATION AND SUBMISSION

"He who believes and is baptized will be saved."

—Mark 16:16

M r. MacDonald asked the inhabitants of St. Kilda island how to be saved.

An old man replied, "We shall be saved if we repent, forsake our sins, and turn to God."

"Yes," said a middle age lady, "and with a true heart too."

"Ay," rejoined a third, "and with prayer."

A fourth added, "It must be the prayer of the heart." "And we must be diligent," said a fifth, "in keeping the commandments."

After each had spoken, they looked to the preacher for congratulations, but they had only aroused his deepest pity. The carnal mind always maps out a way in which self can work and become great, but that is not the Lord's way. Believing and being baptized have no merit or glory. "Where is boasting then? It is excluded" (Romans 3:27).

It may be that you are unsaved. Why? Do you think the plan of salvation laid down in our text is untrue? How can that be, when God has pledged His own word? Do you think it is too easy? Why then are you not saved?

To believe is simply to trust, to depend, and to rely on Christ Jesus. To be baptized is to submit to the ordinance that our Lord fulfilled at the Jordan River (John 1:33). The outward signs do not save, they merely set forth our death, burial, and resurrection with Jesus. Like the Lord's Supper, it is not to be neglected.

Do you believe in Jesus? Then dismiss your fears. You will be saved.

Are you still an unbeliever? Remember there is only one door. Jesus said, "I am the door. If anyone enters by Me, he will be saved" (John 10:9).

THIRSTING FOR MORE
OF HIM

"But whoever drinks of the water that I shall give him will never thirst."
— John 4:14

We who believe in Jesus find enough in our Lord to fully satisfy and make us "content with such things as we have" (Hebrews 13:5).

The believer's days are not weary for lack of comfort, and their nights are not long from absence of heart-cheering thought. Believers find in Christ a spring of joy, and a fountain of consolation. They are content and happy.

Put believers in a dungeon, and they will find good company. Drive them away from friends, and "there is a friend who sticks closer than a brother" (Proverbs 18:24). Blast all their shade trees and they find "the shadow of a great rock in a weary land" (Isaiah 32:2). Destroy the foundation of their earthly hope and their hearts will still be fixed, trusting in the Lord.

The heart is as greedy as the grave until Jesus enters, and then it becomes a cup, full to overflowing. There is such fullness in Christ that He alone is the believer's all. The true saints of God "drink of the water that He gives and never thirst. The water He gives becomes a fountain, springing up into everlasting life" (John 4:14).

A long time ago someone said, "I have been sinking my bucket down into the well often, but now my thirst for Jesus has become so insatiable that I want to put the well itself to my lips and drink." Is that the feeling of your heart this morning? Your only need is to know more of Him.

Come to the fountain and drink freely of the water of life. Jesus will never think that you took too much, He will welcome you saying, "Drink, drink abundantly My beloved."

A BRIDE FOR MOSES

"He had married an Ethiopian woman."

—Numbers 12:1

The leader of Israel married a foreign woman. What a strange choice for Moses to have made, yet stranger is the choice of Him who is a prophet like Moses (Deuteronomy 18:15). Our Lord, who is as fair as the lily, entered into a marriage with one who confesses herself to be dark because the sun has tanned her (Song of Solomon 1:6). It is the wonder of angels that the love of Jesus should come to poor, lost, and guilty sinners.

Believers are overwhelmed and astonished that Jesus' love is lavished on objects so utterly worthless. They know their secret guilts, their unfaithfulness, and their sinful hearts, but these are dissolved in grateful admiration at the unmatched sovereignty of grace.

The cause of Jesus' love must be in His own heart because it is not found in me. Holy Rutherford said, "His relation to me is that I am sick and He is the Physician I need. Alas, how often I play fast and loose with Christ. He binds, I loosen. He builds, I tear down. I quarrel with Christ, and He agrees with me twenty times a day."

Most tender and faithful Husband of our souls, continue Your gracious work of conforming us to Your image until You have "a glorious church without spot or wrinkle" (Ephesians 5:27).

Moses and his wife met with opposition because of their marriage (Numbers 12:1). Is it any wonder that the world opposes Jesus and His bride, especially when great sinners are converted?

The objection of the Pharisee is that Jesus is "a friend of . . . sinners" (Matthew 11:19). Yet the old cause of the quarrel is revived, because He "married an Ethiopian woman."

OCTOBER 6, EVENING

HEAVEN-BORN FAITH

"Why have You afflicted Your servant?"

—Numbers 11:11

Our heavenly Father sends frequent troubles to test our faith, and if our faith is of any value, it will stand the test. Imitation gold is afraid of fire, but pure gold is not.

It is a poor faith that can trust God only when friends are true, the body healthy, and the business profitable. True faith grasps the Lord's faithfulness when friends are gone, when the body is sick, when spirits are depressed, and when the light of our Father's countenance is hidden. A faith that can say in desperate trouble, "Though He slay me, yet will I trust Him" (Job 13:15) is heaven-born faith.

The Lord also afflicts His servants to glorify Himself, for He is greatly glorified in the graces of His people. "We also glory in tribulations, knowing that tribulation produces perseverance; and perseverance character, and character hope" (Romans 5:3). The Lord is honored by these growing virtues.

We would never hear the music of the harp if the strings were not touched. We would never enjoy the juice of the grape if it were not crushed. We would never discover the sweet perfume of cinnamon if it were not pressed and beaten. We would never feel the warmth of the fire if the logs were not consumed.

The wisdom and power of the great Workman is discovered by the trials that He permits His vessels of mercy to pass through. Present afflictions heighten future joy. There must be shading in the painting to bring out the beauty of its lights.

Would we be so supremely blessed in heaven if we did not know the curse of sin and the sorrow of earth? Will not peace be sweeter after the conflict, and rest more welcome after working? Will not the recollection of past sufferings enhance the peace of the glorified?

There are many other comforting answers to the question that opened our brief meditation. Think on this all through the day.

OCTOBER 7, MORNING

TRUST

"Now in whom do you trust?

—Isaiah 36:5

What an important question! Listen to the Christian's answer and see if it is the same as yours.

"In whom do you trust?" "I trust," says the Christian, "in the triune God. I trust the *Father,* believing that He chose me before the foundations of the world. I trust Him to provide for me, to teach me, to guide me, to correct me, and to bring me home to His own house where there are many mansions."

"I trust the *Son,* who is very God of very God, though He is the man Christ Jesus. I trust Him to take away all my sins by His own sacrifice and to cover me with His perfect righteousness. I trust Him to be my Intercessor, to present my prayers and desires before His Father's throne. I trust Him to be my Advocate at the last great day, to plead my cause and justify me. I trust Him for who He is, for what He has done, and for what He has promised to do."

"I trust the *Holy Spirit,* who has begun to save me from inbred sins, and whom I trust to drive out all sin. I trust Him to curb my temper, to subdue my will, to enlighten my understanding, to check my passions, to comfort my depression, to help my weakness, and to illuminate my darkness. I trust Him to dwell in me as my life, to reign in me as my King, to completely sanctify me, soul and body, and to take me to dwell with the saints in light forever."

What a blessed trust! To trust Him whose power will never be exhausted, whose love will never wane, whose kindness will never change, whose faithfulness will never fail, whose wisdom will never be perplexed, whose perfect goodness will never be insufficient.

If this trust is yours, you are happy and blessed. You enjoy sweet peace now and lasting glory hereafter. The foundation of your trust will never be removed.

OCTOBER 7, EVENING

FISHING

"Launch out into the deep and let down your nets for a catch."

—Luke 5:4

This narrative teaches that we are instruments of God. The catch was miraculous, yet the fishermen, the boat, and the fishing tackle were required.

It is the same in personal evangelism. "For since, in the wisdom of God, the world through wisdom did not know God, it pleased God through the foolishness of the message preached to save those who believe" (1 Corinthians 1:21). No doubt when God works without instruments He is glorified, but He also selects the plans and the instruments who will magnify Him on the earth.

Human effort alone is totally worthless. "Master, we have toiled all night and caught nothing" (Luke 5:5). Why? They were skilled, experienced fishermen who understood their work. They were not lazy; they had toiled all night. Was the sea fished out? Certainly not, as soon as the Master came the fish swam into the net in schools.

Why? It is because there is no power apart from the presence of Jesus Christ. Without Him we can do nothing, but with Him we can do all things (Philippians 4:13). Christ's presence guarantees success. Jesus sat in Peter's boat and His will, by divine influence, drew fish into the net.

When Jesus is lifted up in His church, His presence is the church's power. "And I, if I am lifted up from the earth will draw all people to Myself" (John 12:32).

Go out this morning and in faith fish for souls. Let us work until night and we will not labor in vain. He who tells us to let down the net will fill it with fish.

PRAYING IN THE SPIRIT

"Praying in the Holy Spirit."

—Jude 20

Mark the great characteristic of true prayer: in the Holy Spirit. The seed of acceptable devotion must come from heaven's storehouse. Only the prayer that comes from God can go to God. The desire that He writes on our hearts will move His heart and bring a blessing. The desires of the flesh have no power with Him.

Praying in the Holy Spirit is praying with fire. Cold prayers may as well ask the Lord not to hear them. If you do not pray with warmth, you are not praying. It is as well to speak of a lukewarm fire as a lukewarm prayer. It is essential that prayer be red hot.

Praying in the Holy Spirit is praying with persistence. The true prayer warrior gathers force and grows more fervent when God delays the answer. The longer the gate is closed, the more vehemently the door knocker is used. Beautiful in God's sight is tearful, agonizing, unconquerable insistence.

Praying in the Holy Spirit means praying humbly, because the Holy Spirit never puffs us up with pride. It is His work to convince of sin and to make us broken and repentant in spirit. We shall never sing *Gloria in excelsis* unless we pray to God *De profundus*. If we do not cry out of the depths, we will never behold glory in the highest.

Praying in the Holy Spirit is a loving prayer. Prayer should be perfumed and saturated with love, love to our fellow saints and to Christ.

Praying in the Holy Spirit is a prayer full of faith. We prevail only as we believe. The Holy Spirit is the author of faith and strengthens our faith so that we pray, believing God's promise. Oh that this blessed combination of excellent graces, as priceless and sweet as a merchant's spices, would be found in us because of the Holy Spirit in our hearts.

Most blessed Comforter, exert Your mighty power and help our infirmities in prayer. Amen.

OCTOBER 8, EVENING

KEPT FROM FALLING

"Able to keep you from stumbling."

—Jude 24

The path to heaven is safe, but in some respects no road is as dangerous, for it is beset with difficulties. One false step (how easy it is to take that step if grace is absent), and down we go. What a slippery path some of us have to walk. Many times have we exclaimed with the psalmist, "My feet had almost stumbled; my steps had nearly slipped" (Psalm 73:2).

If we were strong, sure-footed mountaineers, this would not matter. But we are weak, and even on the best roads we may stumble. These feeble knees of ours can scarcely support our tottering weight. A straw may throw us, a pebble wound us. We are like children, wobbling as we take our first steps in the walk of faith. Our heavenly Father holds us or we quickly fall. If we are kept from falling, how much we should bless the patient power that watches over us day after day. "Your words upheld him who was stumbling and You have strengthened the feeble knees" (Job 4:4).

Think how likely we are to sin, how inclined to choose danger, how strong our tendency to fall down. These thoughts should make us sing, "Glory to Him who is able to keep us from falling."

We have many foes, the road is rough, and we are weak. Enemies lurk in ambush, and they rush out when least expected and try to push us down. Only an Almighty arm can protect from these unseen foes. His arm is our defense. He is faithful in His promise that He is able to keep us from falling (Jude 24). Therefore we can say with joyful confidence:

> Against me earth and hell combined,
>   But on my side is power divine;
> Jesus is all, and He is mine!

No Answer

"But He answered her not a word."

—Matthew 15:23

If you have not received an answer to your prayers, there is comfort in this evening's text. The Savior did not immediately answer this woman, though she had great faith. Jesus intended to answer, but He waited.

Were her prayers good? None better. Was her case needy? Very. Did she feel her insufficiency? She was overwhelmed with it. Was she earnest? Intensely so. Was she lacking faith? No, for her faith was so powerful that Jesus said, "O woman, great is your faith" (Matthew 15:28).

It is true that faith brings peace, but not always instantaneously. There are many reasons we are called to the trial of faith rather than to the immediate reward of faith. Genuine faith may be hidden in the soul like a seed that has not budded and blossomed into joy and peace.

Silence from the Savior is the painful trial of many praying saints, but even heavier is the harsh, cutting reply, "It is not good to take the children's bread and throw it to the little dogs" (Matthew 15:26).

Many in waiting on the Lord find immediate delight, but that is not always the case. Some, like the Philippian jailer, are in a moment turned from darkness to light (Acts 16:34), while others are plants of slower growth. A deeper sense of sin may be given to you, and you will need patience to bear the heavy blow. "Though He slay me, yet will I trust Him" (Job 13:15). But even if he gives you an angry word, believe in the love of His heart.

I urge you, do not give up seeking or trusting my Master if you have not obtained the conscious joy you are seeking. Throw yourself on Him, and depend on Him even more when you cannot rejoice.

OCTOBER 9, EVENING

A PRELUDE TO ECSTACY

"Faultless before the presence of His glory."

—Jude 24

Think about that wonderful word, *faultless!* We are a long way from it, but our Lord never stops short of perfection in His works of love. One day we will be faultless. The Savior keeps His people, "that He might present her to Himself a glorious church, not having spot or wrinkle or any such thing" (Ephesians 5:27).

All the jewels in the Savior's crown (Revelation 14:14) are flawless. But how will Jesus make us faultless? He will wash our sins in His blood until we are as white and fair as God's purest angel. "Though your sins are like scarlet, they shall be as white as snow; though they are red like crimson they shall be as wool" (Isaiah 1:18). We will be clothed in His righteousness, the righteousness that makes the saints who wear it faultless.

The work of the Holy Spirit will be complete in us. We will be blameless and above reproach. His law will have no charge against us, but will be magnified perfectly in us. He will make us so thoroughly holy that we will have no lingering tendency to sin. Judgment, will, memory, and every power and passion will be emancipated from the bondage of evil. We will be holy, even as God is holy. Saints will not be out of place in heaven. Their beauty will be as great as that of the place prepared for them.

Oh the rapture of that hour, when the everlasting doors shall be lifted up and we, having been made for the inheritance, will dwell with the saints in light (Acts 26:18). Sin will be gone and Satan shut out. Temptation will have run its course forever, and we will be faultless before God. This will be heaven indeed.

Be joyful. Rehearse the song of eternal praise that will soon roll in a full chorus from all the blood-washed host before the throne (Revelation 14:3).

"David danced before the Lord with all his might" (2 Samuel 6:14). Let us imitate David, as a prelude to the ecstacies of heaven.

OCTOBER 10, MORNING

DELIVERED

"I will deliver you from the hand of the wicked. And I will redeem you from the grip of the terrible."

—Jeremiah 15:21

Look at the glorious personality of this promise: "I will," and "I will." The Lord Jehovah intercedes to redeem and deliver His people, personally promising to rescue them so that He will have all the glory.

There is not a word in our text about any effort on our part. Our strengths and weaknesses are not considered, but the lone *I*, like the sun in the heavens shines resplendently as all-sufficient.

Why then do we calculate on our power and consult with mere flesh and blood? Jehovah has power enough without borrowing from our puny strength. The Lord commences the work alone. He has no need for human arms to assist Him.

It is ridiculous to look for friends and relatives to help, for they, as we, are only broken reeds. If we try to lean on them, they are often unwilling when able, or unable when willing. Since the promise comes from God alone it is best to wait on Him alone, and when we do He never fails.

Who are the wicked, that we should fear them? The Lord will utterly consume them; they are to be pitied rather than feared. As for the terrible ones, they are terrors only to those without God. When the Lord is on our side, whom shall we fear? If we run into sin to please the wicked, we have cause to be alarmed, but if we hold fast to our integrity the rage of tyrants will be overruled for our good.

"Beloved, do not think it strange concerning the fiery trial which is to try you, as though some strange thing happened to you: but rejoice to the extent that you partake of Christ's suffering that when His glory is revealed you may also be glad with exceeding joy" (1 Peter 4:12–13).

OCTOBER 10, EVENING

PRAYER

"Let us lift our hearts and hands to God in heaven."

—Lamentations 3:41

Prayer teaches us our unworthiness. It brings about a sound condition by correcting evil in such proud beings as ourselves. If God gave us favors without constraining us to pray for them, we would never know how poor we are. True prayer is an inventory of needs and necessities, a revelation of our hidden poverty. While it is a request for divine wealth, it is also a confession of human emptiness.

The healthiest condition for a Christian is to be empty of self and constantly dependent on the Lord for everything; to be poor in self but rich in Jesus, as weak as water, personally, but mighty through God to do great exploits. Hence the use of prayer. While it adores God, prayer puts the creature where it should be—in the dust.

Apart from the answer it brings, prayer is also a great benefit to the Christian. Just as a runner gains strength for the race by daily exercise, we acquire energy for the great race of life by the hallowed labor of prayer.

Prayer plumes the wings of God's young eaglets, who thus learn to fly above the clouds. Prayer girds the loins of God's warriors and sends them into combat with sinews braced and muscles firm. An earnest pleader comes out of the prayer closet rejoicing like a strong athlete about to run a race.

Prayer is the uplifted hands of Moses, which rout the Amalekites more than the sword of Joshua (Exodus 17:11). Prayer girds human weakness with divine strength, turns human folly into heavenly wisdom, and gives troubled mortals the peace of God. We do not know what prayer can do.

We thank You, great God, for the mercy seat, which is a choice proof or Your marvelous lovingkindness. Help us to use it throughout this day! Amen.

THE TEST

"Whom He predestined, these He also called."

—Romans 8:30

In 2 Timothy 1:9, we read, "Who has saved us and called us with a holy calling." This is a touchstone by which we may test our calling.

It is a holy calling, not according to our works but according to God's purpose and grace. This calling prohibits all trust in our own actions, and it conducts us to Christ alone for salvation. Afterward, it purges us from dead works to serve the living and true God.

"We should be holy and without blame before Him" (Ephesians 1:4). If you are living in sin, you are not called. But if you are truly Christ's, you can say, "Nothing pains me as much as sin. I want to be rid of it. Lord help me to be holy." Is this your heart's desire? Is this the continual purpose of your life toward God and His divine will?

Again, in Philippians 3:13–14, we are told about "the upward calling of God in Christ Jesus." Is your calling an upward calling? Is your heart set on heavenly things? Has it elevated your hopes, your tastes, and your desires? Has it raised the purpose of your life so that you spend it with and for God?

Another test is found in Hebrews 3:1, "Partakers of the heavenly calling." *Heavenly* means a call from heaven. If man alone called you, you are not called. Is your calling from God? Is it a call to heaven as well as from heaven? Unless you are a stranger here and heaven is your home you have not been called with a heavenly calling. Those with a heavenly calling declare that they wait for a city which has foundations, whose builder and maker is God (Hebrews 11:10). They confess that they are strangers and pilgrims on earth (Hebrews 11:13).

Is your calling holy, high, and heavenly? Then, beloved, you have been called of God, for this is the calling whereby God calls His people.

MEDITATION NEGLECTED

"I will meditate on Your precepts."

—Psalm 119:15

There are times when solitude is better than company and silence is wiser than speech. We would be better Christians if we were alone more often, waiting on God and gathering, through meditation on His Word, spiritual strength for His service. We are spiritually fed when we think on the things of God.

Truth is like a cluster of grapes. If we want wine we must bruise, press, and squeeze it many times. The bruiser's feet must come down joyfully on the grapes, or else the juice will not flow. They must tread the grapes well, or else much of the precious liquid will be wasted. So must we by meditation tread the clusters of truth if we would get the wine of consolation.

Our bodies are not supported merely by taking food into the mouth, for it is the process of digestion that supplies the muscle, nerve, sinew, and bone; it is this process of digestion that causes outward food to become assimilated to the inner life.

Our souls are not nourished merely by listening briefly to this, that, and the other part of divine truth. Hearing, reading, marking, and learning all require inward digesting to complete their usefulness. This inward digesting of truth lies for the most part in meditation.

Why is it that some Christians, although they hear many sermons, make little progress in the divine life? They neglect their prayer closets and do not meditate on God's Word. They love wheat, but they do not grind it. They would have corn, but they will not go in the fields and gather it. The fruit hangs on the tree, but they will not pick it. The water flows at their feet, but they will not stoop to drink it.

From such folly deliver us, Oh Lord. Help us to resolve this morning to "meditate on Your precepts."

OCTOBER 12, MORNING

A COMFORTING SPIRIT

"The Helper, the Holy Spirit."

—John 14:26

This age is exclusively the dispensation of the Holy Spirit, in which Jesus cheers us, not by His personal presence, but by the indwelling and constant abiding of the Holy Spirit.

It is the Holy Spirit's function to console God's people, to convict of sin, and to illuminate and instruct. But the main part of His work lies in making glad the hearts of the renewed, in confirming the weak, and in lifting up those that are bowed down. The Holy Spirit does this by revealing Jesus.

The Holy Spirit consoles, but Christ is the consolation. If I may use this example, the Holy Spirit is the Physician, but Jesus is the medicine. The Holy Spirit heals the wound by applying the holy ointment of Christ's name and grace, for the Spirit takes not of His own things, but of the things of Christ.

If we give the Holy Spirit the Greek name *paraclete,* then our blessed Lord becomes the *paraclesis.* The former is the Comforter, the latter is the Comfort. Now with such rich provisions, why should we be sad or depressed?

The Holy Spirit has graciously engaged to be your Comforter. Can you imagine, weak and trembling believer, that He will be negligent of this sacred trust? Do you suppose that He has undertaken what He cannot or will not perform? If it is His special work to strengthen and comfort, do you suppose that He has forgotten this, or that He will fail to sustain you?

No! The blessed Spirit, whose name is *the Comforter,* delights to give "the oil of joy for mourning and the garment of praise for the spirit of heaviness" (Isaiah 61:3).

Trust in Him. He will surely comfort you until the house of mourning is closed forever and the marriage feast has begun.

OCTOBER 12, EVENING

REPENTANCE

"For godly sorrow produces repentance."

—2 Corinthians 7:10.

Genuine spiritual mourning for sin is the work of the Spirit of God. Repentance is too choice a flower to grow in nature's garden. Pearls grow naturally in oysters, but repentance never shows itself in sinners unless divine grace works it in them. If you have one particle of real hatred of sin, God must have given it to you, for human nature's thorns never produced a single fig. "That which is born of the flesh is flesh" (John 3:6).

True repentance has a distinct reference to the Savior. When we repent, we must have one eye on sin and another on the cross. But even better is to fix both eyes on Christ and see our transgressions only in the light of His love.

True sorrow for sin is eminently practical. People may not say they hate sin if they are living in it. Repentance makes us see the evil of sin, not merely as a theory but experientially, as a burnt child dreads fire.

We should be as afraid of sin as the victim of a mugger is afraid of thieves. We must shun sin, and shun it in everything, in great and little things, as we shun little vipers as well as great snakes.

True mourning for sin will make us guard our tongues, lest we say a wrong word. It will make us watchful over our daily actions, lest we offend in anything. Each evening, let us close the day with painful confessions of our short-comings. Each morning, let us wake with an eager prayer that God will hold us back from sinning against Him.

Sincere repentance is continual. Believers repent until their dying day. Repentance is not intermittent. Other sorrows yield to time, but repentance grows with spiritual growth. Repentance is so bittersweet that we thank God we are permitted to experience it until we enter our eternal rest.

STRONG AS DEATH

"Love is as strong as death."

—Song of Solomon 8:6

Whose love is as mighty as the conqueror of monarchs? It would sound like satire if it were applied to my poor, weak, and scarcely living love for Jesus my Lord. I do love Him, and perhaps by His grace I could even die for Him, but my love for Him can scarcely endure a scoffing jest, much less a cruel death.

Surely it is my beloved's love which is spoken of in our text, the love of Jesus, the matchless lover of souls. His love was indeed stronger than the most terrible death, for it triumphed over the cross. It was a lingering death, but love survived the torment. It was a shameful death, but love despised the shame. It was a penal death, but love bore our iniquities. It was a forsaken and lonely death, from which the eternal Father hid His face, but love endured the curse and gloried over it. Never such love. Never such death. It was a desperate duel, but love was victorious.

Answer my heart. Are your emotions excited when you contemplate such heavenly affection? Yes, my Lord, I desire to feel Your love flaming like a furnace within me. Come in Your fullness and excite the love of my spirit:

> For every drop of crimson blood
> Thus shed to make me live,
> O wherefore, wherefore have not I
> A thousand lives to give?

I need to love Jesus with a love as strong as death. He deserves it: I desire it. The martyrs felt such love, and they too were flesh and blood. They mourned their weaknesses and out of them were made strong (2 Corinthians 12:9–10). Grace gave the martyrs unflinching faithfulness, and the same grace is available for me.

Jesus, lover of my soul, shed Your love in my heart this evening. Amen.

OCTOBER 13, EVENING

KNOWLEDGE

"Yes indeed I also count all things loss for the excellence of the knowledge of Christ Jesus my Lord."

—Philippians 3:8

Spiritual knowledge of Christ is personal knowledge. I cannot know Jesus through another person's acquaintance with Him. It is a conscious knowledge, for I must know Him not as the visionary dreams of Him but as the Word reveals Him. I must know His natures, divine and human. I must know His offices, His attributes, His works, His shame, His glory.

I must meditate on Him until I "may be able to comprehend with all the saints what is the width and length and depth and height—to know the love of Christ which passes knowledge" (Ephesians 3:18–19).

It will also be an affectionate knowledge. Indeed, if I know Him at all, I must love Him dearly. An ounce of heart knowledge is worth a ton of head learning. My knowledge of Him will be a satisfying knowledge. When I know my Savior, my mind will be full to the brim, of Him. I will feel that I have what my soul has longed for. "This is that bread of life. He who comes to Me shall never hunger" (John 6:35).

It is an exciting knowledge. The more I know about my Beloved, the more I want to know. The higher I climb the loftier the summits that invite my eager footsteps. I will want more as I get more. Like the miser's treasure, my gold will make me covet more of Him.

This knowledge of Christ Jesus will be a most happy one. It will be so elevating that sometimes it will completely carry me above all trials, doubts, and sorrows. It will make me something more than "man who is born of woman is of few days and full of trouble" (Job 14:1). This knowledge will surround me with the immortality of the ever-living Savior and gird me with the golden bands of His eternal joy.

Come, my soul, sit at Jesus' feet and learn about Him all this day.

THE NONCONFORMIST

"And do not be conformed to this world."

—Romans 12:2

I f a Christian can possibly be saved while conforming to this world, it must be as by fire (1 Corinthians 3:15). Such salvation is almost as much to be dreaded as desired. Reader, if you want to leave this world and enter heaven as a shipwrecked mariner then be worldly.

Would you have a heaven below as well as a heaven above? Can you "comprehend with all the saints what is the width and length and depth and height—to know the love of Christ which passes knowledge" (Ephesians 3:18–19)? Do you want an abundant entrance into the joy of your Lord? "Then come out from among them and be separate . . . Do not touch what is unclean, and I will receive you" (2 Corinthians 6:17).

Will you strive for the full assurance of faith? You cannot have it in communion with sinners. You cannot be a great Christian, you can never be perfect in Christ Jesus, while you yield yourself to the maxims and modes of this world. It is ill for an heir of heaven to be a great friend with the heirs of hell. A member of the king's family should never be intimate with the king's enemies.

Even small inconsistencies are dangerous. Little thorns make great blisters. Little moths destroy fine garments. Little frivolities, a little dishonesty, will rob Christianity of a thousand joys. When you are too close to the world, the tendons of your strength are cut, and you can only creep where you ought to run.

For your own comfort, for the sake of your growth in grace, if you are a Christian then be a Christian. Be a marked and distinct Christian.

WHO CAN ENDURE?

"But who can endure the day of His coming?"

—Malachi 3:2

Jesus' first coming was without external pomp or show of power, yet there were few who endured its testing. Herod and all Jerusalem were stirred at the news of the wondrous birth, but many who were waiting for Him showed their hypocrisy by rejecting Him when He came.

His life on earth was a separating fan, and when it tried the great heap of religious profession, few endured the process. But what will His second advent be like? What sinner can endure to think of it? "He shall strike the earth with the rod of His mouth, and with the breath of His lips He shall slay the wicked" (Isaiah 11:4).

When in His humiliation He only had to say, "I am He," and the soldiers fell to the ground (John 18:6), what, then, will it be like for His enemies when He shall be fully revealed as "I AM" (Exodus 3:14)?

His death shook earth and darkened heaven (Luke 23:44). What, then, will be the dreadful splendor of that day when, as the living Savior, He shall summon the living and the dead before Him (2 Timothy 4:1)?

Oh that the terrors of the Lord would persuade you to forsake your sins and "kiss the Son lest He be angry and you perish in the way" (Psalm 2:12). Though a lamb, He is also "the lion of the tribe of Judah" (Revelation 5:5), "breaking them with a rod of iron: He shall dash them to pieces like a potter's vessel" (Psalm 2:9).

None of His foes will stand before the tempest of His wrath, none shall be able to hide from the sweeping hail of His indignation. But His beloved and bloodwashed people look for His appearing with joy and hope. "He will sit as a refiner and a purifier of silver" (Malachi 3:3) for "when He has tested me I shall come forth as gold" (Job 23:10).

Let us search ourselves this morning and "be even more diligent to make your call an election sure" (2 Peter 1:10).

OCTOBER 15, MORNING

THE SUBSTITUTE

"But the firstborn of a donkey you shall redeem with a lamb. And if you will not redeem him, then you shall break his neck."

—Exodus 34:20

Every firstborn creature is the Lord's. Since a donkey was unclean, however, it could not be presented in sacrifice to God. Should it, then, be exempt from the universal law? By no means, for God has no exceptions. The donkey is His, but He will not accept it. He will not reduce the claim, but yet He cannot be pleased with the victim. No way of escape remained but redemption. The donkey must be saved by the substitution of a lamb in its place. If not redeemed, it must die.

My soul, here is a lesson for you. You are that unclean animal. Though you are the property of the Lord who made and preserves you, you are so sinful that God will not, cannot, accept you. It has come to this, the lamb of God must stand in your place, or you will die eternally.

Let the world know of your gratitude to that spotless Lamb who has already bled to redeem you from the law's fatal curse.

Sometimes, it must have been difficult for an Israelite to decide what should die, the donkey or the lamb. Would not the owner stop to estimate and compare? Assuredly there was no comparison between the value of the soul of man and the life of the Lord Jesus. Yet the Lamb dies and man, the donkey, is spared.

My soul, admire the boundless love of God toward you. Worms are bought with the blood of the Son of the Highest! Dust and ashes are redeemed with a price far above silver and gold (1 Peter 1:18–19). What doom was mine, but what plenteous redemption was found!

The breaking of the donkey's neck was but a momentary penalty, but who can measure the wrath to come? Yet precious beyond that measure is the glorious Lamb who has redeemed us from such doom.

OCTOBER 15, EVENING

COME AND EAT

"Jesus said to them, 'Come and eat breakfast'."

—John 21:12

With these words the believer is invited to a holy nearness with Jesus. *Come and eat* implies the same table and food. Sometimes it means to sit side by side and lean our head on the Savior's arm, but it is always to be "brought into the banqueting house where His banner over me is love" (Song of Solomon 2:4).

Come and eat gives us a vision of our union with Jesus, and the only food that we can feast on when we dine with Jesus is Jesus Himself. Oh, what union! That we feed on Jesus is a depth which reason cannot fathom. "He who eats My flesh and drinks My blood abides in Me, and I in him" (John 6:56).

It is also an invitation to enjoy fellowship with the saints. Christians may differ on a variety of points, but they have one spiritual appetite. If we cannot all feel alike at least we can all feed alike, "for the bread of God is He who comes down from heaven and gives life to the world" (John 6:33). At the table of fellowship with Jesus, we are one bread and one cup.

Get nearer to Jesus and you will be linked more and more in spirit to all who are sustained by the same heavenly manna. If you are closer to Jesus, you will be close to other believers.

We also see in these words the source of strength for every Christian. To look at Christ is to live, but for strength to serve Him we must come and eat. We are unnecessarily weak when we neglect this precept.

We do not need to be on a diet. Rather, we should "feast on choice pieces, a feast of wines on the lees, of fat things full of marrow, of well-refined wines on the lees" (Isaiah 25:6). From this feast we will build up strength for the Master's service.

If you desire nearness to Jesus and a love for His people, and strength from Him, then by faith, come and eat with Him.

THE FOUNTAIN

"For with You is the fountain of life."

—Psalm 36:9

There are times in our spiritual experience when human counsel, or sympathy, or religious ordinances fail to comfort or help. Why does our gracious God permit this? Perhaps it is because we have been living too much without Him. He therefore takes everything that we have been depending on in order to drive us to Him.

It is a blessed thing to live at the fountain head. While our skin bottles are full, we are, like Hagar and Ishmael, content to go into the wilderness (Genesis 21:14), but when they are empty, nothing will do but "Him who sees me" (Genesis 16:13).

We are like the prodigal: We love the swine pens and not our Father's house. Remember, we can even make swine pens and husks out of religious forms. They may be blessed things, but we may put them in God's place and then they become valueless. Anything becomes an idol when it keeps us from God. Even the bronze serpent (Numbers 21:9) is to be despised and called Nehushtan (a piece of brass) (2 Kings 18:4), if we worship it instead of God.

The prodigal was never safer than when he was driven to his father's home. Our Lord brings famine to make us seek Him.

The best position for a Christian is to be living fully on God's grace, to be abiding where we first stood, "as having nothing, and yet possessing all things" (2 Corinthians 6:10). Never think that your standing is in your sanctification, humility, accomplishments, or feelings. Your salvation is only because Christ offered a full atonement. You are complete in Him and have nothing of your own to trust in. Rest only on the merits of Jesus, for He is the only ground of confidence.

Beloved, when you are made thirsty, be sure to turn eagerly to the fountain of life.

OCTOBER 16, EVENING

FALSE WORDS

"And David said in his heart, 'I shall perish someday by the hand of Saul.'"

—1 Samuel 27:1

David's thoughts were false. He certainly had no ground for thinking that God's anointing was an empty act. The Lord had never deserted His servant. David was frequently in danger, but in every incident divine intervention had delivered him.

David's trials were many and varied, but in every case He who sent the trial graciously ordained a way of escape. David could not put his finger on any entry in his diary and say, "Here is evidence that the Lord will forsake me." Rather, David should have recognized that because of what God had already done, He would continue to be his defender.

But don't we also doubt God's help? Is this not mistrust without cause? Have we ever had even the shadow of a reason to doubt our Father's goodness? Is His lovingkindnesses not marvelous? Has He once failed to justify our trust in Him?

No! Our God has never left us. We have dark nights, but His star of love shines in the blackness. We have hard conflicts, but over our head He holds the shield of defense. We have gone through many trials, but never to our detriment, always to our advantage.

The conclusion from our past experience is that He who has been with us in six trials will not forsake us in the seventh. What we have known of our faithful God proves that He will keep us to the end. "Now to Him who is able to keep you from stumbling and to present you faultless before the presence of His glory with exceeding joy" (Jude 24). Do not reason contrary to the evidence. How can we ever be so ungenerous as to doubt our God?

Lord, throw down the Jezebel of our unbelief and let the dogs devour it (2 Kings 9:36).

OCTOBER 17, MORNING

MY SHEPHERD

"He will gather the lambs with His arm."

—Isaiah 40:11

The sheep in the good Shepherd's flock have a variety of experiences. Some are strong in the Lord and others are weak in faith, but Jesus is impartial in His care for His sheep. The weakest lamb is as precious to Him as the most advanced of the flock.

Lambs lag behind, prone to wander and grow weary. But from all such dangers the Shepherd protects them with His arm of power. He finds new-born souls, like young lambs ready to perish, and He nourishes them until their life becomes vigorous. He finds weak minds ready to faint and die, and He consoles them and renews their strength.

All the little ones He gathers, for it is not the will of our heavenly Father that one of them should perish (Matthew 18:14). What a quick eye He must have to see them all! What a tender heart to care for them all! What a far- reaching and powerful arm to gather them all!

In His lifetime on earth He was a great gatherer of weak sheep. Now that He dwells in heaven His loving heart yearns toward the meek and contrite, the timid and feeble, the fearful and fainting here below.

How gently He gathered me to Him, to His truth, to His blood, to His love, and to His church! With what effectual grace did He compel me to come to Him! Since my conversion, how frequently He has rescued me from wandering and enclosed me in His everlasting arms!

But best of all, He does it personally. He does not delegate the task of love but personally condescends to rescue and preserve even His most unworthy servants. How can I love Him enough or serve Him worthily? I would eagerly make His name great to the ends of the earth, but what can my feebleness do for Him?

Great Shepherd, add to Your mercies one more, a heart to truly love You. Amen.

ABUNDANCE

"Your paths drip with abundance."

—Psalm 65:11

Many are the paths of the Lord that "drip with abundance," and the path of prayer is exceptionally abundant. A praying believer will never have to cry, "My need, my need. Oh woe is me." But starving souls live at a distance from the mercy seat and become like parched fields in times of drought.

Prevailing with God in wrestling prayer makes the believer strong. The nearest place to the gate of heaven is the throne of grace. If you are much alone with Jesus, you will have much assurance. If you are alone with Him but a little, your religion will be shallow, polluted with doubts, filled with fears, and not sparkling with the joy of the Lord.

Since the enriching path of prayer is open to the weakest saint, since no high attainments are required, since you are freely invited if you are a saint at all, then see to it, my dear reader, that you are often in private devotion. Be much on your knees.

Another path that is especially abundant is the secret walk of communion. Oh the delights of fellowship with Jesus! Earth has no words to calm a believer like leaning on Jesus.

Few Christians understand it. They live in the lowlands and seldom climb to the mountain top. They live in the outer court and never enter the holy place. They never take up the privilege of priesthood. At a distance they see the sacrifice, but they do not sit close to the priest to eat and enjoy the burnt offering.

Reader, always sit under the shadow of Jesus. Come up to that palm tree and take hold of the branches. Let your beloved be as an apple tree among the trees of the forest (Song of Solomon 2:3). Then you will be satisfied with abundance.

Oh Jesus, visit us with Your salvation.

OBEY

"Behold to obey is better than sacrifice."

—1 Samuel 15:22

Saul had been commanded to slay all the Amalekites and their cattle (1 Samuel 15:3). Instead, he spared their king and told the Israelites to take the best oxen and sheep for themselves (1 Samuel 15:9). When called to account, he declared that he had done it to offer a sacrifice to God (1 Samuel 15:21). But the prophet Samuel told him that sacrifices were not excuses to justify acts of rebellion.

Our text should be printed in letters of gold and hung before the eyes of this present idolatrous generation, for it is a generation fond of self-will in worship, but utterly neglectful of God's laws.

Never forget that to keep strictly in the path of our Savior's commands is better than any outward form of religion. To hear and obey His precept is better than bringing the fat of rams, or any other precious thing, to lay on His altar.

If you are failing to keep the least of Christ's commands, be disobedient no longer. All your pretensions to serve your Master and all your devout actions are no payments for disobedience. *To obey* even in the slightest and smallest thing "is better than sacrifice," regardless of how pompous the sacrifice is.

Don't talk to me about Gregorian chants, sumptuous robes, and incense and banners; the first thing God requires of His child is obedience. It is a blessed thing to be as teachable as a child, but it is more blessed when one has been taught to carry it out to the letter. How many adorn their churches and decorate their ministers but refuse to obey the Word of the Lord!

My soul, obey.

RICH AS THE RICHEST

"Babes in Christ."

—1 Corinthians 3:1

Are you weak in the Christian life? Is your faith little, your love feeble? Cheer up, you have a reason to be thankful.

Remember that in some things you are equal to the greatest and most mature Christian. You are as much bought with blood and as much an adopted child of God as any believer. An infant is as much a child of its parents as a full grown adult.

You are completely justified, for justification is not a thing of degrees. Your little faith has made you totally clean. You have as much right to the precious things of the covenant as the most advanced believers do, because your right to covenant mercies does not lie in your growth but in the covenant itself.

Your faith in Jesus is not the full measure but the token of your inheritance. You are as rich as the richest, if not in enjoyment at least in real possession. The smallest star that gleams is still set in the heavens. The faintest ray of light still has affinity with the sun. In the family register of glory, the small and the great are written with the same pen. You are as precious to your Father's heart as the greatest in the family.

Jesus is tender with you. You are like the smoking flax, and a rougher spirit than God would say, "Put out that flax, it fills the room with an offensive odor!" But "a smoking flax He will not quench" (Matthew 12:20). You are like a bruised reed, and a less tender hand than Jesus would throw you away. But "a bruised reed He will not break" (Matthew 12:20). Instead of being downcast because of what you are, you should triumph in Christ, who "made us sit together in the heavenly places" (Ephesians 2:6).

Are you poor in faith? In Jesus you are heir of all things. I will rejoice in the Lord and glory in the God of my salvation.

SONGS IN THE NIGHT

"God my Maker, who gives songs in the night."

—Job 35:10

We can all sing during the day. When our cup is full we are inspired. When wealth rolls in we praise God, who gives a bountiful harvest or sends us a ship fully loaded. Chimes whisper music when the wind blows; the difficulty is for the music to sound when there is no wind.

It is easy to sing when we can read the notes by daylight, but one is skillful who sings from the heart when there is no light to read by. None can make a song in the night by themselves. We may attempt it, but a song in the night must be divinely inspired.

Let everything go well and I can weave songs, fashioning them from the flowers along my path. But put me in a desert where nothing green grows, and how will I frame a hymn to God there? How can a mere mortal make a crown for the Lord where there are no jewels?

Let my voice be clear, my body full of health, and I can sing God's praises. But lay me on a bed of pain and you will silence my tongue, unless God gives me a song. It is not in my power to sing when all is adverse, unless an altar coal touches my lips.

It was a divine song that Habakkuk sung in the night. "Though the fig tree may not blossom, nor fruit be on the vine; though the labor of the olive may fail and the fields yield no food; though the flock may be cut off from the fold and there be no herd in the stalls—yet I will rejoice in the Lord, I will joy in the God of my salvation" (Habakkuk 3:17–18). Since our Maker gives songs in the night, let us wait on Him for the music.

Oh Lord, let us not remain silent because of affliction. Tune our lips to the melody of thanksgiving. Amen.

OCTOBER 19, EVENING

GROWING

"Grow up in all things into Him."

—Ephesians 4:15

Many Christians remain spiritually stunted and dwarfed. Year after year they show no signs of growth. They exist, but they do not "grow up in all things into Him."

Should we be content with being the "green blade," when we could advance to "the ear" and eventually ripen into the "full ear of corn?" Should we be satisfied to believe in Christ without wanting to experience the fullness that is found in Him? No. We should be good traders in heaven's market, desiring to be enriched in the knowledge of Jesus.

Why should it always be wintertime in our hearts? We must have our seed time; but oh for springtime and also a summer season that gives the promise of an early harvest. If we are to ripen in grace, we must live near Jesus, in His presence, ripened by the sunshine of His smile.

We must have sweet fellowship with Him. We must leave the distant view of His face and like John pillow our head on His bosom (John 13:23). Then we will find ourselves progressing in holiness, in love, in faith, in hope, and in every precious gift.

A most charming sight to the traveler is the sun gilding the mountain tops with its light. But a more delightful scene is the glow of the Spirit's light in a saint who has risen in spiritual stature until, like a mighty snow-capped Alp, this believer reflects the light of the Sun of Righteousness. Here is a believer brilliantly beaming brightness for all to see, glorifying His Father in heaven.

Do Not Keep Back

"Do not keep them back."

Although this message was sent to the south and referred to the seed of Israel, it may profitably be a summons for us. We are naturally backward to all good things. It is a lesson of grace to learn to go forward in the ways of God.

Reader, are you unconverted but desirous of trusting in the Lord Jesus? Then do not keep back. Love invites you, the promises secure you, and the precious blood prepares the way. Do not let sin or fear hinder you. Come to Jesus just as you are. Do you long to pray? Would you pour out your heart before the Lord? Do not keep back. The mercy seat is prepared for those who need mercy. A sinner's cry will prevail with God. You are invited, no you are commanded, to pray. Come, come with boldness to the throne of grace.

Dear friend, are you already saved? Then do not keep back from fellowship with the Lord's people. Do not neglect the ordinances of baptism and the Lord's Supper.

There is a sweet promise made to those who confess Christ. By no means miss it, lest you come under the condemnation of those who deny Him.

If you have talents, do not keep back from using them. Do not hoard your wealth, or waste your time, or let your abilities rust or your influences lay unused. Jesus did not keep back. Imitate Him by being first in self-denial and self-sacrifice.

Do not keep back from close fellowship with God, from boldly appropriating covenant blessings, from advancing in the divine life, and from prying into the precious mysteries of the love of Christ.

My beloved friend, do not be guilty of keeping others back by your coldness, harshness, or suspicions. For Jesus' sake go forward and encourage others to do likewise. Hell and the combined bands of superstition and infidelity are forward to the fight. Soldiers of the cross, keep not back.

OCTOBER 20, EVENING

COMPELLING LOVE

"The love of Christ compels us."

—2 Corinthians 5:14

How much do you owe your Lord? Has He ever done anything for you? Has He forgiven your sins? Has He covered you with a robe of righteousness? Has He set your feet on a rock? Has He established your steps? Has He prepared heaven for you? Has He written your name in His book of life? Has He given you countless blessings? Has He laid up for you a store of mercies that eye has not seen nor ear heard? Then do something for Jesus that is worthy of His love, something more than a mere wordy offering.

When your Master comes, how will you feel if you have to confess that you did nothing for Him, that your love was shut up like a stagnant pool that refused to flow to His poor or to His work. What do people think of a love that never shows itself in action? Why do they say, "Open rebuke is better than secret love"? Who will accept a love so weak that it does not actuate a single deed of self-denial, generosity, heroism, or zeal!

Think how He has loved you and given Himself for you! Do you know the power of that love? Then let it rush like a mighty wind to your soul and sweep out the clouds of worldliness and clear away the mists of your sin.

For Christ's sake let this be the tongue of fire that shall sit upon you. For Christ's sake let this divine rapture carry you aloft from earth and empower you to be as bold as a lion and as swift as an eagle in your Lord's service.

Love should give wings to the feet of service and strength to the arms of labor. Be fixed on God with a constancy that is not to be shaken. Resolve to honor Him with a determination that can not be turned aside, and press on with an intensity that will never weaken.

DIRECT AND PERSONAL

"Why are you troubled? And why do doubts arise in your heart?"

—Luke 24:38

"Why do you say, O Jacob, and speak, O Israel: 'My way is hidden from the Lord, and my just claim is passed over by my God'?" (Isaiah 40:27).

The Lord cares for all things, and even the lowest creatures come under His universal providence. But His special providence is over His saints. "The angel of the Lord encamps all around those that fear Him" (Psalm 34:7). "Precious shall be their blood in His sight" (Psalm 72:14). "Precious in the sight of the Lord is the death of His saints" (Psalm 116:15). "And we know that all things work together for good to those who love God, to those who are the called according to His purpose" (Romans 8:28).

Jesus is the Savior of all who believe. Let this fact cheer and comfort you. You are in His special care, "He keeps you as the apple of His eye (Deuteronomy 32:10). "My own vineyard is before Me" (Song of Solomon 8:12). "The very hairs of your head are all numbered" (Matthew 10:30).

Let the thought of His special love to you be a spiritual pain killer, a balm to your troubles. "I will never leave you nor forsake you" (Hebrews 13:5). God says as much to you as to any saint of old, "I am your shield, your exceedingly great reward" (Genesis 15:1).

We lose much comfort by reading His promises for the church instead of taking them as direct and personal. Believer, grasp the divine Word with a personal, appropriating faith. Think that you heard Jesus say, "I have prayed for you that your faith should not fail" (Luke 22:32). Can you see Him walking on the waters of your troubles? He is there saying, "Be of good cheer! It is I; do not be afraid" (Mark 6:50).

Oh those sweet words of Christ! May the Holy Spirit make you feel they are spoken directly to you. Jesus whispers consolation. Do not refuse it. Sit under His shadow in delight.

OCTOBER 21, EVENING

WITHOUT MERIT

"I will love them freely."

—Hosea 14:4

This sentence is a body of divinity in miniature. If you understand it you are a theologian. If you can dive into its fullness, you are a true master of Scripture.

Our text is a condensed version of the glorious message of salvation. The meat of this text is the word *freely.* This is the glorious, the suitable, and the divine way in which love streams from Christ Jesus the Redeemer to us. It is a spontaneous love, flowing to those who neither deserved it, purchased it, nor sought it. Indeed, it is the only way God can love us.

The text is a death blow to all sorts of personal merit. If there were any merit necessary in us, then He would not love us freely. At the very least, such love would have a condition. But it stands, "I will love you freely."

Even when you complain, "Lord, my heart is so hard," Jesus still says, "I will love you freely."

Even if you say, "But I do not feel my need of Christ as I should," Jesus still says, "I will not love you because you feel your need, for I love you freely."

"But I do not feel that softening of spirit that I desire." Remember, even the softening of spirit is not a condition, for there are no conditions in the covenant of grace. The covenant of grace is unconditional to the point that without merit we may venture on the promise of God made to us in Christ Jesus. "He who believes in Him is not condemned" (John 3:18). It is a blessing to know that the grace of God is free at all times, without preparation, without merit, without money, and without price (Isaiah 52:3; 55:1).

The words, "I will love them freely," is also a precious promise inviting backsliders to return. Indeed the text was written for such, for "I will heal their backsliding, I will love them freely" (Hosea 14:4). Backslider, surely the generosity of the promise will at once break your heart and you will turn to seek your Father's face.

APPLIED BY GRACE

"He will take of Mine and declare it to you."

—John 16:15

All the promises and doctrines of the Bible are useless unless a gracious hand applies them, for our condition is such that though we are thirsty, we are too weak to crawl to the brook. When a soldier is wounded in battle, it is of little use to know that there is a physician behind the lines if no one is there to take the wounded to the hospital.

It is the same with our souls. To meet our need there is one, the Spirit of Truth, who takes the things of Jesus and applies them to us. Do not think that Christ has placed His joys on heavenly shelves that we have to climb to reach. No, He draws near to us and sheds His peace in our hearts.

Oh Christian, if tonight you are distressed, your Father does not give you promises that are out of reach at the bottom of a well. The promises in the Word He Himself will write on your heart. He will manifest His love to you; and by His blessed Spirit, He will dispel your cares and troubles. Remember, it is God's prerogative to wipe every tear from the eyes of His people (Revelation 21:4).

The good Samaritan did not say, "Here is the wine and oil, take it." He actually poured in the oil and the wine (Luke 10:34). So Jesus gives you the sweet wine of the promise, holding the golden chalice to your lips and pouring the life-blood into your mouth. Even the poor, sick, and way-worn pilgrim is not merely strengthened to walk but is borne on eagle's wings.

Glorious gospel! It provides everything for the helpless. It comes to us when we cannot reach it. It brings us grace before we seek it. Here there is as much glory in the giving as in the gift.

Happy are the people who have the Holy Spirit to bring Jesus to them.

OCTOBER 22, EVENING

WHY GO AWAY

"Do you also want to go away?"

—John 6:67

Many have forsaken Christ and no longer walk with Him. If this includes you, dear reader, what reason do you have to make a change? Has there been any reason in the past? Has not Jesus proven Himself to be all-sufficient? When your soul simply trusted Jesus, were you ever confused? Have you not found the Lord to be compassionate and generous? Has not your faith in Him given you all the peace your spirit could desire? Can you dream of a better friend than Jesus? Then don't change the old and tried for the new and false.

As for our present circumstances, can those justify forsaking Christ? When we are hard beset with this world or severe trials within the church, it is blessed to pillow our head on the Savior's bosom. This is the joy we have: *today* we are saved in Him. And if this joy is satisfying, why would we ever think of changing? Who trades gold for dross? We will not forswear the sun until we find a better light. We will not leave our Lord until a brighter lover appears. And since this can never be, we will hold Him with a grasp immortal and bind His name as a seal on our arms.

As for the future, can you imagine anything that could legitimize our mutiny, that we should go and serve under another leader? I think not. If life is long, still He never changes. If we remain poor, still Christ makes us rich. If we are sick, what more could we want than for Jesus to make our bed during our sickness.

When we die it is written, "Neither death nor life, nor angels nor principalities nor powers, nor things present nor things to come, nor height nor depth, nor any created thing shall be able to separate us from the love of God which is in Christ Jesus our Lord" (Romans 8:38–39).

Let us say with Peter, "Lord to whom shall we go?" (John 6:68).

OCTOBER 23, MORNING

SLEEPY

"Why do you sleep? Rise and pray, lest you enter into temptation."

—Luke 22:46

When is the Christian most likely to sleep? Usually it is in times of prosperity. Have you found this to be true? When you had daily troubles to take to the throne of grace you were more wakeful than when you were on an easy road which makes travellers sleepy.

Another dangerous time is when all goes well spiritually. Bunyan's Christian did not sleep when lions were in the way, or when he was wading through the river or fighting Apollyon. But after he had climbed halfway up the Hill Difficulty and come to a delightful garden, he sat down, and to his great sorrow and loss, he fell asleep.

Enchanted ground is a place of balmy breezes, fragrant perfumes, and soft influences that lull pilgrims to sleep. Bunyan describes it like this, "Then they came to an arbor, warm and promising much refreshing to the weary pilgrims; for it was finely wrought above head, beautified with greens and furnished with benches and settees. It had also in it a soft couch where the weary might lean . . . The arbor was called the Slothful's Friend and was made on purpose to allure, if it might be, some of the pilgrims to take up their rest there when weary."

Depend on it. In easy places we shut our eyes and wander into the dreamy land of forgetfulness to God. Old Erskine wisely remarked, "I like a roaring devil better than a sleeping devil." There is no temptation half so dangerous as not being tempted. The distressed soul does not sleep. It is after we are peacefully confident and fully assured that we are in danger of slumbering.

Take heed joyous Christian, material blessings are near neighbors to temptation. Be happy, but be watchful.

THE LIFE WITHIN

"The trees of the Lord are full of sap."

—Psalm 104:16

Without sap a tree cannot flourish or exist. Vitality too is essential to a Christian. There must be life, a vital principle infused in us by God the Holy Spirit, or we cannot be trees of the Lord. Being a Christian is but a dead thing unless we are filled with the Spirit of divine life.

This life is mysterious, a sacred mystery. Regeneration occurs by the Holy Spirit's entering and becoming our life. This life in us then feeds on the flesh and blood of Christ and is sustained by divine food. But who can explain how it all happens?

What a mysterious thing sap is! The roots go searching through the soil, but we cannot see them absorb or transmute the minerals into their life. This work is done down in the dark. Similar is our root, Christ Jesus, for our life is hid in Him. This is the secret of the Lord. The source of the Christian life is as mysterious as the life itself.

The sap in the tree is active. In the Christian, the divine life is always full of energy, not always in fruit bearing but in inward operations. The believer's graces are in continual motion, not always working for God but always living on Him.

Just as the sap produces the tree's foliage and fruit, the life of Christ is manifested in healthy Christians. In their talk they speak of Jesus, and in their actions it is obvious that they have been with Jesus. They have so much sap that it fills their conduct and conversation with life.

OCTOBER 24, MORNING

RECURRING FORGIVENESS

"He poured water into a basin and began to wash the disciples' feet."

—John 13:5

The Lord Jesus so greatly loves His people that He is still doing much that is analogous to washing their soiled feet. Their poorest actions He accepts; their deepest sorrows He feels; their slenderest prayers He hears, and their every transgression He forgives. He is still their servant as well as their Friend and Master.

He performs majestic deeds for them. He wears the miter on His brow and the jewels on His breastplate as He stands to plead for them.

Humbly and patiently He goes among His people with basin and towel. He does this everyday as He takes our infirmities and sins. Last night you prayed and confessed that much of your conduct was not worthy of your position. Tonight you may mourn again that you have fallen in the same folly and sin from which grace once delivered you.

Yet Jesus has great patience. He will hear your confession and say, "I am willing, be clean" (Mark 1:41). He will again apply the blood of sprinkling, speak peace to your conscience, and remove every spot.

It is a great act of eternal love when Christ, once for all, absolves the sinner and places him in the family of God. But what condescending patience when the Savior, with long-suffering, bears the recurring follies of a wayward disciple. Day by day, hour by hour, He washes away the multiplied transgressions of His erring but beloved children.

To dry a flood of rebellion is marvelous, but to endure the constant dropping of repeated offenses, to bear with a perpetual trying of patience, this is indeed divine.

As we find comfort and peace in our Lord's daily cleansing its influence on us will increase our watchfulness and our desire for holiness.

OCTOBER 24, EVENING

TRUTH

"Because of the truth which abides in us and will be with us forever."

—2 John 2

Once the truth of God enters the human heart, no power, human or infernal, can dislodge it. We entertain the truth not as a guest but as the master of the house. This is a Christian necessity.

Those who feel the vital power of the gospel and know the might of the Holy Spirit as He opens, applies, and seals the Lord's Word would sooner be ripped to pieces than torn from the gospel of their salvation. There are a thousand mercies wrapped in the assurance that the truth will be with us forever. Truth will be our living support, our dying comfort, our rising song, and our eternal glory. This, then, is also the Christian privilege, and without it faith is of little value.

Although this divine truth is sweet food for babies it is, in the highest sense, strong meat for the mature. The truth that we are sinners is painfully with us, to humble us and keep us watchful. Yet the more blessed truth that whoever believes in Jesus shall be saved (John 3:16) is with us as our hope and joy.

Experience does not loosen our hold on the doctrines of grace, but it knits us more firmly to it. Our reasons and motives for believing are now stronger and more numerous than ever, and we have every reason to expect it will be so until in death we clasp the Savior in our arms.

Wherever this abiding love of truth can be discovered, we are bound to exercise our love. No narrow circle can contain our gracious sympathies. The communion of our hearts must be as wide as the election of grace. But above all let us love and spread the truth ourselves.

NOT LUCK

"She gleaned in the field and after the reapers, and she happened to come to the part of the field belonging to Boaz, who was of the family of Elimelech." —Ruth 2:3

It seemed accidental, for she only happened to come, but for believers there are no accidents.

Ruth had gone to work in the fields, and the providence of God was guiding her every step. She had no idea that in the barley fields she would find a husband and that he would make her the joint owner of those broad acres. But more than that, Ruth, a poor foreigner, was to become a progenitor of the Messiah.

God is good to those who trust Him. He often surprises them with unexpected blessings. Little do they know what may happen to them tomorrow, but this sweet fact comforts them: "No good thing will He withhold from those who walk uprightly" (Psalm 84:11).

Luck is banished from the faith of Christians who see the hand of God in everything. The trivial events of today and tomorrow may involve consequences of the highest importance. Oh lord, deal as graciously with us as You did with Ruth.

How blessed it would be if, in wandering in the field of meditation tonight, our next Kinsman would reveal Himself to us. Oh Spirit of God, guide us to Him. We would sooner glean in His field than own the entire harvest of another. Oh for the footsteps of His flock that will lead us to the green pastures where He dwells.

This is a weary world while Jesus is away. We could do better without the sun and moon than without Him. But how divinely fair all things become in the glory of His presence! Our souls know the virtue that dwells in Jesus, and we can never be content without Him.

We will wait in prayer tonight, until on a part of the field belonging to Jesus He manifests Himself to us.

INDEBTEDNESS

*"You looked for much, but . . . it came to little; and
. . . I blew it away. Why?" says the Lord of hosts.
"Because of My house that is in ruins, while every-
one of you runs to his own house."* —Haggai 1:9

The miserly limit their contributions to the ministry and to missions and call the savings good
economy. Little do they realize they are impover-
ishing themselves. Their excuse is that they must care
for their families, but they forget that to neglect the
house of God is a sure way of bringing ruin on their
homes.

Our God can prosper our endeavors beyond our
expectations, or He can defeat our plans to our confusion and dismay. He can steer our vessels into a profitable channel, or run them aground in poverty and
bankruptcy.

From much observation I have noticed that the most
generous Christians are the happiest and invariably the
most prosperous. I have seen the liberal giver rise to
undreamed-of wealth, and I have as often seen the
ungenerous descend to poverty by the very stinginess
they thought would make them wealthy.

People trust good stewards with larger and larger
sums, and so it is with the Lord. He gives by the car-
loads to those who give by the bushels. When wealth
is not bestowed, the Lord makes the little multiply
through the contentment that a sanctified heart feels
in proportion to the tithe that has been dedicated to
the Lord.

Selfishness looks first at home, but godliness "seeks
first the kingdom of God and His righteousness" (Matthew 6:33). In the long run selfishness is loss and godliness is great gain (1 Timothy 6:6).

It takes faith to act towards God with such an open
hand, though surely He deserves it. Furthermore, all
that we do is only a poor acknowledgment of our
amazing indebtedness to His goodness.

GIVING

"All the rivers run into the sea, yet the sea is not full; to the place from which the rivers come, there they return again."

—Ecclesiastes 1:7

Everything earthly is on the move. Time knows no rest. The solid earth is a rolling ball, and the great sun a star obediently fulfilling its course around some greater luminary. Tides move the sea, winds stir the ocean, and friction wears away the rock. Change and death rule everywhere. The sea is not a miser's storehouse for the wealth of waters, for as by one force waters flow into the ocean, by another they are lifted from it. We are born to die, and everything is hurry, worry, and stress.

Friend of the unchanging Jesus, what a joy to reflect on our changeless heritage. Our sea of heavenly joy will be forever full because God will pour eternal rivers of pleasure into it. We expectantly seek a city beyond the skies, and we will not be disappointed.

This passage may well teach us gratitude. Father Ocean is a great receiver, but he is also a generous distributor. What the rivers bring him, he returns to the earth in the form of clouds and rain. When we take all and give nothing in return we are out of step with the universe. Giving is but sowing seed for ourselves.

If you are a good steward, willing to use your substance for the Lord, you will be entrusted with more. Friend of Jesus, are you giving to Him according to the benefit received? Much has been given to you. Where is your fruit? Have you done all? Could you do more?

To be selfish is to be wicked. If the ocean gave up none of its watery treasure, it would bring ruin to the world. God forbid that any of us should follow the ungenerous and destructive policy of living for self.

Jesus lived for others and "in him all the fullness should dwell" (Colossians 1:19). Oh for Jesus' spirit, that we not live for self.

OCTOBER 26, EVENING

FAITHFUL SAYINGS

"This is a faithful saying."

—2 Timothy 2:11

Paul has four faithful sayings. The first is found in 1 Timothy 1:15: "This is a faithful saying and worthy of all acceptance, that Christ Jesus came into the world to save sinners."

The next is in 1 Timothy 4:9: "Godliness is profitable for all things, having promise of the life that now is and of that which is to come. This is a faithful saying and worthy of all acceptance."

The third is in 2 Timothy 2:11–12: "This is a faithful saying: if we endure we shall also reign with Him."

The fourth is in Titus 3:8, "This is a faithful saying . . . that those who have believed in God should be careful to maintain good works."

There is a connection between these faithful sayings. The first one lays the foundation of our eternal salvation in the free grace of God as shown in the mission of the Redeemer. The next affirms the double blessing we obtain through this salvation, the blessings of time and eternity. The third shows one of the duties of the chosen people. We are called to endure for Christ, with the promise that "if we endure we shall also reign with Him" (2 Timothy 2:12). The last sets the active form of Christian service, urging us diligently to maintain good works.

Thus we have the root of salvation in free grace. Next, the privileges of that salvation, in the life which now is and which is to come. We also have the two great branches of enduring and serving with Christ. Both branches are loaded with the fruit of the Spirit.

Treasure these faithful sayings. Let them be the guides for your life, your comfort and your instruction. The apostle of the Gentiles proved these sayings to be faithful, and they are faithful today.

Let us accept them and prove their faithfulness.

INDWELLING SIN

"But we are like an unclean thing."

—Isaiah 64:6

Believers are "a chosen generation, a royal priesthood, a holy nation" (1 Peter 2:9). The Spirit of God is in us, and we are far removed from the natural man. But despite all that, we are still sinners from the imperfection of our nature, and we will continue as sinners to the end of this earthly life.

The black fingers of sin leave soot on our cleanest robes. Sin mars our repentance before the Potter has finished with us on the wheel. Selfishness defiles our tears; unbelief tampers with our faith. The best thing we ever did, apart from the merit of Jesus, only swells the number of our sins; for when we have been most pure in our own sight, we were not pure in God's sight. If He charges His angels with error (Job 4:18), how much more must He charge us, even when we are in the most angelic frame of mind.

The song that thrills to heaven and seeks to emulate seraphic strains has human discord in it. The prayer that moves the arm of God is still a bruised and battered prayer. God's arm moves only because the sinless One, our Mediator, has stepped in to take the sin of our supplication.

The purest degree of sanctification a Christian ever attained on earth has so much dross that it is only worthy of the flames. Every night when we look in the mirror we see a sinner. We need to confess, "We are all like an unclean thing. And all our righteousnesses are like filthy rags" (Isaiah 64:6).

Oh how precious the blood of Christ to such hearts as ours! How priceless a gift is His perfect righteousness! How bright the hope of perfect holiness hereafter! Even now, though sin dwells in us, sin has no dominion. We are in bitter conflict with sin, but it is a vanquished foe.

Just a little while and we will enter victoriously into the city where nothing defiles.

OCTOBER 27, EVENING

CHOSEN

"I chose you out of the world."

—John 15:19

Here is distinguishing grace and discriminating consideration. Some people become the special object of divine affection. Do not be afraid to dwell on this high doctrine of election. When you are depressed, you will find it to be a bottle of the richest cordial.

Those who doubt the doctrines of grace miss the richest clusters of grapes. They lose "a feast of choice pieces, a feast of wines on the lees, of fat things full of marrow, of well refined wines on the lees" (Isaiah 25:6). There is no balm in Gilead comparable to it. If the honey in Jonathan's wood enlightened the eyes (1 Samuel 14:26), this is honey that will enlighten your heart to love and learn the mysteries of the kingdom of God. Eat it abundantly. Live on this choice food. Enlarge your mind to comprehend more and more of the eternal, everlasting, and discriminating love of God.

When you have climbed the high mountain of election, linger on its sister mountain, the covenant of grace. Covenant engagements are the ammunition of the massive rock behind which we lie entrenched. Covenant engagements, with the bond of Christ Jesus, are the quiet resting places of trembling spirits:

His oath, His covenant, His blood,
    Support me in the raging flood;
When every earthly prop gives way,
    This still is all my strength and stay.

If Jesus undertook to bring me to glory, if the Father promised that He would give me to the Son as part of the infinite reward for the work of His soul, then, my soul, until God Himself shall be unfaithful, until Jesus shall cease to be the truth, you are safe.

When David danced before the ark, he told Michal that election made him do so (2 Samuel 6:21). Come, my soul, rejoice before the God of grace and leap for joy.

OCTOBER 28, MORNING

PRECIOUS LORD

"His head is like the finest gold; His locks are wavy and black as a raven."

—Song of Solomon 5:11

Comparisons fail in attempting to describe the Lord Jesus, but the spouse in our text tries to the best of her ability.

The head of Jesus refers to His deity. "The head of Christ is God" (1 Corinthians 11:3). Thus the ingot of purest gold is the best conceivable metaphor to describe one so precious, so pure, so dear, and so glorious. Jesus is not a grain of gold but a vast globe of it, a priceless treasure that earth and heaven cannot excel.

The creatures are mere iron and clay; they will all perish like wood, hay, and straw. But the ever-living Head of the creation will shine forever and ever. In Christ there is no mixture, not even the smallest taint of alloy. He is forever infinitely holy and totally divine.

The bushy locks depict his manly vigor. There is nothing effeminate in our Beloved. He is the manliest of men, bold as a lion, laborious as an ox, swift as an eagle. Every conceivable and inconceivable beauty is found in Him even though "He is despised and rejected by men" (Isaiah 53:3).

The glory of His head is not cut away. He is eternally crowned with peerless majesty. The black hair indicates youthful freshness, "You have the dew of Your youth" (Psalm 110:3). Others grow weak, but "He is a priest forever according to the order of Melchizedek" (Psalm 110:4).

Others come and go, but he abides as God on His throne, world without end. We will behold Him tonight and adore Him. Angels are gazing on Him, and His redeemed must not turn their eyes from Him. Where else is there such a Beloved?

Oh for an hour's fellowship with Him! Be gone intruding cares! Jesus calls me and I run after Him.

OCTOBER 28, EVENING

THE DISCIPLES' PRAYER

"In this manner, therefore pray: Our Father in heaven,"

—Matthew 6:9

This prayer begins where all true prayers must commence, with the spirit of adoption, "Our Father." There is no acceptable prayer until we can say, "I will arise and go to my Father" (Luke 15:18).

This childlike spirit soon perceives the majesty of the Father "in heaven" and ascends to devout adoration, saying, "Hallowed be Your name." The child lisping, "Abba, Father," grows into the cherub crying, "Holy, Holy, Holy."

It is only a step from rapturous worship to the glowing missionary spirit, which is an outgrowth of love and reverent adoration, "Your kingdom come, Your will be done on earth as it is in heaven."

Next comes heartfelt dependence on God, "Give us this day our daily bread." Then, with further illumination from the Spirit, we discover that we are not only dependent, but sinful, and we ask for mercy, "Forgive us our debts as we forgive our debtors."

Being pardoned, having the imputed righteousness of Christ and knowing our acceptance with God, we humbly ask for holy perseverance, "Do not lead us into temptation." The person who is really forgiven is anxious not to sin again.

The possession of justification leads to a keen desire for sanctification. "Forgive us our debts," that is justification. "Do not lead us into temptation, but deliver us from the evil one," that is sanctification. As a result there follows a triumphant ascription of praise, "For Yours is the kingdom and the power and the glory forever. Amen." We rejoice that our King reigns. "To Him be glory and dominion for ever and ever" (Revelation 1:6).

Thus from a sense of adoption to fellowship with our reigning Lord, this short model of prayer conducts the soul. Lord may we pray like this.

OCTOBER 29, MORNING

OPEN OUR EYES, LORD

"But their eyes were restrained, so that they did not know Him."

—Luke 24:16

These disciples should have known Jesus. They had often heard His voice and gazed on His face. It is amazing that they did not recognize Him. Yet it may be the same with us. We may not have seen Jesus lately. We may even be in deep trouble this evening, and although He plainly says, "It is I; do not be afraid" (Matthew 14:27), we do not recognize Him.

Our eyes are veiled. We know His voice. We have looked on His face. We have leaned our head on His breast. Yet though He is near, we say, "Oh, that I knew where I might find Him" (Job 23:3). We should know Jesus, because the Scripture reflects His image. Yet it is possible for us to open the precious book and not see our Savior.

Dear child of God, are you in that condition? Jesus feeds His flock "among the lilies" (Song of Solomon 2:16), and yet you do not see Him. Just as the Father walked with Adam in the garden (Genesis 3:8), Jesus walks through Scripture and fellowships with His people.

How can we be in the garden of Scripture and not see Him? In our case, as in that of the two disciples, it is unbelief. Evidently they did not expect to see Jesus, and therefore they did not know Him. As a general rule in spiritual things, we get what we expect from the Lord. Faith alone lets us see Jesus.

Make this your prayer. "Lord, open my eyes that I may see my Savior." It is a blessed thing to want to see Him, but it is far better to see Him. To those who seek Him He is kind (Luke 6:35), but to those who find Him, He is precious beyond expression.

PRAISES

"I will praise You, O Lord."

—Psalm 9:1

Praise should always follow answered prayer, just as the mist of earth rises when the sun warms the ground.

Has the Lord been merciful and gracious to you (Psalm 103:8)? Has He inclined to you and heard your cry (Psalm 40:1)? Then praise Him. Let the ripe fruit drop on the fertile soil from which it drew life. Sing to Him who has answered your prayer, for "He shall give you the desires of your heart" (Psalm 37:4).

To be silent about God's mercies is ingratitude. It is to act as base as the nine lepers, who after being healed did not give thanks to God (Luke 17:17). To forget to praise God is to refuse a benefit; for praise, like prayer, is one great means of spiritual growth.

Praise helps to remove our burdens, excite our hopes, and increase our faith. Praise is a healthy and invigorating exercise, quickening the pulse and giving added strength for the Master's service.

Blessing God for mercies received also benefits non-believers, who hear it and are glad (Psalm 34:2). Others in similar circumstances will be comforted if we say, "Oh, magnify the Lord with me, and let us exalt His name together" (Psalm 34:3). "The poor man cried out and the Lord heard him and saved him out of all his troubles" (Psalm 34:6).

Weak hearts will be strengthened and tired saints will be revived as they listen to our "songs of deliverance" (Psalm 32:7). Their doubts and fears will vanish as we "teach and admonish one another in psalms and hymns and spiritual songs" (Colossians 3:16). "Yes, they shall sing of the ways of the Lord" (Psalm 138:5), when they hear us magnify His holy name.

Praise is the most heavenly of Christian duties. "The angels, the living creatures and the elders sing with a loud voice, Worthy is the lamb" (Revelation 5:11–12).

OPEN OUR EARS, LORD

*"You who dwell in the gardens, the companions
listen for Your voice—Let me hear it."*

—Song of Solomon 8:13

My sweet Lord Jesus remembers well the garden of Gethsemane. Although He has left that garden, He now dwells in the garden of His church, where He fellowships with those who keep His blessed company. He speaks to His beloved with a voice of love and a depth of melody that is more musical than the harps of heaven and leaves all human music far behind.

Tens of thousands on earth and millions above are indulged with its harmonious accents. Some whom I well know and whom I greatly envy are at this moment listening to that beloved voice. Oh that I were a partaker of their joys! Though some of these are poor, some bedridden, and others near the gates of death, I would gladly starve, grow weak, or die with them if I could only hear Your voice.

Once I heard it often, but I have grieved Your Spirit. Return to me in compassion, and once again say, "I am your salvation" (Psalm 35:3). I am content with no other voice. I know Your voice and cannot be deceived by another. I pray to hear it. I do not know what You will say, nor do I make any condition. Oh my Beloved, speak to me, and if it is a rebuke I will bless You for it.

Clean my dull ears. Let it cost what it may, I will not turn from my one consuming desire to hear Your voice. Pierce my ear (Exodus 21:6). Pierce it with Your harshest notes, only do not let me remain deaf to Your call.

Tonight, Lord, grant Your unworthy servant his desire, because I am Yours. You have bought me with Your blood. You have opened my eyes to see You, and the sight has saved me. Lord, open my ears. I have read Your heart, now let me hear Your lips. Amen.

RENEW STEADFASTNESS

"Renew a steadfast spirit within me."

—Psalm 51:10

A backslider, if there is a spark of life left, will groan after restoration, and in this renewal grace is required the same as at conversion. As repentance and faith were necessary then, it is needed now. Only the same grace that first came can bring a backslider back to Jesus.

No one can be renewed without a manifestation of the Holy Spirit's energy as real and true as was felt at conversion. Flesh and blood are as much in the way now as then.

Let your personal weakness be an argument to make you pray for help. When David felt powerless he did not fold his arms or close his lips. He hastened to the mercy seat, saying "Renew a steadfast spirit within me."

Let the doctrine that you can do nothing drive you with an earnestness to Israel's strong Helper. Oh for grace to plead with God as though you were pleading for your very life, "Lord renew a steadfast spirit within me."

If you sincerely pray for God to do this, you will prove your honesty by using the means of grace through which God works. Be much in prayer. Live much on the Word of God. Kill the lust that has driven your Lord from you. Be careful to watch over the future uprisings of sin.

The Lord has His own appointed ways. Sit by the wayside, and you will be ready when He passes. Continue in the blessed ordinances that foster and nourish your dying graces. Know that all power must proceed from Him. Continually cry, "Renew a steadfast spirit within me."

A FRIEND IN TROUBLE

"I knew you in the wilderness, in the land of great drought."

—Hosea 13:5

Yes, Lord, You knew me in my fallen condition and still You chose me. When I was loathsome and self-abhorrent You received me as Your child and satisfied my needs. May Your name be blessed forever for Your rich and boundless mercy.

Since then, my inward experience has often been a wilderness. But You own me as Your beloved. You poured streams of love and grace into me, to gladden me and to make me fruitful.

When my outward circumstances were at their worst and I wandered in a land of drought, Your presence comforted me. People have forsaken me, but You have known my soul in adversities, because no affliction of mine dims the lustre of Your love.

Most gracious Lord, I magnify You for all Your faithfulness in my difficult circumstances. I deplore it when my exalted heart forgets you. I owe everything to Your gentleness and love. Have mercy on Your servant.

My soul, if Jesus acknowledges you in difficulty, be certain to follow Him and His cause now that you are prosperous. Do not let worldly success lift you up so that you are ashamed of the truth. Follow Jesus into the wilderness: bear the cross with Him when persecution grows hot. He was with you in poverty and shame; never be so treacherous as to be ashamed of Him. Oh for more shame at the thought of being ashamed of my Beloved. Jesus, my soul clings to You:

> I'll turn to Thee in days of light,
>   As well as nights of care,
> Thou brightest amid all that's bright!
>   Thou fairest of the fair!

HOUSE CHURCH

"The church in your house."

—Philemon 2

Is there a church in your house? Are parents, children, friends, or neighbors members of it, or are some still not saved? Take a moment and let the question go around, "Am I a member of the church in this house?"

How your heart would leap for joy and your eyes fill with holy tears if from the oldest to the youngest all were saved. Let us pray for this great mercy until the Lord grants it.

It was probably the cherished object of Philemon's heart that all his household would be saved, but that request was not immediately granted. He had a wicked servant, Onesimus, who, having wronged his master, ran away. Yet Philemon's prayers followed him, and by the grace of God, Onesimus heard Paul preach, and his heart was changed. Onesimus returned to Philemon, to be not only a faithful servant, but also a beloved brother, adding another member to the church in Philemon's house.

Are there unconverted neighbors or children absent this morning? Pray that they will return home and gladden your heart with the good news of what grace has done. Are there any unsaved present in the home? Petition the Father for them.

If there is a church in your house, move in the common affairs of life with deliberate holiness, diligence, kindness, and integrity. More is expected of a church than an ordinary household. Family worship must be more devout and hearty, internal love must be warmer and unbroken, and external conduct must be sanctified and Christlike.

We need not fear that the lack of size will remove us from the list of churches, for the Holy Spirit has enrolled a family church in the inspired book of remembrance.

As a church, let us draw near to the great Head of the one church universal and pray that He will give us grace to shine in this world to the glory of His name.

NOVEMBER 1, MORNING

SAFE

"And did not know until the flood came and took them all away, so also will the coming of the Son of Man be."

—Matthew 24:39

The penalty was universal. None escaped, not the rich or the poor, the educated or the illiterate, the admired or the abhorred, the religious or the profane, the old or the young. All sank in one common ruin. No doubt some ridiculed the patriarch Noah. But where are their merry jokes now? Others probably threatened him for his zeal, which they considered madness. But where are their boastings and hard words now? The critics who judged the old man's work drowned in the same sea that covered their sneering companions.

Even those who spoke well of the good man's convictions but did not share them have sunk to rise no more. And the workers who were paid to help build the wondrous ark are also lost. The flood swept them all away; there were no exceptions.

Final destruction is sure. No rank, possession, or character can save a single soul who has not believed in the Lord Jesus. My soul, look at this wide-spread judgment and tremble. How astonishing was the general apathy. "In the days before the flood they were all eating and drinking, marrying and giving in marriage," until the awful morning dawned (Matthew 24:38). The only wise persons on earth were in the ark. Folly duped the rest of the human race, folly as to self-preservation, the most foolish of all follies, and folly in doubting the true God, the most malignant of foolishness.

Isn't it strange that all neglect their souls until grace gives them a reason to leave their madness and act like rational beings? Blessed be God, all were safe in the ark. From the huge elephant to the tiny mouse, all were safe. The timid rabbit was equally secure with the courageous lion. The helpless prairie dog was as safe as the laborious ox. All are safe in Jesus.

My soul, are you safe in Him?

NOVEMBER 1, EVENING

CHANGELESS

"I am the Lord, I do not change."

—Malachi 3:6

It is well that in the midst of all the variableness of life there is One who does not change, One whose heart never varies. All things have changed and are changing. The sun is aging and "the earth will grow old like a garment" (Isaiah 51:6). The folding up of this worn out tent has commenced. The heavens and the earth will soon grow old and wear out. There is only One who is immortal, only One whose years have no end, only One who never changes.

The joy of a sailor as he steps on the solid shore after being tossed about is the satisfaction of the Christian. In the midst of all the changes of this troubled life, the believer secures the foot of faith on the truth, "I am the Lord, I change not."

The stability that an anchor gives a ship, when it grips the solid rock, is similar to our hope when we grasp our glorious text. With God, "there is no variation or shadow of turning" (James 1:17). Whatever His attributes were, they are the same today. His power, His wisdom, His justice, and His truth are unchanged. He has always been the refuge of His people. He has always been their stronghold in the day of trouble, and He is still their sure helper.

He is unchanged in His love. He loves us with "an everlasting love" (Jeremiah 31:3). He loves us as much as He ever did, and when all earthly things melt in the last conflagration (2 Peter 3:10), His love will still wear the dew of youth. Precious is the assurance that He changes not! The wheel of providence revolves, but its axle is eternal love:

> Death and change are busy ever,
>   Man decays, and ages move;
> But His mercy waneth never;
>   God is wisdom, God is love.

NOVEMBER 2, MORNING

EVIDENCE OF HOLINESS

"Indignation has taken hold of me because of the wicked who forsake Your law."

—Psalm 119:53

Do you feel a holy shudder when others sin? If not, you lack inward holiness. David's cheeks were wet with rivers of water because of prevailing unholiness (Psalm 6:6). Jeremiah desired eyes like fountains of tears to lament the iniquities of Israel (Jeremiah 9:1). Lot was enraged with the conversations of the men of Sodom (Genesis 19:7). Those on whom the saving mark was set in Ezekiel's vision were those who sighed and cried for the abominations of Jerusalem (Ezekiel 1:1).

It can only grieve gracious souls when they see what pains people take to go to hell. Christians know the evil of sin, and they are alarmed to see others flying like moths into the blaze. Sin makes the righteous shudder because it violates a holy law that is in our highest interest to keep, for sin pulls down the pillars of nations.

Sin in others horrifies us because it reminds us of our own baseness. When we see a transgressor, we cry along with the saint mentioned by Bernard, "He fell today, and I may fall tomorrow." Sin to us is horrible because it crucified our Savior. In every iniquity, we see the nails and the spear. How can a saved soul behold sin without abhorrence?

It is an awful thing to insult God. The good God deserves better treatment. The great God claims it. The just God will have it, or He will repay His adversary. An awakened heart trembles at the audacity of sin and stands alarmed at the contemplation of its punishment. How monstrous a thing is rebellion. How terrible a doom is prepared for the ungodly.

My soul, never laugh at sin's folly, lest you eventually smile at sin. Sin is your enemy. Sin is your Lord's enemy. Detest it. This is the evidence that you possess holiness.

NOVEMBER 2, EVENING

ACCEPTED PRAYER

"Behold, he is praying."

—Acts 9:11

Prayers are instantly noticed in heaven. The moment Saul began to pray the Lord heard him. Here is comfort for the distressed but praying saint.

Often when the broken-hearted kneel to pray, all they can do is sigh and sob through tears. Yet those sighs make the harps of heaven thrill with music. And the tears? The tears are caught and treasured by God. "You put my tears into Your bottle" (Psalm 56:8) implies that they are caught as they flow.

Beseeching one, even when fear holds back your words, you will be understood by the Most High. You need only look up with moist eyes, for "I have heard your prayer, I have seen your tears" (Isaiah 38:5). Tears are the diamonds of heaven, and sighs are in the music of Jehovah's court. Your prayer, no matter how weak or trembling, will be answered. Our God loves to hear your prayer: "He does not forget the cry of the afflicted" (Psalm 9:12).

True, the Lord "will bring down haughty looks" (Psalm 18:27), and "everyone who exalts himself will be humbled" (Luke 18:14). God does not care for the pomp and pageantry of kings. "Your pomp is brought down to Sheol" (Isaiah 14:11). Nor does God regard the swell of military music from the pride of man. But wherever there is a sorrowful heart, or a lip quivering, or a deep groan, or a guilty sigh, to that person Jehovah's heart is open.

He registers our prayers in His memory. He puts them, like rose petals, between the pages of His book of remembrance; and when the volume is opened, a precious fragrance will arise:

> Faith asks no signal from the skies,
> To show that prayers accepted rise,
> Our priest is in His holy place,
> And answers from the throne of grace.

TRUE PRAYER, TRUE POWER

"Their prayer came up to His holy dwelling place, to heaven."

—2 Chronicles 30:27

Prayer brings God's unfailing support to the Christian in any situation and circumstance. When you cannot use your sword, take the weapon of all-prayer (Ephesians 6:18). Your powder may be damp, your bow string may be loose, but the weapon of all-prayer is always ready. Swords and guns need refurbishing, but prayer never rusts. When we feel that our prayers are dull, it is then that they cut the best.

Prayer is an open door that no one can shut. Devils may surround you, but the way upward is always open. As long as the upward road is unobstructed, you will never fall into the enemy's hands. You can never be taken by blockade, attack, violence, or storm as long as heaven's relief is free to come down in time of need.

Prayer is never out of season. In summer or winter, its merchandise is precious. Prayer gains an audience with heaven in the dead of night, in the midst of business, in the heat of the day, or in the shadows of evening. In poverty, in sickness, in obscurity, in slander, in doubt, and in every other condition, our covenant God will welcome our prayers and answer from His holy place.

Prayer is never futile but powerful. You may not always get what you ask for, but you will always have your need supplied. When God does not answer according to the letter, He does so according to the Spirit. If you ask for coarse grain, will you be angry because He gives fine flour? If you seek physical health, will you complain if He makes sickness the method of healing your spiritual disease? Is it not better to have the cross sanctified instead of removed?

This evening, offer Him your petition and request. The Lord is ready to give you the desires of your heart (Psalm 37:4).

NOVEMBER 3, EVENING

COURAGE IN WEAKNESS

"My strength is made perfect in weakness."

—2 Corinthians 12:9

A qualification for serving God with any degree of success, for doing God's work well and triumphantly, is a sense of our weaknesses.

When God's warriors enter the battle confident of their own strength, when they boast about conquering and obtaining victory, their defeat is certain. God does not go with believers who march under their own power. Those who count on their own victory have calculated incorrectly, for it is "not by might nor by power, but by My Spirit says the Lord of hosts" (Zechariah 4:6). Those who go to battle in their own power will return with their banners trailing in the dust and their armor stained with disgrace.

We must serve God in His strength and in His way, or He will not accept our service. What we do on our own, unaided by divine strength, is not from God. The fruits of this earth He throws away. He reaps corn only when the seed was sown from heaven, watered with grace, and ripened by the sun of divine love.

God will take all that you have before He fills you. He will empty your storehouse before He fills it with the finest of wheat. The river of God is full of water, but not a drop flows from earthly springs. The only strength used in God's battles is the strength He alone imparts.

Are you mourning over your weakness? Take courage! You must be conscious of weakness before the Lord gives you the victory. Your emptiness is the preparation for being filled with God's strength. Being cast down is the making ready for your lifting up:

> When I am weak then am I strong.
> Grace is my shield and Christ is my song.

IN HIS LIGHT

"In Your light we see light."

—Psalm 36:9

Christ's love for unbelievers cannot be fully expressed until Jesus speaks to their hearts. All descriptions of it fall flat and are uninteresting unless the Holy Spirit gives them life and power. Until Immanuel reveals Himself, sinners cannot see Him.

If you wanted to see the sun, would you put on your house lights and say, "Here is the light of the day?" Of course not! The sun must reveal itself in its own blaze. It is the same with Christ. "Blessed are you, Simon Bar-Jonah," said He to Peter, "for flesh and blood has not revealed this to you but My Father who is in heaven" (Matthew 16:17).

Improve human nature by any education process, elevate mental faculties to the highest degree, and still none of these can reveal Christ.

The Spirit of God must come with power. Then in that mystic holy of holies the Lord Jesus will reveal Himself to the sanctified eye, but not to the near-sighted world. Christ must be His own mirror. This weak-sighted world can see nothing of the sacred glories of Immanuel. He stands before it without form or beauty, a root out of dry ground, rejected and despised (Isaiah 53:2,3).

Only when the Spirit has touched the eye with salve, quickened the heart with divine life, and educated the soul to a heavenly taste, only then is He understood. "To you who believe He is precious, He has become the chief cornerstone" (1 Peter 2:7). But to others "He has become a stumbling stone and rock of offense" (Romans 9:33).

Oh Jesus, our Lord, our heart is open. Show Yourself to us now. Grant us a glimpse of Your all-conquering charm. Amen.

OUR HERITAGE

"No weapon formed against you shall prosper."

—Isaiah 54:17

This day is notable in English history for two reasons. The papal plot to destroy the House of Parliament was discovered in 1605:

> While for our princes they prepare
> In caverns deep a burning snare,
> He shot from heaven a piercing ray,
> And the dark treachery brought to day.

And today is also the anniversary of King William III's landing at Torbay, which resulted in religious liberty being secured in 1688. Our Puritan forefathers made this a special time of thanksgiving, and there is a museum copy of the sermon Matthew Henry preached on this day.

Our Christian feeling and our love of liberty should make us regard this anniversary with holy gratitude. Let our hearts and voices proclaim, "You are great and do wondrous things; You alone are God" (Psalm 86:10).

You have made England a home for the gospel, and when enemies have risen, You have shielded her. Help us to offer songs for repeated deliverance. "Sing to Him, sing psalms to Him; talk of all His wondrous works" (1 Chronicles 16:9). We believe the promise, "No weapon formed against you shall prosper."

Today, every lover of the gospel of Jesus Christ should plead for overturning false doctrines and extending divine truth. It would be well for us to search our hearts and throw out any false doctrine concealed there.

HIGH THOUGHTS

"Be thankful to Him and bless His name."

—Psalm 100:4

Jesus is not content for His children to think poorly of Him. Our Lord wants all His people to be rich in high and happy thoughts concerning Him. He desires that His chosen ones should delight in Him.

We should not consider Him a bare necessity, like bread and water, but a delicacy that is a ravishing delight. He has revealed Himself as the pearl of great price (Matthew 13:46), as a fragrant "bundle of myrrh" (Song of Solomon 1:13), as the "rose of Sharon" with lasting perfume, and as the "lily" in its purity (Song of Solomon 2:1).

To think high thoughts of Christ, remember how they esteem Him beyond the skies. God regards His only Begotten as "His indescribable gift" (2 Corinthians 9:15). The angels think of Him as the worthy Lamb (Revelation 5:12). Consider also what the blood-washed think of Him as they sing, "Amen! Blessing and glory and wisdom. Thanksgiving and honor and power and might" (Revelation 7:12).

High thoughts of Christ will help us act more consistently toward Him. The more loftily we see Christ enthroned, the more lowly we bow before the throne.

Our Lord wants us to think well of Him so that we may submit cheerfully to His authority. High thoughts of Him increase our love. Love and esteem go together: therefore, think about your Master's excellence. Meditate on His glory before He took on our nature. Think of the mighty love that drew Him from His throne to the cross. Admire Him because He conquered all the powers of hell. See Him risen, crowned, and glorified! Bow before Him as the Wonderful Counselor, Mighty God, Everlasting Father, Prince of Peace" (Isaiah 9:6).

These thoughts will make your love for Him complete.

DRENCHING RAIN

"I will pour water on him who is thirsty."

—Isaiah 44:3

When believers become depressed, they often chastise themselves with dark and fearful thoughts, but this action only increases depression. It is as well to expect a chained eagle to fly as to expect fear to increase grace.

It is not the law, but the gospel that saves the seeking soul. It is not legal bondage, but gospel liberty that restores the depressed believer. It is not slavish fear, but the sweet calling of Jesus' love that returns the backslider to God.

Have you lost the joy of Christianity? Is your prayer, "Restore to me the joy of Your salvation and uphold me by Your generous Spirit" (Psalm 51:12)? Are you barren like dry ground? Are you fruitless? Do you fall short in usefulness for Jesus Christ?

Then here is the promise you need, "I will pour water on him who is thirsty." You will receive from God the required grace and have it to the full. As water refreshes the thirsty, you will be refreshed. Your desires will be satisfied.

Water activates dry vegetable life, and your life will be revived by fresh grace. Water swells the buds and makes the fruit ripen. You will have fruit-bearing grace in the ways of God.

All the good qualities and riches of divine grace you will enjoy in abundance. You will be drenched, your meadows will be flooded, and your fields will be turned into pools. Your thirsty land will be springs of living water: "I will pour water on him who is thirsty."

POWER IN THE BLOOD

"This is the blood of the covenant which God has commanded you."

—Hebrews 9:20

There is a strange power about blood. The sight of it always has an effect. A kind heart cannot bear to see a sparrow bleed. Unless we are used to it, we turn away with horror at the slaughter of an animal.

As for human blood, it is consecrated. It is murder to shed blood in anger, and it is a dreadful crime to squander it in war. I believe this is because blood is life, and its shedding is death.

When we think of the blood of the Son of God, our reverence is increased. We shudder to think of the guilt of sin and the terrible penalty the Sinbearer endured. Blood, always precious, is priceless when it flows from Immanuel's side.

The blood of Jesus seals the covenant of grace and makes it forever sure. Covenants of old were made by sacrifices, and the everlasting covenant was ratified the same way. What a delight to be saved on the sure foundation of divine engagements that cannot be dishonored! Salvation by works of the law is a broken vessel, while the everlasting covenant vessel fears no storms because the blood of Jesus ensures it.

The blood of Jesus made His testament forever valid. Wills are of no power until the testator dies. In this light the soldier's spear is a blessed aid, because it proved our Lord to be really dead. Thus we may boldly appropriate the legacies He has left for His people. Happy are we who see our title to heavenly blessings assured by a dying Savior.

Does His blood still have a voice? Does it call us to sanctify ourselves to Him by whom we have been redeemed? Does it call us to newness of life? Does it incite us to entire consecration to the Lord?

Oh that the power of Your blood might be known and felt in me this night. Amen.

NOVEMBER 6, EVENING

INSCRIBED

"See, I have inscribed you on the palms of My hands."

—Isaiah 49:16

Part of the wonder of this text is in the word *see*. Verse fourteen of this same chapter reads, "The Lord has forsaken me, and my Lord has forgotten me." How amazed the divine mind seems to be at such wicked unbelief! What could be more astounding than the unfounded doubts and fears of God's favored people?

The Lord's loving words of rebuke should make us blush. He cries, "How could I forget you when I have inscribed you on the palms of my hands? How dare you doubt My vigilance when your very name is written on My flesh?"

Oh unbelief, how strange you are! We do not know if the greater wonder is the faithfulness of God or His people's unbelief. He keeps His promise a thousand times, and yet at the next trial, we doubt Him. He never fails. He is never a dry well, never a setting sun, a passing meteor, or a melting vapor. Yet we continually worry with anxieties, and are molested with suspicions and disturbed with fears as if our God were a desert mirage.

See is a word to excite admiration. Here indeed is a theme to astonish. Rebels obtain such closeness to the heart of infinite love so as to be written on the palms of His hands.

"I have inscribed you." It does not say I have inscribed your name, but your name is there because you are. See the fullness: "I have inscribed your person, your image, your case, your circumstances, your sins, your temptations, your weaknesses, your needs, your works. I have inscribed everything about you. Everything that concerns you I have put on the palms of My hands."

Don't ever say that God has forsaken you, for He has inscribed you on His own palms.

WITNESSES

"You shall be witnesses to Me."

—Acts 1:8

To learn how to fulfill your duties as a witness for Christ, look at His example. He is always witnessing; by the well of Samaria, in the temple at Jerusalem, by the lake of Gennesaret, or on the mountain's brow. He is witnessing night and day. His mighty prayers are as vocal to God as His daily services.

He witnesses under all circumstances. Scribes and Pharisees cannot shut His mouth. Even before Pilate He gives a good confession (John 18:38). Jesus witnesses so clearly and distinctly that there is no mistaking Him.

Christian, make your life a clear testimony. Be like a clear brook, where every stone is seen at the bottom. Be not like a muddy creek; be clear and transparent. Let your love of God and humanity be visible to all.

Don't merely say "I am true." Be true. Don't boast of integrity. Be upright. Let the world see your testimony. Never, for fear of feeble man, restrain your witness. Your lips have been warmed with a coal from off the altar, so speak with heaven touched lips (Isaiah 6:6). "In the morning sow your seed, and in the evening do not withhold your hand" (Ecclesiastes 11:6). Don't watch the clouds, don't consult the wind. In season or out witness for the Savior.

And if for Christ's sake and the gospel's you endure suffering, rejoice that the honor was conferred on you. "Count it all joy when you fall into various trials" (James 1:2). Your suffering, your losses, and your persecutions will be a platform from which you will witness with more vigor and greater power for Jesus Christ.

Study your great Example. Be filled with the Spirit (Ephesians 5:18). Remember you need much teaching, much upholding, much grace, and much humility if your witnessing is to be for your Master's glory.

NOVEMBER 7, EVENING

RECEIVING CHRIST

"As you therefore have received Christ."

—Colossians 2:6

The life of faith is represented as one of receiving, an act implying the very opposite of anything like merit. It is simply accepting a gift. As the earth drinks rain, as the sea receives streams, as night accepts light from the stars, so we, giving nothing, partake freely of the grace of God. The saints are not wells or streams, but empty tanks into which the living water of God's salvation flows.

Consider what the very idea of receiving implies. One cannot receive a shadow, but only that which is substantial. So it is in the life of faith: Christ becomes real. Without faith, Jesus is only the name of a person who lived a long time ago. By faith, however, Jesus becomes real in the consciousness of our hearts.

Receiving also means grasping or getting possession. The thing I receive becomes my own. I appropriate that which is given. When I receive Jesus, He becomes my Savior to the point that neither life nor death can rob me of Him. All this happens when I receive Christ and take Him as God's free gift.

Salvation may be described as the blind receiving sight, the deaf receiving hearing, and the dead receiving life. We have received not only these blessings, but we have received Christ Jesus Himself. It is true that He gave us life from the dead, pardoned our sin, and imputed righteousness. These are all precious, but we are not content with them alone. We have received Christ Himself. The Son of God has been poured into us, and we have received and appropriated Him.

What a heartful Jesus must be, for heaven itself cannot contain Him!

A BLESSED GUEST

"The Teacher says, 'Where is the guest room in which I may eat the Passover with My disciples?'"

—Mark 14:14

Jerusalem at passover time was like a large hotel. Every home-owner invited friends, but no one invited the Savior. Since He had no dwelling of His own, it was by His own supernatural power that He found an upper room in which to keep the feast.

Even to this day Jesus is not received except by His supernatural power and grace. All doors are open to the prince of darkness. But Jesus must find a place to lodge, or else stay in the streets.

It was through Christ's mysterious power that the owner of the upper room opened his guest chamber to Jesus. Who this person was we do not know, but still he offered this room to the Redeemer.

This is how we know who are the Lord's chosen and who are not. When the gospel comes to some people, they fight it off. But when it is received and welcomed, this indicates that a secret work occurred in the soul, and that God has chosen them for eternal life.

My dear reader, are you willing to receive Christ? Then there is no difficulty; Christ will be your guest. His own power is working in you to make you willing. What an honor to entertain the Son of God! The heaven of heavens cannot contain Him, and yet He condescends to find a home in our hearts!

We are not worthy that He should come under our roof, but what an unutterable privilege when he condescends to enter. He makes a feast, and we feast with Him on royal food. We sit at a banquet where the food is immortal and gives eternal life to those who eat it.

Blessed among the children of Adam are those who entertain the angels' Lord.

NOVEMBER 8, EVENING

WALKING

"So walk in Him."

—Colossians 2:6

If we have received Christ in our hearts, the new life we have will manifest itself in a walk of faith with Him.

Walking is action. Our religion is not to be confined to the prayer closet. We must put into practice what we believe. If we walk in Christ, then we act as Christ would act. Christ is our hope, our love, our joy, and our life. We are to be the image of Jesus to a world that will say, "You are like your Master; you live like Jesus Christ."

Walking indicates progress. "So walk in Him." Proceed from grace to grace. Go forward until you reach the uttermost degree of knowledge concerning your Beloved.

To walk is a sign of continuance. There must be a perpetual abiding in Christ. Many Christians have fellowship with Jesus in the morning and evening but give their hearts to the world all day. This is poor living. We should always walk with Him, following His steps and doing His will.

Walking implies habit. When we speak of our walk, we mean our habits, the tenor of our lives. If we sometimes enjoy Christ, sometimes call Him ours, but then disown Him, that may be a habit, but it is not walking with Him. We must have a habit of keeping close to Him, clinging to Him, never letting Him go, "for in Him we live and move and have our being" (Acts 17:28). "As you therefore have received Christ Jesus the Lord, so walk in Him." Hold fast to Him.

Jesus Christ is the trust of your faith, the source of your life, the principles of your actions, and the joy of your spirit. Let Him be this until life's end, when you will enter into the joy and rest of heaven.

Oh Holy Spirit, enable us to obey this heavenly instruction.

NEVER DOUBT HIM

"He will dwell on high. His place of defense will be the fortress of rocks: bread will be given him, his water will be sure."

—Isaiah 33:16

Do you ever doubt that God will fulfill His promises? Will the fortress of rocks be carried away by a storm? Will the storehouses of heaven fail? When your heavenly Father knows you have need of food and clothing, do you think He will forget you? There is not a sparrow "that falls to the ground apart from your Father's will" (Matthew 10:29). "The very hairs of your head are all numbered" (Matthew 10:30), so trust and never doubt Him.

Perhaps your afflictions will continue until you trust God. There are many who have been tried and plagued until desperation has driven them to exercise faith in God, and with that faith has come instant deliverance. They have seen God keep His promises.

Oh, I pray, doubt Him no longer! Do not please Satan by indulging any more hard thoughts of God. It is not a laughing matter to doubt Jehovah. It is sin, and not a little sin but the highest degree of crime. The angels never doubt Him, nor the devils either. We alone, out of all the beings God has fashioned, dishonor Him by unbelief and tarnish His honor by mistrust. Shame on us. Our God does not deserve to be suspect.

We have proved Him true and faithful to His Word in our pasts. There are many instances of His love and kindness that we have received. And are still receiving, so doubt is inexcusable. From this moment on, wage constant war against doubts about God, for they are enemies to our peace and to His honor.

Go forward with an unstaggering faith. "Be fully convinced that what He had promised He is also able to perform" (Romans 4:21). "Lord I believe, help my unbelief" (Mark 9:24).

NOVEMBER 9, EVENING

AT HOME

"The eternal God is your refuge."

—Deuteronomy 33:27

The word *refuge* may be translated *mansion* or *abiding place*. Thus the thought that God is our abode or home. Fullness and pleasure encompass this metaphor. Our earthly home, whether it is the humblest cottage or the barest attic, is precious to us. But dearer by far is our blessed God, "for in Him we live and move and have our being" (Acts 17:28).

At home we feel safe. We shut out the world and dwell securely. So too when we are with God, we "fear no evil" (Psalm 23:4). He is our shelter and retreat (Psalm 61:3), our abiding refuge (Psalm 62:8).

At home we rest. We find sleep after the fatigue and toil of the day. Our hearts also find rest in God when, wearied with life's conflicts, we turn to Him, and so our souls dwell peacefully.

At home we let our hearts loose, for we are not afraid of being misunderstood or misconstrued. When we are with God, we can also commune freely with Him, laying open our hidden desires. "The secret of the Lord is with those who fear Him" (Psalm 25:14).

Home is the place of our truest and purest happiness. It is also for our homes that we work and labor. This gives us strength to bear daily burdens, and quicken the fingers to perform our tasks.

In all of this, we may say that God is our home. It is in God that our hearts find their deepest delight. We have joy in Him that far surpasses all other joy. Love to Him strengthens us. As we think of Him in the person of His dear Son, glimpsing the suffering face of the Redeemer, we feel that we must work, for there are many yet to be brought home.

Happy are those who have the God of Jacob for their refuge (Psalm 146:5)!

NO FRIENDSHIP WITH THE WORLD

"It is enough for a disciple that he be like his teacher."

—Matthew 10:25

No one disputes this statement, for it could not be that a servant is above his Master.

When our Lord was on earth, what kind of treatment did He receive? Were His claims acknowledged, His instructions followed, and His perfection worshiped by those He came to bless? No, He was despised and rejected (Isaiah 53:3). His place was outside the camp, and cross bearing was His occupation.

Did the world offer Him comfort and rest? No, for "foxes have holes and birds of the air have nests, but the Son of Man has nowhere to lay His head" (Matthew 8:20). This inhospitable country offered Him no shelter. It cast Him out and crucified Him.

If you follow Jesus, maintaining a consistent, Christlike walk and conversation, you must expect similar treatment. The world will despise you. Don't imagine that the world will admire you, or that the more holy and Christlike you are, the more peaceably people will act toward you. If they did not prize the polished gem, how will they value the uncut jewel? "If they have called the master of the house Beelzebub, how much more will they call those of his household" (Matthew 10:25).

If we were more like Christ, we would be more hated by His enemies. It is a dishonor for a child of God to be a favorite of the world (James 4:4). It is terrible to hear the wicked world applaud and shout "Well done" to a believer.

Let us be true to our Master, and have no friendship with a blind and evil world that scorns and rejects our Savior. Far be it from us to seek a crown of honor when our Lord found a crown of thorns.

NOVEMBER 10, EVENING

LEANING ON THE EVERLASTING ARMS

"Underneath are the everlasting arms."

—Deuteronomy 33:27

God, the eternal God, is our support at all times, especially when we are sinking into deep trouble. There are seasons when we sink quite low, perhaps under a deep sense of sin. We are humbled before God and we scarcely know how to pray, because we feel worthless.

Dear child of God, even when you are at your lowest, "underneath are the everlasting arms." Sin may drag you ever so low, to the depths, but even to the uttermost Jesus saves (Hebrews 7:25).

You may sink into trials in which every earthly support is cut away. Still, "underneath are the everlasting arms." Regardless of the degree of affliction, the covenant grace of an ever-faithful God will encircle you. You may sink into fierce conflict within, but you are never beyond the reach of the "everlasting arms." While they hold you, all of Satan's efforts will not avail. This assurance of support is a comfort to any weary, but dedicated worker in God's service. Implied in our text is a promise of strength for each day, grace for each need, and power for each duty.

Furthermore, even at death this promise is valid. When we stand in the middle of Jordan, we will be able to say with David, "I will fear no evil; for You are with me" (Psalm 23:4). We will descend to the grave, but no lower, because the "everlasting arms" prevent our falling further. Throughout life and at its close, we will be upheld by the "everlasting arms," which never lose their strength.

"Have you not known? Have you not heard? The everlasting God, the Lord, The Creator of the ends of the earth, neither faints nor is weary" (Isaiah 40:28).

CIRCUMSTANCES

"He will choose our inheritance for us."

—Psalm 47:4

Believer, if your inheritance is small, be satisfied. Rest assured that this is best. Unerring wisdom ordained your lot and selected the safest and best condition.

A large ship being brought up the river must navigate around sandbars. If someone asked the captain, "Why do you steer through the deep part of the channel and not head directly for the dock?" his answer would be, "I could not get my vessel to the harbor if I did not keep to the deep channel." It is the same with us. We would run aground and suffer shipwreck if our divine Captain did not steer us into the depths of affliction, where waves of trouble follow each other in quick succession.

Some plants die with too much sunshine. You may be planted where you get little sun. But you were put there by a loving Gardener because only in that situation will you produce the perfect fruit He desires. If another condition were better for you, divine love would have planted you there. You have been placed by God in the most suitable circumstances.

If you could choose your lot in life, you would soon cry, "Lord, choose my inheritance for me, for by self-will I have pierced myself with many sorrows" (1 Timothy 6:10). Be content with what you have, for the Lord has ordained all things for your good.

"If anyone desires to come after Me, let him deny himself, and take up his cross and follow Me" (Matthew 16:24). Your cross is the burden best suited for your shoulders, and it will "make you perfect in every good work to do His will, working in you what is well pleasing in His sight through Jesus Christ to whom be glory forever and ever" (Hebrews 13:21):

> Trials must and will befall—
> But with humble faith to see
> Love inscribed upon them all;
> This is happiness to me.

NOVEMBER 11, EVENING

TESTED FAITH

"The genuineness of your faith."

—1 Peter 1:7

Untried faith may be true faith, but it will be little faith and probably remain so as long as there are no trials. Faith prospers when all things are against you. The tempest is your trainer, the lightning your illuminator.

When the sea is calm, you can hoist all the sails, but the ship will not move. On a slumbering ocean, the keel sleeps. But let the winds blow and the waters rise, let the vessel rock and the deck be washed with waves, let the masts creak under strain and the sails swell, and it is then that the ship makes headway.

No flowers have so lovely a blue as those that grow at the foot of a glacier. No stars gleam so brightly as those in the polar sky. No water tastes so sweet as in the desert. And no faith is so precious as that which lives and triumphs in adversity.

Tried faith brings experience. You would never have believed your own weaknesses had you not been compelled to pass through deep rivers. You would never have known God's strength had you not been supported in the floods. Faith increases in stability, assurance, and intensity the more it is tried. Faith is precious, and its trial is precious (1 Peter 1:7).

If you are young in the faith, don't let this discourage you. You will have trials enough without seeking them. Your full portion will be measured out in due season. Meanwhile, if you cannot claim the result of long experience, thank God for the grace you have. Praise Him for the degree of holy confidence you have reached. Walk according to His way, and you will have more and more blessings from God until your faith will remove mountains and conquer impossibilities.

AN EXAMPLE OF PRAYER

"Now it came to pass in those days that He went out to the mountain to pray, and continued all night in prayer to God."

—Luke 6:12

If ever anyone could have lived without prayer, it would have been our spotless and perfect Lord. Yet no one prayed as much as He. Such was His love for fellowship with His Father.

His love for His people was so great that He was in continual intercession for them. This eminent prayer life of Jesus is a lesson for us, for He has given us an example to follow.

The time He chose was admirable. It was the hour of silence when the crowd would not disturb Him. It was the time of rest when all but Jesus had ceased laboring. While others slumbered through their problems and ceased approaching Him for relief, Jesus refreshed Himself in prayer.

The place was well selected. He was alone. No one would intrude or observe. He was free from Pharisaic ostentation and vulgar interruptions. Those dark and silent hills were a proper chapel for the Son of God. Heaven and earth in midnight stillness heard the groans and sighs of the mysterious Being in whom both worlds were blended.

His continual pleading is remarkable. The long night watches were not too long. The cold wind did not chill His devotions. The grim darkness did not darken His faith. The loneliness did not check His supplications.

The timing of this prayer is notable. It was after His enemies had been enraged that prayer was His refuge and comfort. It was before He sent out the twelve apostles that prayer was the gate of His enterprise, the herald of His new work.

Learn from Jesus and resort to special prayer when you are going through a difficult trial or contemplating a new endeavor for the Master's glory.

"Lord, teach us to pray" (Luke 11:1).

NOVEMBER 12, EVENING

BEARING FRUIT

"The branch cannot bear fruit of itself."

—John 15:4

When did you begin to bear fruit? It was when you came to Jesus and cast yourself on His great atonement and rested in His finished righteousness. Ah, what fruit you had then! Do you remember those early days? The vine flourished, the tender grapes appeared, the pomegranates budded, and the beds of spice gave forth their fragrance.

Are you still bearing fruit? If not, remember your first love, and repent. Do the first works. Work hardest at that which has proven to draw you closer to Christ, because it is from Him that all your fruit proceeds.

Any exercise that brings you to Him will help bear fruit. No doubt the sun is splendid at creating fruit among the trees of the orchard, but Jesus is greater among the trees of His garden of grace.

When have you been the most fruitless? It was when you lived farthest from the Lord Jesus Christ. When you slackened in prayer, when you departed from the simplicity of faith, when the world engrossed you, when you forgot the source of your strength, when you said, "My mountain stands firm, I will never be moved," then you ceased to be fruitful.

Some of us have learned that we have nothing outside of Christ. When we saw the utter barrenness and death of all creature power, we cried in anguish, "In Him all my fruit must be found, for no fruit can come from me."

Past experience teaches that the more we depend on the grace of God in Christ and wait on the Holy Spirit, the more we will bear fruit.

Oh, today, trust Jesus for fruit as well as for life.

LET THE CHURCH PRAY

"Men always ought to pray and not lose heart."

—Luke 18:1

Jesus sent His church into the world to fulfill His purpose, and that mission includes intercession. The church is the world's priest. Creation is mute, but the church is to be its mouth.

It is the church's highest privilege to have its prayers accepted. The door of grace is always open for her petitions, which never return empty. The veil was rent for her, the blood was sprinkled on the altar for her, and God invites the church to ask what she wills.

Can the church refuse the privilege that angels would envy? Is the church not the bride of Christ? May she not go to her King at any hour? Will she allow the precious privilege to be unused?

The church always has need for prayer, for there are always some who are declining or falling into open sin. There are lambs to be prayed for, that they may be carried in Christ's bosom. The strong also need prayer, lest they grow presumptuous. The weak need prayer, lest they despair.

If we had prayer meetings twenty four hours a day, every day of the year, we would still never be without prayer requests. There are always the sick, the poor, the afflicted, and the wavering. We are always seeking the conversion of relatives, the reclaiming of backsliders, and the salvation of the lost.

With congregations gathering, with ministers always preaching, with millions of sinners remaining dead in sin, in a country where darkness is descending, in a world full of idols, cruelties, and devilries, if the church does not pray, how can she excuse this neglect?

Let the church be in prayer always. Let all believers cast their mites of prayer into the treasury.

NOVEMBER 13, EVENING

ALL OR NOTHING

"I will cut off . . . those who worship the host of heaven on the housetop; those who worship and swear oaths by the Lord, but who also swear by Milcom." —Zephaniah 1:4–5

These people thought they were safe because they worshiped both parties. They went with the followers of Jehovah and at the same time bowed to Milcom. God considers duplicity abominable, and He hates hypocrisy. Idolaters who give themselves fully to false gods have only one less sin than those who bring "sacrifices of idols" to the Lord's temple.

In the daily matters of life, a double-minded person is despised, but in religion it is loathsome to the worst degree (James 1:8). The penalty in our text is terrible, but well deserved. How can divine justice spare the sinners who know, approve, and profess to follow the truth and yet love evil and give it a place in their hearts?

My soul, search this morning and see if you are guilty of dual allegiances. You profess to be a follower of Jesus, but do you really love Him? Is your heart right with God? To have one foot on the land of truth and another in the sea of falsehood will involve a terrible fall and a total ruin. Christ will be all or nothing. God fills the whole universe, and there is no room for another god. If Jesus reigns in my heart, there is no space for another power.

Do I rest alone on Jesus crucified and live only for Him? Is this my desire? Is my heart set on this? If so, blessed be the mighty grace that has led me to salvation.

If not, Lord, pardon my sad offence, and may my heart fear Your name. Amen.

FIRST THINGS FIRST

"And Laban said, 'It must not be done in our country to give the younger before the first-born'."

—Genesis 29:26

There was no excuse for Laban's dishonesty, but we can learn from the custom he quoted.

Some things must be taken in order. If we would win the second we must secure the first. The second may be more lovely, but the rule of heaven must stand. For example, many desire the beautiful and well-favored Rachel of joy and peace in believing, but first they must marry the tender-eyed Leah of repentance.

Everyone falls in love with happiness, and many would cheerfully serve twice the seven years to have it. Yet, according to the rule of the Lord's kingdom, the Leah of holiness must be our soul's beloved before the Rachel of happiness can be attained.

Heaven stands not first, but second, and only by persevering to the end do we win a portion of it. The cross must be carried before the crown can be worn. We must follow our Lord in His humiliation, or we will never rest with Him in glory.

What do you say, my soul? Are you so vain that you hope to break the heavenly rule? Do you hope for reward without labor or honor without toil? Dismiss this idle expectation and be content to take the ill-favored things for the sake of the sweet love of Jesus.

In such a spirit, working and suffering, you will find that bitter grows sweet and the hard become easy. Like Jacob, your years of service will seem but a few days because of your love for Jesus (Genesis 29:20). And when the hour of the wedding feast comes, all your toil will be as though it had never been. An hour with Jesus will make up for ages of pain and labor:

> Jesus, to win Thyself so fair,
>   Thy cross I will with gladness bear;
> Since so the rules of heaven ordain,
>   The first I'll wed the next to gain.

NOVEMBER 14, EVENING

OWNED

"For the Lord's portion is His people."

—Deuteronomy 32:9

The Lord's people are His by His own sovereign choice. He set His love on them, and He did this apart from any goodness He foresaw in them. "I will be gracious to whom I will be gracious and I will have compassion on whom I will have compassion" (Exodus 33:19). He ordained a chosen company for eternal life, and they are His by His unconstrained election.

They are not only His by choice, but also by purchase. He has bought and paid for them to the final penny. "Knowing that you were not redeemed with corruptible things, like silver and gold . . . but with the precious blood of Christ, as of a lamb without blemish and without spot" (1 Peter 1:18,19).

There is no mortgage on His estate, no lawsuits can be raised by opposing claimants. The price was paid in open court and the church is the Lord's absolute ownership forever.

See the blood-mark on all the chosen. Though it is invisible to the human eye, "the Lord knows those who are His" (2 Timothy 2:19). He never forgets His redeemed. He counts the sheep for whom He laid down His life. He remembers the church for whom He died.

They are also His by conquest. What a battle He had with us before we would be won. How long He laid siege to our hearts. How often He sent us terms of capitulation. But we barred our gates and shut Him out. Can you remember that glorious hour when He won your heart? He placed His cross against the wall, scaled our ramparts, and planted on our strongholds the blood-red flag of His omnipotent mercy.

Yes, we are indeed the conquered captives of His omnipotent love, chosen, purchased, and subdued. The rights of our divine possessor are inalienable. We rejoice that we never can be our own. We desire, day by day, to do His will and to show forth His glory.

NOVEMBER 15, MORNING

OH GOD, STRENGTHEN

"Strengthen O God, what you have done for us."

—Psalm 68:28

It is necessary to beseech God to strengthen what He has done in us. If we fail to do this, unbelief will arise, and with it trials and afflictions.

Satan seeks to flood our heart's garden and make it desolate. It is also true that many Christians leave the floodgates open, and through lack of prayer, the dreadful deluge comes in.

We forget that the Author of our faith is also the Preserver of our faith. The lamp that burned in the temple was never allowed to go out. It had to be replenished daily with fresh oil. Likewise, our faith lives by being sustained with the oil of grace, and we can obtain it only from God. Foolish virgins we will be, if we do not secure the oil necessary for our lamps (Matthew 25:2).

He who made the world upholds it, or it would fall in one tremendous crash (Colossians 1:16). He who made us Christians must maintain us by His Spirit, or our ruin will be speedy and final.

Let us then, evening by evening, go to our Lord for our grace and strength. We have a strong argument to plead. It is for His own work of grace that we ask, "Strengthen, O God, what You have done for us." Do you think He will not honor that request? Let your faith take hold of His strength, and all the powers of hell cannot cast a cloud or shadow over your joy and peace.

Why faint when you are strong? Why suffer defeat when you can conquer? Take your wavering faith and drooping graces to Him who can revive and replenish.

Earnestly pray, "Strengthen, O God, what You have done for us." Amen.

NOVEMBER 15, EVENING

ALL-SUFFICIENT

"The Lord is my portion, says my soul."

—Lamentations 3:24

Our text does not say, "the Lord is partly my portion," or "the Lord is in my portion." It states that He Himself is the total sum of my soul's inheritance. Within the circumference of that circle lies all that we possess or need.

"The Lord is my portion," not only His grace, His love, or His covenant, but Jehovah Himself. He has chosen us and we have chosen Him. If we are called according to the purpose of electing love, we can sing:

> Lov'd of my God for him again
> With love intense I burn;
> Chosen of Him ere time began,
> I choose Him in return.

The Lord is our all-sufficient portion. God fills Himself, and if He is all-sufficient in Himself, He must be all-sufficient for us. It is not easy to satisfy human desire. When we think that we are satisfied, it is not long before we perceive that something is missing.

But all that we can wish for is found in our divine portion. We ask, "Whom have I in heaven but You? And there is none upon earth that I desire beside You. My flesh and my heart fail; but God is the strength of my heart and my portion forever" (Psalm 73:25–26). "Delight yourself also in the Lord, and He shall give you the desires of your heart" (Psalm 37:4). Our faith stretches its wings and mounts up like an eagle to its proper dwelling place, to the heaven of divine love.

"The lines have fallen to me in pleasant places; yes I have a good inheritance" (Psalm 16:6). "Rejoice in the Lord always. Again I say rejoice" (Philippians 4:4). Show the world that you are happy and blessed. Induce them to exclaim, "We will go with you, for we have heard that God is with you."

UNTIL THE DAY BREAK

"Your eyes will see the King in His beauty."

—Isaiah 33:17

The more you know about Christ, the less you will be satisfied with a superficial view of Him. The more deeply you study His transactions in the eternal covenant, or His engagements as your eternal Surety, or the fullness of His grace in all His offices, the more you will see the King in His beauty. Look and long to see more of Jesus.

Meditation and contemplation are like windows of semitransparent quartz and gates of emeralds through which we see our Redeemer. Meditation puts the telescope to the eye. It enables us to see Jesus better than we could have seen Him if we had lived in the days of His flesh.

Would that our conversation were more heavenly. Would that we were more taken with the person, the work, and the beauty of our incarnate Lord. Through meditation, the beauty of the King flashes on us with resplendence.

Beloved, it is possible that just before we die we will see our glorious King. Many dying saints have looked up from the stormy waters and have seen Jesus walking on the waves. They have heard Him say, "Be of good cheer! It is I; do not be afraid" (Mark 6:50). Ah, yes, when our old house begins to shake and the clay falls away, we will see Christ through the cracks; between the rafters the sunlight of heaven will come streaming in.

If we want to see Him face to face, we must go to heaven, or the King must come here in person. Oh that He would come on the wings of the wind! He is our husband, and we are widowed by His absence. He is our dear brother, and we are lonely without Him. Thick veils and clouds hang between our souls and true life, "until the day breaks and the shadows flee away" (Song of Solomon 2:17).

Oh, long expected day, begin!

NOVEMBER 16, EVENING

TO GOD BE THE GLORY

"To whom be glory forever. Amen."

—Romans 11:36

This should be the single desire of every Christian. All other wishes must be subservient and tributary.

We may wish for prosperity in business, but only to help promote the glory of God. We may desire more gifts and more graces, but it should only be for God's glory. We are not acting properly if we are moved by any motive other than our Lord's glory.

As a Christian, you are of God and through God and therefore ought to live for God. Let nothing set your heart beating faster than your love for Him. Let this ambition fire your soul. Let it be the foundation of your every enterprise. Let it be your sustaining motive when zeal grows cold. Make God your only object.

Where self begins, sorrow begins. But if God is my supreme delight and only object:

> To me 'tis equal whether love ordain
> My life or death—appoint me ease or pain.

Let your desire for God's glory grow. You blessed Him in your youth, do not be content with the praises you gave Him then. Has God prospered you in business? Give Him more glory. Has God given you experience? Praise Him with a stronger faith.

Does your knowledge of Him increase? Then sing His praise more sweetly. Do you enjoy happier times than you once did? Have you been healed? Has your sorrow been turned to peace and joy? Then give Him more music. Put more coals and sweeter frankincense in the censer of your praise.

Experience the joy of glorifying your great and gracious Lord. Sing the Amen to this doxology, by your service and increasing holiness.

DAILY DANGERS

"He who splits wood may be endangered by it."

—Ecclesiastes 10:9

Oppressors may get their way with the poor and needy as easily as they can split wood. But they had best watch out, because log splitting can be dangerous and many a lumber jack has been injured or killed.

Jesus is persecuted in every injured saint, and He is mighty to avenge His beloved. Abusing the poor and needy is a thing to fear. If there is no danger to the persecutors here, there will be in the hereafter.

Splitting wood is a common business, and it is the same with you, for there are dangers connected with your calling and daily life. I am not talking about the hazard of flood and disease, or sudden death, but of spiritual perils.

Your occupation may be quite humble, yet the devil can still tempt you as you work. You may be an employee who is screened from gross temptations and vices, and still some secret sin may damage you.

Even those who stay at home and do not mingle with the rough world may be endangered by being secluded. They may think they are safe, but they are not. Pride may enter even a poor person's heart. Greed may reign in a tenant farmer's soul. Uncleanness may venture into the quietest home. Anger, envy, and malice may insinuate itself into the most rural abode. Even in speaking a few words, people may sin, or a little purchase at a shop may be the first link in a chain of temptations. Merely looking out a window may be the beginning of evil.

Oh Lord, how exposed we are! How can we be secure? To keep ourselves is a work too hard for us. Only You are able to preserve us in such a world of evil. "Keep me as the apple of Your eye; hide me under the shadow of Your wings" (Psalm 17:8).

NOVEMBER 17, EVENING

A SECRET SPRING

"A spring shut up, a fountain sealed."

—Song of Solomon 4:12

This metaphor refers to the secret inner life of a believer. In the Middle East there were springs over which an edifice was built to make the water inaccessible to all except those who knew the secret entrance. Like the heart of a believer renewed by grace, there is a mysterious life within that no human skill can touch, a secret no one else knows.

Our text includes not only secrecy, but also separation. This is not a common spring from which every passerby may drink. It is preserved from all others. It is a fountain that bears the king's royal seal. All can perceive it is not a common fountain, but a fountain owned by the king for his use only.

It is the same in our spiritual life. The chosen of God were separated by eternal decree in the day of redemption. They are separated by the possession of a life that others do not have, and it is impossible for them to feel at home with the world and its pleasures.

There is also the idea of sacredness. The spring shut up is reserved for use by a special person. This is a picture of the believer's heart, which is a spring kept for Jesus. All Christians should feel God's seal on them and be able to say with Paul, "From now on let no one trouble me for I bear in my body the marks of the Lord Jesus" (Galatians 6:17).

Another idea is prominent, security. Oh how sure and safe is the inner life of the believer. If all the powers of earth and hell could combine against it, that immortal principle will still exist, because He who gave it pledged His life for its preservation.

Who can harm you when God is your protector?

ALWAYS

"Your throne is established from of old; You are from everlasting."

—Psalm 93:2

Christ is Everlasting, and so we may sing with David, "Your throne is established from of old." Rejoice believer! "Jesus Christ is the same yesterday, today, and forever" (Hebrews 13:8).

Jesus always existed. The babe born in Bethlehem was the Word. "In the beginning was the Word, and the Word was with God, and the Word was God. He was in the beginning with God. All things were made through Him, and without Him nothing was made that was made" (John 1:1–3).

The title that Christ revealed to John on Patmos was "Him who is and who was and who is to come" (Revelation 1:4). If He were not God from everlasting, we could not devoutly love Him. We could not feel that He had any share in eternal love, which is the fountain of all covenant blessings. But because He is from all eternity with the Father, we can trace the stream of divine love as equally to Jesus as to His Father and the blessed Holy Spirit.

"He always lives to make intercession" (Hebrews 7:25). Go to Him in your time of need, for He is waiting to bless you. Jesus our Lord exists forever. If God should spare your life to fulfill seventy years, you will find His cleansing fountain still open. His precious blood will not have lost its power. Your High Priest who filled the healing fountain with His precious blood always lives to cleanse you from all sin.

When only your last battle remains, you will discover that the hand of your conquering Captain has not grown feeble. The living Savior will cheer the dying saint.

Through eternity the Lord Jesus will remain the perennial spring of joy, life, and glory to His people. You may always draw living waters from the sacred well. Jesus always was, He always is, and He always will be. He is eternal in all His attributes, in all His offices, and in all His might.

NOVEMBER 18, EVENING

FOOLISH QUESTIONS

"Avoid foolish disputes, genealogies, contentions, and striving about the law; for they are unprofitable and useless."

—Titus 3:9

Our days are few and are better spent in doing good than in disputing matters of minor importance. The old scholars did a great deal of harm by incessant discussions on subjects of little or no practical importance. Our churches suffer from petty wars over abstruse points and trivial questions, for after everything that can be said is said, no one is any wiser. The discussions do not promote love or knowledge but only sown seed in a barren field.

Questions on points where the Scripture is silent, or on mysteries that belong to God alone, or on prophecies of doubtful interpretation, or on methods of observing human ceremonies are usually foolish and best avoided.

Our business is not to discuss foolish questions, but to avoid them. "This is a faithful saying and these things I want you to affirm constantly, that those who have believed in God should be careful to maintain good works. These things are good and profitable" (Titus 3:8). If we observe this precept, we will be far more occupied with profitable things than in paying attention to unworthy, contentious, and needless striving.

There are, however, some questions that are the opposite of foolish, and these we must not avoid but fairly and honestly answer. Do I believe in the Lord Jesus Christ? Am I renewed in the spirit of my mind? Am I walking after the flesh or the Spirit? Am I growing in grace? Does my conversation adorn the doctrine of God my Savior? Am I looking for the coming of the Lord, watching as a servant who expects the Master? What more can I do for Jesus? Questions like these demand our attention.

Let us be peacemakers and endeavor to lead others, both by our action and example, to avoid foolish questions.

WHERE IS HE?

"Oh, that I knew where I might find Him."

—Job 23:3

In Job's worst moment he cried to the Lord, for the great desire of an afflicted child of God is to see the Father's face.

Job's first prayer was not to be healed of that festering disease, or to see his children raised from the grave, or for his property to be returned. Job's foremost cry was, "Oh, that I knew where I might find Him. That I might come to His seat!" God's children run home when the storm comes. It is a heaven-born instinct of believers to seek shelter beneath the wings of Jehovah, as "a refuge from the storm" (Isaiah 25:4).

A hypocrite, when afflicted by God, resents the infliction and runs from the Master who has punished him. But not the true heirs of heaven. We kiss the hand that disciplines us and seek shelter from the rod in the heart of God.

Job's desire to commune with God was intensified by the failure of all other comforts. The patriarch turned away from his so-called friends. He looked to the celestial throne in the same way a traveler hurries from his empty bottle to a well. Job bids farewell to earthly hopes and cries, "Oh that I knew where I might find Him."

Nothing teaches the preciousness of the Creator like the emptiness of life. We turn with bitter scorn from earth's sharp, stinging, and honeyless hives to rejoice in Him whose faithful Word is sweeter than honey.

In every trouble, realize that God is present. Enjoy His smile and bear your daily cross with a willing heart for His dear sake. "God is our refuge and strength. A very present help in time of trouble" (Psalm 46:1).

PLEADING THE CASE

"O Lord, You have pleaded the case for my soul."

—Lamentations 3:58

Observe how positively the prophet speaks. He does not say, "I hope, I trust, I sometimes think that God pleads the case for my soul." Instead, he speaks of it as an indisputable fact.

With the aid of the gracious Comforter, shake off the doubts and fears that mar your peace and comfort. Let this be your prayer: "O Lord, You have pleaded the case for my soul." Let there be no more surmise or suspicion. Speak with the clear, melodious voice of full assurance.

Notice how gratefully the prophet speaks, ascribing all the glory to God. There is not a word concerning himself or his own pleading. He does not assign his deliverance in any measure to man, much less his own merit. It is God alone who has pleaded the case for his soul and redeemed his life.

A grateful spirit should always be cultivated by Christians. After God answers prayer, we should sing to Him. This earth should be a temple filled with the songs of grateful saints. Everyday should be a censer smoking with the sweet incense of thanksgiving.

Jeremiah is joyful as he triumphantly sings. He has been in a terrible dungeon and now, more than ever, is the weeping prophet. Yet in the book of Lamentations, we hear Jeremy singing as clearly as Miriam with her tambourine (Exodus 15:20). He is bellowing like Deborah when she met Barak with her shouts of victory (Judges 5:1). Jeremiah's song rises heavenward, "O Lord, You have pleaded the case for my soul; You have redeemed my life."

Child of God, seek a vital experience of the Lord's lovingkindness, and when you have it, speak positively, and sing gratefully and shout triumphantly.

THE HIDING PLACE

"The rock badgers are a feeble folk, yet they make their homes in the crags."

—Proverbs 30:26

Conscious of their own defenselessness, the rock badgers burrow in the rocks and are secure from their enemies. My heart, learn from these feeble folk. You are as weak and as exposed to peril as the timid rock badger. Follow their example and seek shelter.

My best security is in the stronghold of an unchanging Jehovah. His unalterable promises stand like giant walls of rock. All will be well if I hide in the bulwark of His glorious attributes, which are guarantees of safety for those who trust in Him.

Blessed be the name of the Lord, for I have found the joy of trusting in Him. Like David in the caves of Adullam, I find myself safe from the cruelty of the enemy. Long ago, when Satan and my sins pursued me, I fled to the cleft of the rock Christ Jesus. There, in His riven side, I found a delightful resting place. My heart, run to Him again tonight. Whatever your grief may be, oh my soul, Jesus feels for you, and He will console and help you.

No monarch in an impregnable fortress is more secure than the rock badger in his rocky burrow. The master of ten thousand chariots is no better protected than the little dweller in the cleft of the rock.

In Jesus the weak are strong and the defenseless are safe. The weak could not be stronger if they were giants, and the defenseless could not be safer if they were in heaven, for faith gives them the protection of the God of heaven on earth. What more do they need?

The rock badgers cannot build a castle, but they avail themselves of what is already there. I cannot make a refuge, but Jesus has provided one. His Father has given it, His Spirit has revealed it, and again tonight I enter my refuge and am safe from every foe.

NOVEMBER 20, EVENING

THE MIGHTY SPIRIT

"Do not grieve the Spirit of God."

—Ephesians 4:30

Everything a believer has must come from Christ, through the channel of the Spirit of grace. Just as all blessings flow to you through the Holy Spirit, nothing good can come out of you in holy thought, devout worship, or gracious act apart from the sanctifying operation of the Spirit. Even when the good seed is sown in you it lies dormant unless He "works all things according to the counsel of His will" (Ephesians 1:11).

Do you desire to speak for Jesus? How can you unless the Holy Spirit touches your tongue? Do you desire to pray? What dull work that will be unless the Spirit makes intercession for you.

Do you desire to subdue sin? to be holy? to imitate your Master? Do you desire to rise to superlative heights of spirituality? Do you want to be like the angels of God, full of zeal and eagerness for the Master's cause? You cannot be any one of these without the Spirit, for "without Me you can do nothing" (John 15:5).

Oh, branch of the vine, there is no fruit without the sap. Oh, child of God, there is no life in you apart from the life God gives through His Holy Spirit. Do not grieve Him or provoke Him to anger by sin. Do not quench Him in even the faintest motions in your soul. Foster every suggestion and be ready to obey every prompting.

Because the Holy Spirit is so mighty, attempt nothing without Him. Do not begin a project, or carry on an enterprise, or conclude a transaction without imploring His blessing. Honor Him by acknowledging your entire weakness apart from Him.

Dear Lord, open my heart and my whole being to Your incoming Holy Spirit. Uphold me with Your generous Spirit (Psalm 51:12). Amen.

SITTING WITH JESUS

"Lazarus was one of those who sat at the table with Him."

—John 12:2

Lazarus is to be envied. It was good to be Martha and serve but better to be Lazarus and fellowship. There is a time and a place for each, but none of the trees of the garden yield such clusters as the vine of fellowship. To have been able to sit with Jesus, to hear His words, to watch His actions, and to receive His smiles was so great that it must have made Lazarus as happy as the angels. When it has been our delight to feast with our Beloved in His banquet hall we would not have given half a sigh for all the kingdoms of the world, even if such a breath could have bought them.

Lazarus is to be imitated. It would have been strange if he had not been at the table with Jesus; after all, Jesus had raised him from the dead. If the risen one would have been absent, when the One who gave him life was there, that would have been ungrateful indeed.

We too were once dead, yes, and like Lazarus, stinking in the grave of sin. Jesus raised us, and by His life we live. Therefore, can we be content to live at a distance from Him? Do we forget Him at His table, where He stoops to feast with His children? Oh, this is cruel! It behooves us to repent and do as he has asked. His wish should be our law.

For Lazarus to have lived without the fellowship of the One of whom the Jews said, "See how He loved him" (John 11:36), would have been disgraceful. Is it then excusable in us whom Jesus has loved with an everlasting love? To have been cold to Him who wept over his lifeless corpse (John 11:35) would have shown brutishness in Lazarus. What does this say to us, for whom the Savior has not only wept, but died?

Come, let us return to our heavenly Bridegroom and ask for His Spirit that we may be closer and sit at His table.

SHEEP WATCHING

"Israel served for a spouse. And for a wife he tended sheep."

—Hosea 12:12

Jacob, when trying to reason with Laban, said, "These twenty years I have been with you . . . that which was torn by beasts I did not bring to you; I bore the loss of it, you required it from my hand whether stolen by day or stolen by night. There I was! In the day the drought consumed me, and the frost by night, and my sleep departed from my eyes" (Genesis 31:38–40).

Even more difficult was the earthly life of our Savior, as He watched over all His sheep. In His last account He said, "I kept them in Your name. Those whom You gave Me I have kept; and none of them is lost . . . that the Scripture might be fulfilled" (John 17:12).

His "head was covered with dew and His locks with the drops of night" (Song of Solomon 5:2), because He was in prayer, wrestling for His people. Peter must be pleaded for, and another claims His tearful intercession. No shepherd sitting under that cold sky, looking up to the stars, could ever complain that his work was as difficult as the work of Jesus Christ. Jesus faced such difficulties because of His love for His church:

> Cold mountains and the midnight air,
> Witnessed the fervor of His prayer;
> The desert His temptations knew,
> His conflict and His victory too.

It is good to dwell on the spiritual parallel of Laban, who required an accounting of Jacob's sheep. If the sheep were injured by wild animals, Jacob must make it good. If any died, Jacob had to pay. The work of Jesus was an obligation to bring every believer safely to the Father.

Look at Jacob and you see a representation of Him of whom it was said, "He shall feed His flock like a shepherd" (Isaiah 40:11).

RISEN

"The power of His resurrection."

—Philippians 3:10

The doctrine of a risen Savior is exceedingly precious, for the resurrection is the cornerstone of Christianity, the keystone of salvation. It would take a large volume to tell about all the streams of living water that flow from the resurrection of our dear Lord and Savior Jesus Christ. But to know that He has risen, to have fellowship with Him, to commune with the risen Savior by possessing a risen life, to see Him leave the tomb by leaving the tomb of worldliness ourselves, this is even more precious.

The doctrine of a risen Lord is the basis of this experience, but just as the flower is lovelier than the root, the experience of fellowship with the risen Savior is lovelier than the doctrine. I want you to be so certain that Christ rose from the dead that you will sing about it. I want you to derive all possible consolation from this well-witnessed fact. But do not stop there. Although you cannot see Him visibly, I implore you to see Christ Jesus through the eye of faith. Although you cannot touch Him, you are privileged to talk with Him. You will know that He is risen, because you are risen in newness of life.

To know that a crucified Savior has crucified all my sins is priceless knowledge. But to know that a risen Savior has justified me, bestowed new life on me, and made me a new creature through His own newness of life, this is a noble experience. Anything less cannot satisfy. May you "know Him and the power of His resurrection."

Why should souls who are alive in Jesus wear the grave cloths of worldliness and unbelief? Rise, for your Lord is risen. He is risen indeed!

NOVEMBER 22, EVENING

FELLOWSHIP

"Fellowship with Him."

—1 John 1:6

When we were united by faith to Christ, we were brought into complete fellowship by being made one with Him. His interests and our interests became identical.

We have fellowship with Christ in His love. What He loves, we love. He loves the saints, and so do we. He loves the sinners, and so do we. He loves the poor perishing human race and wants the earth's deserts transformed into the garden of the Lord, and so do we.

We have fellowship with Him in His desires. He desires the glory of God, and we also work for that. He desires that we be with Him, and we also desire that. He desires to drive out sin, and we fight under the same banner. He desires that His Father's name be loved and adored by all His creatures, and we pray daily, "Your kingdom come. Your will be done on earth as it is in heaven" (Matthew 6:10).

We have fellowship with Christ in His sufferings. We are not nailed to a cross, or die cruel deaths, but when He is reproached, we are reproached. It is a sweet thing to be blamed for His sake, to be despised for following the Master. After all, "a disciple is not above his teacher, nor a servant above his master" (Matthew 10:24).

We commune with Him in His labors by ministering to people through the Word of truth and deeds of love. We agree with Him: "My food is to do the will of Him who sent Me and to finish His work" (John 4:34). We have fellowship with Christ in His joys. We are happy in His happiness; we rejoice in His exaltation.

Believer, have you tasted that joy? There is no more thrilling or purer delight this side of heaven than having Christ's joys fulfilled in you, "that your joy may be full" (John 15:11).

HIGHER GROUND

"Get up into the high mountain."

—Isaiah 40:9

Believer, you should be thirsting for the living God. You should be longing to climb the hill of the Lord, desiring to see Him face to face. Do not be content with the mists of the valley when the summit awaits you.

My soul thirsts to drink deep of the cup reserved for those who reach the mountain top. I long to bathe my brow in heaven. How pure are the dews of the hills, how fresh is the mountain air, how rich is the food of the lofty dwellers, whose windows look into the New Jerusalem!

Many saints are content to live in coal mines and not see the sun. They eat dust like serpents, when they could taste the heavenly meat of angels. They are content to wear miner's clothing, when they could wear the king's robes. Tears mar their faces, when celestial oil could anoint them. Many believers languish in dungeons, when they could walk on the palace roof and view the good land.

Wake up, believer, and realize your low condition. Get rid of your laziness, your lethargy, your coldness, and anything that interferes with a chaste and pure love for Christ. Make Him the source, the center, and the circumference of your soul's range of delight.

What keeps you in a pit, when you could sit on a throne? The mountain of liberty is there for you. Stop living in the lowlands of bondage; stop resting on the satisfaction of your diminutive attainments. Press forward to things more sublime and heavenly. Aspire to a higher, a nobler, a fuller life. Upward to heaven! Nearer to God!

> When wilt Thou come unto me Lord?
> Oh come, my Lord most dear!
> Come near, come nearer, nearer still,
> I'm blest when Thou art near.

NOVEMBER 23, EVENING

A RIVER GLORIOUS

"There the majestic Lord will be for us a place of broad rivers and streams, in which no galley with oars will sail, nor majestic ships pass by."
—Isaiah 33:21

Broad rivers and streams produce fertility and abundant harvests. Places near broad rivers are remarkable for their variety of plant life and plentiful harvests.

God is all this to His church. In having God the church has abundance. What can she ask for that He will not give? What can she mention that He will not supply? "In this mountain the Lord of hosts will make for all people a feast of choice pieces" (Isaiah 25:6). Do you want the bread of life? It falls like manna from the sky. Do you want refreshing streams? The rock follows you, and that Rock is Christ (1 Corinthians 10:4).

If you are suffering from want, it is your own fault. If you are distressed, you are not distressed in Him, but in yourself. If you are suffering financial hardship, your hardship is not in Him, but in you.

Broad rivers and streams point to trade. Our glorious Lord is a place of heavenly merchandise. Through our Redeemer, we have exchange with the past. The wealth of Calvary, the treasures of the covenant, the riches of the ancient days of election, and the stores of eternity all come to us down the broad stream of our gracious Lord.

We have business with the future. Ships, full to the water's edge, come to us from the millennium, visions of the days of heaven on earth! Through our glorious Lord, we have exchange with angels and communion with the bright spirits washed in blood, who sing before the throne. But better still, we have fellowship with the Infinite One.

Broad rivers and streams are especially intended to show security, because in old days rivers were a defense. Oh, my beloved, what a defense God is to His church. The devil cannot cross this broad river of God. Satan may worry us, but he cannot destroy us, for "no galley with oars will sail, nor majestic ships pass by."

NOVEMBER 24, MORNING

SLEEPY

"A little sleep, a little slumber, a little folding of the hands to rest; so shall your poverty come like a prowler, and your need like an armed man."
—Proverbs 24:33–34

The laziest only ask for a little slumber, and they would be indignant if accused of being thoroughly idle. A little folding of the hands to sleep is all they crave, and they can give you a thousand reasons why this is proper. Yet little by little their day ends, the time to work is gone, and the field is not weeded.

By a little procrastination, souls are ruined. They begin with no intention to delay for years. Tomorrow they will attend to serious things. A few months will bring a more convenient time. The present hour is so occupied and unsuitable that they ask to be excused. Then like sand in an hour-glass time passes and life is wasted by drops. The season of grace is lost in a *little* sleep.

Be wise. Catch the flying minutes to use at this very moment. May the Lord teach you this sacred wisdom; otherwise, a worse poverty awaits, an eternal poverty that will seek a drop of water and beg in vain (Luke 16:24). Like a traveler steadily journeying, poverty overtakes the idle, and ruin overthrows the undecided. Each moment brings the dreaded pursuers closer. Like an armed man who enters with authority and power, want will come to the idle and death to the unrepentant. There will be no escape.

Oh that we would diligently seek the Lord Jesus before that solemn day dawns and it is too late to plow, too late to plant, too late to repent, and too late to believe. It is too late at harvest time to regret that you failed to plant.

This evening, faith and holy decisions are timely. May you obtain them tonight.

LIBERTY

"To proclaim liberty to the captives."

—Luke 4:18

No one but Jesus can deliver the captives. True liberty comes only from Him.

This liberty is righteously bestowed because the Son, who is heir of all things, has the right to free us. It is a liberty that has been dearly purchased by His power and with His blood. He makes us free by His own bonds. We have no burdens, because He carries them.

We have liberty because He suffered. We are purchased, but He freely gives the purchase price. Jesus asks nothing from us as a preparation for our liberty. He finds us in sackcloth and ashes and invites us to put on the beauty of freedom. He saves us just as we are, without our help or merit.

When Jesus sets you free, your liberty is a perpetual, unrestricted inheritance. There are no chains to bind you again. When the Master says, "Captive, I have delivered you," it is done forever. Satan may plot to enslave, but "if God is for us, who can be against us" (Romans 8:31)? The world and its temptations may seek to ensnare, but "He who is in you is greater than he who is in the world" (1 John 4:4).

The machinations of our deceitful hearts may harass and annoy, but be "confident of this very thing, that He who has begun a good work in you will complete it until the day of Jesus Christ" (Philippians 1:6). The foes of God and the enemies of the believers may gather their hosts together and come with concentrated fury against us, but "who is he who condemns" (Romans 8:34)? The soul that Christ delivers is as free to soar as the eagle that leaves its nest and flies beyond the clouds.

"You are not under law but under grace" (Romans 6:14). Therefore, let your liberty be exhibited in a practical way by serving God with gratitude and delight.

NOVEMBER 25, MORNING

THE JOY OF ELECTION

"For He says to Moses, I will have mercy on whom I will have mercy, and I will have compassion on whomever I will have compassion."

—Romans 9:15

With these words the Lord in the plainest manner claims the right to give or withhold His mercy according to His own sovereign will. As the prerogative of life and death was vested in the monarch, so the Judge of all the earth has a right to spare or condemn the guilty.

People by their sins have forfeited all claims on God. They deserve to perish, and if they all did there could be no grounds for complaint. But if the Lord steps in to save, He may rightly do so. Or if He judges it best to let the condemned suffer the righteous sentence, none may indict Him at their bar. Foolish and impudent are discourses about equal rights before God, and ignorant, if not worse, are those contentions against discriminating grace. These are nothing but the rebellions of proud human nature against the crown and scepter of Jehovah.

When we see our utter ruin and the justice of the divine verdict against sin, we no longer find fault that the Lord is not bound to save us. We do not murmur if He chooses to save others, as though in so doing He were injuring us. We feel that if He looks on us it will be His own free act of undeserved goodness, for which we will forever bless His name.

How can those who are divinely elected sufficiently adore the grace of God? They have no room for boasting because sovereignty excludes it. The Lord's will alone is glorified, and the very idea of human merit is cast out in everlasting contempt.

There is no greater, humbling doctrine in Scripture than election. There is no doctrine more promotive of gratitude, and consequently none more sanctifying. Believers, do not be afraid of the doctrine of election. Simply rejoice in it.

SUCCESS

"Whatever your hand finds to do, do it with your might."

—Ecclesiastes 9:10

This text refers to works that are humanly possible. If you are to be eminently useful, you must carry out with might "whatever your hand finds to do."

One good deed is worth more than a thousand brilliant theories. Don't wait for greater opportunities or for a different kind of work. Just do the things you find to do day by day.

There is no other time in which you will live. The past is gone, the future has not arrived, and you have only the present. Do not wait until your experiences have matured before serving God. Endeavor to produce fruit now, but be careful to "do it with your might."

Do it promptly. Do not waste your life thinking about what you intend to do tomorrow. No one ever served God by doing things tomorrow. If we honor Christ and are blessed, it is with the things we do today.

Whatever you do for Christ, put your entire soul in it. Do not give Christ a little glossed-over effort now and then. When you serve Him, do it with all your heart, soul, and strength.

Where is the Christian's power? It is not in our efforts, because Jesus says, "My grace is sufficient for you, for My strength is made perfect in weakness" (2 Corinthians 12:9).

Your power is in the Lord of Hosts. Seek His help, and then proceed with prayer and in faith. Then when you have done "whatever your hand finds to do," wait on the Lord for His blessing. The work will be well done, and your efforts will not have failed.

THE PLUMB LINE

"For who has despised the day of small things?
For these seven rejoice to see the plumb line in
the hand of Zerubbabel."

—Zechariah 4:10

Small things marked the beginning of Zerubbabel's work. The Lord had raised up someone who would persevere. The plumb line was in good hands, which is a comfort for every believer.

At the beginning, regardless of how small the work of grace, the plumb line is in good hands. A master builder greater than Solomon is building the heavenly temple. He will not fail or be discouraged until the highest spire is in place.

If the plumb line were in the hand of a mere mortal, we might fear for the building. But the pleasure of the Lord will prosper in Jesus' hand. The work will not be shoddy, but true. It will be well done because the Master's hand holds a good instrument.

If the walls were carelessly erected without proper supervision, they would be out of square. But the plumb line is used by the chosen superintendent. Jesus is always watching over the construction of His spiritual temple to insure that it is built securely and well. He will use the plumb line, and every stone in the wall that is out of line must come down. Hence the failure of many flattering works, the downfall of many glittering ministries.

It is not our place to judge the Lord's church, for Jesus has a steady hand and a true eye, and He uses the plumb line well. Aren't you glad the judgment is left to Him?

Lord Jesus, how happy we would be if we could see You at Your great work. Oh Zion, your beautiful walls are still in ruins! Oh glorious Builder, make our desolation rejoice at Your coming. Amen.

A PRIEST, STANDING

"Joshua the high priest standing before the Angel of the Lord."

—Zechariah 3:1

J oshua the high priest is a picture of every child of God made perfect by the blood of Christ and taught to minister in the holy things within the veil. Jesus has made us priests and kings of God (1 Peter 2:9). On earth we exercise the priesthood of consecrated living and holy service.

This high priest, however, is "standing before the Angel of the Lord" to minister. This should be the perpetual position of true believer. Every place is now God's temple, and His people can truly serve Him in their daily employment as well as in His house. We are to minister by offering the spiritual sacrifice of prayer and praise, "presenting our bodies a living sacrifice, holy, acceptable to God" (Romans 12:1).

Note where Joshua stands to minister; it is before the Angel of Jehovah. Only through a mediator can we defiled ones ever become priests unto God. We present what we have before the messenger, the Angel of the covenant, the Lord Jesus. Through Him our prayers find acceptance as they become wrapped in His prayers. Our praise is made sweet as it becomes wrapped with bundles of myrrh, aloe, and cinnamon from Christ's own garden. And if we bring Him only tears, He will put them with His tears in His bottle (Psalm 56:8), for "Jesus wept" (John 11:35). Or if we bring Him nothing but groans and sighs, He will receive them as an acceptable sacrifice, because He once was broken in heart and "bowed down heavily as one who mourns for his mother" (Psalm 35:14).

Standing in Him I am accepted in the Beloved. My polluted works are received, and God smells a sweet aroma. He is content and I am blessed. This is the position of the Christian: "a priest standing before the Angel of the Lord.

ALTOGETHER FORGIVEN

"The forgiveness of sins, according to the riches of His grace."

—Ephesians 1:7

Is there a sweeter word in any language than *forgiveness,* especially when spoken in a guilty sinner's ear? Blessed, forever blessed, is this dear pardon that shines in the condemned one's cell, to give the perishing hope in the midnight of despair.

Can it be that such sin as mine can be forgiven, altogether forgiven, forever forgiven? Hell is my portion as a sinner. There is no possibility of escape while sin remains on me. Can the load of guilt be lifted, my crimson stain removed? Can the manmade stones of my prison be broken, the doors be lifted from their hinges? Yes! Jesus tells me that I may be forgiven, that I may be blessed by atoning love.

I believe in the appointed propitiation, Jesus crucified. Thus my sins are now and forever forgiven by the virtue of His substitutionary pain and death. What joy! What ecstasy to be a perfectly pardoned soul! My soul dedicates everything to Him, who with His freely given love became my surety and redeemed me through His blood. What riches of grace free forgiveness exhibits. To forgive all, to forgive fully, to forgive freely, to forgive forever! What a constellation of wonders!

When I think of how great my sins were and how cherished the cleansing drops of blood are, I am lost in wonder, love, and praise. How gracious the pardon! I bow before the throne that absolves me and clasp the cross that delivers me. From this moment I will serve the Incarnate God, through whom I am pardoned.

INNER LIGHT

"For I rejoiced greatly when brethren came and testified of the truth that is in you, just as you walk in the truth."

—3 John 1:3

The truth was in the beloved Gaius (3 John 1:1), and Gaius walked in the truth. If the truth was not in Gaius he would have been a pretender.

Truth must enter, penetrate, and saturate the soul, or else it is personally ineffectual. Doctrines held as a creed are like bread in the hand that gives no nourishment. But doctrine accepted by the heart is like digested food that builds up and sustains the body.

Truth must be a living force, engaged energy, an indwelling reality, the fiber of our being. If it is, then we may lose our clothes or even our limbs, but not the truth. A Christian can die, but a Christian cannot deny the truth.

It is a rule of nature that the inward affects the outward, just as light from a lantern shines out through the glass. Thus the truth is kindled within us, and its brightness shines forth in our outward life and conversations. It is said that the food of certain worms colors the silk cocoons they spin. In the same way our inward nature tinges our every word and deed.

Walking in the truth shows a life of integrity, holiness, faithfulness, and simplicity—the natural products of the principles of truth the gospel teaches. The Holy Spirit enables us to receive these truths. We may judge the secrets of the soul by their manifestations in an individual's conversation.

Today, Oh gracious Spirit, rule and govern us by Your divine authority, so that nothing false or sinful may live in our hearts and extend its malignant influence to our daily walk. Amen.

NOVEMBER 28, MORNING

THE COMMON GOOD

"Seeking the good of his people."

—Esther 10:3

"Mordecai the Jew was second to King Ahasuerus, and was great among the Jews and well received by the multitude of his brethren, seeing the good of his people and speaking peace to all his countrymen" (Esther 10:3). Mordecai was a true patriot and used his high office to promote the prosperity of Israel. In this position, Mordecai was a type of Jesus, who on His throne of glory spends His power for His people.

It would be good if every believer could be a Mordecai to the church, striving for its prosperity. Those who are placed in positions of affluence and influence should honor their Lord in the high places of earth and testify for Jesus before the great and the mighty.

Others have what is far better, a close fellowship with the King of kings. Let them plead daily for the Lord's people who are in doubt, who are tempted, and who have little comfort. It will be to their honor to make much intercession for those who sit in darkness and dare not approach the mercy seat.

Instructed believers may serve their Master greatly if they lay out their talents for the general good and teach their wealth of heavenly learning to others.

The very least in our Israel may seek the welfare of our Lord's people. It is the most Christlike and happy course for a believer to cease from living for self. If you bless others, you will be blessed. On the other hand, to seek personal greatness is a wicked and unhappy plan, and its end will be fatal.

My friend, are you using the best of your power for the good of the church in your neighborhood? Unite with the Lord's poor, bear their cross, do all the good you can, and you will not miss your reward.

NOVEMBER 28, EVENING

GOSSIP

"You shall not go about as a talebearer among your people . . . You shall surely rebuke your neighbor and not bear sin because of him."
—Leviticus 19:16,17

Malicious talkers produce poison in three ways, for it injures the teller, the hearer, and the accused. Whether the report is true or false, God's Word forbids it. The reputation of the Lord's people should be precious and protected. It is disgraceful to help the devil dishonor the church and the Lord.

Some tongues need a tight bridle. "Indeed, we put bits in horses' mouths that they may obey us and we turn their whole body. Look also at ships: although they are so large and are driven by fierce winds, they are turned by a very small rudder wherever the pilot desires. Even so the tongue is a little member and boasts great things. See how great a forest a little fire kindles! And the tongue is a fire, a world of iniquity" (James 3:3–5).

Many delight in pulling down their fellow saints in order to raise themselves. Noah's two wise sons covered their father's nakedness, but the son who exposed him earned a fearful curse (Genesis 9:23).

Some dark day we ourselves may be in need of understanding and silence. Let us then cheerfully give it to those who need it now. Let it be our family rule and personal bond to speak evil of no one.

The Holy Spirit, however, does permit us to censure sin, and He prescribes the method for doing it. We correct the fallen to their faces, not behind their backs. This action is Christlike, and under God's blessing it will be redemptive. Hundreds have been saved from gross sins by the timely, wise, and affectionate warning of faithful ministers and saints.

In Jesus' warning to Peter, in the prayer that preceded that warning, and in the gentle way He listened to Peter's boastful denial (Matthew 26:33), our Lord Jesus has given us a gracious example of how to deal with friends who have committed error.

NOVEMBER 29, MORNING

THE ANOINTING

"Spices for the anointing oil."

—Exodus 35:8

Under the law, much use was made of this anointing oil, and what it represents is of primary importance to the gospel.

If we want our service for the Lord to be acceptable, the Holy Spirit who anoints is indispensable. Without the Spirit's aid, our religious services are in vain and our inner experience is dead. Whenever our ministry is without the Spirit's unction, it becomes miserable, including our prayers, praise, meditations, preaching, and other efforts.

The Spirit's anointing is the soul and life of holiness. Its absence is disastrous. To go before the Lord without anointing is like some common Levite thrusting himself into the High Priest's office. It is a ministry of sin instead of service.

May we never venture to our Master's work without a sacred anointing that drops from our glorious Head. From His anointing, we who are the skirts of His garments partake of an abundant unction.

Choice spices were mixed with pharmacist's skills to produce the anointing oil. This is a picture of the influential riches of the Holy Spirit, in whom all good things are found. Matchless comfort, infallible instruction, immortal quickening, spiritual energy, and divine sanctification are compounded with excellent skill to produce the heavenly anointing oil of the Holy Spirit.

This anointing oil imparts a delightful fragrance to the character of the individual on whom it is poured. Nothing like it can be found in all the treasuries of the rich or the secrets of the wise. It cannot be duplicated, for it comes only from God and is freely given to every waiting soul through Jesus Christ. Seek it. It is available this evening.

Oh Lord, anoint Your servant. Amen.

TREASURE THAT CANNOT BE LOST

"'. . . what shall we do about the hundred talents which I have given to the troops of Israel?' And the man of God answered, 'The Lord is able to give you much more than this.'" —2 Chronicles 25:9

This was an important question asked by the king of Judah. And it may be more important for the tried and tempted Christian.

The loss of money is never pleasant, and when principle is involved, we are not always ready to make the sacrifice. We ask, "Why should we lose money that we could use? Perhaps the truth is too expensive. What can we do without funds? What about the children and our already limited income?"

These questions and a thousand others can tempt Christians to unrighteous gain. The possibility of serious financial loss can keep us from carrying out our convictions. All cannot view this matter in the light of faith. And even with the followers of Jesus, the notion that "we must do whatever we need in order to live" carries a lot of weight.

"The Lord is able to give you much more than this," is a most satisfactory answer to this anxious question. Your Father holds the purse strings. What we lose for His sake He can repay a thousand times. If you obey His will, rest assured that He will provide.

A grain of heart's ease is of more value than a ton of gold. A thread-bare coat wrapped about a good conscience is far more desirable than anything that has been lost. God's smile in a dungeon is enough for a true heart, but His frown in a palace would be hell to a gracious spirit. Let the worst come, let all our resources go, and we have not lost our treasure. Our treasure is above, where Christ sits at the right hand of God.

"Blessed are the meek, for they shall inherit the earth" (Matthew 5:5). "No good thing will He withhold from those who walk uprightly" (Psalm 84:11).

ARMED

*"Michael and his angels fought with the dragon;
and the dragon and his angels fought."*

—Revelation 12:7

War will rage between two great powers until one or the other is crushed. Peace between good and evil is impossible. Even the pretense of it would be a triumph for the powers of darkness.

Michael will always fight evil because his holy soul hates sin and will not endure it. Jesus will always be the dragon's foe. Jesus will actively, vigorously, and with full determination exterminate evil. All His servants, whether angels in heaven or messengers on earth, will and must fight. They are born to be warriors, for at the cross they enter into a covenant never to make peace with evil. They are a warlike company, firm in defense and fierce in attack. The daily duty of every Christian soldier is to fight wholeheartedly against the dragon.

The dragon and his angels will not stop fighting. They are incessant with their onslaughts and they spare no weapons, fair or foul. We are foolish if we expect to serve God without opposition. The more zealous we are, the more certain we are to be assailed by hell. The church may become lazy, but the restless spirit of our antagonist never stops fighting. The servants of Satan partake of the old dragon's energy and are usually active. War rages, and to dream of present peace is not only futile, but dangerous. But glory be to God; we know the end. The great dragon will be cast out and forever destroyed (Revelation 20:10).

Let us sharpen our swords tonight, and pray that the Holy Spirit will strengthen us for the conflicts. Never was a battle as important; never was a crown so glorious. Warriors of the cross, to your battle stations! And may the Lord tread Satan under your feet!

WINTER LABORS

"You have made summer and winter."

—Psalm 74:17

My soul, begin this winter month with your God. Let the cold snows and piercing winds remind you that He keeps His covenant with day and night. Thus you are assured that He will keep the glorious covenant that He made with you in Christ Jesus. He who is true to His Word, in the seasonal cycles of this sin polluted world, will not prove unfaithful in His dealings with His own well-beloved Son.

Winter in the soul is not a comfortable season. It can be painful, but it is comforting to know that the Lord makes winter. He sends the sharp blasts of adversity to nip the buds of false expectations. He scatters frost over the green meadows of joy. His ice freezes the streams of delight. He does it all. He is the Winter King, and He rules the realm of frost. Therefore, let us not complain.

Losses, crosses, depression, sickness, poverty, and a thousand other ills come from the Lord with wise design. Frost kills noxious insects and stops raging diseases. Frost breaks the hard ground and sweetens the soil. Oh that such good results would always follow our winters of affliction!

How we need a fire in winter. How pleasant is its cheerful, warming glow. In the same way, let us desire our Lord. He is the constant source of warmth and comfort in time of trouble. Let us draw close to Him to find joy and peace.

Wrap yourself in the warm garments of His promises, and go forth to the labors befitting the season. It is bad for the lazy not to plow because of the cold, for without plowing they will be forced to beg in the summer.

NEW SONGS

"Oh that men would give thanks to the Lord for His goodness, and for His wonderful works to the children of men!"

—Psalm 107:8

If we complained less and praised more, we would be happier and God would be glorified. Let us daily praise God for common mercies (as we frequently call them), mercies which are yet so priceless that, when deprived of them, we are ready to perish.

Let us bless God for eyes to see the sun, for health and strength to walk, for the bread we eat, and for the clothes we wear. Let us praise Him that we are not hopeless or guilty. Let us thank Him for liberty, for friends, for family, and for comforts. Let us praise Him for everything we receive from His bountiful hand. We deserve little, yet He gives so much.

But beloved, the sweetest and the loudest note in our songs of praise should be redeeming love. God's redeeming acts toward His chosen ought to be the favorite theme of our praise. If we know what redemption means, let us sing our song of thanksgiving.

We have been redeemed from the power of corruption and lifted from the depths of sin. We have been led to the cross of Christ, and our shackles of guilt have been broken. We are no longer slaves to sin but children of the living God. Should we not unceasingly give thanks to the Lord our Redeemer?

Child of God, can you be silent? Awake, awake you heirs of glory, and lead captivity captive. Cry with David, "Bless the Lord, O my soul; and all that is within me, bless His holy name" (Psalm 103:1).

Let the new month begin with new songs.

CHRIST VIEWS THE CHURCH

"Behold you are fair, my love."

—Song of Solomon 4:1

The Lord's admiration for His church is wonderful. His description of her beauty glows. She is not merely fair but *all fair,* which is a closer rendering of the text.

He views her in Himself, washed in His sin-atoning blood and clothed in His meritorious righteousness. He considers her beautiful, and no wonder, for it is His own perfect excellence that He admires in her. The holiness, glory, and perfection of His beloved spouse are His own glorious garments.

She is not simply pure, or well-proportioned: she is positively lovely and fair! She has actual merit! Her deformities of sin are removed. She has, through her Lord, obtained a meritorious righteousness that confers real beauty on her. Believers have been given a positive righteousness, which makes them "accepted in the Beloved" (Ephesians 1:6). Nor is the church barely lovely; she is superlatively lovely. Her Lord calls her the "fairest among women" (Song of Solomon 1:8).

She has a worth and excellence that cannot be rivaled by all the nobility and royalty of the world. Jesus would not exchange His elect bride for all the queens and empresses of earth or even for the angels in heaven. He puts her first and foremost, the fairest among women. Like the moon, she outshines the stars.

Behold is a special note of exclamation, inviting and arresting attention, "Behold, you are fair my love! Behold, you are fair." This opinion He holds even now, and one day from the throne of His glory He will openly declare before the assembled universe, "Come, you blessed of My Father" (Matthew 25:34). This will be His solemn affirmation of the loveliness of His elect.

NOTHING

"Indeed, all is vanity."

—Ecclesiastes 1:14

Nothing can satisfy but the Lord's love and presence. Saints have tried other anchorages but have been driven from those fatal refuges. Solomon, the wisest of men, was permitted to experiment for us. Here is his testimony.

So I became great and excelled more than all who were before me in Jerusalem. Also my wisdom remained with me. Whatever my eyes desired I did not keep from them. I did not withhold my heart from any pleasure. For my heart rejoiced in all my labor; and this was my reward for all my labor. Then I looked on all the works that my hands had done and on the labor in which I had toiled. And indeed all was vanity and grasping for the wind. There was no profit under the sun (Ecclesiastes 2:9–11).

Solomon even begins Ecclesiastes by saying, "Vanity of vanities, all is vanity." What! Everything is vanity? Favored monarch, is there nothing of worth in all your wealth? Is there nothing in all your wide land, which reaches from the river to the sea? Is there nothing in Palmyra's glorious palaces, nor in your house in the forest of Lebanon? Is there nothing in all your music, dancing, wine, and luxury?

"Nothing," he says throughout the book, "but grasping for the wind." That was his verdict after he had trodden the whole round of pleasure.

To embrace our Lord Jesus, to dwell in His love, and to be fully assured of union with Him, this is worth something.

Dear reader, there is no need to try other forms of life to see if they are better. If you could have all the comforts of life but lost your Savior, you would be wretched. If you have Christ and if you were to waste in a prison you would find it a paradise. Should you live in obscurity or die in famine, with Christ you will be fully satisfied with favor and goodness.

WITHOUT SPOT

"There is no spot in you."

—Song of Solomon 4:7

After pronouncing His church positively full of beauty, our Lord confirms her with a precious negative, "There is no spot in you." It is as if the thought occurred to the Bridegroom that the complaining world would insinuate that He mentioned only her beauty and purposely omitted those features that were deformed or defiled. But Jesus sums it up by declaring His church universally beautiful and utterly free from stain.

A spot is quickly removed and is the least thing that can disfigure beauty, but even from a spot the believers are delivered. Had Jesus said only that there was no hideous scar, no horrible deformity, no deadly cancer, we would have marvelled. But when He testifies that His church is free from even the slightest stain, then our wonder is increased.

If He had promised to remove all the spots in the future, we would have had an eternal reason for joy. But when He speaks of it as already done, we have intense emotions of satisfaction and delight. Oh my soul, here is spiritual meat; eat and be satisfied.

Jesus Christ has no quarrel with His spouse. Though she often wanders from Him and grieves His Holy Spirit, He does not allow her faults to lessen His love. He sometimes chastens her, but it is always in a tender manner and with kind intentions. He does not remember her foolishness. He does not think uncaring thoughts. He pardons and loves her after the offense.

It is good that Jesus is not as mindful of being injured as we are. Many a believer will get out of sorts with the Lord because of some slight turn in providence. But our precious Husband knows our silly hearts too well to take any offense at our ill manners.

CONQUERING

"The Lord mighty in battle."

—Psalm 24:8

God is glorious in the eyes of His people because He has worked miracles for them, in them, and through them. The Lord Jesus on Calvary routed every foe and broke all the weapons of the enemy by His finished work of satisfactory obedience. Through His triumphant resurrection and ascension, He completely overturned the hopes of hell. Leading captivity captive (Ephesians 4:8), He openly triumphed over His enemies by defeating them on His cross (Colossians 2:15).

Every arrow of guilt that Satan might shoot has been broken, because "who shall bring a charge against God's elect" (Romans 8:33)? Useless are the swords of the devil, for in the church the lame are victorious and the weakest warrior is a crowned victor.

The saved adore their Lord because He conquered them. The arrows of our natural hatred were snapped and the weapons of our rebellion were broken. What victories grace has won in our evil hearts! How glorious is Jesus to us when our will is subdued and sin is dethroned.

As for our remaining corruptions, they will meet with an equally certain defeat. Every temptation, doubt, and fear will be utterly destroyed.

In the Salem of our peaceful hearts, the name of Jesus is beyond comparison. He has won our love and He shall wear it. With this security we look for future victories, for "we are more than conquerors through Him who loved us" (Romans 8:37). We will cast down the powers of darkness by our faith, zeal, and holiness. We will win sinners to Jesus. We will overturn false systems. We will convert nations. "If God is for us, who can be against us" (Romans 8:31)?

This evening, as a Christian warrior, chant the war song and prepare for tomorrow's fight. "He who is in you is greater than he who is in the world" (1 John 4:4).

DECEMBER 3, EVENING

AN ELECT PEOPLE

"I have many people in this city."

—Acts 18:10

Here is encouragement to evangelize. Among the vilest, the most reprobate, and the most debauched and drunken, God has an elect people who must be saved.

When you take the Word to them, you do so because God has ordained you to be the messenger of life to their souls. They must receive it because of the decree of predestination. They are as much redeemed by blood as the saints in heaven.

They are Christ's property, and yet perhaps they may love the taverns and hate holiness. But if Jesus Christ purchased them, He will have them. God is not unfaithful to forget the price His Son paid. God will not permit Jesus' substitution to be ineffectual for them.

Tens of thousands of redeemed ones are not regenerated yet, but regenerated they must be. This is our comfort when we go to them with the quickening Word of God. These ungodly ones are prayed for by Christ before the throne. "I do not pray for these alone, but also for those who will believe in Me through their word" (John 17:20).

These ignorant souls know nothing about prayer, but Jesus prays for them. Their names are on his breastplate, and before long they will bow their stubborn knees and say a penitential prayer before the throne of grace.

"It was not the season for figs" (Mark 11:13). The predestinated moment had not struck. But when it comes, they must obey, for God will have His way. They must obey, for the Spirit will not be withstood when He comes with fullness of power. They must become the willing servants of the living God.

"Your people shall be volunteers in the day of Your power" (Psalm 110:3). "He shall see the labor of His soul and be satisfied. By His knowledge My righteous Servant shall justify many. For He shall bear their iniquities and He shall divide the spoil with the strong" (Isaiah 53:11).

DECEMBER 4, MORNING

GROANS AND SIGHS

"Even we ourselves groan within ourselves, eagerly waiting for the adoption, the redemption of our body."

—Romans 8:23

This groaning is universal among the saints. To a greater or lesser degree, we all groan. But it is not the groan of murmur, complaint, or distress; rather, it is the sound of desire. Having received a promise, we desire the full portion.

We sigh that our entire humanity, in its trinity of spirit, soul, and body, will be set free from the last vestiges of the fall. We groan to put off corruption, weakness, dishonor, and to wrap ourselves in incorruption, immortality, glory, and the spiritual body which the Lord Jesus will give us. We long for the manifestation of our adoption as the children of God. And so we groan inwardly, not with the hypocrites' groan, which leads people to believe they are saints, but with sacred sighs, too hallowed to talk about. And so we tell our longings only to our Lord.

Then the apostle says we are waiting. We learn not to be peevish like Jonah or Elijah when they said, "Let me die" (Jonah 4:3) (1 Kings 19:4). We learn not to whimper and sigh for the end of life because we are tired of work or want to escape our present suffering before the will of the Lord is done.

We also groan for glorification, but we are to wait patiently for it because what the Lord appoints is best. Waiting implies being ready. We are to stand at the door expecting the Beloved to open it and take us away.

Groaning is a test. You may judge people by what they groan after. Some groan for wealth, and thus worship money. Others groan about the troubles of life and are impatient. But those who sigh after God, who are not content until they are made like Christ—they are blessed.

May God help us to groan for the coming of the Lord and the resurrection which He will bring.

DECEMBER 4, EVENING

THE HOSPITAL

"Ask and it will be given to you."

—Matthew 7:7

We know a place in England where bread is served to everyone who asks. All you have to do is knock on the door of St. Cross Hospital and bread is offered.

Jesus Christ so loves sinners that He has built His own St. Cross Hospital, where all hungry sinners have to do is knock. No, even better, Jesus has attached a bath to this Hospital of the Cross. Whenever souls are dirty and filthy, all they need to do is go there and be washed. The fountain is always full and effectual. Every sinner who ever came found that this bath washed away their stains. Sins that were scarlet and crimson disappeared and the sinner became whiter than snow.

As if this were not enough, a wardrobe is also attached to this Hospital of the Cross. Simply by asking, sinners may be clothed from head to foot. If they want to be soldiers, they are not given ordinary garments, but armor to cover them fully, and a sword and a shield.

Nothing good will be denied. They will have spending money as long as they live, and they will find an eternal heritage of glorious treasure when they enter into the joy of the Lord.

If all these things are to be had by merely knocking at mercy's door, Oh my soul, knock hard this morning, and ask large things of your generous Lord. Do not leave the throne of grace until all your wants have been spread before the Lord and until by faith you are persuaded that they will be supplied.

Do not be bashful when Jesus invites. No unbelief should hinder when Jesus promises. No cold heart should restrain when such blessings are to be obtained.

RAISING UP DEFENDERS

"Then the Lord showed me four craftsmen."

—Zechariah 1:20

In this vision the prophet saw four terrible horns pushing this way and that, dashing down the strongest and the mightiest. When the prophet asked what the horns were, he was told, "These are the horns that have scattered Judah, Israel and Jerusalem" (Zechariah 1:19).

Zechariah saw a representation of the powers that had oppressed the church. There were four horns, because the church is attacked from all quarters. The prophet had every right to be dismayed, but suddenly four craftsmen appeared. When he asked what they were coming for, he was told, "The craftsmen are coming to terrify them, to cast out the horns of the nations that lifted up their horn against the land of Judah to scatter it."

God will always find people for His work, and He will find them at the right time. At first, the prophet did not see the craftsmen. He saw the horns and then the craftsmen. Moreover, the Lord finds enough people. He did not find three craftsmen, but four. There were four horns, and so there must be four workmen. God also finds the right people. He did not choose four scribes with pens to write nor four architects with plans to draw. He found four craftsmen to do rough work.

Rest assured, you who tremble when the horns grow troublesome, the craftsmen will be found. Don't worry about the weakness of the church. Growing up in obscurity may be the valiant reformer who will shake the nations. Another Chrysostom may come from our ragged schools; another Augustine from the darkness of urban poverty. The Lord knows where to find His servants.

God has a multitude of mighty soldiers waiting in ambush, and at His word, they will start the battle, because "the battle is the Lord's" (1 Samuel 17:47). Be faithful and in the right time Christ will raise our defense.

DECEMBER 5, EVENING

HEAVENLY HONOR

"As is the heavenly Man, so also are those who are heavenly."

—1 Corinthians 15:48

The head and members of the church are one nature and not like that monstrous image Nebuchadnezzar saw in his dream. "The head was of fine gold, its chest and arms of silver, its belly and thighs of bronze, its legs of iron, its feet of iron and clay" (Daniel 2:32–33).

Christ's mystical body is no absurd combination of opposites. The members are mortal, and thus Jesus died. The glorified head is immortal, and thus the body is now immortal. The record shows, "Because I live, you will live also" (John 14:19). As is our loving head, so is every member of the body: a chosen Head and chosen members, an accepted Head and accepted members, a living Head and living members. If the head is pure gold, all the parts of the body are pure gold. There is a double union of nature as a basis for the closest possible communion.

Pause here, devout reader, and see if you can contemplate the infinite condescension of the Son of God in exalting your wretchedness into the blessed union with His glory. We are so unworthy that we say to corruption, "you are my father, and to the worm, you are my sister" (Job 17:14). Yet in Christ we are so honored that we can say of the Almighty, "Abba Father" (Romans 8:15), and to the Incarnate God, "My Maker is my husband" (Isaiah 54:5).

Surely if relationships to ancient and noble families make people think highly of themselves, then we have the right to glory over the heads of them all. Let the poorest and most despised believer claim this privilege. Do not let lethargy make you forget your pedigree. Let no foolish attachments to present-day vanities occupy your mind to the exclusion of this glorious, this heavenly, honor of union with Christ.

DECEMBER 6, MORNING

A GOLDEN BAND

"Girded about the chest with a golden band."

—Revelation 1:13

"One like the Son of Man" appeared to John in Patmos, and the beloved disciple noted that He wore a golden band.

While on earth Jesus was always ready to serve. Now, before the eternal throne, He maintains this holy ministry as our great High Priest (Hebrews 4:14). It is good that He has not ceased to fulfill this office of love. Our assurance and safeguard of this fact is that "He always lives to make intercession" for us (Hebrews 7:25). Jesus is never idle. His garments are never loose, as though His duties were ended. He diligently works for the cause of His people.

The golden band is the symbol of the superiority of His service, the royalty of His person, the dignity of His state, and the glory of His reward. No longer does He cry out of the dust. Now He pleads with authority, a King as well as a Priest. Our cause is safe in the hands of our enthroned Melchizedek.

Our Lord thus presents all His people with an example: Never loosen your band. This is not the time to lie down; this is the season of service and warfare, and we need to bind the band of truth more tightly. It is a golden band, our richest ornament, and we greatly need it. A heart that is not bound tightly with the truth of Jesus and the faithfulness of the Spirit will be easily entangled in the things of this life and tripped by the snares of temptation.

It is useless to possess Scripture unless we bind it around our entire nature, character, and being. If in heaven Jesus does not take off His band, how on earth can we?

"Stand therefore, having girded your waist with truth" (Ephesians 6:14).

DECEMBER 6, EVENING

CHOSEN SINNERS

"The base things of the world and the things which are despised God has chosen."

—1 Corinthians 1:28

Walk the streets at night, if you dare, and you will see sinners. Watch when the night is dark, when the wind is howling, and you will see sinners.

Go to a jail, and walk the cell blocks. Look at the prisoners and note their hardness. These are people you would not want to meet on the streets at night; they are sinners. Go to the juvenile halls and note the depravity; they are sinners.

Go where you will. You do not need to ransack the earth to find sinners; they are common enough. You can find them on every road and street of every city, town, village, and hamlet. But note also that for these Jesus died. If you find the most sinful, I have hope for them, for "Jesus Christ came into the world to save sinners" (1 Timothy 1:15).

Electing love has selected some of the worst to be made the best. Pebbles in the brook Grace turn into jewels for the royal crown. Worthless dross He transforms into pure gold. Redeeming love has set apart many of the worst to be the reward of the Savior. Effectual grace calls many of the vilest to sit transformed at the table of mercy. Therefore, let no one despair.

Sinner, by the love in Jesus' tearful eyes, by the love streaming from those bleeding wounds, by that faithful, strong, pure, and abiding love, we urge you not to turn away as though it were nothing. "For God so loved the world that He gave His only begotten Son, that whoever believes on Him should not perish but have everlasting life" (John 3:16).

Trust in Him, and He will bring you to His Father's right hand in everlasting glory.

DECEMBER 7, MORNING

THE OBJECTIVE

"I become all things to all men, that I might by all means save some."

—1 Corinthians 9:22

Paul's objective was not merely to instruct and improve, but to save. Anything less would have disappointed him. He wanted people renewed in heart, forgiven, sanctified, in fact, saved.

Have our Christian efforts been aimed at anything below this objective? Then let us amend our ways. What will it avail in the last day for us to have taught and moralized people if they appear before God unsaved? Blood red will be our skirts if through life we have sought inferior objects and forgotten that people need salvation.

Paul knew the ruin of our natural state and did not try to educate, but to save. Paul saw humanity sinking to hell and did not talk of refining, but of saving them from the wrath to come. With untiring zeal he spread the gospel, warning and beseeching sinners to be reconciled to God.

Paul's prayers were urgent and his labor incessant. Saving souls was his consuming passion, his ambition, and his calling. He became a servant to all, saying, "Woe is me if I do not preach the gospel" (1 Corinthians 9:16).

He laid aside his preferences to prevent prejudice against the gospel. He submitted his will to the nonessentials. If people received the gospel, Paul raised no questions about forms or ceremonies, for the gospel was the one all-important business. Through this, if he could save some, he would be content. This was the crown for which he strove, the only sufficient reward for all his labor and self-denial.

Dear reader, have you and I lived to win souls? Are we motivated by the same all-absorbing desire? If not, why not?

Jesus died for sinners; cannot we live for sinners? Where is our tenderness? Where is our love for Christ if we do not seek His honor in the salvation of sinners? Oh that the Lord would saturate us through and through with an undying zeal for souls.

DECEMBER 7, EVENING

WHITE ROBES

"You have a few names even in Sardis who have not defiled their garments and they shall walk with Me in white, for they are worthy."
—Revelation 3:4

We may understand our text to refer to justification. They shall walk in white, and so enjoy a constant sense of their own justification by faith. They will understand that the righteousness of Christ is imputed to them, that they have been washed and made whiter than the new fallen snow.

It also refers to joy and gladness, for white robes were the Jews' holiday dress. They who have not defiled their garments will have bright faces. They will understand what Solomon meant when he said, "Go, eat your bread with joy, and drink your wine with a merry heart: for God has already accepted your works. Let your garments always be white" (Ecclesiastes 9:8). Those who are accepted of God will wear white garments of joy and gladness as they walk in sweet fellowship with the Lord Jesus.

Then why so many doubts, why so much misery and sadness? It is because many believers defile their walk with sin and error. They lose the joy of their salvation and the comfort of fellowship with the Lord Jesus.

The promise also refers to walking in white before the throne of God. Those who have not defiled their garments here will certainly walk in white up where the hosts sing perpetual hallelujahs to the Most High (Revelation 19:1). They shall possess joys inconceivable, happiness beyond dreams, ecstasy beyond imagination, and blessedness that even the stretch of desire has not reached.

The undefiled will have all of this, not from merit or work, but because of grace. They will walk with Christ in white, for He has made them worthy. In His sweet company they will drink from the living fountains of waters (Revelation 7:17).

KNOWN FUTURE NEEDS

"You, O God, provided from Your goodness for the poor."

—Psalm 68:10

All God's gifts are prepared in advance and reserved for wants foreseen. He knows our future needs, and out of the fullness of Christ Jesus He provides from His goodness. You may therefore trust Him for all your future needs. He has infallible foreknowledge about every one of them. He can say to you in any condition, "I knew that you would need this."

A traveler journeying across a desert may pitch the tent only to find that some essentials were not bought along. "Ah!" says the traveler, "I did not foresee this. If I could start this journey over I would bring these necessary items."

But God has foreknowledge of all that His wandering children require. And when those needs arise, the supplies are ready. It is goodness that He has prepared for the poor in heart. Goodness, and goodness only. "My grace is sufficient for you" (2 Corinthians 12:9). "As your days, so shall your strength be" (Deuteronomy 33:25).

Reader, is your heart heavy this evening? God knew it would be. The comfort your heart wants is treasured in the sweet assurance of our text. You are poor and needy, but He knows your need and has the exact blessing you require. Plead this promise. Believe it, and you will obtain fulfillment.

Do you feel that you were never so consciously vile as you are now? Behold, the crimson fountain is still open with all its former power to wash your sin away.

You will never be in a position where Christ cannot help you. There will never be a bind in your spiritual life where Jesus Christ will not be equal to the emergency. Your history has all been foreknown and provided for in Jesus.

DECEMBER 8, EVENING

DELAYED ANSWERS

"Therefore the Lord will wait that He may be gracious to you."

—Isaiah 30:18

God often delays answering prayer. There are several instances of this in Scripture. Jacob did not get the blessing from the angel until near the breaking of day. He had to wrestle all night (Genesis 32:24). The poor Syrian woman from Phoenicia was not answered for a long time (Mark 7:26). Paul pleaded with the Lord three times that "a thorn in the flesh" would be removed. It was not, but he received a promise that God's grace was sufficient (2 Corinthians 12:8).

If you have been knocking at the gate of mercy and have not received an answer, shall I tell you why the Almighty has not opened the door? Our Father has reasons to keep us waiting that He alone knows. Sometimes it is to show His power and His sovereignty, so we may know that Jehovah has a right to give or to withhold.

Frequently, the delay is for our benefit. Perhaps you are kept waiting so that your requests will become more fervent. God knows that delays accelerate and increase desire. If He keeps you waiting, you will see your need more clearly, and you will seek an answer more earnestly. You will value the mercy all the more because of the wait.

There may also be something wrong in you that needs to be removed before the joy of the Lord is given. Perhaps your view of the gospel is confused, or you may be placing a little reliance on yourself instead of trusting simply and entirely on the Lord Jesus. Or, God may make you wait so that He may more fully display the riches of His grace.

Prayers that are filed in heaven, if not immediately answered, are certainly not forgotten. In a little while they will be answered to your delight and satisfaction. Do not let despair make you silent. Continue earnestly in supplication.

DECEMBER 9, MORNING

PEACE

"My people will dwell in a peaceful habitation."

—Isaiah 32:18

Peace and rest are the special possession of the Lord's people. "You will keep him in perfect peace whose mind is stayed on You" (Isaiah 26:3). Before man fell, God gave him the lush gardens of Eden as his quiet resting place. But how quickly sin blighted that fair home of innocence.

In that day of universal wrath, when the flood swept away a guilty race, the chosen family were quietly secured in the resting place of the ark. They floated from the old condemned world to the new earth of the rainbow and the covenant (Genesis 8:1). This foreshadowed Jesus, the ark of our salvation.

In the wilderness, the shadow of the pillar of cloud (Exodus 13:21) and the rock from which water flowed (Exodus 17:6) gave the weary pilgrims sweet rest.

At this hour we rest in the promises of our faithful God, knowing that His words are truth and power. We rest in the doctrines of His Word, which are true comfort. We rest in the covenant of His grace, which is a haven of delight.

We are more favored than David in Adullam (1 Samuel 22:1) or Jonah under his plant (Jonah 4:7), because nothing can invade or destroy our shelter. Jesus Christ is the quiet resting place of His people. When we draw near to Him in the breaking of bread, in the hearing of the word, in the searching of the Scriptures, or in praise and prayer, we find our approaches to Him bring peace to our spirits:

I hear the words of love, I gaze upon the blood,
I see the mighty sacrifice, and I have peace
with God.
'Tis everlasting peace, sure as Jehovah's name,
'Tis stable as His steadfast throne, for evermore
the same:
The clouds may go and come, and storms may
sweep my sky,
This blood sealed friendship changes not,
The cross is ever nigh.

DECEMBER 9, EVENING

FACE TO FACE

"We shall always be with the Lord."

—1 Thessalonians 4:17

Even the sweetest visits from Christ are short and transitory. One moment our eyes see Him, and we "rejoice with joy inexpressible and full of glory" (1 Peter 1:8). Then we do not see Him. Our Beloved withdraws. Like a gazelle or a young deer, He leaps over the mountains of division. He is gone to the land of spices and feeds no more among the lilies:

> If today he deigns to bless us
>   With a sense of pardoned sin,
> He tomorrow may distress us,
>   Make us feel the plague within.

How wonderful the thought that soon we will not see Him from a distance but face to face. Then He will not be a traveler stopping for a night, but He will eternally fold us in the center of His glory. We will not see Him for a little while, but then for:

> Millions of years our wondering eyes,
> Shall over our Savior's beauties rove;
> And myriad ages we'll adore,
> The wonders of His love.

In heaven there will be no care or sin. No weeping will dim our eyes. No worldly business will distract our happy thoughts. We will have nothing to hinder us from gazing forever on the Sun of Righteousness.

If it is wonderful to see Him here now and then, how marvelous it will be to gaze on His blessed face forever. Never a cloud to come between, never to turn away and look at a world of weariness and woe! Blessed day! When will you dawn? Rise unsetting sun!

Here, the sense of joys may come and go, but this will one day be changed gloriously. If to die is to enter into uninterrupted communion with Jesus, then death is indeed gain and the black drop is swallowed up in a sea of victory (1 Corinthians 15:54).

AN OPENED HEART

"The Lord opened her heart."

—Acts 16:14

There are many interesting points in Lydia's conversion. It was brought about by providential circumstances. "Lydia was a seller of purple from the city of Thyatira" (Acts 16:14), but at just the right time to hear Paul, we find her at Philippi. Providence, the attendant of grace, led her to the right place at the right time. Grace was preparing her soul for the blessing, grace preparing for grace.

Lydia did not know the Savior, but as a Jew she knew many truths that were stepping stones to knowing Jesus. On the Sabbath she went to pray and her prayer was heard. Never neglect the means of grace. God may bless us when we are not in His house, but we have greater reason to hope that He will bless us in fellowship with His saints.

Note the words: The Lord opened her heart. Lydia did not open her own heart. Her own prayers did not do it. Paul did not do it. The Lord alone must open the heart if one is to receive the things that make for peace. He alone can put the key in the door, open it, and gain admittance. He is as much the heart's master as He is its maker.

The first outward evidence of her opened heart was obedience. As soon as Lydia believed she was baptized. It is a pleasing sign of a humble and broken heart when the child of God is willing to obey a command that is not essential for salvation, that is not forced by a selfish fear of condemnation, but is a simple act of love to the Master.

The next evidence was love manifesting itself in acts of kindness to the apostles. Love for the saints has always been the mark of a true convert. Those who do nothing for Christ or His church show no evidence of an opened heart.

Lord, forever give me an opened heart. Amen.

SECURITY

"He who calls you is faithful, who also will do it."

—1 Thessalonians 5:24

Heaven is a place where we will never sin. It is a place where we will cease our constant watch against an indefatigable enemy. In heaven there will be no temptations to ensnare our feet. The wicked will not trouble us, and the weary will be at rest. Heaven is the incorruptible and undefiled inheritance (1 Peter 1:4). It is the land of perfect holiness and complete security.

Can the saints on earth taste the joys of security? The doctrine of God's Word is that all who are in union with the Lamb are safe, that all who have committed their souls to Christ will find Him a faithful and permanent preserver. Sustained by such a doctrine, the saints can enjoy security even on earth. This is not the high and glorious security that renders them free from every slip; it is a holy security that arises from the sure promise of Jesus, that all who believe in Him will not perish but have everlasting life (John 3:16).

Believer, frequently reflect with joy on the doctrine of the perseverance of the saints, and honor the faithfulness of our God with your holy confidence in Him. May God give you a sense of your safety in Christ Jesus. May He assure you that He has inscribed you on the palms of His hands (Isaiah 49:16). May He whisper in your ear the promise, "Do not fear" (Luke 12:32).

The great Surety of the covenant is faithful and true. He has promised to present you, perhaps the weakest of the family, before the throne of God as holy, blameless, and above reproach in His sight (Colossians 1:22). In sweet contemplation you will drink the spiced wine of the Lord's pomegranate (Song of Solomon 8:2) and taste the fruits of Paradise.

If with unstaggering faith you believe that "He who calls you is faithful, who also will do it," you will have an appetizer of the enjoyments that ravish the souls of the perfect saints above.

ALL WORK, GOD'S WORK

"You serve the Lord Christ."

—Colossians 3:24

To whom was our text spoken, to kings who boast of a divine right? No, for far too often they serve themselves or Satan and forget the God who permits them to mimic majesty for their little hour.

Does the apostle speak to those so-called right reverend fathers in God, the bishops, or the honorable archdeacons? No indeed. Paul knew nothing of these inventions of man. Not even to pastors and teachers or to wealthy and esteemed believers was this word spoken. It was spoken to servants, yes, and even to slaves.

Among the toiling multitudes, the journeymen, the day laborers, the servants, and the drudges of the kitchen, the apostle found the Lord's chosen. To them he says, "Whatever you do, do it heartily, as to the Lord and not to men" (Colossians 3:23). This saying gives honor to the weary routine of earthly employment and sheds a halo around the most humble occupations.

To wash feet may be the job of slaves, but to wash His feet is royal work. To loosen shoe strings is terrible employment, but to loosen the great Master's shoes is a royal privilege. The barn, the shop, and the factory all become temples when men and women do all to the glory of God. Then divine service is not a thing of a few hours and a few places, but all of life becomes holiness unto the Lord, and every place and thing is as consecrated as the tabernacle and its golden candlestick:

> Teach me, my God and King,
>   In all things Thee to see;
> And what I do in anything,
>   To do it as to Thee.
> A servant with this clause
>   Makes drudgery divine;
> Who sweeps a room, As for Thy laws,
>   Makes that and the action fine.

DECEMBER 11, EVENING

CONSISTENT

"His ways are everlasting."

—Habakkuk 3:6

Human ways are variable, but God's ways are everlasting. There are many reasons for this comforting truth.

The Lord's ways result from His wise deliberations. He orders all things according to the counsel of His own will (Ephesians 1:11). Human action is frequently the hasty result of passion or fear and is followed by regret and a change of mind.

Nothing can take the Almighty by surprise. Nothing can happen to you that He has not foreseen. His ways are the outgrowth of an incorruptible character, and in them the fixed and settled attributes of God are clearly seen.

Unless the Eternal One can change, His ways must remain forever the same. Is He eternally just, gracious, faithful, wise, and tender? Then His ways must ever be distinguished with the same excellences. Humans act according to their nature, and when their nature changes their behavior changes. With God "there is no variation or shadow of turning" (James 1:17). His ways will everlastingly be the same. Moreover, there is no reason from without that could reverse the divine ways, since they are the embodiment of irresistible might.

All the nations of the earth are counted as nothing (Isaiah 40:17). God does according to His will, both in the army of heaven and among the inhabitants of the earth. No one can restrain His hand or say to Him, "What have You done?" (Daniel 4:35). But it is not might alone that gives stability. God's ways are the manifestation of the eternal principles of right, which therefore can never pass away. Wrong breeds decay and involves ruin, but the true and the good have a vitality that ages cannot diminish.

This morning, let us go to our heavenly Father with confidence, remembering that "Jesus Christ is the same yesterday, today and forever" (Hebrews 13:8) and that He is gracious (1 Peter 2:3).

DECEMBER 12, MORNING

TREACHEROUS

"They have dealt treacherously with the Lord."

—Hosea 5:7

Believer, this is a sorrowful truth. You are the beloved of the Lord, redeemed by blood, called by grace, preserved in Christ Jesus, accepted in the Beloved, and on your way to heaven. Yet, you "have dealt treacherously with the Lord." You have dealt treacherously with God, your best friend, and treacherously with Jesus, who owns you. You have dealt treacherously with the Holy Spirit, who has made you alive to God.

How treacherous you have been in the matter of vows and promises. Do you remember the love of your adoption, that happy time, the springtime of your spiritual life? How closely you clung to your Master! You vowed, "He will never charge me with indifference. My feet will never be slow in His service. I will not let my heart wander after other loves. In Jesus, the store of sweetness is indescribable. I give up all for my Lord's sake." Have you kept these commitments?

If your conscience speaks, it will say, "You who promised so much, have performed so little. Your prayers have been slurred and short, but not sweet; they have been brief, but not fervent. Fellowship with Christ has been forgotten.

Instead of being heavenly minded you have had carnal cares, worldly vanities, and thoughts of evil. Instead of service, there has been disobedience. Instead of fire, there has been lukewarmness. Instead of patience, anxiety. Instead of faith, confidence in the arm of flesh. Though a soldier of the cross, there has been cowardice, disobedience, and desertion. You have dealt treacherously.

Treachery to Jesus! What words can be used in denouncing it? Words avail little. Let our penitent thoughts execrate the sin that is so surely in us. Treacherous to thy wounds, Oh Jesus, forgive us and let us not sin again! How shameful to be treacherous to Him who never forgets us. Who stands even now before the eternal throne—our names engraved on His breastplate.

DECEMBER 12, EVENING

SALT WITHOUT LIMIT

"Salt without prescribed limit."

—Ezra 7:22

S alt was used in every fire offering made to the Lord. The preserving and the purifying properties of salt are emblems of divine grace in the soul.

When Artaxerxes gave salt to Ezra the priest, he set no limit to the quantity. We may be quite certain that when the King of kings distributes grace among His royal priesthood, the supply is never short.

Often in ourselves we are destitute, but never in the Lord. Those who choose to gather manna will find they have as much as they desire. There is no famine in Jerusalem, that bread and water should be rationed.

Some things in the economy of grace are measured. For example, vinegar and gall are given with such exactness that we never have a single drop too much. But of the salt of grace there is no limit. "Ask and it will be given you; seek, and you will find; knock and it will be opened to you" (Matthew 7:7). A person may have too much money, or too much honor, but not too much grace.

Jeshurun grew fat and kicked, and then he forsook God who made him (Deuteronomy 32:15). But there is no fear of a person becoming too full of grace. A plethora of grace is impossible. More wealth brings more care, but more grace brings more joy. Increased wisdom is increased sorrow, but abundance of the Spirit is fullness of joy.

Believer, go before the throne for a large supply of heavenly salt. It will season your afflictions, which are tasteless without salt. It will preserve your heart, which corrupts if salt is absent. It will kill your sins, just as salt kills reptiles.

You need much. So seek much, and have much.

WINDOWS

"I will make your pinnacles of rubies, your gates of crystal and your walls of precious stones."

—Isaiah 54:12

The church is symbolized as a building erected by heavenly power and designed by divine skill. Such a spiritual house must not be dark. There must be windows to let the light in and to allow the residents to look out. The windows are as precious as semitransparent quartz, the most transparent of precious stones. From these windows, the church beholds her Lord, heaven, and spiritual truth, for

> Our knowledge of that life is small,
> Our eye of faith is dim.

Faith is one of those precious windows, but it is often so misty and cloudy that we see darkly and mistake much of what we do see. If we cannot gaze through windows of diamonds and know even as we are known (1 Corinthians 13:12), it is still a glorious thing to behold the altogether lovely One, even if the glass is clouded.

Experience is another of these dim but precious windows that yield a subdued religious light. Through our afflictions we see the sufferings of the Man of Sorrows. Our weak eyes could not endure the Master's glory through windows of transparent glass. But when our eyes are dimmed with weeping, the beams of the Sun of Righteousness are tempered and shine through the windows with a soft radiance that is inexpressibly soothing.

Sanctification, as it conforms us to our Lord, is another window. Only as we become heavenly can we comprehend heavenly things. The pure in heart see a pure God. Those who are like Jesus see Him as He is. Because we are so little like Him, the windows are semitransparent; because we are somewhat like Him, the windows are semitransparent.

We thank God for what we have, but we long for more. When shall we see God and Jesus, and heaven and truth, face to face?

DECEMBER 13, EVENING

STRENGTH TO STRENGTH

"They go from strength to strength."

—Psalm 84:7

There are various translations of this text, and all of them contain the idea of progress. "They go from strength to strength," that is, they grow stronger and stronger.

If we are walking, we go from strength to weakness. We start fresh and strong, but as the road becomes rough and the sun grows hot we are forced to sit and rest. Then once again, we pursue our weary way.

Christian pilgrims, however, having obtained a fresh supply of grace, are as vigorous after years of toilsome travel and struggle as when they first started. They may not be quite so elated and buoyant, perhaps not so hot and hasty in their zeal; but they are stronger in all that constitutes real power. Although they travel more slowly, they travel more surely. Some gray-haired veterans have been as firm in their grasp of truth and as zealous in diffusing it as they were in their youth.

Unfortunately, for others it is different. Their love grows cold and iniquity abounds. This is not the fault of the promise, which remains true. "Even the youths shall faint and be weary. And the young men shall utterly fall. But those who wait on the Lord shall renew their strength. They shall mount up with wings like eagles. They shall run and not be weary. They shall walk and not faint" (Isaiah 40:31–32).

Anxious believer, stop worrying about the future. You say, "But I go from affliction to affliction." Oh you of little faith. You also go from "strength to strength." You will never find a bundle of affliction that has not been wrapped in sufficient grace. God will give you the strength of youth with the burden allotted to full grown shoulders.

DECEMBER 14, MORNING

THE LIVING DEAD

"I have been crucified with Christ."

—Galatians 2:20

The Lord Jesus Christ in His dying on the cross represents the effective death of all His people. The apostle to the Gentiles delighted to think that in Christ he had died on the cross.

Paul did more than believe this doctrinally; he confidently accepted it and rested his hope on this truth. Through Christ's death Paul knew that divine justice had been satisfied and that he had found reconciliation with God.

Beloved, what a blessed thing when you can stretch yourself on the cross of Christ and say, "I have been crucified with Christ; it is no longer I who live, but Christ lives in me; and the life which I now live in the flesh I live by faith in the Son of God, who loved me and gave Himself for me" (Galatians 2:20). The law has slain me; therefore, I am free from its power, because in Jesus I have suffered the curse.

But Paul meant even more than this. He not only believed and trusted in Christ's death, but he actually felt its power crucifying his old corrupt nature. When Paul saw the pleasures of sin he said, "How shall we who died to sin live any longer in it?" (Romans 6:2). This is the experience of every true Christian. Having received Christ we are utterly dead to this world.

Yet, while conscious of death to the world, we can at the same time exclaim with the apostle, "I live by faith in the Son of God who loved me and gave Himself for me" (Galatians 2:20).

The Christian's life is a matchless riddle. No unbeliever can comprehend it, and even believers cannot fully understand it. Dead, yet alive! Crucified with Christ, yet at the same time risen with Christ in newness of life!

Union with the suffering, bleeding Savior and death to the world and sin, are soul-cheering. Oh for more enjoyment of them!

THE CHOICE

"Orpah kissed her mother-in-law, but Ruth clung to her."

—Ruth 1:14

Orpah and Ruth loved Naomi so much that they were willing to return to Judah with her, but Naomi urged them to return to the comfort and pleasure of their Moabite friends. At first, both Orpah and Ruth said they would go with Naomi and live with the Lord's people. After further consideration Orpah, with much grief and a respectful kiss, left her mother-in-law, her family and her God and went back to her idolatrous friends. While Ruth, with all her heart, gave herself to the God of her mother-in-law.

It is one thing to love the ways of the Lord when all is well and quite another thing to cling to them during discouragement or difficulty. The kiss of outward profession is cheap and easy, but practical clinging to the Lord, which is apparent in our decisions for truth and holiness, is difficult.

How is it with you? Is your heart fixed on Jesus? Is the sacrifice bound with cords to the horns of the altar (Psalm 118:27)? Have you counted the cost? Are you ready to suffer all worldly loss for the Master's sake? If so, your gain will be abundant. "Greater riches than the treasurers in Egypt are not to be compared with the glory to be revealed" (Hebrews 11:26).

Orpah is never heard from again. In false comfort and idolatrous pleasure her life melts into the gloom of death. Ruth, however, lives in history and in heaven. Grace has placed her in the noble line of the King of kings. Blessed are those who for Christ's sake can renounce all. But forgotten, and worse than forgotten, are those who, during temptation, turn back to the world.

Oh that this morning we would not be content with a form of devotion that is no better than Orpah's kiss. May the Holy Spirit help us to cling with whole hearts to our Lord Jesus.

DECEMBER 15, MORNING

THE JEWELED FOUNDATION

"And lay your foundations with sapphires."

—Isaiah 54:11

Foundations are hidden, and as long as they support the building, it is not expected that they will be noticed.

In the church, however, not only that which is seen, but that which is unseen is beautiful and precious. In Jehovah's work everything is a masterpiece, nothing blemished, nothing meager. The deep foundations of the work of grace are as precious as sapphires. No human mind is capable of measuring their glory. We build on the covenant of grace, which is firmer than diamonds and as enduring as jewels. Sapphire foundations are eternal, and the covenant stands through the lifetime of the Almighty.

Another foundation is the person of the Lord Jesus (1 Peter 2:6). He is as clear, spotless, everlasting, and beautiful as the sapphire. Like the sapphire, His beauty blends the deep blue of earth's rolling ocean and the radiance of the embracing sky.

Our Lord can be compared to the ruby, because He stood covered with his own blood. But now we see Him radiant with the soft blue of love, love abounding, deep, and eternal.

Our eternal hope is built on the justice and the faithfulness of God, which is as clear and cloudless as the sapphire. We are not saved by compromise, nor by mercy defeating justice, nor by law suspending its operations. No, we defy the eagle's eye to detect a flaw in the ground work of our confidence, for our foundation is sapphire and will endure the fire. The Lord Himself has laid the foundation of His people's hopes. We must determine if our hopes are built on this foundation.

Good works and ceremonies are a foundation of wood, hay, and straw. They are not laid by God but by our own conceit. Anguish will be yours when your lofty tower crashes because you built on sand.

You who built on sapphires can await the storm with calmness. You will stand the test.

DECEMBER 15, EVENING

COME

"Come to Me."

—Matthew 11:28

The cry of the Christian religion is the gentle word, "Come."

The Jewish law said harshly, "Go, but watch your step. Break the commandments and you will perish. Keep them and you will live." The law was a dispensation of terror that drove people with a whip.

The gospel draws with love. Jesus is the good Shepherd (John 10:11) calling His sheep to follow and leading them onward with the sweet word, "Come."

The law repels. The gospel attracts. The law shows the distance between God and mankind. The gospel bridges this awful chasm and brings the sinner across.

From the first moment of your spiritual life, until you are ushered into glory, Christ's words will be, "Come, come to me." He will always be ahead of you, urging you to follow Him. He will always lead, paving your way and clearing your path. You will hear His animating voice calling you throughout your life.

In the solemn hour of death, He will usher you into the heavenly world with the sweet words, "Come, you blessed of my Father" (Matthew 25:34).

This is not only Christ's cry to you, but if you are a believer, this is your cry to Christ, "Come! Come!" You long for His second coming. You say with John, "Come quickly Lord Jesus" (Revelation 22:20). You crave closer fellowship with Him.

As He calls "Come," respond by saying, "Come Lord and live in me. Come and occupy the throne of my heart. Reign there alone, without a rival, and consecrate me completely for Your service."

THE HEARING EAR

"Surely you did not hear. Surely you did not know; Surely from long ago your ear was not opened."

—Isaiah 48:8

It is painful to think that this is an accusation against believers who are spiritually insensitive. We should regret that we do not hear the voice of God as we should.

There are gentle motions of the Holy Spirit in the soul that often go unheeded. There are whispers of divine commands and of heavenly love that are ignored by our leaden intellects. We have been carelessly ignorant. There are situations we should have seen, iniquities that went unnoticed, sweet feelings that became blighted flowers in the frost, left unattended. We missed glimpses of the divine face because we walled up the windows of our soul. We did not hear or know.

As we think about it, we are deeply humbled, but we adore the grace of God as we learn from our text that all this folly and ignorance was foreknown by God. He is pleased to deal with us in mercy!

Admire the marvelous sovereign grace that chose us even when knowing all this. Wonder at the price that was paid even though Christ knew what we would be like. He who hung on the cross foresaw us as unbelieving, backsliding, cold of heart, indifferent, careless, and negligent in prayer, and yet He said, "I am the Lord your God, The Holy One of Israel, your Savior . . . Since you were precious in My sight, you have been honored and I loved you; Therefore I will give men for you and people for your life" (Isaiah 43:3–4).

Oh redemption, how wonderfully resplendent you shine when we think of how sinful we are! Oh Holy Spirit, give us the hearing ear and the understanding heart. Amen.

DECEMBER 16, EVENING

REMEMBERED

"I remember you."

—Jeremiah 2:2;

Christ delights to think about His own. Like a bird returning to its nest or a traveler hurrying home, our minds follow the object of our choices. We cannot look too often on the face we love. We want to have only precious things in sight.

It is so with our Lord Jesus. From all eternity "His delight was with the sons of men" (Proverbs 8:31). His thoughts rolled onward to the time when His elect would be born in the world. He viewed them in the mirror of His foreknowledge. "In Your book they all were written. The days fashioned for me. When as yet there were none of them" (Psalm 139:16). "He was in the beginning with God" (John 1:2). He was there. He set the bounds of the people according to the number of the children of Israel (Exodus 19:12).

Many times, before His incarnation, He descended to the earth. On the plains of Mamre (Genesis 18:1), by the brook of Jabbok (Genesis 32:24), beneath the walls of Jericho (Joshua 5:14), and in the fiery furnace of Babylon (Daniel 3:24), the Son of Man visited His people. His soul delighted in them. His heart longed after them.

Never were they absent from His heart. "See, I have inscribed you on the palms of my hands: Your walls are continually before Me" (Isaiah 49:16). As the breastplate, naming the tribes of Israel was the most brilliant ornament worn by the high priest (Exodus 28:29), so the names of Christ's elect are His most precious jewels and glitter on His heart.

We may often forget to meditate on the perfection of our Lord, but He never ceases to remember us. Let us be reprimanded for past forgetfulness and pray for grace to fondly remember Him.

Lord, paint on the eyes of my soul the image of Your Son. Amen.

DECEMBER 17, MORNING

THE ENTRANCE

"I am the door, if anyone enters by Me, he will be saved and will go in and out and find pasture."

—John 10:9

Jesus, the great I AM, is the entrance to the true church, the way of access to God. He gives those who come to God by Him choice privileges.

1. *He will be saved.* The fugitive murderer entered the gate of a city of refuge and was safe (Numbers 35:11). Noah entered the door of the ark and was secure (Genesis 7:13). Entrance through Jesus into peace is the guarantee of entrance by the same door into heaven. Jesus is the only door, open, and safe (John 10:9). Blessed are you who rest all hope of admission to glory on your crucified Redeemer.

2. *He will go in.* We will be privileged to go in with the divine family, to share the children's bread, and to participate in all their honor and joy. We will enter the chambers of fellowship, the banquets of love, the treasures of the covenant, and the storehouses of the promises. We will go unto the King of kings in the power of the Holy Spirit, and the secret of the Lord will be with us.

3. *He will go out.* This blessing is often forgotten. We go in the world to work and suffer, but what a mercy to go in the name and power of Jesus! We are called to bear witness to the truth, to cheer the depressed, to warn the careless, to win souls, and to glorify God. As the angel of the Lord said to Gideon, "Go in this might" (Judges 6:14), so the Lord would have us go as His messengers in His name and strength.

4. *He will find pasture.* We who know Jesus will never want. In fellowship with God we will grow, and in watering others we will be watered. Having made Jesus our all, we will find all in Jesus. Our souls "will be like a watered garden. And like a spring of water whose waters do not fail" (Isaiah 58:11).

DECEMBER 17, EVENING

HEART-RENDING

"Rend your heart, and not your garments."

—Joel 2:13

Outward signs of religious emotion are easily accomplished and are frequently hypocritical. True repentance is difficult and consequently far less common. The performance of many and minute ceremonial regulations is pleasing to the flesh, for true religion is too humbling, too heart-searching, too thorough for carnal tastes. The falsely religious prefer the ostentatious, the flimsy, and the worldly show.

Outward observations are temporarily comfortable. The eye and ear are pleased, self-conceit is fed, and self-righteousness is puffed up. But this is deception. At death and at the day of judgment, the soul needs something more substantial than ceremonies and rituals. Apart from a vital godliness, all religion is utterly vain. When offered without a sincere heart, every form of worship is a sham and a mockery of the majesty of heaven.

Heartrending, on the other hand, is divinely worked and seriously felt. It is a secret grief that is personally experienced as a deep work of the Holy Spirit moving upon the heart. It is not a matter merely to be talked about and believed; it is keenly and deeply felt in every living child of the living God.

Heartrending is powerfully humiliating and completely sin-purging. It is sweetly preoperative for those gracious comforts that the falsely religious are unable to receive. It is distinctly discriminating because it belongs to the elect of God, and only to them.

Our text commands us to rend our hearts, but our hearts are naturally hard as marble. How then can this be done? We must take them to Calvary. A dying Savior's voice split the rocks (Matthew 27:50-51), and His voice is just as powerful this morning.

Oh blessed Spirit, let us hear the death cries of Jesus and our hearts shall be split easier than men tear their clothing in the day of lamentation.

DECEMBER 18, MORNING

SPIRITUAL INVENTORY

"Be diligent to know the state of your flocks, and attend to your herds."

—Proverbs 27:23

Every business takes inventory. The books are reviewed, the stock examined, and a determination is made of the company's financial condition.

Every believer who is wise in the Kingdom of heaven will cry, "Search me, O God, and know my heart. Try me and know my anxieties" (Psalm 139:23). We frequently need to take a personal inventory to determine if things are right between God and our hearts.

The God we worship is a great heart searcher. His servants know Him as "a righteous God who tests the hearts and minds" (Psalm 7:9). In His name, let me inspire you to examine your condition diligently, lest you miss the promised rest (Hebrews 4:1).

Let the oldest saints look at the fundamentals of their spirituality. How biblical are they? Even grey heads may cover sinful hearts. Young believers ought not to despise this warning because the greenness of youth may contain the rottenness of hypocrisy. Every now and then a cedar falls in our midst. The enemy still sows weeds among the wheat (Matthew 13:25).

It is not my aim to introduce doubt and fear to your mind. No, truly no. It is my hope that the rough wind of self-examination will drive away doubt and fear. It is not security but carnal security we must kill; not confidence but fleshly confidence we must overthrow; not peace but false peace we must destroy.

The precious blood of Christ was not shed to make you a hypocrite but to enable sincere souls to praise Him. I implore you to search and look, so that at the end of your life it will not be said, "Tekel: You have been weighed in the balances, and found wanting" (Daniel 5:27).

CONFIDENCE

"The lot is cast into the lap. But its every decision is from the Lord."

—Proverbs 16:33

If the decision of the dice is the Lord's, who do you think arranges your entire life? If the simple throwing of dice is guided by Him, how much more the events of your life, especially when you are told by your blessed Savior, "The very hairs of your head are all numbered: not a sparrow falls to the ground apart from your Father's will" (Matthew 10:28–30)?

It will bring peace to your mind, dear friend, if you remember this. It will so relieve your anxiety that you will be able to walk untroubled, with patience, and in joy.

When you are anxious, you cannot pray with faith. When you are troubled about the care of this world, you cannot serve your Master; you think only of serving yourself. But Jesus says, "Seek first the kingdom of God and His righteousness, and all these things shall be added to you" (Matthew 6:33).

You are meddling with Christ's business and neglecting your own when you worry about your fate and circumstances. In trying to "provide," you may have forgotten that it is your business to obey. Wise up, obey, and let Christ provide.

Come and survey your Father's storehouse. Do you think He will let you starve when He has so great an abundance? Look at His heart of mercy. Could He ever be unkind? Look at His inscrutable wisdom. Could He ever be wrong? Above all, look to Jesus Christ your Intercessor, and ask yourself this question. While Jesus pleads, can my Father be ungracious to me?

If He remembers even the sparrows, will He forget one of His children? "Cast your burden on the Lord and He shall sustain you; He shall never permit the righteous to be moved" (Psalm 55:22).

THE SEA

"There was no more sea."

—Revelation 21:1

It is hard to rejoice at the thought of losing the glorious old ocean. The new heavens and the new earth are none the fairer in our imaginations if, indeed, they lack a great and wide sea, with gleaming waves and sandy shores.

Our text is to be read as a metaphor tinged with the old Oriental prejudice regarding the sea. A physical world without a sea is sad to imagine. It would be like a ring missing the sapphire that made it precious. There must be a spiritual meaning here.

John on the isle of Patmos saw the deep waters as prison walls shutting him off from other believers and from his work (Revelation 1:9). But there will be no such barrier in the world to come.

Miles of rolling billows lie between us and many a loved one, who tonight we prayerfully remember. In the bright world to which we go, however, there will be unbroken fellowship for all the redeemed family. In this sense there will be no more ocean.

The sea is the emblem of change. It ebbs and flows. It moves from glassy smoothness to mountainous billows, from gentle murmuring to tumultuous roaring. It is always changing. The sea is a slave to the fickle winds and the changing moon. The ocean's instability is proverbial.

In this mortal state, we have too much of this. Earth is constant only in her inconstancy. But in the heavenly state, all sad changes will be unknown. Gone will be the fear of storms that wreck our hopes and drown our joys.

The sea of glass glows with a calm glory unbroken by waves. No tempest howls along the peaceful shores of paradise. Soon we shall reach that happy land where partings, changes, and storms will be ended! Jesus will guide us there.

Are we in Him? That is the question.

DECEMBER 19, EVENING

LOVE THOUGHTS

"Yes, I have loved you with an everlasting love."

—Jeremiah 31:3

Sometimes the Lord Jesus tells the church His love thoughts. "You are fair, my love" (Song of Solomon 4:7). But this is not His only method, for Jesus is a wise lover and knows when to keep back the intimation of love. Yet there are times when He makes no secret of His love. As Erskine preached, "There are times when He will put it beyond all dispute in the souls of His people."

In a gracious manner, the Holy Spirit will witness to our spirits the love of Jesus. He takes the things of Christ and reveals them to us. No voice is heard from the clouds, no vision is seen in the night, but the testimony is surer than either of these. If an angel were to fly from heaven and inform us of the Savior's love, the evidence would not be one particle more satisfactory than that which is carried to the heart by the Holy Spirit.

Ask the Lord's people who have lived closest to the gates of heaven. They will tell you that there have been seasons when the love of Christ was so clear and sure to them that they could no more question it than they could doubt their own existence.

Yes, beloved believer, you and I have had times of refreshing from the presence of the Lord. Our faith has mounted to the utmost height of assurance. We have had confidence to lean on our Lord.

We have no more questioned our Master's affection to us than John did when he asked the dark question, "Lord, who is it that will betray You?" (John 13:21,25). That question has been put far from us. He has kissed us with the kisses of His mouth (Song of Solomon 1:2) and killed our doubts by the closeness of His embrace. His love is better than wine (Song of Solomon 1:2).

DECEMBER 20, MORNING

REWARDS

"Call the laborers and give them their wages."

—Matthew 20:8

God is a good paymaster. He pays His servants while they work and when they are finished. One of His payments is a clear conscience. Today, if you have spoken faithfully of Jesus to one person, you may fall asleep with joy thinking, "I discharged my conscience of that person's blood." There is great peace in doing something for Jesus. There is great happiness when placing jewels in His crown.

There is also a great reward in watching the first budding of conviction in a soul. To say of that girl in the class, "She has a tender heart, I hope the Lord is at work in her;" to go home and pray over that boy who said something that makes you think he might know more of the divine truth that you thought; this is the joy of hope.

But the joy of success is unspeakable. This overwhelming joy is hunger; you want more of it. Being a soul winner is the happiest thing in this world. Every soul you bring to Christ gives you a new heaven on earth.

Who can conceive the ecstasy that awaits us above! How sweet is that sentence, "Enter into the joy of your Lord" (Matthew 25:21). Do you know what the joy of Christ is over a saved sinner? This is the same joy we will possess in heaven. Yes, you will sit with Him on His throne (Revelation 3:21). When the heavens ring with, "Well done, well done" (Matthew 25:21), you will partake in the reward.

You have worked with Him, you have suffered with Him, and you will reign with Him. You have sown with Him, and you will reap with Him. Your face was covered with sweat like His, and your soul was grieved for sinners as His soul was. Thus your face, like His countenance, will be bright with heaven's splendor, and your soul will be filled with heavenly joys, even as His soul is.

DECEMBER 20, EVENING

THE EVERLASTING COVENANT

"Yet He has made with me an everlasting covenant."

—2 Samuel 23:5

This covenant is divine in origin: "He has made with me an everlasting covenant." Oh, that great word *He!* Stop and think about it. God, the everlasting Father, has positively made a covenant with you. God, who spoke the world into existence, stoops from His majesty, takes hold of your hand and makes a covenant with you. The stupendous condescension of this act would overcome our hearts if we could understand it.

Not just any king made a covenant with me. He is the Prince of the kings of the earth, Shaddai, the Lord All-sufficient, the Jehovah of ages, the everlasting Elohim. "He has made with me an everlasting covenant."

Note that this covenant is specific in its application, for it is made with *me*. It is nothing to me if He made peace for the world; I need to know if He made peace with me! It is not important that He made a covenant; I want to know if He has made a covenant with me. Blessed is the assurance that He has made a covenant with me! If the Holy Spirit gives me this assurance, then God's salvation is mine. His heart is mine, and He is mine. He is *my* God.

This covenant is also everlasting. An everlasting covenant had no beginning and will never end. In the middle of all the uncertainties of life, how sweet to know that "the solid foundation of God stands" (2 Timothy 2:19). How trustworthy to have God's promise, "My covenant I will not break, nor alter the word that has gone out of My lips" (Psalm 89:34).

Like dying David, I will sing, "Although my house is not so with God, yet He has made with me an everlasting covenant" (2 Samuel 23:5).

DECEMBER 21, MORNING

ROYAL CLOTHING

"I clothed you in embroidered cloth and gave you sandals of badger skin: I clothed you with fine linen and covered you with silk."
—Ezekiel 16:10

What matchless generosity the Lord provides for His people's clothing. They are dressed with divine skill that produces an unrivalled embroidered cloth, where every attribute of divine beauty is displayed. There is no art form equal to that of our salvation, no skillful workmanship like the righteousness of the saints.

Justification has engrossed educated writers in all ages of the church, and it will be the theme of admiration in eternity. God has skillfully worked it. Here, utility and durability are mixed, comparable to sandals of badger skin. The skin of the badger, one of the finest and strongest leathers known, covered the tabernacle (Exodus 26:14). Thus, the righteousness of God endures forever (Psalm 111:3). You who have sandals of badger skin will walk the desert safely. "You shall tread upon the lion and the cobra" (Psalm 91:13).

In our text the purity and dignity of our holy attire is illustrated in the fine linen. When the Lord sanctifies His people they are clothed as priests in pure white. Not even new fallen snow exceeds their whiteness. In the eyes of men and angels they are beautiful. In the Lord's eye they are without spot or wrinkle (Ephesians 5:27). Their royal clothing is as delicate and rich as silk, for no expense was spared, no beauty withheld, no exquisiteness denied.

What then? Is there no inference to be drawn from this? Surely there is gratitude to be felt and joy to be expressed. Come, my heart, shout hallelujah! Tune your voice to sing His praise:

> Strangely, my soul, art thou arrayed
>   By the Great Sacred Three!
> In sweetest harmony of praise
>   Let all thy powers agree.

PROMISES KEPT

"I will strengthen you."

—Isaiah 41:10

God has a strong reserve and can fulfill this promise. He is able to do exceedingly abundantly above all that we ask or think (Ephesians 3:20).

Believer, until you can drain dry the ocean of omnipotence, until you can break into pieces the towering mountains of almighty strength, you never need to worry. Do not think that human strength will ever be able to overcome the power of God.

While the earth exists, you have plenty of reasons to be strong in your faith. The same God who directs the earth's orbit, who feeds the burning furnace of the sun, and who trims the lamps of heaven has promised to supply your daily strength. He who is able to hold the universe together by His power is able to fulfill His promises to you (Colossians 1:17).

Remember what He did in the days of old. Remember how He spoke and it was done, how He commanded and the sun stood still and the earth stopped (Joshua 10:13). Do you think that He who created the world will grow weary? "He hangs the earth on nothing" (Job 26:7). Is He who does this unable to sustain His children? Will He be unfaithful to His Word because He lacks power?

He stops the storms. He flies on the wings of the wind (Psalm 18:10). He makes the clouds His chariots and holds the ocean in the hollow of His hand (Isaiah 40:12).

He cannot fail you when He has put such a faithful promise as this on record. Do you think for one moment that God has outpromised Himself? Ah, no! Doubt no longer.

Oh Thou my God and my strength, I do believe that Your promises will be fulfilled. The boundless reservoir of Your grace can never be exhausted. The overflowing storehouse of Your strength can never be emptied. Amen.

DECEMBER 22, MORNING

EVERLASTING CERTAINTY

"Because of their blemish."

—Deuteronomy 32:5

What is the blemish that corrupted? It would be presumption to decide this ourselves, but God's word reveals it, and we are on solid ground when divine revelation is our guide.

We are told that "as many as received Him, to them He gave the right to become children of God, to those who believe in His name" (John 1:12). If I have received Christ Jesus in my heart, I am a child of God. And that reception is described in the same verse as believing on the name of Jesus Christ.

If I believe on Jesus Christ's name, that is, if from my heart I trust the crucified but now exalted Redeemer, I become a member of the family of the Most High. Whatever else I may not have, if I have this, I am a child of God.

Our Lord Jesus puts it in another way. "My sheep hear My voice, and I know them, and they follow me" (John 10:27). Here is the matter in a nutshell. Christ appears as a shepherd to *His* sheep but not to the sheep of others. As soon as He appears to them, His sheep perceive who He is and they trust Him; they follow Him. He knows them and they know Him. There is a mutual recognition and ongoing connection between them. Thus the one sure infallible mark of regeneration and adoption is a hearty faith in the appointed Redeemer.

Reader, are you in doubt or uncertainty about bearing the secret mark of God's child? Then don't let an hour pass until you have said, "Search me, O God, and know my heart" (Psalm 139:23).

I plead with you not to trifle here. If you must procrastinate, let it be about some secondary matter, like your health or business. About your soul, be serious. I implore you to be serious about your never-dying soul and its eternal destiny. Make certain where you will spend eternity.

DECEMBER 22, EVENING

CALLED HIGHER

"Friend, go up higher."

—Luke 14:10

When the life of grace begins, we draw near to God with fear and trembling. Conscious and humbled by guilt, we are astonished to be in the presence of Jehovah.

Although we will never forget the seriousness of our position or lose the holy reverence that encircles us when we are in the presence of God, our fear loses its terror. As we grow in grace, our fear becomes a holy reverence, not an overshadowing dread, of the God who creates and destroys. We are called up higher to greater access to God in Christ Jesus.

Then we walk in the splendor of Deity, veiling our faces like the glorious twin winged cherubim at each end of the mercy seat (Exodus 25:18). Covered by the blood and righteousness of Jesus Christ, reverent and bowed in spirit, we approach the throne. There we see a God of love, of goodness, and of mercy, and we realize the covenant character of God rather than His absolute Deity. We see in God His goodness rather than His greatness. We see more of His love than His majesty. Bowing in humility, we enjoy a greater sacred liberty of intercession.

While prostrate before the glory of the infinite God, we are sustained by the refreshing consciousness of being in the presence of boundless mercy and love. We realize we are accepted in the beloved (Ephesians 1:6). Thus the believer is asked to come up higher, to exercise the privilege of rejoicing in God and drawing near to Him in holy confidence, saying, "Abba, Father."

> So may we go from strength to strength,
>   And daily grow in grace,
> Till in Thine image raised at length,
>   We see Thee face to face.

NIGHT

"The night also is Yours."

—Psalm 74:16

Yes, Lord, You do not abdicate Your throne when the sun goes down. During these long winter nights, You do not leave Your children to become the victims of evil. Your eyes watch us like stars shining. Your arms embrace us like the planets surround the sun. The dew of gentle sleep and all the influences of the moon are in Your hands. The fear and depression of the night disappear when You are present.

This is precious to me as I lie awake through the midnight hours tossing and turning in anguish. There are precious fruits put forth by the moon as well as by the sun. Lord, grant me the favor of being a partaker of them.

Our nights of affliction are as much under Your control and arrangement as the brightest summer days, when all is happiness. Jesus is in the tempest. His love wraps the night like a coat. To the eye of faith, the sable robe is not a disguise. From twilight to daybreak, the eternal Watcher observes us. He overrules the shadows and dew of midnight for our highest good. We hear the voice of Jehovah saying, "I form the light and create darkness, I make peace and create calamity. I, the Lord, do all these things" (Isaiah 45:7).

Gloomy seasons of moral indifference and social sin are not exempt from the divine purpose. When the altars of truth are defiled and the way of God forsaken, the Lord's servants do not despair. The darkest eras are governed by the Lord and will end at His command. What may seem defeat to us is victory to Him:

> Though enwrapt in gloomy night,
>   We perceive no ray of light;
> Since the Lord Himself is here,
>   'Tis not right that we should fear.

DECEMBER 23, EVENING

IMPARTED RICHES

"Yet for your sakes He became poor."

—2 Corinthians 8:9

The Lord Jesus Christ was eternally rich, glorious, and exalted. "Yet for your sakes He became poor."

Rich Christians cannot have true fellowship with poorer brethren, unless the rich minister to their needs. This is true between Christ Jesus and the members of His church. It is impossible that our divine Lord could have fellowship with us, unless He became poor to make us rich.

Had He remained on His throne of glory and had we continued in the ruin of the fall, fellowship would have been impossible. Our position after the fall, apart from the covenant of grace, made it impossible for fallen humanity to communicate with God.

In order to establish communion it was necessary for the rich ancestor to give the estate to His poor relatives. The righteous Savior gave His sinning children His perfection, and we, the poor and guilty, receive of His fullness, grace for grace. Thus, in giving and receiving, One descended from the heights and the other ascended from the depths to embrace in true and fervent fellowship.

Poverty must be enriched by Him in whom are infinite treasures before it can venture into fellowship. Guilt must be lost in imputed and imparted righteousness before we can walk in fellowship with purity. Jesus must clothe His people in His own garments, or He cannot admit them to His palace of glory. He must wash them in His own blood, or else they will defile the embrace of His fellowship.

Oh believer, this is love! For your sake the Lord Jesus "became poor," that He might lift you up into communion with Him.

DECEMBER 24, MORNING

CHOOSING SIDES

"The glory of the Lord shall be revealed, and all flesh shall see it together."

—Isaiah 40:5

We anticipate the happy day when the entire world will be converted to Christ. When the gods of the heathen will be thrown to the dogs. When false religions and cults will be exploded. When kings will bow before the Prince of Peace, and all nations will call their Redeemer blessed.

Some despair. They look on the world as a vessel breaking up and going to pieces, never to float again. We know that "the day of the Lord will come as a thief in the night, in which the heavens will pass away with a great noise and the elements will melt with fervent heat: both the earth and the works that are in it will be burned up" (2 Peter 3:10). But we cannot read our Bible without the conviction that

> Jesus shall reign where'er the sun
> Does his successive journeys run.

We are not discouraged by the length of His delays. We are not disheartened by the long period He allocates to the church to struggle with little success and much defeat. We believe that God will never permit this world, which once saw Christ's blood shed on it, to forever remain the devil's stronghold. Christ came to deliver this world from the detested sway of the powers of darkness.

What a shout when with the angels we cry, "Hallelujah, hallelujah, for the Lord God Omnipotent reigns" (Revelation 19:6)! What satisfaction in that day to have had a share in the fight, to have helped break the arrows, and to have aided in winning the victory for our Lord! Happy are those who trust in the conquering Lord, and who fight side by side with Him, doing their little bit in His name and by His strength.

How unhappy are those on the side of evil! It is a losing side, where to lose is to be lost forever.

On whose side are you?

DECEMBER 24, EVENING

IMMANUEL

"Behold, the virgin shall conceive and bear a Son, and shall call His name Immanuel."

—Isaiah 7:14

Let us go down to Bethlehem in the company of wondering shepherds and adoring Magi. Let us see Him who was born King of the Jews. By faith we can claim an interest in Him and can sing, "Unto us a Child is born. Unto us a Son is given" (Isaiah 9:6). Jesus is Jehovah incarnate, our Lord, our God, our brother, and our friend. Let us adore and admire Him.

In our text we immediately notice His miraculous conception. That a virgin should conceive a child was unheard of. The first Messianic promise, however, was about "the seed of the woman" not the offspring of the man (Genesis 3:15). Since adventurous woman led the way in the sin, which brought forth Paradise lost, it is a woman who ushers in the Regainer of Paradise.

Our Savior, though truly man, was the Holy One of God. Let us reverently bow before the holy Child whose innocence restores humanity to its ancient glory. Let us pray that He may be formed in us as the hope of glory (Colossians 1:27).

Don't miss His humble parentage. His mother was described simply as a virgin, not a princess, or prophetess, nor the heiress of a large estate. True, the blood of kings ran in her veins (Luke 3:23), and her mind was taught of God, but how humble was her position. How poor was the man she was engaged to marry. And how miserable were the accommodations for the newborn King!

Immanuel: God with us now in our nature, our sorrow, our lifework, our punishment, and our grave; and with us, or rather we with Him, in resurrection, ascension, triumph, and Second Advent splendor.

DECEMBER 25, MORNING

ENDING CHRISTMAS

". . . when the days of feasting had run their course, . . . Job . . . would rise early in the morning and offer burnt offerings . . . . For Job said, 'It may be that my sons have sinned . . . .'"—Job 1:5

What the patriarch did early in the morning after the family festivities might be good for us to do before we fall asleep this Christmas evening.

In the midst of cheerful family gatherings, it is easy to slide into sinful frivolity and forget our Christian walk. It should not be this way, but our days of feasting are seldom days of sanctified enjoyment. Too frequently they degenerate into sinful flippancy.

There is a way of joy as pure and as sanctifying as bathing in the rivers of Eden. Holy gratitude should be as purifying an element as grief. Unfortunately for our poor hearts, the evidence proves that the house of mourning is more sanctifying than the house of feasting.

Believer, in what way have you sinned today? Did you forget your high calling? Have your words been idle and your speech loose? Confess the sin and fly to the sacrifice that sanctifies. The precious blood of the Lamb slain removes the guilt and purges the defilement of our sins of ignorance and carelessness.

The best ending for a Christmas day is to wash again in the cleansing fountain. Believer, come to this sacrifice continually. If it is good tonight, it is good every night.

Living at the altar is the privilege of the royal priesthood. Sin, as great as it may be, is not a reason to despair. Draw near again to the sin-atoning victim and your conscience will be purged from dead works.

OUR REPRESENTATIVE

"The last Adam."

—1 Corinthians 15:45

Jesus is the federal head of His elect. Every heir of flesh and blood has a personal interest in Adam because he is the covenant head and representative of the race under the law of works. Under the law of grace, every redeemed soul is one with the Lord of heaven, for He is the second Adam, the Sponsor and Substitute of the elect in the new covenant of love.

The apostle Paul declares that Levi was in the loins of Abraham when Melchizedek met him (Hebrews 7:9–10). So, too, the believer was in the loins of Jesus Christ, the Mediator, when in old eternity the covenant settlements of grace were decreed, ratified, and made sure forever. Thus, whatever Christ has done He has done for the entire body of His church.

We were crucified with Christ (Galatians 2:20) and buried with Him (Romans 6:4; Colossians 2:10–12). Still more wonderful, we are risen with Him and even ascended with Him to the seats on high (Ephesians 2:6).

Thus the church has fulfilled the law and is "accepted in the Beloved" (Ephesians 1:6). The just Jehovah views the church in Jesus Christ and does not look on her separate from Him. As the anointed Redeemer of Israel, Christ Jesus is not distinct from His church. All that He has He holds for her.

Adam's righteousness was ours as long as he maintained it, and Adam's sin was ours the moment he committed it. In the same manner, all that the second Adam is or does is ours because He is our representative. This is the foundation of the covenant of grace.

This gracious system of representation and substitution moved Justin Martyr to cry out, "O blessed change, O sweet permutation." It is the ground work of the gospel of our salvation. It is to be received with strong faith and rapturous joy.

DECEMBER 26, MORNING

HIS PRESENCE

"Lo, I am with you always."

—Matthew 28:20

The Lord Jesus is in the midst of His church. He walks among the golden candlesticks (Revelation 2:13). His promise, "Lo, I am with you always," is as effectual now as it was the morning He prepared breakfast for His disciples at the lake (John 21:9).

Not physically but truly Jesus is with us. What a blessed truth! Where Jesus is, love becomes inflamed. There is nothing like the presence of Jesus! A glimpse of Him so overcomes us that we are ready to say, "Turn Your eyes away from me for they have overcome me" (Song of Solomon 6:5).

Even the smell of the aloes, myrrh, and cassia, which drop from His perfumed garments, strengthen the sick and weak. Let your head lean for a moment on His gracious bosom. Discover His divine love flowing into your cold heart, and you will be cold no longer. You will become equal to every labor and capable of any suffering.

If we know that Jesus is with us, every power will be developed and every grace will be strengthened. We will throw ourselves into the Lord's service with heart, soul, and strength. Thus the Lord's presence is to be desired above everything else.

His presence will be realized by those who are most like Him. If you desire to see Christ, you must grow in conformity to Him. When you bring yourself, by the power of the Spirit, into consolidation with Christ's desires, you will be favored with His company. His presence is available. His promise is as true as ever. He delights to be with you.

If He does not come, it is because we hinder Him with our indifference. He will reveal Himself to our earnest prayers and will graciously stay if we only ask. Prayerful tears are the golden chains that bind Jesus to His people.

DECEMBER 26, EVENING

DYING REEDS

"Can the reed flourish without water?"

—Job 8:11

Reeds are like hypocrites, spongy and hollow. There is no substance or stability in them. They are shaken to and fro by every wind. They are like liturgists who yield to every influence. This is why the reed is not broken in the storm, and why hypocrites are not troubled with persecution.

I do not want to be a deceiver or be deceived. Today's text may help me determine if I am a hypocrite. The reed lives in water and owes its existence to mud and moisture. Let the mud become dry, and the reed quickly withers. It's greenness is absolutely dependent on its circumstances. An abundance of water makes it flourish. A drought destroys it.

Am I like this? Do I serve God only when I am in good company or when religion is profitable and respectable? Do I love the Lord only when material comforts are received from His hands? If so, I am a base hypocrite, and like the withering reed, I will perish when death deprives me of outward joys.

If I can honestly claim that I have held fast to my integrity when bodily comforts have been few and life has been adverse, then there is hope that a genuine, vital godliness is in me. Though the reed cannot grow without mud, the Lord's plants can and do flourish even in drought. A godly person often grows best when worldly circumstances decay around him.

Those who follow Christ for gain are like Judas. Those who follow Him for bread and fish are children of the devil (John 6:26–27; 8:44). But those who serve Him out of love are His own beloved ones.

Lord, let me find my life in You and not in the mud of this world's favor or gain. Amen.

DECEMBER 27, MORNING

A GUIDE

"The Lord will guide you continually."

—Isaiah 58:11

The Lord will guide you. Not an angel, but Jehovah will guide you. God told Moses that an angel would lead the people through the wilderness. But Moses said, "If Your Presence does not go with us, do not bring us up from here" (Exodus 33:15).

Christian, God has not left you to an angel's guidance. He Himself leads you. You may not see the cloudy, fiery pillar, but Jehovah will never forsake you.

Notice the word *will,* "the Lord *will* guide you." How certain this makes it! How confident that God will not forsake us! His precious *shalls* and *wills* are better than others' oaths. "I will never leave you nor forsake you" (Hebrews 13:5).

Observe also the adverb *continually.* We are not merely guided at certain times; we have a perpetual monitor. "Trust in the Lord with all your heart, and lean not on your own understanding; in all your ways acknowledge Him and He shall direct your path" (Proverbs 3:6–7). We are never left to our own understanding, but we continually hear the guiding voice of the Great Shepherd.

If you have to change your position in life, if you have to emigrate overseas, if you become poverty stricken, if you are given a promotion, if you are thrown among strangers or cast among foes, do not fear, because "the Lord will guide you continually." You will be delivered from every dilemma if you live near God, if your heart is kept warm with His holy love. You will not go astray if you go in the company of God.

Like Enoch, walk with God (Genesis 5:22), and you cannot mistake the road. You have infallible wisdom to direct you, permanent love to comfort you, and eternal power to defend you.

AS ONE

"The life which I now live in the flesh I live by faith in the Son of God."

—Galatians 2:20

When the Lord in mercy saw us in sin, He said, "Live." He did this first because life is an absolute essential in spiritual matters. Until life is given, we are incapable of participating in the things of God's kingdom.

The life that grace confers at the moment of belief is the life of Christ. Like sap from a tree, it runs into us, the branches, and establishes a living connection between our souls and Jesus.

Faith is the grace that perceives this union. Faith is the neck that joins the body of the church to its all-glorious Head. Faith holds the Lord Jesus with a firm and determined grasp. Faith knows Jesus's excellence and worth. No temptation induces faith to trust anyone or anything but Christ.

Christ Jesus is so delighted with this heavenly grace that He never ceases to strengthen and sustain our faith with His loving embrace and the all-sufficient support of His eternal arms. A living, sensible, and delightful union is established where streams of love, confidence, sympathy, and joy flow.

When the soul can perceive its oneness with Christ, His pulse may be felt as beating for both, and His blood as flowing through the veins of each. Then the heart is as close to heaven as it can be on earth, and it is prepared to enjoy sublime and spiritual fellowship.

WAR AND PEACE

"I did not come to bring peace but a sword."

—Matthew 10:34

Christians will make enemies. If doing right and believing the truth causes us to lose every earthly friend, it will be only a small loss, for our great heavenly Friend will be friendlier and more gracious than ever.

You who have taken up His cross know what your Master said: "I have come to set a man against his father, a daughter against her mother, . . . and a man's enemies will be those of his own household (Matthew 10:35–36).

Christ is the great peacemaker, but before peace He brings war. When the light comes the darkness must depart. Where truth is, the lie must flee. If the lie remains, there will be a severe conflict, because truth cannot and will not lower its standard.

If you follow Christ, all the hounds of the world will yelp at your heels. Count on this, if you live for Jesus Christ, the world will not speak well of you. "Do you not know that friendship with the world is enmity with God?" (James 4:4). If you are true and faithful to the Most High, people will resent your unflinching devotion because it is a testimony against their iniquity.

Regardless of the consequences, you must do what is right. You will need the courage of a lion to pursue a course that could turn your best friend into your fiercest foe. For the sake of Jesus Christ, you must be courageous.

Risking your reputation and emotions for the truth requires a degree of moral principle that only the Spirit of God can work into you. Do not turn back, do not be a coward; be a hero of the faith. Follow in your Master's steps. He walked this rough way before you.

Better a brief warfare and eternal rest than false peace and everlasting torment.

DECEMBER 28, EVENING

PASSAGES

"Thus far the Lord has helped us."

—1 Samuel 7:12

The word *thus* is like a finger pointing to the past. Be it twenty years or seventy years, "thus far the Lord has helped us." Through poverty, through wealth, through sickness, through health, at home and abroad, on land and sea, in honor and dishonor, in perplexity, joy, trial, triumph, prayer, and temptation, "thus far the Lord has helped us."

You delight to look down a long avenue of trees, to gaze from end to end at the long vista. It is a verdant temple, with branching pillars and arches of leaves. Look down the long aisle of your years, at the green branches of mercy overhead, at the strong pillars of lovingkindness and faithfulness that lift your joy. Many birds sing in those branches, and they all sing of mercy received "thus far."

But the Word also points forward. When you reach a certain location and write *thus far,* you have not reached the end. There is still a distance to travel. More trials and joys, more temptations and triumphs, more prayers and answers, more work and strength, more battles and victories, and only then sickness, old age, disease, and death.

Is it over? No! There is more, the awakening in Jesus' likeness. Thrones, harps, songs, psalms, white raiment, the face of Jesus, the society of saints, the glory of God, the fullness of eternity, and the infinity of ecstasy all await.

Be of good courage, believer, and with grateful confidence raise your "Stone of Help" (1 Samuel 7:12) because:

> He who hath helped thee hitherto
> Will help thee all thy journey through.

When read in heaven's light, *thus far* will be glorious and marvelous to our grateful eyes!

DECEMBER 29, MORNING

YOUR THOUGHTS ABOUT JESUS

"What do you think about the Christ?"

—Matthew 22:42

The real test of your soul's condition is "What do you think about the Christ?" Is He "fairer than the sons of men" (Psalm 45:2)? Is He "the chief among ten thousand" (Song of Solomon 5:10)? Is He "altogether lovely" (Song of Solomon 5:16)?

It takes all the faculties of the spiritual saint to appreciate what Christ is. Judge your holiness by this barometer: Does Christ stand high or low with you? If you seldom think of Christ, if you are content to live without His presence, if you do not cherish Him, if you neglect His laws, then your soul is sick. May God grant that it is not sick unto death!

Or is your first thought, "How can I honor Jesus?" Is your daily wish, "O that I knew where I might find Him" (Job 23:3)? If so, let me tell you that, although you may have a thousand infirmities and scarcely know if you are a child of God, I am persuaded beyond doubt that you are safe, because you cherish Jesus.

I do not care if you are in rags. What do you think of His royal garments? I do not care if you are wounded and bleeding. What do you think of His wounds? Do His wounds glitter like rubies in your mind?

I would not think less of you if you were like the beggar Lazarus, lying at the gate looking for crumbs, full of sores with only the dogs to lick your ulcers (Luke 16:19–21). I would not judge you by your poverty but by what you think of His beauty. Does He have a glorious high throne in your heart? Would you lift Him higher if you could? Would you be willing to die if you could add another note to the choir that proclaims His praise?

Ah, then, it is well with you. Whatever you think of yourself is not important. If you exalt Christ, you will soon be with Him.

DECEMBER 29, EVENING

THE END IS BETTER

"The end of a thing is better than its beginning."

—Ecclesiastes 7:8

Look at David's Lord and Master. See His beginning. "He is despised and rejected by men. A Man of sorrows and acquainted with grief" (Isaiah 53:3). See the end. "The Lord said to my Lord, 'Sit at My right hand. Till I make Your enemies Your footstool'" (Matthew 22:44).

Like our Lord, you must bear the cross, or you will never wear the crown. You must wade through the mire, or you will never walk the golden pavement. Cheer up, Christian, for "the end of a thing is better than its beginning."

See the creeping worm; its appearance is contemptible. It is the beginning of a thing. Mark the insect with gorgeous wings, playing in the sunlight, sipping at the flowers, full of happiness and life. The end of that thing was better than its beginning.

You are that caterpillar. Until you are wrapped in the chrysalis of death, be content to follow your Master. "It has not yet been revealed what we shall be, but we know that when He is revealed we shall be like Him for we shall see Him as He is" (1 John 3:2). You will be satisfied when you wake in His likeness.

The rough diamond is put on the wheel of the lapidary. It is cut on all sides; it loses much that seems costly. Yet a glittering ray flashes from the diamond that was so roughly cut. Compare yourself to such a diamond, for you are one of God's people, and this is the time of the cutting process.

Let faith and patience have their perfect work. In the day when the crown will be set on the head of the King—Eternal, Immortal, Invisible (1 Timothy 1:17)—one ray of glory will stream from you. "'They shall be Mine,' says the Lord of hosts. 'On the day that I make them My jewels'" (Malachi 3:17).

"The end of a thing is better than its beginning."

THE BITTER END

"Do you not know that it will be bitter in the latter end?"

—2 Samuel 2:26

Dear reader, if you are only a professing Christian and not a true possessor of the faith that is in Christ Jesus, then our text accurately describes your end. You are a respectable attendant at a place of worship, but you go because others go and not because your heart is right with God. This is your beginning, and I suppose that for the next twenty or thirty years, you will be spared to go on professing Christianity with an outward appearance, but not with your heart.

Walk softly. Gaze gently. I want to show you your deathbed scene. A clammy sweat is on your face, and you wake and cry, "Oh God, it is hard to die. Did you send for my minister?" "Yes, he is coming." Then to the minister you plead, "Sir, I am dying in fear. I cannot say I have hope. I am afraid to stand before God. Oh pray for me."

The minister prays with sincere earnestness. The way of salvation is explained for the ten thousandth time. But before you can grasp the rope, you sink. The minister closes your cold eyelids, and you will never see anything here again.

But where are your true eyes now? Jesus said, "And being in torments in Hades he lifted up his eyes" (Luke 16:23). Why didn't you lift up your eyes before? Because you were so accustomed merely to hearing the gospel that your soul slept. Alas! When you lift your eyes up now, how bitter it will be. Let the Savior's own words reveal the woe. "Father Abraham, have mercy on me, send Lazarus that he may dip the tip of his finger in water and cool my tongue for I am tormented in this flame" (Luke 16:24).

There is frightful meaning in these words. May you never have to experience Jehovah's wrath.

COME DRINK

"On the last day, that great day of the feast, Jesus stood and cried out, saying, 'If anyone thirst, let him come to Me and drink'."

—John 7:37

Patience had its perfect work in the Lord Jesus. On the last day of the feast, He pleaded with the Jews. On the last day of this year, He pleads with us to be reconciled to Him.

"We implore you on Christ's behalf," said the Apostle, "as though God were pleading through us" (2 Corinthians 5:20). How deep is the love that makes the Lord weep over sinners! Surely at this call our willing hearts will come.

The provision is abundant, for all is provided to quench the thirst of our souls. To our conscience the atonement brings peace. To our understanding the gospel brings rich instruction. To our heart the person of Jesus is the worthy object of affection. To the entire person, the truth in Jesus is pure nourishment.

The proclamation is made freely to all. Every thirsty one is welcome. Whether it is the thirst of selfishness, ambition, pleasure, knowledge, or rest, all who suffer from thirst are invited. It is not goodness in us that brings the invitation. The Lord Jesus sends it freely and without reservation.

No waiting or preparation is required. A fool, a thief, or a prostitute can drink. No sinful character is barred from the invitation to believe in Jesus.

We do not need a golden cup or a jewelled chalice to bring water to the thirsty. All are welcome to stoop and drink from Jesus, the flowing fountain of hope. Blistered, leprous, and filthy lips may touch the stream of divine love. They cannot pollute it but will themselves be purified.

Dear reader, hear the Redeemer's loving voice as He cries to you, "If any one thirsts, let him come to Me and drink."

DECEMBER 31, MORNING

Are You Saved?

"The harvest is past. The summer is ended. And we are not saved."

—Jeremiah 8:20

Not saved! Dear reader, is this your situation? You know the way of salvation. You read it in the Bible. You heard it from the pulpit. It has been explained by friends. Yet you neglect it and are not saved. You will have no excuse when the Lord will judge the living and the dead (2 Timothy 4:1).

Years have followed one another into eternity and your last year will soon be here. Your youth has gone, life is going, and you are not saved.

Let me ask you, will you ever be saved? Is there any possibility? Already the most advantageous seasons have left you unsaved. Can other occasions change your condition? Affection and prosperity have failed to impress you. Tears, prayers, and sermons have been wasted on your barren heart.

A convenient time never has come. Will it ever come? It is logical to fear that it never will arrive, and like Felix (Acts 24:24–25), you will find no convenient season and find yourself in hell.

I want to startle you. Oh be wise. Be wise in time. Before another year begins, believe in Jesus, who is able to save to the uttermost (Hebrews 7:25).

Consecrate these last hours of the year to private thoughts, and if deep repentance comes, it will be well for you. And if it leads to a humble faith in Jesus, that will be best of all.

Oh see to it that you are forgiven before this year passes away. Let not the new year's midnight celebrations sound on a joyless spirit. Now, now, now, believe and live.

"Escape for your life! Do not look behind you nor stay anywhere in the plain. Escape to the mountain, lest you be destroyed" (Genesis 19:17).

DECEMBER 31, EVENING

INDEX

Mar. 16 E; **22:1,** *Apr. 14 M; Apr. 15 M;* **22:7,** *Apr. 14 M;* **22:11,** *May 25 M;*
22:14, *Apr. 11 M; Apr. 12 M; Apr. 15 M;* **22:22,** *Mar. 24 E;* **23:2,** *Feb. 3 E;*
Apr. 29 M; Aug. 22 E; **23:4,** *Feb. 4 M; Feb. 7 M; Apr. 8 E; Nov. 10 M; Nov.*
11 M; **23:5,** *Jan. 9 M;* **23:6,** *Jul. 8 M;* **24:4,** *Jul. 4 E;* **24:8,** *Dec. 3 E;* **25:5,**
Jul. 8 E; **25:6,** *Jan. 25 M;* **25:10,** *Sep. 18 E;* **25:14,** *Jun. 24 M; Nov. 10 M;*
25:18, *Apr. 11 E;* **26:9,** *Sep. 21 E;* **27:1,** *Jun. 16 E;* **27:9,** *May 25 M;* **27:14,**
Aug. 30 M; **28:1,** *Jul. 2 E;* **28:6,** *Feb. 6 M;* **28:9,** *Apr. 15 E;* **29:2,** *Aug. 16*
M; **30:5,** *May 13 M;* **30:6,** *Mar. 10 M; Mar. 10 E;* **30:7,** *Jul. 25 E;* **31:4,** *Aug.*
19 E; **31:5,** *Aug. 27 E;* **31:10,** *Jun. 14 E;* **32:3,** *Sep. 14 E;* **32:4,**
Sep. 14 E; **32:5,** *Sep. 14 E;* **32:7,** *Oct. 30 M;* **32:8,** *Feb. 9 M; Apr. 27 M; Sep.*
1 M; Sep. 28 M; **33:13,** *Sep. 28 M;* **33:21,** *Jul. 2 M;* **34:1,** *Feb. 1 M; Sep. 30*
M; **34:2,** *Oct. 30 M;* **34:3,** *Oct. 30 M;* **34:4,** *Feb. 19 M;* **34:6,** *Oct. 30 M;*
34:7, *Oct. 3 M; Oct. 21 E;* **35:3,** *Mar. 5 E; Oct. 30 E;* **35:14,** *Nov. 27 M;*
36:8, *Mar. 4 E;* **36:9,** *Oct. 16 E; Nov. 4 E;* **37:4,** *Jun. 14 M; Oct. 30 M; Nov.*
3 E; Nov. 16 M; **37:23,** *Apr. 29 M;* **38:21,** *May 25 M; Jun. 13 E;* **39:1,** *Mar.*
14 E; **39:12,** *Mar. 16 M;* **40:1,** *Oct. 30 M;* **40:2,** *May 30 E; Jun. 9 M;* **40:3,**
Jun. 9 M; **40:7,** *Jan. 23 E;* **40:17,** *Sep. 28 M;* **41:3,** *Oct. 1 M;* **41:4,** *Aug. 30*
E; **41:9,** *Aug. 20 M;* **42:1,** *Jan. 4 M;* **42:5,** *Sep. 13 M;* **42:9,** *Jul. 21 E;* **43:4,**
Sep. 22 M; **45:1,** *Jan. 28 E;* **45:2,** *Jun. 21 M; Dec. 29 E;* **45:6,** *Jun. 4 E;*
45:7, *May 29 M;* **45:8,** *Feb. 8 M; Feb. 15 E; Aug. 25 M;* **45:9,** *Apr. 22 M;*
46:1, *May 3 E; Nov. 19 E;* **46:4,** *Mar. 24 E; Sep. 26 M;* **47:4,** *Nov. 11 E;*
50:10, *Mar. 17 M;* **51:5,** *Aug. 29 M;* **51:7,** *Jul. 30 E;* **51:8,** *Jun. 24 M; Jun.*
14 E; Sep. 14 E; **51:9,** *Jul. 30 E;* **51:10,** *Oct. 31 M;* **51:11,** *Jun. 29 E;* **51:12,**
Nov. 6 M; Nov. 21 M; **51:14,** *Apr. 7 E; Jun. 29 M; Nov. 3 M; Nov. 27 M;* **52:8,**
Aug. 17 M; **55:6,** *May 2 M;* **55:22,** *Mar. 7 E; May 26 M; Dec. 19 M;* **56:3,**
Mar. 4 M; **56:8,** *Mar. 29 E; Nov. 3 M; Nov. 27 M;* **56:9,** *Jul. 13 E;* **59:16,**
Feb. 6 M; **61:1,** *Sep. 9 M;* **61:2,** *Sep. 22 E;* **61:3,** *Aug. 30 M; Nov. 10 M;*
61:4, *Mar. 4 E; Aug. 30 M;* **62:2,** *Feb. 26 M;* **62:5,** *Feb. 28 M;* **62:8,** *Nov.*
10 M; **63:5,** *Mar. 18 E;* **65:9,** *Aug. 1 E;* **65:11,** *Aug. 1 E; Oct. 18 M;* **66:2,**
Sep. 30 M; **66:12,** *Jun. 9 M;* **66:20,** *May 24 M;* **67:6,** *Apr. 27 M;* **68:10,**
Dec. 8 E; **68:13,** *Apr. 15 E; Jun. 3 M;* **68:17,** *Oct. 3 M;* **68:28,** *Nov. 15 E;*
69:9, *Mar. 15 E;* **71:9,** *Jun. 9 M;* **72:14,** *Oct. 21 E;* **72:19,** *Aug. 6 E;* **73:2,**
Oct. 9 M; **73:3,** *Jul. 28 M;* **73:7,** *Jan. 9 M;* **73:22,** *Jul. 26 E; Jul. 28 M;*
73:23, *Jul. 29 M;* **73:24,** *Sep. 1 M;* **73:25,** *Mar. 19 E; Nov. 16 M;* **73:26,**
Nov. 16 M; **74:16,** *Dec. 23 E;* **74:17,** *Dec. 1 M; Jun. 11 E;* **77:8,** *Jul.*
5 E; **78:1,** *Sep. 28 M;* **78:23,** *Feb. 24 M;* **78:25,** *Jan. 1 M;* **78:45,** *Jul. 24 E;*
80:12, *Jul. 20 E;* **84:3,** *Sep. 29 E;* **84:6,** *Sep. 13 M;* **84:7,** *Dec. 14 M;* **84:11,**
Apr. 27 M; Oct. 1 E; Oct. 25 E; Nov. 30 M; **86:10,** *Nov. 5 M;* **87:6,** *Apr. 30*
E; **88:7,** *Apr. 13 E;* **89:19,** *Jan. 23 M;* **89:34,** *Dec. 21 M;* **91:3,** *Jan. 24 M;*
91:4, *May 25 M;* **91:5,** *Apr. 22 M;* **91:9,** *Feb. 27 M;* **91:11,** *Oct. 3 M;* **91:12,**
Oct. 3 M; **91:13,** *Dec. 21 M;* **91:15,** *May 3 M;* **92:4,** *Aug. 14 M;* **93:2,** *Nov.*
18 E; **94:19,** *Feb. 20 M;* **95:1,** *Jan. 1 E;* **97:1,** *Aug. 12 M;* **97:10,** *Jun. 7 M;*
Jul. 13 M; **100:2,** *Jan. 9 E;* **100:4,** *Nov. 5 E;* **100:5,** *Sep. 16 M;* **101:1,** *Sep.*
12 E; **102:5,** *May 27 M;* **102:7,** *Jul. 16 E;* **102:13,** *Jul. 16 E;* **102:14,** *Jul.*
16 E; **103:1,** *Dec. 1 E;* **103:2,** *Feb. 6 M; Jul. 9 M;* **103:3,** *Feb. 6 M; May 31*
E; Aug. 30 E; **103:4,** *Feb. 6 M; May 16 E;* **103:5,** *Jun. 25 E;* **103:8,** *Oct. 30*
M; **103:13,** *Feb. 24 E;* **103:14,** *Apr. 29 E; Sep. 28 M;* **104:16,** *Jan. 2 E; Aug.*
13 M; Oct. 24 M; **104:30,** *Jan. 2 E;* **105:2,** *Jun. 11 E;* **107:7,** *May 22 M;*
107:8, *Dec. 1 E;* **107:23,** *Jul. 19 M;* **107:24,** *Jul. 19 M;* **107:29,** *Sep. 7 E;*
107:30, *May 22 M;* **108:2,** *May 16 M;* **109:4,** *Jan. 15 E;* **109:9,** *Aug. 26 M;*
110:3, *Oct. 28 E; Dec. 4 M;* **110:4,** *Oct. 28 E;* **111:3,** *Dec. 21 E;* **111:9,**
Aug. 26 M; **111:10,** *Sep. 25 E;* **112:7,** *Sep. 15 M;* **113:8,** *Jul. 26 E;* **115:1,**
Aug. 16 M; **116:7,** *Jan. 29 E;* **116:15,** *Oct. 21 E;* **116:16,** *May 17 E;* **118:8,**
Mar. 7 E; **118:12,** *Apr. 6 E;* **118:27,** *Dec. 15 M;* **119:15,** *Oct. 12 M;* **119:35,**
Jan. 25 E; **119:37,** *Jan. 20 E;* **119:49,** *Apr. 28 M;* **119:53,** *Nov. 2 E;* **119:57,**
May 13 E; **119:103,** *Aug. 25 M;* **119:105,** *Jul. 4 M;* **119:116,** *Mar. 14 M;*

119:117, *Mar. 14 E;* *May 25 M;* **119:127**, *Mar. 5 E;* **120:5**, *Sep. 5 M;* **121:3**, *Apr. 22 E;* *Jul. 29 M;* **121:4**, *Apr. 22 E;* **122:6**, *Jul. 16 E;* **126:3**, *Jun. 9 E;* **130:1**, *Feb. 12 M;* **133:2**, *May 8 E;* **137:2**, *Apr. 29 M;* *Sep. 30 M;* **138:5**, *Feb. 1 M;* *Oct. 30 M;* **138:6**, *May 12 M;* **138:8**, *May 23 M;* **139:7**, *Apr. 30 E;* **139:12**, *Apr. 21 M;* *Apr. 22 E;* **139:16**, *Jan. 4 E;* *Dec. 17 M;* **139:17**, *Apr. 30 E;* **139:23**, *Aug. 18 M;* *Dec. 18 E;* *Dec. 22 E;* **142:3**, *Sep. 28 M;* **146:5**, *Nov. 10 M;* **147:4**, *Feb. 24 E;* **148:9**, *Aug. 13 M;* **148:14**, *Sep. 15 E;* **149:2**, *Sep. 22 M;* **149:4**, *Apr. 22 M;*

Proverbs 1:26, *Apr. 8 M;* **1:33**, *Jul. 6 M;* **3:6**, *Dec. 27 E;* **3:7**, *Dec. 27 E;* **3:9**, *May 23 E;* **3:17**, *Jan. 28 E;* *Apr. 29 M;* *Jun. 14 M;* **4:18**, *Apr. 29 M;* **6:18**, *Mar. 6 E;* **7:13**, *Mar. 25 M;* **7:21**, *Mar. 25 M;* **8:17**, *Mar. 13 M;* **8:31**, *Jan. 7 E;* *Sep. 21 M;* *Dec. 17 M;* **11:25**, *Aug. 21 M;* **13:15**, *May 30 E;* **15:17**, *Jun. 24 E;* **15:33**, *Apr. 5 E;* **16:5**, *Jan. 3 E;* **16:18**, *Mar. 6 E;* **16:20**, *May 5 E;* **16:33**, *Dec. 19 M;* **18:12**, *Mar. 6 E;* **18:14**, *Apr. 12 M;* **18:24**, *May 11 M;* *Oct. 6 M;* **21:31**, *Sep. 13 M;* **22:6**, *Jul. 11 E;* **24:33**, *Nov. 24 E;* **24:34**, *Nov. 24 E;* **25:14**, *Sep. 13 M;* **27:6**, *Mar. 25 E;* **27:23**, *Dec. 18 E;* **30:8**, *Jun. 13 E;* **30:26**, *Nov. 20 E;* **30:27**, *Jul. 18 E;*

Ecclesiastes 1:2, *Jun. 25 M;* **1:7**, *Mar. 1 E;* *Oct. 26 E;* **1:14**, *Dec. 2 E;* **2:9**, *Dec. 2 E;* **2:10**, *Dec. 2 E;* **2:11**, *Dec. 2 E;* **7:8**, *Dec. 30 M;* **9:4**, *Sep. 30 M;* **9:7**, *Dec. 8 M;* **9:10**, *Nov. 26 M;* **10:7**, *May 19 M;* **10:9**, *Nov. 17 E;* **11:6**, *Sep. 20 E;* *Nov. 7 E;* **11:7**, *Jan. 5 M;* **12:6**, *Mar. 18 E;*

Song of Solomon 1:2, *Jan. 8 E;* *Apr. 1 M;* *Dec. 20 M;* **1:3**, *Aug. 25 M;* **1:4**, *Jan. 1 E;* *Jan. 23 E;* *Aug. 7 M;* **1:6**, *May 9 E;* *Oct. 6 E;* **1:7**, *Feb. 3 M;* *Sep. 3 M;* **1:8**, *Dec. 2 M;* **1:12**, *Sep. 9 E;* **1:13**, *Apr. 13 M;* *Dec. 20 M;* **1:16**, *May 22 E;* **2:1**, *May 1 E;* *Jun. 15 E;* *Nov. 5 E;* **2:3**, *Aug. 25 M;* *Oct. 18 M;* **2:4**, *Jan. 12 M;* *Aug. 26 M;* *Oct. 16 M;* **2:6**, *Sep. 9 E;* **2:8**, *Mar. 20 M;* **2:10**, *Apr. 25 M;* **2:12**, *Mar. 20 M;* *Apr. 24 E;* *May 30 M;* **2:16**, *Mar. 20 M;* *Jun. 19 E;* *Oct. 29 E;* *Dec. 10 M;* **2:17**, *Jun. 19 E;* *Aug. 6 M;* *Nov. 16 E;* **3:1**, *Jan. 9 M;* **3:4**, *Sep. 29 E;* **4:1**, *Dec. 2 M;* **4:6**, *Jan. 25 M;* **4:7**, *Dec. 3 M;* *Dec. 20 M;* **4:8**, *May 22 M;* **4:10**, *Feb. 15 E;* **4:12**, *Jan. 7 E;* *Nov. 18 M;* **4:16**, *Mar. 1 M;* *Apr. 12 E;* **5:1**, *Jun. 18 E;* **5:2**, *Feb. 29 M;* *Sep. 24 E;* *Nov. 22 M;* **5:4**, *Sep. 27 E;* **5:6**, *Mar. 29 E;* **5:8**, *Aug. 22 M;* **5:10**, *Mar. 20 M;* *May 1 E;* *Dec. 29 E;* **5:11**, *Mar. 9 M;* *Oct. 28 E;* **5:13**, *May 1 M;* **5:16**, *Mar. 9 M;* *Mar. 19 E;* *Sep. 3 M;* *Dec. 29 E;* **6:5**, *Dec. 26 E;* **7:11**, *May 9 E;* **7:13**, *Oct. 1 M;* **8:2**, *Mar. 9 E;* **8:6**, *Jul. 29 M;* *Oct. 13 E;* **8:7**, *Jul. 29 M;* **8:12**, *Oct. 21 E;* **8:13**, *Oct. 30 E;*

Isaiah 1:18, *Jan. 15 M;* *Feb. 1 E;* *Apr. 16 M;* *Aug. 1 M;* *Oct. 10M;* **2:3**, *Apr. 4 E;* *Nov. 4 E;* **3:10**, *Apr. 14 E;* **5:1**, *Mar. 20 M;* **6:6**, *Oct. 3 M;* *Nov. 7 E;* **6:7**, *Mar. 2 E;* **7:14**, *Dec. 25 M;* **9:6**, *Jan. 26 E;* *Feb. 8 M;* *Mar. 25 M;* *Nov. 5 E;* *Dec. 25 M;* **11:4**, *Oct. 15 M;* **14:10**, *Jun. 26 E;* **14:11**, *Nov. 3 M;* **14:12**, *Mar. 6 E;* **21:11**, *Aug. 6 M;* **24:16**, *Jul. 3 M;* **25:4**, *Nov. 19 E;* **25:6**, *May 17 M;* *Aug. 22 E;* *Oct. 16 M;* *Nov. 24 M;* **25:10**, *Jul. 21 M;* **26:3**, *May 26 M;* *Dec. 9 M;* **26:4**, *Jul. 5 E;* **27:3**, *Jan. 26 E;* *Jun. 29 E;* **30:18**, *Dec. 9 M;* **32:2**, *Feb. 3 E;* *Oct. 6 M;* **32:18**, *Dec. 9 E;* **33:16**, *Feb. 28 E;* *Aug. 22 M;* *Nov. 9 E;* **33:17**, *Nov. 16 E;* **33:21**, *Nov. 24 M;* **33:24**, *Aug. 9 M;* **35:2**, *Jun. 1 E;* **35:8**, *Jan. 31 E;* **36:1**, *Jul. 21 M;* **36:5**, *Oct. 7 E;* **37:22**, *Jul. 21 M;* **38:5**, *Nov. 3 M;* **40:5**, *Jan. 27 M;* *Dec. 24 E;* **40:9**, *Jun. 25 M;* *Nov. 23 M;* **40:11**, *May 14 E;* *Oct. 17 E;* *Nov. 22 M;* **40:12**, *Jan. 27 E;* *Apr. 11 E;* *Dec. 22 M;* **40:15**, *Jan. 27 E;* **40:17**, *Dec. 12 M;* **40:25**, *Jul. 5 E;* **40:27**, *Oct. 21 E;* **40:28**, *Oct. 11 M;* **40:29**, *Apr. 28 M;* **40:31**, *Jan. 2 M;* *Jan. 31 E;* *Dec. 14 M;* **41:1**, *Jan. 2 E;* **41:9**, *May 17 E;* **41:10**, *Mar. 2 E;* *Jul. 2 M;* *Dec. 22 M;* **41:13**, *Jun. 17 M;* **41:14**, *Jan. 16 M;* *Aug. 1 M;* **42:3**, *Mar. 27 M;* *May 24 E;* *Aug. 1 M;* **42:15**, *Sep. 13 M;* **43:2**, *Mar. 7 M;* *Sep. 19 M;* *Oct. 1 M;* **43:3**, *Dec. 16 E;* **43:4**, *Dec. 16 E;* **43:6**, *Oct. 20 E;* **43:21**, *Sep. 30 M;* **43:24**, *May 23 E;* **43:25**, *Apr. 28 M;* **44:3**, *Nov. 6 M;* **44:22**, *Feb. 1 M;* *Feb. 10 E;* *Aug. 1*

M; Aug. 11 E; **45:7**, *Dec. 23 E;* **45:9**, *Jul. 21 M;* **45:19**, *Aug. 21 E;* **45:22**, *Aug. 25 M;* **46:10**, *Aug. 2 M;* **48:8**, *Dec. 16 E;* **48:10**, *Mar. 3 M; Mar. 8 M;* **49:8**, *Jan. 3 M;* **49:14**, *Nov. 7 M;* **49:15**, *Jun. 16 M; Jul. 29 M;* **49:16**, *Apr. 30 E; May 5 M; Jun. 16 M; Jul. 29 M; Aug. 13 E; Nov. 7 M; Dec. 11 M; Dec. 17 M;* **51:3**, *Jun. 1 E;* **51:5**, *Aug. 321 M;* **51:6**, *Nov. 2 M;* **52:3**, *Oct. 22 M;* **52:7**, *Jul. 21 M;* **53:3**, *Mar. 17 E; Mar. 24 E; Jun. 4 E; Oct. 28 E; Nov. 10 E; Dec. 30 M;* **53:5**, *Mar. 31 M; May 7 M; Jun. 21 E;* **53:6**, *Apr. 3 M;* **53:7**, *Mar. 26 M; Apr. 2 M;* **53:10**, *Feb. 5 M; Apr. 2 E;* **53:11**, *Dec. 4 M;* **53:12**, *Mar. 30 M;* **54:1**, *Aug. 28 E;* **54:5**, *Jun. 18 M; Dec. 6 M;* **54:7**, *Apr. 28 M;* **54:10**, *Apr. 28 M; Jun. 16 M; Sep. 19 M;* **54:11**, *Dec. 15 E;* **54:12**, *Dec. 13 E;* **54:17**, *Nov. 5 M;* **55:1**, *May 6 M; Jun. 13 M; Oct. 22 M;* **55:3**, *Aug. 25 M; Aug. 26 M;* **55:10**, *Mar. 2 E;* **55:13**, *May 7 M;* **57:18**, *Aug. 30 E;* **58:11**, *Dec. 17 E; Dec. 27 E;* **59:5**, *Aug. 8 M;* **60:20**, *Jul. 10 E;* **61:3**, *May 11 E; Oct. 12 M;* **62:4**, *Mar. 26 E; Sep. 21 M; Oct. 4 M;* **62:5**, *Sep. 21 M;* **62:12**, *Mar. 11 E;* **63:1**, *Jan. 14 E; Jun. 4 E;* **63:3**, *Mar. 21 M;* **63:7**, *Jan. 25 M;* **63:9**, *May 31 M;* **64:6**, *Oct. 27 E;* **65:19**, *Aug. 23 M;* **65:24**, *Mar. 19 M;* **66:1**, *Apr. 5 E;*

Jeremiah 2:2, *Dec. 17 M;* **2:13**, *May 4 M; May 26 M; Sep. 12 M;* **2:18**, *Jul. 20 E;* **3:12**, *Jan. 24 M; Mar. 13 E;* **3:14**, *Mar. 26 E; Jul. 22 M;* **5:22**, *Sep. 16 E;* **8:20**, *Dec. 31 E;* **8:22**, *Feb. 20 M;* **9:1**, *Nov. 2 E;* **12:9**, *Mar. 16 M;* **15:19**, *Jan. 5 M;* **15:21**, *Oct. 10 E;* **16:20**, *May 4 M;* **17:9**, *May 3 M; Jun. 7 M; 17:14**, *Aug. 30 E;* **17:17**, *Apr. 29 M;* **23:6**, *Jan. 31 M;* **29:13**, *Jan. 19 M;* **30:17**, *Aug. 30 E;* **31:3**, *Feb. 1 M; Feb. 29 M; Mar. 18 E; Apr. 26 M; May 5 M; May 17 E; Jul. 17 M; Nov. 2 M; Dec. 20 M;* **32:17**, *Jun. 30 E;* **32:38**, *Jan. 9 M;* **32:41**, *Sep. 21 M;* **33:3**, *Sep. 9 M;* **49:23**, *Sep. 7 E;* **51:51**, *Aug. 18 M;*

Lamentations 3:20, *May 28 E;* **3:21**, *Jan. 25 M; Jan. 29 E; May 28 E;* **3:22**, *Jan. 25 M; May 16 M;* **3:23**, *May 16 M; Oct. 1 M;* **3:24**, *Nov. 16 M;* **3:33**, *Apr. 30 M; Aug. 17 E;* **3:40**, *Mar. 30 E;* **3:41**, *Oct. 11 M;* **3:44**, *Mar. 29 E;* **3:58**, *Nov. 20 M;*

Ezekiel 1:1, *Nov. 2 E;* **3:7**, *Apr. 28 E;* **15:2**, *Jan. 22 M;* **16:6**, *Jul. 7 E;* **16:10**, *Dec. 21 E;* **18:32**, *Feb. 22 E;* **20:41**, *Mar. 28 E;* **33:22**, *Jan. 6 E;* **34:14**, *Feb. 3 E;* **34:26**, *Feb. 24 M;* **35:10**, *Feb. 17 E;* **36:26**, *Aug. 15 E;* **36:37**, *Feb. 19 M;*

Daniel 2:18, *Febb. 21 E;* **2:32**, *Dec. 6 M;* **2:33**, *Dec. 6 M;* **3:16**, *Jun. 24 E;* **3:18**, *Jun. 24 E;* **3:24**, *Mar. 3 M; Mar. 9 E; Dec. 17 M;* **3:25**, *Mar. 3 M;* **3:27**, *Apr. 11 M;* **4:33**, *Mar. 6 E;* **4:35**, *Dec. 12 M;* **5:26**, *Dec. 18 E;* **5:27**, *Jun. 12 M; Dec. 18 E;* **6:5**, *Sep. 5 M;* **9:8**, *Jun. 14 E;* **9:26**, *Jan. 16 E;* **10:8**, *Apr. 11 M;* **10:10**, *Jan. 6 E;* **10:11**, *Jan. 6 E; Oct. 2 E;* **11:32**, *Aug. 4 M;*

Hosea 2:18, *Mar. 26 E;* **3:1**, *Feb. 4 M;* **5:7**, *Dec. 12 E;* **5:15**, *Jul. 25 E;* **7:8**, *Jun. 23 M;* **8:7**, *Feb. 25 E;* **10:12**, *Apr. 1 E;* **11:4**, *May 20 M;* **12:3**, *Sep. 9 M;* **12:4**, *Sep. 9 M;* **12:12**, *Nov. 22 M;* **13:5**, *Oct. 31 M;* **14:4**, *Jul. 30 M; Oct. 22 M;* **14:8**, *Sep. 8 M;*

Joel 1:3, *Jul. 11 E;* **2:8**, *Jul. 18 E;* **2:11**, *Jul. 24 E;* **2:13**, *Dec. 18 M;*

Amos 2:13, *Aug. 27 M;* **4:11**, *Sep. 13 M;* **9:9**, *Jun. 20 M;*

Obadiah 1:11, *Jul. 23 M;*

Jonah 1:3, *Feb. 25 M;* **1:17**, *Jul. 24 E;* **2:9**, *Feb. 26 M;* **3:9**, *Mar. 13 M;* **4:3**, *Dec. 4 E;* **4:6**, *Jan. 11 M; Mar. 7 E;* **4:7**, *Dec. 9 E;* **4:9**, *Jul. 13 M;*

Micah 2:10, *Feb. 7 M;* **2:13**, *Aug. 24 M;* **5:2**, *Feb. 27 M;* **5:4**, *Aug. 19 M;* **7:19**, *Sep. 23 M;*

Nahum 1:2, *Sep. 12 M;* **1:3**, *Feb. 22 M;*

Habakkuk 1:8, *Sep. 10 E;* **3:6**, *Dec. 12 M;* **3:17**, *Jun. 22 E; Oct. 19 E;* **3:18**, *Jun. 22 E; Oct. 19 E;*

Zephaniah 1:4, *Nov. 18 M;* **1:5**, *Nov. 14 M;* **3:17**, *Sep. 21 M;*

Haggai 1:9, *Oct. 26 M;* 2:17, *Aug. 4 E;* 2:23, *Sep. 29 E;*

Zechariah 1:8, *Sep. 26 M;* 1:12, *Feb. 24 E;* 1:13, *Feb. 24 E;* 1:19, *Dec. 5 E;* 1:20, *Dec. 5 E;* 2:5, *Apr. 22 E;* 3:1, *Nov. 27 M;* 4:6, *Nov. 4 M;* 4:7, *Aug. 2 M;* 4:10, *Jul. 1 M; Nov. 26 E;* 6:6, *Sep. 12 E;* 6:13, *Jun. 22 M;* 11:2, *Sep. 26 E;* 14:7, *Oct. 4 M;* 14:8, *Jul. 1 M;*

Malachi 2:16, *May 17 E;* 3:2, *Jul. 1 E;* Oct. 15 M; 3:3, *Oct. 15 M;* 3:6, *Nov. 2 M;* 3:7, *Apr. 28 E;* 3:17, *Feb. 26 M; Sep. 13 E; Dec. 30 E;*

Matthew 1:21, *Feb. 8 M; Feb. 8 E; Oct. 4 E;* 3:7, *Feb. 25 M;* 3:16, *Mar. 3 E; May 8 E;* 4:1, *Feb. 20 E;* 5:3, *Apr. 5 E;* 5:5, *Nov. 30 M;* 5:6, *Apr. 28 M; Aug. 16 E; Aug. 22 M;* 5:8, *May 16 M; Jul. 4 E;* 5:9, *Mar. 17 E;* 5:13, *Jun. 10 M;* 5:14, *Jan. 12 E;* 5:15, *Jan. 12 E;* 5:16, *Sep. 20 M;* 5:43, *Mar. 12 M;* 5:48, *Jan. 25 E; Aug. 31 E;* 6:1, *Jul. 3 E;* 6:9, *Jan. 26 M; Oct. 29 M;* 6:10, *Jan. 30 M; Apr. 2 E; Jun. 7 E; Jul. 10 M; Oct. 29 M; Nov. 23 M;* 6:11, *Apr. 2 E; Jul. 16 M; Aug. 4 E; Oct. 29 M;* 6:12, *Oct. 29 M;* 6:13, *Mar. 16 E; Oct. 29 M;* 6:19, *Mar. 10 E; May 11 M; Sep. 11 M;* 6:20, *Mar. 10 E; May 11 M;* 6:21, *May 11 M;* 6:26, *Jan. 6 M; Jan. 26 M;* 6:33, *Jun. 24 E; Oct. 26 M; Dec. 19 M;* 7:7, *Dec. 5 M; Dec. 13 M;* 7:13, *Aug. 18 M;* 7:14, *Aug. 18 M;* 7:15, *Sep. 10 E;* 7:23, *Jan. 4 E;* 7:24, *Mar. 7 E; May 11 M;* 7:25, *Mar. 7 E;* 8:17, *Apr. 12 M;* 8:20, *Nov. 10 E;* 9:6, *Aug. 10 M;* 9:20, *Aug. 25 M;* 9:21, *Feb. 4 E;* 10:16, *Mar. 3 E; Mar. 25 M; Jul. 25 M;* 10:24, *Nov. 23 M;* 10:25, *Nov. 10 E;* 10:28, *Dec. 19 M;* 10:29, *Nov. 9 E; Dec. 19 M;* 10:30, *Apr. 11 E; Apr. 29 E; Aug. 2 M; Aug. 17 E; Sep. 28 M; Oct. 21 E; Nov. 9 E; Dec. 19 M;* 10:34, *Dec. 28 E;* 10:35, *Dec. 28 E;* 10:36, *Dec. 28 E;* 11:19, *Oct. 6 E;* 11:25, *Feb. 5 M;* 11:28, *Jan. 25 M; Feb. 1 E; Apr. 19 E; Aug. 1 M; Sep. 15 E; Dec. 16 M;* 11:30, *Feb. 23 E;* 12:15, *May 7 M;* 12:20, *Apr. 19 E; Jul. 19 E; Oct. 19 M;* 13:22, *Apr. 4 E;* 13:25, *Dec. 18 E;* 13:30, *Sep. 21 E;* 13:46, *Jan. 7 M; Nov. 5 E;* 14:20, *Mar. 19 M;* 14:27, *Aug. 5 M; Oct. 29 E;* 14:30, *Jan. 14 E;* 15:22, *Mar. 27 E;* 15:23, *Oct. 9 E;* 15:26, *Oct. 9 E;* 15:27, *Mar. 4 E; Mar. 27 E;* 15:28, *Jan. 15 M; Oct. 9 E;* 15:37, *Mar. 19 M;* 16:17, *Nov. 4 E;* 16:18, *Jul. 21 M;* 16:23, *May 29 M; Nov. 11 E;* 17:20, *Feb. 4 E;* 18:14, *Oct. 17 E;* 19:16, *Jun. 2 E;* 19:17, *Jun. 2 E;* 19:26, *Mar. 21 E; Sep. 23 E;* 20:6, *Aug. 5 E; Dec. 20 E;* 20:16, *Aug. 18 E;* 20:28, *Jan. 16 E;* 21:12, *May 29 M;* 22:30, *Jul. 22 M;* 22:37, *Jan. 25 E;* 22:42, *Dec. 29 E;* 22:44, *Apr. 19 M; Dec. 30 M;* 23:14, *May 29 M;* 23:27, *Sep. 18 M;* 24:35, *Apr. 19 E;* 24:38, *Nov. 1 E;* 24:39, *Nov. 1 E;* 25:2, *Nov. 15 M;* 25:6, *Dec. 24 M;* 25:8, *Aug. 28 M;* 25:11, *Jun. 5 M;* 25:12, *Jun. 5 M;* 25:21, *May 2 M; Sep. 26 E; Oct. 2 M; Dec. 20 M;* 25:34, *Feb. 28 M; May 9 M; Dec. 2 M; Dec. 16 M;* 25:40, *Mar. 17 M;* 25:41, *May 29 M; Jun. 26 M;* 26:7, *Feb. 15 E;* 26:26, *Feb. 26 M;* 26:27, *Feb. 26 M; Apr. 8 M;* 26:33, *Nov. 29 M;* 26:36, *Mar. 21 M;* 26:39, *Mar. 22 M; Nov. 22 M* 26:41, *Mar. 24 M;* 26:43, *Mar. 24 M;* 26:53, *Mar. 27 M;* 26:56, *Mar. 27 M;* 26:67, *Apr. 8 M;* 27:14, *Apr. 2 M;* 27:31, *Apr. 8 M;* 27:45, *Jun. 3 E;* 27:46, *Apr. 8 M;* 27:50, *Dec. 18 M;* 27:51, *Apr. 19 M; Dec. 18 M;* 28:1, *Jul. 14 E;* 28:18, *Apr. 21 E;* 28:20, *Apr. 20 E; May 11 M; Dec. 26 E;*

Mark 1:18, *Jun. 20 E;* 1:30, *Apr. 9 M; Sep. 2 M;* 1:40, *Sep. 4 M;* 1:41, *Sep. 4 M; Sep. 15 E; Oct. 24 E;* 2:4, *Sep. 7 M* 3:13, *Sep. 10 M;* 3:35, *Feb. 5 M;* 4:11, *Jan. 19 E;* 4:36, *Sep. 14 M;* 4:39, *Apr. 20 M;* 6:50, *Oct. 21 E; Nov. 16 E;* 7:26, *Dec. 9 M;* 8:38, *Mar. 26 E;* 9:15, *Aug. 26 E;* 9:17, *Sep. 23 E;* 9:19, *Sep. 17 M;* 9:22, *Sep. 23 E;* 9:23, *Mar. 19 M; Aug. 8 E; Sep. 23 E;* 9:24, *Sep. 23 E; Nov. 9 E;* 9:25, *Sep. 23 E;* 10:21, *Feb. 23 E;* 11:13, *Dec. 4 M;* 11:22, *Mar. 7 M;* 12:10, *Aug. 2 M;* 12:42, *May 23 E;* 12:44, *Feb. 15 M;* 14:14, *Nov. 8 E;* 14:21, *Mar. 25 M;* 14:72, *Jul. 30 M;* 15:15, *Mar. 31 M;* 15:23, *Aug. 18 E;* 16:9, *Apr. 9 M; Jul. 15 E; Aug. 9 E;* 16:16, *Oct. 5 E;*

Luke 2:17, *Jan. 26 E;* 2:18, *Jan. 26 E;* 2:19, *Jan. 27 E; Jun. 24 M;* 2:20, *Jan.*

28 E; 2:25, Aug. 11 E; 2:28, Feb. 14 E; 3:4, Jan. 3 M; 3:23, Dec. 25 M; 4:2, Feb. 20 E; 4:18, Nov. 25 M; 4:26, Aug. 21 M; 5:4, Oct. 8 M; 5:5, Oct. 8 M; 5:19, Sep. 7 M; 6:12, Nov. 12 M; 6:35, Oct. 29 E; 6:38, Feb. 24 M; Aug. 21 M; 7:15, Apr. 9 M; 7:37, Jan. 27 E; 7:38, Jan. 27 M; Apr. 1 M; 7:50, Feb. 14 E; 8:13, Jan. 11 M; 8:42, Aug. 3 E; 8:47, Feb. 14 E; 9:23, Apr. 5 M; 9:48, Jul. 18 E; 10:20, Jan. 9 M; Jul. 10 M; 10:21, Mar. 24 E; 10:34, Oct. 22 E; 10:38, Apr. 9 M; 10:39, Apr. 1 M; 10:40, Jan. 24 E; 10:41, May 20 E; Jun. 18 E; 10:42, May 9 E; 11:1, Nov. 12 E; 11:4, Feb. 9 E; 11:27, Jun. 24 M; 11:28, Jun. 24 M; 12:32, Jul. 2 M; Dec. 11 M 12:48, May 23 M; 13:7, Feb. 1 E; 14:10, Mar. 14 M; Dec. 23 M; 15:2, Sep. 13 E; 15:7, Jul. 10 M; 15:10, Oct. 3 M; 15:17, Feb. 18 E; 15:18, Feb. 18 E; Jul. 25 E; Oct. 29 M; 15:20, Feb. 29 M; 16:13, May 4 M; 16:20, Dec. 29 E; 16:21, Dec. 29 E; 16:23, Dec. 30 E; 16:24, Nov. 24 E; Dec. 30 E; 17:17, Oct. 30 M; 18:1, Nov. 13 E; 18:5, Mar. 22 M; 18:11, May 24 M; 18:14, Nov. 3 M; 18:27, Jan. 13 E; 19:40, Mar. 23 E; 22:31, Aug. 6 M; 22:32, Jan. 11 E; Oct. 21 E; 22:33, Jul. 30 M; 22:40, Feb. 9 E; May 5 M; 22:41, Mar. 21 M; Mar. 22 M; 22:44, Mar. 15 E; Mar. 21 M; Mar. 23 M; Apr. 12 E; 22:46, Oct. 23 E; 22:48, Mar. 25 M; 22:61, Jul. 30 E; 22:62, Jun. 14 E; 23:34, Feb. 11 M; 23:26, Apr. 5 M; 23:27, Apr. 9 M; 23:31, Apr. 8 M; 23:33, Apr. 10 M; 23:43, Jun. 29 M; 23:44, Oct. 15 M; 24:5, Jun. 26 E; 24:16, Oct. 29 E; 24:27, Jan. 18 E; 24:29, Jan. 27 E; May 25 E; 24:31, May 25 E; 24:32, Mar. 9 M; Mar. 16 M; 24:33, May 25 E; 24:35, May 25 E; 24:38, Oct. 21 E; 24:45, Jan. 19 E;

John 1:1, Jun. 10 E; Nov. 18 E; 1:2, Jun. 10 E; Nov. 18 E; Dec. 17 M; 1:3, Mar. 28 M; Jun. 10 E; Nov. 18 E; 1:10, Mar. 16 M; 1:11, Mar. 16 M; 1:12, May 9 M; Dec. 22 E; 1:14, Jan. 10 M; May 10 E; Jun. 21 E; 1:16, Jan. 27 M; Mar. 15 M; 1:17, Mar. 15 M; 1:29, Jan. 17 M; 1:32, Jun. 19 M; 1:33, Oct. 5 E; 1:41, Feb. 19 E; 3:3, Jul. 4 M; 3:6, Oct. 13 M; 3:7, Mar. 6 M; 3:8, Mar. 6 M; Jun. 19 M; 3:13, Mar. 25 E; 3:14, May 31 E; 3:16, Feb. 2 E; Feb. 3 M; Apr. 8 M; May 9 M; Jun. 3 E; Sep. 2 E; Oct. 25 M; Dec. 7 M; Dec. 11 M; 3:18, Oct. 22 M; 4:5, Jan. 12 E; 4:14, Feb. 21 M; Oct. 6 E; 4:34, Feb. 20 E; Nov. 23 M; 4:48, Sep. 2 E; 5:8, May 7 E; 5:13, May 8 M; 5:15, May 8 M; 5:39, Jun. 9 E; Jun. 10 E; 6:26, Dec. 27 M; 6:27, Dec. 27 M; 6:33, Oct. 16 M; 6:35, Oct. 14 M; 6:37, Jul. 17 M; Jul. 29 E; Jul. 30 E; Sep. 2 E; Sep. 29 M; 6:45, Aug. 9 M; 6:50, Aug. 10 M; 6:53, Aug. 25 M; 6:56, Oct. 16 M; 6:67, Oct. 23 M; 6:68, Oct. 23 M; 7:37, Dec. 31 M; 7:46, Apr. 2 M; 8:12, Jan. 5 E; 8:23, Apr. 6 M; Jun. 5 M; 8:36, Jan. 25 M; 8:44, May 19 M; Dec. 27 M; 10:9, Jul. 31 M; Oct. 5 E; Dec. 17 E; 10:11, Mar. 26 M; Dec. 16 M; 10:14, Jan. 20 M; 10:15, Jan. 20 M; 10:27, Jun. 16 M; Sep. 18 E; Dec. 22 E; 10:28, May 11 M; Jun. 16 M; Jul. 29 M; Jul. 30 E; 10:29, May 11 M; Jun. 16 M; 11:4, Aug. 17 E; 11:35, Nov. 21 E; Nov. 27 M; 11:36, Nov. 21 E; 11:43, Aug. 10 M; 11:44, Aug. 17 E; 12:2, Nov. 21 E; 12:21, Apr. 17 E; 12:32, Oct. 8 M; 13:5, Jun. 3 E; Oct. 24 E; 13:23, Feb. 14 M; Sep. 9 M; Oct. 20 M; 13:25, Dec. 20 M; 13:34, Jan. 25 E; 14:1, Jun. 22 M; 14:2, Jun. 24 M; 14:16, Feb. 12 E; 14:17, Jan. 4 E; 14:19, Sep. 8 E; Dec. 6 M; 14:21, May 12 M; 14:26, Oct. 12 M; 14:27, Sep. 15 M; Sep. 26 M; 15:1, Sep. 8 M; 15:2, Jan. 22 E; Sep. 8 M; 15:4, Feb. 26 M; Mar. 9 E; Sep. 9 E; Nov. 13 M; 15:5, Nov. 21 M; 15:9, Mar. 18 E; 15:10, May 30 M; 15:11, Feb. 20 M; May 14 M; Nov. 23 M; 15:15, Jun. 24 M; Aug. 14 E; 15:17, May 24 E; 15:19, Oct. 28 M; 16:12, Mar. 19 E; 16:15, Oct. 22 E; 16:24, Aug. 21 E; 16:27, Feb. 1 M; 16:32, Mar. 21 M; 16:33, Mar. 8 M; Apr. 5 M; May 3 M; 17:4, Feb. 5 M; 17:9, Mar. 20 E; 17:10, Feb. 1 E; 17:12, Nov. 22 M; 17:15, May 2 M; Sep. 5 M; 17:17, Jul. 4 M; 17:20, Dec. 4 M; 17:22, May 14 M; Jun. 30 M; 17:23, Jul. 31 M; 17:24, Mar. 22 E; May 2 M; 18:6, Oct. 15 M; 18:8, Mar. 26 M; 18:9, Jan. 21 M; 18:28, Jul. 30 M; 18:38, Nov. 7 E; 18:40, Apr. 7 M; 19:5, Jul. 22 E; 19:16, Apr. 3 M; 19:28, Apr. 7 M; 19:29, Apr. 7

M; **19:30,** Jan. 31 M; Feb. 3 M; Jun. 11 E; Jun. 12 E; **20:11,** Jul. 14 E; **20:16,** Jul. 15 E; **20:28,** May 5 M; **21:9,** Dec. 26 E; **21:12,** Oct. 5 M; Oct. 16 M; **21:17,** Oct. 5 M; **21:19,** Oct. 5 M; **21:22,** Sep. 18 E;

Acts 1:8, Nov. 7 E; **1:9,** Jun. 4 E; **2:4,** Jun. 19 M; **2:33,** Aug. 10 E; **3:6,** Jan. 12 E; **4:13,** Feb. 11 M; Mar. 12 E; **4:36,** Aug. 11 E; **5:31,** Apr. 22 M; Aug. 10 E; **7:43,** May 4 M; **8:13,** Aug. 8 M; **8:30,** Feb. 21 E; Sep. 6 M; **8:37,** Aug. 25 E; **9:5,** Feb. 25 E; **9:11,** Nov. 3 M; **10:38,** Jul. 28 E; **13:39,** May 15 M; **14:22,** Mar. 8 M; May 22 M; May 26 E; **16:5,** Mar. 18 M; **16:14,** Dec. 10 E; **16:34,** Oct. 9 E; **17:18,** Sep. 25 E; **17:26,** Mar. 12 M; **17:28,** Feb. 17 M; Aug. 1 E; Nov. 9 M; Nov. 10 E; **18:10,** Dec. 4 M; **20:28,** May 5 M; Sep. 18 E; **22:10,** Jul. 7 E; **24:24,** Dec. 31 E; **24:25,** Dec. 31 E; **26:18,** Oct. 10 M; **27:23,** Apr. 10 E;

Romans 1:4, May 10 M; **1:7,** Jul. 5 M; **3:4,** Apr. 18 E; **3:26,** Sep. 25 M; **3:27,** Oct. 5 E; **3:31,** Jan. 25 E; **4:5,** Jun. 6 M; **4:20,** Mar. 19 M; **4:21,** Nov. 9 M; **4:25,** May 10 M; **5:1,** Feb. 14 E; Sep. 25 M; **5:3,** Oct. 7 M; **5:8,** Feb. 10 E; **5:9,** Feb. 10 E; **6:2,** Feb. 8 E; Dec. 14 E; **6:4,** Sep. 8 E; Dec. 26 M; **6:6,** May 30 E; **6:8,** Jan. 31 E; **6:13,** Jan. 26 M; **6:14,** Feb. 8 E; Nov. 25 M; **7:13,** Mar. 11 M; **7:21,** Aug. 9 M; **7:22,** Aug. 9 M; **7:23,** Aug. 9 M; **7:24,** May 15 E; Jun. 12 M; **8:1,** Jan. 27 M; Feb. 13 E; Apr. 4 M; May 15 M; **8:11,** May 10 M; **8:12,** Feb. 3 M; **8:14,** Jun. 19 M; **8:15,** Jun. 19 M; Jul. 30 E; Aug. 25 E; Sep. 27 M; Dec. 6 M; **8:17,** May 3 E; May 14 M; Jun. 30 M; **8:18,** Mar. 29 M; **8:23,** Jun. 23 E; Jul. 20 M; Aug. 16 E; Dec. 4 E; **8:28,** Mar. 4 M; Aug. 5 M; Oct. 21 E; **8:30,** May 28 M; Oct. 11 E; **8:31,** Feb. 25 E; Jun. 16 E; Jul. 13 E; Nov. 25 M; Dec. 3 E; **8:32,** Apr. 8 M; Jul. 8 M; Jul. 26 E; Aug. 14 M; Oct. 2 E; **8:33,** May 15 M; Jul. 27 E; Sep. 25 M; Dec. 3 E; **8:34,** Apr. 4 M; Apr. 21 M; Jul. 6 E; Sep. 25 M; Nov. 25 M; **8:35,** Mar. 20 M; **8:36,** Mar. 20 M; **8:36,** Mar. 20 M; **8:37,** Mar. 20 M; Apr. 23 M; Apr. 26 E; Jun. 2 M; Jul. 12 M; Sep. 26 M; Dec. 3 E; **8:38,** Feb. 4 M; Mar. 20 M; Oct. 23 M; **8:39,** Mar. 20 E; Oct. 23 M; **9:15,** Nov. 25 E; **9:33,** Nov. 4 E; **11:26,** Jan. 21 M; **11:36,** Nov. 17 M; **12:1,** Feb. 3 M; Aug. 14 M; Nov. 27 M; **12:2,** Oct. 14 E; **12:10,** Aug. 14 M; **12:20,** Feb. 11 M; Mar. 12 M; **14:8,** Jun. 10 M; **14:9,** May 10 M; **14:23,** Aug. 29 E;

1 Corinthians 1:2, Jul. 12 M; **1:21,** Oct. 8 M; **1:23,** Sep. 11 E; **1:28,** Dec. 7 M; **1:30,** Apr. 4 M; Sep. 25 E; Oct. 25 E; **2:2,** Mar. 2 E; **2:9,** Jun. 4 M; **2:12,** Feb. 29 M; **3:1,** Oct. 19 M; **3:12,** Jul. 11 M; **3:21,** Jan. 30 E; **3:23,** Jan. 12 M; Jan. 30 E; **3:23,** Jul. 26 M; **6:11,** Jun. 7 M; **6:15,** Sep. 27 M; **7:20,** Jun. 27 M; **7:23,** Sep. 18 E; **9:16,** Dec. 7 E; **9:22,** Dec. 7 E; **10:4,** Nov. 24 M; **10:12,** Mar. 14 E; **10:13,** Jul. 30 E; **10:31,** Sep. 11 M; **11:3,** Oct. 28 E; **11:24,** Apr. 26 M; **11:29,** Aug. 25 M; **11:31,** Jun. 12 M; **13:12,** Jun. 4 M; Jun. 10 E; Dec. 13 E; **15:14,** May 10 M; **15:17,** May 10 M; **15:20,** May 10 M; **15:25,** May 2 M; **15:31,** Apr. 26 M; **15:45,** Dec. 26 M; **15:48,** Dec. 6 M; **15:54,** Apr. 20 M; Dec. 10 M; **15:55,** Apr. 20 E; **16:13,** Sep. 5 M;

2 Corinthians 1:3, Feb. 20 M; **1:5,** Feb. 12 M; **2:11,** Feb. 9 E; **3:2,** May 17 E; **4:7,** Jan. 5 E; Jul. 7 M; **4:17,** Apr. 5 M; Jul. 3 E; Sep. 4 E; Sep. 12 E; **4:18,** Jan. 29 M; Apr. 5 M; **5:6,** May 2 M; **5:7,** May 2 E; Jun. 24 E; **5:8,** Apr. 20 M; May 2 M; **5:14,** Jan. 31 M; Jun. 5 E; Oct. 21 M; **5:17,** Mar. 30 M; Jul. 4 M; Aug. 16 E; **5:19,** Jun. 21 E; **5:20,** Dec. 31 M; **5:21,** Apr. 3 M; Apr. 4 M; Apr. 13 E; Jun. 21 E; Sep. 4 M; **6:2,** Jun. 6 M; **6:10,** Oct. 16 E; **6:14,** Jan. 5 M; Jan. 13 M; **6:15,** Jan. 29 M; **6:16,** May 5 M; **6:17,** Jun. 27 M; Sep. 11 M; Oct. 11 M; Oct. 14 E; **7:6,** Feb. 20 M; **7:10,** Oct. 13 M; **8:9,** Feb. 13 E; Sep. 3 M; Dec. 24 M; **9:15,** Mar. 1 E; Mar. 21 M; Nov. 5 M; **10:17,** Mar. 6 M; **11:22,** Jun. 6 E; **11:24,** Apr. 26 M; **12:2,** Sep. 9 M; **12:8,** Dec. 9 M; **12:9,** Jan. 14 M; Feb. 4 M; Mar. 4 M; Oct. 4 M; Oct. 13 E; Nov. 4 M; Nov. 26 M; Dec. 8 E; **12:10,** Oct. 13 E; **13:5,** Jun. 26 M;

Galatians 1:12, May 12 M; **1:16,** May 9 M; **2:10,** Mar. 17 M; **2:20,** Feb. 26 M;

Mar. 6 M; Mar. 18 E; Apr. 23 M; Jun. 5 E; Sep. 3 M; Dec. 14 E; Dec. 26 M; Dec. 28 M; 3:1, Apr. 23 M; 3:2, Apr. 23 M; 3:9, Mar. 8 M; 3:13, Mar. 27 E; 3:26, Mar. 18 M; 5:1, Apr. 17 E; Sep. 19 M; 5:11, Sep. 11 E; 5:17, Jun. 2 M; 5:18, Sep. 6 E; 5:25 Sep. 18 M; 6:7, May 12 M; 6:9, Jun. 28 E; 6:17, Nov. 18 E;

Ephesians 1:3, *May 9 M; Sep. 27 M;* **1:4**, *Feb. 2 E; Apr. 3 M; Oct. 11 E;* **1:6**, *Jan. 28 M; Sep. 23 M; Dec. 2 M;* **1:7**, *Nov. 27 M;* **1:9**, *Mar. 29 M;* **1:11**, *Jan. 30 E; Aug. 2 M; Nov. 21 M; Dec. 12 M;* **1:14**, *Jul. 20 M;* **1:18**, *Apr. 25 E; Sep. 27 M;* **1:19**, *Sep. 8 E;* **1:20**, *May 9 M; Sep. 8 E;* **1:21**, *May 9 M;* **1:22**, *May 9 M;* **2:1**, *Mar. 6 M; Jul. 7 E; Aug. 10 M;* **2:6**, *Jul. 26 E; Oct. 3 M; Oct. 19 M; Dec. 26 M;* **2:10**, *Jul. 12 M;* **2:13**, *Sep. 15 E;* **2:18**, *Jul. 26 M;* **2:19**, *Jul. 10 M;* **3:8**, *Mar. 2 E; Jun. 6 E; Aug. 22 E;* **3:17**, *Jul. 11 M; Aug. 23 E;* **3:18**, *Jan. 28 M; Feb. 14 M; Feb. 14 E; Apr. 25 E; Oct. 14 M;* **3:19**, *Jan. 28 M; Feb. 14 E; Mar. 18 E; Mar. 28 M; Apr. 25 E; Apr. 29 E; Jun. 25 M; Oct. 14 M;* **3:20**, *Aug. 16 M; Dec. 22 M;* **4:1**, *Sep. 11 M;* **4:3**, *Jul. 18 E;* **4:7**, *Jan. 27 M;* **4:8**, *Aug. 10 E; Dec. 3 E;* **4:13**, *Jan. 3 M;* **4:14**, *Feb. 21 E;* **4:15**, *Oct. 20 M;* **4:26**, *May 29 M;* **4:30**, *Nov. 21 M;* **5:11**, *Sep. 11 M;* **5:18**, *Nov. 7 M;* **5:19**, *Sep. 11 M;* **5:25**, *Mar. 20 E;* **5:27**, *Jul. 12 M; Oct. 6 E; Oct. 10 M; Dec. 22 M;* **6:11**, *Jun. 2 M;* **6:14**, *Dec. 6 E;* **6:16**, *Mar. 14 E; Oct. 2 M;* **6:18**, *Feb. 6 M; May 24 M;*

Philippians 1:6, *Jan. 14 M; May 23 M; Nov. 25 M;* **1:21**, *Jan. 7 M; Jun. 12 M; Sep. 11 M;* **1:27**, *May 24 E;* **2:8**, *Jun. 3 E;* **2:10**, *Aug. 19 M;* **2:15**, *Sep. 6 M;* **3:8**, *Mar. 19 E; Oct. 14 M;* **3:9**, *Jan. 31 M; Jan. 31 E; Mar. 19 E;* **3:10**, *Nov. 22 E;* **3:13**, *Oct. 11 E;* **3:14**, *Oct. 11 E;* **4:4**, *Nov. 16 M;* **4:6**, *Mar. 7 E; May 26 M; Aug. 10 E; Sep. 26 M;* **4:8**, *Mar. 3 E;* **4:11**, *Feb. 16 M;* **4:12**, *Feb. 10 M;* **4:13**, *Aug. 6 M; Oct. 8 M;*

Colossians 1:5, *Oct. 2 M;* **1:9**, *Jan. 18 M; Feb. 21 E;* **1:16**, *Nov. 15 E;* **1:17**, *Mar. 28 M; Dec. 22 M;* **1:19**, *Jan. 27 M; Apr. 27 E; Oct. 26 E;* **1:22**, *Dec. 12 M;* **1:27**, *Apr. 9 M; Dec. 25 M;* **1:28**, *Jan. 28 M; Jan. 31 M;* **2:2**, *Sep. 27 M;* **2:3**, *Sep. 25 E;* **2:6**, *Nov. 8 M; Nov. 9 M;* **2:9**, *Jan. 3 M; Apr. 13 M; May 18 M; Aug. 30 E;* **2:10**, *Jan. 28 M; May 18 M; Dec. 26 M;* **2:11**, *Feb. 26 M;* **2:12**, *Aug. 25 M: Dec. 26 M;* **2:14**, *Feb. 3 M;* **2:15**, *Dec. 3 E;* **3:2**, *Mar. 10 E;* **3:3**, *Mar. 6 M; Sep. 8 E; Sep. 16 M;* **3:4**, *Aug. 10 M;* **3:5**, *Mar. 16 E;* **3:16**, *Jul. 26 M; Oct. 30 M;* **3:23**, *Dec. 11 E;* **3:24**, *Dec. 11 E;* **4:2**, *Jan. 2 M;*

1 Thessalonians 1:4, *Jul. 17 M;* **2:18**, *Aug. 7 E;* **4:14**, *Jun. 29 M;* **4:17**, *Jan. 1 M; Apr. 6 M; Dec. 10 M;* **4:18**, *Aug. 23 M;* **5:5**, *Jan. 5 M; Jul 10 E;* **5:15**, *Feb. 11 M;* **5:17**, *Apr. 15 E;* **5:22**, *Mar. 11 M;* **5:24**, *Dec. 11 M;* **5:25**, *Jul. 7 M;*

2 Thessalonians 2:13, *Feb. 2 E;* **2:16**, *Aug. 11 E;*

1 Timothy 1:15, *Jul. 17 M; Sep. 25 E; Oct. 27 M; Dec. 7 M;* **1:17**, *Dec. 30 M;* **3:16**, *Jun. 4 E;* **4:8**, *Oct. 27 M;* **4:9**, *Oct. 27 M;* **6:6**, *Jun. 24 E; Oct. 26 M;* **6:10**, *Nov. 11 E;* **6:17**, *May 16 M;* **6:18**, *Sep. 11 M;*

2 Timothy 1:9, *Jun. 17 M; 1:12, May 21 M; Jun. 25 M; Jul. 17 M; Sep. 3 M; 2:1, Mar. 15 M; 2:3, Sep. 5 M; 2:11, Oct. 27 M; 2:12, Mar. 29 M; Jul. 3 E; Oct. 27 M; 2:19, Jan. 4 E; Jan. 5 E; Jun. 21 E; Nov. 15 M; Dec. 21 M; 4:1, Oct. 15 M; Dec. 31 M; 4:7, Mar. 14 M; 4:8, Jan. 10 M; Mar. 14 M; 4:18, Jul. 12 E;*

Titus 3:4, *Jun. 4 M;* **3:8**, *Oct. 27 M; Nov. 19 M;* **3:9**, *Nov. 19 M;*

Philemon 2, *Nov. 1 M;*

Hebrews 1:2, *May 14 M;* **1:3**, *Apr. 4 M; Apr. 22 M;* **1:9**, *Mar. 24 E; May 29 M; 1:13, May 11 M; 1:14, Oct. 3 M; 2:10, Apr. 20 E; 2:14, Jan. 27 M; Apr. 20 M; 2:18, Oct. 3 E; 3:1, Feb. 8 M; Oct. 11 E; 4:1, Jan. 1 M; Dec. 18 E; 4:9, Jan. 1 M; Jan. 10 M; Jan. 18 M; 4:14, Dec. 6 E; 4:15, Jan. 23 M; Mar. 29*

M; May 31 E; Oct. 3 E; 4:16, Feb. 13 E; Jul. 26 E; Sep. 19 M; 5:7, Mar. 24 M; 5:8, Mar. 29 M; 5:10, Feb. 15 M; 6:6, Mar. 27 M; May 30 M; 6:20, Jan. 30 E; 7:9, Dec. 26 M; 7:10, Dec. 26 M; 7:25, Jan. 27 M; May 9 M; Nov. 11 M; Nov. 18 E; Dec. 6 E; Dec. 31 E; 8:5, Feb. 21 E; 9:4, Jan. 27 E; 9:20, Nov. 6 E; 9:22, Feb. 2 M; 9:24, Jan. 30 E; 10:19, Apr. 19 M; 11:10, Feb. 7 M; Sep. 18 E; Oct. 11 E; 11:13, May 2 E; Oct. 11 E; 11:26, Feb. 23 E; Dec. 15 M; 12:2, May 2 E; Jun. 2 M; Jun. 28 M; 12:4, Jan. 9 E; Feb. 8 E; Mar. 23 M; 12:6, Apr. 30 M; 12:11, May 18 E; Sep. 27 M; 12:15, Feb. 8 E; 12:23, May 15 E; Jul. 10 M; Jul. 26 E; 12:24, Apr. 17 M; 12:27, Jun. 22 E; 12:29, Jul. 17 M; 13:2, Oct. 6 M; 13:5, Feb. 23 M; Mar. 1 E; Mar. 23 E; Apr. 6 M; May 11 M; Oct. 6 M; Oct. 21 E; Dec. 27 E; 13:8, May 11 M; Nov. 18 E; Dec. 12 M; 13:13, Apr. 6 M; Jul. 9 M; 13:14, Jul. 9 M; 13:21, Nov. 11 E;

James 1:2, *May 22 M; Nov. 7 E; 1:4, May 18 E; 1:6, Mar. 19 M; 1:8, Jun. 23 M; Nov. 14 M; 1:12, Apr. 22 M; 1:17, Feb. 27 M; Sep. 28 E; Nov. 2 M; Dec. 12 M; 1:21, Aug. 2 E; 2:23, Feb. 8 M; 3:3, Nov. 29 M; 3:4, Nov. 29 M; 3:5, Nov. 29 M; 3:17, Mar. 17 E; 4:2, Sep. 28 E; 4:4, May 3 M; Aug. 20 E; Nov. 10 E; Dec. 28 E; 4:7, Jul. 25 M; 4:8, May 5 M; 5:15, Sep. 2 M; 5:16, Feb. 6 E; Jul. 15 E; Sep. 28 E; 5:17, Sep. 28 E;*

1 Peter 1:2, *Jul. 12 M; 1:3, Jan. 27 M; May 10 M; Sep. 15 M; 1:4, Dec. 11 M; 1:7, Nov. 12 M; 1:8, Jan. 31 M; May 10 E; Jun. 15 M; Aug. 25 E; 1:18, Oct. 15 E; Nov. 15 M; 1:19, Apr. 16 M; Oct. 2 E; Oct. 15 E; Nov. 15 M; 1:22, May 4 E; 1:23, May 4 E; 2:3, May 21 M; Jul. 20 M; Dec. 12 M; Dec. 15 E; 2:7, Mar. 1 E; Nov. 4 E; 2:9, Feb. 29 E; May 4 E; May 14 M; Jul. 29 E; Oct. 26 E; Oct. 27 E; Nov. 27 M; 2:21, Jul. 28 M; 2:24, Jun. 21 E; 3:18, Jun. 21 E; 4:12, Oct. 10 E; 4:13, Mar. 21 M; Oct. 10 E; 5:4, Apr. 22 M; 5:7, Jan. 6 M; Sep. 1 E; 5:8, Feb. 9 M; Mar. 14 E; May 3 M; 5:10, Jul. 11 M;*

2 Peter 1:4, *Jun. 26 E; Jul. 27 M; Sep. 16 M; 1:5, Jul. 26 M; 1:6, Jul. 26 M; 1:8, Aug. 4 M; 1:10, Oct. 15 M; 2:1, Sep. 10 E; 2:7, Mar. 16 E; 3:10, Feb. 25 M; Nov. 2 M; 3:12, Feb. 25 M; 3:18, Jan. 4 M; Feb. 15 M; Jun. 18 E;*

1 John 1:3, *Jul 26 E; 1:5, Aug. 31 E; 1:6, Nov. 23 M; 1:7, Jan. 27 M; Feb. 18 E; Apr. 16 M; May 31 E; Jul. 23 E; Aug. 31 E; 2:1, Mar. 30 M; Jul. 30 E; Oct. 4 E; 2:6, May 17 M; 2:20, Aug. 4 M; 3:1, Feb. 13 M; 3:2, Jan. 10 E; Feb. 13 M; Feb. 28 M; Apr. 22 M; Jun. 23 E; Aug 3 M; Dec. 30 M; 3:14, Jul. 9 M; 4:4, Jul. 25 M; Nov. 25 M; Dec. 3 E; 4:7, Sep. 16 M; 4:8, Jun. 5 E; Sep. 16 M; 4:13, May 6 M; 4:14, Feb. 5 M; 4:18, Mar. 18 M; 4:19, Jun. 5 M; Jun. 11 E; Sep. 3 M;*

2 John 2, *Oct. 25 M;*

3 John 1, *Nov. 28 M; 3, Nov. 28 M;*

Jude 1, *Jul. 12 M; 20, Oct. 8 E; 24, Jan. 28 M; Mar. 14 M; Mar. 16 E; Oct. 9 M; Oct. 10 M; Oct. 17 M;*

Revelation 1:4, *Nov. 18 E; 1:6, Feb. 15 M; Oct. 29 M; 1:8, Feb. 4 M; 1:9, Dec. 19 M; 1:11, Jun. 10 E; 1:13, Dec. 6 E; 1:18, Apr. 27 E; 2:4, Feb. 11 E; 2:10, Jan. 10 M; 2:13, Dec. 26 E; 2:24, Feb. 11 E; 3:4, Dec. 18 M; 3:5, Jan. 4 E; 3:7, Apr. 19 M; Jun. 15 E; 3:11, Sep. 26 E; 3:14, Apr. 19 E; 3:15, Feb. 20 E; 3:16, Feb. 20 E; Jun. 5 M; Jun. 29 E; Jul. 15 M; 3:17, Feb. 20 E; Mar. 6 E; 3:19, Jun. 7 E; 3:20, Apr. 25 E; Jul. 1 E; Sep. 27 E; 3:21, Jun. 4 E; Dec. 20 E; 4:2, Apr. 22 M; 4:4, Apr. 22 M; Sep. 9 E; 4:8, Feb. 16 E; Jul. 10 M; Aug. 9 M; 4:10, Jul. 10 M; 5:4, Feb. 21 E; 5:5, Feb. 8 E; Feb. 21 E; Oct. 15 M; 5:6, Apr. 23 E; 5:9, Jun. 4 E; 5:10, Apr. 22 M; 5:11, Oct. 30 M; 5:12, Jun. 4 E; Oct. 30 M; Nov. 5 E; 6:5, Aug. 4 E; 7:9, Jul. 6 E; 7:12, Nov. 5 E; 7:13, Jul. 27 E; 7:17, Dec. 8 M; 9:11, Feb. 18 E; Jun. 13 E; 11:12, Feb. 7 E; 11:15, Jun. 7 M; 12:7, Nov. 30 E; 12:11, Apr. 16 M; 13:8, Feb. 8 M; 13:18, Apr. 13 E; 14:1, Jan. 17 M; 14:3, Oct. 10 M; 14:13, Jun. 29 M; 14:14, Oct. 10 M; 16:15, Apr. 26 E; 17:14, Feb. 8 M; 19.1, Dec. 8 M; 19:6,*

Jun. 29 M; Dec. 24 E; **19:7,** *Jul. 22 M; Sep. 16 M; Sep. 27 M;* **19:9,** *Jul. 22 M;* **19:12,** *Apr. 22 M;* **20:10,** *Mar. 25 M; Nov. 30 E;* **20:13,** *Sep. 7 E;* **21:1,** *Sep. 7 E; Dec. 19 E;* **21:2,** *Feb. 8 M;* **21:3,** *Sep. 15 E;* **21:4,** *Jan. 17 M; May 28 M; Oct. 2 M; Oct. 22 E;* **21:5,** *Aug. 2 E;* **21:9,** *Apr. 22 M;* **21:21,** *Jul. 10 M;* **21:23,** *Jul. 10 M; Aug. 3 M; Aug. 9 M;* **21:27,** *Oct. 2 M;* **22:1,** *Jul. 10 M;* **22:2,** *Jan. 9 M; Jul. 10 M;* **22:5,** *Jun. 1 M; Jul. 26 E;* **22:12,** *May 13 M;* **22:17,** *Jun. 13 M; Aug. 1 M; Sep. 2 E;* **22:20,** *Jan. 2 M; Jul. 10 M; Sep. 15 E; Dec. 16 M.*